RELOADING FOR SHOTGUNNERS

4th Edition

**by Kurt Fackler
&
M.L. McPherson**

DBI BOOKS
a division of Krause Publications, Inc.

STAFF

SENIOR STAFF EDITOR
Harold A. Murtz

ASSOCIATE EDITOR
Robert S.L. Anderson

PRODUCTION MANAGER
John L. Duoba

EDITORIAL/PRODUCTION ASSOCIATE
Karen Rasmussen

ASSISTANT TO THE EDITOR
Lilo Anderson

ASSISTANT TO THE PUBLISHER
Joyce Gately

ELECTRONIC PUBLISHING MANAGER
Nancy J. Mellem

ELECTRONIC PUBLISHING ASSOCIATE
Laura M. Mielzynski

MANAGING EDITOR
Pamela J. Johnson

PUBLISHER
Charles T. Hartigan

About the Cover

For over three decades, the byword at Ponsness/Warren has been, "We don't reload—we remanufacture!" So good are their machines that the quality of reloaded ammunition is difficult to tell from factory production.

The Ponsness/Warren 900 Elite Grand shotshell reloader featured on our covers is considered the ulitmate package for the serious shooter with higher production requirements. The machine uses specially designed full-length sizing dies to securely hold and resize each shell throughout the loading process.

A fully progressive machine with eight stations, the 900 has a smooth and quiet center shaft index system that automatically indexes shells to the next station of operation. With each cycle of the operating handle, the 900 Elite completes the loading cycle and kicks out a finished shell.

This high-quality reloader comes with the P/W Bushing Access Top Plate, which allows the reloader to change shot and powder bushings in seconds, and its 25-pound shot tube means less downtime for refilling the reservoir. The Grand package also includes a canvas dust cover, die cleaner bracket with die brush and swab, automatic shell counter, bushing kit with ten of the most popular sizes, shot and powder measure kit to check weights, PENX lubricant, and P/W's STOS grease.

The Ponsness/Warren 900 Elite Grand is available in 12, 20, 28 and 410-bore, and is said to be the machine by which all others are judged. Quality is built into each part of this beautifully crafted reloader, and we're confident it will last for a number of generations.

ISBN 0-87349-197-1

Library of Congress Catalog #81-65119

FOREWORD

SOME RELOADERS assemble shotshells with an almost cavalier attitude. If the components of a specific set of loading data cannot be matched exactly, then a misinformed reloader might substitute a case, primer or wad. And too often, some forget that powder and shot bushings are not absolutes which throw some specified charge weight as shown in manufacturer's literature. The exact components shown in any loading recipe must always be used. And both propellant and shot charge weights must always be verified with an accurate avoirdupois scale. Anything less may result in very serious grief.

Simply opening a data book and selecting a load does not qualify one to reload shotshells. Take the time to read all of the material in this book before making any attempt to assemble your own ammo. The information contained herein is essential, though admittedly it is not possible for us to foresee every problem or question. Also, always follow all the warnings and cautions of your component manufacturer. This is critical, especially with propellants. Finally, double-check every load you wish to assemble with the data supplied by the propellant manufacturers.

Shotshell reloading is not a difficult undertaking, if all instructions are followed. For the most part, shotshell loading tools are self-contained units, and the need for accessories is very limited, except for the mentioned powder and shot scale.

The other essentials are a good source of loading data and an adequate record-keeping system.

It is hoped that this book will supply much of the needed information for both the novice and experienced reloader. But, it is important to remember that no single source can answer every question. Whenever doubt exists, contact the manufacturer of the component in question. Never, I repeat never, continue to reload when even the slightest doubt is present. If your ammo does not look and perform as well as factory shells, then there is a problem; the responsible reloader will not use such ammo and will refrain from further assembly for any ammo until the problem is corrected.

Shotshell reloading can be a safe and rewarding hobby. It can allow the shooter to save up to 50 percent, or more, of the cost of ammo. This, in turn, can allow the reloader to shoot a great deal more. And more shooting is what makes for a proficient shotgunner and enjoyable hunting and target shooting. Follow the rules and you will gain a lot of satisfaction from shotshell reloading. Ignore the rules and a serious accident might serve to point out that the rules were not there just to make things difficult.

There is a new format for the data in this issue of RFS. We have endeavored to make loads easy to find based on gauge, chamber length and shot charge.

Kurt Fackler

WARNING: *Never use lead shot with steel shot data and never use steel shot with lead shot data. Lead and steel pellets have drastically different ballistic properties and to mistakenly use one for the other can cause serious property damage and/or personal injury—even death.*

CONTENTS

Introduction

THE ESSENTIAL DESIGN of the shotshell cartridge has remained with us for 150 years with the same objective: to improve the shooter's chances of hitting a moving target by shooting multiple projectiles. How we have achieved that objective over the years has evolved with several monumental changes to basic components of the loads.

The shotshell industry is a fiercely dynamic, science-based one. Every once in a while, the design of a shotshell component is tweaked and this change spurs an entirely new philosophical approach to making a load. While this is uncomfortable to large-scale shell manufacturers who kick and scream before changing their systems, most innovations are gladly accepted by handloaders who put them into production as soon as the components are available.

Centerfire shooters and reloaders deal with a single, usually streamlined, projectile. Centerfire objectives are generally limited to accuracy at a given range, though hunters often consider transferred energy, too. Shotguns, on the other hand, are a multi-application tool. If we choose to do so, shotshell handloaders can load a large single projectile, too, and take big game effectively at moderate ranges. In another load, we may decide to completely alter the ingredients and make a grouse load. Try that with a 30-30! Because there are so many variables to play with, an individual loader's personality is often reflected in his or her loads.

As an example, let's consider Mary: She is petite, loves to shoot Sporting Clays, but cannot tolerate the recoil produced by $1^1/_8$-ounce factory target loads. These loads were created for the manufacturer's vision of a "typical" target shooter, that is, an average-size male. By loading her own shells and applying an understanding of specific shotshell ballistics, Mary can utilize different amounts or different types of key elements of the load to reduce recoil. The reduced recoil will help keep her shooting competitively all day long.

It is not cost-effective for factories with high-speed loading machines to offer many different types of target loads. They would not be price competitive because there are not enough Marys out there to make manufacturing light recoil loads economically feasible. Manufacturers prefer, instead, that shotgunners alter their shooting style to accommodate the factory-made "everyday" shotshell with its less specialized, less expensive ingredients.

Specialization is one advantage of loading your own shotshells. Mary can easily buy specific load data—light recoil loads are listed in this very publication. There are shot bushings that will drop proper powder and shot charges for lighter recoil, and she can take advantage of specialized powders and specialized wads. Chances are, her custom combination of components will exceed the performance of a standard factory load, and without the punishing recoil. It wouldn't be surprising if John, her teammate, begged a few shells from her toward the end of the day.

Loads can also be created to accommodate special guns. Do you have a fine lightweight English double barrel weighing about $6^1/_2$ pounds? With just that information we know you have a very specialized shotgun, never intended to shoot heavy magnum hunting loads. It is built on a very light frame and the barrels are thin and fine. This is a carrying gun, meant to travel easily and swing on a bird with grace. The loads that shotgun was designed for are game loads, different than those we are used to shooting. This gun was designed to shoot $1^1/_8$-ounce loads without shotcups. A handloader will be able to closely follow the design intent of this fine English double, understanding design objective and form, where someone using off-the-shelf ammo may compromise the shotgun's design.

By handling all the individual components that collectively make a load, a shooter will become more in touch with the requirements of shooting conditions. Picking up a box of shells off the shelf keeps pellet sizes and their applications abstract. Studying the various sizes and parts of a shotshell, and considering the conditions under which they will be used, connects a shooter with all the elements of the sport—the game, environmental conditions, shotgun and, of course, ammunition.

I have been a part of shotgun ammunition's growth since the 1970s. I watched the industry deftly adapt to a fundamentally different design philosophy when steel shot was mandated late in that decade. Ammunition and the shotguns themselves had to change overnight, and did. That result took bright and innovative people who, by their very nature, tend to squabble over their principles and axioms. Those squabbles are part and parcel of the dichotomy between a rapidly developing science and established manufacturing procedures. Both sides speak the truth as they know it on particular issues, but, luckily, the proof is always in the pudding.

Better loads, coincidentally, go hand in hand with better shooting. Certainly you have pondered a missed shot somewhere along the way, looked the empty case over and wondered whether that miss was the ammunition's fault. Maybe the target was outside of the effective pattern. Maybe you should have shot sooner. However, what if we changed the odds and adopted ammunition that accommodated *your* style of shooting? Improved ammunition is certain to increase your odds, and in any percentage game, such as shotgunning, that's an advantage.

We have outlined several performance advantages of specialized handloads. I am sure there are several readers, maybe even you, who are wondering when we will get down to the cost issues. Saving money is terrific, and you are going to recoup your investment in this book just by creating your own loads, but why not apply yourself a little and get a lot more return? This book is your vehicle. Once you have grasped the reasons why each component exists, and exactly what it does, you will have a better understanding of all shotshells and what they will accomplish, even if you never make a single load. Perhaps you now use one type of load for all of your shotgunning; are you one of those who "just aims" better than the next guy? Then maybe you are just a good shooter when you could be a great shooter. "I just aim better" means easy pickings for accomplished shooters who load their own. Bring your money when we shoot together, especially under extremely difficult conditions. Using one load for all your shooting is like a carpenter using a crow bar as a hammer. Using the proper tools will make you a better shooter (or carpenter if you finally start using a hammer).

Inexperienced shooters commonly view the shotshell as a plastic, sausage-like casing containing mysterious, unidentifiable elements. It isn't. Each component of a shotshell serves a purpose, and together these components create what we know as a *load*. The components of a load can be changed to improve the performance of that load. Usually this is accomplished by utilizing specific components best suited for a particular condition. For instance, pellet energy at long ranges can be increased with component manipulation. What if your "everyday load" were rated on an arbitrary scale at 50 percent effective beyond 40 yards, and 50 percent effective at less than 40 yards. Now, let's say that a great majority of your day's shooting is going to be beyond 50 yards. What if you could influence your loads toward increased effectiveness at longer range, perhaps 80 percent effective at 40 yards and beyond? Would you consider giving up some effectiveness at shorter ranges for 80 percent effectiveness at longer ranges? By reloading, you have the power to manufacture ammunition for specialized use.

Using and understanding proper applications of specialized ammunition not only does you a favor, but also your game as well. The hunter's goal is to kill game humanely; that is, quickly and effectively. Understand the hunting conditions and understand what you need to do in order to compensate for those conditions. Familiarity, in the case of shotshells, will breed a smarter shooter. We promise.

Start-Up Costs

You are going to have to purchase and set up a certain amount of equipment to manufacture handloads. Start-up costs are the barrier most beginning handloaders have the hardest time overcoming. Tools and equipment add expense up front, so if you are a person who likes to itemize your hobbies and interests, you may have difficulty amortizing the cost of a reloading tool over the first four or five boxes of shells. "The Tool," however, is a vital part of the creation process and a large part of the fun. Tools are good. Reloading presses are tools requiring setup, maintenance, repair and adjustment—kind of like a bass-boat without the nuisance of a trailer, stickers or seaweed. Moreover, reloading presses provide more than low cost ammunition. They provide a hobby—an excuse to "egress." This is an invaluable pretext best utilized when you see unwelcome in-laws darken your front doorstep. Try putting a price tag on that! Just be sure your domestic associate is fully aware of the considerable amount of "uninterrupted train of concentration" required for handloading shotshells. Whilst you lurk in the lair that is your reloading room, others who also reside in your home are obliged to entertain the unentertainable.

The Reloading Hobby

Is reloading a lifestyle choice? Yes, no, maybe—I don't know. Reloading is an escape from a world that offers fewer and fewer opportunities to create tangible goods. As such, reloading is an endeavor of craftsmanship. Reloading produces a tangible product, one that you can hold in your hand and proclaim to anyone who will listen: "Hey, I made this." And unlike other hobbies, you get to go have fun with the product you created. Think about it: If you build custom bird houses, who gets to enjoy them? The birds, of course. The architect of the home is not the one living within and has no reason to improve the functionality of his creation. He will not be the little bird bumping her head on an ill-placed nail. He will probably build the next bird house with a nail in exactly the same unfortunate spot. Whether the birdhouse can be improved or not is lost on the designer/builder; he has lost a direct connection to his product.

Handloads, on the other hand, offer built-in improvement potential, allowing the reloader to consider changes during use. You can use that product, make note of its performance, good or bad, and make the next one better. When improvements are discovered, you get to decide whether or not to tell friends how to improve their shooting. Sometimes it's just good to be an "ace." Celebrate selfish luxury and your ammunition. That's not a bad feeling in a world where creativeness is often abstract and end products are hardly seen or touched.

Now, to achieve these relative plateaus of Nirvana, both on and off the range, we are going to have to learn what actually comprises a functioning shotshell. Keep in mind that sometimes things won't work out so well. But at other times you will see results that will make you proud and astonish your friends. Besides, hobbies are a wonderful way for one to express an obsession, center conversations upon and make you feel alive. Everyone starts at the beginning, and as a shotshell reloader, here is your beginning.

1

The reasons for loading your own ammo are numerous. And all of them are personal.

Why Reload?

ONE OF THE best reasons to reload shotshells is simply to learn how and why ammunition is put together, so that an informed decision can be made on exactly what load is needed to get the job done with the shooting conditions at hand. It does not matter if the shotshells are factory-made or custom-made — an informed shooter will know what shell is best for every situation.

The shotgun is a limited-use, specialized firearm. Under most circumstances, a shotgun is effectively limited to 50 yards or less. Within that range lies our universe of shooting. Functioning within this universe requires physical skill, a mastery of timing, a certain domination over reactive response, a modicum of physical conditioning and specific cognitive skills.

Several of these skills are self-explanatory. It's pretty obvious to most that good timing will help the shooter track a speeding target. A modicum of physical conditioning will help you carry your shotgun to the field, lift it to your shoulder and absorb recoil without wilting you into a puddle. Domination over a reactive response involves a couple of factors. First, you are going to have to smoothly follow-through with your shot even though every fiber of instinct screams at you to clutch up and flinch. Our bodies, conditioned like Pavlov's dogs, know there is going to be a loud bang followed a millisecond later by an unpleasant recoil jolt. Not clutching up and flinching is a trick of mind over instinct, but physical conditioning will also help as you will be able to maintain a higher level of concentration for longer periods of time. Cognitive skills refer to those of the brain. A knowledgeable shooter goes out into the field prepared to do the best job possible by way of familiarity with his firearm. This level of heightened familiarity is where certain steps of the firing process become automatic.

Automatic familiarity is a level requiring little conscious thought to perform a task. Operating your television's remote control is a good example. For most of us, our thumb makes its way to the "channel up" button with little conscious directive. However, I'll bet the first few times you used that remote you had to *consciously* find the buttons then plod up and down the meager program offerings before becoming completely familiar with the gizmo's operations. Similar rules apply to your shotgun and its use.

The remaining item, cognitive skills as they pertain to your loads, yes, *your* loads, is one of great importance, because proper loads are the connection between you and your target. By planning your loads and using the best possible combination of ingredients, you improve your chances of connecting with the target.

How does one gain enough experience to know which shells work best under specific conditions? By reloading. Reloading teaches you why this load or that one works best. It also pushes the shooter down a pathway of experience by permitting more shooting for less money. I once had a reloader tell me that he never saved a dollar by reloading, but he shot a lot more. Perhaps this fellow said it all. Load more, shoot more. You will become a better shot, and you will make and use better loads.

Become a Thinking Reloader

The shooter who understands and utilizes the better load in each and every situation has an advantage over an unprepared shooter. Learn from your loads. From the start, the reloader is faced with decisions. First, what load do you want to make? This means you need to know something about hulls, powders, wads, primers and shot. You need to know how to bundle these items together to make a safe, predictable load that shoots in the manner you expect and intend.

Because there are multitudes of variables that can affect exactly how your loads will work, I will make several assumptions prior to describing your load's effect in certain situations. For instance, choke may be listed in our text as Improved Cylinder, but we know that not everyone is going to use Improved Cylinder for all their shooting. If you use Modified, instead, bear in mind that your final outcome generally will be a tighter pattern than we describe.

Being prepared with the right ammunition can go a long way toward shooting success. I have heard of no one fast enough to unscrew and replace a choke tube for a follow-up shot at the same target. However, we can accommodate single-barrel shooters with loads designed for looser or tighter patterns at a given range. This is an easy advantage, requiring only preparation and understanding of your equipment. No

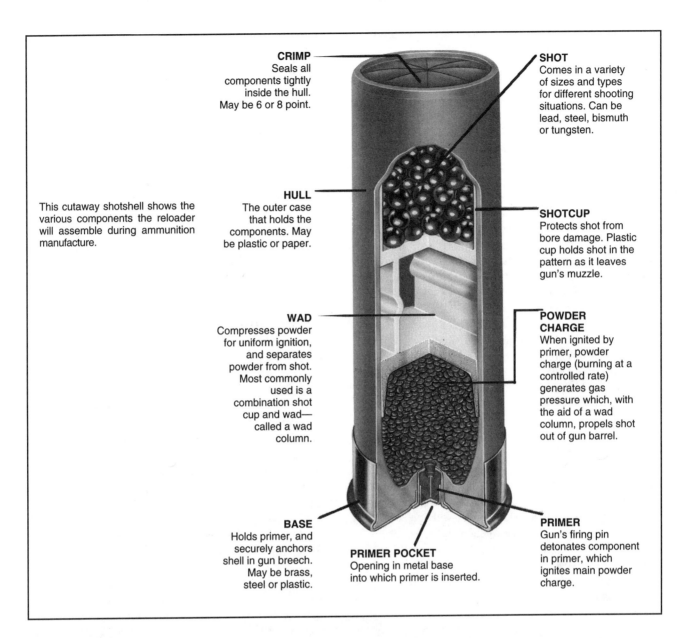

CRIMP
Seals all components tightly inside the hull. May be 6 or 8 point.

SHOT
Comes in a variety of sizes and types for different shooting situations. Can be lead, steel, bismuth or tungsten.

This cutaway shotshell shows the various components the reloader will assemble during ammunition manufacture.

HULL
The outer case that holds the components. May be plastic or paper.

SHOTCUP
Protects shot from bore damage. Plastic cup holds shot in the pattern as it leaves gun's muzzle.

WAD
Compresses powder for uniform ignition, and separates powder from shot. Most commonly used is a combination shot cup and wad— called a wad column.

POWDER CHARGE
When ignited by primer, powder charge (burning at a controlled rate) generates gas pressure which, with the aid of a wad column, propels shot out of gun barrel.

BASE
Holds primer, and securely anchors shell in gun breech. May be brass, steel or plastic.

PRIMER POCKET
Opening in metal base into which primer is inserted.

PRIMER
Gun's firing pin detonates component in primer, which ignites main powder charge.

one can say for sure how many more targets you will hit, but you will hit more.

A lot of shooting school time is dedicated to target anticipation, expectation and gun control. This is reactive shooting: dealing with the target after it has been presented to you. Thus, "reaction" entails the associated skills that deal with the presented target. The point is, preparation works hand in hand with shooting skills, and it's not just one or the other.

Active Shooting

Active shooting, as we will deal with it in these pages, refers to factors one can control prior to ever seeing a target. Perhaps an analogy will help you understand my use of the term "active": The active suspension used in ultra-high-tech Grand Prix race cars predicts bumps in the road and deals with them prior to contact. This allows drivers to go faster than they otherwise could. Less stress is placed upon the suspension since the system softens the spring and shock absorber. If that wheel is allowed to move upward an instant before it takes the full hit of

a bump, less energy is transferred through that wheel to the frame.

In shotgunning, we should rely slightly less on our cat-like reflexes and eagle eyes to deal with targets. We should prefer to hone our skills as predictors of the forthcoming targets. If we can plan ahead for specific shooting situations, even a little bit, we can greatly reduce the burden on our reactive shooting skills. Think of it as a balancing act—you want to get as much over to the active side as possible in order to have fewer worries when your time to shoot comes.

Using specific-application components to better suit a target will, likewise, create conditions for a more desirable outcome—namely hitting your target.

Your shotgun, no matter how well designed for the task, cannot overcome second-rate ammunition, and you cannot make ill-suited loads shoot beyond their potential. A crummy load can make a good shooter look like an amateur. Deny the importance of quality and varied ammunition and you will shoot all the years of your life with a high handicap. Ammunition is the shooter's least expensive yet most important variable. With knowledge, it can be put to your advantage.

Who's Going to Help?

Reloading is one of those endeavors about which nearly everyone will offer a dabble of advice. There are many "experts." In my daily contact with reloaders I have learned to first patiently let them tell me about handloading. This can be time-consuming because reloading involves shooting, and conversations tend to digress. Often, I have to be careful to preserve fragile egos as finding answers to reloading questions becomes a detective game. Before ever asking me if two particular components are compatible, a caller is compelled by some sort of unseen shotshell inquiry momentum to describe why a particular component is exactly what he needs for his particular application. He wants to know why the rest of the components cannot be forced to accommodate that singular product. My muted response: "Arrggh!"

To become a knowledgeable loader, you first have to be willing to learn and to trust. Choosing who to trust is your first task. Remember the golden rule of shotshell reloading: There are no fixed variables that create the "perfect load." The perfect load, as hopefully you have ascertained by now, is an elusive character, forever in company and utterly dependant upon the circumstances of your shooting.

Identify Your Needs

Consider your shooting. To get started, make a list of your shooting objectives and circle the category that represents your greatest interest, but not necessarily your greatest expenditure of shells. By narrowing the field a bit, you will be able to focus your questions about that type of shooting. Asking specific questions will net specific answers, the information you need right now. Soon you will be able to generalize these skills for use with your other loads. Rome was not built in a day, and you cannot learn everything with one telephone call.

Understand, right off the bat, that you will not make one type of powder, hull, wad or pellet work for all of your hunting and target shooting. As you begin reloading, the temptation will be great to use only those components you thoroughly understand. If you try to do this, someone, somewhere, will give you the answers you want to hear; you may wind up using #7½s on geese just because you had that shot left over from your trap

loads. Be willing to try some new things. It's fun and interesting to find load data using new and different components.

Sources of Information

Shotshell component manufacturers are usually a good place to start in your quest for information. They have tested most conceivable combinations of components and have a wealth of data available. For the most part, they will be willing to share their experiences with you, and all you have to do is ask.

Start by selecting a certain component that, according to test reports or advertisements, seems to suit one or more of your shooting needs. Perhaps this will be a particular hunting wad found to be effective for wind-driven pheasants. You see this and think that it might be just the ticket for your late season hunt in South Dakota, where the cover is sparse and the birds fly fast.

To find out more about this product, take another look at the reports and then contact the writer or manufacturer. Magazines usually list sources of particular products, sometimes with an address or a phone number, usually at the end of articles. Next, organize your questions into a specific order. Trust me, nothing is harder for a technical assistant to deal with than someone on the other end of a phone saying: "I want to make a load." That's usually the beginning of that terrible, protracted game of "reload detective." Instead, try this approach: "I saw your product, the X-19 Field Wad featured in the May issue of 'A Lot of Shotguns.' I am going to South Dakota to shoot pheasants and would like to know how to best use your product."

If you present this request, I will just about guarantee that you'll wind up with excellent load advice, from powder and shot selection right up to optimum payload. If you ask a tech rep to find a load that accommodates your on-hand components, he will try his best to find a fit, but I can't guarantee those results. Load for your conditions.

Dealers operate under similar scenarios as manufacturers. More often than not, they are enthusiasts and have tried everything in the store. Walking into a reloading shop and bluntly asking for the best load for a particular condition is not the worst way to go. You will certainly gain more respect from the store personnel than if you begin with your own limited opinion.

Reloading involves personal selection of various components. I have only one sure-fire way to qualify the expertise of someone dispensing advice: Is that person scratching his head

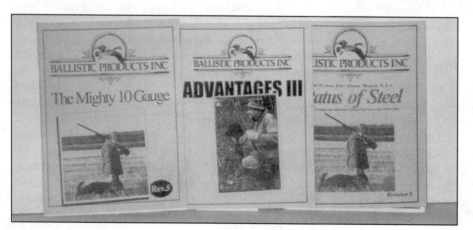

Shotshell component manufacturers are usually an excellent place to start in your quest for load data information.

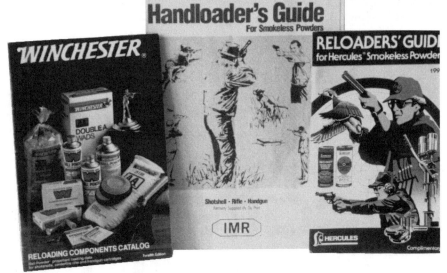

At least two data sources are required to confirm the load you select and prevent the potential of using a load that was printed with an error. Check the loads found in this book against the powder manufacturer's data.

and mumbling various component names and configurations while getting a slightly glazed look in his eyes when answering your questions? If you're looking to find a particular load, you've found your guy. Basing your conversation on the knowledge you've gained here, in combination with his specific advice, you will be set up with some great loads.

Your best option is to first read this book, understand the components as we present them, and select some loads from the over 14,000 presented in our load data section. Most modern configurations are listed in these pages, so maybe you won't have to go very far after all. All the loads use components that are currently available or recently popular.

Building Great Hunting Loads

The reloading bench can define the quality of your shotgunning. To become a better shooter an average reloader can learn specific load recipes for specific applications. By using these loads, a reloader will come to understand the nature and ingredients of higher quality loads.

To the shooter who has never reloaded a shotshell, reloading may seem complicated and offer small returns for the investment. Those who do reload can identify better shells by their components, realizing that reloading is far from complicated. Instead, the process is a series of logical steps to produce a most efficient product. Having the means at your disposal to create very, very good loads, and especially those which have a specific function in your hunting, is an automatic shooting advantage. You can produce loads in your basement that far exceed what you can buy off the shelf.

Handloading provides you with superior ammunition because each load is hand-crafted, each load given the attention and scrutiny no machine can duplicate. Many special handloading components cannot be run through high-speed factory-type loading machines. But you can select individual components that provide payload and pellet speeds that are suited to your type of shooting. Because you are aware of the components within your shotshells, reloading ammunition provides you with insight into the world of ballistics, and that makes you a better judge of what loads to use in any given situation.

Of course, money can be saved by loading your own shotshells. You have the opportunity to select components that offer the best value for your applications. During many years of hunting, I have noticed that some hunters will try to save money by using cheap, inappropriate ammunition. When you have waited months for the season to arrive, scrimped and saved to go hunting, tweaked your gun to perfection, trained your dog in everything except algebra, and enveloped yourself in the finest outdoor wear, why would you let your ammunition be a weak link in your chain of success? High quality ammunition appropriate to the hunting conditions is a minor percentage of your total cash outlay, but can make the difference between getting skunked or filling out. Many times I have been asked, "How did you make that shot?" The question should be, "How did you make that shell?" We do shoot well with better loads.

As you become a better handloader you will become more mindful of the area you will be hunting, the weather conditions, terrain and ranges. You become more successful more often. Your shotshells become a source of personal pride. When pride is involved so is a great deal of personal satisfaction when your loads work well for you.

The major point is that you can do better in the field by reloading. Reloading is a lot like hunting. If it were easy, you would probably find it very boring. High-quality reloads are similar to all things in this world of high quality: Hard work, skill, knowledge and care are as important as any of the tangible parts.

On the other hand, many things can go wrong with a sloppy, poorly constructed handload. Ammunition is a fairly accurate mirror of the person who assembled it. Each skill level you attain will produce slightly better loads. After a certain point, each improvement may add just a tiny bit more, but then, many times, the advantage you are seeking is just as minute.

A number of factors come together to make one load perform better than another. Some items can be measured and some can't. Patterns can be measured, but I have seen loads that pattern great on paper then perform poorly in the field. Lethal content of a load is more difficult to measure, because at various ranges and with different shot sizes, a good load can become a poor load. Also, different shotguns can turn a great load upside down and even cause a poor load to perform better (I want that shotgun). What works well in one 12-gauge gun may not perform well in another.

2

Over the centuries, the science of shotguns and loads has come a long way, but the fundamentals haven't changed.

Scattergun and Shotshell Evolution

PRESUMABLY, CLOSE UPON the heels of discovering the possibilities of using multiple projectiles on moving targets, some early flintlock shooter became an anonymous pioneer of waterfowling. Multiple projectiles have the advantage of increasing the likelihood of hitting a moving target, making shotgunning a game of percentages. Luckily, unlike fortress walls, waterfowl require a bit less than several hundred tons of transferred energy in order to be harvested, allowing the use of smaller projectiles. Since the earliest days, shotguns have found various, specialized niches and sub-categories.

Early flintlock smoothbores were often handmade works of art. Each was an individual endeavor of a particular craftsman that adhered to his particular notions of the perfect firearm. Gun-making in this tradition, perhaps viewed as primitive now, is a relatively lost art. The number of living craftsmen with the patience, skill and ability to apply these skills are few and far between. If you have the opportunity to visit the firearms museum in Cody, Wyoming, spend a moment with some of their examples and try to imagine the tools, or lack thereof, used to manufacture the exacting mechanisms found in these pieces. I guarantee, there was no cement-floored, brightly lit shop with CNC tools. With the hours of craftsmanship involved, I have often wondered how anyone could have afforded a flintlock smoothbore.

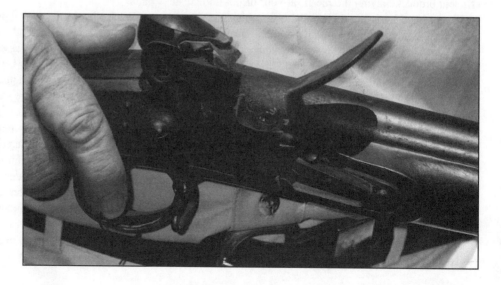

This is an early flintlock shotgun. Note the powder pan, touch hole, flint and frizzen. Many flintlock smoothbores were handmade works of art.

The percussion shotgun followed the flintlock in shotgun design evolution. It proved more reliable since the powder charge was contained within the bore and protected from the elements.

Like many mechanical devices that technology has passed by, the flintlock may seem charming now, but evolution happens for reasons of practicality. The percussion cap brought with it reliability and convenience. It was not uncommon for a flintlock to require several strikes before igniting. The pan of powder sat more or less out in the elements just waiting for that raindrop to render it ineffective. Percussion caps were much more reliable and, for the most part, watertight. They also brought the added advantage of faster loading cycles. From these caps have evolved our modern-day primers.

The History of Chokes and Bores

Early muzzle-loading shotguns had constrictions at the rear of the barrels which offered a narrower channel for powder and greater wall thickness for a thicker chamber section without altering the exterior barrel dimensions. Thicker chamber sections improved strength in this critical area of the firearm. Of course, for better sighting, one prefers the barrel plane (the outside of the barrel) to be flat and level—hence the interior alterations. Until the mid-19th century, everyone used Cylinder bores (no constriction) and thought nothing of it.

Cylinder barrels, those without a choke, were the only thing available and necessary in the early years. Why? Because in the days of muzzleloaders, there were no pattern disrupters built into the equation. First, there was no hull; combustion took place inside the chamber itself. Second, there was no forcing cone, or funneled transition area, between the larger chamber and the narrower barrel itself.

Without a hull and without a forcing cone, our muzzle-loaded round continues down the smooth bore without disruption or areas of transition to deform otherwise round pellets, saving their roundness for straight flight. It should also be noted that payloads were not excessive (the 12-gauge often did not exceed $1^1/_8$ ounces) and velocities were less than hurried; initial setback forces were not enough to deform the pellets. Balanced muzzleloaded charges, constructed as such, would make the owner of a modern $15,000 shotgun cry if he made pattern comparisons. At 35 to 40 yards, patterns from those old muzzleloaders can be things of beauty. With progress comes complexity.

Most folks, especially the English, have credited the English as the source of choking a barrel. This is based upon Englishman W.R. Pape's 1866 patent of the boring technique. Whether it was applied as a pattern control device at that time, no one seems to know for sure. Nonetheless, an American market hunter may have played a more practical role in developing a workable application of bore constriction.

Noting the increased range effect of water by constricting the nozzle of a firehose, Fred Kimble, a market hunter out of Illinois, took a new look at his 6-bore shotgun and considered the similarities between a stream of water and a payload of birdshot. After re-working his shotgun and giving the barrel a heavy taper at the muzzle end, he took the firearm out to the field and conducted (probably one of the earliest) pattern tests. Unfortunately, results were not very good. Mr. Kimble had overdone it. The acute taper ruined the pattern, sending pellets all over the place. Noting that the taper did affect the pattern, he removed a goodly amount of the constriction and tried again. Aha, there it was! One of shotgunning's very first choke-controlled patterns. After some more fiddling he found he could eventually put all of his 6-bore's $1^1/_2$-ounce lead charge within a 30-inch circle at 40 yards.

Choke and Shot Volume

Kimble's first escapade into choke engineering demonstrates a problem we have seen with heavily choked, modern-day turkey guns. Muzzle constriction can and does reach a point of diminishing returns. Usually a tip-off to this condition is concurrent use of overly-heavy loads with a very tightly choked shotgun. A load of $1^3/_8$ ounces in the 12-gauge occupies considerably less space than does a 2-ounce load. If both are fired through the same choke, the $1^3/_8$-ounce load offers a greater likelihood of compliance without undue disruption as there is simply less shot to move around. If, however, the shooter decides to use the heavy-duty 2-ounce load, all those pellets, like the $1^3/_8$-ounce load, reach the choking area as a collective glob. Well, we know each pellet will interact more strongly with each other pellet. Confusion ensues, and likely as not a larger percentage of pellets will react to the directional influences of each other rather than to the choke. Try to imagine sending varying numbers of marbles down a long ramp and through a narrowing chute. Even more analogous is a row of toll booths. Your car is a pellet, and as additional cars/pellets are funneled through the gates, things slow down. Similarly, large payloads require less constriction than a lighter load to achieve similar patterns. Though he did not know it during

13

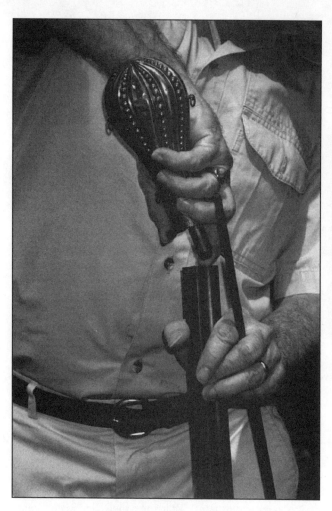

The loading procedures for modern and blackpowder percussion shotguns are quite different, but the components are still similar. In this sequence, David Fackler shows the loading sequence. First a powder charge is metered from the powder flask. The flask is tipped to move powder from the flask chamber into the neck of the flask. The gate of the powder flask is shut and the finger removed from the mouth to allow the powder to fall into the chamber. Next, an overpowder wad is rammed down over the powder charge and then an exact amount of birdshot dropped from the shot carrier. The charge is rammed home, an overshot wad is inserted, a percussion cap is placed on the nipple and the shotgun is ready to fire.

those first experiments, this problem of interior ballistics affected Mr. Kimble's results.

Mr. Kimble learned that the best way to build a choked barrel was to bore out the barrel to a larger specific diameter behind the muzzle, then slowly remove material from the muzzle area until he had the choke and, thus, patterns he desired.

The relationship between bore diameter and the amount and size of shot Mr. Kimble used had as much, if not more, effect upon the patterns as the careful metal cutting to achieve an improved pattern. Chokes can be reamed out to perfectly accommodate specific loads, but change the load and some other choke constriction may become "optimal." Same holds true today. With the advent and popular use of screw-in chokes, bore constriction, luckily, has become a variable we can change upon a whim. However, prior to the era of a pocketful of chokes, the burden of pattern accommodation fell solely upon the shooter and his ammunition. Later, you will see some of the specific load recommendations for a specific bore and say to yourself, "Geez, the factories don't even offer those kinds of loads." Well, you're right. That's why you have taken ammunition matters into your own hands.

As Mr. Kimble improved his skills as a choke maker, he made several replicas of his Full-choked (tightest possible pattern) designs and sent them out into the world. One went to a Mr. Schaefer of Boston, Massachusetts, and another to a Mr. W.W. Greener in England. That's the significant one we hinge

our argument upon, because shortly thereafter Mr. Greener came out with his famous choked-bore shotguns and cleaned up at English shooting trials. But it is Fred Kimble's design, with only slight refinements, that remains as the fundamental model we use for our chokes today. And, I will be happy to argue this point with English friends in their favorite pub over thick, dark beer.

Shotgun Gauge and Evolution

The English were already an industrialized nation in the 19th century, and as such, they created many of the standards we continue to use in shotgunning. One of these is gauge. Since bore diameter is a portion and product of ballistics and predictable shooting results, it is natural that ballistics were utilized in a bore-sizing formula. This thinking is an early and important step in placing the ballistic horse before the ballistic cart. This classical and intriguing relationship boiled down to a rule of thumb that lives on today: The weight of a round lead ball, if it is the same diameter as the inside of the barrel, is likely the most efficient and, therefore the best, lead charge weight for that bore to shoot in multiple pellet form. A logical step of evolving this formula was to designate a common means of describing a common function.

A 1-pound unit of lead was used. The pound of lead was cast into a certain number of round balls. Of one size, you can make twelve balls. Of another size, you will get twenty balls out of

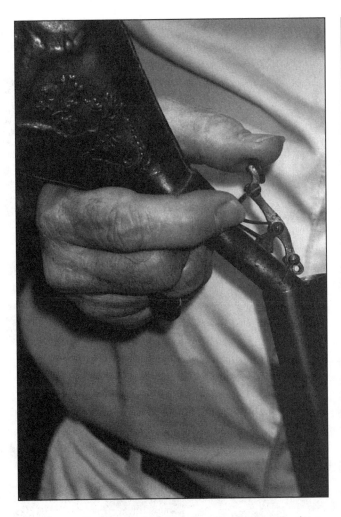

that pound of lead. One particular diameter got exactly sixteen rounds (1-ounce each) out of that pound of lead. Can you guess which gauge this was? If you said 16 you are right. It also just so happens that 1-ounce loads are typically optimal for the 16-gauge. Other gauges require higher math skills and as such we leave them to you and your calculator.

Thus was created a system of standard bore definition. Somehow along the way, the ballisticians decided to stay on the even count—although a few odd sizes have been made—sticking us probably forever with the term "odd-ball."

Where did the 410-gauge come from then? It didn't. Gauge is simply a handy moniker in the case of the 410. If we were to apply the system of gauge to this particular caliber, we would come up with the 36-gauge. The 410 refers specifically to the caliber (about one-tenth under a half-inch).

You may be interested to know that the 410 evolved not as a beginner's gun, the status it has today, but rather as the choice of at least one standout expert, Annie Oakley. In order to accommodate the confines of Buffalo Bill's Wild West Shows, Annie Oakley used the 410-bore. By using extremely light loads and fine pellets, the projectiles would not carry sufficient energy to cause harm nor damage, yet held enough energy to accomplish the feats for which she became a legend.

European Shotguns

Around the beginning of the 20th century, $2\frac{1}{2}$-inch car-

tridges containing $1\frac{1}{16}$ ounces of lead were the 12-gauge standard in England. English game is usually middling in size (pheasants and such) and ranges are not exceptional, so this standard was not without merit. England was also home for many of the finest smoothbore gunmakers. Furthermore, being the home of industrialization that it was, we see little reason why English influences should not have swayed acceptance of the 12 as the "standard" gauge. Modern shotgunning has redefined the 12-gauge, but English doubles were its roots.

On the European continent, particularly amongst Belgian and German shooters, the 16-gauge was favored for its long-distance versatility. The 16 shoots a very effective 1-ounce game load, and is very comfortable to carry over the long haul.

European 16s have been traditionally manufactured with light frames and thin, fine barrels, mainly to keep the guns as light as possible. Most of these lighter doubles weighed around 6 pounds.

Unlike the smallest gauges that sometimes wind up mismatched to hunting conditions, the 16 is a capable shooter and will not leave one under-gunned when loaded properly. Purveyors of the 16 know these attributes well. They also know their 16 will encourage a lady into learning shotgun skills where she might otherwise be afraid of the larger, harder recoiling guns. Moderate recoil will inspire confidence in young or beginning shooters, improve accuracy and reduce flinch in the experienced shooter, and give an old man a chance to fire parting shots.

All shotgun gauges have a range of optimal payloads. We can work into the gray area of light and heavy, but should not overdo it. Payloads above optimum become subject to the scattergun's particular brand of diminishing returns: At a certain point with every gauge, velocity drops dramatically, pressures climb quickly and patterns become uncontrollable.

The light-framed doubles should be reserved for upland game and hunts where there is a lot of walking; that is their intended purpose on this world. Light 16-gauge shotguns will move swiftly into shooting position, similar to a good 20-gauge gun. The 16-gauge's agility is complemented by very hard hitting 1-ounce loads. This is where the 16 holds an advantage over the 20: 1-ounce loads are heavy in a 20-gauge, patterns become difficult to control and the shotgun as well as shooter are stressed by excessive recoil. At 1 ounce, the 20-gauge is overloaded and delivers diminished returns. However, we find that the 20-gauge is in its realm with $7/8$-ounce payloads.

We know most folks have used large-capacity loads in these various gauges. Fine. What we are observing is the optimum capacity for the various gauges. If you insist on running heavy magnum loads through a light upland double, it is akin to pushing a motor to its limits. It will do it, but not as long as it would at a moderate pace. Use your light double as it was intended, and you will be able to use it for a very, very long time. If you want to exceed the performance of a certain gauge, use a bigger gauge, not a bigger shell.

North American Influences

North American shooters introduced scattergun applications that were quite different than the Europeans. We had these great big open spaces where the curvature of the earth is contemplated when gazing upon the horizon. Our shotguns have to accommodate these great distances on the plains. A secondary and rather uniquely North American influence was the predicament of game acquisition. Since wild game was in abundance on the frontier, and the frontier was the frontier, shooters went after it as a staple for dinner. Wild game harvesting made economic sense at that time in our history, whether it was headed directly to the table or turned into income at the market.

To accommodate these shooting conditions, American shooters developed a preference for larger gauges and more powerful ammunition. From the late 1800s into the turn of the century, the 10-gauge became more or less accepted as the standard North American waterfowler. Early 10-gauge loads contained $1^{1}/_{4}$ ounces of shot inside cases that were $2^{7}/_{8}$ inches long. Today, this seems very light, but sheds some light on how the 10 was used in those days. The larger bore, as discovered with overboring these days, offers improved patterns throughout the effective range, to perhaps 50 yards.

American Gauge Applications

My father uses the 10-gauge for prairie waterfowling. He selects loads ranging between $1^{1}/_{4}$ ounces for small ducks on up to ultra-heavy 2-ounce loads for very nasty conditions. By taking advantage of specific load selections, effective ranges run between 35 and 80 yards. His kills are clean and he does

A fine example of an old blunderbuss. Blunderbusses were specifically designed for multi-projectile loads.

not tolerate crippling birds. More often than not, he uses the 10 as a tool for clean up, particularly on the occasions that a 12-gauge shooter has overestimated his effective range and only touched a bird. The 10-gauge can push tighter patterns of larger shot faster and with more energy than a 12-gauge. The reasons are a formula of bore diameter and ballistic principles that are inarguable. There was a gent who accompanied us, once, on a trip to the prairie lands for an annual foray into the Central Flyway. This fellow was certain that his skills with a 12 were equal to anyone's with a 10—gauge differences and specialization be damned. Well, my father quietly tolerated this chap's drivel for the duration of the 480 miles to our destination, and then into the evening. The next day, while hunting, my father spotted an incoming flock of snow geese. He took a moment to calculate and took aim. I knew what to expect next:

SUGGESTED GAUGE, SHOT SIZE AND CHOKE FOR VARIOUS GAME AND HUNTING CONDITIONS

Game	Gauge	Shot size	Choke
Ducks	10,12,16,20	2,4,5 or 6	Full to Mod.
Crows	10,12,16,20	2,4,5 or 6	Full
Geese	10 or 12	BB,2,4,5	Full
Pheasant	12,16,20,28	5,6,7½	Full to Mod.
Partridge or Grouse	12,16,20,28	6,7½,8	Mod. to Imp. Cyl.
Quail	12,16,20,28 or 410	6,7½,8.9	Mod. to Imp. Cyl.
Dove/Pigeons	12,16,20,28, or 410	6,7½,8	Mod.
Woodcock	12,16,20,28, or 410	6,7½,8	Mod. to Imp. Cyl.
Rabbits	12,16,20,28, or 410	4,5,6,7½	Full to Imp. Cyl.
Squirrels	12,16,20,28, or 410	4,5,6	Full to Imp. Cyl.
Rail	12,16,20,28, or 410	7½,8,9	Mod. to Imp. Cyl.
Turkeys	12,16 or 20 3″ mag.	BB,2,4,5	Full
Fox	12,16 or 20	BB, 2 buck	Full
Coyotes	12,16 or 20 3″ mag.	3 or 4 buck	Full
Deer or Black Bear	12	Rifled slug	Cyl. bore

A baritone bark of the mighty 10 and one of the geese did a forward roll (executing an excellent imitation of a sack full of potatoes), landing with a whoosh-thud in Mr. Know It All's blind. From that blind, all I could see were eyeballs. Mr. Know it All spent the rest of the hunt watching the sky for feathered 10-12-pound bombs.

Extended Chambers

An excellent development in 10-gauge shooting was the 3½-inch chamber. The larger 10-gauge bore easily handles this ratio of length and diameter, and solidified the 10's reputation as North America's range shotgun. Preferred loads for the 3½-inch magnum 10 run between 1½ and 1⅞ ounces. Configurations ranging between these weights take full advantage of the powder, velocity and pattern density relationship.

Other gauges also have utilized extended chamber lengths to accommodate heavier payloads; some, in my opinion, with mixed results. Most recently, the 12-gauge has also been extended to the 3½-inch length. Whether that additional space should automatically be filled with extra shot is a question most often put to us as ballisticians. Hull length, by itself, does not make for a sudden, extraordinary shift in performance or capabilities. At 3½ inches, the same overall length as a 10-gauge, there is space inside the hull for an exceptionally heavy payload. In using a 3½-inch 12-gauge, the shooter has to remember the limitations of bore diameter. In any payload equating that of a 10-gauge, the 12-bore, because it is narrower, is going to have an extended payload length. As payloads become elongated, internal ballistics become increasingly complicated.

The trick with the 3½-inch 12-gauge is to find its domain, create loads suitable for that application, and utilize all of its potential. It is not, alas, an all-around shotgun for all of your

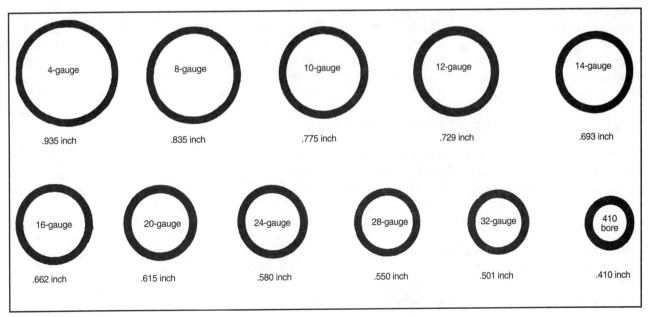

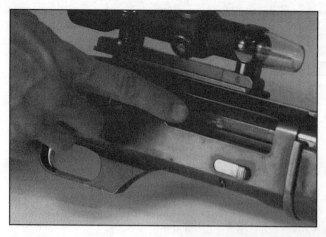
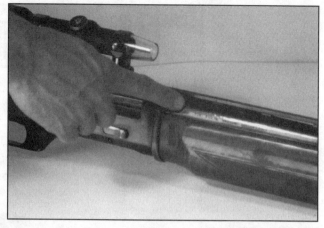

The receiver, chamber and choke on a modern-day shotgun.

shooting needs. That goes back to our carpenter mentioned earlier, the guy using the crowbar for all his carpentry needs.

Emergence Of The 12-Gauge

The 10-gauge is not for everyone. It requires definite commitment on the part of the shooter. The ammunition, whether reloaded or purchased, is expensive. You use a lot of slow-burning powder, generally larger shot charges, and the wads are specially made to take advantage of the long-range shooting. Furthermore, it makes a terrible Skeet gun for Wednesday night league shoots.

Physically, not everyone is up to the demands of the 10-gauge. Shooting a box of shells can be punishing, leaving a shooter with a 10-gauge hangover. This monster pushes the threshold of comfortable shooting.

As for comfort level, the 12-bore is probably the universal favorite. Most people can shoot the 12-gauge all day long and suffer little to no ill effect. Of course, your load choice will greatly affect your comfort level. If you shoot an entire box of $1^1/_2$-ounce magnum loads, you will suffer. However, if you instead choose a box of $1^1/_8$-ounce loads and head out to the trap range, you can shoot many rounds before wobbling your brains.

You'll note that the comfortable-shooting $1^1/_8$-ounce 12-gauge load is one we have naturally gravitated toward over the years. No matter what other specialized loads we may use, when it comes to firing a shotgun all day long we usually choose that configuration. The 12-gauge can be described as riding the fence between pleasure and pain, while maximizing effectiveness with a reasonably sized bore diameter. It is ineffective at nothing, and outstanding for many types of shooting. With specialized loads and equipment, we have managed to stretch the range of 12-gauge effectiveness to cover almost all types of hunting and shooting. Understanding the loads we feed it and the conditions we use it in can make this gauge a master of most situations.

In understanding the intricacies of the various shotgun gauges, accomplished shotgunners usually own a number of smoothbores. Though the 12 can be extended toward nearly universal applications, there are situations where you may prefer to take advantage of another gauge and its realm of "expertise." You need more than one shotgun to have a first-hand understanding of firearm diversity. Knowing the differences and which niche each gauge occupies is what makes us smarter shooters and more likely to use specialized loads and firearms correctly. I must warn you though, owning several shotguns quickly becomes very much like Imelda Marcos maintaining her closet full of shoes; you gotta have a few more. Where do you stop? When does Imelda have enough shoes? Or, in our case, when does the hunter have enough shotguns? Perhaps only when the Chevy Suburban no longer has room for the dog!

For the most part, it is not yet a crime to buy and own several shotguns (watch that arsenal legislation). The average hunter needs to own and learn to best apply several gauges and types of shotguns.

When selecting the foundation of your reloading operation, carefully define all of your objectives and needs.

3

Selection, Care And Use of Your Reloading Tools

OVERWHELMED WITH THE great variety of reloading tools available today, the new handloader generally goes to a shooting friend and asks, "What should I buy?" More often than not, the advice is valuable because both partake in the same type of shooting and everyone is happy. Sometimes, though, the new handloader suffers with a machine completely inappropriate for his requirements. He might wonder if his friend is perhaps not so bright after all.

There are as many types of reloading requirements as there are shooters. Two shooters may use their loads for exactly the same type of shooting, but that's where their similarities end. Surely they'll be using different shotguns. Perhaps one uses a gas-operated semi-automatic and his experienced friend uses a double barrel. In this case, the first guy will want to select a reloading tool particularly adept at resizing shells. Since resizing is not of particular concern for the double barrel user, he will not consider resizing in his evaluation of reloading tools.

However, interests change, new guns come along and shooters graduate to different shooting disciplines. This means different tools may be needed to accommodate these changes, so try to anticipate future needs when purchasing equipment.

Reloading Tool Basics

There are no "bad" reloading tools. Perhaps you are ready to jump into reloading, but, in terms of quality and price, would like to have your cake and eat it too. MEC has made the 600 Junior in its basic single-stage form for many years. They almost never wear out, and they're easy to adjust and set up. They are, after all, one of the world's most popular reloaders.

Maybe you're ready to move into some heavy 3-inch loads that require a strong press so you can fully resize your hulls for ultimate dependability. You can't afford to miss a shot because you don't get very many. Maybe you just like the look and feel of cast and machined parts, and don't mind paying a few extra dollars. Then your choice is the Ponsness/Warren Model 375 press.

Are you ready to step up to the ultimate progressive reloader? This one offers top speed as well as superb fit and finish, and you almost hate to get it dirty. It will produce the finest target loads you can imagine. It represents a commitment though. Just getting one means waiting in line until others get theirs. We refer to the Spolar Power Loader.

Make your decisions based on what type of shooting you plan to do and build your set-up accordingly. So, what do you need?

There are two main divisions of reloading presses, the progressive and the single-stage. The differences between the two lie in degrees of operational speed versus load variety.

The Single-Stage Loader

Single-stage presses can assemble just about any hull type with almost any combination of ingredients. Minor adjustments have to be made, but they are few. For your first loading tool, the single-stage calls to you. These presses can be retrofitted to reload almost any gauge and any length hull. Usually the manufacturer can supply kits or individual accessories for the tool, enabling it to accommodate any practical reloading combination.

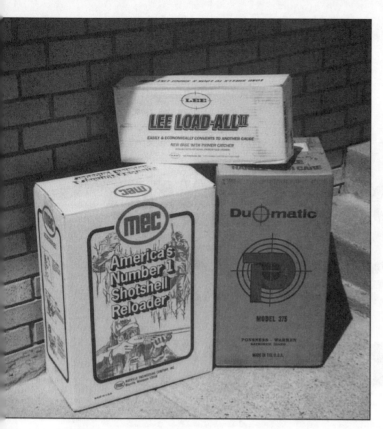

Shotshell reloaders, as delivered from the factory, come boxed with comprehensive assembly instructions.

Single-stage presses require the operator to manually move a hull from station to station until it is finished. When a load is completed, the process is begun again with an empty hull. It may sound boring, but as you craft each shotshell it becomes a form of therapy and in no time a full box of ammunition is loaded. Creating handloads, one at a time, slows a frenetic metabolism and gives you a chance to reflect on the good things in life and the fun these shells will bring, like time in the field, resolution of the physical world's certain mysteries, improved shooting and doing something for yourself. And, of course, not in the least, negotiation skills with your Domestic Associate.

Author Robert Persig used his motorcycle as a metaphor for philosophical discoveries in *Zen and the Art of Motorcycle Maintenance*. You need only go to your reloading room to have a similar experience. It is Zen and the art of handloading!

Single-stage reloading tools come in many varieties. Each will separately reflect its creator's vision of how to create handloads. Take the time to decide what kind of loads you want to make. How many of them do you want, and how quickly? How much cash do you want to lay out to try it? The least expensive machine costs little more than a few boxes of shells, which certainly makes reloading accessible for anyone with the inclination to give it a try.

Remember, single-stage tools don't produce ammunition as fast as progressive reloaders. If you need to produce large volumes of similarly outfitted loads, go with a progressive machine. Otherwise, you may never get out of the reloading room.

Single-stage reloaders can make any type of hunting load while progressive machines are somewhat limited in scope. Also, single-stage presses are easily adjustable and reasonably easy to adapt to other gauges, etc.

There are a couple of single-stage loaders that make excellent training tools. One, the Lee Load-All II, costs little more than ten boxes of target loads. It is a ready-to-go, versatile little machine, and many reloaders have kicked off their hobbies with it. When we were researching machines for this book, an experienced reloader looked at the gleaming new Lee machine we were evaluating and told us about his experiences with one. He bought it as a teenager, and still uses it for some of his loads today, 15 years later. A quick comparison with our new one showed only superficial changes over the years. Remember our comparison of reloaders to cars in terms of reliability? Since first starting out, this handloader has worked his way through several types of machines and currently uses a Ponsness/Warren Model 900 Elite for his target loads. The evolution taught him well, and he has had fun throughout the process.

The Progressive Loader

The progressive reloader is designed to load more than one hull at a time, in stages. It works like an assembly line. As the shell is brought to each station, a particular step is performed until, ultimately, a finished shell is produced.

There are usually ten steps involved in loading a shotshell: hull-insert; resizing; depriming; repriming; powder drop; wad insertion, shot drop; crimp start; crimp finish; finished load and exit. Progressive reloaders are juggling at least eight functions at a time with every pull of the handle. To do this, the device is limited in its range of adjustments. These adjustments may or may not include:

(1) A slight accommodation for manufacturing variations of hulls. In the 12-gauge, most progressive machines are set up for $2^3/_4$-inch hulls. Many companies offer 3-inch, and even $3^1/_2$-inch kits for their progressive reloaders. It is my experience that magnum loads must be assembled on a single-stage reloader because of the specialized component and length requirements. Trying to load hunting loads on any type of progressive machine is an absolute exercise in frustration—no matter what the sales brochure or instruction manual may say. It becomes the ultimate act of compromise, like entering your Harley-Davidson in a motocross.

(2) Wad ram adjustment to accommodate most standard length (target) wads. If you have any notion about using a two-piece wad or any other type of specialized wad, a progressive machine will give you fits. Presume that you will be using standard target wads. Access to the wad insertion station is limited. Remember that makers of progressive machines assume that your intent is to rapidly assemble a large volume of basic shells.

(3) You are limited to the size of shot that a particular manufacturer's bushings will accurately measure. Generally, the most accurate drops come with #5 or smaller pellets. Stay in this range and loading should go smoothly. If you go with larger pellets, you will have to battle the mechanics of the machine itself.

Lyman's Pro 1000 beam scale and LE 1000 digital scale can be used for measuring shot and powder throws from the press.

(Below) The zeroing weight for the Lyman LE 1000 scale lies hidden inside a compartment. Before using this scale, be sure to zero it as well as verify the accuracy.

An Expert's Machine

Most manufacturers do their best to set up the progressive machines before they leave the factory. However, because of the very nature of the machine, handloaders find that adjustments will need to be made. Eight or more functions are occurring at the same moment, and this can be a thrilling exercise. Even an advanced handloader may let slip a vulgar phrase or two during this procedure. While you adjust one station, another one may go out of whack. It's a balancing act. Keep the user's manual close at hand and read it before you even start, then several more times after you have had some time with the machine. The manual will make more sense after a bit of loading experience, so never throw it away. You will also need the manual for the proper manufacturer part numbers when ordering additional or replacement parts.

• Remember, if you have a flaming temper do not buy a progressive loader.

• If this is your first loader do not buy a progressive loader.

• If you plan to reload for hunting (other than the most simple of loads) do not purchase a progressive loader.

• Your first box of shells on a progressive reloader will have two characteristics: 1) It will be your most expensive box of shells ever; 2) It will be the slowest box of shells produced, ever. If you plan on loading a large number of target loads and then add a few hunting loads, plan to buy both a progressive loader and a single-stage tool. Life is sweet if you exercise this option!

• If you already have a single-stage loader and want to load faster, you are ready for a progressive loader. Proceed to local authorized dealership.

• Progressive loaders can very quickly turn out boxes and boxes of finely made target loads. Do not try to change what the loader was designed to do, even if retro-fit kits are available.

• Progressive presses can turn out boxes and boxes of mistakes, too. Verify all measurements.

Which Press Type Is Right for Me?

What kind of shotgunner are you? This will determine the kind of press you choose. In reloading presses, there is no good or bad—only specific applications. Reloading tools run the price gamut from little more than a box of really expensive shells, right on up to second mortgage category. The range is reflective of the manufacturer's anticipation of their product's use.

A good way to pigeon-hole loading tools is to divide them by application. For certain jobs and certain circumstances one loader will clearly stand out. Based on the facts we present, you will be the judge of which is best suited for the task at hand. It is our job to help handloaders determine what kind of loading they intend to do.

So, you bought an economy model reloader and have spent six months using it and learning the fundamentals of reloading. Maybe, after many boxes of shells, you decide you have outgrown that particular machine's potential. That's not a problem because used tools have value. They can benefit experienced and beginning reloaders alike. That tool has given you the opportunity to experience a new hobby and has taught you the fundamentals of load assembly with a minimum of muss and fuss. Also, it probably clarified the direction you would like to take in your handloading. If this is the point you have reached, maybe you are ready to graduate to another level. Over the course of a couple months the machine has probably paid for itself. Now is the time for that tool to be passed on to another novice reloader or to be kept for its practicality. Clubhouses are a terrific place to post sales notices, should you decide to sell your press.

It's hard to recommend that you burden your local gun dealer with selling your used machine. Undoubtedly, he will also be selling new machines and may prefer to better utilize

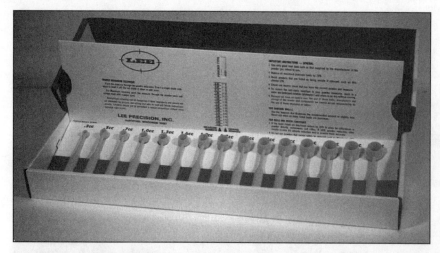

(Left) Lee manufactures this series of dippers for measuring powder. Each holds a specified amount measured in cubic centimeters. Inexpensive and surprisingly accurate, the set includes a reference chart for proper usage.

Here is a shot bushing filled with shot. The exact number of pellets contained in the bushing will be the same number dropped into the hull.

(Above) Most reloading presses use a bushing system for metering powder and shot. Bushings come in various sizes, the internal diameter determining the amount of powder or shot dropped.

MEC's powder/shot metering system utilizes a bar. Powder is metered through a powder bushing; shot through the bar itself. If you forget to insert a powder bushing, powder will spill from the hole in the bar and onto your reloading bench.

his time with the higher margin inventory he has on hand. If you want your dealer to sell it, be sure to work out a mutually beneficial arrangement. A consignment fee of 20 percent would be reasonable, especially considering the enjoyment you have already gotten from the machine. Did reloading bring you anything? Enjoyment, relaxation, a new hobby? Better ammunition, even? If it has brought you any one of these things, you have gotten your money's worth. Pass it on with a smile.

Buying a Used Reloader

I have a secret for those thinking about buying a used machine: Reloading presses suffer about the same rate of wear as your average shovel. Unless you really abuse them, they are really difficult to break. They are simple machines, really. If you do break a part, there are OEM replacement parts available for any of the machines. Parts are reasonable enough in cost that most dealers will be able to inventory enough parts to satisfy customers' needs.

Reloading tools have reliability records pretty much unequaled in any other machinery. If our cars were as good, we would certainly not be making payments on anything new—unless we chose to upgrade our Ford Model As. Unless specialization requires change, reloaders can pretty much last forever. Don't tell that to a fiscally conservative spouse—all rationalization for new toys is then diminished. Don't presume that he/she will forget either. Permission, though it may hinge upon longevity of the tool, is not without future consequence.

Obsolete machinery is the used reloading tool's giant, singu-

lar caveat: Make absolutely certain, without a shadow of a doubt, that the manufacturer of the tool you consider is still in business. There are a couple (Texan and Bear come to mind) that have been out of business for years. Testament to their reliability is that there are a few guys still using the things out there. However, unless you have access to your own machine shop, parts are unavailable. Bushings are unavailable. Instruction manuals are unavailable.

Most of the machinery currently manufactured has been around in basic form for about 20 years. If you look hard enough, you will be able to dig up a used example. Ask your friends, check around the club, see your local dealer. You may just decide to buy a new machine from the dealer to take advantage of warranties, dealer support and dealer advice—utterly invaluable as you begin reloading. This is particularly true of progessive machines.

Other Tools You'll Need

Shot/Powder Scales

It's to the handloader's advantage to have, and use, an accurate 1000-grain or larger scale. Smaller capacity scales, such as a 500-grain model (just over 1-ounce capacity), are fine if the handloader only wants to measure powder charges.

By using a scale, you have the opportunity to verify the charge drops of your bushings so you can check for variations or inaccuracies in weight per volume. Various lots of powder can fluctuate; not significantly, but a little. The best handloaders use scales for both powder and shot measurement and verification. In the last few years electronic scales have become

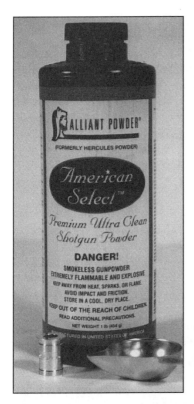

Before loading begins, cycle the powder/shot bushings and weigh the results to make sure your machine is throwing the correct weight of shot and powder.

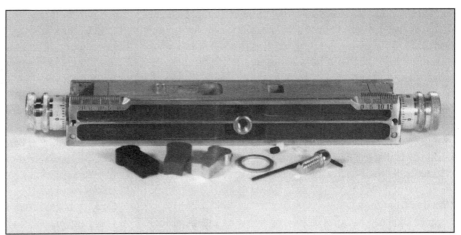

(Above) The Universal Charge Bar from Multi-Scale has calibrated settings for adjustments. Confirm your loads with a scale, then go up or down until you have exactly the right weight.

Ballistic Products makes roll-crimping tools for most available gauges.

very reasonably priced. For the accuracy and easy readout they offer, these units have become a superb value.

Here's a handy tip that every reloader needs to know: 437.5 grains equals 1-ounce. Now you can figure out exactly how much of every component you will need to assemble a certain number of loads.

For example, if the load calls for 30 grains of powder, you will get around fifteen loads out of every ounce of powder (437.5÷30=14.58). With 16 ounces to the pound, 15 (rounding up) times 16 equals 240 loads from 1 pound of powder.

Shot and Powder Bushings

Bushings are the most common method used in loading presses to meter propellant and shot. They are reasonably priced, available from your local dealer and are manufacturer-specific. Bushings are shaped like a cylinder with a hollow center. The hollow center of each size bushing has a different internal diameter. Bushings use this internal space to *volumetrically* measure powder, and usually shot charges, even though the load recipes will call for a specific *weight* of propellant and shot. Data charts telling you which bushing will correspond to the desired charge of propellant or shot are published by the various tool makers. Mostly, they are happy to send you a copy of these bushing charts upon request, or for a small fee. Always refer to these charts for proper bushing selection. Charts for many popular bushings are listed at the back of this book.

Occasionally, propellants will reflect a change in density. In these cases, there are minor adjustments that have to be made to the bushing charts. These charts are updated as necessary.

It is up to you, as a responsible reloader, to verify your propellant and shot charges. The only accurate way to do so is to weight the charge on an accurate scale.

Shot and powder bushings are usually stamped with a code in the form of a letter, a number, or an inside diameter measurement, which is, by tradition, seemingly barely visible to the naked human eye. I have found that a permanent marker can clear this up in a jiffy so you can identify bushings with ease and certainty. Mark the numbers as large as possible to avoid mistakes.

Shot Bushings

The careful handloader will use a scale to verify the shot charge. It is possible even with the same bushing to drop varying weights. There are several characteristics of shot that affect an otherwise straight-forward process. The first is the size or diameter of the pellet. Most shot bushings are cut to meter #$7\frac{1}{2}$ (.095-inch) pellets most accurately. Any change in diameter from this size will tend to change the charge weight of the drop, either up or down. Usually, smaller shot results in heavier charges, larger shot in lighter charges, but this is not necessarily true in all instances—reversals do occur.

Second, the material a pellet is made of affects metering. Steel shot is around 70 percent the weight of lead, and therefore occupies 30 percent more space for the same weight. Bismuth is about 85 percent the weight of lead. Do not expect lead shot bushings to drop an equal amount of steel or bismuth. Furthermore, the exterior surface of steel or bismuth pellets presents a friction coefficient sufficient to inhibit accommodation and sometimes reduce stacking potential. In other words, bushings designed for lead will be less accurate when used for steel or bismuth.

While close counts in horseshoes and artillery, there are times when shells such as 28-gram loads are checked and verified during competitive events. A reloader using a standard 1-ounce lead bushing may find his reloads will have just a tad too much weight—1 ounce equals 28.35 grams. Oops! This may be grounds for disqualification. There are super-accurate shot bushings available for 32-gram, 30-gram and 28-gram loads in selected and specific target shot sizes. Use the correct bushing.

Powder Bushings

Since shotshell powders suffer a bit from volume distortions, it should not be news that a bushing volume drop of powder is suspect. This is another chance for a reloader to use his grain-weight scale to check the amount of powder being dropped. The only solid reference point we have is the exact weight of the drop. You cannot check the energy level of the powder, but you can be sure of the weight dropped. After normally cycling the machine a few times, always check dropped charges before starting to load and each time you add powder to your reservoir.

Neatness Counts

This is as good a time as any to mention a few safety tips to observe around the loading bench.

An intrinsic part of reloading is maintaining the area you use. Schedule clean up sessions as part of your reloading process. If you have a giant pile of clutter surrounding your machine, remembering the particulars of your job at hand become more difficult and you are more likely to make mistakes. Once every session, take a few moments to clean up. Make sure you are not loading the garbage can with an excessive amount of flammable materials. Spread spilled powder granules out, don't let them pile up. Loose powder is not explosive, but it is highly flammable. Primers, on the other hand, *are* explosive. Don't let them sit around in little piles. Save your old primer boxes and use them for proper storage. Don't let flammable materials gather in vacuum cleaner bags; clean them out regularly.

To keep track of exactly what powder and shot bushings are in your machine, label a Post-It Note or marking tape and stick it on the press. You will be glad you did when the phone rings and you forget where you are. This is an exceptionally good idea if you leave the machine ready to go for a couple days at a time.

The reason manufacturers do not sell powder reservoirs in a 25-pound size, as they do for the shot container, is that they prefer you not contain this much propellant in one space. They recommend that you use great big reservoirs for shot only.

Shotshell Presses

On the following pages is a brief review of some of the shotshell reloading presses currently offered. The comments about each machine are based on the author's personal experiences (with one exception), so bear in mind that what works well for me may or may not be satisfactory for you. All of the tools are

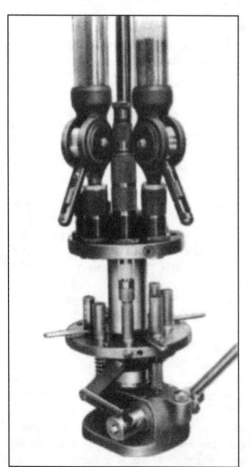

(Left) Hollywood's Progressive Press came set up for one gauge and could crank out 400 rounds per hour.

(Right) Progressive reloading presses, like this Hornady 366, are designed to produce a finished shell with each pull of the handle. It works like an assembly line. As each shell is brought to a station, a different step in the loading sequence is performed. The last station final crimps the loaded round and then ejects it.

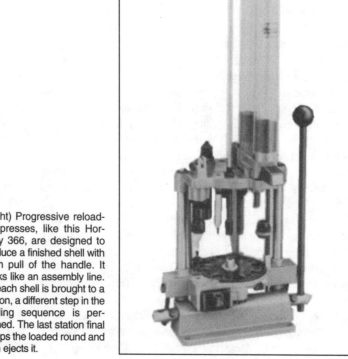

good, and are capable of turning out reloaded ammunition as good as factory loads, and sometimes better in terms of specific performance.

The world of shotshell presses is not a large one, unlike metallic cartridge tool offerings. Here, there are just seven manufacturers, but they have reloaders for nearly every need and budget—from about $49.98 to about $3600.

Once you decide on just what kind of shotgunning you'll be doing, then and only then can you make an intelligent decision about which tool you need. Do your homework well and you won't have any regrets later in your shooting/reloading career.

Dillon
Model/Type: SL 900, progressive
Options: None

The SL 900 has a lot of moving parts; it is the loader of choice for tinkerers looking for automation. We noted in watching Dillon personnel operating a prototype that the machine requires very standardized target-only components; you may not be able to assemble hunting loads. The best use appears to be loading copious amounts of standard trap loads. The machine must be specifically set up to a singular case design.

Hollywood Engineering
Models/Type: Automatic, Progressive, Senior Turret
Options: None

Though Hollywood reloading presses have been around for what seems like forever, I have not yet had the chance to work

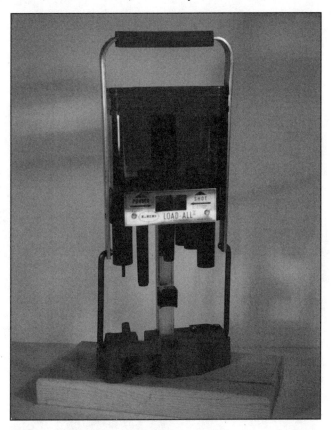

The Lee Load-All II single-stage is an excellent press for the beginner. It's inexpensive, comes ready-to-go from the box and will give the reloader many years of service.

with one. They have an excellent reputation and are built to last. With a weight of 100 pounds, the Automatic and Progressive presses have a lot of well-engineered metal in them.

The Hollywood Automatic is said to turn out 1800 rounds per hour, on average, and is fully automated with shell pick up and ejector. It comes completely set up for one gauge and is, theoretically, ready to go out of the box.

The Progressive model can load about 400 rounds per hour and uses the same basic construction as the Automatic. It comes completely equipped for one gauge—10, 12, 16, 20, 28 or 410. The price is high, but the quality is there.

The Hollywood Turret multi-stage press is capable of making about 200 rounds per hour, and it, too, comes ready to go for one gauge, as above. These are robust machines that will outlive most owners.

Hornady
Models: Single-stage and/or progressive: 366 Auto, Apex 3.1 Auto, Apex 3.1 Assist Auto
Options: Fully progressive conversion

The Hornady Apex models present an interesting feature in that they are at once a single and progressive machine. Optionally, the buyer can purchase the Apex Auto which comes equipped with automatic carrier advancement, automatic powder and shot dropper and automatic primer feed. Should you decide to start with the standard model, it can be updated later.

In being able to choose between multi-shell loading and one at a time, the decision of whether the load is too complex for progressive loading can be made at the bench, during loading. This gives you a chance to try any load both ways on the same machine.

The Apex has a solid, cast frame. The cost is higher than most single-stage machines, but less than other progressive machines. Being one machine suitable for almost all applications is the Apex's best feature. You will have to purchase a bushing set to get started.

Lee Precision, Inc.
Model/Type: Load-All II, single-stage
Options: Automatic primer feeder

The Load-All II is for the person who wants to try handloading without selling the farm to do so. This machine will cost you about the same as a few boxes of shells. Especially good for the beginner, everything (except components) required for loading your first box of shells is included. Lee utilizes plastic bushings with a unique tab that both identifies the bushing and keeps neophytes from confusing shot and powder charges. A set of these bushings is found in Lee's storage bin/lid. Very handy. Using the Load-All II is simplicity itself: work your way from left to right and follow the illustrated instructions. Loading advice is, well, abbreviated. Adjustments are primitive, but straight forward; you will understand the fundamentals of each by not having to muddle through extraneous clutter.

The investment will not break the bank. The Load-All II, if used patiently, can make fine reloads. Do not push the machine beyond its limited output and you will have a reloader to enjoy for years.

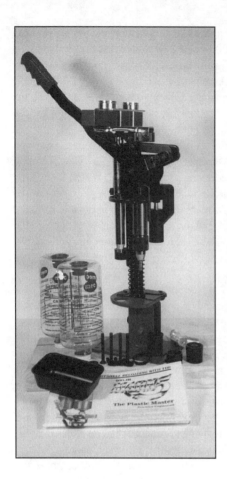

The MEC 600 Jr. single-stage press as delivered from the factory is basically ready to go. Just bolt it to the table, then fill and install the powder and shot hoppers. It's all set up and adjusted from the factory for Winchester AA hulls.

MEC's Steelmaster is very similar to the Sizemaster, except it is set up by the factory to load steel shot. Although, the steel shot accessories won't prevent you from being able to load lead shot.

MEC's 650, a progreesive reloading tool, works six shells simultaneously and is indexed from station to station by hand.

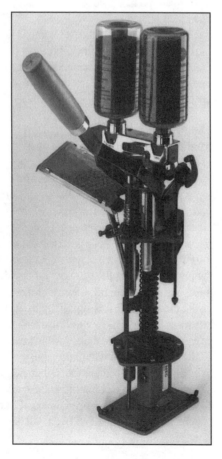

MEC's 9000H, another progessive, operates on a 110-volt hydraulic pump—neither lever nor elbow grease required.

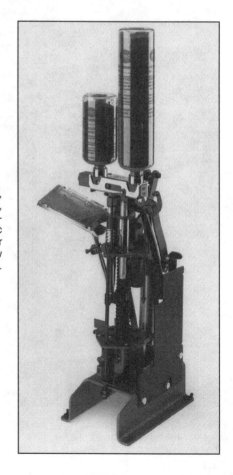

Mayville Engineering Co.

Models/Type: Single-stage: 600 Junior Mark V, Sizemaster, Steelmaster. Progressive: 650, 8567 Grabber, 9000G, 9000H-Hydraulic

Options: Gauge conversions for most models; steel shot conversions for all single-stage and certain progressive models; primer feeders for machines not already so equipped; covers; extended handles.

MEC is probably the best known shotshell reloader manufacturer in the world. Quiet improvements over the last several decades have made a good machine better. The single-stage presses operate on a straight-forward approach, and setup is easy, sometimes too easy—new owners rarely consult the owner's manual.

By utilizing some of MEC's extensive line of accessories, any type of shotshell in any gauge can be manufactured on the 600 Junior. The price is reasonable. You will have to purchase a set of bushings before you get started. The Sizemaster offers a collet-type resizer (as opposed to a sleeve on the 600 Junior) which will squeeze the brass section of hulls back into shape. A sturdier frame and simple conversions between 2³/₄- and 3-inch hulls may encourage those who are going to put an emphasis on hunting loads to opt up to this particular model. The Steelmaster is just like a Sizemaster with MEC's steel shot acces-

sories already installed. The steel accessories will not get in your way should you decide to load lead pellets.

MEC also manufactures several types of progressive reloaders. The progressive line starts with the 650, which is indexed from station-to-station by hand and can work six shells at once. The 8567 Grabber works six shells at once, too, but includes a resizing station, similar to that of the Sizemaster's. A neat feature is that when the shell is removed from the final station, the carrier automatically indexes for the next cycle.

Fully automatic indexing, as well as finished shell ejection, are features of the 9000G. Finally, should you not want to, or are unable to operate the lever, MEC offers the 9000H. The operator inserts the hull and the wad and a 110-volt hydraulic pump does all the grunt work.

The single-stage machines are excellent choices for any type of handloading. Because of short clearance, the wad guide fingers may have to be removed for hunting-type wads in these machines. As usual, we recommend that you use only single-stage machines for hunting loads.

Ponsness/Warren

Models/Type: Progressive: L/S-1000, Du-O-Matic 375C, Hydro-Matic, Size-O-Matic 900 Elite, Size-O-Matic 900 Elite Grand, 950 Elite, 950 Elite Grand.

Ponsness/Warren's L/S-1000 can handle both lead or steel because of its specially designed bushing system that prevents hung-up pellets.

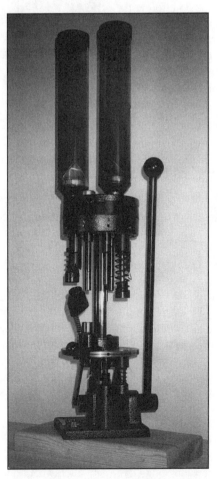

A well-used Ponsness/Warren Model 375 progressive reloader. If it were a car, it would have 120,000 miles on it. Kept adjusted and maintained, it will continue to produce excellent reloads.

Ponsness/Warren's 950 Elite is an eight-station progressive press that will handle both high and low brass cases without alteration.

Options: Length and gauge conversions; metal crimp starters; all kinds of things for the progressive machines and retrofit items going back to the earliest models.

The very best feature of any of the Ponsness/Warren machines is their unique, full-length sizing die. The shell is pressed into a sizing die at the very first station and rides through all the rest of the process contained within this hardened steel ring. Rarely with this system will a hull distort, and as much pressure as necessary can be applied for proper crimp closure. It's really hard to make a bad shell on the 375C loader. The shell is brought up to the fully adjustable tooling by a rolling lever. All operations happen directly in front of you, and shells can be fiddled with during any part of the operation. Ponsness/Warren reloaders are manufactured with a cast frame and most parts are machined. Fit and finish are excellent. If you are buying a 375, get a steel crimp starter as an accessory and your reloading world will be in order.

The progressive machines are sturdy and provide reliable service. The 900 Elite is the only progressive model that takes advantage of full-length sizing dies. All of the rest use an abbreviated collar to hold the shell in place during the reloading process.

The 950 is the sister model (without the sizing dies) to the 900. Resizing is accomplished at the final station. Shells are held loosely in the collars and require little or no effort at the knock-out station. Some loaders will see this as reason enough to go with the 950's retaining plates while others will prefer that the shell is held steady by the 900's full-length sizing dies.

The L/S-1000 was designed to progressively load both lead and steel shot. It also uses the short collar. Though you can manufacture hunting loads with an L/S—it's even available with 10-gauge dies—you will probably be happiest using a single-stage machine for hunting loads. Steel pellets flow well through Ponsness/Warren's specially designed bushing system for the L/S series, saving handloaders from frustrations of hung-up pellets.

Spolar Powder Loader
Model/Type: Progressive: Gold Premier
Options: None

With an anodized finish and handsomely crafted construction, the Gold Premier is almost as much fun to look at as it is to use. Rarely will you come across such workmanship in this modern world. The Gold Premier is very expensive; most parts are machined from billet. Whether the cost will be worth it to you will be dependent upon what you expect from this machine.

If quality of construction is an important factor, you will enjoy the fluid movements made possible by close tolerances and sealed ball bearings in many of the moving parts. As a left-hander, I appreciated the fact that the Gold Premier is ambidextrous. Switching the handle to the (correct) other side was easy and made loading more natural for me. It's a right-handed world, and lefties appreciate such little considerations. An exceptional feature of the Gold Premier is that it can be "disarmed" and everything stopped during a loading cycle. Dies are removable and the charge bar can be unhooked. Carefully read-

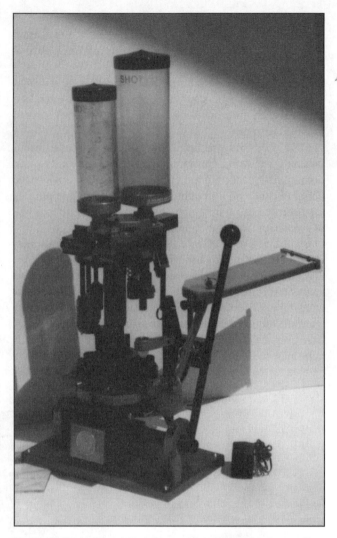

Because of its high level of craftsmanship and close tolerances, Spolar's Gold Premier is an expensive progressive reloader.

ing the manufacturer's instructions will help lift the fog surrounding these procedures because they are somewhat complicated. A thorough visual study of the complexities of the machine will help, too.

The Gold Premier is designed to manufacture a lot of one load type. Set the machine up and go. It is almost to the machine's detriment that it is literally ready to go out of the box because the temptation is great to get started without reading the manual. One of the first instructions is to just cycle the empty machine quite a few times to become familiar with each moving part.

Consistency seems to be the Gold Premier's watchword. Many problems of reloading have been examined and addressed from an engineer's standpoint. Some parts, like an electric primer vibrator, even seem overly engineered. Getting consistent loads from your Gold Premier requires consistent and practiced manipulation of the operating handle. The Gold Premier is not set up to work quickly. Start jerking the handle and you will wind up with powder all over the floor. However, once a steady pace is achieved, consistently good loads are easily produced.

It's the only part of the load chain that is reused, but to do so safely and properly requires understanding certain considerations.

4

Shotshell Hulls

JUST GETTING STARTED in reloading can be an intimidating affair, especially to one who may be unfamiliar with the firearms industry's array of available components. As a start, hulls are a good component to use as a stepping stone to becoming a reloader. Commitment to reloading can be easy as not throwing empty hulls into a big garbage barrel. Instead, empty your pockets into a cardboard box, and soon enough it will be full. Find another box and fill it up, too. No matter which types, collect whatever good hulls you come across. With each succeeding box, you are doing exercises that will help you to become either a reloader or a demented scavenger, depending upon your spouse's point of view. If you ask your friends to save their empties, you will soon find that you have tubs full. When you have enough hulls or you have displaced the family car, you are ready for the next step, sorting out these treasures.

Hulls are probably the most expensive component, and if you have to purchase the first big batch of them, it will add significantly to your start-up costs. However, if you do decide to buy instead of suffering the indignities of eyeing dumpsters in a different way, you will get presorted hulls, saving time you otherwise will be spending sorting hulls yourself.

To sort, begin by grabbing a couple of big plastic buckets. Nothing invented is handier for sorting hulls. If you must, purchase several 5-gallon buckets of joint compound from the hardware store and finish that back room wall. Otherwise, find a restaurant owner and ask him/her to hand over the pickle buckets. Small bribes and politeness seem to be the more effective means. Of course, you can also buy them at the local hardware store.

All hulls begin a fatiguing process with the first loading. Repeated reloading and firing eventually breaks the seal between the base and the brass head. In some hull types, the process of base degradation is extreme, and therefore more

Shotshell case variations are many. Gauge, length and brand differences are often obvious. But, inner construction variations in otherwise similar cases can demand notable changes in loading data.

noticeable than in others. Other symptoms of hull fatigue include the plastic walls of the hull becoming very brittle near the top and finally developing cracks.

Exaggerated hull expansion can sometimes be traced to origins other than hull fatigue. Note that some reloading tools do not resize the base as thoroughly as other machines, so take a before-and-after measurement with a caliper if you have any doubts. Some shotgun chambers are more sensitive to hull uniformity than others. Chamber standards and hull standards are close, or approximate, measurements, but inexact due to machining, measurement and tooling differences. Know your equipment—what will make it work, and what makes it work the best.

Many reloading problems are the direct result of hull failures of one type or another, usually stemming from fatigue. Some hulls have been known to totally separate or crack lengthwise while firing loads that have otherwise performed well for many years. The failure is in the individual hull. Component failures proportionally become more frequent as hulls are recycled. Unfortunately, reloaders tend to blame every other component before they look at their overly tired hulls.

One reloader sent in a load with which he had experienced hull failures. Every time he fired the load he had cracked or sheared away part of a hull. "Because of the deterioration, the load must be too hot," was his conclusion. We matched the load by taking his components out of his shells, verified correct weights and types, and loaded them into less tired or brittle cases. These same loads with fresher hulls performed flawlessly and, needless to say, without undo hull failures. Plastic hulls will harden with age.

Hull Types

Hulls come in different colors, lengths and crimps, variations that are apparent from the outside. But there are also internal differences that affect your loads. Just because you are holding a 12-gauge hull doesn't mean that you can load it with just any 12-gauge recipe. Seemingly small, but ballistically significant differences in hull material, design, capacity and wear affect loads profoundly. Sometimes you will find slight differences in the "standard" internal dimensions of hulls. Shotshell makers may create specialized loads by altering hull dimensions, perhaps making a hull "deeper" by using a lower base height. There are other differences that will be outlined later in this chapter. For now, though, your initial sorting will be to separate gauges. Then you can sort for length, then brand and, finally, type. It is best to sort and grade hulls as the first stage of a reloading session. Toss away any hulls that are torn or split, burnt, disfigured, dirty or misshapen; be ruthless. The number of hulls you throw away corresponds directly to your happiness while reloading.

Length Differences

The 12-gauge shotshell comes in several lengths. All are measured by *uncrimped length*. This means that, if the hull has been fired and you are looking at an unfolded tube, measuring from top to bottom will give you the correct measurement.

The longest hull, in relation to dimension, is the 12-gauge 3^1/$_2$-inch shell. This particular length first showed up in the 10-gauge, where the additional length, as a factor of bore diameter, was not quite such a radical departure from conventional wisdom. In the 12-gauge, however, the additional ^{1}/$_2$-inch over the already existing 3-inch magnum creates new ballistic variables to deal with. Chambering modern shotguns for this longest of the 12s was utilized more as a tool of reconciliation for the higher pressures produced (purposely) by the factory 3^1/$_2$-inch loads and the popular 12-gauge bore. Driving steel pellets at high velocity demands higher operating pressures, and the pellets require more room per ounce.

To verify integrity of the equipment being utilized by shotgunners, manufacturers created an entirely new class of shotguns. The 3^1/$_2$-inch shotshells retain, however, largely the same specifications as any other hull. The diameter remains the same

Each hull type offers different internal volume. This Activ hull offers generous space for a bulky powder below the wad.

as any other 12-gauge hull. Payloads in the 3^1/$_2$-inch 12-gauge are longer than within the larger diameter of a 10-gauge, like a test tube versus a water glass. Remember, for this reason loads should be lighter than those in the 10-gauge and should also utilize smaller pellets. I say this only because I have seen folks attempting to ballistically compare the 3^1/$_2$-inch 12-gauge to the 10-gauge. The physical laws of the universe do not lie and cannot be superseded.

Give 3^1/$_2$-inch hulls an extra look for deficiencies resulting from elevated pressures. They are allowed a higher pressure level than the shorter shells, and hull life is shortened. Look for black soot around the primer pocket, a separated plastic tube, cuts in the tube caused by the tube expanding into the top edge of the brass, or damaged crimps. These are the main signs of accelerated wear. If one area is bad, it is likely other areas of the hull are none too good either.

If you want to shoot the heavier loads peculiar to the 3^1/$_2$-inch 12-gauge, buy a modern gun made for it. With the additional pressure of the loads, it is imperative that you do not, under any circumstances, extend the chambers of an existing, shorter-chambered shotgun—a recipe for disaster.

The 3-inch magnum appears in the 12- and 20-gauge, and the 410-bore. The 3-inch chamber, in each, creates additional room for larger volumes of bulky, slow-burning powder as well as larger shot payloads. Almost all 3-inch hulls will have six-point crimps. Because of the slower burning powders used in the heavy loads typically found in them, these hulls will wear out faster than the shorter 2^3/$_4$-inch hull.

Each gauge has a standard length that you will see used most often. The 2^3/$_4$-inch hulls in 12-, 16-, 20- and 28-gauge are utilized either for game or target loads. The 410-bore uses 2^1/$_2$-inch hulls. Even though a certain hull is identified as having a certain overall length, there are slight variables due to differing manufacturing tolerances. More often than not, the differences are slight, but any difference will change the internal working volume as well as crimping adjustments.

Straight-Walled and Compression-Formed Hulls

There are two types of plastic cases with which we must contend. One is a straight-walled hull, and the other is a tapered type. Though they may look the same from the outside, they are very different on the inside. The straight-walled hull has the same inside diameter from the top to the bottom. Examples of straight-walled types are the Activ, Federal Gold Medal and Fiocchi hulls. The tapered hull becomes increasingly thicker toward the primer pocket. Examples of tapered hulls are the Winchester AA, Peters Blue Magic and Remington STS. In general, the internal capacity of a straight-walled hull is greater than that of a taper-walled hull. Furthermore, in general, the pressure created (from the same load recipe) by a taper-walled hull is greater than that from a straight-walled hull.

Straight, thin-walled hulls are an excellent choice for reloaders looking for as much space as possible for their magnum loads. The advantage of this design for hunting loads is two-fold: First, straight, thin hulls more easily accept the heavy, stiff components that comprise hunting loads; hunting wads do not like to flex and therefore need a hull with a straight tube for consistent seating. Second, the thin wall flexes from the pressure and the crimp tends to open more easily; in big heavy hunting loads, we are looking for the minimal amount of component-induced pressure. Thick hull walls or a tapered design add needed pressure to light loads. However, when we are working against a pressure ceiling, additional hull-induced pressure is at odds with our objective.

Hulls for Hunting Loads

When you are in the field and chasing critters, said critters usually will not give you a chance to "re-shoot." For this reason, and because of the low volume of hulls used for hunting, I look at my hunting hulls a little more carefully than everyday shooters. The hulls I choose for hunting are clean, dry and in very good shape. No cracks, splits or dents. Everyone saves and puts to use too many poor hulls, even for hunting. I plead guilty as well. It does take a little extra effort to pitch them out, especially when I have made a home for the little things all winter long. But in the end, if I am going to invest time, effort and good components on a hull and then expect it to perform perfectly, I should hold my serious hunting hulls to a higher standard.

Most hunting loads call for the straight-sided hull because of the additional space. It offers thinner sides and less wall material occupying valuable chamber space. Less hull means more space for the load ingredients—more powder, and an accompanying greater payload of shot, take up additional space which is often not available in compression-formed hulls. If the hull design doesn't give the space or cannot be squeezed under pressure, such as with the compression-formed hull, we are forced to use smaller volumes of faster burning powders resulting in higher operating pressures.

Certain components are put together to give predictable results. If your objective is to manufacture a load that does not use a great deal of powder, then your smart choice is a fast burning powder in a higher pressure hull. This is the combination for driving any 12-gauge load of $1\frac{1}{8}$ ounces or less. This same idea may not be so good for the person designing a good hunting load and who is looking for lower pressure and/or more space in which to place shot and cushioning agents. Just because a target wad can be jammed down into a light-load hull (with excessive wad pressure) does not mean that filling the resulting space with shot creates a hunting load of any performance value. It is possible to stress the wad so that the gas

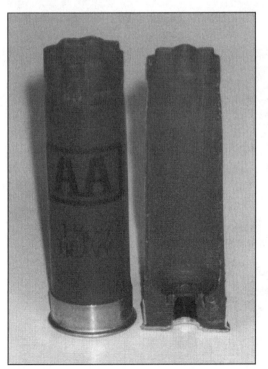

(Left) An example of Winchester's venerable AA hull. The base wad is tapered into a rounded cup and is actually part of the wall's structure. Space is limited for large payloads and bulky powders, but the tighter confines are excellent for lighter loads and low volumes of high-energy powders.

(Right) Even though the left hull is marked "Light" and the right one says "Heavy," these two hulls are identical. It's best to sort your hulls by their physical makeup rather than by what's marked on the tube.

seal cants, releasing pressure and gases during firing, and maybe even breaking up the wad. Ever wonder about particularly poor patterns? Maybe your wad is self-destructing from an ill-conceived load. A heavy hunting load is a heavy hunting load and a light weight load is just that. Keep them apart. Utilize components to their greatest advantage and don't compromise their character by demanding things they weren't designed to do.

Target Hulls

A target hull is built with the overall objective of efficient use of very little powder. As such, the design reduces the powder's combustion area in order to accommodate the lesser amounts of powder required for lighter loads, allowing a combustion space that will create the best conditions possible for augmenting a specific powder's peak pressure. Generally, it is a stiff hull that assists the manufacturer in achieving a higher level of uniformity as well as boosting the pressure. The Winchester AA fits this profile exactly. AA hulls are of high quality and can be reloaded with good hunting loads by carefully working with and understanding the design. We can actually design fairly heavy hunting loads by making careful concessions. But remember, target-type hulls will reach a maximum capacity sooner than would a straight, thin-walled hull with a flat plastic disk base. Hull types should not be vilified nor put into a position of exaltation for their effect on pressures. Rather, take them as they are, just another factor that can influence the final outcome.

In some instances, the handloader will want a higher chamber pressure to ensure positive ignition of the very slow burning powders. Slow burning powders are like a poor quality fuel oil. Similar to a diesel engine, these powders require heat and pressure to gain complete burns. A fast burning powder (see the powder section), as in trap and Skeet powders, requires little care in obtaining the proper heat and pressure conditions.

High Brass, Low Brass and No Brass Hulls

When referring to a hull's brass, we are talking about the metal section along the base that contains the primer, makes a lip for the hull's rim, and then wraps up the side of the hull. At one time, when all-brass cases were being phased out and paper/brass combinations were emerging, the heavy loads utilized an extra length of brass for strength. Lighter loads only needed a shorter section of brass. This worked quite well and was applied to specific loads on an as-required basis. The appellation attached to shorter brass loads was "low base," which has little or nothing to do with the internal base we will be looking at later on.

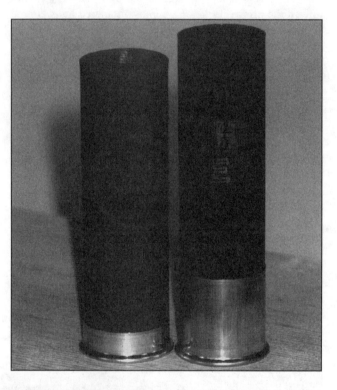

(Above) Both of these 12-gauge hulls are made by Fiocchi. At left is a 2³/₄-inch low brass version, at right a 3-inch high brass.

Evolution of the shotshell, left to right: all-brass hull; very high brass; low brass; and the Activ no brass.

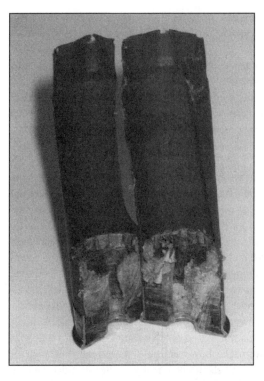

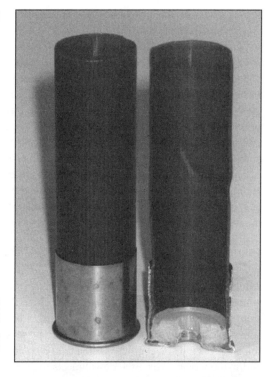

(Left) A Winchester hull with fiber base wad. Note the route the primer flash must take with this arrangement. This hull works well, but is hampered by problems associated with the composite base.

(Right) Remington uses a plastic disk base wad in many of their hunting shells. It's a yellow plastic and easily recognized.

Since loads are contained entirely by the shotgun's chamber, brass height, in almost every hull design, has become little more than a slave of fashion. The purpose of the brass that remains on modern shells is to create a strong rim to seat the shell in the chamber and to give the extractor something to grab. In addition, it lends a modicum of strength to the base of the load and increases the hull's overall effectiveness at containing the pressurized gases. Automatic and slide-action shotguns extract shells with great force, so the rim must be of a reasonably strong material and attached with some conviction.

If you were to listen to the old guy at the trap range, he will help you sort your hulls into "hunting hulls" (high base) and "target hull" (low base). Interestingly, some loads, which are exactly the same ballistically and every other way, are made in both high and low brass styles. The most prominent examples are the Winchester AA Target and Winchester XX Hunting hulls (in both eight- and six-point crimp). The target hull has a low brass head, and the hunting version has a high brass head. There are no differences in the reloading capacities of these cases or the associated ballistics they produce. In addition, the brass is always brass. Some hulls have heads which are zinc-plated steel, brass-washed steel, copper-colored, black-dyed, and even solid brass. Brass length, by itself, will not change ballistics, but it may be indicative of internal variables.

One hull maker uses no visible brass on the outside. Activ brand hulls are a unitized plastic design incorporating a metal ring moulded into the base to grip the primer. It's hard for some old-timers to accept hulls without brass, and they assume Activ hulls are not as strong as other brands. Nothing could be further from the truth. The plastic used is a special linear material, which actually does not require resizing. Furthermore, in a unitized design such as Activ's, there is no seam between tube and base where gases might otherwise escape. The only disadvantage I have encountered with Activ's design is that an overly

fatigued hull may come apart at midriff. This is the downside of how the linear plastic is oriented in manufacturing.

Keep an eye on the hulls that contained bargain factory loads. Hull quality does play a part in the cheap price you paid for the original loads. Some shotshells are manufactured with such blemishes that it becomes obvious the manufacturer never intended for anyone to reload the empties. The only way for a handloader to guarantee type uniformity is to purchase and use new, unfired hulls. Often, these come with primers already seated, and if you add up the real costs, they become a real bargain.

Hull Interior Base

This used to called the interior base wad, but over the years so much confusion has occurred by the use of the word "wad" that it has been dropped. The interior base of a hull can be an integral part of the hull or a separate portion. Years ago, and in a few remaining hulls today, the interior base was made of a compressed fiber material—in some cases, asbestos. You are cautioned against reloading any hull with interior base material that might be loose. As a rule, I do not reload any hulls that contain fiber base materials. Usually, these are the super-cheap "Sparrow and Coot" loads. The concern is that this fiber material might pop loose, end up in the barrel and become an obstruction. Furthermore, it may have become a sponge, absorbing moisture like crazy and falling apart even faster. This mess waits to ruin your handloads. Do not reload hulls with loose fiber bases, even if you have a recipe. I have handloaded them in the past, and believe me, they are not worth your time unless you get the hulls so very cheap that you are willing to throw a dozen away for every one you load. You had also better be so familiar with loose base symptoms that you are able to identify the dozen bad hulls.

Modern hulls are made with plastic interior bases as either a part of the one-piece hull or as a separate item sandwiched between the case head and tubing material. The latter is referred to as a three-piece hull, or Riefenhauser design. Modern hulls sometimes use a plastic disk base in the same manner as the old fiber bases, but with a large difference—they work great for reloading. Fiocchi, a popular hull in the United States and Europe, utilizes the Riefenhauser design. Unlike the AA, where the walls and base are made in a singular unit, base height is adjustable by substituting a taller or shorter section during assembly. By the varying base thickness, a huge variety of load combinations and heights are matched without mandating extreme measures in component adjustments. Instead of making huge adjustments in component heights, ammunition manufacturers logically utilize this method of design to facilitate many different load types with just a few part changes in the hull's construction.

It is easy for manufacturers to make plastic disk bases in several heights. Since identical hulls with different volumes will create headaches for reloaders, it's a good idea to make a simple jig to verify the depth of the bases. Go to the hardware store and buy a 3/8-inch dowel rod. Establish a baseline measurement with one of the hulls, preferably one set up for your reloader. Put the dowel inside the hull until it contacts the base, and make a mark where the dowel meets the top edge of the crimp. With a permanent pen, mark that dowel for that particular hull type and use it forever. What we are doing is establishing a baseline measurement for comparative purposes, not creating an exact standard of measurement. Understanding and identifying hull base height will save you great frustration during loading sessions, particularly if you are using a progressive reloading tool.

Since you are taking the time to establish base height, take the extra moment to visually inspect the base for any flaws that could cause it to come loose. Poke it. Look at it. If it passes, go ahead. If the base is loose, it can't be fixed—the seal between the hull base and brass is ruined. Throw it away and move on.

Learning to Let Go

As shooters, we are always looking for every advantage in the field and at the range. Most of the time, though, advantages are weighed against our checkbook balance, and we look for areas to economize our loading and better rationalize our passion for creating handloads. The most basic component of shotshell performance, the hull, is often the object of greatest fiscal responsibility—mostly due to the fact that it can be picked up and used over again and again. A fact of life is that most shotshell reloaders use hulls well past their prime and wind up trading performance for economy. Part of our conditioning as reloaders has us repeating a mantra that says, "Nothing must ever be thrown away." Performance, however, is also a great rationalization for creating loads and should be equally applied as a determining factor in component selection. Our objective in this information is for you to be able to distinguish between a hull ready for another loading and one that will diminish the performance of your loads, thereby handicapping your shooting.

Shotshell cases showing these and any other defects must be culled from reloading stock. When 10 percent of the cases in a given lot have been rejected, it is time to discard the entire lot. Cases do have finite safe and useful reloading life.

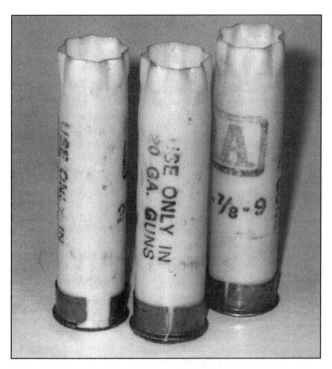

The brass on these hulls is broken or cracked. Do not use hulls in this condition because their structural integrity is compromised, which could lead to a high pressure gas leak.

These hulls have been exposed to a lot of moisture, which has caused extensive corrosion. It's not worth trying to use hulls like this.

Before you can say for sure whether a hull is past its prime, you must be able to recognize hull condition by the sometimes-subtle clues it offers. A hull cannot speak and therefore will not pull you aside to say, "I cannot be shot again." Rather, hulls offer visual signs of readiness for their retirement to the happy place that is a 55-gallon circular file.

Hull retirement is difficult for handloaders; learning to release that poor little shotshell with which you have become so familiar is tough and requires intestinal fortitude. However, just as Elsa needed to go live with the other lions, there comes a time when the little AA needs to go live with the other garbage. I know it may look on the surface like it could be reloaded one more time, but if you take the time to review the evidence, you will probably think otherwise.

Sending pellets out to meet the target in a consistent pattern and velocity is going to help you hit and improve your score. The most significant effect worn-out hulls have on your shooting is in the area of shot-to-shot consistency, as patterns and velocities are especially affected by pressure fluctuations.

It is a simple matter to demonstrate (in the laboratory) that a worn-out hull will produce great fluctuations from the norm in pressure and velocity readings. For a target shooter, a variation of 100 fps (or more) is going to make that lead a little more difficult to determine, take away some sure hits and ascribe an undeservedly poor reputation to your otherwise fine handloads. To be better shooters, we need to identify the factors that create inconsistencies in our loads and weed them out. With the hull, we have one of the basics.

Even in a normal firing cycle, the entire hull is exposed to tremendous heat and pressure. In addition to receiving its share of the initial abuse, the crimp section is unfolded and ironed out against the walls of the shotgun's chamber, understandably becoming the first area to begin breaking down. Just as continual bending back and forth will weaken a spoon to a point where it lops over, a hull is also slightly weakened every time it is crimped, ultimately to a point where little structural integrity remains. Keep in mind that the heat generated by your load has also toasted the crimp, making it brittle and prone to cracking within the recesses of the seams.

A worn-out hull's effect on a load can run the gamut from a small influence upon the powder's burning cycle in its rise to peak pressures to a complete breakdown of combustion. The embarrassing consequence of this is your favorite shotgun making little flatulent noises and dribbling pellets out the end of the barrel. More than annoying, it's a complete waste of components as well as somewhat dangerous with the risk of components lodging in an unchecked barrel.

We live in a world of objectivity. Every shooter would like to be provided with a specific number of firings that he or she can get out of a hull. Sorry, friends, that answer just isn't available. Load type, hull brand and type, shooting conditions and a multitude of other factors create conditions where giving a specific answer to that question is nearly impossible. Rather, it is better to learn how to read your hulls. The following criteria can be applied to any hull, so grab a random example from the pile in your reloading room and let's check it out.

Hull Inspection

Look at the crimp. Are there any signs of excessive heat damage? Is there ash residue or a brittle, hard feel to the plastic? Are there any visible cracks in the recesses of the crimp? Can you see daylight through any area of the crimp? Are there any sections of the crimp altogether missing? I have seen hulls missing an entire $1/4$-inch section of crimp actually being fired at Sporting Clays tournaments. Talk about handicapping yourself!

Know the brand. Is this a hull brand pre-disposed toward problems with weak crimps? Certain brands use thinner and more brittle plastics in hull manufacturing than others. Learn to recognize these brands. Don't necessarily avoid them, but remember to check them closely after each firing.

Check for structural integrity of the hull's walls. Is there any obvious sign of damage? Sometimes, the repeated intense heat and pressure of multiple firings will weaken a hull just above the powder's chamber. If you cut a hull apart, you will notice that this area of the interior is pock-marked from the heat and pressure to which it has been exposed. Sometimes these pock-marks can turn into little pin holes that can leak gas. Holes are a valid reason to toss out a hull. Also, I know of way too many reloaders who are likely as not to try and salvage a crushed hull. Don't. Try twisting the plastic tube in the brass. Hulls do not have pivot points. If the tube moves, trash the hull. Finally, here's an obvious one: Does the silk-screened printing on the outside of the hull correspond to others of the same type? This may tell you how much the plastic has stretched in previous firings. The tube will stretch to a certain point, then simply come apart. Activ hulls are known to be susceptible to this phenomenon.

Take a moment to visually examine the brass. Has it seen too many resizings? Is it cracked? Does it look as if it is about to crack? Is there any possibility that the brass may separate from the tube? Test it by holding the hull by the brass end and giving the tube a little twist. If it turns or comes apart, pitch it. You have just detected a ruptured seal. In a condition related to the firearm from which it was last shot, is the brass so oversized that it is almost impossible to resize? How is the rim? Will it allow proper headspacing or be a problem for locking up your semi-automatic or pump? If you shoot a Browning BPS 10-gauge, pay particular attention to any rim abnormalities. Does the base show any carbon deposits from a leaking primer pocket? Is the base either concave or convex (dished in or dished out)? If you answer yes to any of these questions, toss the hull.

Despite the fact your hulls passed all of the inspection criteria, if they've been reloaded too many times you probably are operating under a sense of false economy. Though everything about the shotshell *looks* all right, it reaches a point where the "ballistic integrity" is no longer there because the hull is just plain worn out. The real effects of a tired shell can be telling, and the sooner you realize those things just don't last forever, the better off you'll be. It is generally accepted that you can safely and practically reload a hull *about* six times before it should be retired. You should be keeping good records on your reloads that tell you how many times they've been used (in addition to all the other pertinent data, of course).

Just how does a well-used hull affect shotshell ballistics? Here's a scenario that spells it out:

You are at your league shoot. You position yourself, get mentally prepared and holler "Pull." The target flies, you naturally swing though the bird and squeeze the trigger at the exact

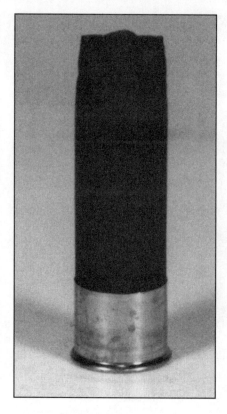

A bit difficult to see, perhaps, but this hull is unusable because the crimp area has holes at the folds. This shell couldn't hold a tight crimp and would deliver sub-standard performance or a squib that might leave an obstruction in the barrel, which could lead to diaster.

moment you know will create a connection between your gun's pattern and the target. What happens next, inside your shotgun, is a series of mechanical and chemical events utterly dependent upon the collective quality of your equipment, especially your load.

The firing pin strikes the primer, and primer begins ignition of the powder charge. Quite obviously, up to this point in the firing sequence, hull condition has no ballistic effect. However, from this point on, the effect becomes considerable, especially when you consider how many more things are going to happen before you either hit or miss the target.

The powder charge begins burning, and pressure builds rapidly as the solid powder is converted to a gas. Sooner or later, something has to give way to the pressure, and the wad column offers the least resistance. How soon the wad column moves is critical to the load's performance and, ultimately, downrange pattern performance. Ideally, we would like for the wad column to start giving at a very *consistent* time during the firing cycle, the point that creates optimum burning pressure. This pressurized combustion cycle inside a shotshell is much like that of an internal combustion engine with similar possible failures. Have you ever heard or felt the consequences of an engine that is missing on one cylinder? If, during the flame cycle, there is a sudden drop in pressure, the burn becomes much less intense and may not be complete, creating a miss and poor performance. The reasons for an incomplete burn in a shotshell powder charge are similar to an engine's valve not seating properly, allowing it to sputter and lose power. In either a shotshell or an engine, we have a similar term for the condition's result: a miss.

In a shotshell, at the critical moment when combustion begins, the crimp must hold the load back momentarily to

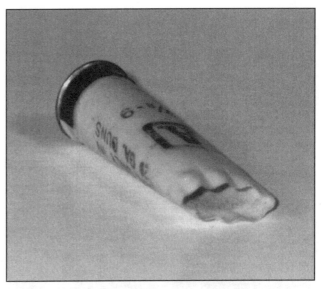

This hull was stepped on at the range. If you *really* have to use it again, be sure to inspect the base wad carefully because even though the tube can be ironed out there may be some internal damage.

The hull on the left is an "extra crispy" AA that's burned and cracked and ready for retirement. The hull on the right has been fired once and is in prime condition.

assure proper powder burn. If the crimp is cracked and weak, containment is compromised and the payload moves forward too early, giving the powder too large of a chamber in which to work for proper combustion (remember, part of our formula is compression). Under these conditions, powder cannot attain a level of optimum burning pressure and the burn is incomplete. The partially converted energy source sends the load out the end of the barrel slower than Grandpa driving home from the bank. That hollow "poompy" sound associated with a dud is powder robbed of compression, burning ineffectively somewhere in the barrel.

Repetitive testing makes it clear that solid crimps are a highly important ingredient to an effective shotshell. In order to have a solid crimp, the shotshell must have structural integrity.

What do you think? Is that hull you're looking at up to another firing or not? Have you felt a tug on the sleeve? Weigh the benefits of another firing against the importance of hitting the next target. Proper equipment is an opportunity to improve your shooting before you ever set foot on a course or go afield.

Hull Resizing and Preparation

All reloading devices have some means of resizing the metal head of the hull. The remainder of the hull does not require squeezing back into shape because the plastic is pliable enough to work into the chamber. The brass section is our concern, as the metal will retain its new expanded shape. Hulls acquire their figures from the chambers they were fired in. All shotgun chambers are not equal. Some chamber diameters are smaller, some are larger, and some are plainly oversized. When it's fired, the shell's brass section will attempt to expand to the same diameter as the shotgun chamber. Trying to resize overly

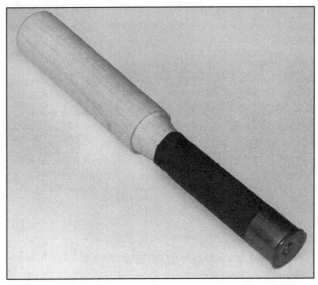

This simple tapered dowel helps to open up the case mouth on those hulls that have stiff crimps.

expanded heads can be difficult. Cracks, bulges and stiff resistance can make the reloading process far more difficult than it should be. Overly expanded cases are increasingly at risk for rupture on the next firing.

Difficult resizing, either related to a reloading press or oversized hulls, sometimes leaves reloaders hanging ape-like from the reloading tool's handle. Activ hulls are good for avoiding just such a situation. These hulls are made of linear plastic that flows very nicely through shotguns and reloading tools alike. Activ's claim that their hulls require no resizing seems to stand up. In all their configurations, they require little to no resizing effort even after many firings. This feature can be very important to the reloader who has an older reloading machine with worn parts or a cantankerous autoloading shotgun.

I have found that using a little bit of dry lubricant on the outside of the casing, or the inside of the die, helps in resizing dif-

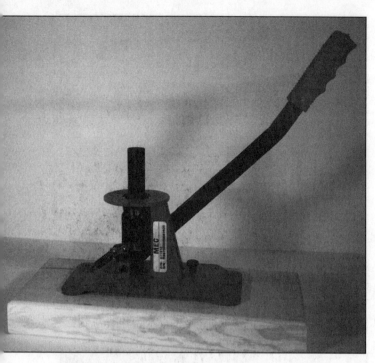

The MEC Super-Sizer tool resizes the brass of the shotshell back to factory specifications. It's available in all popular gauges.

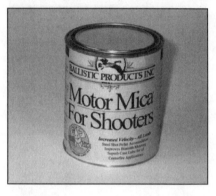

Motor Mica is a powdered friction-reducing compound that can speed up loads by making the pellets and wad more slippery.

comparatively rather thick. Resizing is a good demonstration of differences in base metal materials because some whistle through the process while others are quite the bear.

A magnum shotshell reloader can save himself time and effort by preparing hulls *before* they hit the reloading machine. MEC makes a device called a Super-Sizer that will resize the base with a quick downstroke of the tool's handle. For those of you with a resizing collar attached to your reloader, this pre-effort will save a lot of arm work and time. The hulls you may save, by not snagging and ruining the brass, can eventually pay for the device. The Super-Sizer is adaptable to accommodate all popular gauges.

Presorted hulls, especially if brought in from a cold garage, should be laid out to dry for several days. Condensation should have a chance to leave as it came (slowly) before you introduce the moisture-sensitive powder to your hull. You can sort them into small paper bags and put them into a warm place for however long it takes to make sure they are dry. I can't recommend putting hulls into the oven because if the heat is turned up too high you will have more problems than solutions. Once you are sure the hulls are completely dried out, they can be put into plastic bags and sealed with a twist-tie. Never place hulls in a plastic bag until they have first been dried out completely.

Crimping

In the world of fold-crimping, there are two types: eight-point and six-point. Ballistically, they are exactly the same. Appearance-wise, and according to your reloading press's crimping dies, they are different. This requires that you know the difference between the two. If you don't differentiate, your reloading press will reward you with the ugliest crimps you can imagine. The eight-point crimp is usually used on target loads that feature smaller shot. The six-point crimp is usually found on hulls intended for hunting and smaller gauges. The latter requires less material from the hull, folding flatter and better with bigger shot. Small-gauge hulls are generally closed with six-point crimps. The 10-gauge is always fixed with a six-point crimp.

When you work with new hulls, consider using a six-point crimp starter. A new hull does not have a memory of a former crimp embedded in the plastic. The new hull has to be shown the way, and often the best results are found with less. Working the hull into the crimp starter several times will introduce folds into the material properly. Often the handloader will only tap the new hull into the crimp starter, whizzing though this station as if it were only the warm-up to the event. That's the wrong approach. Crimp starting is part one of a two-act play. An impatient handloader, after attempting to finish the load, finds that the closure in the center of the hull mouth is incomplete, leaving a hole in the center where the crimp does not meet. Pellets sometimes dribble out, rendering the ugly load useless. This is the result of rushing through the crimping process.

Crimp Shaping On The Press

You can always use a chisel handle to reshape the mouth of the hull. The heat of the previous load may have shrunk the mouth, and you may need to round it out a little to insert the

ficult batches of shells. I stole this idea from metallic loaders, though shotgunners don't suffer the hazards of a stuck case. Try using a Teflon spray (available from Hoppe's) or a molybdenum disulfide concoction—available, perhaps, at your local hardware outlet. I use a dry mica powder because it has no affect on propellants (and vice versa). Also, it is easy to use and not hazardous.

Many reloading devices have been in the field for a number of years, and there are many machines approaching four decades of service. Do you think the resizing rings and dies may be worn? Every time you pass another hull through the device, the resizing rings and dies are pressed into action. By the very nature of their job, they will, over time, succumb to the stresses of their environment and lose their shape; rings and dies wear like rocks at the bottom of a river. Replacement parts are available for most tools, but if yours is totally out of date, think about replacing the entire machine.

After resizing the hull you should inspect the brass for cracks or distortions. Any base or rim gouges, chips, cracks or imperfections are enough to disqualify that hull from being reloaded. Some metal heads are made of very thin material, and some are loading press's tooling. Lightly loaded rounds do not shrink much on first firing because the gases from fast burning powders are "cooler" and easier on the hull mouth. However, light loads sometimes leave the crimp not fully opened, and the edges can be difficult to work around. Expanding the crimp opening to facilitate your loading machine is standard operating procedure.

If you use *new* Fiocchi, Federal or Activ hulls, note that these hulls benefit from lowering the crimp starter about $1/16$- to $1/8$-inch since memory is being introduced to the hull, and extending the pre-crimp process makes the possibility of a hole in the center of the crimp much less likely. This procedure is not necessary on subsequent reloadings.

The Primer Pocket

Located at the base of the hull, directly in the center, is the hole that holds the shotshell primer. Almost every primer on the market today is standardized to the 209 size. The primer pocket's job is to hold the primer tightly, because if there's a loose fit, there will surely be leakage around the primer during firing.

Primer Pocket Resizing

If the hull is in otherwise good condition, but the primer pocket is too loose, the pocket can be resized with a custom tool made by William's Gun Sight. It's called the Primer Pocket Peener, consisting of an anvil and a punch. The punch is inserted through the empty primer hole and lightly tapped with a hammer. The downward force slightly squashes the base, and the base expands to fill in the area around the punch. That usually is enough to repair the hull for another reloading or two. Make sure you are dealing with a flat-based hull because the shape of some hulls is not conducive to this process.

Fiocchi 616 (magnum) and Fiocchi 615 (soft) primers are .001-inch larger in diameter than most 209-type primers. That

The primer pockets of some shells need to be brought back to the correct size, and this Primer Pocket Peener tool handles that job easily.

little bit can make a difference in older hulls with slightly oversize primer pockets. I have opted for the Fiocchi primers on many occasions to save the hulls for another firing.

Paper Hulls

Paper hulls are similar in construction to plastics, with a couple differences in materials, of course. Paper impregnated with wax comprises the basic tube and crimp section. The cardboard base (separate disk) is secured to a brass head of varying height. The base of a paper hull is roughly the same height as the primer pocket, and some of the hulls, Winchester in particular, utilize a thin cardboard seal seated into the base of the hull.

Paper hulls were used for a long time, coming into use after the all-brass shell proved too costly and short lived. Federal manufactures a paper hull to this date, as do some European firms. Paper shotshells are not very common these days, and reloading them requires different techniques and components. I provide this information only for your enlightenment of shotshell history and evolution.

Brass length factors were related to the brass/paper composite hulls and getting the best of both worlds: a strong brass base to contain the load and prevent gas leakage or a rupture; then on top, a pliable paper section which contains the pellet charge in a flexible tube that would roll over and hold a crimp to contain the pellets. Roll crimps worked well in that they yielded to the pressure build-up in a predictable fashion, allowing workable loads to be created.

Paper hull walls are about as thick as a dime and were usually coated with wax to give some protection against moisture. They are only suitable for a couple firings, since the wax, which supports the paper, breaks down rather quickly—certainly sooner than our modern, pliable plastic hulls.

Paper Crimping Considerations

Just like the plastics, paper hulls require a crimp. Most, though, came from the factory with a roll crimp. MEC and Ponsness/Warren both manufacture a special crimp starter to use on paper hulls. Essentially, it is a cone-shaped device without the insets that align with the plastic hulls' crimp pleats.

Old reloaders used to use a special trick for getting one more firing out of paper hulls: They would heat the crimp area slightly, just enough to melt the wax and make the case mouth pliable enough to take another crimp. There was even a reloading tool made by a company called ACME (no association with Wile E. Coyote) that had a heater accessory just for paper crimps. Handle the problem as you will, but it is our recommendation that you throw away hulls with worn case mouths. By the time the crimp is going bad, it is almost certain that the base has disintegrated too, and the consequences of a problem in the base are more likely than crimps to adversely affect your shooting.

Paper Hull Bases

The Winchester paper hull, as an example of such construction, has a cardboard base shaped quite like an edible taco salad bowl which restaurants use to serve 50-calorie salads smothered in 1200-calorie dressings. The top edges of this cardboard seal flair out and contain, to a small degree, some of the propellant's

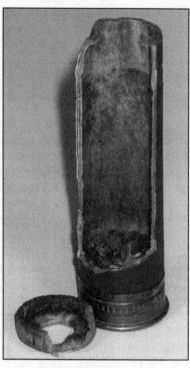

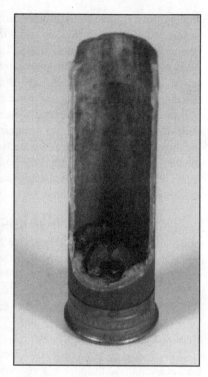

Federal paper hulls are still widely available and are an excellent choice for certain applications.

A Winchester paper hull with the cardboard "disk" removed. This disk can become loose and fall out on its own. Don't get these hulls wet!

This paper Winchester hull shows a lot of debris down in the base, any or all of which can come loose and block the primer hole. Worse, it could lodge in the bore.

gases. These bases sit rather loosely in the hull and have been known to create headaches for shotshell handloaders. Somewhere around the second reload, this gas seal will sit askew and loosely on the base. One of two things may happen, and as a handloader, it is your job to watch for them: First, it is possible for the base to cover the primer hole and thereby disrupt the firing cycle, causing a blooper; second, the base may dislodge and either exit the barrel with the shot, or become stuck inside the barrel, causing an obstruction. As shooters, we know that obstructions can burst the barrel, and they are to be avoided. With paper hulls, part of the reloading process is to carefully inspect the base: Verify its placement and structural integrity.

I caution against removing the thin cardboard base and then using the hull anyway. Removing the seal creates a larger volume, but also removes an element of the hull's intrinsic strength. The companion to increased volume will be the possibility of ruptured brass. This "salad bowl" does a very good job of containing gases.

Looking back, it's understandable why paper gave way to plastic. Plastic hulls, as opposed to paper, offer quite a few benefits to the shotgunner. Plastic is more water resistant and more pliable, while maintaining a superior memory for crimps. Furthermore, plastic is reasonably resistant to heat and stronger for the amount of material used, and it also does an excellent job of sealing. Add lower cost to this list and the motive for the evolution becomes obvious.

The cost of producing plastic hulls has become so reasonable that it is cheaper to produce this better performing product. When it comes to the loads you utterly rely upon in the field, weigh the cost/benefits of using paper and consider giving them away as mementos of yesteryear.

Hull Identifications And Descriptions

The world of shotshells can be a confusing one because of the dizzying array of hulls available to the handloader. And because there are so many variables, the component makers take a fair amount of blame when certain load recipes don't work as planned. There is a certain amount of juggling of components to be done to come up with safe, workable and efficient loads.

To further complicate matters a bit, various component sources sometimes use different names for the same hull. There is really no way to stop this practice, so the best way to identify hulls is to thoroughly understand which ones have what features.

As an example of silly nomenclature, the old Winchester reloading guide called an old Federal hull, commonly known as the League-type, the "Federal Polyformed Plastic Field." Nobody else called it that, but it is an excellent description. Lyman referred to the same hull as the "Federal Plastic Hi-Power 12-gauge 2³/₄-inch Hull." Thus, the handloader must be sharp and get to know exactly what comprises a specific type of shotshell hull.

Winchester AA-Type Hulls

Winchester makes a very basic compression-formed hull known as the AA. They also make the AA in a high-brass model called the Super-X. Upland and AA Handicap are also the same hull. I identify these hulls as "Winchester Compression Formed Hull," a descriptive name that suits my particular needs.

Winchester's Polyformed hull in both 2¾ and 3-inch lengths is quite another hull altogether. Modern configurations of Polyformed hulls have a plastic disk base. The old Polyformed cases used fiber bases of varying heights. These very different hulls shared the Polyform name. Some folks now use Polyform to describe a hull with a non-unitized base.

Because nearly everybody in the shooting world has at one time or another used Winchester's AA hull, I'll describe in detail the form and function of this design. Of course, when we talk about compression-formed hulls and their design characteristics, this information can be applied to hulls with a similar design, such as the Remington RTL.

Designed and manufactured by Winchester, the AA hull is, and has been for many years, an enduring favorite with handloaders. Often one will see an old shooter rooting about the grass in search of these prizes. There are reasons a grown man will do this.

The AA is easy to load in a shotgun. The plastic will slide into the action without sticking and tends to hold its shape without lateral expansion during the wad-compression phase of loading. The thick and concave plastic base prevents the AA from spreading excessively during the firing cycle. Consequently, resizing the hull back to original shape is easy and often not necessary.

The plastic of this hull is a bi-directional (biaxial) compression-formed material that is very strong. The tube has a good memory and reforms the original crimp with ease. Although traditionally red in color, I have seen and used some of the Silver Anniversary (special handicap) editions with various applications. These have no ballistic differences whatsoever from the red ones. However, since they are distinctive, you may want to set the silver ones aside to be used for special loads.

The AA compression-formed hull design is carried over to 3-inch 12-gauge, the 2¾-inch 20-gauge, the 28-gauge and the 410-bore. The 12-gauge 2¾-inch AA is made with the stan-

dard eight-point crimp for trap and Skeet loads, and the six-point crimp (always with higher brass) is used in the hunting series.

The length of the brass is inconsequential to performance of the AA hull. The factory uses this feature more as an identifier between the field and target loads. The brass head comes in several lengths according to the hull's description and designation and/or age. Some of the very old AAs have a short brass base, while the more modern versions are a little bit taller. The highest brass head that I have noted is on the XX hunting loads closed with a six-point crimp. Some reloaders do not recognize this hull as being the AA, but it is, and it can be reloaded with all the same target or field recipes.

Compression-formed hulls, such as the AA, are tapered inside. The inside diameter of the hull decreases as you move from the top of the crimp toward the base of the hull. This design permits the hull to be loaded and fired without undue expansion of the base, and permits easy resizing when the hull is subsequently reloaded.

The inside taper also allows the hull to be loaded with less powder and still generate good speed and power. The design maximizes pressure and gets the load moving *right now*. The taper area uses up interior volume, minimizing the need for space-occupying components, like felt wads or the cushion area of a typical target wad.

The more you fill the hull's chamber area (the space occupied by wad and components) with solids, the greater the resulting pressure will be when the powder is ignited. This situation is compounded when expansion is further limited by the inflexible walls of compression-formed hulls. In essence, less space + no flexibility = more pressure.

For the handloader creating target loads, this is mostly good news. Your very light loads (⅞ to 1 ounce) are most effective in compression-formed hulls for a couple of reasons: First, light loads can take advantage of the minimal interior space's increased operating pressure; second, the tapered base, in occupying volume, saves the handloader the trouble of using spacer wads. Usually, you will find enough space is occupied within the AA design that your crimps will sit at the proper depth of ⅛-inch. In a situation where there is too much internal space, spacer wads must be used or the crimp will collapse inward or not offer firm enough closure to maintain firing pressure.

The features of compression-formed hulls that are favorable to target loads are not always good for the typical hunting load. Hunting loads are designed for a completely different outcome and use components that are incompatible with target load design.

Because of the sheer volume occupied by payload and components, many hunting loads are difficult to place in a compression-formed hull. Certain bulky hunting powders such as SR-4756, PB, and a few others occupy so much space they are difficult to put into a hull designed for reduced capacity. I get many requests for SR-4756 loads in the AA using 1½ ounces of lead. However, such a configuration demands the use of large-capacity hulls like the Remington Type VI (SP12 type) or the Activ numbers. Even if an overweight configuration is

Here's a Winchester hull with a plastic disk base. This hull has thin walls and a large internal capacity—an excellent choice for high-performance loads.

jammed into a AA, the hull design will limit performance, thereby producing a mediocre load.

I utilize specially designed computer programs to model prototype load combinations. However, even model design is the result of cognitive inspiration. As handloaders, we have a great many more component choices to deal with than the big ammo manufacturers, so our world of load development is vastly wider and more difficult. To our advantage, though, a wide selection of components offers us the opportunity to use the very best combinations, regardless of manufacturer. This specialization, when applied correctly, offers us great advantages.

For each major component, such as a hull type, a set of working factors can be described that steer the load designer into utilizing component combinations that can produce outstanding results. In other words, if you fit together components that correspond with each other, you will usually wind up with a load that's a winner for a specific application.

Please do not assume that because the AA hull is not designed for most hunting load applications that it cannot be a great starting point for certain hunting loads. If you utilize the AA's design qualities and don't try to run against them, you can create excellent combinations. Start from the perspective of, "I want the best load possible," as opposed to the old, "I have these components on hand and want a load that does..." (fill in the blank with superlatives).

Winchester also makes a 3-inch version of the AA hull for larger capacity field loads. These have a six-point crimp and have a little less than average internal load capacity compared to straight-walled 3-inch hulls. Generally, they will run higher pressures than other 3-inch hulls with disk bases or deep unitized construction, such as Federal and Activ 3-inch hulls. Using this design to your advantage means they are candidates for high velocity, lighter field loads and should be loaded as such.

Winchester Fiber-Based Hulls

These hulls were not the greatest ones ever created for handloading. The main fault lies in the soft fiber material used for the base. It tends to disintegrate very quickly from the stresses of normal powder burns and, if exposed to moisture, falls completely apart. If for some reason you feel absolutely compelled to use Winchester fiber-based hulls, inspect them very carefully. Shine a light down the tube and verify the integrity of the base. It is quite common for a piece of the base to separate, which will consequently alter the load height. Furthermore, the entire base may let loose, and you certainly don't want that lodged in your barrel!

Winchester Plastic Disk Base/Polyform Hulls

The other version of the Polyform type is the plastic disk-based Winchester hulls. These little beauties are quite often overlooked by reloaders and really shouldn't be. The tube is a very thin, resilient plastic with a very large internal volume for components. The base is a plastic disk, red, yellow or gray in color. The low-brass Polyformed Winchester hull has a high internal base. The high-brass Polyformed hull has a low base.

Reason? The high brass is meant for magnum loads and needs more room inside the hull. The only weak area of the Polyform is at the crimp. The tube material is so pliable that crimps have to be extra deep and an overshot card should be placed on top of the shot to ensure a proper powder burn.

Users of autoloading shotguns should be wary of older Winchester Polyformed hulls. They are well known to separate (brass head from the tube) at the absolutely most inopportune moment, leaving the shooter standing in the field probing his gun with little sticks. Pump and double-gun shooters will have no trouble with the old all-brass heads. The extractors on fast cycling autoloaders though, will rip right through the soft brass rim. Newer Winchester Polyform hulls use a brass-washed steel which is much stronger and will hold up to the autoloader. You will be able to tell the difference between the two by squeezing the brass head between your fingers—the older brass heads are softer than most any other shell.

Federal Gold Medal Hulls

Federal Cartridge makes the Gold Medal hull for a huge variety of loads, including some field loads. This is a dandy hull for the reloader in that it offers a large internal volume to be filled up with components. More often than not, handloaders wind up with insufficient space, so more is better. The Gold Medal hull replaced the older, similar Federal League hull, which used a composite base but had less internal capacity. The Gold Medal has thin walls that extend straight down to a very flat base of the same material.

Federal also makes a hunting version with an exceptionally deep base. The primer actually sits higher than the base, looking

New primed and unprimed hulls are readily available to reloaders, so it doesn't pay to keep your old hulls beyond their useful life.

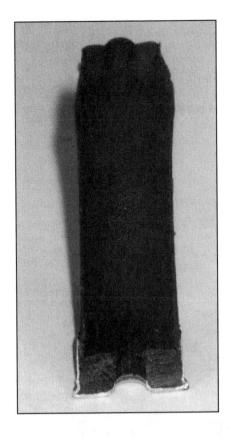

The base wad of the Federal Gold Medal is deep and flat, which is excellent for most target or hunting loads in the 12-gauge.

somewhat like Devil's Tower butte. These hulls will have a six-point crimp which deserves a cautionary note: The material in this hull's walls is laminated, and these layers can separate, even after the first firing. You will notice, as a handloader, that about one in six of these hulls have damaged crimps and should be thrown away.

Remington 2³/₄-inch 12-Gauge Hulls

Remington produces several types of hulls for both target and hunting. Those designated SP use a plastic disk base of varying heights and are of the three-piece (tube, base and brass) design. The SP hulls have evolved over the years, and each produces unique ballistics. These differences make load development frustrating at best. I have taken to assigning a number to each type. It's our system and it works for our needs. We are now up to Type VI which is a green SP12-type hull with comparatively stiffer, thicker walls and a plastic disk base. Prior to that was the smooth-walled, light green Type V. It also used a plastic disk base. Before that was the Type IV with a very thick, stiff wall that not even light could penetrate. These hulls had a unitized base. Type IIIs were very similar to Type IVs. Very few hunting loads were created for either one since pressures were very high. Type II SP hulls had a fiber base wad, as did Type Is, the difference being that the Type I used a Remington 57 primer. There were some decent hunting loads for both, but the last Type II was produced many years ago. It's not likely that you will run into these antiques.

Remington also makes a compression-formed hull, currently called the STS. I have seen this hull in gold and a handsome metal-flake green color. The STS supersedes the former RTL

of very similar design. These are excellent hulls for any type of lighter 12-gauge load and offer dependable platforms for us to design loads on. You will be seeing many new loads for this type of hull in the future and may want to get used to them.

Peters Blue Magic Hulls

The Blue Magic hull took aim at the Winchester AA in hopes of getting some of the target reloading business. The venerable Blue Magic is (was) very similar to the AA. If you are color-blind, you may have to read the inscription on the brass. They load very similarly, but certain characteristics do show up in the laboratory, especially as 12-gauge loads go over 1¹/₈ ounces. Be sure to follow tested loads specific to the hull. If you are a dedicated Blue Magic loader, consider the new STS hull when replacement time comes around.

Activ Hulls

An all-plastic exterior construction is the most conspicuous feature of the Activ hull. Activ has developed a design where the strength of the hull comes from a construction advancement utilizing a steel plate (washer) running the circumference around the primer pocket. Gone, but once quite a dazzling fixture of Activ hulls, is the artwork that graced the older Rainel-Activ tube; it lent a very sophisticated touch. Handloaders will also notice that the tube of the hull is very slick in appearance, with no ribbing either on the outside or inside. At the end of the hull, at the mouth, it is skived, making it a snap to fold or roll crimp, even on the most stubborn loading machine. A hull without crimp memory is partial to a six-point crimp, but will easily accept an eight-point crimp if the loader is willing to spend an extra moment at the crimp start station.

MEC sells a special tool to adapt their 600 JR. loaders to the Activ hull. As the Activ has a huge internal capacity and a very low base, unmodified MEC loaders (single-stage series) will sometimes leave an unseated portion of the primer protruding from the finished load. With MEC part number #8111 (Activ spacer tool) installed under the collar of the priming cup, adequate pressure can be applied to fully seat the primer.

Activ hulls have a smooth, nearly polished exterior. When finished with a rounded, tapered crimp end, the hull should whiz through any shotgun's feed mechanism, including autoloaders with really fussy systems. With no transition area between the hull tube and a brass section, ejector pins and feed mechanisms are much less likely to catch on the hull and put a frustrating stop to the action. Any fussy shotgun that usually resists should function better with Activ hulls.

Activs do not require resizing. This is most handy for the handloader utilizing roll crimps and/or no resizing equipment. The Activ 12-gauge has a large internal capacity suitable for the heaviest magnum loads and is very similar to Federal's high capacity hulls, both in 2³/₄- and 3-inch sizes. However, we cannot extrapolate this information into loading data between the two hulls since pressures change from load to load.

Fiocchi Hulls

Fiocchi is the largest ammunition maker in Europe. Fiocchi

Maker	Type	Gauge	Length (ins.)	Base Wad	Tube Material	Tube Type	Crimp Type	Suitable Applications	Capacity—Relative to Type	Comment
Federal		10	3½	Paper	Plastic	Ribbed/straight	6 point	Hunting	Large	Large capacity—thin walled
Remington	SP	10	3½	Compressed fiber	Plasic	Ribbed/straight	6 point	Hunting	Medium	Taller basewad
Remington	SP	10	3½	Plastic disk	Plastic	Ribbed/straight	6 point	Hunting/heavy magnum	Large	Large capacity—thin walled
Winchester		10	3½	Plastic disk	Plastic	Smooth/straight	6 point	Hunting	Large	Large capacity—thin walled
Federal	Premium	12	3½	Unitized, below primer	Plastic	Ribbed/straight	6 point	Hunting/heavy magnum	Large	Large capacity—thin walled
Remington	SP	12	3½	Plastic disk	Plastic	Ribbed/straight	6 point	Hunting/heavy magnum	Large	Thin walled
Winchester		12	3½	Plastic disk	Plastic	Ribbed/straight	6 point	Hunting/heavy magnum	Large	Thin walled
Activ	No brass	12	3	Unitized, below primer	Plastic	Ribbed/straight	6 point	Heavy field	Large	New hulls available
Federal	Premium, etc.	12	3	Unitized, below primer	Plastic	Ribbed/straight	6 point	Heavy field	Large	Large capacity—thin walled
Fiocchi		12	3	Flat, plastic disk	Plastic	Ribbed/straight	6 point	Heavy field	Large	New hulls available (clear)
Remington	SP	12	3	Plastic disk	Plastic	Ribbed/straight	6 point	Hunting/magnum loads	Large	Thin walled
Winchester	AA, Super-X	12	3	Unitized, tapered	Plastic	Smooth/tapered	6 point	Field	Medium	Excellent for lighter magnums
Winchester		12	3	Plastic disk	Plastic	Ribbed/straight	6 point	Field	Large	Thin walled
Activ	No brass	12	2¾	Unitized, below primer	Plastic	Smooth/straight	8 point	Heavy field/target	Large	New hulls available
Federal	Gold Medal	12	2¾	Flat	Plastic	Ribbed/straight	8 point	Heavy field/target	Large	Large capacity—thin walled
Federal	Hi-Power	12	2¾	Paper, tapered	Plastic	Ribbed/straight	8 point	Light field/target	Medium	
Federal		12	2¾	Paper,flat	Paper	Smooth/paper	6 point	Field/target	Medium	Paper hull
Federal	Top Gun	12	2¾	Paper	Plastic	Ribbed/straight	8 point	Target (weak crimps)	Medium	Large capacity—thin walled
Fiocchi		12	2¾	Plastic disk/high	Plastic	Ribbed/straight	8 point	Target	Small	New hulls available
Fiocchi		12	2¾	Plastic disk/low	Plastic	Ribbed/straight	8 point	Field/target	Large	New hulls available (clear)
Remington	STS/Premier	12	2¾	Unitized, tapered	Plastic	Smooth/tapered	8 point	Target/light hunting	Small	
Remington	Unibody	12	2¾	Unitized/tapered	Plastic	Smooth/tapered	8 point	Target/light field	Small	Stiff plastic material
Winchester	AA	12	2¾	Unitized, tapered	Plastic	Smooth/tapered	8 point	Target/light field	Small	Different brass heights
Winchester	Polyformed	12	2¾	Plastic disk	Plastic	Ribbed/straight	8 point	Field/target	Large	Large capacity—thin walled
Activ	No brass	16	2¾	Unitized, below primer	Plastic	Smooth/straight	6 point	Heavy field/target	Large	New hulls available
Federal	Premium, Hi Power, etc.	16	2¾	Paper	Plastic	Ribbed/straight	6 point	Hunting/target	Large	
Fiocchi		16	2¾	Plastic disk	Plastic	Ribbed/straight	6 point	Hunting/target	Large	New hulls available
Remington		16	2¾	Plastic disk		Ribbed/straight	8 point	Hunting/target	Large	
Remington		16	2¾	Plastic disk	Plastic	Ribbed/straight	8 point	Hunting/target	Large	
Winchester	AA	16	2¾	Unitized, tapered	Plastic	Smooth/tapered	8 point	Light field/target	Medium	
Activ	No brass	20	3	Unitized, below primer	Plastic	Smooth/straight	8 point	Hunting	Large	New hulls available
Federal	Premium Hi Power	20	3	Paper	Plastic	Ribbed/straight	6 point	Hunting	Medium	
Fiocchi		20	3	Plastic disk	Plastic	Ribbed/plastic	6 point	Hunting	Large	New hulls available
Remington	SP	20	3	Plastic disk	Plastic	Ribbed/straight	6 point	Hunting	Large	
Remington	STS	20	3	Unitized, tapered	Plastic	Smooth/tapered	6 point	Hunting	Small	
Winchester	Super-X	20	3	Unitized, tapered	Plastic	Smooth/tapered	8 point	Hunting	Small	
Activ	No brass	20	2¾	Unitized, flat	Plastic	Smooth/straight	8 point	Unitized, below primer	Large	New hulls available
Federal	Premium, Gold Medal etc.	20	2¾	Paper	Plastic	Ribbed/straight	8 point	Hunting/target	Medium	
Federal		20	2¾	Paper	Paper	Smooth/paper	8 point	Hunting/target	Medium	
Fiocchi		20	2¾	Plastic disk	Plastic	Ribbed/plastic	8 point	Hunting/target	Large	New hulls available
Remington	Target/RTL	20	2¾	Unitized, tapered	Plastic	Smooth/tapered	8 point	Target/light hunting	Small	
Winchester	AA/Super-X	20	2¾	Unitized, tapered	Plastic	Smooth/tapered	8 point	Light hunting/target	Small	
Federal	Gold Medal	28	2¾	Paper	Plastic	Ribbed/straight	6 point	Hunting/target	Medium	
Fiocchi		28	2½	Plastic disk	Plastic	Ribbed/straight	6 point	Hunting/target	Medium	New hulls available
Remington		28	2¾	Plastic disk	Plastic	Ribbed/straight	6 point	Hunting/target	Large	
Remington	SP	28	2¾	Plastic disk	Plastic	Ribbed/straight	6 point	Hunting/target	Large	
Winchester	AA/Compression formed	28	2¾	Unitized, tapered	Plastic	Smooth/tapered	6 point	Hunting/target	Small	
Federal		410	3	Paper	Plastic	Ribbed/straight	6 point	Hunting	Medium	
Remington	SP	410	3	Plastic disk	Plastic	Ribbed/straight	6 point	Hunting	Large	
Winchester	Compression formed	410	3	Unitized, tapered	Plastic	Smooth/tapered	6 point	Hunting	Medium	
Federal		410	2½	paper	Plastic	Ribbed/straight	6 point	Hunting/target	Medium	
Remington	SP	410	2½	Plastic disk	Plastic	Ribbed/straight	6 point	Hunting/target	Large	
Winchester	Compression formed	410	2½	Unitized, tapered	Plastic	Smooth/tapered	6 point	Hunting/target	Small	

of America manufactures hulls under the Fiocchi name in Ozark, Missouri. The hulls are a Riefenhauser design; a separate tube, brass base and plastic disk base are brought together to form a large capacity, high performance unit.

Fiocchi hulls are good for many reloadings as the plastic is heat-resistant and resilient. Uniquely, Fiocchi makes the 12-gauge hulls with a clear plastic tube. I like this feature for load identification in the field. There's no doubt about your load when you get to look directly at the components. The brass section of the hull is not actually brass, but cold rolled steel with a brass plating. The "brass" is very strong and operates well in autoloaders, pumps and double barrels.

Since Fiocchi hulls are usually brand-new when a handloader gets them, I usually recommend a six-point crimp for introducing crimp memory to the tube. If the handloader so chooses, roll crimps can also be easily applied.

The chart above illustrates the differences in recognizable hulls most commonly available to American shotgunners. You should be able to use it as a guide for identifying hulls in your inventory.

Big things come from small
packages, and the smallest
component in a shotgun shell
is what really gets things going.

5

Shotshell Primers

EARLIER WE DESCRIBED how shotshell ignition and the reactions that follow are not all that different from those in an internal combustion engine. In shotshells, the primer is most like the spark plug, delivering fire to combustibles. In both shotshell and engine, we have a compressed charge that requires spark to begin the transformation. Bringing the analogy closer, there have been experimental electronically ignited shotshells, eliminating the mechanical connection between the shooter's input and ignition. These loads reduce shotgun lock time by replacing slower mechanical locks with an electrical switch (the trigger). However, electronic ignition, by itself, does not supply everything needed for proper ignition. Unlike internal combus-

tion engines, compression is not a pre-existing condition. Chemical primers supply heat, showering the propellant with tiny white-hot particles. Chemical primers, as such, achieve complete ignition and the necessary and sudden rise of pressure in a reliable fashion. Other than the chemicals used to do the job, primers have changed little since their inception.

Consistency in burn rate and heat is important for the primer to function properly. Insufficient fire can break a firing cycle by inadequately igniting a propellant charge. Bulky, slow-burning powders require a specific type of flame to ignite and burn properly. Too much heat and flame unnecessarily raises early chamber pressure, "pushing the cycle." Insufficient heat and flame do not ignite a large enough portion of the propellant for pressure to rise sufficiently before the chamber is decompressed by the load's movement.

Other factors besides primers can also affect early hull condition: powder chamber shape, payload weight, type of gas seal and composition, and others. Primers cannot be analyzed on their own, but rather as a contributor to the personality of the entire load.

Historical Information

Historically, we look to the year 1807 for the first patent of a cap-style primer and have to thank the Reverend A. J. Forsyth, a Scottish hunter and inventor. He found that certain mixtures of chemicals produced an explosion when impacted. If contained, the reaction could be used to ignite powder charges. Forsyth used the knowledge to create the pill lock ignition system.

In Philadelphia during 1814, Captain Joshua Shaw found that fulminate of mercury inside a copper cap was easier to work with than a "pill." Joseph Manton of England also worked on the same arrangement. The next step was to combine the primer with the other components and create a cartridge. Further primer improvements occurred when U.S. ordnance officer

PRIMER CUP

PRIMING MIX

BATTERY CUP

PRIMER FOIL

ANVIL

BOTTOM FOIL

This cutaway view shows the typical construction of a shotshell primer. Some older open-end primers do not have a bottom foil or seal.

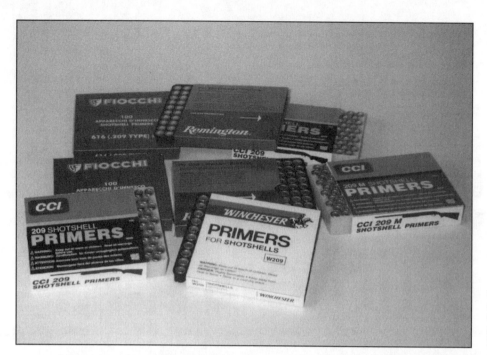

There are a variety of primers, each formulated for a specific use. Do not substitute indiscriminantly.

(Below) This primer is not properly seated and protrudes from the base of the hull. When running your finger across the base, the primer should feel flush with the hull.

Hiram Berdan developed a cartridge that contained a receptacle for a primer. British Colonel Edward Munier Boxer then implemented further internal primer changes by placing a pointed bit of metal inside the primer that struck against a base after being whacked by a firing pin. The result was, as now, that the primer ignited and blew fire/sparks forward into the shell.

Early primers were composed of horrendously corrosive chemicals. Fulminate of mercury causes brass cases to become brittle. Potassium chlorate leaves deposits like common table salt in the firearm, making bore cleaning within hours a requirement. Lead styphnate has been successfully used in primers for many years and is non-corrosive, but the current fears of lead compounds may eliminate its use. Once again, primers are changing not for performance but consequence.

All primers are not the same. Primers by themselves are not significant pressure generators, though different primers, by type and brand, produce varied results and cause distinct reactions as the other shotshell components change. While one primer produces minimal pressure in one load, another type might not. Same goes for maximum pressure. Don't generalize. Don't substitute. Primers, and the energy they produce, are a part of every load's individual ballistic composition.

Powders react differently to the various primer types and brands, so load testing becomes a study in reactive engineering. Factors affecting primer influence include the weight of the load, the type of hull and its shape. When a reloader asks, "What's a strong primer?" the question is loaded (forgive the pun). My answer must be, "What's the combination of ingredients?"

There are certain generalities we can apply to primers and their relationship with pressure. There is one principal rule of all reloading: All arbitrary component swapping creates new and unpredictable situations. Even if the pressure does not increase or decrease a great deal, the balance created by a good working, specific combination of components suddenly is thrown off balance and the load is now a below-average per-

The base of the hull on the left has been crushed concave. This happens when you try to prime a hull that still has a primer in it—a very dangerous practice with live primers.

former. On the other hand, the pressure can and often does move upward, which is the least desirable change from a handloader's standpoint.

Component substitution is a sticky business, otherwise we would not invest so much capital in testing equipment. It is quite possible to crank up the pressure of a particular load to well over the acceptable and safe pressures with just a primer swap. Don't do it. How much can a primer swap change a 12-

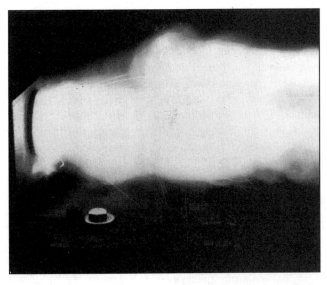
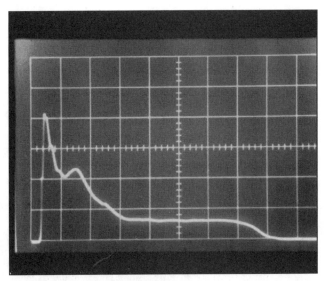

Each primer has a unique set of characteristics that make it useful for a specific application. The same primer detonation is shown in both photographs: White-hot gas (left) is discharged upon firing, while electronic measurement shows the flash intensity over time in milliseconds.

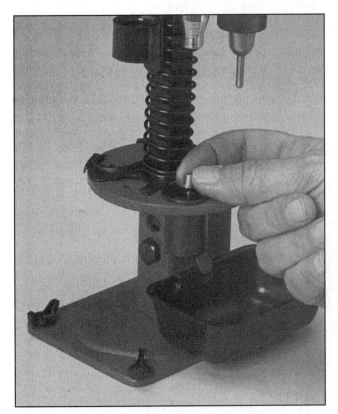

To increase safety and prevent possible contamination, handle primers one at a time with clean, dry hands.

gauge load? Tests indicate that a common target load can change by as much as 3500 psi with only a change of primer. It's dramatic. You have been warned.

There are reloaders who will swear on a stack of duck stamps that a Winchester 209 primer is a low-pressure primer. Not true. Research indicates that the Winchester 209 is often found in the middle of the pressure pack at the 1¹/₈-ounce lead shot level, but zooms to the top of the list for pressure production when used

with light loads such as the 1-ounce 12-gauge with certain powders. How's that for predictability? A light primer? I wouldn't hang my hat on it.

Primers, like powders, have character. Some burn longer and some burn with greater intensity. Some have a longer spark and produce heat over a much longer time period; we refer to this as the flame's duration. In general, target loads do not need much spark, because the propellants are in the fast-burning, easily ignited category. Hunting loads, however, may require a great deal of primer boost and heat to get the slow-burning propellants cooking. On bitterly cold days, the need for tight crimps and warm primers can become critical for proper ignition. For these loads, magnum primers were developed, an appellation that sometimes seems contrary to their typical applications. Magnum primers are hot. Generally, heavy-duty magnum loads seek minimal effect from the primers and shy away from using magnum primers, opting instead for the lower chamber pressures offered by milder primers. Now you understand an important distinction: Magnum loads do not necessarily require magnum primers.

Seating the Primer

Primers must be seated flush with the base of the shotshell. Unlike centerfire primers, which look like little cylindrical disks, shotshell primers come with their own battery cup, replacing a similarly shaped portion of centerfire cartridges. The battery cup holds the primer in the case. Handloaders can assure themselves of proper seating by running a finger over the junction of primer and hull base. If it is reasonably smooth, and no area below the rim of the battery cup is visible, your primer is properly seated. Flush and flat with the head is the only acceptable way.

If, however, the bottom of your shell is concave, or dished inward, you are applying too much seating pressure. Readjust your press before proceeding to another shell—the seating stem has too much protusion.

Primer Problems

Sometimes a poorly adjusted reloading tool will not correctly seat the primer, either hanging it out the back or seating it too deep. A correctly seated primer is level with the hull base. If the primer is not fully seated, a couple of things can happen. The worst-case scenario is that somewhere in the loading cycle some part of the gun could strike the high primer hard enough to cause it to go off before the action (auto, pump or break-open) is closed. This is not only highly unsafe, but it's also cause for an underwear change. Also, a high primer can cause a misfire by actually cushioning the firing pin blow to the point that there's an indent but no ignition. This one is tough to diagnose.

Enlarged primer pockets will allow a primer to back out even if it has been properly seated. Air pressure from seating a tight-fitting wad can work back through the powder to the primer and push it out, usually about one-quarter of the way. Absolutely do not press the primer back in. It just might go off, and the uncon-fined explosion would be disastrous for you and those around you. If the primer is seated too hard, it can push in the base of the hull enough that the firing pin may not be able to bridge the gap. Pay attention to primer seating depth—it will affect your loads.

A Clear Path

Good ignition depends upon the primer's flame having a clear path to the powder charge. Fiber or cardboard bases inside hulls can shift, blocking the primer pocket and snuffing the load. This is most common in certain types of Winchester paper and plastic hulls. Also, it is possible for debris (a spider web, mud, etc.) to find its way into a hull. As you deprime your hulls, it's a good idea to verify that the primer flash has a clear path to the powder. (See Hull Inspection.)

Primer Care and Storage

Do not let oils or moisture get near your primers. If you spray oil on your reloading tool, make sure the primers are covered or somewhere else. Primer dust and loose particles of powder should be mopped up with a damp paper towel. Primer dust is very explosive, so do not fill the vacuum bag with it. Unsealed primers, like the old Remington #57s, really should no longer reside in your reloading room. Take particular care if you have them because the chemicals may spill out and collect near your storage area.

Do not leave primers sitting about. Open one pack at a time and leave the others in a separate, safe area. Use up that pack or put it away. Manufacturers pack primers in those little plastic holders for rational reasons of safety. Never repack primers in jars, bags or other containers—keep primers in the original packaging until used. A jar of primers has about the same explosive potential as a hand grenade. Think about that before you throw away the original packaging. Wear safety glasses when loading or handling primers. Impact detonation is a possibility worth considering.

Become mindful of where you store your primers and how many you have on hand. Although it's OK in some municipalities to store 500 gallons of gasoline on premises, you usually only get to have 10,000 primers on hand before you may be in danger of violating codes. Check it out before you go above this number.

There are some obvious areas where you should not store your primers, like near the furnace or in a damp basement. Furthermore, take a look at the positioning of the shelf you put them on. It is not, I hope, below your collection of ballpeen hammers, if you get my drift. Keep primers away from a place where impact, heat or moisture is probable or imminent.

(Above) This shotgun shell was manufactured in the former Soviet Union. Do not mix or match components, especially those from unknown sources. Stick to accepted data when loading your own ammo.

The primer in the center has been correctly seated flush with the base, while the others either have been seated too deep (left) or not deep enough (right).

CCI makes standard and magnum 209 primers. Avoid getting caught up in the nomenclature and what you think it means. Follow load recipes exactly.

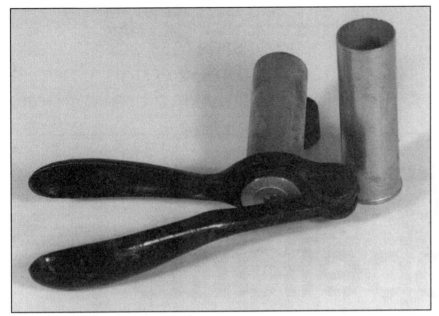

This antique priming tool has seen generations of use—and is still perfectly serviceable.

The primer on the left has a white cover, while the one on the right is of the open-holed variety. Powder can enter the open hole and cause problems for the shooter.

Covered And Open-Hole Primers

Modern primers have either a lacquer or paper covering over the flash hole. Usually, it's colored and easily identifiable.

The old open-hole primers are not compatible with modern equipment, modern powders or modern loads. If you happen to have some around, use them with only specifically recom-

mended loads utilizing bulky, large-granule powders. Remington #57 primers were open, which means fine-granule powders, like Winchester Ball powders, can filter down inside. The resultant problem is that too much pressure can build inside the primer, which could leak out of the primer pocket. Furthermore, the increased pressure increases the risk of a ruptured case. It can also result in a squib load.

Primers and Reloaders

Automatic primer feeders on modern reloading presses are carefully designed with safety in mind. But, in order to be as safe as possible, you must use the protective devices and equipment exactly as it comes from the manufacturer. First, I recommended that you omit open-hole primers from your modern loads. This is especially so with automatic primer feeders. Usually, the primers shake around a bit in the machine, and explosive dust has a tendency to collect in crevices. The problem here is not one of a faulty reloader, but, rather, obsolete components used in an inappropriate manner.

If a primer jams up in your tool, put on an extra pair of safety glasses and do not force the tool in any way. Remove the remaining primers from the hopper and slowly and easily disassemble as much of the reloading press as necessary to get to the little rascal. If you force or jolt the press, as one is wont to do with a stuck progressive machine, you risk detonating the stuck primer and causing a nasty chain reaction.

Primer Sizes and Types

The 209 "size" primers vary by several thousandths of an inch in either diameter or length. The real anomaly of shotgun primers is the older and smaller #57 primer intended for older Remington hulls. It is the smallest diameter shotshell primer. The Remington #57 and CCI 157 (a closed-hole version) are no longer manufactured. The industry has standardized primers by effectively accepting the 209 size across the board.

Primer Summary

Remington 97* 209 size for target use in 12- 20- and 28-gauge with plastic base wad hull.

Remington 97-4 410-bore with solid plastic base wad hulls.

Remington #57* Used in all field loads, SP 10, SP 12, SP 16, SP 20 and SP 28 gauge hulls except certain target hulls with plastic base wads. It has an open hole—no fine grained powder loads.

Remington 209-T Closed flash hole. Used as target load primer.

CCI 209SC (Sporting Clays) Target load primer.

CCI 209 Trap and Skeet general application primer (nickel-colored base).

CCI 209M A longer burning field primer for magnum loads.

CCI 157 Closed flash hole. An alternate field load primer to the Remington #57.

Federal 410 410-bore primer—209 size.

Federal 209 Magnum field load primer.

Federal 339 Target primer.

Winchester 209 Field load primer.

220 Max-Fire Magnum field load primer; archaic and very strong (Alcan).

Shotshell Propellants

I BELIEVE ROGER Bacon (English philosopher and scientist) laid the foundation for handloaders when he said in about 1242: "When the flame of powder touches the soul of man, it burns exceedingly deep."

Blackpowder in its earliest form was created by combining saltpeter (it's the white stuff on your basement walls), charcoal and sulfur. Proper combinations of these elements provide a controlled, high-speed burn creating gas and heat.

Propellants, as we know them, require confinement for their high-speed deflagration, converting the powder into much larger volumes of hot gas. High explosives, by definition, do not require containment for an explosion. There is a huge difference between the two, and taking advantage of a propellant's relative stability and controlled burn is the fundamental component of internal ballistics.

Smokeless powder had the benefit of clearing smoke from the field of fire, allowing shooters to see what was going on around them, a development objective. Besides that, the energy level of a given volume of powder was greatly increased. The terminal velocity of the projectile, and thus the energy and accuracy, were also greatly increased.

Powder Composition & Characteristics

Nitrocellulose is a pulpy or cotton-like material derived from cellulose treated with sulfuric and nitric acids. The first term used to describe any nitrocellulose-base powder is that it's either single-base or double-base. All smokeless powders have a nitrocellulose base; the addition of nitroglycerin makes it a double-base powder. Nitroglycerin is an additive that is adsorbed into the nitrocellulose base.

Nitroglycerin is comprised of oxygen-rich molecules that decompose very, very quickly. The molecule, and the energy contained within, can be best described as a wound spring, waiting for an opportunity to unwind. Double-based powders,

thanks to the nitroglycerin, produce tremendous energy for their volume. Alliant Red Dot is an example of a double-based powder. It provides a lot of energy for the amount of powder used for a particular load. Because of this, shooters use less volume and save money. Powders are also made up of other ingredients, like igniters, fillers, taggants (the red in Red Dot), coatings and retardants.

Modern nitrocellulose-based powders, whether single- or double-based, are best defined by their own unique and identifiable character. A given powder's character becomes a dynamic force dependent on the situation in which we place the powder. Some characteristics must be recognized in order to utilize powders with any degree of effectiveness. Using a certain powder, just because it's what you happen to have on hand, is giving up a lot of potential advantage. By only using one type of powder you are certain to be working outside its realm of effectiveness sooner or later. At that time, that powder's character will work against you by providing inconsistent results.

Powders demonstrate their character in a given situation when, as a result of a certain combination of components, an unrelated portion of the main character changes. For example, a substitution of hulls in otherwise duplicate loads using the same powder and identical amounts and types of all components may produce quite different powder burns in terms of effectiveness. This reaction may result in either higher or lower chamber pressure, a better or poorer load in terms of lethality, or a gain or drop in velocity.

The art here is learning to predict specific swings of powder character. Long ago, I began placing loads and powders on computer databases, charting the test results. Since then, a great number of different powder characteristics have been tracked. I found that nothing is completely predictable. If it were, we would have a formula for creating loads without testing. But there are too many variables for that formula to exist. As it is, to

Shotshell propellants are sold in various size containers, and like many things in life, the more you buy the more you save. However, some municipalities govern the amount of propellant you may have on hand at any time. Check with the authorities!

The author recomends rolling the powder container before pouring the contents into the powder hopper on the reloading machine. This mixes the propellant for more consistent energy levels.

ensure a safe and consistent load, a series of ballistic tests must be done for every new load combination.

Powder Formulations

Powder character is defined by the formula and individual granular shape of a particular powder. Inert retarding chemicals that alter the burn speeds and energy levels of powders are mixed with the base elements in order to stabilize each batch or lot of powder. This brings individual lots of powder into a standard performance range associated with that powder. Most often we refer to rate of burn, measured in .000001-second (milliseconds), to determine performance parameters.

The reloader utilizes the standardized performance measurement for dropping a specified amount of powder with a particular ratio of other components, ultimately creating the load. All this means is that when a shooter runs out of his favorite powder and orders another can of it, he can expect *similar* performance from his favorite load recipe without changing the amount of powder.

All powders are tested during manufacture and must operate within the manufacturer's specified tolerances. But given the nature of the beast, it is not realistic to expect each lot will always be exactly the same. Many other variances occur during the manufacture of powder that impart slight character differences from batch to batch. For this reason, powder lots are numbered and batch-tested for adherence to their performance standard.

Powders will vary from lot to lot in energy levels, ignition quality and bulk density. These minor fluctuations are all part of any manufacturing process, so don't lie awake worrying about it. As a handloader, you affect your particular canister powder's energy more by whether or not you redistribute the powder inside the can. Powder should be re-mixed by rolling the can on its side for a moment or two before you use it.

Don't overdo this mixing because if you get overzealous you could end up reducing the size of too many granules through friction. This would alter the burning rate of that powder, making it unsafe to use.

Moreover, powder can be vibrated hard enough during shipping so as to break down the granules into finer units. Part of a

powder's burn rate is determined by the size and shape of the granules. In general, powder character will be altered toward a faster burn rate and increased bulk density as the granules are broken down because more surface area is exposed. Metering may get a little strange too. Weigh your powder charges and trust your scale. Change your bushings if you need to stay in bounds; the charts you get with your reloading tool are not carved in stone. The world is not perfect, and trucks bounce when they hit bumps.

Chemical Retardants

Chemical retardants are just that; they chemically control the burning speed of the compound by reducing the speed of the burn. Without them, powder energies would be difficult to control. The basic nitro product may be too powerful in a particular lot, exceeding its required performance parameters. However, with more retardant, the correct level of burn speed and power can be achieved and the lot certified for use.

It may have occurred to you that, if you were manufacturing smokeless powder, you could create a whole new powder slower in burn rate than your original base powder by adding additional amounts of retardant. Or you might not use as much retardant to create a new powder that is faster in burn rate. Do powder makers do this? Of course they do, and we shooters appreciate it. We would not have nearly the number of available powders we see on our shelves if the manufacturers were not so clever with chemical retardants.

Burning Clean

Which is cleaner burning, single- or double-base powders? That depends. A direct answer means ignoring important variables. Shooting conditions vary, and so do the retardants and chemicals used in various powders. Clean burning depends upon how you are using a specific powder and when you are using it. Some powders will leave more unburned residue clinging to barrels than others used in the same circumstances, but a small change in environmental conditions might reverse the results.

Any comparison of powders at the "hotter" end of the burn rate spectrum (high energy, low volume) against slower burning powders is not very scientific. It ignores application. It would be like comparing a dump truck to a Porsche. One hauls a lot and the other hauls. Faster burning types do not have as high a per-

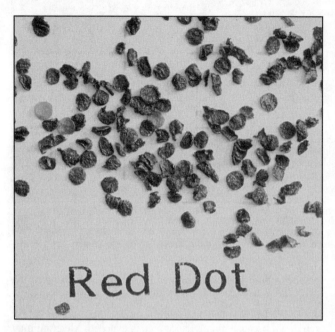

Red Dot

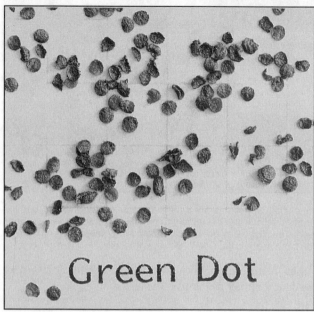

Green Dot

Hercules' Red Dot is, perhaps, the most popular shotshell reloading powder and is used primarily for 12-gauge target loads. It has small quantities of red-colored wafers, hence the Red Dot name.

Green Dot is a slightly slower burning propellant than Red Dot with a granulation of similar size and shape. It is generally used for standard and medium shothell loads from 12- to 20-gauge. It has a small quantity of identifying green wafers.

centage of the inert retardants found in slower burning powders. Will a slow burning magnum powder leave more residue in your barrel? Heck yes. Do you want to use target powder for high-speed magnum-weight loads? Heck no. Buy a particular powder for the shooting results it gives and don't experiment.

Ignition Quality

Depending on a huge number of variables, shotshell powders have wide variations in ignition quality. In freezing temperatures, one powder may be harder to light off than others. Some smokeless powders will operate far better in one gauge than in

another. Certain hulls are better hosts for specific powders than other hulls. The Winchester AA, with its "studio-sized" tapered interior, is a hull designed for the efficient energy produced by small volumes of dense double-based powders. Ignition with this combination can be counted upon.

Powder ignition character is altered by other components and factors too. Wads, their sealing qualities (as well as compatibility with the hull) and payload weight alter ignition. Furthermore, so do crimps and hull condition. If all 12-gauges were fired at 70 degrees F, and at a pressure of 10,500 psi, any functional load combination could be expected to operate rea-

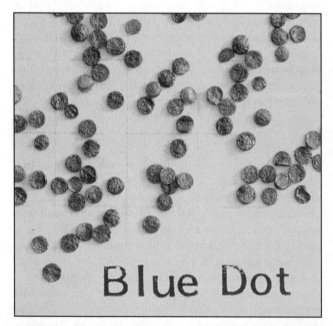

Blue Dot

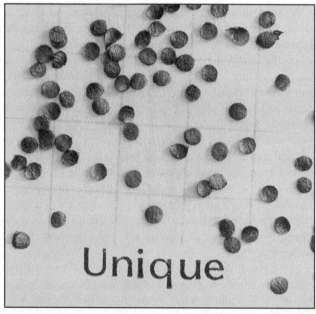

Unique

Blue Dot's primary use tends to be magnum loads from 10- to 28-gauge, and it has limited applications. A small number of blue granules are included for identification.

Unique is a very versatile propellant used for the 12-, 16-, 20-, and 28-gauge. It's a handy choice for the reloader who wants to load multiple gauges with a single propellant.

sonably well. However, we take our powders to places where ignition character could be a surprise rather than as expected. These factors are why load design is a complex, expensive and long-term procedure.

For the new handloader, ignition problems can be frustrating. Usually, the source is a small problem of misapplied components, but we need first be aware of how components relate to a proper burning cycle.

Shotshell Ballistics and Powder

To initiate and sustain a powder burn, shotshell propellants require compression. This does not mean crushing the wad on top of the powder, but rather that compression will produce a contained area necessary for the process. Diesel fuel is basically an oily glop, yet under compression it takes on a new character that combusts with energy enough to power eighteen-wheelers. Like diesel fuel, in order to burn properly propellants need to be contained to generate pressure and useful energy.

The sequence of events inside a firing shotshell takes place in under three milliseconds. The following outlines these events in order:

1) The primer ignites the propellant by showering it with white-hot gases and incandescent particles.

2) The powder undergoes a chemical change, transforming from a solid to a high volume of hot gas. The powder continues to burn at an increasing rate as the resulting pressure increases.

3) More gases add to the compression and the cycle accelerates—a chain reaction.

4) Something must give way to the expanding gases, and, of course, this is the wad and shot column. They're driven from the barrel like a spitball through a straw.

Any loss of pressure during the burning cycle diminishes the chances of a complete and efficient powder burn. A small interruption could be a collapsed gas seal, for example. If load components are breaking down, it will be reflected to the ballistician in the form of inconsistent pressures and velocities.

Irregularities in the pressure curve, perhaps caused by an inappropriate component shift, reduce the effectiveness of the propellant burn as compression is lowered in that moment. Unpredictable component shifts have several identifiable origins: weak cushion sections in wads, weak seals or worn-out hulls with poor crimps. Many substandard loads are fired that "sound" OK. However, they are producing inferior results and velocity compared to a more perfect load. Your loads may be getting out there, but not as they should.

An all-out load failure is a "blooper," a poor quality load that the shooter should identify by its distinctively peculiar tone and lack of recoil when fired. Should you encounter a blooper load that does not sound as it should, stop everything. Do not fire another round through that barrel until the chamber and barrel are checked and rendered free of obstruction! It's entirely possible that the wad is lodged inside the barrel. Another round fired behind it will not blow it out the end of the barrel; instead, it'll rupture the barrel, more than likely hurting you and those around you.

Remember that shotshells are operating, fundamentally, at the very low end of the pressure spectrum. All powders, particularly slow burning ones, are sensitive to pressure, and with improper containment burning is less than complete. Also, a lighter than average load may reduce pressure to a point where the proper burning cycle cannot be initiated.

Cold weather, which we will define as below the freezing temperature of water, demands special loads and consideration for your powder's complete and proper burn. Your powder is going to need all the help it can get to produce a usable load. Use medium burn rate powders. Also, look to use heavier loads and new hulls for stronger crimps. You may want to look for a load using a magnum primer. These hotter primers are more

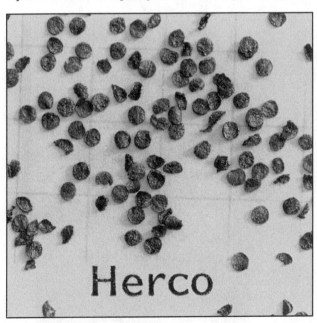

Herco is of moderate burning speed. Its major applications are in heavy loads from 10- to 28-gauge.

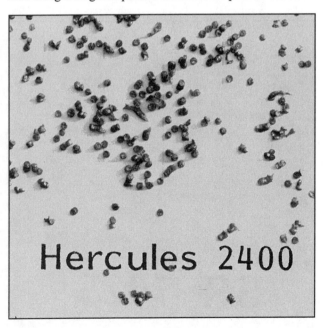

Hercules' 2400 is a very slow burning powder in shotshell applications. It is limited to 410-bore loads, but serves well there.

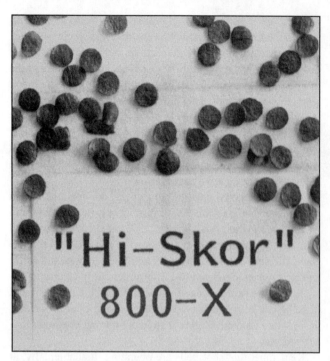

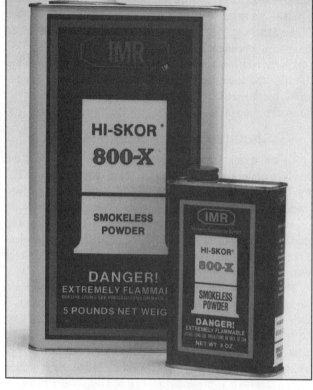

IMR's Hi-Skor 800-X is a bit slower burning than 700-X, but has the same disc-like shape. It's a very versatile powder for a variety of loads.

likely to get things going in the cold, because these are the conditions they were created for.

Burn Rates

For the sake of categorization and definition, let's divide smokeless powders into three categories: fast, medium and slow burn rates. Powder character and application are defined by burn rate. Understanding burn rate, as related to other powders, helps you control the power of your loads. If the reloader understands the aspects of the medium burn rate powders, then understanding the other two categories becomes simple.

Often, the first and best application for medium burn rate powders will be an extended range load. Trap clubs sometimes stage "Annie Oakley" events or some other super-long-range handicap shoot-off. The standard trap load, using a fast powder and producing standard velocities, no longer cuts the mustard here. How do you increase velocity and make pellets effective at longer range? How about stretching the slope of the pressure

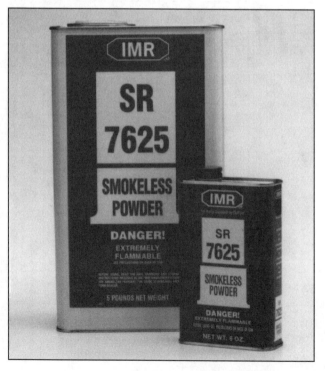

IMR's SR-7625 is of medium burning speed and is a versatile shotshell powder for field and other loads in 10- to 28-gauge.

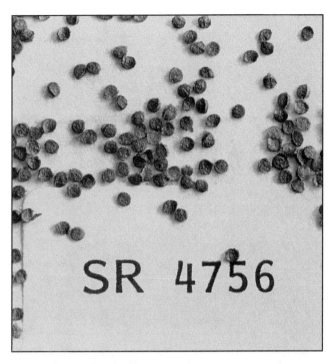

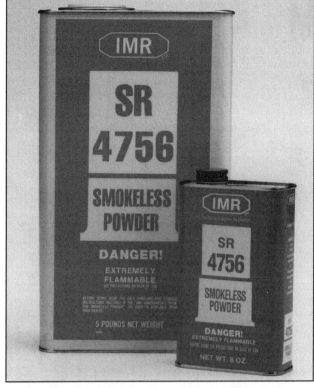

IMR's SR-4756 is used mostly for magnum loads—a rather slow burning powder for most shotshell loading.

curve to apply a greater total push to the shot charge? A switch to medium burn rate powders will fire a heavier load—with more velocity—while generating safe levels of pressure. In general applications, medium burn rate powders are often overlooked, misunderstood or ignored by reloaders. Mediums I have enjoyed with great success include Alliant's Unique and Herco; IMR's SR-7625 and 800-X; Scot Solo-1250; Winchester's WSF (Winchester Super Field) and 540; and Hodgdon's International Clays. Herco is the most overlooked of them all. It can make both light and heavy loads go very fast, consistently and without dramatic pressure peaks.

Medium burn rate propellants have great character. Once the handloader learns to stay within the wide limits of medium burn rated propellants, he is well on the way to propellant understanding.

Burn rate is not printed on canisters of powder because of the concern that someone might wish to calculate (rather than have tested) a load based upon only partial information. Also, relative

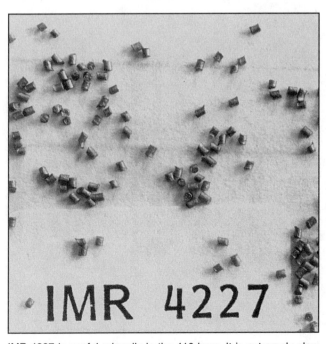

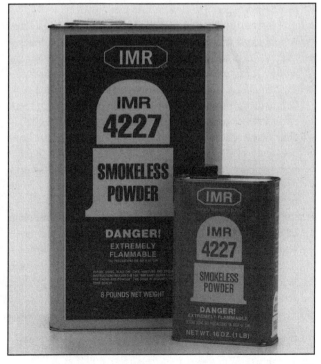

IMR-4227 is useful primarily in the 410-bore. It is extremely slow burning and has limited applications here.

Winchester's Super-Lite (WSL) Ball powder is a fast burning propellant best suited to 12-gauge target loads.

Super-Field (WSF) by Winchester generally replaces the older 473AA powder, but *data is not interchangeable.* This is another Ball powder.

burn rate depends upon the conditions of use. However, understanding that there are differences in powder burn rates and how powders are applied is critical to the handloader. Here are some basic facts, rules and tips concerning powder.

- Fast burn rate powders are only used with light payloads as more shot weight will make the pressure climb very high.
- Everything with powders is relative, one to the other. Fast burn means faster than others which are "slower."
- With fast burn rate powders, it is harder to detect imperfect burns than with slower burn rate powders. Fast burn rate powders cover up more defects.
- Fast burn rate powders are less elastic in application and forgiveness compared to slower burn rate powders.
- Fast burn rate powders are usually associated with the lightest weight loads for a gauge, usually the trap and Skeet loads.
- Faster powders are generally useful in larger gauges. Assuming an equal charge of shot is used, the difference is dramatic.
- In the smaller gauges, only medium and slow burn rate powders can be put to best use. Smaller chambers generate excessive pressures with faster burn rate powders. Smaller-chambered shotguns use relatively very slow burn rate powders and usually generate higher chamber pressures than the larger gauges. The 410-bore further demonstrates this principle in its unique (among scatterguns) ability to utilize certain rifle powders.
- Cold temperatures retard all propellant burn rates to some degree. Slow burn rate powders may not ignite well under severe conditions.
- There is not a parallel relationship between the potential velocity of a load and the relative burn rate of the powder, but the two are related.
- More powder does not mean additional velocity. In fact, a drop in velocity can occur.
- Light payloads of shot combined with slow burn rate pow-

ders can result in a great amount of unburned powder and fluctuations in pressures.
- Weak crimps, especially in older hulls, can result in unburned powder or bloopers. Crimps are important to proper combustion.
- Air pockets left in the powder area may result in a blooper.
- Use nominal wad pressure when loading, just enough to force out all the air and seat the wad. That's all that is required for proper combustion—no more!

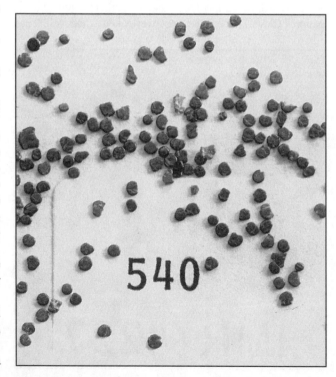

Winchester's 540 is mostly used for heavy field loads. It's also popular for 28-gauge reloads.

Winchester Super-Target (WST) is relatively fast burning and replaces the old Winchester 452 AA. Again, *data is not interchangeable.* It's used mostly for 12-gauge target loads.

- Store powders in original containers. These containers are designed to burst at very low pressures, only allowing the propellant to burn quickly. Solid containers could create bombs. Your propellant does not know the difference. And keep the containers tightly closed.
- Never put one type of powder in another type of powder container. I don't care how well you mark the can, you could miss seeing the label.

- Become familiar with the ordinances pertaining to home storage of powder and the amounts that are allowable.

Powder Elasticity

New reloaders always seem to yearn for a "universal load." One powder, one weight, one component—all easy to load and a dream to shoot. We all might like that load, but even if the loads were simplified—the targets and hunting conditions are not. Game bird hunters have many different ammunition needs, maybe even more than have been considered thus far. Weather conditions impose additional requirements, and if we are to become super-specialized for best results, the handloader will want to fire refined shells specifically designed for the game, weather and shotgun(s) utilized. Powder has a great influence on the overall picture.

Most powders are developed for a specific purpose and then are stretched to be used in other applications. For instance, did you know that the SR in IMR's excellent SR-7625 powder stands for "small rifle?" Yet, this propellant works exceedingly well in most shotshell applications. Shotguns and pistols share several powders. I know that several of Hodgdon's powders I like in my shotguns are also favorites of pistol loaders. Rifle powders do not have much crossover. They just burn too slowly for anything except a few 410-bore loads. If it's an extruded tube-type powder, it probably will not work well in a shotgun.

Even the shotgun-specific powders are stretched in different directions. Alliant Blue Dot is an excellent magnum load powder. I like it for most hunting loads and stretch its application in many directions. In steel loads, its particular burning quality is nearly perfect for the individual nature of steel loads. However, I find that in temperatures below 32 degrees F it loses its per-

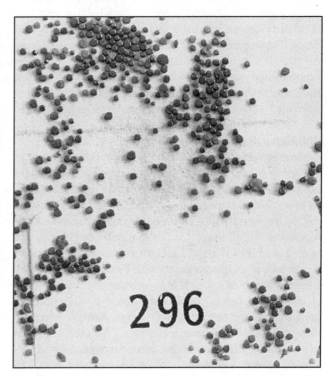

Winchester's 571 is relatively slow burning and is useful for 3-inch shells in both 12- and 20-gauge.

Winchester's 296 is the slowest burning of the Winchester powders in shotshell applications and is used only in 410-bore shells.

formance edge. Consequently, I pull out another powder for cold weather and use different loads.

Some medium burn rate powders can be stretched both ways. IMR's SR 7625, for example, drives my fastest $1^1/_{16}$-ounce Sporting Clays loads as well as my all-time favorite pheasant loads using $1^3/_8$ ounces of nickel-plated #5s.

To better understand stretching a powder application, especially in terms of burn rate, let's grab a golf club, a golf ball, a croquet mallet and a croquet ball. A golf club represents a fast burning powder, while a croquet mallet is a slow burning powder; a golf ball will serve as a light load, and a croquet ball is a heavy hunting load. Our analogy is easy enough and similar to what happens with our loads.

Now, if you are handed the golf club and the two balls, reactions are somewhat predictable: You can whack that little, light golf ball at least 300 yards (sure, but we're imagining anyway) with a solid and fast swing. Now line up and do the same with the croquet ball. Take a good fast swing and really impart a lot of energy to the ball. Went about 5 feet didn't it?

Now take the croquet mallet and give a big, energy-laden (but slow) swing. How'd that golf ball do? Forty feet? Better than expected. Now whack the croquet ball. Maybe not 300 yards, but our analogy becomes clear.

Fast burning powders impart energy very quickly and count on getting a lighter mass moving fast. Slow burning powders build to a crescendo of energy, transferring it to the mass over a longer period of time. When playing golf, use a golf club. When shotgunning, use a powder specialized to the load used.

For a powder to have great elasticity, it must have good ignition quality through a wide range of loads with no sharp increases or drops of pressure.

When certain powders are stretched over a wider range of loading applications (lighter to heavier loads), the powder will reveal particular qualities that may reduce its usefulness or efficiency. The original reason for choosing a powder may become less clear. It is knowledge of powders and their individual characteristics that allow handloaders to make better load choices, using powders that are best suited for the conditions at hand or anticipated—I do not use Blue Dot for cold weather goose loads.

Hull Capacity/Powder Measurement

Some powders are bulky and will occupy a large amount of hull space. We talked earlier about the development of high-energy double-based powders and how for the same energy levels as single-based powders they can occupy less space. Powder volume has a great influence upon the wad column height and which wad will fit best. This factor operates both for us and against us in our efforts as handloaders because it may either give or take away component options. Powder is measured by weight in our loads. As such, little consideration is given to the volume a given type of powder may occupy. If you insist upon using compression-formed hulls with single-based powders and heavy payloads, I hope your arm is strong. You will need a lot of strength to crush your loads closed. A combination of volume and weight measurements, for our purposes, would be nifty, but not very convenient. It is smarter for you as a hand-doader to become familiar with different powder types and how

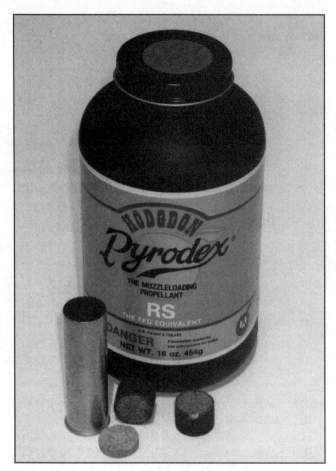

Hodgdon's Pyrodex RS is ideal for shooters who want to go the old-timey blackpowder route with their shotguns.

they occupy space, as well as their energy levels, relative to other powder types. Remember to follow tested load recipes and do not substitute components.

Pressure Management

The means of measuring shotgun chamber pressures, whether in pounds per square inch (psi) or lead units of pressure (LUP), represent the maximum reasonable and allowable internal pressures for that gauge/load. What relieves chamber pressure is the movement of the mass within the shotshell: the wad and the shot. If the load is somewhat heavy for use with a fast burn rate powder, the powder charge may generate gases that achieve higher pressure than recommended as safe for use. Since the amount of the powder can be regulated, we have control over pressure. Excessive pressure will wreck the gun's pattern, and might wreck the gun and shooter.

However, regulating the amount of powder only goes so far. As the payload weight increases, at some point the load is going to require a different powder; the powder's burn time needs to be extended to lower the peak pressure value and spread it over a longer period. This will increase the velocity of the mass being propelled.

So why not load the slowest burn rate powder available and go for screaming speed? Slow burn rate powders are really slow. They need to push heavy loads and sustain a certain level of resistance or they will not burn cleanly or consistently. A

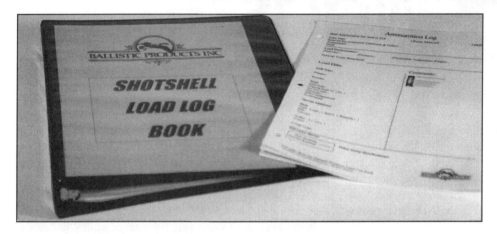

Verify your load recipes by checking manuals and guides distributed by powder companies.

Keep accurate records of all your loading and shooting. Take copious notes in your load book.

very light load combined with a slow powder is almost an automatic dud. Such a load might test OK on a shimmering August day, but in October when the frost is on the pumpkin—"Poop!"

Outside temperatures affect all shotshells, and on marginal loads the effect is even more profound. Hot weather increases the burn rate of shotshell powders, and cold weather reduces it. Rifle shells are less affected because they fire at perhaps three times our operating pressures.

If you doubt that slow burn rate powders really burn all that slowly, then take a heavy magnum load and fire it at night. You will note a heavy blue flame extending 6 inches beyond the end of your barrel. These are burning gases. Even shotguns with long barrels, such as 34-inch hunting shotguns, display burning gases when slow burn rate powders are utilized.

Steel Shot and Powders

Given two pellets of the exact same size, one of lead and one of steel, the steel pellet weighs about 30 percent less than the lead one. Therefore, if you have an ounce of steel shot and an ounce of lead, you will have a greater number of steel pellets. We have found that steel pellets demand the powder character offered only by the medium-slow to slow burn rate powders. There is little give to steel payloads, and the volume of payload is higher for the weight. While no clear-cut path can be made for all the possibilities, we note that IMR's SR-4756 and Alliant's Blue Dot function extremely well with steel shot

loads. Several types of powder by Scot/Accurate promise to be exceptional. Also, look for loads with Hodgdon's HS-7.

Data Books

Every powder company issues a brochure listing the most recent information and data concerning their powders. Powders change slightly over time, evolving into different types, volumes, energies, etc. In these guides, information is detailed on how to store and treat powders. Do yourself a favor: If you are seriously thinking of reloading shotshells, you should have every one of these instructional guides. I encourage you to contact the manufacturers and obtain their manuals. If you limit your inquiries to their specific brands, I think you will find each manufacturer more than helpful in creating better handloads. The powder and primer manufacturers have knocked themselves out to gather the information printed in these guides. It is all there for you to take advantage of. The guides are usually free upon request.

Any load alterations or substitutions are the perfect and fastest way to screw up an otherwise effective load. Component alterations are similar to trying to increase engine power by substituting various types of fuels; say kerosene instead of gasoline. Would you get mad at your car because it won't perform with stuff that ought to be powering camp lights? Well, don't blame the load, components or recipes if you have used substitutions and your loads are not performing.

7

As the heart of the load,
the modern wad seals
the bore, protects the shot,
and does so much more.

Shotshell Wads

ALL SHOTSHELL LOADS require an individual component, the wad, to be placed between its propellant and pellets. In metallic cartridges, the bullet itself (since it's a solid object) serves as the gas seal. However, a stack of multiple projectiles offers plenty of spaces between each other and, therefore, cannot contain the propellant gases, and so the load chain requires a gas-scaling platform.

The shotshell wad is a study unto itself, and not enough handloaders take the time to consider this vital link between propellant and payload. Wads serve two functions in shotshells: as a gas seal and also as a platform and carrier for the shot payload. Over time, the lowly wad has evolved into a technologically advanced component.

Cardboard Wads

In an earlier time, cardboard disks served as shotshell wads. The disks varied in thickness and were stacked according to the capacity/payload needs of the load. But the cardboard

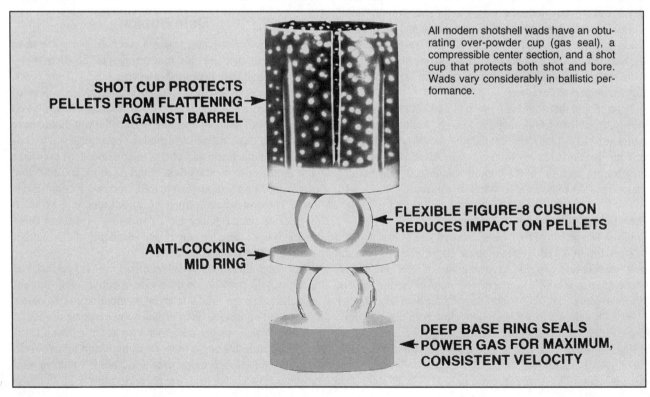

SHOT CUP PROTECTS PELLETS FROM FLATTENING AGAINST BARREL →

All modern shotshell wads have an obturating over-powder cup (gas seal), a compressible center section, and a shot cup that protects both shot and bore. Wads vary considerably in ballistic performance.

→ FLEXIBLE FIGURE-8 CUSHION REDUCES IMPACT ON PELLETS

ANTI-COCKING MID RING →

← DEEP BASE RING SEALS POWER GAS FOR MAXIMUM, CONSISTENT VELOCITY

This is a collection of fiber and felt wads and gas seals from older loads that are biodegradable components. They don't leave unsightly plastic debris around the fields. Using these could earn the hunter an invitation to return to a hunting spot.

Wads can have large (left) or small shotcups to accomodate different payloads. The larger shotcup has less cushioning at the mid-section.

disk's intrinsic sealing qualities are poor, and gases escape easily around the sides. This reduces shot velocity, decreases shot-to-shot uniformity and tends to enlarge the pattern. To overcome leaking seals, more powder is used, increasing the potential energy of the load. Basically, a level ten powder charge is placed into the load, but by the time the excess gas leaks around a cardboard seal it may be down to a level six pressure/velocity payload. Thus, to create a level ten load, we have to increase the charge dramatically. However, this is not always the case. Sometimes the seal will hook up tighter than usual and result in, let's say, a level eight load. Perhaps it now becomes clear why wad efficiency is so critical to consistent ballistics.

Modern Plastic Wads

Blackpowder shotguns and early shotshell cartridges had straight-walled combustion chambers. Gas seal design only required a disk of proper diameter and construction. Modern gas seals have to conform to the dimensions of modern hulls.

In 1960, Remington Arms came out with the first plastic shotshell and plastic wad combination. The slickness of plastic on plastic helped resolve a ballistic conundrum: how to achieve a near leak-proof seal while allowing the "give" necessary to oblige rapidly expanding gases. As the powder burns, pressure builds. And if relief is not found, the tremendous pressure will seek another source of escape. That's usually a weak spot in the barrel. Consistent and easy payload movement reduces the wad's role as a variable, allowing the load designer to focus on performance-oriented variables.

As soon as gas seal design emphasis turned toward performance, specialized gas seals began to appear for specific hull types. Winchester's compression-formed AA hulls have interior walls that taper toward the base. Winchester and a few other companies make wads with a smaller, angular base wad to fit

these hulls. Were a shooter to use a taper-design wad in a straight-walled hull, he may be a bit disappointed with the results; powder migration past the seal as well as significant blow-by reduces load pressure and velocity.

Variances in gas seal design, and the different pressures they produce, are just one reason not to substitute wads. There will probably be recipes for just about every conceivable combination, but a casual substitution of wads can cause loading, performance and safety problems. Don't do it!

Federal manufactures specific wads for their Gold Medal hulls. The wads have a pretty big gas seal to fit the hull's thin straight walls. Other hulls with a straight-walled design work well with Federal wads as well as other wads with large gas seals. However, when you decide to load wads with large gas seals into compression-formed hulls, you are going to encounter some serious resistance during seating.

If you measure taper- and straight-walled wads, you will not see be a great deal of difference, but we are dealing with close tolerances and high pressure gas containment (around 10,000 psi). What happens when we plop a taper-walled wad into a straight-walled hull? The gas seal does not fit snugly to the sides of the hull, resulting in gas blow-by, a poor pattern and possibly a blooper load.

What if a wad with a larger gas seal is placed in a taper-walled hull? According to load data I have, this is done frequently. The fit may be a bit tight, but you will note that such loads usually call for bulky powders that do not permit the gas seal to be pushed deep into the tapered section. Measurably higher pressures are not a result of this combination. Loading manuals often describe straight-walled wads being placed in taper-walled hulls, but hardly ever the other way around.

Most modern wads are designed to obturate, wherein a bell-shaped gas seal flares outward under pressure to create a self-sustaining seal. A similar principle made Minie balls effective

There are wide choices to be had with wads, like these from Pattern Control. They're available in 12 ($1^{1}/_8$, 1 ounce), 20 ($^{7}/_8$-ounce), 28 ($^{3}/_4$-ounce) and 410 ($^{1}/_2$-ounce) in seven styles for trap, Skeet and field loads.

in the muzzle-loading rifle. Here, the hollowed-out base of a lead slug expands outward under pressure from the gases, conforming tightly to the confines of the bore. A tight, consistent seal gives maximum drive and consistent ballistic performance.

High-velocity loads require a tight gas seal both in the hull and in the shotgun's bore to achieve quality results. The application of back-boring or overboring (a technique where standard bore diameters are enlarged) has become popular without much consideration of the procedure's effect on plastic gas seals. Back-boring places additional pressure upon the gas seal, requiring the seal to be as tight-fitting as possible to continue normal obturation past the hull. If the gases are allowed past the seal, velocity as well as patterns suffer.

The problems of an inadequate gas seal grow exponentially when an overbored barrel meets with a tapered gas seal. Even though a load may show a reasonable velocity in the ballistic laboratory, this mismatched application of gun and load leave inexperienced shotgunners shaking their heads and misunderstanding the true nature of their problem. As long as a gas seal is well matched to the barrel, offering complete powder burning capabilities, matching the hull type becomes a secondary consideration since performance is a higher priority than loading conveniece.

As shot loads become heavier than $1^{1}/_8$ ounce in the 12-gauge, propellant charges become bulkier because larger amounts of slower burning powders are required. As such, the powder charge sits above the tapered base, rendering a tapered-base wad irrelevant; in such a load, tapered-base wads increase the risk of a poor load without any potential advantage. Consider, instead, using a wad with a larger, tighter fitting seal.

The Cushion Section

The cushion section of a target wad is located just above the gas seal. Its job is three-fold: to compress uniformly, progressively and without tipping the gas seal.

In the reloading press, the cushion section of the wad must compress without collapsing. A full collapse would compro-

A good gas seal is a very important part of the wad. Without it, blow-by causes sub-standard performance.

mise its interior ballistic value during the firing cycle. A collapsed cushion section may also damage the gas seal. So, under the slow pressure of the wad ram, the cushion section must compress to accommodate various powder heights, a few alterations in shot charges and a few minor differences between otherwise similar hulls, and it must do so predictably without failure.

There are several levels of "adjustment" in handloads. The powder, and the specific amount used in a load, can alter the load height. Changes in shot size, even if all the other components remain the same, can also change the height of a load. Manufacturers use the compressible section of the wad to allow a somewhat "universal" wad to be successfully placed in several different load configurations. Also, certain powders are highly compressible.

Of course, the broad applications of modern wads can be taken to extremes. Though it would be nice to only have to use one type of wad for all types of shooting, from hunting to target, it's not very smart. In heavier hunting loads, the cushion section may be crushed to a point where it is twisted and damaged. Once you have mangled it, you have an increased chance of a leaking seal and an inconsistent load. Just because heavy loads are listed does not mean they will always be effective. It

(Right) As the shot-filled wad travels through the bore, it protects the shot from deforming and holds it in one group; (below) after exiting the bore, the shotcup begins to open; and (bottom) a few feet farther the petals open fully, allowing the shot to continue to the target. The wad drops to the ground within a few yards.

might mean, rather, that the wad manufacturer is pushing the envelope of reasonable performance to find more applications. This can be handy if you cannot find a better wad, but is a poor choice nontheless.

The cushion section should compress progressively during the initial firing sequence. Though its overall effect inside the shotshell is somewhat limited by the extreme forces put upon it, it is designed to work like a shock absorber in a car. As the expanding gases build (within a millisecond or so) behind the seal, it moves forward as if it were struck by a sledge-hammer. In absorbing this sudden burst of energy, the column must remain straight and not let the gas seal tip, even a little bit.

The shock wave imparted to the shot column is terrific. In a millisecond, pressure builds to nearly 10,000 psi and, within a few inches of travel, the load achieves the vast majority of its velocity. The tremendous pressure moves up the wad column in a wave; first through the gas seal, the cushion, then into the shotcup. The bottom layers of pellets begin to move forward before the pellets above them, and something has to give.

Usually what gives is the bottom layers of pellets, squashing themselves against the upper layers. Our ballistic goal, via the cushion section, is to draw out the wave of energy moving through the wad column. A progressively collapsing wad column is the equivalent of wrapping a towel around a hammer: Energy is dampened progressively before the full force is imparted. Any carpenter knows that even a thin pair of leather gloves will save a thumb from a crushing blow. Energy dispersal inside a shotshell is similar.

As loads get heavier, the cushion section offers diminishing returns inside the shotshell. First, the cushion is crushed by the larger pellet payload. In doing this, valuable space is removed, causing the energy wave to come into more direct contact with the lower layers of pellets. Second, what's left of the cushion has to do more work. In the 12-gauge, it's much easier for the cushion to absorb energy and ease the load forward if the payload is $1^1/_4$ ounces or less. Payloads greater than that exceed the design intent of plastic wad columns, requiring specially designed hunting wads and compressible felt or cushion wads placed directly below the shot charge.

The Shotcup

Modern wads, with a container for the pellet charge, are important for pattern enhancement. We have already talked about protecting the bottom layer of pellets from being crushed as the load moves forward. To further improve the pattern, we also need to protect the outer layer of pellets from scrubbing against the barrel, which would remove material and deform the pellets. The thin petals attached to the wad platform are designed to take the punishment given to the load by the barrel. Although the petals are usually not thick enough to absorb lateral energy, eliminating the scrubbing effect demonstrably improves pattern evenness and density.

The petals, upon leaving the barrel, open up and allow the pellets to go free. If a wad without slits was used, the pellets tend to remain inside the shotcup, acting like a slug and producing a very dangerous load. Unslit wads are sold only to offer a chance to slit shotcups in various ways to alter pattern performance.

Patterns for Target Shooting

The focus of the target wad industry is tailored toward the 12-gauge $1^1/_8$-ounce lead load. This makes a lot of sense, because that's exactly what most shotgunners use almost all the time. For this type of load, there is a wad to suit everybody— and each, used in accordance with its design, works well. And there are many other types of shots clay target shooters encounter. Skeet shooters do not want tight patterns. Sporting Clays shooters want many different patterns and load types for the varying situations they encounter on the course.

Many shooters go through patterning agonies attempting to shoot the tightest of all possible patterns, but perhaps they should be looking at developing a load that demonstrates a stronger fringe or even a wide-open spread. If we were all 27-yard handicap trap shooters, then the tight center pattern would be our objective.

Some Sporting Clays shooters spend a lot of time switching chokes when, to get much the same effect, they could have just used a different load. By using different types of wads, we can affect our patterns. And by understanding the patterns that different loads produce, we can use these loads to our advantage on the Sporting Clays course.

To get tighter patterns, you'll want to keep all the pellets within the shotcup because the thickness of the wad petal adds to your choke constriction. Many reloaders have unknowingly followed this custom for some time, regardless of their pattern objective. A wad petal .030-inch thick adds about double that amount to the choke constriction. If you shoot handicap or international trap, take note. Thicker wad petals should mean tighter patterns. Don't use a thick shotcup if you are attempting to load middle- or short-range loads.

European shooters, more accustomed to multi-range applications for their target loads, have long made use of shorter shotcups as part of a carefully planned pattern-control design.

Shotcup proportions are carefully maintained to provide adequate center pattern densities and allow a controlled number of pellets to work a greater portion of the pattern on the fringe. These percentages are designed into the wad in the form of petal height. The fringe pellets, the outer "doughnut" of the pattern, are important for maximizing short-range use of a shotgun.

European shotgunners have also designed wads that place a portion of the lead pellets in a fixed non-petalled shotcup for a dense center pattern, while the remainder of the pellets become

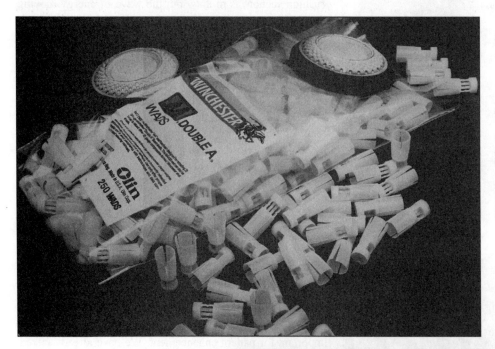

Some think that the 16-gauge seems to be on its way to becoming an orphan chiefly because wads for it can be difficult to locate in some areas. When choices are limited, it pays to stock up on components when they are found.

A wide variety of wad styles is available to suit individual load designs and requirements. Use the proper wad for the load and performance will be enhanced.

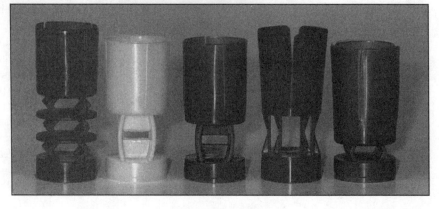

the outer fringe doughnut. It's a completely different philosophy of shooting than we long-ranging Americans are accustomed to, but in multi-range target shooting, it works effectively. Allowing the bore of your shotgun to control a portion of the load can create very successful field and target loads.

Spreader Wads

Some modern wads, by design, are made with no shotcup at all. These are brush or spreader-type wads. Though the outside pellets will be deformed by barrel scrub, your pattern will function very close to the true choke of your shotgun. Used in shotguns with highly polished bores, brush wads will surprise you with some exceptional results. Other short-range wads may have a vertical "X" section moulded into the center. These actively push the pattern wider than the bore's marked constriction.

Specific Loading Instructions

Quality wad makers spend a lot of time and effort assembling loads for their specific wads. The exact design and resins used to manufacture the wads are proprietary and, therefore, not shared with manufacturers of "copycat" designs.

I am against using target wads marketed as "substitutes" for established designs. Usually, no specific data is supplied with these wads, and you are directed to just use another manufacturer's data. A statement like this should signal you, the thinking handloader, that perhaps the manufacturer is less than familiar with the subtleties of shotshell ballistics.

Not long ago, I talked with an established wad maker whose original design was "borrowed" by a substitute manufacturer. He spoke to a customer on the phone one day, trying to sort through a load fitting problem. They went around and around the problem, and he offered a few suggestions that should have put the fellow on the right track. As they were closing their conversation, the manufacturer commented that he had not had this kind of fit problem with that particular wad. The caller said, well, no, it wasn't that wad. The one he had was a substitute, manufactured by so-and-so. It seems that he couldn't make contact with the manufacturer of that particular wad, so he called the company that made the wad it was *supposed* to duplicate.

Also, since target wads are manufactured by the ton, there are bound to be moulding errors—rejects that didn't get rejected. It may behoove you to inspect your wads before you drop them into a shell. Problems we have seen include petals that are not fully formed; tiny (and some not so tiny) pinholes in the plastic, which may weaken the structure; malformed or partially miss-

Filler wads (these are cork) are placed into the base of the hunting wad to control payload height. You can use as many as necessary for proper crimping.

Wool felt cushion wads are available in many sizes and gauges for hunting loads. They can perform a number of ballistic functions.

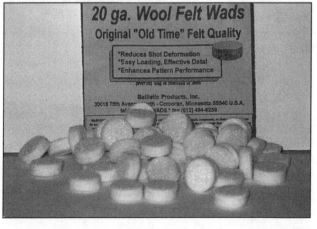

When using hunting wads, the MEC wad guide fingers must be removed. Otherwise, the rammer sits too high to properly seat the wad.

ing gas seals; or even plastic that "just doesn't feel right" to the touch, usually due to a high or low mould temperature setting during the manufacturing process. Wads may have gotten crushed during transport or storage—maybe even enough to go beyond the plastic's original memory. If that's the case, you will see distortions of the wad's shape.

Wads are as specific as any other component. You know by now not even to consider arbitrarily switching hulls for a particular load. Neither should you substitute wads, for the exact same reasons.

Hunting Wads

When load capacities exceed a nominal amount (I use 1¼ ounces of lead in the 12-gauge as a threshold), target wads become ineffective as carriers, and special procedures must be utilized in order to properly contain the load and control the pattern at typical hunting ranges. The second wad in our two general categories of wads is the special-purpose hunting wad. Because the loads are required to dispatch live game rather than simply break a clay target, special demands are placed upon hunting loads. Sufficient numbers of pellets must be driven with enough energy to penetrate the game and kill cleanly.

Lethal energy requires velocity. Introducing the velocity factor to magnum payloads requires components sometimes completely different than target loads to achieve maximum effectiveness.

Hunting Wad Capacities

Shot column heights in hunting wads are varied by placing filler wads under the pellet payload. The filler wads serve essentially the same purpose as the cushion area of a target wad, only on a larger scale. Filler wads are usually made of felt, cork or fiber material, and are available in various thicknesses. Most reloading data will specify a certain type of filler configuration; consider this to be a suggestion. Changes in shot size will affect your column height, and you may need to use different thicknesses to get the right height for that perfect crimp.

In the 12-gauge, the shot charge should be raised to the top edge of the shotcup by placing 20-gauge card wads into the base of the shotcup. I prefer to use 20-gauge fillers that are precut to ⅛- or ¼-inch thickness. Wool felts are very dense, but light, and they may be used liberally to raise the shot column. Cork wads are just as light, but provide a firmer platform. Felt or cork wads may be used interchangeably; their minimal mass allows the handloader to use them without measurably affecting load pressures.

Cutting Petals to Change Pattern

Handloaders can influence a magnum load's pattern by varying the number and length of wad slits. A shotgun pattern can be made tighter by cutting fewer full-length slits into the shotcup. A minimum of three petals, two-thirds the length of the shotcup, is required for all loads. A general rule of thumb is that the greater the number and length of the slits, the quicker the load's pattern will open up. Please note, however, that insufficient numbers of petals and/or insufficient petal length

This looks like too much shot to fit into this target wad shotcup, but it goes in nicely.

Although a target wad by definition, Activ's T-42 is an exception to a general rule. It makes an excellent heavy payload hunting wad with a large shotcup and short cushion section.

will defeat the intent by giving increasingly inconsistent patterns or creating the same problem as no slits. The wad "holds" pellets in the base, flips over and becomes a shuttlecock for a "slug" load; ineffective for waterfowl shooting as well as dangerous to fellow shooters. Experiment with wad slits and pattern controls, but remain reasonable in the applications for best results.

I recommend that the handloader begin with four long slits to establish a baseline from which to work. Then try different numbers and lengths of slits to achieve, at a given range, best results on the pattern board. Look for *consistency* with the size pellets you will be using in the field. Make and keep notes concerning each shotgun and load type so you can duplicate the load later. The great part of this kind of experimentation is that you have the perfect excuse to go crack off a few magnum hunting loads during the off-season.

Teflon-Wrapped Loads

Specialized Teflon-wrapped loads offer the shooter an opportunity to utilize every bit of space within the shotshell and

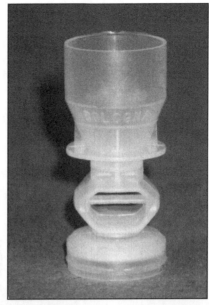

This wad is designed for tight patterns at extreme range, as in International Trap. Note that the payload sits in an unslit cup.

A wad is inserted into this angled wad slitter and an X-Acto knife is used to cut the petals. The snapring is moved up or down to control slit height.

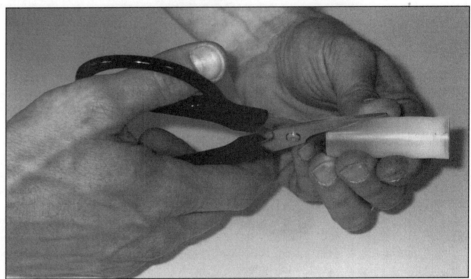

Sometimes shotcups need to be modified for optimum performance, and here stainless steel snips are used to cut petals into a wad.

protect the shot column (or slug) from deformation and barrel scrub. Teflon wrap is a very thin, material applied as a long-range carrier for large capacity 10- and 12-gauge loads. The wrap allows the handloader to create certain space-consuming loads that would not otherwise be possible due to volume limitations within a shotshell. Always use proper recipes and loading instructions for Teflon-wrapped loads.

Do not substitute any other wrap for Teflon sheets. Mylar, used to contain steel shot loads, does not offer the lubricity of Teflon and will not give satisfactory results in those applications. Mylar wraps are used exclusively inside a steel pellet shotcup. Mylar's sole purpose is to offer an extra measure of protection for your barrel from the deleterious effects of contact with steel pellets. Recipes for these types of loads are available from Ballistic Products, Inc.

Steel Pellet Shotcups

In the days of lead shot, the shotcup protected the pellets from the barrel. With steel shot, the wad has exactly the opposite mission. It did not really matter if the lead cup allowed a

few pellets to become deformed, because each load had many pellets and the very next load gave you a fresh batch of pellets to muck up. However, most shooters prefer not to replace their barrel following every steel shot round.

Because barrel and steel pellets are made of the same material, direct barrel/pellet contact is a no-no. A protective shotcup is the standard measure of prevention. Steel pellets place terrific stresses on shotcups, so the need for specialization and integrity is imperative. Materials used in manufacturing steel shotcups are specialized and very different than those used to make lead shot wads.

The design of the shotcup and the load must incorporate a protective material and deliver expected ballistic objectives. With this dual-purpose design, each load is going require a special kind of harmony between the components. Only certain combinations can really work well, and due to the specific nature of the loads and components necessary to create them, the handloader *must* use only the components and recipes that have proven to be safe. What it all boils down to is that when loading steel shot, only use wad columns or shotcups (or anything else) specifically made for steel.

8

With shot available in myriad sizes, alloys and finishes, the correct choice will separate also-ran loads from top-performing "wonder-shells."

Shotshell Pellets

LEAD IS AN excellent element from which to make shotshell pellets. Unlike car keys in the morning, lead is readily available. It is dense and therefore an excellent carrier of energy. It is malleable, so it absorbs energy put upon it during the firing sequence. It becomes a liquid at a reasonably low temperature and, therefore, re-solidifies quickly. Since lead pellets are manufactured in a process that involves melting ingots then letting surface tension shape the pellet, re-solidification, and the speed with which it is accomplished, becomes a factor.

Lead Shot

The manufacturing process of lead shot involves bringing lead ingots to the top of a drop tower, around 100 feet high, where the lead is then melted and poured through a sieve. The sieve has specifically sized holes for specific pellet sizes; the resulting droplets coming through are the actual size of the finished pellet. The droplets, as they leave the sieve, are still molten, and it is the manufacturer's desire to maintain pellets size and roundness. To this end, the droplets take a 100-foot freefall, ending up in a tub of water. What keeps the pellets round is the principle of surface tension—equal atmospheric pressure on all sides creates a spherical shape. A 100-foot drop is adequate to solidify most shot sizes.

As a quality control measure, pellets are then put through a roundness test. Right after being dried, the pellets are rolled down a series of carefully spaced plates. If the pellet is perfectly round, gravity gives it enough speed to jump the carefully measured crevasse between the plates. Out-of-round pellets, like Evel Knievel trying to jump the Snake River, fall in. Later, the misshapen pellets are re-melted and get to try again.

SHOT SIZES.

	9	8½	8	7½	6	5	4	3	2	1	BB	BBB	T
PELLET DIAMETER													
INCHES	.08	.085	.09	.095	.11	.12	.13	.14	.15	.16	.18	.19	.20
MM	2.03	2.16	2.29	2.41	2.79	3.05	3.30	3.56	3.81	4.06	4.57	4.83	5.08

BUCKSHOT.

	No. 4	No. 3	No. 2	No. 1	No. 0	No. 00	No. 000
PELLET DIAMETER							
INCHES	.24	.25	.27	.30	.32	.33	.36
MM	6.10	6.35	6.86	7.62	8.13	8.38	9.14

All American brand chilled lead shot is available in very small sizes like #10, #11 and #12 for special applications. Chilled shot's best features are lower price and wider patterns due to deformation of the pellets. For close-in targets this can be an advantage.

Lawrence Brand high antimony Magnum lead shot is harder than chilled lead and offers improved long-range patterns in many loads.

The almost perfectly round pellets are then, usually, coated with graphite to reduce friction when in contact with each other and when used in metering devices.

Lead pellets are classified by their alloy content. Pure lead ingots (formerly with just a dash of arsenic to give the pellet some additional surface tension) created soft or "drop shot." Modern drop shot is alloyed about .5 percent antimony for the same purpose. Lead, when alloyed with antimony, becomes a rounder pellet.

Chilled shot has an antimony content from about .5 to around 2 percent. Magnum shot runs 3 to 6 percent antimony content, depending upon size. Smaller pellets have higher percentages, while larger sizes have lower percentages. It's hard to guess the exact antimony content, as manufacturers purchase their ingots in "premixed" lots, and it would be unreasonable to test all the batches. In addition, rejected pellets, when re-melted and added to a new batch, alter the original lot's antimony content, so to have an exact reading we would have to exclude all the rejects.

Winchester introduced copper-plated Lubaloy shot to hunters in 1929. The flash coating of copper created several advantages for shotgunners. First, the harder pellets held a much better pattern because they retained their spherical shape better. Second, the copper plating provides a slippery surface for improved flow and pellet metering. This is especially helpful with larger pellets, which tend to get in each other's way. The copper coating, as any hunter will tell you, resists getting wadded up in feathers, making its way instead to vital organs and resulting in cleaner kills.

Nickel-plated lead shot, originally developed for high-stakes live pigeon shoots, is the pellet of choice for the world's best shooters. While the surface of copper-plated shot is hard, nickel-plated shot is even harder. It is used by the Olympic shooting teams because their targets move so fast and are so distant only the tightest possible patterns will do the job. It is also the ulti-mate game pellet as penetration and energy transfer are unequaled. The difference is difficult to phrase in objective terms, but everyone who has tried it knows it's the best. If you are willing to pay the extra cost of admission, the nickel-plated shot club is for you.

Pellet Roundness And Flight

As far as aerodynamic shapes go, spherical is OK. Considering the nature of a shotshell—random shot placement, multiple projectiles, low manufacturing costs—it's the best we are going to do. Round pellets push a lot of air in front of them compared to the slim long projectiles our centerfire compadres use, but they only shoot one projectile at a time and we average around 300. If pellets remain perfectly spherical, and pressure on the pellet remains equally proportioned, the pellet flies straight and true with a given level of energy. However, should that pellet become deformed during the firing sequence, air pressure will be higher on one part of the pellet and lower on the other. In this situation, the pellet does several undesirable things. First, the course is altered; lower pressure on one side allows the pellet to be pushed in that direction, like an airplane wing altering its course. Second, the pellet expends valuable energy in its course alteration. Deformed pellets show up on the outside fringes of patterns. The number of deformed pellets can be directly related to the quality of the pellets in the load.

Regardless of which choke constriction you are using, softer pellets will spread more than harder pellets. The choice between a Modified choke and Full choke is quite often less of a pattern factor than the difference between soft chilled shot and high-antimony magnum shot. Conversely, if you are shooting at extended ranges, you can deliver tighter patterns with increased energy by using the hardest lead pellets possible. Ridiculous? Try it.

Shoot the densest pattern that brings maximum energy to the target. For geese on the prairie, T buck or larger shot might be the minimum size applicable.

(Below) It pays to match the shot size to the game being hunted, otherwise you'll just be shooting holes in the sky. Large shot would be overkill for these small birds.

From what you now know about deformed pellets, you may have gathered that you could increase the spread of a pattern by using softer shot. Right. Clay targets also require little energy to break. Even though you will be giving up some energy and velocity, you can improve your very close-range shooting by using softer, chilled pellets on clay targets. Think of it as improving your odds by strengthening the outside fringes of the patterns, utilizing probability in the form of that golden, misshapen pellet. However, because you are giving up lethal energy with misshapen pellets, I do not recommend using chilled lead for game applications.

Pellet Energy And Size Selection

Shot size selection controls the energy your load will deliver at a given range. There are reams of information on specific shot size selection, and everyone has an opinion. However, the rule of thumb, as it pertains to shot size, is to shoot the densest pattern that brings sufficient energy to the target. If your target

is made of clay and taken at under 25 yards, # 9 shot will be great. If your targets are big geese on the prairie in a screaming north wind, T buck or larger might be the minimum size applicable. As long as you understand that larger pellets will carry a diminished pattern farther, with lethal energy, you have the qualifications necessary to make your own shot size selection.

For taking game, I would like to influence you toward larger pellets. Too many hunters choose pellets based strictly upon pattern board results. Paper is easy; game is tough. It is better if a lesser number of lethal hits occur than a larger number of non-lethal hits. Of course, I do not encourage you to use #2 shot for your next pheasant hunt, but perhaps consider a one-size increase when in doubt. Let the conditions, range and game dictate your choices.

What follows is a guideline and only that. Use the shot size that works for you, your equipment, conditions and game. This chart is a starting point for someone who may need a place to begin.

Pellet Sizing Applications for Game		
Shot Size (ins.)	Effective Range (yards)	Optimum Conditions
T Buck (.20)	65 to 100	Heavy 40+ mph winds; extreme range; 10-gauge size
BB (.18)	60 to 90	Heavy 30+ mph winds; very long range; largest 12-gauge lead pellet
#1 (.16)	50 to 90	Windy 30+ mph; very long range
#2 (.15)	45 to 75	Windy 25+ mph; very long range; larger waterfowl (geese)
#3 (.14)	35 to 70	Windy; medium to long range; penetrates brush
#4 (.13)	30 to 65	Windy; decent patterns; medium to long range
#5 (.12)	30 to 60	Some wind; excellent pattern/ penetration; normal ranges
#6 (.11)	25 to 55	Very dense patterns; excellent for most pheasant shooting and turkey (for head shots)

Sporting Clays Pellet Applications

The pellet energy range of #9 (.080-inch), #8$\frac{1}{2}$ (.085-inch), #8 (.090-inch), #7$\frac{1}{2}$ (.095-inch) and #7 (.100-inch) is quite adequate to break clay birds even under extreme conditions. The better Sporting Clays shooter will want to have available a selection of loads using these sizes of shot during a tour of any Sporting Clays course. The shot sizes selected will depend upon the course, conditions and the station of fire.

Successful Sporting Clays shooting is generally accomplished by firing many different kinds of shells, including light, low-recoil rounds. The less felt recoil your body absorbs in a round of Clays, the better your accuracy and concentration are in the long run. On a hot day, a fifty-bird shoot-off could be lost because your ammunition took too much of a toll on your tired body. Therefore, on as many targets as possible, shoot light 1-ounce, or even $\frac{7}{8}$-ounce, load configurations. There are enough pellets in a 1-ounce, #9 load to destroy a half-dozen targets, and you only need to break a target once. If you drive loads with sufficient velocity, the smaller pellets will carry plenty of energy to the target.

I have already mentioned that soft pellets can be used to your advantage in close-range shooting. I don't recommend taking this to an extreme, though. Drop shot, or utterly soft lead pellets, hardly functions as a pellet at any range. Chilled shot, with at least a small percentage of antimony, remains above the threshold of functionality. Choose a small size and make that pattern wide!

You probably would like to know which size I recommend for "utility" shooting. Number 8 shot is the average size for most Sporting Clays shooters. Bear in mind that the quality of the lead shot does vary and will control effective range. Reaching out for long shots with softer lead pellets may not break the clays because so many pellets have deformed and flown in different directions. The need for hard magnum lead shot on all long-range Sporting Clays shots becomes obvious when you experiment with different pellet hardnesses and quality. Top target shooters even disregard the extra cost and opt for the ultra-high performance of copper- or nickel-plated shot. Longer shots require the additional pellet energy and pattern uniformity found only by using hard shot.

If hardness alone is not quite doing the trick, a move up in size might help. Long-range clay target shooting may require #7$\frac{1}{2}$, or even #7, pellets. The heavier weight of the pellet will carry the energy to the target over the straightest and quickest path. If the pellets you are using are made of hardened lead, your probability of a break has just been improved. For long-range work, it may be better to use a 1$\frac{1}{16}$- or 1$\frac{1}{8}$-ounce load in order to maintain the dense pattern with the large shot.

Pellets by the Gauge

The 10-Gauge

Not surprisingly, the most effective 10-gauge waterfowl loads are those with the most lethal payloads. But lethal payloads are not necessarily maximum payloads. A survey of accomplished 10-gauge shooters revealed that their favorites were 1$\frac{7}{8}$-, 1$\frac{3}{4}$-, and 1$\frac{1}{2}$-ounce payloads. The 10-gauge can be loaded upwards of 2$\frac{1}{2}$ ounces, but just because this can be done does not mean

that is where peak performance is found. The aforementioned loads maintained the best overall balance in terms of pattern density, pattern uniformity, speed, felt recoil (important during long days of shooting) and overall load lethality.

Cutting back a bit on the shot payload can sometimes become the high performance option. Inside your shotgun barrel, large masses of shot tend to create internal conflict—crowding—that will inhibit the efficient focusing of downrange patterns. Although easy for consumer comparison to other load types, super-magnum-weight payloads are usually very much overrated.

The 12-Gauge

Similar to the lessons learned with the 10-gauge, the 12 is found to operate best when emphasizing downrange energy. By slightly reducing the mass of the load and driving it faster, 12-gauge magnum load performance can be significantly improved.

Although there are plenty of heavy artillery advocates in the field, no 12-gauge 3-inch load over 1$\frac{7}{8}$ ounces compares to the positive results demonstrated by the high velocity 1$\frac{5}{8}$-ounce lead shot combination. Even with very large pellets, this load provides outstanding pellet coverage, and with a velocity that keeps the pellets lethal, even at extended ranges. A large mass of slow moving pellets cannot be substituted for velocity and thoughtful load construction.

Magnum marketing has become part of the shotgunner's world. However, keep in mind that less can be more with lead shot loads and, now, non-toxic pellet loads. Choose your loads carefully, study and understand the ballistics of what you are shooting, and remain cognizant of what you intend to accomplish. Doing this will help you zero in on the shooting you do and where to put high performance loads to best use in the field. Don't revert to the caveman mentality of carrying the biggest stick just because you can. While a pheasant will not trample you like a cape buffalo, the wrong ammunition will ruin your hunt by hobbling your performance. Avoid overloading, a condition certain to ruin your ammunition's performance potential.

The 16-Gauge

Smaller shot sizes in the 16-gauge seem to provide superior performance on upland game, even at longer ranges. I have used #5 through #8 with excellent results. Anything larger than #5 begins to compromise the ballistics of this bore size, and while it will function, ballistic results drop off rapidly. This illustrates the principle that the best shot sizes for a specific gauge are directly proportional to the bore size (i.e., the smaller the gauge, the smaller the shot that can be used effectively). Shotguns in this bore size seem to crave plated shot. Their patterns come alive and push farther more effectively.

If I had to pick a favorite shot size for the 16 in the field it would probably be #6 nickel-plated. In terms of a lethal load with high pattern density and a high pellet count, this is king! If you cannot kill consistently with proper applications of 1$\frac{1}{8}$ ounces of #6 plated shot, perhaps the problem lies with the nut that connects the gunstock to the trigger. With a fast-driving

71

For a given weight, steel shot (right) occupies a larger amount of space than does lead. Special components are needed to load steel to protect the gun's barrel.

This old timey shot measure is adjustable for a number of loads. Since the tool measures by volume, it is unsuitable for use with steel shot.

1¹/₈-ounce load, you have a utility pheasant gun throughout the season.

The 20-Gauge

One of the beauties of the 20-gauge is that is can be chambered in a smaller and lighter gun compared to the 12-gauge. This, of course, means better handling on fast-rising birds and less bulk to lug around the game fields all day. This bore size offers sufficient ballistic "oomph" to reliably bring down most sporting fowl, and is completely competent on the clay bird field, to include Sporting Clays.

The 3-inch magnum here practically duplicates the performance of the top 16-gauge loads. Current factory loadings range from 1 to 1¹/₄ ounces of shot and include several buckshot combinations and the ⁵/₈-ounce slug. Steel shot loadings up to 1 ounce are useful and popular. By a wide margin, the 20-gauge is the second most popular U.S. chambering.

I have killed a lot of ducks with this gauge, using the 3-inch magnums, of course. Early on, when lead was legal, I thought #4s would be just the ticket for the web-footed fliers, but had a lot of trouble bringing them down reliably and cleanly. No matter what the range, too many escaped either unscathed or as cripples, which I hate to see. After some informal patterning, I tried slightly smaller shot, moving to #5s at first (and seeing some improvement), then to #6s. Voila! I had found my load for ducks over decoys. With steel shot, #4s work the best as long as the range is 40 yards or less (which applies to *all* gauges when steel shot is used).

The 28-Gauge

Contrary to what a lot of folks think, the 28-gauge is perfectly adequate for use in hunting upland birds and is at home breaking clay pigeons. To be most effective, this bore size needs to be fed small size shot. Remember, as bore size is reduced, smaller shot (#6, #7¹/₂, #8) provide optimum patterns. Obviously, this axiom holds true for the 20-gauge and 410-bore as well.

Back in the days of paper hulls, 1-ounce loads from Win-

chester were available, but disappeared for a while. Sometime in the 1960s that payload returned to dealer shelves and has been a real plus for the upland gunner. Handloads using this charge weight should be quite effective.

I have always been fond of the 28 because of the minimal recoil, reasonable muzzle blast, and the light easy-handling and graceful guns in which it's chambered. These guns are a welcome relief from the seemingly ponderous (comparatively) 12-gauge cannons I sometimes carry when I don't really need to. They are pure delight to swing on a rising pheasant or outgoing ruffed grouse.

I have found that #6 or #7¹/₂ works extremely well in the 28, but #8s can also be deadly. My personal preference is one of the former sizes, and I leave the #8s for woodcock and clay birds.

For some reason, game hit with the 28 comes out of the sky as if it were hit by a lightning bolt...I suppose it should since the 1-ounce loading duplicates a favorite upland load in the 20-gauge.

The 410-Bore

This dimimutive shotshell has a small but loyal following with hunters, and it's still used for breaking clay birds. Because of its small shot payload, the 410 is best used in the hands of a seasoned gunner when it comes to taking feathered game. While available in 2¹/₂-inch length, it kills best with 3-inch loads. Woodcock hunters using this bore size generally load #7¹/₂s, #8s and #9s for best patterns, but must be very good shots to reliably bring the little speedsters to bag.

The guns chambered for this smallest of our current shotshells are delightful to carry into the field or dense woods where the timberdoodle and ruff hang out. Some might even describe the guns as toy-like because they're so light and handy. That's part of the draw here—small guns, small shot swarms and fast moving targets.

Pellet Enhancements

Buffered Loads

All shotgunners—and especially handloaders—are always

seeking better control of their patterns, which becomes increasingly difficult as distance grows. Exterior ballistic influences increase as the payload slows and the barrel's influence becomes a distant memory. To take better control of exterior ballistics, many specialized long-range loads will use additives within the shot column called buffers, for the lack of a more inclusive and descriptive name. These substances can take many forms, depending upon the effect desired by the handloader. A number of different materials have been tried in order to achieve the desired pattern results. Some of the substances used have achieved high performance, but with a cost: extreme load pressures. These higher load pressures have restricted the use of most buffers.

Some buffers have a very short shelf life or change character while packed in the load. Flour, or any cereal product, is guilty here. Flour is too finely grained and tends to pack into some areas of the shot column while leaving gaps here and there. Flour also absorbs moisture over time and becomes harder and heavier, thus changing the buffering characteristic and increasing the curve of pressure. Don't use it. You will ruin your gun and maybe hurt yourself. Stick with buffering additives listed in recognized load data.

The ideal buffering compound is one that moves into the spaces between the shot pellets with ease, has an extremely long shelf life without any change in character, and does the best job of providing pattern improvement and reflecting the actual choke constriction of the shotgun.

Additionally, such a buffer provides support for the pellets to prevent setback forces from exerting too much of a crushing impact upon the soft pellets, thereby changing their shape. A pellet that becomes out-of-round will have an independent flight characteristic, something we don't want. The perfect buffer also carries a positive action up into the choke by providing the pellets a better basis for the "liquid physics" required for the shot mass to move smoothly through the choke.

The amount of buffer that can be placed in a load is confined by the open area between the pellets. Since the amount of space will vary when different pellet sizes are used, it's impossible to give an exact amount needed. Other factors such as the amount of shot in the load, the density of the buffer material and the method used by the handloader to insert the buffer material also come into play. It boils down to using whatever it takes to fill the spaces between the pellets.

The pressure differences generated in certain loads by adding buffers do not follow a general rule. Many loads reflect very small changes when buffered. However, buffer only those loads that have been tested with buffer. In some instances, I have seen a pressure influence of 1000 LUP. One always has to assume a rise in chamber pressure whenever adding mass to a load.

Friction Reducers

Testing shows that direct application of a dry lubricant helps the pellets crowd through a choke and exit the barrel a bit easier. I always dust pellets with a dry friction-reducing medium. You may recall that lead shot is coated with graphite. There is no reason other pellets, especially steel and bismuth, will not benefit from a similar application of dry lubricant.

Non-Toxic Pellets

The hardest, most expensive part of introducing a new, non-toxic pellet for taking waterfowl is getting approval from the U.S. Fish and Wildlife Service. Although every rational reason may give compelling evidence for a particular pellet's immediate approval, the governmental bureaucracy has a habit of working with deliberation—meaning it is slow.

Nevertheless, certain inroads in the form of alternate non-toxic pellets have been made in the U.S. Bismuth was the first pellet, other than iron, approved for use on migratory waterfowl in the United States. The 1995-1996 season was the first year it was used, on a temporary approval basis.

The ultimate stamp of permanent U.S. approval was granted for bismuth in mid-1997. How nice. It seems that the product, comprised of an element that is a major ingredient of antacid tummy medicine, has finally been approved for shooting ducks and geese. Some shooters have wondered why non-toxic ammunition is expensive. Well, subsidizing insipid research such as stuffing game farm mallards with shot and studying fourth-generation genetic outcomes requires a lot of in-depth research, and that means a ton of money.

How did the U.S. get here? In the mid-1970s, research led to conclusions that ducks were ingesting lead pellets and dying of its toxic effects. Of course, this is not a good thing, and we do not endorse poisoning ducks. However, it was immediately assumed that the birds were gobbling lead pellets, but the researchers did not consider run-off from chemicals used to treat crops. There are other possibilities, but you get the point. Unless studies are done that eliminate all the possible variables, that research is inconclusive at best.

Leaping to a conclusion, the government phased out lead shot. Even this is OK, if we have some evidence that it was doing harm to wildlife. However, the blunder, in my opinion, is that the legislation leaned on research, conducted by "expert opinion" who determined that steel pellets were the ultimate solution. As such, steel was approved as the singular non-toxic pellet. Now, for another pellet to gain approval it must prove itself innocent. Apparently, in our mad dash away from lead pellets, we have run over all other alternatives.

By mandating steel only, we took younger smallbore shooters out of the sport. We placed a burden of expensive and time-consuming research upon small manufacturers. We relegated fine older shotguns to the backs of closets and had to completely re-think modern gun design to facilitate the ballistics of steel shot. Hopefully, new non-toxic pellet alternatives will bring smallbore shooters and fine shotguns back to our sport.

Canada, on the other hand, states that pellets must not be lead. That's it. Needless to say, they are way ahead of the U.S. in alternate non-toxic pellet development. Insofar as the U.S. has made some progress, check your state's individual regulations, then either lobby or say thank you to the lawmakers involved.

Steel Shot

Steel shot loads have had the benefit of over twenty years of research and development. Many fine steel loads have been developed that give excellent patterns and superior penetration. With some thought and experimentation, steel shot has been turned to a shooter's advantage. Currently, steel shot load technology is at its peak—loads have never been better in regard to velocity, patterns and lethality. Modern components and shotguns specifically designed to utilize steel shot are now the norm, and shooters have adopted steel's particular shooting requirements and load applications. A comment I've heard from more than a few hunters goes like this: "Geez, my current steel recipes are better than my lead loads ever were; I'm happy with what I have!"

Steel shot handloading has become a very good value, and development of loads and components will continue for a very long time into the future. Many excellent steel loads will continue to be used in the field because many hunters have developed incredible prowess with them.

Steel shot will be around for many years because it can be used to your benefit—both economically and performance-wise. Excellent steel loads and recommendations will continue to be developed and used in the fields. While alternative non-toxic shot brings new and exciting technology, it does not supersede past achievements. As technology is further tested and understood, it will serve to improve specific areas of our shooting.

Handloading shotshells provides a great advantage to the shotgunner. Just as one can only hand-assemble grand-prix race cars to achieve extraordinary performance, the high performance shotshell requires the attention only thoughtful and knowledgeable handloaders can provide.

Are steel handloads cheaper than factory ammunition? Sometimes, sometimes not, depending upon the specialized components you choose to use. However, cost is not the only consideration here—the high quality hunt is our reward. Considering the great cost of just getting out in the field in the first place, a hunter's goal should be to bring along the best equipment possible.

Using Steel Shot in Your Shotgun

The hunter who uses steel pellets in a shotgun must face various realities of the medium.
- Steel pellets are nearly as hard as your barrels, and special measures must be taken to protect these barrels.
- Do not use steel shot in older guns that were not designed for such use. This could ruin the gun or, worse, the shooter. Be advised and be careful.
- Steel pellets are fundamentally different from lead or bismuth pellets. Steel pellets require steel-specific loading procedures.
- When a handloader exceeds or disregards published guidelines, the loads he manufactures may not produce the intended results and may even be dangerous.
- An understanding of the basic principles of shotshell ballistics will benefit a handloader when it comes time to make judgments concerning his loads.
- If you decide that you cannot follow or understand written directions, please do not handload steel. Leave high-performance load production to those who are qualified.

Non-toxic shot has improved to the point where it's almost as effective as lead. As shooters gain more experience with steel, they'll learn to adapt to its nature.

You are responsible for the loads you assemble. Do you substitute almond for vanilla in a cake mix then get mad at Betty Crocker? No. So follow loading guidelines exactly as published by whomever. Failing to follow guidelines can contribute to the scoring of the barrel or even more extensive damage to equipment and/or people.

Load guidelines are concrete. Don't even waste your time asking for any variations on published recipes. I can save you a phone call to the data's publisher and give you the answer right now: *Do not deviate from published guidelines.*

Regardless of what your past experiences may be, you can indeed shoot steel shot successfully. However, true high-performance loads require the reloader/hunter to commit to learning how to properly assemble high-quality components to produce the performance suited for the various field conditions encountered.

We all have heard stories of steel shot bouncing off large birds. What people may be noting are slow moving pellets not carrying sufficient energy to penetrate feathers and body. Watching game fly away makes a shooter acutely aware that insufficient loads will always prove to be the most expensive/wasteful loads in any hunt. It is important, for game conservation, that your loads are properly designed and functional for specific weather and game. As with all pellet types, specialized loads will put you on a higher plane of shooting performance.

If you understand the basic principles of handloading lead shot, then handloading steel shot will require that you learn only a few additional things.

Too many people have been given the wrong impression that handloading steel is difficult. Fundamentally, though, it is very

This young hunter limited out using reloads and the proper load recipe to bring down these nice Canadas. His Remington autoloader worked perfectly because he was careful to size and crimp the shells properly.

similar to making high-quality lead loads. Of course, there are some people who should not reload ammunition of any kind. Under similar circumstances of personal responsibility, we see daily examples of people who shouldn't drive cars. Steel handloading is a commitment to good procedures and excellence, or it is a commitment that should not be made.

The handloader needs to look at the steel shot—handloads and factory stuff alike—put through his shotgun with a critical and informed eye. Just because someone else closed the shell does not mean the contents are good. Open up a shell once in a while and inspect the pellets. Are they what you want to send through your barrel? Handloaders should select only high quality steel shot manufactured under specific component guidelines.

What constitutes the most effective steel shot? First, the outside surface of the pellets should be polished. Polishing removes the rough coating left on the pellet during annealing (part of a softening process). With a reduced drag coefficient, the polished pellet has a much longer, straighter flight, delivering more of its retained energy to the target. Also, the shot will pass through the choke easier.

Modern steel shotgun barrels, on the diamond pyramid hardness (DPH) scale, register at about 115 to 117. For comparative purposes, the standard acceptable hardness for steel shot pellets is 90 DPH. Steel pellets for shotshells are pure iron, rated at dead soft. Yes, "steel" is a misnomer, but that is what it has been called for twenty years and I am not going to make waves.

Steel shot must work in concert with steel shot wads. To operate otherwise will wreck your shotgun. The increased velocity necessary for effective steel shot loads places addition-al stress on shotshell components. This is not necessarily bad, it's just that the components have to be carefully designed and properly used. High quality, protective wads are readily available for handloaders. Their special design and materials absorb the brutal impact of steel pellets, not allowing the pellet to come into contact with the barrel.

Pellets must have rust protection, and handloaders need to properly store steel pellets. Rusty pellets will continue to rust. Extensive corrosion can actually bind the pellets together inside the shell. An unyielding glob of steel shot bullying its way down your barrel is guaranteed to tear up things. Just like milk, steel pellets have an expiration date. Do not use rusty pellets unless you are indifferent toward your shotgun.

Bridging describes an in-barrel pellet scenario. During the firing process, the payload of shot and wad must, of course, pass through the area of constriction (choke) at the end of the shotgun's barrel. When the steel shot pellets are too large for the particular gauge used, the shot can form into a connecting "bridge" of pellets, perhaps spanning the width of the bore, and beyond. The barrel will give first, usually in the form of a ring bulge or score in the choke area. Only very specific sizes can converge to become greater than the inside diameter of the barrel. Three or more pellets usually will not lock together.

Since bridging consists of a ratio of the shot size to the diameter of the bore of the shotgun, I strongly suggest that the handloader not exceed certain shot sizes in the various gauges. The following parameters are only concerning the bridging phenomenon and not related to sizing recommendations based upon shell performance.

In the 10-gauge, the maximum steel shot size I recommend is F (.218-inch) shot. Most 10-gauge shotguns will benefit further from forcing cone modifications and moderate constriction (no tighter than Modified) to assist in handling large steel shot.

The maximum size pellet for the 12-gauge is somewhere between BB and T, depending on the choke constriction and whether you are shooting an overbored shotgun. The optimum steel setup includes a lengthened forcing cone, slight overbore, and Modified or Improved Cylinder choke.

Using larger steel shot sizes will not automatically cause a problem with your shotgun, as bridging is a factor of probability. With large steel pellets, you increase the risk of interior barrel damage. If you don't mind replacing a barrel every couple of years, don't stay awake at night worrying about shot size selection. Several of the newer single-barrel shotguns have many reasonable barrel replacement options.

Avoid following the simplistic advice of automatically moving to two sizes larger than lead pellets. It's an axiom applicable only to mediocre ammunition. Handloaders have so many more loading options and components to tweak that they use completely different performance criteria.

Learn how to best use all the pellet sizes and know where and when each is most effective, as well as velocity requirements for each size at a given range. A healthy duck requires about 3 foot-pounds of energy for lethal penetration. Use steel pellets that are the correct size for the game and shooting conditions you encounter. Provided your loads are of high quality, the rest will take care of itself.

One of the keys to a successful duck hunt is being able to bring down what you're shooting at. This hunter is serious about the sport and made sure his reloads were effective.

Before you give up on an otherwise effective load because of poor pattern performance, make sure your gun isn't the largest factor in screwing up your patterns. Often, a quick and insightful evaluation is to simply shoot the load in question through a different shotgun.

Shot Metering Procedures

I unequivocally recommend the use of an accurate scale. A 1000-grain powder scale works wonders, adds very little time to the overall loading procedure and permits greater accuracy of weights and measures. Steel shot bushings are available for many shotshell loading tools, but these are really limited-application items. Smaller pellets work as indicated and will flow through bushings well. However, large steel pellets are a pain to volumetrically meter through a bushing as they get hung up wherever they can. Nobody makes so many hunting loads (with large pellets) that they shouldn't weigh each pellet charge.

To make a homemade shot measure, first find the correct number of pellets for the load you want to assemble. Then, find a discarded primer tray with 100 tiny pockets in it. By one method or another, usually glue or tape, fill or cover the holes that you don't require for your pellet count (e.g., if your load calls for seventy-five pellets of #BB, then cover or fill twenty-five of the holes, leaving exactly seventy-five open). If you need more than 100, divide the pellet count by two and fill part of the tray twice. Use the tray as a dipper and make sure each hole has one pellet in it. Unless you enjoy picking up pellets, use a funnel for dropping the shot into the hull.

Forget what you know about the weight of lead shot as applied to various effective payloads. Until you're completely familiar with steel shot payloads, the overall number of steel pellets used in a load should be a handloader's primary measurement. The comparisons hunters make to lead shot loads seem to compel them to overload steel. Hunters have, for many years, assessed load application by payload weight and have associated certain weights with a lethal hunting load. For instance, $1^1/_8$ ounces of lead is a target load. However, $1^1/_8$ ounces of steel shot is a magnum payload—the pellet equivalent of around $1^1/_2$ ounces of lead. In the 12-gauge, a $1^1/_2$-ounce load is a magnum by anyone's definition. This misapplication of low velocity, high volume steel shot loads is largely to blame for steel shot's poor image. Work with sane volumes (convert pellet counts to lead equivalents if you need to) and use steel within a reasonable payload range for effectiveness. A consideration of the total number of pellets in a load is the only practical method of comparative analysis.

Buffers and Steel Shot

The resiliency of steel causes pellets to bounce when energy is exchanged, rather than absorbing energy through deformation, as lead shot does. Specialized steel shot buffers contain ingredients that deaden these interactions. The buffer is used to cushion the shot, reducing the wave of energy passed through the pellets during the initial thrust of the burning cycle. Almost every steel shot load is buffered since the advantages of doing so are essential for high performance.

Large steel pellets such as T shot (.20-inch) or F shot (.218-inch) sometimes do not disperse evenly within the base of a shotcup due to the wad's interior space. Thus, one pellet will be supporting the strain of the entire weight of the load. The pressure placed upon the base of the wad is extreme. If possible, when using either T or F size shot, place a thin cardboard or wool felt in the base of the wad to act as a cushion. This will let the pressure of setback spread over a wider area and ease the strain on the base of the wad. The plastic wad base could be made rhino-tough, but then a great deal of the patterning character would be lost. A compromise must be reached somewhere between rock-hard durability and pattern quality.

I have found that placing an overshot card wad on top of a steel shot load holds the pellets within the shotcup for the journey up the barrel. This is important in reducing the likelihood of

Using the right size shot can mean the difference between a kill and a cripple that escapes. When in doubt about shot, use one size larger to get more energy on target.

a pellet getting ahead of the wad and contacting the barrel. Any thickness .030-inch and under will serve the purpose and get out of the load's way upon exiting the muzzle.

Steel Pellet Shotguns

If you wish to load and shoot heavier steel loads in the 12-gauge, such as $1^1/_4$-ounce (equal in pellet count to $1^5/_8$ ounces of lead shot) or even $1^1/_2$-ounce numbers (equal to nearly 2 ounces of lead), just don't do it with a Full choke, or turn to the 10-gauge. The larger size of the 10-gauge provides the proper conditions necessary for heavier loads to attain adequate speed. Remember, speed is the ingredient that gives a load it's lethal quality. The 12-gauge is simply not suited for heavy steel loads with a Full choke, no matter what the length of the shell. More open chokes seem to work better, though.

If you use a gun with a 3-inch chamber, you should be using 3-inch loads. The $1/_4$-inch difference between the $2^3/_4$-inch hull and the longer chamber will allow a "jump space" before the load (wad and shot) hits the forcing cone area. While this small space was important with lead shot, we find that, with steel shot, some barrels will "jar" the pellets very hard upon entering the forcing cone. All shotguns are not affected. The longer the forcing cone, the less likely that a jarring effect will occur. The result of bouncing around during the firing process creates a chain reaction of bouncing pellets that will disrupt the continuity of the pattern. The choke at the tip of your barrel cannot make everything else right again in the pattern if the load has been battered during the early stages of the firing process. This is something to consider if you are experiencing poor pattern results. Try the longer shell, which properly fits the chamber.

It is best not to use "upland grade" double shotguns for steel shot loads. These guns are usually built on a lighter frame and have thin-walled, lightweight barrels made for light, lead shot loads using small pellets. For steel shot, the better shotgun is the thick, heavy waterfowler type. Most heavy pumps, autos,

doubles and newly made guns with advanced design and metal alloys are completely appropriate for the demands of steel shot.

I recommend that you never use a Damascus-barreled shotgun for any type of steel pellet load. Damascus barrels look like a very long and tightly compressed spring. The metal usually has an intricate pattern that is easily seen. If there is any question about this, take the gun to a gunsmith for inspection. He'll advise you properly. Though these were the high-quality shotgun barrels of the blackpowder era, they were not designed for modern, slow burning powders. High energy steel shot loads have no place in Damascus barrels, either.

Steel Shot Loading on the Press

Most handloading tools can function with steel shot. Some work better than others, some require no modifications whatsoever, others require minor modifications, and still others would be more useful to the steel handloader at the bottom of a lake.

If you can reload with a modicum of patience, there is little reason for your machine not to give decent steel shot loading results. I have worked with every type of single-stage reloader brand. I know they work. When damage occurs to a tool, the blame almost always falls upon the user. One of the main reasons is that steel pellets will not shear at the bushing/loader contact point. Get a little angry while forcing a stuck bushing or bar, and you will have damaged equipment.

The only type of press I don't recommend is a fully progressive machine. These are not built to meter large steel shot, nor are they suitable for the multiple levels of wads necessary for most steel shot loads. Automated powder or shot drops are a sure sign of impending trouble as you will probably have to work the crimp several times for a proper seal. If you have chosen a single-stage press for your steel loads, you have chosen well.

Proper press setup is critical for correct loads. Something seemingly as insignificant as a poorly adjusted crimp tool can affect everything, even chamber pressures. Take the time to properly set up your machine and equip it with what it needs to make steel shot loads. If it needs a special steel shot kit, buy one. It will protect the investment you have made in your loader. Remember that steel shot is 70 percent the weight of lead and volumetric measurements are different. Use the specialized steel shot bushings or charge bars required for metering the pellets.

Comparing Lead And Steel

The traditional and very fine old lead shotshell for duck hunting was $1^1/_4$ ounces of lead #4s. At one time, if you hunted ducks with a 12-gauge in the United States, your load was this one. Nominal velocity was around 1300 feet per second.

If we look at that same load today and want to equate that to a basic load of steel shot, we find that $1^1/_4$ ounces of lead #4s equals 168 pellets; the same $1^1/_4$ ounces of steel #4s has 240 pellets. That's seventy-two additional pellets, which is too many because our goal is an equivalent pellet count.

To get equivalent energies in steel, first let's go pellet for pellet to get the same patterns. How heavy does the load need to be? A steel load of 168 same-size pellets (the same pellet count) weighs $7/8$-ounce! Would you shoot a $7/8$-ounce steel load at a big duck? Why not? You used to shoot that very same pattern count of lead with tremendous success. Perhaps you might say, "Well, from what I've learned so far, #4 steel is fine when the work is close and over decoys, but it does not reach as far as #4 lead." Good observation—you're getting there. Our next goal in this duck load quest is to find a load that will push a dense, lethal pattern to a reasonable duck hunting range, like our old lead favorite did.

It is little wonder that our old lead load was magic on decoyed mallards. That 168 pellets is a very dense cloud of shot, and the old $11/4$-ounce payload was moving at a good clip. The pellets impart a lot of transferred energy—just right for most water-fowling. As we switch to steel pellets, we could retain energy by moving up several shot sizes, but we don't want to lose that pattern density. However, if we shift to only a *slightly* larger pellet, we find that $11/8$ ounces (166 pellets) of steel #3 (.14-inch) will provide the same pattern density as the old #4 lead load.

That lead load when fired at 1325 fps ran out of gas (pellet energy below 2.0 foot-pounds) at about 53 yards. Since it worked, let's establish that as our goal for the steel parity load.

A #3 steel load of 166 pellets launched at 1300 fps runs out of lethal energy at 41 yards. This is not enough to equal our old favorite lead load. However, if we boost our steel #3 load to 1425 fps, it retains lethal energy out to nearly 50 yards. Voila! Only 3 yards short of our old favorite lead load.

You can't swap steel for lead in the same configurations and expect the same performance. Hopefully, you can use the detailed concept above to compare the ballistic qualities of your old lead favorites with steel shot recipes.

Steel Shot Safety

The shooter can expect that at some time while shooting steel shot some scoring will appear in the shotgun's barrel. Until shotguns are part of a physics/design breakthrough, we can expect a certain amount of this to happen. Scoring does not detract from the barrels' ability to shoot well. If you shoot a lot of steel, there are many more opportunities to score your barrel.

Use *only* recommended load weights and measures. Make sure that your reloading equipment is accurate, scaled correctly and in good condition. Accuracy is critical and amounts must be correct. Become familiar enough with your handloads that you know when proportions may not be right.

Properly slit all wads to create petals. Otherwise, you will be effectively shooting a steel slug, which will ruin your choke and go much farther down range than you would expect.

Use only high-quality steel shot of consistent weight and roundness.

If the shell does not fit together correctly, something is probably wrong. Stop! Re-examine and measure everything. Contact the component manufacturer and verify your procedure and components.

Of course, common sense and personal responsibility are factors in loading steel shot, just like they are with lead shot. Use

your head! If you have any doubts, find the solution before blundering ahead with a questionable procedure. More than once, I have been asked about a certain load condition only after a case or two of that load had been assembled. After learning the load is not safe, the first question usually is, "Can I use it anyway?" It's upsetting to have the customer become depressed when he has to take apart 500 incorrectly loaded shells.

Tungsten Shot

Federal Cartridge Company introduced a new pellet comprised of a combination of tungsten and iron. Tungsten, also known as wolfram, is a hard substance used in manufacturing metal-cutting tools, engraving tools and lamp filaments. To make shot pellets, tungsten is broken down to a powder form, as is the iron. The two powders are mixed together in a ratio of 60 percent tungsten, 40 percent iron. This mixture is then pressed together in the spherical shape of a pellet. It is then heated to sinter the elements. Finally, the pellets are coated with a rust preventative.

The advantage of tungsten pellets lies in their density. If lead density is considered at 100 percent, tungsten pellets are 94 percent the density of lead. By way of comparison, bismuth pellets are 85 percent the density of lead; steel is 70 percent. The only non-lead rival in density is Molyshot at 99 percent the density of lead. Both bismuth and Molyshot will be discussed later.

Pellet density is the delivery vehicle of energy. It is akin to comparing an empty wheelbarrow and one full of bricks with

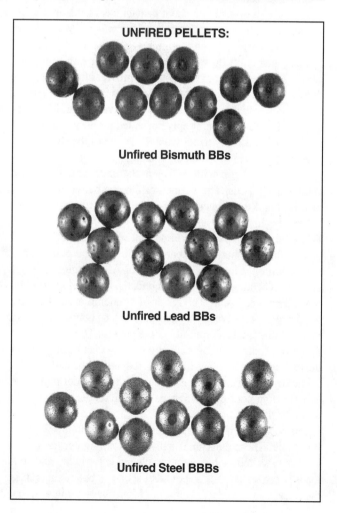

UNFIRED PELLETS:

Unfired Bismuth BBs

Unfired Lead BBs

Unfired Steel BBBs

regard to potential destruction at speed. Losing density, by any percentage, is a loss of effectiveness in both lethality and range. The bottom line is that a denser pellet is a better pellet. If a tungsten pellet is launched at 1300 fps and a bismuth pellet is launched at the same velocity, it's clear that the tungsten pellets will fly farther and straighter.

Under the conditions present within shotguns, the tungsten pellet will not deform, no matter what. That is both its beauty and its predicament. An utterly round pellet will fly as directed by the ballistics of the load and barrel. The net effect will be tighter patterns that will not be influenced by fringe fly-away pellets. The wads Federal uses with their tungsten loads are similar to those used in some steel shot loads over the years, in that the petals significantly overlap each other. To prevent the ultra-hard tungsten from engraving barrels, the wads are thick and dense, and absorb energy. As such, the thick walls will magnify the choke constriction. Modified chokes act like Full chokes, and Full chokes blow patterns. If you are using tungsten, stick with Federal's recommendation of using an Improved Cylinder or Modified choke for your long-range patterns.

In long-range field shooting, tungsten pellets deliver tremendous energy at great ranges. Tungsten exceeds bismuth in long-range effectiveness in both pattern composition (some bismuth pellets come apart during the firing cycle) and retained energy through its higher density.

Tungsten pellets will penetrate. They carry sufficient energy

FIRED PELLETS: RECOVERED FROM STYROFOAM BLOCK

Recovered Bismuth BBs

Recovered Lead BBs

Recovered Steel BBBs

to get the job done and are another step in the right direction. Properly applied, they will increase your range of lethality.

Because tungsten/iron pellets are so hard, they require modern shotguns that have been designed and manufactured in the current steel shot era. Unlike bismuth and Molyshot, tungsten is not compatible with older double-barreled shotguns with tight chokes.

Bismuth

Bismuth is a by-product of industrial combustion, and many South American mines are closed because of a lack of global demand. Should bismuth shotshell production dramatically increase, market forces might compel under-utilized South American mines to reopen, augmenting current supplies. Demand may also drive an effort toward reclamation from other industrial sources, hopefully making bismuth more affordable for hunters.

With a specific gravity of 9.747, bismuth lies a bit higher than midway between lead (specific gravity of 11.34) and raw iron, of which steel shot is made (7.86). Bismuth's melting point is 271.3 degrees Celsius, which is not terribly high, and significant is the fact that, like lead, it is easily smelted for the production of pellets. Carefully alloying bismuth with tin slightly reduces bismuth's problematic tendency toward brittleness, making it acceptable for use as shotgun pellets.

Pellet-to-pellet friction presents a greater problem with bismuth than with comparably sized lead pellets. This kind of contact generates, in some instances, additional chamber pressure, and likely as not, the offending pellet yields by breaking. Under the rules of volume's influence on chamber pressure, bismuth's resistance to deformation and occupation of about 15 percent additional volume, compared to the same weight as lead, generates higher chamber pressure. Furthermore, bismuth presents ballistic questions and problems related to developing loads for an unfamiliar element. Lead, and now steel, have become familiar over the years. We can observe their specific effects on other components and interior ballistics. Developing proper and safe loads for bismuth demands additional time in the ballistic laboratory to analyze many different variables that affect the load's outcome. Every new element will present its own unique set of problems for ballisticians, and bismuth has presented its own. Furthermore, components cannot be arbitrarily applied to untested elements based only upon their relative success with lead and/or steel. The few loads listed in the data section are all that are available at this time.

If we rate bismuth shot and very hard lead shot on a Brinell hardness scale, we will see a rating of about 18 to 22. Steel shot is actually off the scale. Steel shot is generally rated on a Rockwell scale that does not include the lower ratings of lead, as lead is too soft for accurate measurement.

While steel shot has become a suitable waterfowl pellet, bismuth shot provides the hunter with another alternative. The bismuth pellet alloy is about 85 percent of lead's density and softer than the barrels of your shotgun. Softness is bismuth's great advantage, because it is the first non-toxic pellet that permits fine shotguns, currently stashed in closets and safes, to return to waterfowling duty and the general usage for which they were crafted.

As is typical of any type of shotshell ammunition, hand-loaded bismuth is going to be the better performer. The attention you can give your handloads is reflected in the field with improved shooting and greater emphasis on maximum performance as opposed to maximum production.

Loading Fundamentals for Bismuth Shot

Loading bismuth is unlike loading either lead or steel and requires certain unique procedures. Follow directions though, and you will be rewarded in the field. We have field-tested bismuth loads in Canada for quite a few years and are happy to report excellent performance.

- Bismuth is unique unto itself. Bismuth loads cannot use lead or steel shot load recipes or proportions. Bismuth shot has its own unique characteristics and ballistic reactions. To substitute recipes or pellet types is to sacrifice the advantage of using bismuth as well as one's personal safety. Be sure to use only bismuth-specific load recipes and components.
- Although you will see certain components used with lead, bismuth and/or steel, that is not an invitation to create generalized substitution rules, no matter how insignificant it seems. Follow loading guidelines carefully and do not deviate.
- Better loads are produced with specific proportions of a number of different components. Utilizing only components you may have on hand will produce uninspired and possibly dangerous loads. If you want the best, you have to make use of the latest technological breakthroughs.
- Given the same amount by weight, bismuth shot produces higher pressure in a given load than does lead shot. Carefully follow the formulas.
- Note that you cannot use steel or lead shot bushings in your loading machine. Specialized bismuth shot bushings or charge bars are the only accurate volumetric way to measure bismuth pellets for loads. If you do not have specialized bars or bushings, you must weigh out the shot charge on an accurate, calibrated scale or count the pellets.
- Bismuth shot is totally non-toxic. Bismuth can be found as an ingredient in many over-the-counter health products and cosmetics consumed by humans. It should, therefore, be good enough for ducks.
- All gauges can effectively utilize bismuth pellet loads. That alone is great news for younger and smaller shooters who have been excluded from waterfowling by virtue of the equipment requirements of steel. The 28-gauge is a very effective non-toxic upland gauge with bismuth shot. Even 410-bore shotguns can utilize bismuth shot.

Since bismuth pellets are softer than gun barrels, and as ongoing studies continue to reveal the ballistic peculiarities of bismuth, wad design and development continues. Steel shot wads were specifically designed for maximum barrel protection. Wads for bismuth must offer special protection to the pellets. Standard target wads, though most have a well-cushioned section, are not the best choice for hunting applications. They do not adequately encase and protect larger volumes of bismuth required for magnum loads. For the same reason that we buffer and utilize cushion sections to pamper the bismuth shot column, it is greatly beneficial to have protective petals long enough to protect the bismuth pellets from the ravages of contact with barrel, forcing cone and choke.

Since bismuth loads will be used in a broad range of hunting and shooting applications, you will note that there is a wide disparity of volume between various loads. Applications of filler wads will be less specific here than you may have become used to with steel shot loading. Use cork or felt filler wads as necessary to produce the proper shot column height for a good crimp. Remember, filler wads are the only optional components in a load.

The general idea of buffering is to protect the pellets and thus enhance pattern performance. Buffer fills the spaces between each individual pellet. Unless these spaces are filled, the inertia generated by the initial thrust (setback) smashes the pellets into one another, causing pellet imperfections or fractures.

A word of caution is in order: It is extremely important to use only specifically recommended buffers in all loads, including bismuth loads. Specific types of buffers are used in specific load recipes; changing buffer types or brands will alter the load's character, including chamber pressure. Load recipes, when followed exactly, perform as indicated in the guidelines. A buffering agent that is too dense will dramatically increase chamber pressure, sometimes beyond the point of safety.

As with steel shot, the handloader must apply adjusted guidelines for proper bismuth loading. Like the metric system, this altered perspective requires handloaders to forget familiar standards when factoring the most effective load capacities for a given situation. Your volumetric measurements will not be correct. You will need specialized bushings to integrate a new perspective of what weights of bismuth (at 85 percent the density of lead) will fill up different styles of shotcups.

Consider the following for waterfowl *bismuth* loads:

Recommended Bismuth Shot Payloads (ozs.)							
	10-ga.	12-ga. 3½"	12-ga. 3"	12-ga. 2¾"	16-ga.	20-ga. 3"	20-ga. 2¾"	28-ga.
Optimum*:	1½	1½	1⅜	1¼	1¼	1¼	1⅛	¾
Maximum:	1⅞	1¾	1⅝	1⅜	1⅛	1⅛	1	½
Long Range:	1¾	1⅝	1½	1¼	1⅛	1	½	
Mid-Range:	1⅝	1½	1⅜	1⅛	1	1	⅞	⁷⁄₁₆
Short Range:	1⅜	1⅜	1¼	1	1	1	⅞	⁷⁄₁₆
Minimum:	1¼	1¼	1⅛	⅞	⅞	¾	⁵⁄₁₆	

*Based upon 1994 Canadian field shooting tests.

Patterning Bismuth

Bismuth patterns do not look as nice as hard lead, tungsten, steel or Molyshot patterns. If you choose to use bismuth, it's a fact you will have to face. That is not to say that the pellets are not effective at range, they just have a couple basic strikes against them before they get to the patterning board.

Bismuth pellets, due to manufacturing difficulties we are told, are not very round. At the time of this writing, a random sample of bismuth pellets shows about 5 percent of the various sized pellets are misshapen and of inconsistent size. Manufacturing technology should eventually address these problems. Also, bismuth pellets have a tendency, but not always, to come apart under impact and therefore lose lethal energy as they break apart.

To achieve good patterns, bismuth loads require a larger payload and the tender loving care provided by a specialized wad column. The larger payload will require hunting-style wads (those without a cushion section) to provide the extra shotcup volume. I have created successful bismuth patterns by utilizing thick-walled, high density steel shot wads. The thick petals, while not conducive to filling in the outside pattern fringe, will protect a high percentage of the pellets during the firing sequence and barrel transitions. I usually buffer the loads as well to give the broadest base of support for each pellet.

Although pattern boards are a nice, tidy, empirical way to study a load, they are a singular factor of the less definable feature of overall load lethality. Use the strengths of bismuth to your advantage. Properly launched, a bismuth pellet is capable of penetrating hard flesh or even bone without breaking up. It is soft enough to use in any of your shotguns, even the old doubles you felt compelled to stow away and save for a kinder pellet. Bismuth is a kinder pellet, available and legal to use on waterfowl, right now.

Molyshot

Everyone can agree that the ideal lethal load hits with the highest possible number of individual pellets. However, the load must also propel a pellet of adequate size and weight at sufficient velocity to deliver adequate energy at a specific range.

Physics tells us that a pellet will impart its retained energy to the target by transfer of its inertia to the larger body—dissipation of that energy into the target. Ideally, the retained energy in the pellet (forward momentum) drops immediate anchor in the target, delivering its lethal force. This brings to light one of steel's and tungsten's intrinsic weaknesses: Because the pellets are so hard and do not deform, ever, they sometimes transfer energy about as effectively as a very sharp dart. Smaller pellets may pass through the bird rather cleanly, not imparting enough lethal force. Though lead fills these requirements nicely, it is illegal to use on migratory waterfowl.

Molyshot (an appellation that may or may not stick), comprised of a combination of molybdenum disulfide and various non-toxic elements and polymers, is the non-toxic waterfowl pellet on the horizon. Kent Cartridge Company of Canada, Ltd., will be manufacturing this new pellet, already approved for use in Canada for the 1997 waterfowl season.

Purdey, the very sophisticated London gunmakers, have already endorsed Molyshot for use in Purdey shotguns. Purdey has been around for a very long time. Some of the old Purdeys date to the 19th century and have thin muzzles. Nonetheless, the company has given the green light, exclusively, to this product. To me, that indicates some very serious potential.

Molyshot promises some substantial advantages in all areas over all currently available non-toxic pellets. Molyshot pellets are about 99 percent the density of lead, while malleability of the pellet remains controllable. If that works out as planned, it should load and shoot very similarly to lead. Furthermore, it seems that the cost of Molyshot will be only a little more than premium lead shot. Perhaps Molyshot will provide the loads we want to bring with us to the duck blinds. The traits of this new pellet address all of the current problems with the various available types of non-toxic pellets. Given these facts, it is very tempting and very easy to jump to some rapturous conclusions about Molyshot's potentials. However, only the laboratory, the duck blind and time are qualified to judge it. I can only report conclusions at a later date.

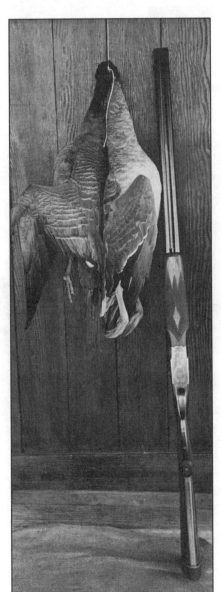

While steel shot is effective on large species, it may be best not to use it in a very valuable gun to avoid barrel damage. Bismuth may be the answer here.

9

Shotshell reloading involves a logical course of events that demands undivided attention. Be careful and follow the recipe.

Step-By-Step Shotshell Reloading

RELOADING A SHOTSHELL follows some very basic principles of assembly. Except for only a very few variables, components have to go into the hull a certain way in order to function. Familiarity with brands allow us to make certain brand-specific comments along the way. Depending on their weight in your personal scheme of things, these comments may help you select a particular machine. As opposed to a brand-by-brand breakdown of every step, I will only point out the exceptional of certain brands' features.

The first step is to have a hull in hand. You will want to have already inspected it for flaws that would waste the other components and your time if you tried to use it. Hull inspection is covered in Chapter 4.

Resizing

Most machines start the process by resizing the hull. When fired, the hull tube expands to fill the shotgun's chamber. This happens to the brass section as well. Even though there is standardization in the industry, shotgun chambers are not all precisely the same size. This results in shotshells that are often a bit oversize to feed properly after firing. Regardless of which gun they were fired in, it's essential to resize.

Reloading tools are designed to resize the hull down to the nominal chamber size. Having been squeezed back down to original size, the shell should easily drop into most chambers, with no nudging nor encouragement on the part of the shooter. Most machines accomplish the resizing step by using a sleeve that is forced around the outside of the hull, down over the brass section to the rim. MEC, notably on their Super-Sizer

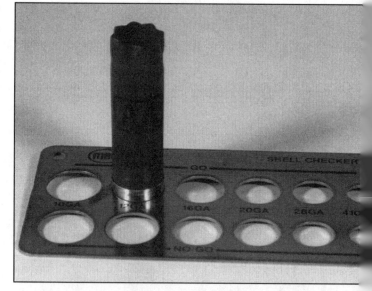

MEC's Shell Checker is a size gauge that helps the handloader determine if a shell has been properly resized. If the shell doesn't fit in the gauge, it may not function in a gun.

accessory tool as well as on their Sizemaster machine, uses a collet with steel fingers to squeeze the brass section of the hull down to size. Ponsness/Warren uses a full-length resizing die into which the shell is inserted at the first station. The die holds the shell throughout the entire loading cycle until it is ejected at the final station. For very large-capacity hunting loads, the support offered by the P/W die is crucial for supporting the hull during the crimping process. Without it, the hull sometimes

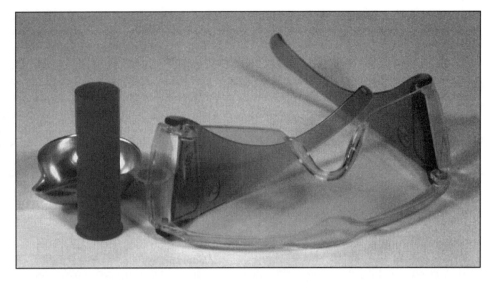

When reloading, be sure to take all safety precautions seriously, including wearing eye protection.

develops a seam just above the propellant area, rendering the load unsafe and useless.

Sometimes you will run into a hull so oversized that resizing is utterly impractical. Rather than possibly damaging your equipment, throw the hull into the garbage. If your shotgun is producing these hulls, your chamber is oversized. It's a gun problem, and you may need a new barrel.

Depriming

Depriming the hull is accomplished in pretty much the same fashion by all the available reloading tools, either simultaneously with resizing or at the very next station as a separate operation. The hull is fed up into the depriming die until the pin contacts the spent primer. Mechanical leverage is then used to push the primer out of the pocket and into a spent-primer container.

The handloader is cautioned to pay particular attention to two details when depriming. First, you will be able to establish a standard feel for how much pressure is required for depriming hulls. If it is too difficult, look for obstructions in the hull. If it is too easy, check the outside surface of the hull's base for black deposits, indicative of gases escaping past the primer. If you see this, that hull is unusable and should be thrown away. In addition, make sure your tool is properly adjusted so as not to crush the hull's base wad. Contortion of the base wad will affect your load's ballistics.

Keep the depriming area neat and don't let spent primers accumulate in a huge pile. They can become a hazard if wedged into the machine somewhere. Also, never deprime live primers from hulls. The potential for a dangerous primer detonation is too great. It's better to discard improperly primed hulls.

Repriming

For repriming, the empty hull is placed on a spring-loaded platform and the primer is forced into the pocket by a primer seater. The process is eased by the leverage provided by the reloading tool. Remember, wear safety glasses when working with live primers. They can explode if subjected to sufficient impact, heat or sparks. Don't take chances with your eyes.

I know this sounds rather silly, but you cannot believe how easy it can be to miss an old primer still in a hull, particularly with progressive machines. Some sort of obstruction may hinder the exit of a spent primer, and the (dead) primed hull will move into the priming station. Again, if you feel abnormal resistance, the repriming station is the first place to look. Not only is this the most hazardous area to have a problem in the reloading sequence, it is also the most likely area for a problem to occur.

Modern shotshell primers have been standardized to the 209 size. Fit in the shell should never be a problem unless there is some other problem. If for some reason your primers are not easily sliding into the empty pocket, stop what you're doing! Do not force primers, anytime, anywhere or for any reason. Primers can expel white hot gas with explosive, dangerous and harmful energy if subjected to sufficient impact, heat or sparks.

Primers come in different levels of energy, and each load calls for a specific primer in order to function properly. Use only the primer recommended in your load recipe. If you do not have that particular primer, get some. Otherwise, choose a different load.

It is not overly difficult to properly seat primers. Too deep or too shallow are the only possible problems. If you are seating the primers too deeply, the hull may become concave at the base, mandating an adjustment of the primer seating post. If this is carried to an extreme, your shotgun's firing pin may not make contact. If the primer is not fully seated, it will not sit flush with the base of the hull. Looking at the base of the hull from the side, you should not see any of the primer's edge protruding.

Adequate seating is particularly important in automatically indexing progressive machines. If the primer is not properly seated, it may catch on the edge of the reloading tool's base plate, halting forward progress. Further, a protruding primer can result in a dangerous shell explosion during action cycling before the gun is properly locked.

MEC Reloader Adjustments for Primers

MEC sells a special tool to adapt their 600 JR. loader to the Activ hull. As the Activ has a huge internal capacity and a very low base wad, unmodified MEC loaders (single-stage series) will sometimes leave a portion of the primer protruding from the finished hull. With MEC part number #8111 (Activ Spacer

Tool) installed under the collar of the priming cup, adequate pressure can be applied to fully seat the primer. The adapter tool is inexpensive.

Another problem specific to MEC single-stage loaders and Activ hulls is the MEC priming tool getting snagged on the hull's base. This happens, again, because the base of the hull is very low and the primer seating base protrudes beyond it. One can either learn to live with this occasional annoyance or use a priming tool for the gauge one size smaller than you are loading. For example, when loading the 12-gauge, you can try the 16-gauge priming tool. This cure will take care of it every time, but this is such a minor annoyance, most folks don't even notice or worry about it.

Automatic Primer Feeders

Use caution when working with automatic primer feeders. First, you are handling a full box (100) of loose primers. Primers are designed to be contained, either in a shotshell or in their specially manufactured storage boxes. Automatic primer feeders must be cared for in several specific ways.

When primers get jammed in the primer feeder, as they inevitably will, remove them carefully and *gently*. Do not force the operating handle because you could cause the stuck primer to explode, which in turn can cause a chain reaction with the remaining primers. Disassemble the mechanism carefully to remove a stuck primer.

Also, be careful of the accumulation of primer dust. This applies if you happen to be using open-holed primers such as the venerable Remington #57. Happily, open-holed primers are a thing of the past, but they seem to keep surfacing. Primer dust is explosive and must be removed from the reloader. Jostling the primers through the primer feeder loosens some of the combustible materials, and it accumulates on the surface of the mechanism. Do not collect the dust in one area or on one rag. Remove it from the area with a damp cloth and dispose of it.

Powder Drop

Powder has to be metered, either by weight or volume, then placed inside the hull. The powder charge sits on top of the primer and below the wad.

Powder is measured in grains. One ounce equals 437.5 grains, and that is your reloaders' mantra. Repeat it when purchasing components and do your own math. Target loads use somewhere around 20 grains. (That is not a loading recipe, but an approximation useful for your component purchasing).

In every reloading machine, there will be a space for a powder bushing. The manufacturer assumes you are smart enough to know that a bushing must go into the bushing space. The proper bushing for each specific load must be placed into this space for controlled measurement of your powder charge. Charts, provided by the manufacturer of your reloader, will

Shotshell Reloading Step-By-Step with

Step 1: Setting Up the Press

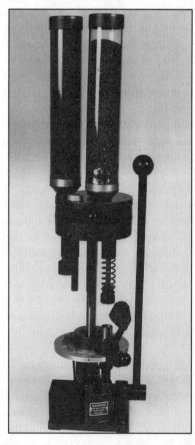

The Ponsness/Warren Du-O-Matic 375C machine can load lead or steel shot. It's of the double-post construction for greater leverage and strength. It's available in 10, 12, 16, 20, 28 and 410.

Before any reloading session, remove the bushing access plug (arrow) to verify the machine is equipped with the correct shot and powder bushing for the load you are building. Replace the access plug and fill the shot and powder reservoirs with the proper grades of each component.

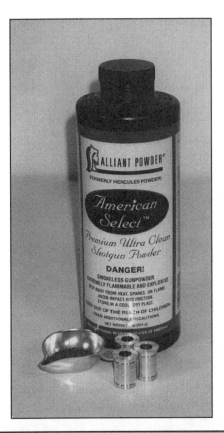

Before dropping powder in the hull, the propellant needs to be metered, either by volume with powder bushings or by weight with a scale.

specify which bushing to use for a specific type and amount of powder. Different powders will drop at different weights through the same bushing, so you must correlate powder bushings with each and every load type you assemble. Verify proper metering every time you change a bushing and/or powder brand or type. You do not know for sure what goes on when you are not with your loader, and it is better to know if Junior has been playing with your stuff before you start. Verify your powder drops with an accurate scale after first settling the powder in the reservoir and then cycling the machine normally through several complete cycles. With the reasonable cost of scales, there is absolutely no excuse for not having one on your bench.

It is imperative that you understand and follow instructions regarding powder drops and measurements. Should you decide not to, quit handloading now. Take up collecting ants so you don't hurt anyone.

Modern smokeless powders are reasonably safe to work with. They are a flammable solid and, as such, do not give off vapors that can ignite. We have always enjoyed the aplomb with which gasoline is treated; pouring gasoline into your hot lawn mower is risky. If done properly, handling modern smokeless powders is much less risky. Be careful, follow the cautions, but do not be so afraid of the substance that it hinders your procedural good judgment. If you must worry about something, worry about mishandling primers.

the Ponsness/Warren Du-O-Matic 375C

Step 2: Resizing

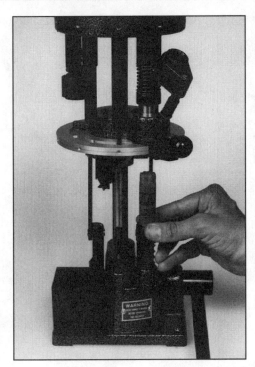

Pull the operating handle all the way down and place an empty shell on the shell seating post.

Move the operating handle to the full up position. This seats the shell in the full-length resizing die, where it will remain throughout the entire reloading sequence.

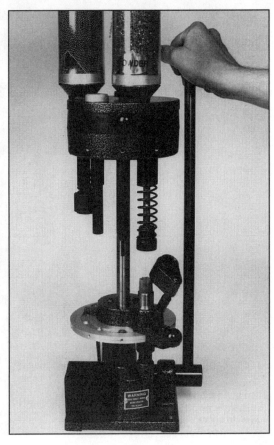

Wad Insertion

MEC provided handloaders with a mixed blessing when they attached a spring-loaded wad pressure scale to their reloading tools. On the good side, it gave the handloader an idea of how much pressure he was applying to the wads. On the bad side, it has, in a tradition that seems like it will go on forever, persuaded handloaders into thinking that every load is "indexed" to some sort of special wad pressure measurement. Oκ, let's get to the truth of the matter by examining the objectives of wad seating and older plastic wads versus newer modern plastic wads. With this information, your loads will improve, as will your attitude every time you load.

Before high quality, specially designed plastic hunting wads were made available to handloaders, reloading data had to accommodate a very few available plastic wads. Because there were only a few wad types, loads as light as 1 ounce and as heavy as $1^7/_8$ ounces used exactly the same component. The only way to accommodate such different pellet payloads was to crush the pedestal section of the wad until such a point was reached where the hull could be properly crimped. By calibrating a spring-loaded measuring device, a numeric scale of pressure was assigned to each payload. This idea worked just fine using only one wad for every load, but became really confusing as other wads were made available to handloaders. Some-

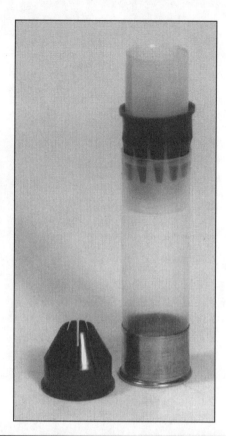

The wad guide fingers act like a funnel for easy insertion of the wad into the case mouth. Without the guide, the wad often catches on the mouth.

Step 3: Depriming and Repriming

Move the die arm to the left, indexing it under the primer knock-out assembly. Then pull the operating handle all the way down to knock out the spent primer.

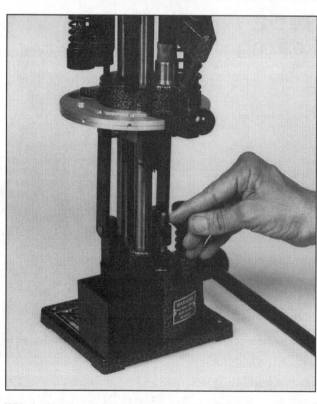

With the handle still fully down, insert a fresh primer on the primer feed assembly post and bring the handle all the way up to seat the new primer.

This wad was crushed in an attempt to create enough space for a large payload. Note the torn gas seal and collapsed shotcup. This load recipe obviously calls for a shorter wad.

how, having that scale in front of you compels you to take some sort of reading from it.

Modern wads are available in specific column heights. You will note in our loading section that there are dozens of different wad types for many different applications, including various payload specialists. We need, these days, to be less concerned with accommodating a specific payload by altering the other components.

Wads do need to be seated correctly on the powder, and there is always a certain amount of "flex" utilized for proper crimp-

ing. To seat a wad, press it firmly into the base of the hull, without so much force as to tear or distort the plastic. With time, you will develop a "feel" for what is right. The spring-loaded scale on a MEC loader only becomes useful when crushing force is applied. If you are into the high numbers as you are loading, consider that as a warning zone.

Crushing a wad causes it to cant in the hull, destroys the mid-section and often ruptures the gas seal. Loads made in this manner are incredibly unreliable. If anyone asks you about how much pressure it takes to seat a wad, there is only one answer: firmly on top of the powder. Crushing a wad to pack in more shot or for any other reason is bad loading practice.

A workable method of wad seating is to note the top of the wad as it relates to the crimp fold on the hull. Make sure the top of the petals sit below the crimping line. In most instances (not all), this will be the proper wad height for your shot drop. If minor adjustments, either up or down, are necessary, you can do so by slightly adjusting the pressure you apply to the press handle. Your arm is generally a better gauge than the spring indicator.

If for some reason the wad protrudes from the top of the hull and you are not even close, or the wad drops out of sight inside the hull, something is wrong with the load. Check all measurements and try again. If you run into the same problem, verify your load data.

Wad guide fingers must be replaced once in a while, putting

the Ponsness/Warren Du-O-Matic 375C

Step 4: Powder Charging

Index the die arm one notch to the left, under the shot/powder drop tube, pull the operating handle down, and move the charge ring to the left, dropping the powder charge.

Step 5: Seating The Wad

Raise the operating handle and place a wad in the wad carrier (arrow), which tips in and out for ease of operation

Tip the wad carrier into position above the shell and pull the operating handle fully down to insert and seat the wad on top of the powder charge.

them on similar status as windshield wipers on your automobile. They serve well for a period of time, but do wear out and then cause problems far beyond their modest replacement costs. I do not know of any manufacturer's wad guide fingers that cost more than a single issue of a popular hunting magazine.

Wad guide fingers sit directly above the hull at the wad placement station. Thin, usually plastic, fingers extend into the mouth of the hull, easing passage of the gas seal. Modern, high performance handloads use very fine gas seals, requiring a bit of care at this stage. Tearing the gas seal here compromises the consistency of your load. If you are using high capacity hunting wads in a MEC loader, disregard wad guide information and ease the wads into the hull by hand.

Hunting loads may require the placement of a filler wad at this point. A filler wad is usually made of felt, cardboard or cork, shaped like a disk in varying thicknesses. Should your load require a filler wad, place it into the wad guide as you would like it to sit in the wad column. Use the wad rammer to gently seat the filler wad, or combination of filler wads, inside and on top of the shotcup's base.

Shot Drops

Most of your shot charges will be metered through a charge bar or bushing. Shot fills a cavity inside the bushing, which is conveniently cut to the specific diameter required to accommodate a cer-

This is the proper amount of shot for a good crimp in this load. The shot goes right up to the very bottom of the crimp area. Payload height can be adjusted with filler wads if necessary.

Shotshell Reloading Step-By-Step with

Step 6: Dropping The Shot

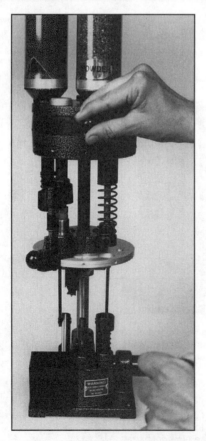

Move the charge ring all the way to the right to drop the shot charge. Then raise the operating handle and index the die arm one more notch to the crimp start station.

Step 7: Crimping

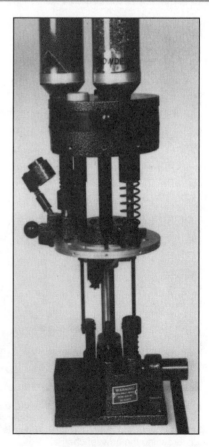

Pull the operating handle fully down to crimp start the shell mouth. Raise the handle, index the die arm another notch to the final crimp station, and pull the handle down to make the final crimp. Sometimes it is necessary to hold the handle down for a few seconds to "set" the crimp.

There are three types of crimps in use today, from left: roll, eight-point and six-point. All have their uses in various shotgun missions.

tain payload. This method works exceptionally well with smaller lead shot, especially pellets sized #4 and smaller. With these, you simply drop in the proper bar or bushing and proceed.

As shot sizes become larger, we run into problems of inconsistency. Larger pellets occupy space, just like smaller pellets, but those larger pellets need more elbow room. As you increase size, inconsistencies increase as well. Largely, you will get a slight weight reduction for every shot size increase. Your scale will reflect this particular phenomenon. When using a bushing, always verify shot weight by pulling a sample after first settling

the shot in the reservoir and then cycling the machine normally through several cycles.

If you find that inconsistencies are beginning to affect your crimping, those inconsistencies are too great. Use your scale to weigh your shot payloads. If you save those little 35mm film containers, you can use them cut to size for holding individual charges and creating batches of loads.

Shot bushings are always intended for metering lead shot only—unless they specifically state otherwise. Remember, the volumetric measurement of a bushing is a relative measurement of a specific weight. That volume represents an approximation of a desired weight of shot. For the sake of efficiency, we go with this system. Measuring every payload by actual weight becomes cumbersome in high-speed reloading.

If your bushing says $1\frac{1}{8}$ ounces, that is for lead. If you were to use that bushing for a volumetric measurement of steel, you will wind up with the wrong weight. Lead is heavier than most other types of pellets and as such occupies less space per weight than any other pellets currently available to shooters.

In the case of non-toxic pellets that are not steel and are softer than the material of which your bushings are constructed, there's little reason you cannot chart a specific weight a given bushing drops. Again, bushings are nothing more than cylinders with varying inside diameters. If drops are consistent and reliable, there's no reason not to use that bushing to drop your non-

the Ponsness/Warren Du-O-Matic 375C

Step 8: Shell Ejection

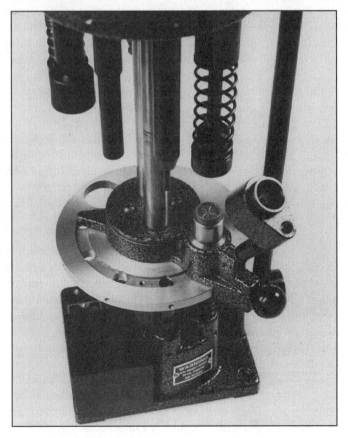

To eject the loaded shell from the sizing die, index the die arm all the way to the right (to the first station) and pull the handle fully down.

toxic pellet charges. I shy away from recommending this procedure for steel pellets because of the pellet's hardness. Indiscreet use may erode the junction area of bushing and reloader, rendering subsequent drops inaccurate.

Some reloader manufacturers will give you the green light for running steel shot through their machines, while others will tell you to stay away from it altogether. MEC offers a steel shot conversion kit to retrofit their loaders, as well as a model specifically designed for steel. Ponsness/Warren allows you to run steel through certain models without modifications (other than specialized shot bushings). Because of specific procedural differences, I only recommend using a single-stage reloader for assembling steel shot loads.

Crimping

Crimping your loads is the final stage. The quality of the crimp may determine whether you have a good load or a bad one—for reasons well beyond cosmetic. If the crimp is not deep enough, the plastic hull's "memory" may partially reopen the mouth, dribbling pellets in your pocket and robbing your load of its ballistic balance. A crimp that is too deep may also lose pellets as the folds have passed the optimum closure spot.

Crimping is accomplished in what is usually a two-stage process, crimp starting and crimp finishing. A good crimp is a balancing act between reloader adjustment and components. It is never a static setup, once achieved never altered. You can spend some serious time monkeying with crimp tools. For every different payload, powder, wad and hull type, whatever, you will probably have to readjust the final crimp station. Knowing what to look for and how to handle it makes the job quite easy, though.

Crimp Starting

Unless roll-crimped, hulls come in either a six-point fold or an eight-point configuration. Tradition has it that six-point crimps are used on hunting loads and eight-pointers are used on target loads. A ballistic lab could not possibly quantify a difference between the two. Either performs well for both applications. The only reason to select one crimp over the other is your hulls. If you are using Winchester AA hulls, for example, they come with an eight-point crimp from the factory. Were you to try to apply a six-point fold to this hull, you would end up with a jumbled mess and look like a moron at the gun club. To determine which type of crimp you have on your once-fired hulls, simply count the little points on the top rim of the hull. Most 2³/₄-inch 12-gauge hulls have eight-point crimps, most 3-inch 12-gauge hulls have six-point crimps, and all 10-gauge hulls have six-point crimps. If there are eight, use an eight-point crimp starter on your machine. All reloading tool manufacturers offer crimp starters in both configurations. To determine which one is on your machine, flip the crimp starter over and count the ridges or valleys. The number you come up with will correspond to the points it will produce.

When using brand-new hulls, handloaders are offered the option of using the crimp that most suits their artistic standards. Which would I recommend? Well, that depends on a couple of

The crimp starter rotates freely to align with the existing points in the case mouth and starts the tube closed for final crimp finishing.

things. Certain hull conditions behoove us to recommend one type of crimp over the other.

First, skived hulls taper to a fine edge at the top rim, allowing folds to be easily introduced to the plastic. Some hull tubes are moulded this way, while others are trimmed as a final production process. Skived hulls work well with 6- or 8-point crimps. However, if the hull is not skived (the end is about as thick as a dime), you may want to use a six-point crimp.

Second, larger pellets have bad manners when it comes to crimps too. The pellets tend to bulge up and make closure difficult, awkward and off-kilter. I have found that, in some instances, pellets have an easier time working into the larger spaces between six-point crimps. On the other hand, the little hole in the center of the crimp, where the edges of the hull converge, can be better controlled with an eight-point crimp. If you are using fine shot, this may enter into your decision.

Third, some machines just crimp better than others. Usually, it is easier for a machine to apply a six-point crimp; hulls more readily accept a six-point memory. For some handloaders, eight points are like graduate school. The easier-to-apply six-point will cure most problems.

Finally, don't agonize over your decision or waste long distance phone calls finding out which is better. You have bigger dragons to slay than crimp starter conundrums.

Once you choose, there is really not much to adjusting a crimp starter. Adjust it downward until you can see that folds have been introduced to the hull. Remember, you are only *starting* the crimp at this station, not trying to close the hull altogether. If you somehow overdo it with this adjustment, the crimp will squash together in the center during the final crimp.

In applying crimps, we often refer to the hull's memory. This means that plastic sometimes has the annoying ability to return to its former shape. New, unfired hulls may have to have folds introduced to the plastic by slowly working the hull into the crimp starter station several times before moving on to the final crimp station. This is especially true of hulls with thick, unskived tubes. When you can plainly see that folds have been introduced to the hull tube, you can proceed to the final crimp station.

Final Crimping

The final crimp station completely closes the hull, leaving what should be a flat level surface across the top. We want the center hole to be as small as possible without being crushed together and forming a spiraled swirl.

In general, the fold-crimp will provide the handloader with a positive closure that is about $1/16$- to $1/10$-inch deep. Overly deep crimp centers contribute to higher pressure loads. However, hulls are not created equally. Some hulls have soft, thin plastic mouths that may not hold the crimp. Other hulls hold like snapping turtles. Proper crimping depth requires some applied judgment by the handloader. Use depth sufficient enough to hold your crimps together. Take notes and refer to them for specific hull applications.

Use the crimp applied to factory ammunition as your guide to quality. The crimp depth quality and finish of factory ammunition is outstanding. Factory shells display beautiful working crimps on just about all loads, and you can learn from their work. Every reloading tool on the market today can be properly adjusted to produce just as good a crimp as factory shells. Factory loads look good because shotshell manufacturers use a formula of perfectly sized components and an exact amount of shot with the component column height set just right to produce a beautiful working crimp. Learn how to make this happen. For starters, most people benefit by reading their machine's operation manual.

Crimping problems most often occur when components are mismatched. For instance, a low-volume, compression-formed hull is not conducive to loading heavy magnum shot and slow burning powders. They become difficult to work with, in general, and are inconsistent, at best, when crimping.

Unfortunately, some people can reload for years without elevating their skills. They mix and match hulls. They don't care if a hull has a high or low internal base—it's a red hull isn't it? An uninformed person may try to jam more or larger sized pellets into a wad not designed for this treatment. He sometimes can't identify wads and doesn't worry about substitution. He sometimes demands loads be created to suit powder he happens to have on hand, rather than utilizing a powder designated for the load.

A change in hull type can undo an otherwise good fitting load, perhaps offering a too deep or too shallow crimp. Modifications to the tool will not provide for the $1/10$-inch (even more in some instances) hull depth differentials found between low-base hulls and high-base hulls. Many hulls, even from the same manufacturer, have quite different internal depths. The internal depths of some 12-gauge $2^3/4$-inch hulls are shown below. No, all hulls are not created equal.

Internal Hull Depths		
Hull	Depth (ins.)	Comment
Activ	2.43	
Federal Gold Medal	2.40	
Fiocchi Hunting	2.40	Low base wad
Winchester AA	2.40	Tapered interior toward base
Eley Plastic Based Hull	2.35	
Fiocchi Target	2.25	High base wad

As you might imagine, the difference of almost $2/10$-inch will affect your loads—both the crimp and the ballistics.

Specific Adjustment Procedure

The final crimp works, fundamentally, in two steps. First, your carefully applied crimp start is now pushed completely closed by a tapered section inside the final crimp die. Second,

This Fiocchi hull was crushed in the final crimp die. Further adjustment to the machine is needed. With improper crimp adjustments, hunting loads tend to fold just above the brass. This hull is weakened and can't be used.

Too much pressure on the hull at the final crimp station crushed this crimp beyond usefulness. The loading machine needs to be adjusted.

This crimp is not deep enough and will not offer adequate pressure for an effective load. Also, it is likely to come open and spill shot.

This crimp is quite functional. Note the taper to the front of the shell, which eases feeding in pumps and autos.

while the crimp is held together by the die, a ram closes the crimp and forces it past the axis, creating a reasonably tight seal and, hopefully, a good looking crimp. The quality of your crimp is determined by the interaction of these two steps. Crimps need to be deep enough to create enough pressure for a complete powder burning cycle. Pay attention to your crimp adjustments.

On the Ponsness/Warren machine, watch the outside housing spring tension on the final crimp station. The spring adjusts the taper placed upon the end of the hull to facilitate proper shell feeding in the shotgun. It's really hard to be too tight with the spring, unless you are using one of the models without sizing dies. Adjusted too loosely though, and you are left with an untapered, flat crimp with a gaping hole in the center. Tightening this spring dramatically affects final crimps.

The cam adjustment on the MEC reloading tool is absolutely critical to producing acceptable shells. This adjustment controls the portion of the crimp that begins the closure and sets up the hull for final closure. When a certain distance has been covered by handle movement, a cam's lobe passes a contact point, removing pressure on the outside housing. Internally, a plunger continues to travel downward, finishing the crimp with a flat surface. Too much tension on the outside housing will bulge the hull just above the brass. Too little and you will have no taper and a big hole in center of the crimp.

In the case of Activ or Winchester AA hulls with unitized walls and bases, hull bulging at the crimp station is not a big problem. However, with thin-walled hull types, adjustment is critical. Additional pressure caused by the outside housing being adjusted too low and the center ram adjusted too high is enough to buckle the hull before the crimp is even closed! Another sign that the final crimp is out of adjustment are hulls that have a been crushed together in the center of the crimp, forming a swirl.

The solution is to locate the cam adjuster for the final crimper. Find it near the base of the handle on the final crimp side. You will want to loosen the Allen screw that secures the cam to the machine, then turn the cam to the right (clockwise, toward the front of the reloader).

Tighten the Allen screw down again. Now, what you have done is to adjust the cam lobe so that it will release the outside housing assembly at an earlier point in the downward stroke of the handle. Hold the outside of the final crimper and watch the point where the cam's lobe passes over the final crimp. If you find that subsequent to that adjustment the shells have a hole in the center of the crimp, make a slight adjustment to the cam in a counter-clockwise direction.

Adjusting crimp depth is a separate procedure. That action is controlled by the screw on top of the final crimp assembly. Start rather loose and then tighten in stages until proper (about $1/8$-inch) depth is consistently achieved.

Forget using the wad guide fingers in MEC reloaders. There simply is not enough adjustment space to bring both the rammer tube high enough to insert a wad and properly seat it in the hull. I recommend you opt for proper seating. Pull the wad guide off, use the stiff plastic of the wad itself to guide it into the hull.

When using filler wads to raise the height of the shot column

for a solid crimp, be aware that the size of the shot used greatly influences the height of the shot column inside the wad. A $1 1/4$-ounce payload of #4s sits much lower in the shotcup than $1 1/4$ ounces of T shot. Filler wads such as $1/8$- and $1/4$-inch 20-gauge, which fit into the base of the shotcup, are for the convenience of the reloader. Many load combinations do not require filler wads of any size to be used.

For steel loads, fold-crimps must be seated tightly on top of the shot column. Worn-out hulls or those made with weak, laminated plastic are not good for loading steel shot. Compression is lost when laminated hulls fall apart, wasting your loading efforts and components. Avoid buying hulls with built-in flaws. Not all hulls are satisfactory for reloading.

Slow burn-rate powders (used in most hunting loads) and weak crimps do not mix. Furthermore, in cold weather, where most hunting loads are used, these factors come together to cause bloopers. Efficient and consistent ignition requires attention to the details, including the crimp.

Crimps must be firm, but the loader must not crimp so deeply that the top of the shotcup is pinched beneath the edges of the crimp. If this happens, the stout plastic shotcup used in heavy hunting loads can lift the hull plastic right out of the brass rim. Failing that, it may stretch or tear the hull in half. Also, chamber pressure may soar dangerously.

If you see this situation cropping up in your loading, add a filler wad under the pellet column, raising it slightly. Come firing time, the crimp will be forced open from the center, as it should be. Most hunting loads should be topped off with a thin .030-inch overshot card wad cut from a manila folder.

Somewhere in the delicate balance between reloader adjustment and component selection you will find crimping nirvana—a place where there are no holes in the center of crimps; no swirled, crushed-together crimps; and no crushed hull midsections. You may find this, but it is temporary. Perfect crimps require a constant accommodation of variables.

Roll-Crimping

Besides the many benefits offered by this nearly lost art form, it has become easy to attain perfect roll-crimps in every practical shotgun gauge. I don't recommend indiscriminately alternating between fold- and roll-crimps. Without tested guidelines,

At left is a near-perfect crimp, next to it an absolutely flawless crimp that's almost too nice to shoot.

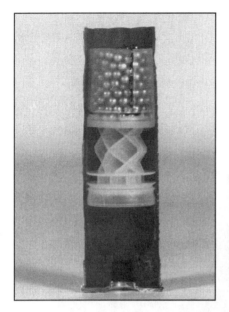

This sequence shows the diferences between the wad/payload that sits too high (left), too low, and just right for proper crimping.

to do so would be component substitution, shotgunning's prime no-no. Of the two types of crimps, however, roll-crimps demonstrate a greater load-to-load consistency of tested speeds and pressures. Load consistency does not translate across the board to lower pressures. The efficiency of the roll-crimp is conducive to producing many new loads and combinations. The length of the hull area required to form a roll-crimp is about half the length required for a fold-crimp. Therefore, much more of the total overall hull volume is available to the handloader who is utilizing the roll-crimp method.

The roll-crimper has gone through several evolutionary changes to reach its current form of refinement. The tool is carefully machined of a special alloy, assuring a smooth and uniformly cut contact area. The roll crimper is about $1\frac{1}{2}$ inches high with an integral bit for the chuck of the power tool used to drive it. It is as easy to change and use as a common drill bit. The bottom of the roll-crimper is specially designed to fold the hull inward and then down, leaving a slight taper on the top edge of the hull for better feeding through shotguns with a magazine.

Modern roll-crimping tools are available as a separate component and are used in conjunction with a power drill. A thin card is first placed over the shot charge, then the tool is used to force the lip of the hull over and roll it down until it meets the card. This is accomplished with a combination of heat from the friction of the spinning tool and moderate downward pressure.

I have found using a separate device to hold the shell while the roll-crimp is being applied to be very helpful. It is possible to secure the hull just with your hand, but it's not overly easy.

Most factory slug loads use roll-crimps to secure the slug. Besides superior seating of the projectile, a benefit of roll-crimped slug loads is load identification. The shooter can see at a glance whether or not the load in hand is a slug load. I doubt if anyone wants to rip a 12-gauge slug through the corn when #6 pellets were the intended payload!

Once-fired hulls, previously having been fold-crimped, are not candidates for roll-crimping without trimming. The plastic memory for the old fold-crimp is difficult to roll away, and the results are universally unsatisfactory.

If you would like to create $2\frac{3}{4}$-inch roll-crimped loads, a 3-inch hull of identical type that's trimmed $\frac{1}{4}$-inch is now a $2\frac{3}{4}$-inch hull ready for new life with a roll-crimp. If the hull is to be trimmed any further, you must follow reloading guidelines for shorter hulls. Of course, a point eventually is reached where the internal components of a particular load can no longer be stuffed inside a shortened hull, making it particularly obvious that the load will not work in that configuration.

Marking Your Loads

Since reloaded shells have little or nothing to do with the original markings or the original boxes, the handloader is often faced with wondering what is in those hulls. Yes, cutting a few open has been done many times. If you can't figure it out with the clues that provides, toss the loads away. You can solve this problem by marking your loads. A permanent marking pen is your friend. There are permanent felt-tip pens available that write on brass and plastics. Purchase new shell boxes and mark them.

You can also use plastic bags and drop in a 3x5-inch file card with the load data. Use medium-sized (you have to lift them, remember) heavy-duty corrugated cardboard boxes with the file card tucked inside for storage. The great number of variables in shotgunning make our lives more complex sometimes. Short range, long range, intermediate range, rabbits, scatter loads, different sizes of shot, this wad and that wad. It's a challenge. Your ultimate choice is to mark them or toss them. Sometimes being neat pays dividends.

Your Reloading Bench

The bench you decide to place under your reloader is largely up to you and your interpretation of comfortable. I can, however, offer a few suggestions that will make the setup process easier for you as well as save you the aggravation of redoing several steps.

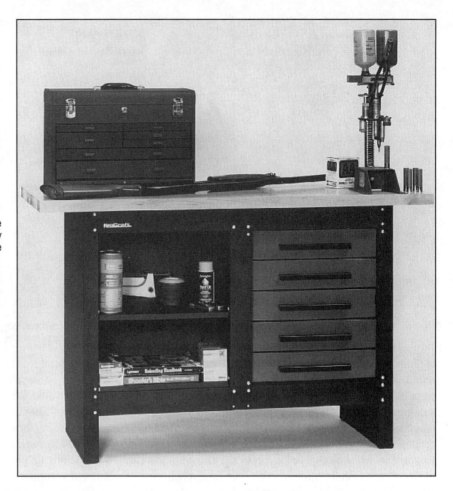

Whether your reloading bench is homemade or commercially purchased like this Kennedy bench from Sinclair International, make sure it fulfills your *personal* reloading needs.

Using C-clamps to hold your reloader to the living room coffee table is not recommended. Coffee tables sit way too low for proper leverage. Besides, the clamps have trouble holding onto most smoothly finished surfaces. If you twist this into a recommendation, then get yourself off the hook with your spouse by showing her this page. Here are some guidelines:

Proper Height

A knee-level living room table is too low. There are a couple of other height considerations when selecting a bench, though. On some of your loads you will have to be applying a fair bit of leverage. Give some thought to how high you want your bench in relation to you and your machine's handle. About belt high works for most folks. You will also have to load and mount the powder and shot reservoirs once in a while, and if your bench is too high you may need a step ladder. Don't forget that you will want a pretty close look at your shells as they go by. Make the height somewhat convenient for inspection.

Give adequate-clearance from the back wall. If the bench is too shallow, it will become quickly cluttered. Moreover, progressive reloaders usually spit finished shells out the back.

Press Mounting

The reloading press has to be mounted fairly close to the front edge of the bench. Different brands require different distances, but most will require a setback of less than 4 inches. Should you forget or, worse, overlook this step, the press handle will clunk down on the table just before the die contacts the shell. Just after that your forehead will clunk on the table.

Bench Strength and Weight

I usually ballast my bench with a couple 25-pound bags of lead shot. However, it's a good idea to use some angle iron, available at your hardware store, to bolt the bench to the wall. If you take this step, make sure you really want the bench in that position.

As odd as it sounds, I know of one $700 reloading tool out there attached to a bench with four different carriage bolts. One bolt has an extra-long unthreaded shank and, as such, cannot be fully tightened. This was remedied by using a short section of brass tubing between a half-dozen washers! It pays to make just one trip to the hardware store, and then buy adequate hardware. Measure the diameter of the mounting holes and get the right bolts.

Storage

As long as you have the hammer and saw out, take some extra time to build storage shelves. Most reloading components will last indefinitely if stored in a dry, ventilated area. Unless you live in the desert, your basement floor does not count when it comes to dry. Keeping supplies off the floor and on a shelf will make you a lot happier and a better handloader. I can't think of any components that would require a shelf deeper than 10 inches. Also, think about where you want to store your shot—overhead is a bad idea. Finally, primers should be stored near the floor, but where nothing can fall on the boxes.

Ambient temperature can
have an adverse affect
on load performance, but the
savvy handloader can compensate.

10

Load Tuning for Performance

THERE ARE MYRIAD variables under which your shotgun must operate. These conditions can include terrain, weather, types of shooting, variations in loads and others. Sometimes we can tip the scales to our advantage by using the optimum combination of components and firearm. Being prepared is half the battle, sometimes.

Hot Weather Shooting

Those who know that their loads will be shot in warm weather (over 75 F.) or really hot weather (over 85 F.) will need to take some special precautions.

Hot days will increase the pressure of your hunting loads. The types of powders used do not have as much influence on increased pressure as does the amount or volume of powder. A 10-gauge load (using the largest volumes of powder) or a 3- or $3^{1}/_{2}$-inch 12-gauge load will knock you very hard when you fire it in 90-degree temperatures. While every load will react somewhat differently to heat, one can expect to find an approximate rise of 1000 psi for every 10 degrees of temperature over 70 F. This describes a big load with a lot of powder and is a worst case scenario. Smaller loads (target and upland), with small charges of powder, have a much smaller rate of rise, possibly as low as 200 psi for every 10 degrees over 70 F. Therefore, you need not make any changes to light loads.

The powder is the problem with excessively high ambient temperatures. We cannot point our fingers at any specific powders, only the volumes used. All powders react to heat and cold, and ambient temperature must be considered if we want our loads operating at peak performance. The more powder in the load, the greater the reaction to temperature. What follows are a few steps a shooter can take to keep loads operating as they should. By the way, most loads are tested in laboratories at a controlled 70 F.

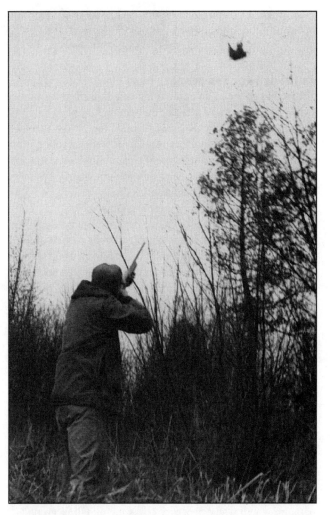

The shotgun must operate efficiently in a variety of conditions. To be prepared for whatever comes your way, load smart and shoot smart—and you'll have a successful day afield.

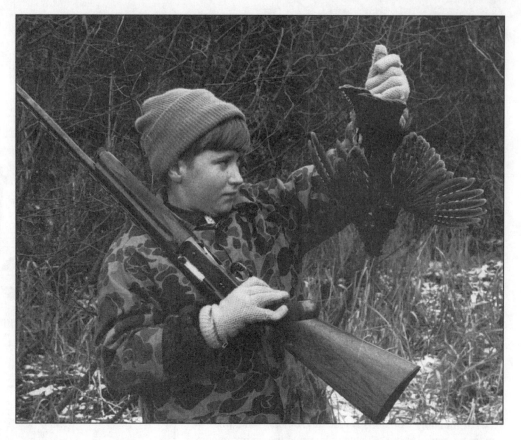

Cold weather shooting requires a bit of foresight to be truly effective at bringing down game. This young shooter's Browning A-5 and winter loads helped bring this nice grouse to bag.

Reducing High Temperature Load Pressure

Primers: If the load you are using calls for a magnum primer (which produces more pressure by burning hotter), switch to a standard primer. If a CCI 209M is called for, switch to a CCI 209. Primer change can affect a load by 1000 psi or more, a fact that should open your eyes regarding random substitutions. However, do not then use such loads indiscriminately in cool or cold weather; bloopers could result.

Powders: If you know the heat is going to be on your loads, you may reduce the powder charge by 5 percent or 2 grains (in the 12-gauge)—whichever is greater in your particular load. This will reduce pressure on a hot day by about 1000 to 1200 psi. Don't do the inverse to accommodate cold weather. Some powders perform at peak at much lower temperatures than others.

Crimps: It is an old reloaders' trick to crimp hulls more deeply on cold days to sustain powder ignition and create some pressure for combustion. You will get the same net result on hot days. A deep crimp is greater than 1/8-inch from rim to surface of the crimp. If your reloading instructions call for a "deep crimp" think about how you are going to use the loads. Some sources may not know that deep crimps are conducive to increased pressure, but now you know! Wisdom helps create better shotshells.

Cold Weather Shooting

Cold weather shooting, by my definition, begins at the temperature where water freezes. Cool is the middling ground of under 40 degrees. Cold weather can be managed, rather than endured, if the handloader makes informed load selections for the conditions and takes several preventative measures.

How do you know if you need cold weather loads? Well, are you going on a hunt north of the Mason-Dixon line after October? If the water around your blind begins freezing, that's nature's way of telling you to pull out the cold weather gear. Of course, I refer specifically to your loads. Your mother and the evening news should both have thoroughly covered the clothing aspects of cold.

Improving Low Temperature Load Pressure

Cold weather is difficult for the hunter, but it can bring a great day in the fields. If you have fortitude for the task, the game will be there and you can have some winter-like fun. For cold weather success, though, the shooter must have shells that hold up to the task despite the falling mercury.

Primers: It may be possible to select a primer that will increase the ignition quality of a particular load. Search through established load data sources for recipes similar to your old favorite, but ones that use hotter primers. CCI manufactures a primer that burns consistently, regardless of weather. They also make a magnum primer, somewhat a misnomer in that it usually is not for magnum loads, but rather is magnum hot as opposed to the "standard" 209. Never use such loads if the temperature or the shell is above 40 degrees F.

Hulls: Just like your garden hose, your hulls become brittle in the cold. Use hulls a reasonable person would consider to be in "excellent" condition. I say this for all your hunting loads, but it becomes especially important for cold weather loads. Cold weather, which exacerbates an already brittle condition, may blow a shabby old crimp right off the top of the hull.

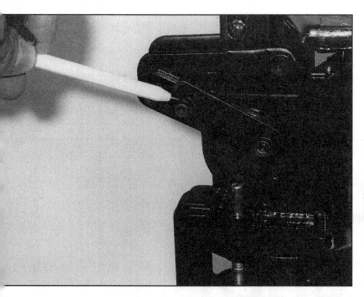

Part of fine-tuning loads involves getting the crimps just right to ensure proper ignition as well as smooth feeding in repeating shotguns. The cam adjustment on the MEC final crimp station is adjustable to provide a perfect crimp. It's a matter of trial and error.

Ponsness/Warren's point of adjustment for the final crimp station is here. It adjusts the hull taper as well as tightness of the closure. This is all part of the load tuning procedure.

Powders: Powder is a key performance variable in all shooting conditions. Various powders have very different ignition qualities, and ignition is only a singular factor of a powder's design intent. In order to accommodate another area of performance, perhaps an extended burn, for example, certain powders may not emphasize cold weather compatibility. Each and every powder has many specific characteristics, which a load designer uses when concocting combinations.

To accommodate medium burn-rate powders, desirable for cold weather, you may want to consider using slightly lighter loads. You want to create conditions conducive to a rapidly rising pressure curve. Heavy payloads are the right choice for cold weather but, more importantly, you want a complete burn. For cold weather, I recommend IMR-7625, IMR-4756, Scot Solo-1250, Hercules Unique and several others of similar disposition. Ultra-slow burn-rate powders, like Hercules Blue Dot, require specialized loading procedures and the best conditions. Certainly they should not be considered for use in cold weather loads.

Wads: Like the fuel/air mixture in an internal combustion engine, powder needs compression to burn properly. For a complete burn cycle, it needs a lot of pressure. If, however, compression (resistance) suddenly drops, the burn cycle is interrupted.

If one substitutes target wads in hunting loads, performance suffers greatly, and even more so in the cold. The weak pillar section (usually designed for $1^1/_8$-ounce loads or lighter) moves forward too quickly, reducing pressure and interrupting the burn cycle. I have always recommended using high-density steel shot wads for extremely cold temperature hunting. A phenomenon of the high density plastic material, necessary for use with steel shot, is that the tough, harder product does not become signifi-

cantly "less flexible" as it gets colder. Use the "Tuff" (or any high-density steel wad) in recommended loads in very cold weather, regardless of pellet type. You will notice improved patterns (yes, I am just goofy enough to have gone patterning in sub-zero conditions). You will also reduce the likelihood of cold weather bloopers, those occasions on which you will have to take off your gloves to verify an unblocked barrel.

Shot: It can be assumed that you have given some velocity away to the cold. Usually compounding the dilemma of lost velocity (let's also call it lost energy) is a ripping wind, working to shred your pattern and slow your pellets.

Compensation begins with pellet size selection. With weight being the pellet's dominant factor of retained momentum, we can change this variable and increase a load's lethality. A single size larger is usually enough, say from a #4 to a #3.

Steel Loads

Steel loads have an advantage over lead in cold weather because of the principle of bulk vs. weight. This describes the relationship between the number of pellets in a given load and the pressure created by it vs. the traditional weight of the pellets in a load. Large volumes of pellets add to the quick generation of combustion pressure, assisting the load in getting a much better burn out of slower burn-rate powders.

Keeping your shells warm in the field will only help performance. One method is to use a plastic shell box "warming house." Throw in chemical heat packs and shut the lid. This will keep your shells in good firing condition. Chemical heat packs (available for a very reasonable cost) are also great inside gloves to keep your fingers warm, of course.

11

Loading Buckshot

FOR MANY YEARS, shooters have demonstrated a wide variety of applications for buckshot loads. Unfortunately, buckshot loads are underrated, misunderstood and often underapplied. Fired at shorter ranges through thick cover, buckshot loads are often the ideal projectiles in regard to energy and on-target coverage. This is why Eastern shooters make such good use of these loads for big game.

Buckshot is defined by most as pellets larger than BB (.180-inch). Practical sizes for the shotgun range on up to #0000 (.380-inch).

Buckshot loads can be made in several ways to serve the purpose of the shooter. The use of lead buckshot pellets implies a scatter load where the shooter wants to flood a target zone with pellets. However, buckshot loads can be engineered to maintain reasonably tight groups of pellets at the target.

The real intent of a buckshot load is to provide a number of high energy hits on the target. It remains in the hands of the buckshot load designer (you) to determine how tightly focused (number of target hits) or open (improved chance of striking target) each load will be. It is up to you to balance the equation with pattern controls.

For the sake of presenting a consistent model, a standard buckshot load is a load of loose confederation, while a special buckshot load will utilize components and a design that guide the load toward a more specific (tighter) outcome.

Well-designed and constructed buckshot loads often utilize a wide range of loading materials. These loads are intended to be utilized over a wide range of applications and therefore often feature many unique designs.

The handloader may be interested to note that finer lead birdshot loads are often convertible to buckshot loads. Many tests indicate that the same weight of buckshot in a load that contains fine lead birdshot will produce the same or slightly less test pressure. However, do not under any circumstances presume

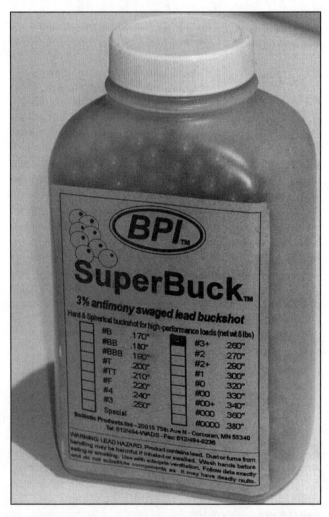

Buckshot is available in many sizes as well as in a high antimony version for high performance loads. It costs more than standard-size shot.

you can make a heavier load. Buckshot may be used in any load as long as the weight of the load does not change and the shotcup has room for the larger sized pellets.

Guidelines for Buckshot Handloads

Putting together proper, functional buckshot loads is best defined by examination of what can fit into a load. Buckshot load volume is defined by the components utilized. Even the powder selected will define a portion of the volume remaining for the other components, including the pellets.

Buckshot loads are assembled and tested in a specific configuration that must not be changed or modified simply because the handloader lacks some certain component or does not wish to purchase a component. Even when some slight change may not disrupt the original load design, testing every possible slight change or alternative is neither possible nor practical. When a tried-and-true recipe calls for a certain type of cooking sherry, an experienced chef does not change the recipe to fit whatever is on hand.

Hard and uniform lead pellets consistently produce higher quality buckshot loads. Since you will be operating with a reduced number of pellets, for pattern's sake you will want to look for the roundest buckshot you can find. Furthermore, to ensure hardness you will want a pellet with at least 3 percent antimony. Copper-plated buckshot, once available, is an excellent product, but just about impossible to find these days. It is important that the buckshot you use is very consistent in size, otherwise the tables supplied in this chapter will become invalid for your loading. Measure the pellets you use and verify they correspond to the baseline data before using them. If you come up with different weights or measurements, weigh each of your loads, trying to stay as close as possible to the payload guidelines.

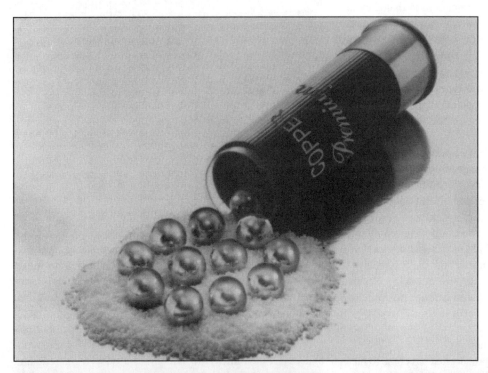

Many premium-grade, factory-loaded shotshells use buffering agents to help prevent some of the shot deformation that occurs during shot acceleration. This improves the patterns.

Shot buffer is used in heavy loads with larger pellet sizes. Not every load needs it, but it can improve patterns dramatically.

The adjustable shot dipper is very useful with large pellets: weigh the desired payload, put it into the dipper and adjust the cup accordingly. This gives an accurate measurement for subsequent loads.

Hulls and Wads for Buckshot Loads

Compression-formed hulls look very much like Winchester's AA. The hull's walls become thicker toward the integral base wad (as opposed to the base wad being a separate part) and the base is generally more bowl-shaped rather than a flat surface.

The tapered wall of compression-formed hulls creates a unique condition, wonderful for lighter loads but difficult for buckshot stacking. Stacking is the careful placement of large pellets in order to best utilize available pellet payload space. If you look carefully on the shelves of your local sporting goods store, you will see that manufacturers of compression-formed hulls do not utilize this particular hull design when making large-size buckshot pellet loads.

Fiocchi's well-known clear hulls make excellent containers for buckshot loads. They are straight-walled with a flat, low, plastic disk base. Even better for reloading is that they are available, new and primed. Generally, you will want to stay with the straight-walled hulls for the best fit and finish with large payloads.

Whatever hull the handloader selects can be made into a fine buckshot load as long as that hull's design limitations (or advantages) are considered. I only mention straight-walled hulls as an advantage because I am often asked, "What hull would you use?" And there you are.

Some factory wads are suitable for loading buckshot, while others negatively affect an otherwise good load. The handloader must remember that the size of buckshot selected for a particular load has a great influence over component options. Some loads are designed in a way to accommodate smaller buckshot sizes. As pellets increase in size, it becomes increasingly difficult to maintain the weight and bulk of the load design. I will later demonstrate buckshot fit (diameter and stacking relative to gauge and components) and how the size of buckshot pellets can either make a load or hinder an otherwise positive load combination.

Teflon-Wrapped Buckshot Loads

Teflon is a wonderful Dupont product that has come to mean a number of things to the consumer, from slick frying pan surfaces that are easy to clean to friction-reducing spray lubricant. Teflon in the form of thin film makes an ideal substance with which to encase lead shot for a ballistic advantage. Relative to barrel diameter, buckshot is quite a bit more imposing than your average bird shot.

In application, the Teflon wrap is rolled into a cylindrical shape and placed into the hull on top of the gas seal. The thin, slick sheathing makes for easier shot charge transition through the barrel and constricting choke area, an area of your shotgun that can destroy unprotected buckshot loads. Easing choke passage allows larger buckshot pellets to retain their shape for better patterns and concentration during the flight to the target. The Teflon wrap allows the handloader to utilize a number of different buckshot pellet sizes in hulls and conditions that may otherwise limit pellet size or configuration.

Teflon-wrapped loads require a gas seal to be placed on top of the powder charge, followed by an appropriate number of

Hunting big game with the shotgun is the only legal method in some states. Good buck loads must be developed to deliver as much energy on target as possible.

filler wads to comprise a column of the needed length. I use either felt or cork wads of the same gauge as the load. Put a coiled Teflon wrap into the hull, on top of a plastic gas seal, and allow it to uncoil inside the hull. Place your filler wads inside the Teflon wrapper. Stack the buckshot according to directions, place an overshot card wad on top of the shot column, and then crimp. Now you have a buckshot load.

Buckshot loads are often made by using multiple components to accommodate specific buckshot sizes. Nitro card wads (nominally .125-inch thick) are sometimes used as a gas seal, and more often as a filler wad, creating more consistent firing conditions and the proper payload length for correct crimp closure.

Buckshot Loading Dynamics

The handloader should note that each buckshot pellet within a given pattern carries by itself an enormous amount of energy. Even the smaller buckshot pellets deliver rather massive downrange energy. Underestimated energy should encourage handloaders to explore what size pellet is really required without going overboard. Often, a small buck pellet will do the job quite nicely, even when a shooter half-expected to need the requirements of about two sizes larger.

It is possible to overwhelm the hull/wad of a load by using oversized pellets and jamming them in a mix of components. The results, as testing and earlier experience tells, was never pleasing. To obtain any good result, the package of individual components must be as balanced as possible. Now, we must remember that very large buckshot pellets have always been

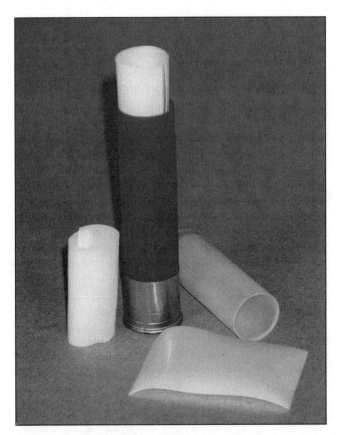

Teflon wrap can be used to protect the buckshot payload against barrel abrasion and ease it through the choke.

difficult to work into available components. Extra care has to be taken in overall load selection when working with larger buckshot pellets. To this end, here are some tips to help the reloader make balanced loads.

When considering a large-buckshot pellet load, there are several planning stages the reloader must make. First, select a combination of components that will accept a stacking arrangement of the chosen pellet size. Utilization of the charts and materials within this book will put you on the right track to determine optimum pellet sizes. This is, of course, only if the handloader cares about stacking the pellets in some sort of orderly arrangement. Many of the smaller-pellet buckshot loads do not require stacking and may be impossible to stack because the pellets refuse to fall into an orderly arrangement. To stack them would require the patience of a cottonwood tree.

Pellet Stacking

Larger pellets require stacking in order to place them into a load without creating a height and crimp-closure problem. In real-world application, buckshot stacking can either be an option or a requirement. Available internal space for a particular payload will make the determination for you.

Stacking does not always produce better groupings of pellets for long-range shooting. As with all types of loading, a large determining factor in downrange patterns is the barrel of each particular shotgun. With tighter chokes, the stack of pellets all ram the constriction as a nearly non-adjustable mass, thereby becoming congested and deformed. Clearly, large buckshot will

flow more easily through a less-constricted choke. For improved long-range patterns, you may want to consider using a Modified choke. Sound strange? Give it a try before you scoff at this notion. Random setting pellets fired through a tighter choke often produce tighter pellet groupings at a longer distance but—caveat—not always.

The principle behind stacking buckshot pellets is that the greater the angle of surface contact between two pellets, the greater the tendency those pellets will impart energy in that direction. In other words, any order given to the buckshot inside the hull will reduce the amount of randomness of the buckshot's flight.

With smaller buckshot pellets, the number of pellets makes up for pattern density and reduces obvious randomness. The compactness and increased surface contact of the greater number of pellets reduces the need for stacking or layering as influences remain more constant on all sides.

Stacking pellets in a load may call for a wooden dowel to tamp the pellets into place. A slight touch of force is OK because many of the buckshot loads will require some firm pressing to get them properly seated. A layer-by-layer approach is suggested. However, only so many buckshot pellets of a certain size can be placed (regardless of the pressure you apply) in a limited cylindrical area.

Simply put, if it is possible to arrange one level of like pellets, using as many as possible while fitting within the inside diameter of your components, it is possible to arrange additional layers of like pellets on top of this first layer. Stacked pellet layers are usually arranged in like numbers with the alternating layers set in the valleys between the pellets of the layer below.

Buckshot Types

#0000 Buckshot
Size: .38-inch
Weight: 85 grains
Comments: The #0000 or quad-buck weighs in at a little more than 1/5-ounce each! In the smaller gauges, these pellets become difficult to work with, but are just fine in 10- and 12-gauge. Certain loads can be assembled in the smaller gauges. It can be used as a slug in the 410-bore. An excellent size for big game, where allowed.

#000 Buck
Size: .36-inch
Weight: 70 grains
Comments: The #000 buck allows arrangment in layers of three in the 10-gauge hull with a thin coating of Teflon wrap as the shot stacking wrap. Twelve of these very large pellets will create a mighty 2-ounce load.

The #000 in the 12-gauge lines up very well in layers of two. Since the #000 buck pellet does not require many layers to exceed the weight that can be reasonably shot in the 12-gauge, this size buckshot has been overlooked in 12-gauge loads. Again, a layer of Teflon wrap around the pellets works as a fine shot carrier. This is also an excellent size for big game, where allowed.

#00 Buck

Size: .34-inch

Weight: 54 grains

Comments: The #00, or double-ought, at $^1/_8$-ounce per pellet is the most frequently used buckshot size for security and tactical loads. It all started when the post office opted to protect the mails and express cars from train robbers back in the 1880s. Fired from 10-gauge double shotguns, #00 buck as a close-quarters load became standard for protection of railway guards and postal workers. This is still the standard for many government ammunition contracts, but in 12-gauge, of course.

This size is on the large end of what reasonably can be loaded in the 12-gauge using standard shotcups and layers of two pellets. With any type of modern plastic shotcup, three-pellet layers cause the hull to dimple outward. This does nothing for the looks or the fit of the load. Only Teflon wrap allows an improved, near-perfect fit for layers of three #00 buck in the 12-gauge.

Grandpa knew what he was doing. A short-barreled 10-gauge with a heavy load of #00 buck was something that made you stop and think before you screwed around with his property. Grandpa was on the leading edge of tactical loading, and here we are, several generations later, using the same basic technology with greatly improved hardware.

The 10-gauge offers a tight layer of four #00 buckshot using Teflon wrap. Yes, it really is tight, but the Teflon will help prevent hull pimples. Five layers of four pellets results in a mighty twenty-pellet load of heavy shot. Six layers of three #00 pellets will fit into a 10-gauge hunting wad, providing eighteen heavy-duty longer-range pellets at a total weight of nearly 2$^1/_4$ ounces.

Four layers of four pellets results in a 2-ounce/sixteen-pellet load that will Swiss cheese nearly anything! The BPD10-Tuff will stack nicely and protect the #00 buck for long-range shooting with layers of three. The Remington SP10 wad will just about contain four layers of three #00 buck pellets for a total of twelve pellets, or 1$^1/_2$ ounces.

The 12-gauge hull and the Teflon wrap will beautifully support layers of three pellets. Cut the Teflon for the right height of layers that you need. In the Activ T-42 12-gauge plastic shotcup, one can fit three pellets per row of #00 buck in three layers (or nine pellets which gives about 1$^1/_8$ ounces).

For a special 410-bore application, a thin shotcup holds two #00 pellets neatly stacked on top of each other.

#0 Buck

Size: .32-inch

Weight: 48 grains

Comments: This often overlooked pellet is a marvel of fit and striking power.

Round balls are an effective payload for smoothbores and rifled shotguns. This can be an excellent choice for the woods and heavy cover.

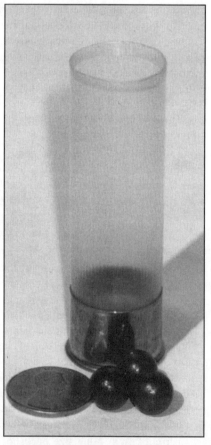

With the penny for size reference, it's easy to see why #000 Buck is an effective game stopper for 12-gauge loads. With buffering and the proper load, the pattern could be quite tight.

With a good load design, #3 Buckshot is a sure killer on a number of game animals. It can also be a good defense/combat load and is useful in the 20-gauge.

The 10-gauge allows a perfect fit of layers of four #0 buck pellets using Teflon wrap. If the load is intended for longer range, stacking pellets is not done. The BPD10-Tuff hunting wad with #0 buck produces an effective hard-hitting long-range load.

In the 12-gauge, the #0 buck pellet will stack into layers of three and calls for Teflon wraps to be used in the load. Nine pellets (three layers of three) result in an excellent 1-ounce load that is low on recoil and hard on hitting. In utilizing the Teflon wrap, the handloader can place four layers of three pellets each to build a 1³/₈-ounce load. Heavier loads may be made using Teflon wrap in 12-gauge combinations with smaller based wads.

The handloader can utilize the Activ T-42, Activ T-35, Federal 12S4, G/BP Magnum 42 or Remington SP12 wads with #0 buckshot. Twelve pellets (four layers of three) fit nicely into the G/BP Magnum 42 and Activ T-42 wads, offering 1³/₈ ounces of a very heavy hitting load.

The 12-gauge plastic shotcup offers a tight but not unreasonable fit. The tight fit may show up as slightly raised pimples on the outside of the hull.

#1 Buck
Size: .30-inch
Weight: 40 grains
Comments: Another overlooked mid-sized pellet, this one is large enough for deep penetration, and even a lighter load will create multiple hits. This shot size allows for utilization of this size in the BPD10-Tuff wad without stacking to create massive, longer-range 10-gauge loads.

This type of load offers exceptional, highly disruptive hitting power. In the 10-gauge hull, the #1 buck pellet size will not permit tight packing, and the loose or mixed arrangement is best suited for the BPD10-Tuff wad combination. The Remington SP10 thin-walled wad offers a good fit for this size buckshot when used with stacked layers of four. The SP10 shotcup will hold sixteen pellets (about 1¹/₂ ounces) in this configuration.

The 12-gauge and the #1 buckshot pellet offer a distinctive fit for large loads in rows of three pellets with a Teflon wrap. This size also is a very fine fit when stacking in 12-gauge plastic wads like the Activ T-42, Federal 12S4, G/BP Magnum 42 or Remington SP12 using layers of three. The Activ T-42 and G/BP Magnum 42 hold rows of three for four layers, a total of twelve pellets. These pellets can also be stacked in layers of four and buffered in a hull with no shotcup.

#2 Buck
Size: .27-inch
Weight: 29 grains
Comments: The 10-gauge offers loose confederations of layers. A double Teflon wrap may work most efficiently in some loads. This size pellet in the Remington SP10 wad will not quite stack itself in concentric rings. However, it is very close and some order is produced, but not layers of pellets. The same can be said for the BPD10-Tuff wad as the #2 buck pellet forms rings, but not layers.

In the 12-gauge, #2 buck is a better fit. Using Teflon wrap,

the pellets adjust themselves into smooth layers of four pellets. The Teflon wrap can support six layers of pellets. The Activ T-42 and G/BP Magnum 42 plastic wads load neatly in layers of four pellets of four rows (or five rows if slightly overfilled).

#3 Buck
Size: .26-inch
Weight: 23.5 grains
Comments: The #3 buck pellet is small enough for random placement into any shotcup or wrap in the 10- or 12-gauge. A 20-gauge wad holds three per layer, and four layers of #3 buckshot (or nearly ³/₄-ounce) make an effective 20-gauge buckshot load. The #3 buck size runs 18.5 to the ounce and is capable of very dense patterns at maximum ranges.

#4 Buck
Size: .24-inch
Weight: 20.5 grains
Comments: There is little point in attempting to stack this pellet in the larger gauges, but random capacities are interesting.

#4 Buck Wad Capacities	
Wad	**Capacity/Approx. Wgt. (ozs.)**
Activ T-42	25 pellets (1¹/₈)
BP-12 Shotcup	26 pellets (1¹/₄)
Turkey Ranger	32 pellets (1¹/₂)
Remington SP10	27 pellets (1¹/₄)
BPD 10-Tuff	49 pellets (2³/₈)

#F Buck
Size: .22-inch
Weight: 16.1 grains
Comments: The Remington 28-gauge shotcup holds layers of three in four stacks for twelve pellets. No other loads require stacking.

#T Buck
Size: .20-inch
Weight: 12.8 grains
Comments: The Remington 28-gauge shotcup holds layers of four pellets in five stacks, a total of twenty pellets. No other loads require stacking.

The handloader should carefully consider pellet size when creating a load. Often, shooters use buckshot far too large to create the required multiple hits. Huge pellets such as .34-inch and larger are often used, but perhaps smaller ones will provide a better load for the day. By following guidelines you can select the pellet size best suited to your needs.

Handloaders should remind themselves that lead buckshot pellets carry significant energy to the target. The size and power of the smallest buckshot pellet, in this case T (.200-inch), is very punishing in multiple hits. Single pellet hits of #4 (.240-inch) buck, and larger, do generate tremendous stopping power (big game levels), but it's the multiple hits on targets that make the shotgun supreme.

12

Unique shooting situations sometimes call for unique ammo, and this is the time to reload highly specialized fodder, but always follow accepted data.

Loading Slugs And Other Special Loads

PROPERLY APPLIED, A shotgun slug is a highly effective, accurate and lethal single-projectile load. Furthermore, with a little effort on the part of the handloader, slug loads can be massaged to a point where their effectiveness can rival (and sometimes exceed) that of certain rifle loads.

To really understand slug effectiveness, a shotgunner must first understand certain components of single-projectile ballistics and transferred energy. There are specific differences between shotguns and rifles, of course, and one of them is velocity. A 30-06 rifle pushes a 180-grain bullet somewhere around 2700 fps. Even though the bullet is very light, especially compared to a shotgun slug, it transfers a tremendous amount of energy to the target. Immediately upon impact, the bullet, by design, begins to deform. This deformation is akin to slamming on the brakes. Of course, the target is the surface absorbing all of the energy. If the bullet is designed properly, all of the energy will be spent before it goes out the other side.

Slugs work in the same way, except that we substitute weight for velocity. Instead of 180 grains, we talk about 437 grains, over twice the weight. Instead of 2700 fps, we talk about 1400 fps. Yet, in a heads-up comparison at an advantageous range for the shotgun, both impart similar energy levels.

If we start monkeying with the ballistics of slug loads, we may gain a couple hundred feet per second, but we lose energy—quickly. Some loads, while extremely accurate on paper, are inappropriate for field use. Long-range shooting is not the forte of your shotgun anyhow. Use it where it works best: in the woods. Keep the range under 50 yards and you will remain happy. If you were hoping to use slugs for some great 300-yard antelope shots, you will be disappointed.

Shooting Slugs

A heavy slug can be analogous to the precision of a bull elephant at full throttle. Very light slugs, on the other hand, can deliver extreme accuracy, so much that they can rival the accuracy of some hunting rifles at 100 yards. However, there is a tradeoff with this that renders fly-weight slugs much less effective than even small-caliber rifles. Mix into this equation a slug

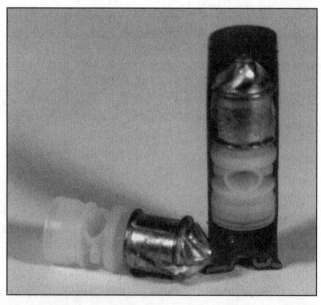

The Ballistic Products G/BP slug comes with an integral gas seal and is shown here in a cut-away Activ hull.

To find the best load for your gun and hunting conditions, you should plan on spending time at the shooting bench to judge the results of your handloading efforts.

design so completely given over to ballistic streamlining and none to target destruction, and you have the hunter's equivalent of blowing pins through a straw. This slug might really drive tacks at 100 yards, but if it passes right through a big tough deer without bringing him down, you have gotten nowhere and failed at making a clean kill.

A heavier slug, by virtue of its weight, carries additional energy into the target, and killing energy is achieved through a combination of velocity and weight. Measurement of this has a kicker: a subjective measurement of imparted energy. Any combination of an increase in velocity or weight of a slug will, however, certainly increase the demonstrable foot-pounds of energy. That's good.

In the 12-gauge, a light slug is considered to be 7/8-ounce or less. Heavy 12-gauge slugs run 1 1/8 ounces or more. Most of the effective designs run somewhere between these weights.

At normal slug ranges of 50 yards or less, where the slug is not yet doing the rainbow arch, the shooter can take advantage of heavy and not-so-aerodynamic designs.

The diameter of the slug works to the advantage of increased energy transfer. Just as weight and velocity are factors of lethality, the large diameter of a shotgun's bore imparts that much more surface area at impact. The goal is to use as much of that bore diameter as possible while still remaining ballistically stable.

I have fired 1 1/4-ounce 12-gauge slugs in various experimental loads with generally disappointing results in terms of speed and distance. Ballistic data points out that a good slug load must have balance for optimum performance. Too much of a good thing (in terms of weight) dramatically reduces launch speed and, therefore, produces an unreasonably arced trajectory. Heavy slugs require slow burn-rate powders, which are unsuit-

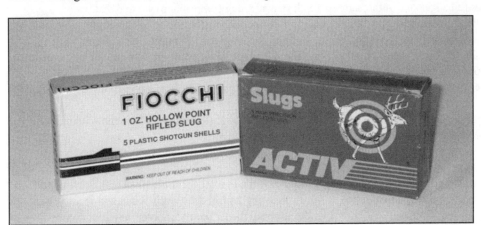

Slug loads are offered by Fiocchi and Activ, but the advantage of handloading is that you can tune your loads for shooting conditions.

The Ballistic Products CSD (Cushioned Steel Driver) steel shot wads have a cushion section, and are designed for most hull and load types. They can be used to create specialized loads.

(Below) Steel shot wads perform the important function of protecting the bore from the steel pellets. The fired example (left) attests to its durability.

able for consistent loads (and consistent accuracy) in cold weather. Sometimes, additional slug weight is another example of too much of a good thing.

For lighter game, and as conditions permit, slug shooters can use lighter slugs that weigh under 7/8-ounce. Don't forget that even a light 12-gauge load carries a terrific amount of energy. One of the benefits of lighter slugs is reduced recoil for shooters who are sensitive to it. Lighter slugs allow handloaders to utilize fast burn-rate powder for better combustion in cold weather. In warmer conditions, you can opt to increase muzzle velocity with slightly slower burn rated powders. In taking advantage of high velocities, the handloader is rewarded with a flatter trajectory to the target as well as an associated increase in delivered energy.

Optimum Slug Weight and Shape

Shotgun gauge is determined by how many round balls (slugs, if you will) can be cast from 1 pound of pure lead in that particular diameter. That is, 1 pound of pure lead cast into twelve round balls produces the diameter of the 12-gauge shotgun bore—.729-inch. A .729-inch round ball of pure lead weighs 1/12-pound, or 583.33 grains. That's a bit over 1 1/4 ounces.

It may be interesting to the handloader to know that, in any given gauge, a lead round ball that fits just into the bore is about the prime computed overall weight for optimum speed and accuracy for that particular barrel diameter. Interestingly, following this formula of slug design, it is also the least susceptible to the effects of tumbling and takes full advantage of the barrel diameter, offering the broadest face possible to the target. Round balls are not a ballistic panacea, but certainly an effective and reasonable solution to many slug-shooting needs. However, never fire a bore-sized ball from a choked barrel.

It is important to keep our eye on the volume a projectile (shot or slug) occupies within the barrel and not wholly fixate upon the projectile's weight. Shotgun gauge/barrel optimums have more to do with volumetric displacement than you would expect. Since slugs are not usually made of pure lead, but often an alloy of metals, the volume displacement becomes greater than an equal weight piece of pure lead. Therefore, the optimum slug will be both slightly larger and lighter than a calculated barrel optimization based upon a pure lead slug.

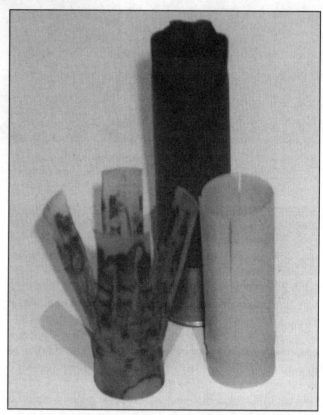

Carrying forward this formula of volumetric measurement (with standard slug composition) we find that:

- The 10-gauge slug optimum is something less than 1 5/8 ounces and close to 1 1/2 ounces.
- The 12-gauge slug optimum appears to be somewhere between 1 and 1 1/8 ounce.
- The 16-gauge slug optimum appears to be just shy of 1 ounce.
- The 20-gauge slug optimum is between 3/4-ounce and 7/8-ounce.
- The 28-gauge slug optimum is about 1/2-ounce.

Most favorite hunting areas are filled with dense cover, usually consisting of tightly woven brush and stunted trees. In order to strike the target, the shooter may have to fire through

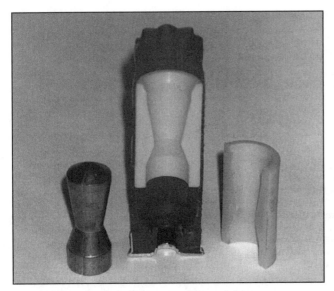

The sabot-type slug rides up bore in a two-piece "case" that falls away upon leaving the muzzle. These slugs can offer rifle-like accuracy, but are lighter than Foster-type projectiles.

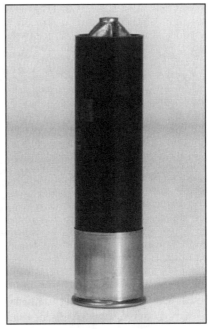

If slugs are used in a gun with a tubular magazine, the handloader must be certain the sharp nose of a slug doesn't protrude from the case mouth. This could initiate a chain reaction in the magazine—recoil could set off all the rounds.

The AQ slug for smoothbores has vanes on the plastic base that are said to induce in-flight rotation. This slug offers the energy of a round ball but with added stability.

branches, twigs and leaves. Unfortunately, there is no such thing as a "brush buster" slug or bullet. Let us not propogate this myth. If a projectile of any type ever hits the intended target after traveling through leaves, blades of grass or anything else other than air, that fact is an accident. The only thing we can say for sure is that tougher projectiles (which are less apt to deform in such encounters) are less deflected.

Rifled vs. Smoothbores

If your shotgun barrel is rifled, you need to take advantage of it by using a slug designed to work harmoniously with such a setup. This type of slug, by design, is useful at extended range. There are several types of slugs designed specifically for rifled shotgun bores. These have rifling pickup rings moulded directly into the body that will grab the barrel's rifling twist. A little

experimentation with slugs designed to work with rifled barrels will lead you to a favorite. Shoot it at various ranges until its performance becomes utterly predictable for you. Practice makes perfect.

The smoothbore purists can, and certainly do, attain high levels of accuracy through the use of specialized slugs. To maintain accuracy, specially designed smoothbore slugs must have proper fit within the barrel. Most often, inaccuracies associated with smoothbores can be directly attributed to slug deflection during its course of travel down the barrel. Deflection is sometimes cured by placing a Teflon wrap around the slug, creating the snug fit between the slug and bore needed for accuracy.

Although smooth barrels will not impart any negative influence upon shotgun slugs, neither will they impart a positive influence. Other factors become critical to high performance loads such as relative bore diameters (individual barrel differences), the general quality of the shotgun bore for slug use, tightness of the barrel's choke, as well as the quality of the gas seal in the loads. These factors add up to the overall efficiency (read accuracy and velocity) offered by an individual shotgun.

Slug Loads and Components

Remember, the conventional American 12-gauge hull measures 2¾ inches in length (open). Hulls loaded with slugs are usually roll-crimped down to the top the outer shoulder of the slug, leaving the correct overall folded length. If the hull is new and unfired, roll-crimping produces a very satisfactory and effective closure. For accuracy and pressure consistency, I recommend that slug handloaders use new hulls for their roll-crimped loads.

With the modern slug's superior design and balanced weight, the handloader can produce some very high-speed, personalized loads for the longer 3-inch chamber. If your shotgun is so chambered, you may wish to use the additional length for a gain in performance as well as conforming to the shot-

The Slugmasters Foster-type slug has a hollow base and a hollow point with fracture lines to promote expansion. It can be an excellent choice for short-range shots.

The muzzleloader's Minie ball is used to good effect in the 10-gauge. The hollow base obturates to seal the bore, and down-range energy is excellent. It's said to be a favorite in Alaska.

gun's design intent. The longer hull also allows a bit more space for powder and other components, including additional gas seals, which can be used to obtain superior consistency and velocity.

On the other side, the handloader may shorten hulls below the usual 2³/₄-inch length for specialty slug loads and increased magazine capacity. Before you make a bunch of these, make sure your shotgun will cycle them properly. Stubbed hulls are a fine way to save previously fired hulls for one more firing. Be sure to follow shortened hull directions, and check the brass heads and base wads for integrity.

Warning: The handloader should note that experimentation in hull length and load concoction is not advised. Often, the chamber pressures of these loads increase in proportion to a decrease in hull length.

For the best results possible, the shooter must take some time to consider important ballistic variables associated with shooting slugs. Two factors affecting what you want to put into a round are the expected temperatures at the time of the hunt (affecting the powder burn and velocity) and the landscape of the hunting area (long or short range).

All of the physical conditions of your hunt are important items that should influence you when selecting slugs and loads that may differ from the laboratory's calculated optimums. To take advantage of your many handloading options, unavailable in factory loaded ammunition, you must examine your shooting and your game to determine which load is most suitable.

Some slugs have a fairly tapered front end. You never ever want a sharp point to stick out beyond the hull's top edge. This is a situation to avoid, especially if you are using a shotgun with a tube-type magazine. Theoretically, it is possible for the protruding slug to contact the primer in the shell ahead in the magazine, creating a dangerous situation. You may wish to add a 12-gauge overshot card to the load before applying a crimp to avoid the problem.

Medium to fast burn-rate powder types have worked extremely well with most slug types and conditions. Although there are many that fall nicely into the category of excellent slug drivers, I especially like IMR-7625, as well as PB. Other really good slug propellants are Alliant's Green Dot, Unique and Herco. Scot/Accurate powders, such as

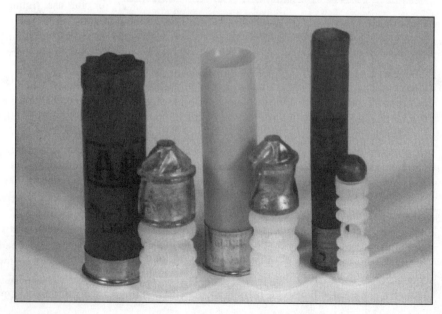

Slugs are available in all practical gauges, including the diminutive 410-bore (far right).

(Left) There are a number of different slugs on the market, some of them novel in design like this one. It's supposed to work with a venturi effect and mushroom like a doughnut on impact.

(Right) This 45-caliber hollow point pistol bullet rides in a colleted sabot. Shotgun velocities are comparable to magnum handguns for this effective slug.

Solo-1000 and Solo-1250, have provided loads with superb consistency.

For long-range shooting in cold weather, I suggest a single-base powder such as the Scot/Accurate or IMR numbers. In colder climates, help your powder burn completely by crimping deeply. Slug wad columns do not require wad pressure for seating, but always need firm crimps to create conditions for proper combustion.

For an accurate slug load, a plastic gas seal should be used, sometimes more than one. Plastic gas seals allow the load to generate maximum energy from the powder burn and place the pressure directly behind the slug, keeping disruptions to a minimum.

Galling and Other Barrel Contamination

Sometimes when shooting slugs, especially one after another at the range, you can look down the barrel and find a large amount of crud. What is it and how did it get there? Sometimes you have to wonder if there is actually more projectile affixing itself to the barrel walls than actually exiting the muzzle. What you see is actually a combination of plastic, powder and lead fouling left behind by any typical slug load, especially tight-fitting, high-performance slugs. More stuff in the load means that the chance of crud building up on the barrel is more likely. There is also a very shotgun-specific reason, one that I will share with you here.

In the spectrum of operating pressures, shotguns are running at the lowest point possible for a combustion cycle. At this low range of pressure, burning cycles are easily interrupted and often incomplete. For this reason, shotgun loads will often leave some ash and residue in the barrels. High-powered rifles can run three and sometimes four times the pressure with specific load examples. Add to the shotgun's equation a big, heavy, tight-fitting slug scraping its way down the barrel, and you are going to find some stuff there. Also different from metallic cartridges, shotshells contain wadding materials, either of plastic or paper. Both types will leave residue on barrel walls. Add this all together, and you will see that a shotgun is fundamentally a quite different animal than a centerfire rifle.

The real problem in cleaning the bore is getting rid of the lead. Layers of it hold all of the other goodies in place with stubborn tenacity. I have found that the best way to remove the lead is with a combination of chemicals and patience. Keep your bore clean and take advantage of the extra accuracy offered by a clean bore.

Standard Slug Dimensions			
Gauge	Slug Type	Weight (grs.)	Dia./Length (ins.)
10	Minie-Type Bullet (Sledgehammer Max-10)	755	.690x1.600
12	Slugmaster (Lite)	384 (7/8 oz.)	.675x.740
12	Slugmaster Fracture	431 (1 oz.)	.675x.740
12	AQ Slug	448 (1 oz.)	.738x1.200
12	Lyman Molded Slug	(463-475)	.710x.800
12	Lyman Round Ball	463 (11/16 oz.)	.690
12	Lyman Foster Mold Slug	475	.710x.800
12	G/BP Dangerous Game Slug	446	.735x.970
	in its plastic mount	487	.735x1.900
16	Slugmaster	370	.635x.685
16	Brenneke	409	.680x1.200
16	G/BP Dangerous Game	386	.670x.910
	in its plastic mount	425	.670x1.865
20	Slugmaster	285	.590x.725
20	Brenneke	373	
20	G/BP Dangerous Game	354	.626x.890
	in its plastic mount	387	.626x1.987
410	G/BP Dangerous Game	92	
410	Slugmaster	120	.385x.450

Specialized Loads

Every once in a while, shooters who own fine English shotguns may want to take them out of the closet and give the little jewels some exercise. Certain load accommodations have to be made, but you can easily create some excellent specialized loads using components that are widely available on the market.

Factory-length 2-inch hulls are rather hard to come by in the United States. If you can find them, they are pricy, and load data to accommodate specific shooting needs is even harder to find. Standard 2¾-inch 12-gauge hulls are sometimes shortened in order to fit English standard shotguns of 2- or 2¼-inch chamber lengths. Another application for 2-inch hulls is packing a greater number of loads in the tube magazines of riot guns.

The handloader has a number of options open when it comes time to make specialized loads in non-standard hulls. From left, 4-gauge, 8-gauge hulls, and 10- and 12-gauge hulls for comparison.

Roll crimping is an excellent choice for slug loads. Since they are easy to identify, there is no mistaking what kind of loads these are.

Shortened hulls bring with them higher chamber pressure. It is logical that a reduced volume would increase pressure and it's true. We see the pressure move upward about 20 percent in the 2-inch hull from loads that were made in the 2³/₄-inch hull. This is similar to the pressure increase found in the change from 3-inch hulls to 2³/₄-inches.

Out of convenience for the handloader, short hull loads should be roll-crimped, a procedure that stabilizes the pressure rise. Roll-crimping also benefits the reloader in that it utilizes the maximum amount of volume in the shorter tube. Since volume is limited and the pressure easily runs up, a smaller amount of shot is a reasonable solution. Most of the shorter loads are around ⁷/₈-ounce. This may seem light, but you have to remember the guns that these loads are used in. They usually are built on lightweight frames, have thin barrels and weigh around 6 pounds. Though this seems very light, the intention was to stretch the 12-gauge into the realm of smaller gauges, bringing with it the advantages of the bigger bore.

Cutting the Hull

For the most part, this job is not an exact science. Measuring from the base, mark the hull at exactly 2 inches, 2¹/₄ inches or whatever you have decided is the right length. Remember, length is determined by the *empty* hull. For cutting, I have had great success using a leveraged, stainless steel snip.

Another method is to place a wooden dowel (available at your hardware store) inside the hull for support and cut the tube with a razor blade or X-acto knife. Be careful and take your time. Remember that sharper blades are safer blades.

Wads

Most of the conventional target wads will be too tall for use in shortened hulls. Since most of the original shorty loads used cardboard gas seals, there is no reason not to fall in line and use this traditional method. I have used a .125-inch nitro card wad as the seal, then stacked an appropriate number of card wads on top of that to take up extra space.

You can use plastic gas seals too. The BPGS (Ballistic Products Gas Seal) offers a complete, finely edged seal for high performance loads. Loads using a plastic gas seal require less powder as you do not have to accommodate leakage.

On top of the gas seal, I place a cork filler wad to create a solid platform for the pellets. The shot charge is then secured by an overshot card, and the shortened hull is roll-crimped by means of a special spinning tool.

Traditionally, these short loads use fine shot like #6 and smaller. Larger shot would use up too much space, negating the advantage of compactness offered by these loads. Short loads use fast burning powders; these are not magnum loads and do not need to be driven with excessive velocity. Shorty loads are poppers, made for a stroll in the countryside, leaving the hunter unburdened by an overly heavy shotgun. Enjoy the walk with the dog and take the occasional pheasant. Use of these loads suggests you slow down and put game acquisition behind your enjoyment of an autumn day.

Just like a round of loaded ammo, every shotgun is made up of a combination of variables. Understanding these factors will lead to better shooting.

Your Shotgun And Your Loads

13

YOU SQUEEZE THE trigger. The primer pops. The propellant is converted to hot gas as it burns. Your carefully applied crimp starts to open under the resulting pressure, and the pellet load begins to make its way down the barrel. In a modern shotgun, the payload, as it leaves the chamber, will encounter the forcing cone, a certain length of barrel and finally the choke. Each section influences load performance in a unique way, and each can be slightly changed in configuration to affect load outcome. Shotgun makers and gunsmiths use these tricks to devise and manufacture special-purpose shotguns. A better understanding of how each section works, and how it can be maintained, will help give you a better understanding of your shotgun and its relationship to your loads.

The Chamber

This is where your shotshell resides when properly loaded into your shotgun. Chambers are not precisely uniform from gun to gun, because there are variances of a couple thousands of an inch from manufacturer to manufacturer—and sometimes from gun to gun. Once in a while, a gun is made with an undersized chamber. If it's an automatic, it probably will refuse to eject shells properly, and furthermore, upon loading a round into the chamber, the action will sometimes not lock and the bolt will have to be set by hand. A good gunsmith should be able to polish out a tight or rough chamber. This effort will improve the mechanical cycling action of an automatic or a pump.

The educated handloader will have a better chance of getting game because he understands all the systems involved in launching a load of shot to the target. A well-trained dog helps, too.

111

Marlin's Model 512 Slugmaster is one of the new breed of bolt-action slug guns for the serious big game hunter.

The Benelli Montefeltro Super 90 autoloader is a sophisticated field gun that has proven extremely reliable.

The slide-action shotgun, here Winchester's Model 1300 Walnut, remains a favorite with many hunters because of its rugged dependability.

An oversized chamber can cause its own havoc. Hot, expanding gases seeking their easiest escape route may find one by coming back between the hull and the chamber, flooding the breach area. The natural seal of the expanding hull against the sides of the chamber won't function properly if the chamber is too big or out of round. A greatly oversized chamber will be even more difficult and will probably require you to replace the entire barrel. If you have a shotgun that consistently produces hulls that are extremely difficult to resize, or are damaged in the form of cracked brass or split plastic, an oversized chamber is probably the culprit. Though you may never have considered chamber size as a factor of your load performance, it is a part of the overall package. Performance is found, and lost, in the details.

The hulls you load for hunting should be the same length as the chamber of your shotgun; if you have a 3-inch chamber, load and shoot 3-inch hulls. The use of shorter 2³/₄-inch hulls may affect pattern quality as pellets bang against the chamber's edge when entering the forcing cone area. This applies to lead, and even more to steel shot loads, since steel has a tendency to deflect energy.

The Forcing Cone

The forcing cone is defined as the transitional area between your shotgun's chamber and the barrel itself. It is conically shaped, hence the name, with the large end toward the chamber. Think of it as a funnel. The dimensions of the forcing cone can have a profound effect on every load.

The forcing cone can be either long or short. Longer is desirable, but short is what you usually have. Long forcing cones run about 1¹/₂ inches in length; short are about ⁵/₈-inch long.

Not every shotgun has long forcing cones because applying a long, sloping taper adds additional machining costs to manufacturing a gun. The pricing of sporting shotguns is always competitive. Customers do not compare guns on the basis of forcing cone length, even though it should be an item to scrutinize. Taking those factors into account, manufacturers invest their time, and manufacturing costs, elsewhere.

Ideally, forcing cones should be a minimum of 1¹/₂ inches long in a waterfowling shotgun. Forcing cones cannot really get too long. Years ago, some fine double barrels were made with what were called taper bores or modified-taper bores. These barrels have a continuous reduction in bore size all the way to the choke.

I have an L.C. Smith 3-inch 12-gauge with a taper bore that was made in the 1930s. The bore is one very long taper—a 34-inch forcing cone/choke if you will. It took a while for me to get around to testing this particular shotgun on paper, and I wish I had done it earlier, because my ignorance cost me some birds. At 60 yards, this particular shotgun shoots patterns like most Full-choked shotguns do at 40 yards. The 60-yard patterns are 3 feet wide.

Larger pellets are more affected by barrel features than smaller ones. To get a regular barrel to shoot as tightly as this one does would require an Extra-Full choke. However, making a choke this tight risks complete disruption of the pattern and sending pellets all over the county. In the taper bore, there was nothing inside the barrel to disrupt the flight of larger pellets. Lesson learned: When shooting long-range patterns with large shot, try to offer as few areas of transition as possible inside the barrel.

As delivered from the factory, many modern shotguns do

not benefit from extended forcing cones for long-range patterns. Mass-produced shotgun bores tend to be machine-finished—correct in size, but a little rough and requiring some finishing for excellent long-range shooting. A little time and money spent here will go a long way toward big improvements of your patterns.

Luckily, lengthening the forcing cones can be accomplished at a very reasonable price. This is standard procedure on my shotguns. I enjoy reduced recoil and improved patterns at all ranges and with all loads. When you shoot steel pellets, your shotgun barrel needs a long, tapered forcing cone or your patterns will be seriously disrupted. Because steel pellets retain energy instead of absorbing it, they require a slick, smooth start down the barrel. Even the best choke in the world cannot reassemble a pattern disrupted by an abrupt forcing cone.

Most gunsmiths are familiar with the procedure and will be happy to do the work. As a final step, I recommend that you have him give the bore a good polish. It's a useful final touch, but you usually have to request it. The polish will help limit corrosion, and offer an even smoother surface for the pellets to ride upon.

The Bore

Beyond the forcing cone is the barrel, and here is a jolly area for discussion in any hunting camp. European bores tend to be slightly smaller than American bores. Europeans tend to work with smaller pellets, and these conform to smaller bores amicably. However, and here is why ours are generally bigger, any shot size larger than American #4 provides less than optimum patterns in smaller bores. As we tend to shoot large payloads at long distance, manufacturers wisely presume that a majority of our loads will be using pellets larger than #4.

As defined within the realm of shotgunning, overbore simply means making the internal diameter of the barrel wider (larger) than what is considered the norm. It would be the same as drilling one hole in a piece of wood then taking a larger drill bit and making the hole wider. The standard inside diameter of a 12-gauge barrel (measured past the forcing cone) is nominally .729-inch. The rub of overbored barrels is that most components are manufactured to accommodate the standard measurement.

Overbored barrels are both good and bad depending upon your shooting. If done correctly, overbores can improve patterns in lighter, competition target loads as the shot charge is better able to take advantage of space and align itself into a more controlled swarm. It is somewhat like getting the advantages of a larger gauge without the recoil. You are wrong, though, if you think that an overbored setup, which works so well at the Clays course, is going to work equally well in every other application. Again, the work must be of the highest quality. It may not *always* be effective.

Shooters have to remember that the wad's relatively fragile gas seal is critical for proper load performance. If expanding gases force past the seal, consistent velocities and pattern performance are compromised. Heavier loads using slow burning powders will make this scenario more likely. Consider these factors before having your shotgun over-bored. There have

Jump shooting waterfowl can be a tough way to bring home dinner, but if the shooter knows how to build a good load, his task will be easier.

been some shooters who have overdone this and failed to improve or ruined otherwise fine shotguns.

There are now a large number of factory overbored shotguns being produced, so you might just have one already. Heavy loads in overbored barrels may require specialized gas seals designed to accommodate the bore. I use one that has concentric rings on the flattened area and is shaped vaguely like an X if you look at it from the side. X seals are very flexible and flair outward with a fine scraper seal. They will handle most overbores in stride.

For those guns with chrome-lined barrels, I do not recommend making modifications. Even though someone may offer this service, it is really not a good idea. After time and a few shells, the chrome lining around the edges of the reworked area begins to peel away. Usually, the metal underneath is rougher and more susceptible to rust and wear. Chrome lining will work best for you without modification. Chrome lining, however, can be stripped and reapplied by such companies as Robar (Phoenix, Arizona).

The Choke

For the purpose of extending the range of multiple hits, chokes compress the pellet payload into a controlled and narrowed stream. Varying the size of the opening will vary the distance attainable by a controlled (dense) swarm of pellets. While one particular choke constriction works well for one fellow, it may not for another. This is because so many other variables enter the equation, including your particular shotgun, shot, shells, wads, and shooting style. Shotgunning is a whole mess of variables poured together, and what comes of it makes the sport a lot of fun.

Everything is relative, and so is measurement. The subjective opinion of measurement assigned to choke constriction is usually a small bit different from manufacturer to manufacturer. However, the following constrictions can serve as a reference tool for the reader.

Nominal Choke Constrictions					
Gauge	Bore Dia. (in.)	Chamber dia. (in.)	Full Choke	Modified Choke	Improved Cylinder
10	.775	.840	.045	.030	.010
12	.729	.795	.035	.019	.009
16	.665	.730	.028	.015	.007
20	.615	.685	.025	.014	.006
28	.550	.615	.022	.012	.005
410	.410	.460	.017	.008	.004

It would seem logical to think that a Cylinder bore, with no constriction whatsoever, would shoot the widest patterns. The answer is both yes and no. Perhaps we have just become used to chokes, but the pattern board seems to tell us that it is a necessary part of our shotgun if we want pattern consistency. Tests with Cylinder bores have demonstrated that even at the shortest of ranges the patterns are wide open indeed, but the patterns are almost predictable in their patchiness. However, certain buckshot loads pattern quite tightly with a Cylinder bore.

When a choke is tightly constricted, the plastic shotcup transmits compression forces of the barrel through to the shot payload. If the payload is not very accommodating, the choke is on the receiving end of a severe strain during its interaction with the load. To withstand these forces, the choke must not be overly constricted. Load variables hampering the longevity of a

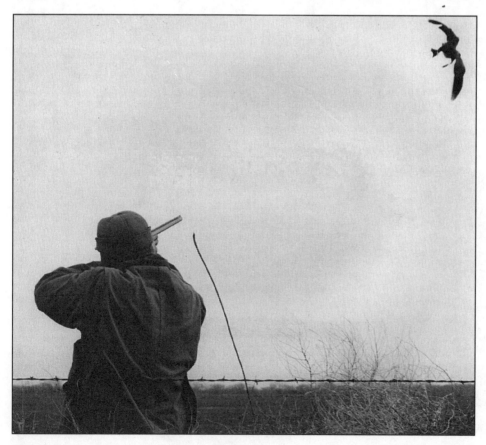

The shooter and reloader must understand that there is no similarity between lead and steel shot, in regard to shotgun choke. Specially designed steel shot chokes will improve steel shot patterns.

Many new and young hunters start with a single shot gun, like this inexpensive Magtech MT-151, and later graduate to a repeater.

The side-by-side double gun has a legion of followers because of the fine handling qualities, quick follow-up shots and pure romance. Shown is the Ferlib Model FVII.

The over/under has become probably the most popular hunting shotgun because it is easy pointing, has a durable action and it's downright good looking. This is the American Arms Silver Sporting with ventilated middle rib.

choke include heavy payloads, high velocity, steel shot and large pellets.

Chokes and Shot Type

A critical factor in the design of a choke is the type of shot that passes through it. The shooter and the reloader must understand that the only similarity between lead shot and steel shot, in regard to shotgun choke, is the roundness of the pellets. Specially designed steel shot chokes will improve your steel shot patterns. Hastings, for example, considers specialized handloads when creating customized screw-in chokes. They offer several types of steel shot chokes to handle specific high performance handloads.

Because of the steel load's character, it pounds into the choke with far more force than lead. If we think of a shotgun as being similar to a fire hose, with the choke as the nozzle, you have a very similar principle of constriction. Water (or pellets) coming down the hose (barrel) gets compressed into a longer and thinner stream (per same volume), and this action causes a strung-out, tighter concentration of the projectiles.

Ballistically speaking, lead is a very accommodating material. Under high pressure, lead provides great slippage (little friction) and offers adjustment through deformation. If pressure exceeds the ability for movement or adjustment, the lead pellets will deform, absorbing excess energy through the alteration of shape. On the other hand, iron (steel) is not forgiving. When pellet-to-pellet pressure is applied to steel, it tends to bind, not slip or compress.

Often a very tight choke will have an inverse effect on steel shot patterns. Steel pellets retain energy and transfer it instead of deforming as lead pellets do. Too much constriction throws your pellets to the fringes of the pattern, making it appear that

you need more choke constriction. Not so. A dead give-away of this condition is a noted lack of density in the very center of the pattern. To get the best patterns possible, steel shot shooters need to experiment with various choke types and constrictions. Somewhere between Improved Cylinder and Full you will find the perfect choke for your shooting conditions. The key is experimentation and having several constrictions available for trial.

I have found the Modified choke to be a good standard for steel shot hunting loads, and patterns can be further enhanced with special loads, using different buffers, shotcups and pellet combinations.

Size is a relative thing for pellets. A #2 steel pellet, good for decoyed geese, big for the 12, is easy stuff for the 10-gauge. More and more hunters are using the bigger gauge in order to accommodate larger and harder (than lead) steel pellets. A larger bore and chamber give the pellets an advantage of pellet accommodation over the next smaller bore size, and chokes have more surface area for pattern manipulations.

Proper chokes are very much related to the particular size or amount of pellets being used. Larger pellets require a more open choke to achieve the same pattern as smaller pellets. Turkey hunters using very heavy loads and wanting fist-sized patterns know these loads will also require reduced choke constriction for pattern results equivalent to lighter loads. These are the basic principles. Some time spent experimenting, gaining practical knowledge with various pellet and choke combinations, will pay off during hunting season.

Screw-In Chokes

Be sure to understand the manufacturer's intended use before you buy and use a new screw-in choke for your shotgun. Some

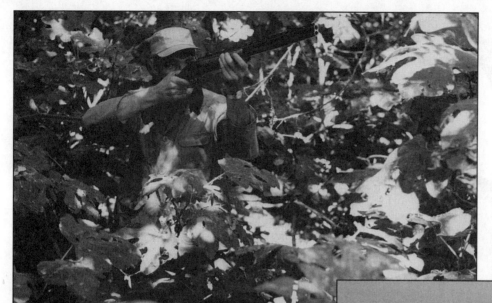

Sporting Clays is a demanding shotgun sport that extracts the most from both shooter and gun. With specialized choke tubes and loads, both can perform at their best levels.

(Below) Aftermarket choke tubes are available from a number of manufacturers. Most are made of the best materials and design, and are an excellent investment for improved shooting.

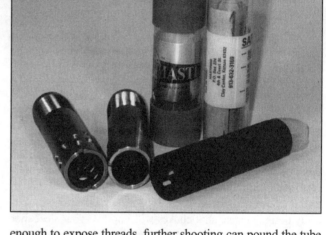

chokes cannot handle the rigors of high performance loads, and the manufacturer will say so somewhere on the label. There are many very specialized screw-in chokes on the market, and when used as the manufacturer intends, most perform superbly at their tasks.

Aftermarket choke manufacturers make their living by improving chokes. Their reputation hangs on the quality of that specific product. On the other hand, shotgun manufacturers, in order to remain price competitive, look at the screw-in chokes they supply as additional manufacturing expense. More importantly, manufacturers look at their potential customers and try to size up which constriction and type would suit the broadest audience. If you partake in any type of specialized shooting, chances are good that you will be able to improve your odds with an aftermarket product. Furthermore, you will more than likely be able to count on an aftermarket manufacturer for advice and product support.

Consider your screw-in chokes to be a shotgunning variable—one which can be changed on a whim to improve your day in the field. Perhaps one of the best features of screw-in chokes lies in the fact that they are made to be replaced. Even high-quality chokes are not prohibitively expensive and are readily purchased and replaced.

Newer application-specific chokes are taking advantage of modern alloys as well as skillful design and manufacturing. Happily, a number of newer steel screw-in chokes will fit the thread pattern of older model guns. This allows for replacement of the original, weaker chokes, thus improving your performance and saving the originals for collectors.

Choke tubes have a way of loosening as more shots are fired. Keep an eye, or better yet, a wrench on them. However, pretending you're a gorilla and over-tightening won't improve matters, so don't do that as a preemptive measure. You'll probably round off the contact area between the wrench and choke, and possibly ruin the threads.

Unwatched and, therefore, probably loose choke tubes have negative effects on the barrel threads. If they become loose enough to expose threads, further shooting can pound the tube so much that the threads will be smashed. Screw-in choke failure is usually the result of thread failure, which in turn is usually a result of neglect. Make it a habit to check choke tube tightness periodically—but be sure to unload the gun before doing so!

Handloaders generally shoot twice the number of shells as an ordinary shooter. Because of this high volume, there will probably be more wear-related shotgun problems to deal with.

Shotgun wear and tear begins with the very first firing, whether you shoot lead, steel or hard candy. Someday, you will wear out your shotgun. It happens. Usually the delicate mechanical item known as the trigger assembly is the first to go. Quite often it has a not-so-subtle way of indicating its ailing condition by allowing an unexpected discharge.

Shotguns are somewhat like refrigerators, dishwashers and other appliances. Sooner or later, you have to buy a new one. It's not torture. Keep in mind that buying a new gun is not like buying a new household water heater, but more like buying a car. There are *many* types, and the price range is pretty wide. You can get the basic gun, just like the basic car, or splurge for an upgrade or even a luxury model. It's fun. This is your hobby, so enjoy it while you can.

Knowing what goes on inside the gun helps the handloader understand load dynamics.

14

The Highlights of Internal Ballistics

THE CHAMBER IS the physical space within your shotgun that contains the shotshell during firing. The metal in the chamber walls is thicker and therefore stronger than that of the barrel, in order to accommodate and contain the considerable forces from a discharging shotshell.

The hull expands to fill the chamber during the initial stages of a firing cycle, and mounting pressure inside the hull rises at a slightly faster rate than it will after the critical moment when the payload begins moving forward. Pressure continues to build, as the propellant completes the burning cycle. This cycle is a balance between an explosive force that will rupture the barrel and a sudden loss of pressure that compromises combustion. If pressure continues to build properly and in a linear fashion, a chemical reaction takes place, creating a large volume of hot gas. Under the forceful push of expanding gases, the wad and shot begin to travel down the barrel, being pushed at an ever-increasing velocity. When the gases no longer affect the wad and shot column outside the barrel, gravity and air resistance take over and influence their path. In a nutshell, this is shotgun ballistics at work.

Pressure Fundamentals and Measurement

Pressure is measured at the chamber, or in the very first part of the barrel. This is done because we are looking for peak load pressure. In the chamber area, gases build behind a static shot charge, and the resulting pressure accelerates it. Less pressure is available as the shot moves down the barrel. (When the payload has moved down the barrel, there is a larger volume for the expanding gases to fill and the powder is already consumed—no new gas.)

LUP (Lead Units of Pressure) measurements have become a familiar yardstick for shotgunners to understand the status and safety of their loads. The shotshell industry has used LUP measurements for more than a century as a reliable gauge for designing guns, shotshell loads and components. At the tail end of the 20th century though, the LUP scale is being relegated to a status similar to the long obsolete dram equivalent; it has little correlation with modern technology, but it's still widely applied. You will see LUP measurements for years to come, but in our science, as load designers, this measurement system is already archaic. Comparisons and misinterpretations of the relationship between the new way and old are hampering, more than helping, modern load design.

LUP measurements are a translation of actual psi (pounds per square inch) measurements. You know how sometimes corporate names sound pretty silly when they are literally translated to another language? When Chevrolet exported the Nova to Mexico, it didn't sell very well. It seems that "nova" literally means "no go" in Spanish. LUP measurements, under certain conditions, are like literal translations of another language. Before the late '60s, when Lyman thankfully coined the phrase "lead units of pressure," measurements obtained with the lead crusher method were recorded as psi. Since these measurements were not literal, as was demonstrated by early electronic measuring devices, "lead units of pressure" more accurately reflected the nature of the loads and the scale by which they were measured. This was a more realistic representation of what was going on with the load. If Lyman had not intervened, psi measurements of old would not correlate with

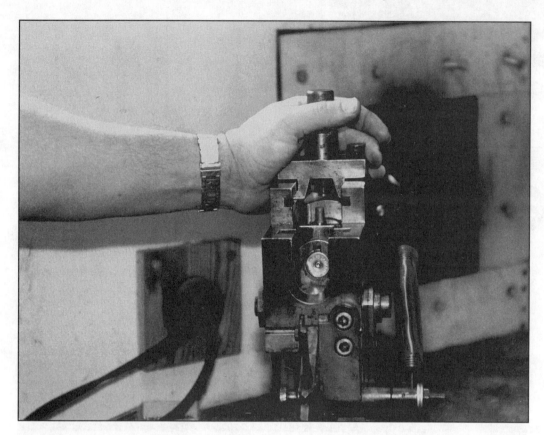

Traditional shotshell ballistics testing uses a heavy barrel mounted in a universal receiver set up for the use of lead crushers.

psi measurements of new, and we would have a real jumble of numbers. But if that were so, at least the old numbers would be rendered obsolete and we would not be trying to correlate numbers that cannot be correlated.

LUP measurement utilizes a barrel with a hole over the chamber. A hole in the shell must align with this hole. A piston fits in this hole and transfers force to a lead cylinder. This force crushes the lead between the piston and an anvil. Total shortening of the lead cylinder is related to peak pressure—more pressure results in a shorter lead cylinder. Owing to inertial effects (the pison has mass and it has to move) and other complications, LUP is not very accurate at representing actual peak chamber pressure. For example, a larger shot charge propelled by a slow powder will show relatively more pressure than a light charge propelled by a fast powder—a longer, softer push on the lead will deform it more than a shorter, harder push.

The industry began a slow evolution toward electronic psi measurements in the late 1960s. Early equipment, like most electronics of the era, was costly and largely inaccessible to smaller manufacturers, so the changeover has been gradual. The electronic measurement devices rely upon electrical pulses and give a fairly accurate reflection of the load's pressure in terms of pounds per square inch. The system also reads chamber pressure throughout the ignition process, offering a better and more direct look at what is happening inside the shotshell. Furthermore, unlike crusher measurements, the test shell need not be physically changed before or during the test process. Data is gathered automatically, and information can be analyzed on a readout without calculations. Several sources of human error are completely removed with this process: First,

there are no worries about the shell being out of alignment, as in a setup requiring a hole in the case. Second, there are no calculations or interpretation of data. Third, there are no doubts about the uniformity of the crusher device itself. The electronic equipment is fast and clean: load the shell, fire the shell, read the data. Repeat.

Why have we not completely converted to electronic pressure measuring? There are several reasons. First, we have become accustomed to the physical consequences of various levels of LUP. We think we know what is high pressure and what is low pressure. Unfortunately for psi measurements, everyone wants to know how it relates to the old, known way of doing things. The short answer is that it doesn't. You will note that most of your psi measured loads will be of a higher numerical value than LUP measurements, even with the exact same load. Unfortunately, even the industry has tried to recognize a non-existent relationship between the two systems and roughly estimates that psi measurements might run "about 1000" more than old LUP standards. I wish they hadn't done that, because now it is accepted as a standard, and nothing could be further from truth. The larger bores have suffered under this misconception the most, particularly the 10-gauge. These loads reflect much higher psi ratings when compared to LUP. Crusher tables were an attempt to represent psi. Ultimately, though, they only measured whatever force, whether it be duration or impact, that crushed a lead pill. Modern electronic measurements exclusively reflect actual psi measurements. To make progress in proper load development and design, a new standard on a different, less linear scale must be observed.

Often psi testing provides new information about old loads.

High pressure spikes most frequently occur early in the firing cycle. Under an LUP system, these peaks were not seen or quantifiable. One advantage of psi measurements is seeing the entire slope of the pressure curve, noting where in the graph line the peak pressure occurs and if a dangerous spike occurs.

You can begin to better understand psi readings by carefully looking at both readings as they pertain to the exact same load. Try to spot trends in their relationship, where they are similar and where they are very different. When the industry stops relating psi to the older LUP, we will be able to make some progress and set new standards for specific loads. Whenever possible, relate psi measurements to the performance of your loads and correspond that measurement to your load's outcome. Unlike many things in the modern world, psi measurements are here to stay.

Guidelines for suggested maximum chamber pressures do change from time to time. The current suggested set is:

Maximum Chamber Pressures			
Shell Length (ins.)	Gauge	LUP	psi*
2⁷/₈	10	10,500	11,000
3¹/₂	10	10,500	11,000
2³/₄	12	11,000	11,500
3	12	11,000	11,500
3¹/₂	12	N/A	14,000
2³/₄	16	11,000	11,500
2³/₄	20	11,500	12,000
3	20	11,500	12,000
2³/₄	28	12,000	12,500
2¹/₂	410	12,000	12,500
3	410	13,000	13,500

*Note that the psi readings are almost uniformly tied to the older LUP measurements. Most industry specialists agree that the numbers have no relationship in practical shotshell applications. With a broader acceptance of psi readings, on their own merits, a re-examination of a "what is acceptable" table would be a very good idea.

The reader may wonder about the wide spread of suggested maximums between the 3¹/₂-inch 10-gauge and the 3¹/₂-inch 12-gauge. The argument is that there are many older 10-gauge shotguns still being used and therefore a reduced upper limit is applied. The 12-gauge 3¹/₂-inch loads get a higher ceiling because these guns are known to be made of modern metals and design. For this reason alone, it is a very bad idea to extend an existing 3-inch-chambered 12-gauge to 3¹/₂ inches. However, the tables leave the impression that the modern 10-gauge is underrated.

For most shotguns, pressures over 11,000 LUP are historically considered high. Most pressure tables were worked up with the 12-gauge as a standard, and the scale was generalized for use with all the other gauges. Actually, each gauge should be tabled by itself. Given ideal conditions, the 10-gauge is barely working up a sweat at 11,000 LUP. However, it is more comfortable to apply lower pressure tables to this gauge, too. If we could control exactly what type of shotgun every load was being fired through, we could increase load performance.

However, the assumption is that the loads will be used in every make and type of shotgun. I cringe when I consider some of the old relics still being dragged out into the field. You may want to relegate grandpa's old shotgun to a special area of museum-like display after you experience the exceptional performance of a modern shotgun. The technology used in manufacturing new hardware, especially compared to the standards of seventy-five years ago, is substantial. You will shoot with greater confidence, hitting more often and enjoying it more.

If we were to assign a pressure spectrum to all firearms, including centerfires, shotshells would operate at the lower end. A large magnum rifle cartridge may operate happily at five times the pressure of your scattergun. If you look at a minimum shotshell operating pressure of 7000 LUP, and consider that most loads are running right around 10,000 LUP, it becomes apparent that our window is small in the relative scheme of things. It also demonstrates why handloaders have to follow

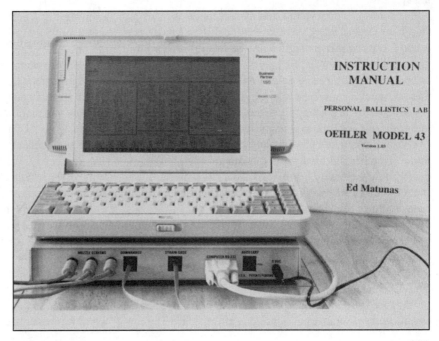

With the Oehler Model 43 Personal Ballistics Laboratory, the serious handloader can gather a lot of information, including pressure and velocity, from rifle, handgun or shotgun. This can help guide him when building a load recipe.

directions so closely; not because shotshells are difficult to control, but rather, we must be precise.

As shotgunners, we do not get to utilize signs of high pressure as centerfire reloaders can (or think they can). Signs of high pressure exist on shotgun hulls, but the indicators are so unreliable and unworthy of examination. The signs do not always show themselves on the hulls or primers of fired shells. A high pressure load may not reveal itself by leaving any sign whatsoever, yet a low pressure load, by virtue of a particular component combination, may leave misleading signs that might be interpreted as high pressure. The only sure way to read and interpret pressure is by using the modern Piezo system.

Dram Equivalent

This is an anachronism applied to modern shotshells.

A dram is the dry unit of volume (apothecaries measurement) equal to $1/8$-ounce or 27.34 grains (avoirdupois). The dram was a standard unit of measurement used with blackpowder loading. Drams of blackpowder were often a volume unit of measurement and not weighed, certainly not on an electronic scale.

With blackpowder's linear character of energy to volume, it is assumed possible to add a given amount of powder to obtain a correlative amount of velocity in a $1^1/8$-ounce load. Powder types considered were limited to one—black, even though there were different brands and granulations. In that simpler time, a given load for the 12-gauge might be $1^1/8$ ounces of lead shot with 3 drams of powder. Because powder was a constant, this load was presumed to develop around 1200 feet per second.

On a modern box of shells, you may also see a 3 dram designation. What it means is that, if you have regularly used blackpowder and have become used to its habits, this box of shells will give you a similar outcome as your old $1^1/8$-ounce blackpowder load with 3 drams of powder. It would be easier and more accurate to say, "12-gauge, $1^1/8$ ounce, 1200 fps." But, manufacturers presume that many of us have deep roots in blackpowder load configurations as well as the archaic metering systems.

Smokeless powder evolved, and manufacturers took advantage of the fact that nitroglycerin content could be altered by percentage, creating immense differences in energy produced by a given volume of powder. Smokeless powder burning rate is even more adjustable and is equally more important. Of course, these changes also mandated more precise measurements of powder charges. In practical application, it was goodbye to dram measurements and hello to grain measurements of propellant.

Because smokeless powders are so dramatically different from each other and blackpowder in energy levels, it tends to overshadow the reality that blackpowders also produce substantially different energy levels. Had tight-fitting gas seals been used with blackpowder loads, instead of leaky fiber seals, large pressure fluctuations between brands and granulations would have been summarily noted. Instead, primitive procedure only made a cursory nod toward pressure variables, enough so that the dram equivelent scale encompassed all blackpowder types and brands in shotshell loads.

Someone in a marketing department, somewhere, created the classification of "dram equivalent" long after the fact. The con-

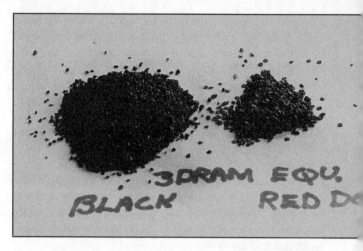

To illustrate dram equivalent, on the left is 3 drams of blackpowder; on the right is a charge of Red Dot smokeless powder that will, under specific conditions, duplicate the velocity that could be obtained with the blackpowder. *Never* use a dram charge by volume of weight of smokeless powder, because it would be extremely hazardous to gun and shooter.

version was used after smokeless powders had established a permanent foothold in shotshell applications. It was used as a prop to create an association to typical blackpowder loads, only now using the new Brand X smokeless powder. It makes sense if you grew up using dram measurements in your blackpowder loads and are familiar with the feel of the various levels, but most of us are more familiar with weight/velocity and have to work backward to apply a dram equivalent chart.

The conversion is still with us, haunting ballisticians everywhere, and we can't seem to get rid of it. That's odd in a world where we have pretty well decided that planet Earth is heliocentric and smokeless powders are here to stay. Let us get rid of the geocentric chart of the universe as well as dram equivalent computations. I doubt if there is anyone still alive who grew up loading blackpowder drams and is still confused by this "smokeless stuff." After all, it is for that person that the dram equivalent is intended.

How Chamber Pressures Affect Shooting

In our consideration of hunting loads, chamber pressure usually figures into all discussions. In our notes concerning chambers, we examined relationships in the chamber area that cause pressure variations. Now, let's look at the pressure.

Pressure can be a problem if it is too high or too low. Obviously, some relationship exists between pressure and velocity, but not directly. Inadequate pressure causes all sorts of problems for the handloader. Consider a similarity between a diesel engine and your shotgun during the firing process.

A diesel engine needs pressure to operate. Your shotshell loads need pressure to operate. Too much or too little pressure causes problems for both the engine and the load.

Inadequate Chamber Pressure

Chamber pressure inadequate for a proper burn cycle can result from several factors: cold temperatures, wrong powder or too little powder, weak hulls and crimps, leaking gas seals, not

10-Gauge

Shot Wt. (oz.)	Dram Equivalent Rating													
	$3^3/_8$	$3^1/_2$	$3^5/_8$	$3^3/_4$	$3^7/_8$	4	$4^1/_8$	$4^1/_4$	$4^3/_8$	$4^1/_2$	$4^5/_8$	$4^3/_4$	$4^7/_8$	5
	Equivalent Velocity													
$1^1/_4$	1200	1225	1250	1270	1295	1315	1340	1360	1385	1405	1430	1450	1475	1495
$1^3/_8$	-	1200	1225	1245	1265	1290	1315	1335	1360	1380	1405	1425	1450	1470
$1^1/_2$	-	1175	1200	1220	1245	1265	-	1310	-	1355	-	1400	-	1445
$1^5/_8$	-	1150	-	1195	-	1240	1265	1285	-	1330	-	1375	-	1420
$1^3/_4$	-	1125	-	1170	-	1215	-	1260	-	1305	1330	1350	-	1395
$1^7/_8$	-	1100	-	1145	-	1190	-	1235	1260	1280	-	1325	-	1370
2	-	1075	-	1120	-	1165	-	1210	-	1255	-	1300	1325	1345
$2^1/_8$	-	1050	-	1095	-	1140	-	1185	-	1230	-	1275	-	1320
$2^1/_4$	-	1025	-	1070	-	1115	-	1165	-	1205	-	-	-	-

12-Gauge

Shot Wt. (oz.)	Dram Equivalent Rating													
	$2^1/_2$	$2^5/_8$	$2^3/_4$	$2^7/_8$	3	$3^1/_8$	$3^1/_4$	$3^3/_8$	$3^1/_2$	$3^5/_8$	$3^3/_4$	$3^7/_8$	4	$4^1/_8$
	Equivalent Velocity													
1	1130	1155	1180	1205	1235	1260	1290	1315	1345	1380	1400	1430	1455	-
$1^1/_8$	1100	1120	1145	1170	1200	1225	1255	1280	1310	1335	1365	1390	1420	-
$1^1/_4$	1055	1080	1110	-	1165	1190	1220	-	1275	-	1330	-	1385	1410
$1^3/_8$	-	-	1075	-	1130	-	1185	1210	1240	-	1295	-	1350	-
$1^1/_2$	-	-	1040	-	1095	-	1150	-	1205	-	1260	-	1315	-
$1^5/_8$	-	-	1005	-	1060	-	1115	-	1170	-	1225	-	1280	-
$1^3/_4$	-	-	970	-	1025	-	1080	-	1135	-	1190	-	1245	-
$1^7/_8$	-	-	-	-	-	-	-	-	-	-	1155	-	1210	-
2	-	-	-	-	-	-	-	-	-	-	1120	-	1175	-

16-Gauge

Shot Wt. (oz.)	Dram Equivalent Rating								
	$2^1/_4$	$2^3/_8$	$2^1/_2$	$2^5/_8$	$2^3/_4$	$2^7/_8$	3	$3^1/_8$	$3^1/_4$
	Equivalent Velocity								
$7/_8$	1145	1170	1200	-	1255	-	1310	-	1365
1	1110	1135	1165	1190	1220	-	1275	1300	1330
$1^1/_8$	1075	1100	1130	1150	1185	1210	1240	-	1295
$1^1/_4$	1040	-	1095	-	1150	-	1205	1230	1260

20-Gauge

Shot Wt. (oz.)	Dram Equivalent Rating								
	2	$2^1/_8$	$2^1/_4$	$2^3/_8$	$2^1/_4$	$2^5/_8$	$2^3/_4$	$2^7/_8$	3
	Equivalent Velocity								
$3/_4$	1145	-	-	-	-	-	-	-	-
$7/_8$	1100	1125	1155	-	1210	1235	1265	-	1320
1	1055	-	1110	1135	1165	-	1220	-	1275
$1^1/_8$	1010	-	1065	-	1120	-	1175	1200	1230
$1^1/_4$	-	-	-	-	1075	-	1130	-	1185

28-Gauge

Shot Wt. (oz.)	Dram Equivalent Rating					
	$1^3/_4$	$1^7/_8$	2	$2^1/_8$	$2^1/_4$	$2^3/_8$
	Equivalent Velocity					
$3/_4$	1115	1160	1205	1250	1295	-
$7/_8$	1070	1115	1160	1205	1250	1295
1	1025	-	1115	1160	1205	1250

410-Bore

Shot Wt. (oz.)	Dram Equivalent Rating		
	$1^3/_8$	$1^1/_2$	$1^5/_8$
	Equivalent Velocity		
$1/_2$	1125	1200	1275
$5/_8$	1050	1140	1210
$3/_4$	-	1080	1155

enough shot weight, and even weak primers or an obstructed flash hole. In the ballistic laboratory, it becomes evident that loads yielding extremely low pressure ratings are unreliable, producing unstable and irrelevant data.

One unit of measurement not often seen by handloaders is the average variation of velocity and pressure. Although many loads are eliminated from recommended data lists because they are unstable, some less than perfectly stable loads do make the lists even though they vary in velocity and pressure.

As a general rule, the lower end of the pressure spectrum (under 7500 LUP) produces the greatest variances in velocity and pressure. Also, at a point around 5500 LUP, most loads become almost non-functional due to a lack of pressure as a companion to heat for proper smokeless powder combustion. If your barrel contains residue of unburned powder after firing, the most likely reason is an incomplete burn due to low or a sudden deprivation of pressure. Large amounts of soot and residue can mean your loads are on the edge of all-out malfunction.

It is interesting that most ballistic engineers would not choose a load with a pressure less than 9000 LUP and, generally, prefer those operating around 10,500 LUP. This area usually yields a very uniform load from shot to shot, giving the shooter a better chance at predicting a proper lead on a target.

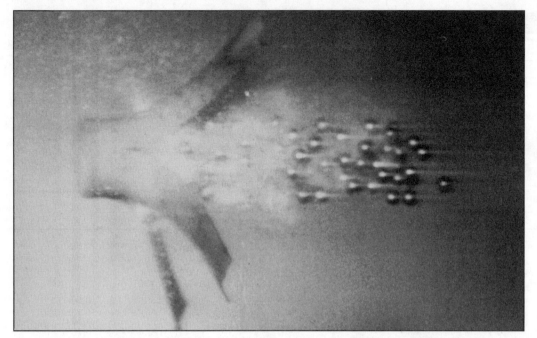

As it exits the muzzle, this charge of #2 pellets from a Federal 10-gauge Premium load speeds ahead of the buffer and wad. Shooters should remember that larger pellets at highest velocity will travel farthest.

By staying within these pressure margins, your chances of a blooper and/or inconsistent loads are greatly diminished. By way of cause and effect, this will also lessen the likelihood of a blue haze of profanity hanging over your blind.

Remember, loads are tested in laboratories at approximately 70 degrees. Great changes occur when the ammo becomes hotter or colder. By controlling this, you can maintain a better level of consistency. Leaving the shells out overnight in the pickup bed when it's 10 degrees below zero will guarantee you a real performance loss, perhaps to a point where you will lose a bird. Low temperatures in the field greatly affect ignition and thereby reduce pressure. This condition becomes even more apparent when using slow burn-rate powders, because the retardants used make the powders more difficult to ignite. To get the fire going, a load using a hotter primer may be required.

A cautionary note: It is incumbent upon you to check your barrel after a shell does not fire correctly. Any blockage, no matter how slight, will rupture a barrel—sending dangerous shrapnel in every direction. The expanding gases produced by burning propellant will find some way out; they must escape. Even a small blockage is enough to turn those burning gases in another direction, and they will find the next weakest link with increasingly explosive energy. Perhaps that outlet will be the weakest part of your chamber, right next to your cheek! Factories do not have enough representatives or personnel to hand-check your barrel for you every time you have a blooper. If you think you have stuck your barrel in the mud, check it. A little glob of dirt is just as hazardous as a wad wedged half-way up the tube.

For what it is worth, note that low pressure loads do not necessarily yield low recoil. Recoil is the product of the mass and velocity of the load. Chamber pressure does not generate recoil. Do not confuse low pressure strictly with amounts of powder. More powder does add to recoil, but is only a contributing factor as a singular component with many other elements influencing the overall outcome.

High Chamber Pressure

Because it is of greater consequence, we are more familiar with the causes of high pressure than low pressure. Hot weather, too much powder, too much shot, a bulky or stiff hull, wrong primers, and other things all have a hand in generating excessive pressure.

With too much pressure, getting a load to fire is not the problem—it is accommodating everything that is already burning, perhaps out of control. Overly high pressures are a direct consequence of the combustion process accelerating at a rate faster than the yielding process (movement of wad and payload). Burning powder has a funny way of increasing pressure more quickly as pressure becomes higher.

Changing components is the usual cause of high pressure loads. It is not possible to substitute components and guess the extent of the reaction. Sloppy reloading, switching compo-

The over-powder cup of plastic wads can affect pressure. These are the deep over-powder cups of the Trapper wad (left) and the efficient Winchester WAA12 (right). Both often produce high chamber pressure compared to other wads, as various reloading manuals indicate.

nents, improper procedures, and inaccurate measuring are the marks of someone who should not be reloading. We all know of cooks who should not cook. They do anyway, and the rest of us suffer. Some handloaders should not reload either.

To avoid high pressures and its associated problems:

- Measure and check everything twice. Similar to the rule of carpentry: "Measure twice, cut once."
- Read the load notes again—before you start loading.
- Verify your shot and powder bushings. President Breshnev, of the Soviet Union, used to say, "Trust, but verify." Something smart actually did come out of Communism.
- Always have a big inventory of components so you will not be inclined to substitute. Again, substitution is the primary cause of pressure-related problems.
- If it does not seem right, check it out. Use your intuition. Look at your loads.
- Nobody is perfect. Everybody can mess up and will sooner or later. When it happens to you, see the above rule.
- When in doubt, dump it!
- High crimp? Dump it!

Component Factors and Chamber Pressure

Some of the components, such as certain hull types, take up more space and thereby reduce the amount of available chamber area to mitigate the gas pressure. Paper hulls are compressible and produce lower chamber pressure than plastic hulls for a given load. Though not overly significant, space occupation and compressibility are pieces of a larger puzzle.

Dangerously high chamber pressure is created when the hull and the internal yield rate of the components cannot accommodate that rapidly mounting gas pressure by moving at a specific moment in the firing cycle. The powder charge has a great deal of additional energy to be released, and the

wad had better start to move at the proper time (becoming the path of least resistance) or trouble is at hand. The greater the pressure, the faster the powder burns and the greater the total energy release.

The wad can accommodate expanding gases by gradually compressing, thereby gaining some time before pressure reaches a critical point. The effect is somewhat like transferring energy through a pogo stick, one with a spring and one without a

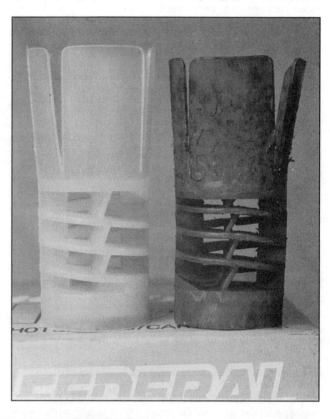

(Above) The wad is supposed to "give" a bit when the shell is fired to cushion the payload. Federal's 12S3 is one of the stiffest wads available, offering little compression on firing setback as shown here.

The market is full of wads of every color and style, but using them indiscriminately changes the chamber pressure of the loads. Use only the wad specified by the load data.

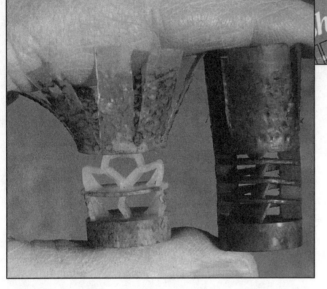

spring. If you're jumping up and down on a cement patio, you might prefer the stick with a spring. Many plastic wads with a crushing section over the gas seal are designed to work just like a spring.

Paper or cardboard wads leak like a cheap rubber raft. With the less than predictable powders in the old days, it was probably a good thing that modern, fine sealing wads were not around.

High pressure is the default blame setting whenever there seems to be a problem with a particular load. Let's consider some other possibilities, too. A paper hull can rupture and send a hot blast out of the breech. When you extract the hull, it looks absolutely terrible. However, that's not always a high pressure problem; it is usually a component failure. Many situations only look like high pressure, when, in fact, components may be failing to contain average pressure. This is why you must choose components carefully, using only high quality items and tossing out damaged or below-par stuff.

Modern, advanced wads have very fine and tight fitting seals. The object is to use as little powder as possible to safely drive the load at the highest possible, most consistent velocity while accomplishing a complete powder burn. Modern loads using these components and minimal charges produce, as well, the lowest possible recoil using roughly 10 percent less powder for the same net results as the earlier paper seals.

Modern wads have very specific applications. If you are a hunter, use wads designed for hunting loads. If you are a target shooter, then use target wads. Just don't try to switch them around. The target components are designed for fast burn-rate powders, while hunting wads are designed to handle slower burn-rate powders and heavy payloads.

Slower burn-rate powders produce a flatter, wider pressure curve, extending right up the barrel. This yields a blow gun effect of constant pressure, rather than a short sharp shock, typical of fast burning propellants.

The ceiling we all must work with when considering load recipes is the overall top pressure generated by a particular combination of components. At a certain point in designing a shotshell load, the combination of components reaches a peak level of performance. There is a certain give and take in the balance between velocity, capacity, pressure and other ballistic variables.

Inconsistencies produce erratic shooting. Fluctuations become obvious as hunters fail to project accurate lead angles on moving targets. When inconsistencies of velocity, pressure or both begin to appear, it is obvious that the load in question has been over-revved, producing inconsistent results. All shotgun loads fluctuate somewhat in velocity and pressure. Most laboratories apply a nominal standard to all load types.

Fluctuations in velocities and/or pressures are often due to the powder not being fully consumed. More powder obviously will not solve the problem if the load is slow, because on another occasion it may burn completely, thus spiking the pressure with a (perhaps unusual) complete burn. If this is a hunting load, a wide range of velocity (and pressure) will have the shooter sending shots all over the sky, behind or in front of intended targets.

Knowing what makes a particular load not work is just as important as understanding what makes a load combination successful. Consistent pressures and velocities must be a factor in all good loads. When components combine to produce exceptional high speed loads with consistent performance, they become favorites in many different applications.

Load testing is a must because efficiency is judged, in part, by how many pellets hit the target at a certain range.

15

Shotgun Patterning

WHAT IS A shotgun pattern, and what does it represent? First, it is important to note that pattern testing produces only a flat, two-dimensional representation of pellets in flight without regard to the length of the shot string, the time it took to get there or the lethality of the pellets. Shotgunning is a dynamic event—not even your target (if you are a sporting person, anyway) stands still. In shooting a dynamic firearm/charge at static paper targets, we are removing shotguns from their natural element and evaluating only a specific segment of their performance potential. This not to say that patterns are not an important part of determining a load's overall potential, but an emphasis on pattern without regard to other factors of lethality is misleading when evaluating shotshell performance.

Now that we have given some perspective to paper pattern results, let's make sure that the pattern results we achieve represent, as accurately as possible, the patterning potential of the shotgun and shell used.

Patterning Basics

Before we get to evaluate a pattern, we first need one to evaluate. So let's take the steps to get going. A pattern board and paper will be the required equipment for patterning. A baseline pattern size I have used for years, and by which everyone will compare ("...my 30 inch pattern is denser than..."), is a 30-inch circle. Judging by the esteem in which it is held, it is evidently a magical size, and must be indicative of nearly every shooting situation. Representations of various species' silhouettes are printed on some commercially available targets. These are used for sighting and are rather irrelevant in pellet percentage. I say this because any movement of a target so small will completely skew your results and perhaps lead you toward dramatic change when none is necessary.

Making a pattern board frame to hold the pattern paper is a simple project that involves a bit of lumber and a few common

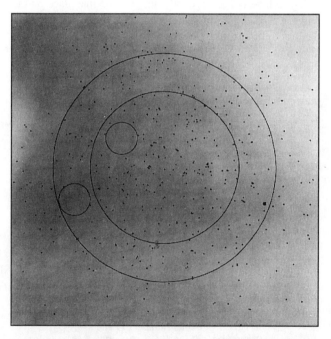

This pattern test indicates a number of holes (circles) that could allow a bird to slip through unscathed. There is also evidence of shot clumping. Not the best load for this gun.

hand tools. It shouldn't take more than a few minutes to bang one together.

As you can see from the nearby photos, all it takes is a few 8-foot 2x4s to make the frame. Use two of them for the legs, spaced 4 feet apart; cut the other 8-footers in half to use as cross braces at the top and again 36 inches down. This is where your pattern paper will be stapled. Use another 48-inch 2x4 about 48 inches from the top, and the last one 2 feet from the bottom. Sharpen the bottoms of the two legs so they can be stuck in the ground and you're ready to hang paper.

125

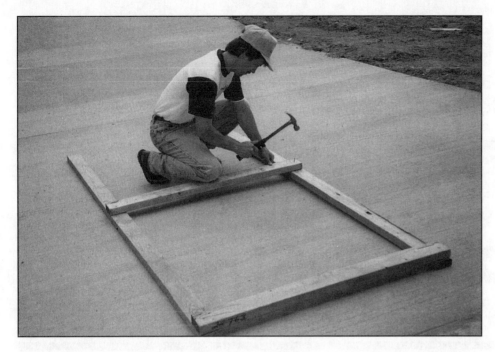

In order to pattern a shotgun, a pattern board frame is needed—and it's easy to build. A few 8-foot 2x4s, some nails and a couple hand tools are all that's necessary.

If you'll be doing your patterning at the same place on the range, it might be easiest to dig a couple of permanent holes for the legs to fit into when you bring the frame out for a test session. Sinking a length of appropriate pipe in the holes to accept the legs would make life even easier.

You can buy pre-printed patterning targets, or you can make your own from white butcher's paper. All you need is a 30-inch circle in the middle for aiming. Use thumbtacks or staples to hold the target to the frame.

A pre-measured string helps to meter out your distances for shooting patterns. I have one pre-measured to 20, 30 and 40 yards. Little strips of duct tape mark the distance intervals; the other end remains affixed to the pattern target frame. Unravel, mark off distance and shoot.

To obtain a pattern percentage, you will need to know approximately how many pellets are contained within your load. For your convenience, we provide the following chart.

Average Pellet Counts Lead Shot					
	—Total Number of Pellets——				
Charge (oz.)	#7	#7$^1/_2$	#8	#8$^1/_2$	#9
1$^1/_8$	388	460	551	658	—
1$^1/_{16}$	—	367	435	521	621
1	345	409	490	585	—
$^7/_8$	302	360	429	512	—
$^3/_4$	259	307	367	439	—
30 grams	365	433	518	619	—
28 grams	341	404	484	578	—
24 grams	292	346	415	495	—

You have several distances to work with. Bear in mind your shotgun's intended purpose. It may be fun to see how your 28-gauge patterns at 40 yards with #9 pellets, but that really isn't very representative of typical 28-gauge shooting. Though turkey hunters may take exception to this rule, start your shooting at 40 yards with big bores and magnum 12-gauge loads.

Shoot at the distance most relevant to your shotgun's design intent, and use loads you intend to bring to the field.

Using a sandbag, for accuracy's sake, squeeze off one round into the target. Just one. Any more will complicate matters and make the mathematic calculations difficult. Count the pellet hits within the 30-inch circle. Multiply your pellet count by 100. Divide that total by the number of pellets in the load. Now you have the pellet percentage and bragging material.

Less than 100 percent of pellets in the cirle is OK. Shoot a string of ten seperate targets and record the pattern percentage of each on a piece of paper.

Rank the numbers lowest to highest and choose the number in the middle as your median. This way we throw out any real "boffo" shots; perhaps you sneezed as you fired round number 8?

Your pattern will give you an idea of how two dimensions of a three-dimensional shot string arrived at the target. As a yardstick, manufacturers state that a Modified choke should deliver 50-60 percent patterns (within a 30-inch circle) at 40 yards. You will see different criteria applied to patterns; a turkey hunter wants 95 percent at a given range, for instance. A full coverage of pellets at a typical operating range is what you are after. Though pellet energy and shot stringing will remain a mystery when patterning, you will become more familiar with your firearm and the pattern spread it develops at a given range. This knowledge, and familiarity, will make you a better shooter.

Pattern Consistency

More than other variables, pattern inconsistencies mean problems. Obvious shot-to-shot differences call for an examination of your loads. If a shotgun is ruining patterns, it usually patterns poorly the same way from shot to shot. Great big inconsistencies are usually traced back to include errors in load assembly or component substitutions. Minor though it may seem, even substituting regular, soft chilled shot for harder magnum pellets will change patterns. More of the softer shot

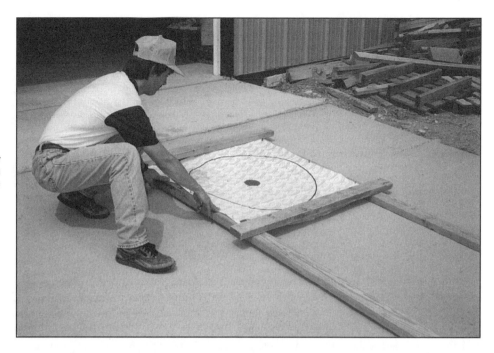

With the frame made, it's an easy matter to staple the 30-inch pattern target to the boards. The frame needn't be pretty, just sturdy.

will deform and fly away from the center of the pattern. Other minor changes can contribute to load inconsistencies, another good reason to document your loads and procedures.

By manipulating your shotgun setup or components, general load trends can be discerned from a longer series of pattern results. There are too many variables involved in pattern testing to make any decisions from only a few shots fired from one shotgun. Trends, rather, will be the best deduction you can make from the results on paper.

Your first decision will concern identifying exactly what you want to evaluate—either the load, and its individual components, or the shotgun, using a baseline load you have found to pattern decently. Trying to evaluate both gun and load in the same day will only confuse you with myriad variables. Only

by eliminating variables will you be able to make any intelligent decisions about improving your patterns. Otherwise, it is, literally, hit or miss.

Over the years, I have discovered many items that individually or collectively can make or break pattern results. These factors create questions concerning the validity of individual pattern results that may not have turned out as expected. I offer the following, so the shooter can change one variable at a time, then hopefully achieve the best pattern possible. Furthermore, the process will help you recognize variables that affect the pattern of a particular load and gun combination.

Identify your shotgun type and its purpose

Shotguns, like dogs, are bred for different purposes. You

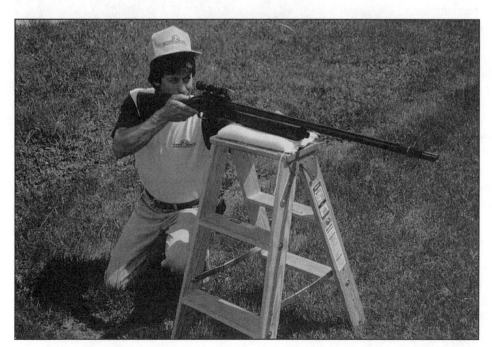

The first order of business is to determine if the shotgun shoots to the point of aim. Test this by resting the gun on a sandbag, aiming for the exact center of the patterning target, and touching off one round.

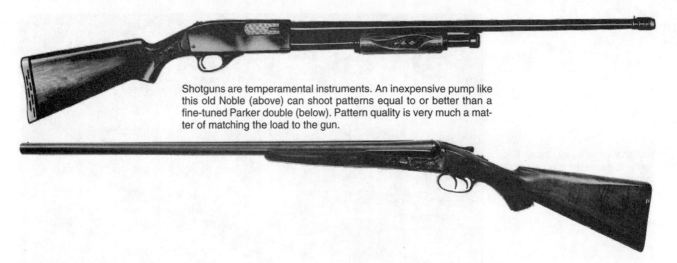

Shotguns are temperamental instruments. An inexpensive pump like this old Noble (above) can shoot patterns equal to or better than a fine-tuned Parker double (below). Pattern quality is very much a matter of matching the load to the gun.

needn't fire a single shot in order to start gathering evidence about your shotgun's potential pattern.

Shotguns are temperamental instruments that all play a different "tune." One less expensive shotgun right off the assembly line and another exquisitely hand-crafted gun can be compared and found to shoot similar patterns. Sometimes, the sum total of parts that comprise a less expensive shotgun come together to create superior patterns at all ranges. Hang onto this shotgun, and don't change a thing. You have gotten very lucky. Individual shotgun variables, even among the same brand and type, include: felt recoil, trigger pull weight, bore alignment, overall balance (less so in very fine handmades, but it happens), sighting plane, and so on. In patterns, sometimes you have a lemon and sometimes you have a Caribbean cruise. Conclusive load pattern testing requires that you use more than one shotgun for your testing just to verify the normalization of your baseline loads.

Shotgun barrel factors—length, chamber, forcing cone, bore diameter, choke and barrel alignment—add up to create your barrel's overall influence on every load fired though your shotgun. To determine the extent of a particular barrel's influence on a load, shoot a long series of different loads at the pattern board. Note the results and how they differ from other shotgun patterns. Are the outside fringes of the circle full of holes while the center remains relatively intact? On the other hand, does the center look like a basket ball blew through it? If so, move back and find that shotgun's favorite patterning range. Make note of this optimum range and use this particular gun for situations that call for that range. If every load comes out with a poor pattern result, you have some work to do. If you find a problem with the gun, fix it and shoot more patterns until you get the desired result. In discovering a problem with your shotgun, and fixing it, your day of patterning was a complete success.

Point of Aim

Although seemingly a basic principle of patterning, one of the more difficult variables to contend with is getting the load to hit the center of the target.

Barrel design and alignment directly influence delivery of the load. Not all shotguns send the pattern along the sight plane. By design, some guns have different points of aim. A rising bird gun, for instance, will shoot 3 feet high at 30 yards. This is very helpful for the pheasant hunter, as it removes an element of anticipation otherwise put upon the shooter, but it's tough for the individual taking pattern readings. His patterns will seem sparse, especially toward the bottom. Don't laugh, but I have spoken to shooters who insist certain loads consistently shoot too high. My advice to them is to turn the hull upside down in the chamber.

Side-by-side double barrel shotguns shoot the right barrel quite differently from the left, even when other factors, such as choke, remain the same. Don't count on consistent point of aim between the barrels, even if all the evidence says it should be so.

Don't even bother shooting a pattern if you intend to do it from the shoulder. Neither you or I are that good. The other extreme would be clamping your shotgun down into a padded

This shooter has taken the time to properly pattern his gun and load to determine exactly how they'll perform on target. Note how even this pattern is.

128

shooting vise (what you see used with rifles). Rest your gun on some sandbags for a modicum of stability. It is important that the point of aim be correct and consistent. Do not rest or clamp the gun against any hard surface—this will dramatically move the center of the pattern with regard to the line of sight, compared to natural shooting conditions.

Component combinations and their placement

Where you place a spacer wad, how many petals in your shotcup, buffering and assembly technique—we spend a lot of time developing specific shot carriers for different patterns and shooting applications. It's hard to believe, but some shooters are completely unaware of the effects of different shot carriers. I outlined applications of different wad types in a separate chapter.

You will achieve the most consistent patterning results by matching hull lengths to your chamber. If, for instance, you have a 3-inch chamber on your 12-gauge gun, use 3-inch loads for patterning. The 2³/₄-inch loads may be disrupted by the transition area between the chamber and the forcing cone.

The quality of the hulls you use for your pattern testing will affect the results. How? The hull, as a container for the load and as the place where the combustion cycle begins, will determine the quality of the combustion cycle. The more rounds put through a hull, the more times the crimp has been stressed. At some point, the crimp will become weak and unreliable, disrupting the load. Inconsistent cycles affect pressures, pressures affect velocities, and velocities affect patterns. You may not even notice the change, but your patterns will show it.

Remember that inferior or worn-out crimps open more easily than firm, flat crimps. Bad crimps alter pressure and velocity. Worn-out hulls, especially those with composition or disk base wads, leak gases around the base wad. Inconsistent gas

containment contributes to shot-to-shot fluctuations in chamber pressure and component distortion. Even with similar loads, different hulls will deliver different patterns. Bad hulls will deliver poor patterns, regardless of the quality of components within.

Primers, by brand, are all over the compass in terms of speed, power and quality of burn. Primers supply approximate reactions, not absolute reactions. Primers will affect your patterns if you are using different types or brands indiscriminately.

When it comes to powder, consider some of the important propellant variables like lot number, age and batch. Every lot burns a little differently. Ambient temperature affects burn rates. I have noted inferior pattern results on the hottest days—when the resulting powder energy is elevated. Changes in strength of the powder can ruin the best of patterns. It helps to note your powder's lot number with your patterning notes. Powder changes become an increasing factor of importance in hunting loads where larger volumes of slow burning powders are combined with heavy shot payloads.

Wads are not always as identical as we would like to have them. The heat of the mould and the relative cooling cycle of the plastic can affect the overall character of a wad. Often, minor differences exist that cannot be seen or measured. Only a plastics engineer knows for sure. Gas seal integrity is critical to patterns, because leakage past it will alter velocity. The shotcup design of all wads affects patterns too. Generally, thicker wads will tighten patterns while thin shotcups will offer a more open pattern.

Larger shot size loads deliver fewer pellets, each carrying more energy. Moreover, the overall percent total attributed to each pellet (either in or out of the magic circle) is greater. Remember, in a load with fewer larger pellets, each one

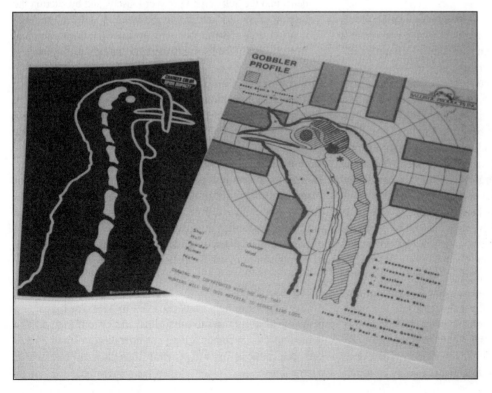

Pre-printed shotgun targets are commercially available for testing different loads, but they can also be made from white butcher's paper and illustrated with various kinds of game.

It takes time to count all the pellet holes in the paper, but that's the only way to tell just how good (or bad) your gun and load are shooting.

becomes a greater part of the 100 percent total; fly-away pellets may be over-represented. Furthermore, swings up and down in percentage are usually regarded with disproportional significance by the shooter. You will need to establish your own baseline for every pellet type and size.

Steel shot is sensitive and reactive. Have you seen that executive toy with the five steel balls that would bounce back and forth until they finally ran out of energy? Like the balls clacking back and forth, steel shot transfers energy rather than absorbing it. That is to say, the harder the pellet, the more the pellet will retain a "memory" of the launch influences and transfer this energy to the next pellet or component in line. Energy transfer has a fundamental effect on steel pellet patterns.

Patterns can be customized by component selection for all shooting conditions. There are pattern-enhancing components such as plastic shot buffers, custom wad slitting techniques, different powders and pellet types, and more. Any of these items can be worked by the handloader for better performance. Each plays a role in providing the best possible pattern for steel shot loads.

The reloading tool's adjustment has an affect on patterns. Excellent and consistent crimps benefit a handloader and his patterns in more ways than aesthetics. Inconsistent crimps, more than any other finishing error, will influence chamber pressure. High pressure has a logical way of increasing load velocity, and low pressure produces the inverse. Usually, you can look at a crimp and predict which way velocity will go. A deep shouldered, concave crimp is a tight one and will increase pressure. A loose crimp, one which is sometimes leaking pellets as you carry it in your pocket, is one that will rob your load of a complete burn cycle at full intended pressure, and therefore proper chamber pressure and load velocity. Consistent load velocity largely determines pattern consistency.

Other tool-related factors that you can verify include:
- Primer seating: Is the primer seated firmly and flush?
- Powder metering: Is the machine and its metering system dropping consistent amounts of powder? You can verify by weigh-

ing a series of drops. Don't forget that some powders meter more accurately than other types.
- Wad seating: Are you seating wads exactly the same each time? If you seat a wad inconsistently, especially when wedged into compression-formed hulls like the Winchester AA, pressure and velocity will vary.
- Pellet metering: Are you happy with your reloader's shot metering ability? If not, weigh or count your shot drops. Smaller pellets flow more easily, and therefore accurately, through volumetric measuring devices like shot bushings. The reloader should note that even arm strength and press manipulation speed can introduce variables to a load by setting the components into the hull either tightly or loosely, and by altering the settling of powder and shot in the metering device. The junction and setup of the various components will influence the final fit and crimp of the load and, therefore, its final performance.

Environmental Conditions and Variables

All weather conditions—including wind speed and direction, air temperature, air density and barometric pressure—affect shooting. Air density affects how well an airplane is able to take off, so do you think it might affect patterns too? It does. In the same manner, altitude also can make a difference in patterns. Thinner air offers less pellet resistance. We have known for years that pellets fired in a near-vacuum will tend to retain the original shape of the charge longer. The more air resistance, the greater the problem in duplicating someone else's results. These outside (no pun intended) influences mostly affect the dynamics of the powder burn and the pellet flight.

Pattern Lethality

The hunter can help stack the odds in his favor by using a pellet of sufficient mass to carry lethal energy to the target. The hunted species becomes a load consideration; a small duck's soft body tissue is easier to penetrate than the rhino-like hide of a large goose.

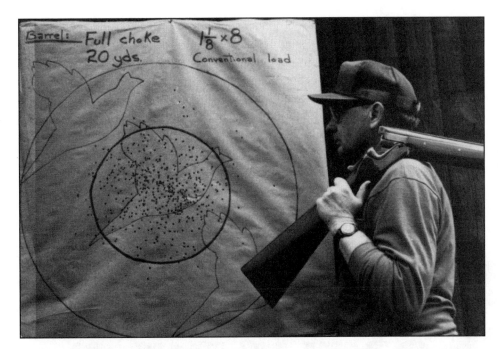

This pattern test shows a very tight and even core that would be deadly—if not destructive—on rising pheasants if the hunter does his part.

In loads using larger pellets, there is a corresponding reduction in the total number of individual pellets. If weight and volume of the load are the same, it just takes fewer pellets to reach a given payload. Now, in this trade-off, we must remember that even the densest patterns do not kill; it is the individual pellets (application) of a pattern that do the work.

The velocity of the load needs to be sufficient for the shooter to make reasonable lead calculations. Target factors are an often-overlooked advantage of high-velocity loads. Slow moving pellets extend the pattern's flight time from the barrel to the in-flight target. Every moment of additional flight time increases the likelihood of a miss.

Energy, the factor that makes little lead spheres so effective, is the critical component of any shotshell load. Shaping the pattern these spheres collectively form is the compromise with which we have to contend. Clearly, if you spend too much time counting holes and shaping your loads exclusively upon that criteria, you are ignoring the primary objective of the pellets. The shotgunner's dilemma is a balance between pattern integrity and pellet velocity. It is difficult to achieve both within the same load. Slow moving loads represent themselves well on pattern paper. However, a load's effectiveness in the field is directly related to the velocity at which its pellets are moving. Fundamentally, it goes something like this: Which is going hurt your hand more, a baseball lobbed by Grandma or a fastball thrown by a major league pitcher? Same baseball, quite different outcome.

Other Ballistic Tools

There are a number of different chronograph kits available to shooters who wish to self-check their loads for velocity. Most of the time, these tools work very well, are reasonable in cost, and help handloaders choose their ammunition. The best use for an at-home chronograph is for comparative purposes. Take readings of several loads out on the same day and look at your results. Good loads, of the exact same recipe, should produce very similar velocities. If that happens with only minor fluctuations, congratulate yourself, you have made some good loads. If, on the other hand, velocities are all over the place, compare your loads to the "Top 11" list below.

Occasionally, I am contacted by someone who has checked their load with a home-use chronograph and is wondering why the measured speed of a particular load is different than the listed velocity. Their chronograph may be showing fluctuations (up or down) of more than 500 fps. The next hour is taken up with a review of many load variables, and I usually find the answer. Many of the problems are obvious to the bystander (me), some are not. Here are eleven points to ponder when searching for consistency.

1. The powder lot you are using has a different energy level than the original test lot.
2. You are using a different lot of primers than was used to make the original test load series.
3. The powder you used was wet (or dry), compared to the test powder.
4. Different wad pressures were applied. Wad pressure is especially critical in taper-base hulls.
5. The crimp height was much higher or deeper than the test lot. A deeper crimp in a load can contribute to higher pressure when fired and, therefore, give additional velocity.
6. Weather conditions were different, either hotter or colder.
7. A quite different shot size or shot hardness was used in the tests.
8. Wads and/or hulls were or were not dusted with a dry lubricant.
9. Shotshells are difficult to track when the chronograph was designed for single objects (bullets). Too many bits and pieces flying past the screens may confuse the electronics.
10. Hulls are not made absolutely identical as to thickness, depth, volume and elasticity.
11. Are you using new hulls or tenth fires? Some hulls can only be described as fragile.

16

Knowing—and heeding—the
laws as they pertain to your sport
will help to keep you out of trouble.

Legal Considerations of Shotgunning

IN THE UNITED States, as well as in a growing number of other countries, there are specific ammunition-related legal considerations one has to ponder before trudging off to the woods, swamps, dunes or whatever.

I can't list every conceivable ordinance covering all the world's shooting areas. That would be silly and would reduce several thousand square miles of forest to paper pulp. Refer, rather, to the reams of funny little publications usually accompanying your license as well as the applications that made it possible for you to obtain your license. Forewarned is foretold, or something like that. What we can do is mention some notable concerns and particular components of ammunition that are most often regulated.

Waterfowl Regulations

The United States enacted federal legislation mandating the use of non-toxic pellets for migratory waterfowl. Of course, waterfowl include all of the basic webbed-foot birds that fly south for winter. Non-toxic pellet laws cover the entirety of the United States without exception.

Before you load up several cases of depleted uranium-based bird shot, you should be aware that any new element to be used in the taking of migratory waterfowl has to undergo an extensive, rigorous process of evaluation. Many people wearing frowns and lab coats will scrutinize, exercise and analyze the pellet and its probabilities until one of two things happen: The entity submitting a substance for approval runs out of money to feed the monster; or, the pellet is approved for use on migratory waterfowl. I am aware of several elements and alloys going

Steel shot is here to stay, but other useful non-toxic shot is already approved for use. Steel shot is a really soft, solid iron and can be gathered by a magnet in the event of a spill.

through this process as I commit this sentence to paper. The crystal ball is foggy, otherwise I could tell you whether there are to be more pellets to choose from next year. Even if we were to decide hard candy would make a dandy non-toxic pellet, that, too, would have to go through the approval process.

Believe it or not, up until a few years ago, there was no exception to the use of steel shot—steel or nothing, kids. The Canadians take a more sane approach to this, as their legislation reads (essentially) "...pellets not containing lead." The United States' poorly written, short-sighted legislation was the result of some questionable studies during the 1970s. Steel by itself is OK; it fulfills requirements of non-toxicity, but it requires spe-

To leave less shooting "residue" around the countryside, many British shooters use loads with cardboard wads and fillers that will rapidly degrade over time. Plastic wads are unsightly, Old Chap, and another excuse for the anti-hunting factions to rally against the sport in the name pollution control.

cialized hardware to use it. Fine older double guns need not apply. Many have lived in dark closets and gun safes over the last few years because of the steel-only laws. The second problem with steel-only is that it leaves little reason for companies to undertake the rigors and expense of research and development. The times, they are a changin' though.

Today your options are expanding, but are still very specific. Bismuth was the first non-steel approved pellet and was legally used during the 1996 hunting season. Before you decide upon a pellet type for your waterfowling, make sure that it is either steel or specifically approved for migratory waterfowl. The United States does not have reciprocity of rules with Canada, so you will have to be nation-specific. Half the fun is getting there isn't it?

Component Restrictions

Certain areas, particularly state refuges, consider the use of shot larger than their favorite bad for yours and everybody else's health. Certainly, if you are using anything bigger than a #BB, you will attempt 250-yard skybusts—so the thinking goes. In any case, be aware that certain areas do have size restrictions. I would hate to have you load up two cases of 3-inch magnum #T steel only to find that you will have to burn it up in Skeet practice.

I have spoken with many hunters over the years who are unclear on certain aspects of non-toxic pellets. Let's clarify a few and hope the information covers most questions.

Lead shot, even if it is plated, is still lead shot and frowned upon by Mr. Game Warden. Whether it is nickel-plated, copper-plated, or encased in little plastic jars with water and snowflakes, you cannot use lead shot.

Steel shot is defined as soft, solid iron—without an alloy. No, you can't compose your own element and use it. Unless, of course, you get it approved by the U.S. Department of Fish and Wildlife.

Each new shot type that does receive specific approval has

to offer several methods of verification—a little periodic table of elements pop quiz, if you will. That way, when Mr. Game Warden slogs into your blind for a visit, he will be able to conduct a little experiment to verify that you are following the straight and narrow. So don't even think about it.

With degradable loads, the shotgunner can appease a landowner who might otherwise close off his property to hunting. Right or wrong, some folks worry about the accumulation of stuff on their property. In the end, it is their land and you have no right to shoot on it without their permission. Perhaps these loads will get you onto property that is otherwise unavailable to shooters.

A solution the British utilize is to build loads with compressed cardboard wads and fillers. Though cardboard wads are ballistically inferior to elegant plastic seals in modern loads, sometimes one does what one has to in order to hunt.

Cardboard wads are completely biodegradable. However, these loads should be limited to the lighter end of the spectrum. Bear in mind that lighter loads are less affected by consequent gas leakage of using cardboard wads. Heavier loads let the gases escape as they offer more resistance than the cardboard seal can contain effectively. Consequently, the heavy loads fluctuate greatly in velocity and pressure. This is another reason that yesterday's loads were lighter in payload.

A hunter's other degradable wad alternative is a new cornstarch-based plastic resin. These wads, when exposed to the sun, will decompose over the course of about two years. Of course, the disadvantage is that you will somehow have to certify the degradability of your "plastic" wads to whomever decides to ask. More folks are familiar with cardboard.

Gauge Restrictions

In the 1930s, it was decided that a certain club's wisdom in selecting the 10-gauge as the largest allowable bore would be good enough to use as a model for the rest of the nation. This survey has to be the absolute pinnacle of casual science. The

Before you stock up on a ton of reloading components—and even loaded ammunition—it's best to check local ordinances to see if they restrict storage to certain quantities. Fire departments tend to get nervous with a lot of certain materials around.

If you'd like to take Granpap's Ol' Betsy to the duck blind, think again before using steel shot in it as that could damage the gun. It's better to leave the older guns behind and save them for lead shot use another day.

British still use the 8-gauge as a long-range waterfowler, but we have not the space to speak wistfully of this monster. If you have British friends coming over for a hunt, have them leave their stout equipment home and bring the pigeon popper to hunt geese on the Great Plains.

So grab that ten and go!? Well, wait a minute, you're still not off the gauge restriction hook, especially Californians. The ballistic wizards there have prohibited the 10-gauge from the Golden State's public lands. The rationale for this clever move was that the gauge, by virtue of diameter, encourages flock shooting and sky-busting (shooting beyond reasonable range). Much of the area in California where the ban has been made into law requires long-range shotguns.

Oddly, the 3½-inch 12-gauge, which was designed to compete with the 10-gauge, somehow does not contribute to sky busting. Was California's action just a door opener for the manufacturers of the longer 12s? It has that appearance. Taking gauge limitation thinking to its logical end, perhaps we should limit hunters to the 410-bore and eliminate sky-busting altogether!

Experienced British shooters put "smaller bores" such as the 12 aside for hard-weather waterfowl hunting. Instead they go to bigger bores such as the 10, the 8 or sometimes even larger. These are Full-choked barrels firing very tight patterns of large pellets. In the United Kingdom, wind figures strongly in ammunition and gauge selection. At Bettyhill, in northern Scotland, the winds tear at you. In August, you have to wear a heavy coat and fight to keep your hat on. In October, when the winds really blow, the 12-gauge, and the finer sized pellets it requires, becomes nothing but a toy. Four hundred miles south of Bettyhill, Scotland, the winds continue to rip into the Yorkshire Dales pushing game at express train velocities. No place here for dinky shotguns and small shot.

In the U.S., waterfowl game officials long ago declared that the 8-gauge "is too big for use on geese." Really? The bore diameter suitable for larger pellets and super-tight chokes makes this gauge excessive? However, given the prospective of a very long walk, smaller upland game and a woodsy environment, we choose a smallbore every time—unless of course it has been prohibited as a game crippler. Think before you decide to let someone else make your hunting decisions for you.

Component Storage

I recommend that you check your local fire ordinances as they might pertain to component storage; particularly with regard to primers and powder.

The National Fire Protection Association (NFPA) refers to the topic of primer storage, and their opinions are largely accepted as a precedent for community regulations. Ordinances as they pertain to you may state that no more than 10,000 primers can be stored at a private residence. This translates to 100 individual boxes of any type of primer. In case of an accident, some insurance companies may not pay off if you have exceeded the NFPA maximum.

The NFPA guidelines state that, under normal storage conditions, no more than 20 pounds of powder may be kept at your house, unless they are stored in a box with walls at least 1-inch thick. Under these circumstances, stored quantities (for individual use) cannot exceed 50 pounds. There is much conflicting information regarding powder storage. Some ordinances don't even reflect common sense. I recommend that you liberally vent a powder storage locker should you decide you need more than 20 pounds of powder. If sealed tightly, ignited powder can generate sufficient pressure for an explosive effect.

INTRODUCTION TO LOAD DATA

FOR MANY DECADES, beginning in earnest with the buffalo hunters who took up the pursuit shortly after the end of the Civil War, the handloaded self-contained cartridge has been part and parcel of the American shooting scene. It would be hard to say when reloading of the first self-contained shotshell or metallic cartridge occurred. However, we can say that in the beginning, and for many decades thereafter, some grade of blackpowder was the propellant used in *all* handloads. There is one overriding thing we can say about that situation: Blackpowder made the handloader's task quite simple. Regardless of the type of cartridge one was loading, the only propellant decisions one had to make were what brand, style and grade (granulation size) of blackpowder to use.

Those who chose to use a poor-quality product found that their handloads produced sub-par ballistics. Those who chose the wrong grade of blackpowder equally compromised their handload's ballistic performance. For example, such a load might have generated barrel leading or sub-par velocity. It might even have resulted in a burst case head (cases were much weaker in those days). In the worst instances it could possibly have burst a gun, although, with a quality gun, this latter result was most unlikely.

I would not claim gun failures did not occur, but I would say a burst gun resulting only from use of the wrong grade of blackpowder in a cartridge handload must have been an exceedingly rare event. If or when this did happen, it had to have been a reflection of a very weak gun design. That is the nature of blackpowder—relatively low energy yield and forgiving.

This is not to suggest blackpowder cannot produce gun-wrecking pressures. Although this misconception will not go away, as many a muzzleloading shooter has discovered the hard way, blackpowder most certainly can destroy a gun. The point is, there is insufficient room to put enough blackpowder in a cartridge case to generate gun-destroying pressures, regardless of grade or brand of powder used.

In the blackpowder era, handloads using blackpowder were quite insensitive to variations in most reloading variables. Primer choice made little difference. Despite claims to the contrary, a "hotter" primer just does not engender a whole lot of ballistic difference in blackpowder loads. This was especially true in days gone by, when the only primer composition was fulminate of mercury—that stuff is hot, hot, hot. By today's standards, all early primers were "magnum strength."

The wadding system used in shotshell loads only had to succeed in sealing the bore and preventing migration of propellant gases into the shot charge while those gases (generated by the burning powder) accelerated the pellet mass through the barrel. It really made very little difference what the wadding material was made of or how much wadding the handloader used (within reason).

The bullet or shot chosen also made little difference. For example, when loading 8-gauge shotgun shells, the handloader generally could use 1/4-ounce, 1/2-ounce, 1 ounce, 1 1/4 ounces or 1 1/2 ounces of shot (or any increment between these amounts). As long as the wadding did the job, the load would perform similarly, regarding developed velocity and pattern efficiency—the handloader did not have to adjust powder charge one iota to safely achieve useful results.

I could go on to list more examples of load details that made very little difference, but that seems unnecessary. My point is, producing safe and effective handloads using blackpowder was relatively simple. Beyond blackpowder's intense inflammability, it really posed few hazards to the handloader.

As noted, for the most part, if the shotshell hull or cartridge case would hold the blackpowder charge, the resulting load would produce safe pressures. This engendered a large margin of safety to the handloader, meaning, in effect, if you could load it, it was safe to shoot!

Beginning just about 100 years ago, after tens (or hundreds?) of thousands of handloaders had plied their trade using only blackpowder, for perhaps thirty years, powder manufacturers introduced dramatic changes onto the handloading scene, in the form of revolutionary new propellants. The first marker of this propellant revolution came with the introduction of various effective and trustworthy bulk smokeless and semi-smokeless powder compositions. The first of these powders provided the handloader the same things offered to those shooting the then-modern factory shells—cleaner loads producing less smoke, less barrel fouling and less barrel corrosion.

Another thing these powders brought was the need for the handloader to pay more attention to component choices. Unlike blackpowder, bulk propellants required specific primers, consistent wadding and consistent crimping to deliver proper shotshell performance. Nevertheless, the handloader could substitute these propellants on a volume-for-volume basis with blackpowder, and for this reason, their adoption was relatively benign.

Then, within a span of a few short years, these bulk formulations began to give way to newer guncotton- and nitroglycerin-based dense propellants. Beginning in the late 1800s, the introduction of these highly energetic substances forever changed the face of handloading.

In what must have seemed an overnight transformation, after an entire generation of old-timers and a new batch of handloaders alike discovered the benefits and pleasures of handloading using blackpowder or blackpowder-interchangeable bulk smokeless powders, an entirely different situation erupted on the handloading scene. For the first time in history, the handloader had to look at his hobby in an entirely new way:

Introduction of the wrong kind of dense smokeless powder or the wrong amount of that powder into a handloaded cartridge carried the very real possibility of creating truly dangerous pressures. We can only guess (however, there is substantial circumstantial evidence to support this supposition) that during this transition era many improper handloads destroyed many guns of all types. Likely, many handloaders and innocent bystanders alike were injured, some fatally, when hapless shooters dropped the hammer on such dangerous overloads.

Why did these bad things happen? Old-time handloaders had all grown accustomed to simply using a volumetric, and relatively large (drams), charge of blackpowder. Then came a period where old-timers and new handloaders alike experienced the advantages of bulk smokeless powders, which they could use in the same manner. Considering this history, it was, no doubt, exceedingly difficult for powder manufacturers to impress upon every one of those experienced handloaders that the then-new dense smokeless powders could not be substituted for blackpowder on a volume-for-volume basis. After all, "Isn't all powder interchangeable?" Further, those new dense smokeless powders were doubly dangerous in this regard. Compared to blackpowder, these formulations were both more energetic and more progressive burning. An overload was vastly more dangerous, compared to an overload with either blackpowder or bulk powder.

However, in a sense, the situation was even worse than that. Not only did the handloader have to use the specific, correct type of powder and in the correct amount, he also had to use the correct type of case, the correct bullet or shot charge, the correct wadding type and the correct primer. In a sense, it was as if suddenly every minuscule load detail was critical—a complete turnaround from the former situation.

This discussion points out the reality of handloading for everybody, shotshell loaders and metallic cartridge loaders alike. It is, after all, very much a matter of following a recipe. *If you do not understand the instructions or if you cannot follow the recipe, do not undertake this hobby.*

In the following data section, we present over 14,000 handloading combinations, including loads for 10-gauge, 12-gauge, 16-gauge, 20-gauge, 24-gauge, 28-gauge, 32-gauge and 410-bore. We list loads for all popular shell lengths (and a few oddballs) and projectile types (lead, steel and bismuth birdshot; lead buckshot; and lead slugs). Each entry includes all pertinent data required for that load: hull, primer, shot charge, shot sizes (if restrictions apply), shot type, powder name and charge, and loaded shell length and crimping depth (where necessary).

I will not detail crimping or wad pressure here. (For a complete discussion, refer to the main text.) However, I will mention that if the crimp on your handload does not look similar to the crimp on a factory load, you should adjust your press until it does. (Depth from the end of the shell to the top of the crimp is quite critical; see the appropriate sections in the introductory text for a complete discussion.) Improper crimping can result in any of the following conditions: squib loads (which can result in an obstructed bore with the potential for a burst barrel), excess and potentially dangerous pressure, and/or blown patterns.

Take the time and effort to learn how to adjust your press to produce consistent and proper crimps. The rewards of developing a correct crimp in your shotshell handloads pose more benefit than any other detail of shotshell handloading.

Data Presentation

Having discussed this question with several in the industry, I have come to the conclusion that I am not alone in the feeling that no presentation system for shotshell data will satisfy all users. There are various reasons for this conundrum, and it deserves some discussion here.

The most obvious problem is that not all shotshell handloaders have the same priorities. Some are looking for the least expensive handloads. These folks often begin the process using once-fired hulls, gathered at the range or in the hunting field. They are also looking for the least expensive powder, primers, wads and shot. For those reasons, the combination of components they are using at any given loading session will likely change from the combination they used at the last loading session. Nevertheless, they want to produce safe, functional and similarly performing handloads, regardless of components used. (It is no small miracle they can often achieve this result!)

Conversely, many shotshell handloaders are quite meticulous. They handload for the pure pleasure of "doing it themselves," but they also fire test patterns and have determined the unique combination of components that launches the desired payload with the desired velocity and produces the desired pattern when fired from a specific shotgun. It is not that these folks are not interested in saving money (in many cases they are); their primary goal is maximum performance.

Similarly, there are groups of handloaders who have identified some specific need that no factory loading can fulfill. For whatever reason, these folks want to produce a certain type of handload. They might or might not care what associated components the load uses, but they will have one (or more) specific priority.

The reality is that each of these, and any other group of shotshell handloaders, will prefer data in a specific presentation format. The trouble is, each group's preferred presentation format is almost certain to differ from that preferred by any other group. A few examples are in order.

One group might want all 12-gauge loads for W-W AA hulls grouped in one section—regardless of charge weight, shot type, primer, wad, powder or velocity. Another group might want all 12-gauge, 1¼-ounce, 1200 fps loads using Unique powder gathered in one section. Another, might want all loads of every type that use CCI-209 primers listed together. The list of variations in presentation preference is essentially endless.

Obviously, we are forced to compromise in the presentation we choose. Acknowledging that no compromise is perfect, we move on to what we can do. We note that any presentation system must fulfill several criteria: foremost, the data must be provided in an understandable, comprehensive and consistent format.

It turns out that the best we can do is provide the information in a way that makes it easy for everyone to find the load for which they are looking. Very likely this approach will amount to "one size fits nobody perfectly." Nevertheless, we hope it will fit everybody acceptably well. Our only assuagement is that nobody else in the industry has yet found a "perfect" presentation format for shotshell data.

Presentation Approach

My approach is as follows: Provide *all* data for a given gauge, shell length, shot type (lead, steel, etc.) and shot charge weight in one continuous table. This means, for example, that we present every 12-gauge, 2³/₄-inch, lead shot, 1¹/₈-ounce loading found in this data manual in one concise and continuous section. This seems a reasonable approach. At the very least, all shotshell handloaders have to know for what gauge and shell length they are handloading. Further, they should know what type of shot and the shot charge weight they intend to load before they set out to handload any shotgun shell. Note that we show component types listed in each column in descending alphanumeric order—names starting with: 0,1,2,3,...,8,9,10,...A,B,C,...,X,Y,Z. The procedure for finding any specific load is then quite straightforward. With our system, the handloader will find every load that fits those criteria conveniently located in one continuous data section. I believe this approach is a big improvement, compared to some systems that have been used. In some other data sources, the handloader has to look all over the place to find every possible similar combination.

Safety Concerns

Be double certain and for sure, positively, that you are referencing the correct column and row when you read the required powder charge! In fact, please, make it a habit to verify the load all the way back to the beginning of the process, which is simplified by looking at the top of the page, where load and hull type are repeated throughout each section. Verify that the powder charge you have selected is actually in the same row as the powder, wad and primer you intend to use. If you make a mistake here, you could find yourself using a powder charge that generates dangerous pressure.

Finally, please note the following additional safety concerns. You cannot assume it is safe to reduce the powder charge shown below that given for the *minimum* velocity loading with that combination of components. For example, in many instances, the data for that combination only shows powder charges for higher velocity loads. Often these charges are in incremental steps so that one could interpolate a lower powder charge that would given some specific, lower velocity.

A lower charge producing a lower velocity should generate lower pressure: Therefore, the load should be perfectly safe, right?...*Wrong!* For myriad reasons, this is not necessarily true. First, the reduced charge might not adequately fill the hull to produce proper and consistent ignition or to ensure a proper crimp. The potential for squib loads is very high. Second, a reduced load might create a partial or delayed ignition, the primer might partially dislodge the shotcup, and then the powder might ignite sometime after the primer's flash, followed by a subsequent minor ignition (which had bathed the remaining powder charge in a superheating flame). It is possible that this could result in the subsequent and almost instantaneous ignition of the entire superheated powder charge. The results could resemble a detonation and could destroy the gun. (See how much things have changed since the blackpowder era?)

The fundamental point: Use the correct components for the load you want; do not try to develop your own data. If the manufacturer has not provided data for a certain higher, or lower, velocity with a certain powder, he likely has a very good reason—for example, that load would not work safely or did not provide acceptable ballistic uniformity, pressure or pattern density.

However, in this regard, it is perfectly acceptable to use powder charges falling anywhere between the minimum and maximum listed loads with that combination. For example, if you find your charge bar drops a charge of given powder that falls between two charges called for in two adjacent velocity listings in this data, a load produced using that charge bar should be perfectly safe. Velocity will be close to what simple mathematical interpolation suggests. That is, if the charge is exactly between the two listed charges, the velocity will be close to exactly between the two listed velocities.

Obviously, never exceed the maximum powder charge shown. In some instances, this could be tempting. For example, if the maximum charge shown is listed as generating a moderate pressure, the handloader might believe he could increase the charge some increment and produce a safe load with increased velocity. However, again, there are myriad reasons not to attempt this. First, it is possible the increased charge will not fit in the hull while allowing proper crimping. Second, it is possible the resulting increase in wad pressure might drive chamber pressure dramatically higher (this potentiality is thoroughly unpredictable). Third, it is likely the resulting load, even if safe, would produce blown patterns. Again, use the correct components for the load you want; do not assume you can do something nobody else can, i.e., produce a safe load with superior velocity and a good pattern! I have something to tell those with such ambitions: If you believe you can accomplish what neither Remington, Winchester nor Federal have managed—unless you have more experience, knowledge, understanding, time, money and equipment to play with than they do—you are probably dreaming.

Equally obvious, never substitute any component without verifying that the resulting load is specifically listed and that it produces the results you want. Never forget this salient fact: Any component substitution is equivalent to an entirely new load. If the required charge weight is sufficiently similar to produce a safe load, that fact is only an accident. Do not assume otherwise and, in so doing, create a less pleasant accident of your own.

This leads to one final caution: *Be absolutely certain you are looking in the correct section for the shot type you are loading.* Data for steel shot (and other exotic types of shot) require very special loading precautions and wad combinations. The handloader must form many of these wad systems by hand and manually insert them into the case at the time of loading. Keep this complication in mind. While it is quite feasible to produce perfectly good loads using exotic shot types, doing so safely requires that one pay special attention to detail. Further, using data for the wrong shot type is bound to lead to catastrophe.

Yes, the shotshell handloader has to follow a recipe, but so does the metallic cartridge handloader. But, the shotshell handloader has thousands of recipes from which to choose. Making the effort to find that one recipe which produces the best results in one gun is half the fun and is one reason the handloader always has a chance of improving his shotgun's performance.

M.L. McPherson

LEAD SHOT LOAD DATA

This data is lead shot-specific; it does not interchange with data used for any other type of lead or other non-toxic shot. Use only the components and amounts listed.

10-GAUGE 3½" — 1¼ OUNCES LEAD SHOT

Primer	Powder Type	Wad	Powder Charge (grains) / Velocity (fps) Minimum	Maximum	Maximum Pressure	Load Notes
FEDERAL: PLASTIC (PAPER BASE WAD)				**1¼ OUNCES LEAD SHOT**		
CCI 209M	Green Dot	Rem. SP10		29.5/1265	8,300 psi	Note 1
Win. 209	Green Dot	Rem. SP10		29.0/1265	8,800 psi	Note 1
REMINGTON: UNIBODY (INTEGRAL PLASTIC BASE WAD)				**1¼ OUNCES LEAD SHOT**		
CCI 209M	Green Dot	Rem. SP10		28.5/1265	8,800 psi	Note 1
CCI 209M	Unique	Rem. SP10		31.0/1265	7,500 psi	Note 1
Win. 209	Green Dot	Rem. SP10		29.0/1265	8,800 psi	Note 1
Win. 209	Unique	Rem. SP10		31.0/1265	7,600 psi	Note 1
WINCHESTER: POLYFORMED (SEPARATE PLASTIC BASE WAD)				**1¼ OUNCES LEAD SHOT**		
CCI 209M	Green Dot	Rem. SP10		28.0/1265	8,500 psi	Note 2
Win. 209	Green Dot	Rem. SP10		28.5/1265	8,600 psi	Note 2

Load Notes: 1 = Add six 20-gauge, 0.135" cards inside bottom of shotcup. 2 = Add five 20-gauge, 0.135" cards inside bottom of shotcup.

10-GAUGE 3½" — 1½ OUNCES LEAD SHOT

Primer	Powder Type	Wad	Powder Charge (grains) / Velocity (fps) Minimum	Maximum	Maximum Pressure	Load Notes
FEDERAL: PLASTIC (PAPER BASE WAD)				**1½ OUNCES LEAD SHOT**		
Fed. 209	IMR 700-X	Rem. SP10		29.5/1230	9,900 LUP	Note 1
WINCHESTER: POLYFORMED (SEPARATE PLASTIC BASE WAD)				**1½ OUNCES LEAD SHOT**		
Win. 209	IMR 700-X	H. Versalite		29.0/1215	9,900 LUP	Note 2
Win. 209	IMR 700-X	Rem. SP10		29.0/1215	9,600 LUP	Note 2

Load Notes: 1 = Add five 20-gauge, 0.135" cards inside bottom of shotcup. 2 = Add four 20-gauge, 0.135" cards inside bottom of shotcup.

10-GAUGE 3½" — 1⅝ OUNCES LEAD SHOT

Primer	Powder Type	Wad	Powder Charge (grains) / Velocity (fps) Minimum	Maximum	Maximum Pressure	Load Notes
FEDERAL: PLASTIC (PAPER BASE WAD)				**1⅝ OUNCES LEAD SHOT**		
CCI 209M	Blue Dot	Rem. SP10		45.0/1285	8,000 psi	Note 1
CCI 209M	Herco	Rem. SP10		36.0/1285	10,300 psi	Note 1

Load Notes: 1 = Add four 20-gauge, 0.135" cards inside bottom of shotcup. 2 = Add three 20-gauge, 0.135" cards inside bottom of shotcup.

Caution: Follow load recipes exactly; do not substitute components, exceed listed maximums or load less than listed minimums.

1⁵/₈ Ounces Lead Shot (cont.)

10-GAUGE 3¹/₂"

Primer	Powder Type	Wad	Powder Charge (grains) / Velocity (fps) Minimum	Maximum	Maximum Pressure	Load Notes
FEDERAL: PLASTIC (PAPER BASE WAD) (CONT.)				**1⁵/₈ OUNCES LEAD SHOT**		
Fed. 209	IMR PB	Rem. SP10		37.5/1295	9,800 LUP	Note 2
Fed. 209	Solo 1500	Rem. SP10		53.0/1430	10,900 LUP	
Win. 209	Blue Dot	Rem. SP10		45.5/1285	8,300 psi	Note 1
REMINGTON: SP (SEPARATE YELLOW PLASTIC BASE WAD)				**1⁵/₈ OUNCES LEAD SHOT**		
CCI 209M	Blue Dot	Rem. SP10		43.5/1285	8,500 psi	Note 1
Rem. 209P	Solo 1500	Rem. SP10		52.0/1430	10,900 LUP	
Win. 209	Blue Dot	Rem. SP10		44.0/1285	8,500 psi	Note 1
WINCHESTER: POLYFORMED (SEPARATE PLASTIC BASE WAD)				**1⁵/₈ OUNCES LEAD SHOT**		
CCI 209M	Blue Dot	Rem. SP10		44.5/1285	8,700 psi	Note 2
CCI 209M	Herco	Rem. SP10		35.5/1285	10,400 psi	Note 2
Win. 209	Blue Dot	Rem. SP10		45.0/1285	8,800 psi	Note 2
Win. 209	Solo 1500	Rem. SP10		53.0/1430	10,900 LUP	

Load Notes: 1 = Add four 20-gauge, 0.135″ cards inside bottom of shotcup. 2 = Add three 20-gauge, 0.135″ cards inside bottom of shotcup.

1⁷/₈ Ounces Lead Shot

10-GAUGE 3¹/₂"

Primer	Powder Type	Wad	Powder Charge (grains) / Velocity (fps) Minimum	Maximum	Maximum Pressure	Load Notes
FEDERAL: PLASTIC (PAPER BASE WAD)				**1⁷/₈ OUNCES LEAD SHOT**		
CCI 209M	Blue Dot	Rem. SP10		45.5/1270	9,900 psi	Note 1
Fed. 209	SR-7625	Rem. SP10		41.0/1260	9,700 LUP	Note 2
Win. 209	Blue Dot	Rem. SP10		45.5/1270	10,200 psi	Note 1
REMINGTON: UNIBODY (INTEGRAL PLASTIC BASE WAD)				**1⁷/₈ OUNCES LEAD SHOT**		
CCI 209M	Blue Dot	Rem. SP10		44.0/1270	9,800 psi	Note 1
Win. 209	Blue Dot	Rem. SP10		44.5/1270	9,100 psi	Note 1
WINCHESTER: POLYFORMED (SEPARATE PLASTIC BASE WAD)				**1⁷/₈ OUNCES LEAD SHOT**		
CCI 209M	Blue Dot	Rem. SP10		45.0/1270	9,800 psi	Note 2
Fed. 209	IMR PB	H. Versalite		37.5/1200	9,700 LUP	Note 3
Fed. 209	IMR PB	Rem. SP10		39.0/1220	10,000 LUP	
Win. 209	Blue Dot	Rem. SP10		45.5/1270	10,200 psi	Note 2

Load Notes: 1 = Add three 20-gauge, 0.135″ cards inside bottom of shotcup. 2 = Add two 20-gauge, 0.135″ cards inside bottom of shotcup. 3 = Add one 20-gauge, 0.135″ card inside bottom of shotcup.

2 Ounces Lead Shot

10-GAUGE 3¹/₂"

Primer	Powder Type	Wad	Powder Charge (grains) / Velocity (fps) Minimum	Maximum	Maximum Pressure	Load Notes
FEDERAL: PLASTIC (PAPER BASE WAD)				**2 OUNCES LEAD SHOT**		
CCI 209M	Blue Dot	Rem. SP10		43.5/1210	9,200 psi	Note 1
CCI 209M	HS-6	Rem. SP10		40.0/1165	9,900 psi	Note 1

Load Notes: 1 = Add two 20-gauge, 0.135″ cards inside bottom of shotcup.

Caution: Follow load recipes exactly; do not substitute components, exceed listed maximums or load less than listed minimums.

Primer	Powder Type	Wad	Powder Charge (grains) / Velocity (fps) Minimum	Maximum	Maximum Pressure	Load Notes
FEDERAL: PLASTIC (PAPER BASE WAD) (CONT.)				**2 OUNCES LEAD SHOT**		
CCI 209M	HS-7	Rem. SP10		43.0/1165	10,200 psi	Note 1
CCI 209M	IMR 800-X	BP BPD		32.5/1200	9,800 LUP	Note 2
Fed. 209	IMR 800-X	Rem. SP10		35.0/1205	9,600 LUP	Note 3
Fed. 209	Solo 1500	Rem. SP10		44.0/1210	10,900 LUP	
Fed. 209	SR-4756	Rem. SP10		46.5/1300	9,800 LUP	
Win. 209	Blue Dot	Rem. SP10		44.0/1210	9,400 psi	Note 1
Win. 209	IMR 800-X	BP BPD		32.5/1195	9,900 LUP	Note 2
Win. 209	IMR 800-X	Rem. SP10		34.5/1190	9,800 LUP	Note 3
REMINGTON: SP (SEPARATE YELLOW PLASTIC BASE WAD)				**2 OUNCES LEAD SHOT**		
CCI 209M	HS-6	Rem. SP10		40.0/1165	11,000 psi	Note 3
CCI 209M	HS-7	Rem. SP10		43.0/1165	11,000 psi	Note 3
Rem. 209P	Solo 1500	Rem. SP10		43.0/1210	10,900 LUP	
REMINGTON: UNIBODY (INTEGRAL PLASTIC BASE WAD)				**2 OUNCES LEAD SHOT**		
CCI 209M	Blue Dot	Rem. SP10		42.0/1210	10,400 psi	Note 1
Win. 209	Blue Dot	Rem. SP10		42.5/1210	10,100 psi	Note 1
WINCHESTER: POLYFORMED (SEPARATE PLASTIC BASE WAD)				**2 OUNCES LEAD SHOT**		
CCI 209M	Blue Dot	Rem. SP10		43.0/1210	9,400 psi	Note 4
CCI 209M	HS-6	Rem. SP10		40.0/1165	10,700 psi	Note 1
CCI 209M	HS-7	Rem. SP10		42.5/1165	10,600 psi	Note 1
CCI 209M	IMR 800-X	BP BPD		34.5/1200	9,700 LUP	Note 5
CCI 209M	IMR 800-X	H. Versalite		37.5/1215	9,300 LUP	Note 1
CCI 209M	IMR 800-X	Rem. SP10		37.0/1215	8,700 LUP	Note 4
Fed. 209	IMR PB	H. Versalite		35.0/1120	9,900 LUP	Note 4
Fed. 209	IMR PB	Rem. SP10		36.0/1155	10,000 LUP	
Win. 209	Blue Dot	Rem. SP10		43.5/1210	9,500 psi	Note 4
Win. 209	IMR 800-X	BP BPD		34.5/1205	10,000 LUP	Note 5
Win. 209	IMR 800-X	H. Versalite		36.5/1205	9,600 LUP	Note 1
Win. 209	IMR 800-X	Rem. SP10		36.5/1215	9,700 LUP	Note 4
Win. 209	Solo 1500	Rem. SP10		44.0/1210	10,900 LUP	
Win. 209	SR-4756	Rem. SP10		48.5/1305	9,900 LUP	
Win. 209	SR-7625	H. Versalite		40.0/1210	9,700 LUP	
Win. 209	SR-7625	Rem. SP10		41.0/1230	10,000 LUP	
Win. 209	W 540	Pacific P		44.0/1210	8,600 LUP	Note 6
Win. 209	W 540	Rem. SP10		44.0/1210	8,700 LUP	Note 7

Load Notes: 1 = Add two 20-gauge, 0.135" cards inside bottom of shotcup. 2 = Add two 20-gauge, ½" fiber wads in bottom of shotcup. 3 = Add three 20-gauge, 0.135" cards inside bottom of shotcup. 4 = Add one 20-gauge, 0.135" card inside bottom of shotcup. 5 = Add one 20-gauge, ½" fiber wad + one 0.135" card in bottom of shotcup. 6 = Add one 20-gauge, ⅜" fiber filler in bottom of shotcup. 7 = Add one 16-gauge, ¼" fiber filler in bottom of shotcup.

Caution: Follow load recipes exactly; do not substitute components, exceed listed maximums or load less than listed minimums.

2 1/8 OUNCES LEAD SHOT

10-GAUGE 3 1/2"

Primer	Powder Type	Wad	Powder Charge (grains) / Velocity (fps) Minimum	Maximum	Maximum Pressure	Load Notes
FEDERAL: PLASTIC (PAPER BASE WAD)				2 1/8 OUNCES LEAD SHOT		
Fed. 209	SR-4756	Rem. SP10		44.0/1230	10,000 LUP	
WINCHESTER: POLYFORMED (SEPARATE PLASTIC BASE WAD)				2 1/8 OUNCES LEAD SHOT		
Win. 209	SR-4756	Rem. SP10		45.0/1240	9,800 LUP	
Win. 209	SR-7625	H. Versalite		39.5/1165	9,900 LUP	
Win. 209	SR-7625	Rem. SP10		38.5/1155	9,900 LUP	

2 1/4 OUNCES LEAD SHOT

10-GAUGE 3 1/2"

Primer	Powder Type	Wad	Powder Charge (grains) / Velocity (fps) Minimum	Maximum	Maximum Pressure	Load Notes
FEDERAL: PLASTIC (PAPER BASE WAD)				2 1/4 OUNCES LEAD SHOT		
CCI 209	SR-4756	H. Versalite		42.5/1180	10,000 LUP	
CCI 209M	Blue Dot	Rem. SP10		42.0/1165	9,800 psi	Note 1
Fed. 209	SR-4756	H. Versalite		40.5/1155	9,900 LUP	
Fed. 209	SR-4756	Rem. SP10		41.0/1160	9,700 LUP	
Win. 209	Blue Dot	Rem. SP10		42.5/1165	10,200 psi	Note 1
Win. 209	HS-7	Rem. SP10		41.0/1165	10,300 psi	Note 1
REMINGTON: SP (SEPARATE YELLOW PLASTIC BASE WAD)				2 1/4 OUNCES LEAD SHOT		
Win. 209	HS-7	Rem. SP10		40.0/1165	10,800 psi	Note 2
REMINGTON: UNIBODY (INTEGRAL PLASTIC BASE WAD)				2 1/4 OUNCES LEAD SHOT		
CCI 209M	Blue Dot	Rem. SP10		40.5/1165	10,400 psi	
Win. 209	Blue Dot	Rem. SP10		41.0/1165	10,500 psi	
WINCHESTER: POLYFORMED (SEPARATE PLASTIC BASE WAD)				2 1/4 OUNCES LEAD SHOT		
CCI 209M	Blue Dot	Rem. SP10		41.5/1165	10,500 psi	
CCI 209M	HS-7	Rem. SP10		40.0/1165	11,000 psi	Note 1
Win. 209	Blue Dot	Rem. SP10		42.0/1165	10,500 psi	
Win. 209	SR-4756	Rem. SP10		42.5/1175	10,000 LUP	
Win. 209	W 571	H. Versalite		48.0/1210	10,000 LUP	
Win. 209	W 571	Rem. SP10		47.0/1210	9,900 LUP	

Load Notes: 1 = Add one 20-gauge, 0.135" card inside bottom of shotcup. 2 = Add two 20-gauge, 0.135" cards inside bottom of shotcup.

2 3/8 OUNCES LEAD SHOT

10-GAUGE 3 1/2"

Primer	Powder Type	Wad	Powder Charge (grains) / Velocity (fps) Minimum	Maximum	Maximum Pressure	Load Notes
FEDERAL: PLASTIC (PAPER BASE WAD)				2 3/8 OUNCES LEAD SHOT		
Fed. 209	SR-4756	H. Versalite		37.5/1150	9,600 LUP	
Fed. 209	SR-4756	Rem. SP10		38.0/1125	10,000 LUP	
Win. 209	SR-4756	H. Versalite		38.5/1155	9,800 LUP	

END OF 10-GAUGE LEAD SHOT LOAD DATA

Caution: Follow load recipes exactly; do not substitute components, exceed listed maximums or load less than listed minimums.

12-GAUGE 2″   ⁷/₈-OUNCE LEAD SHOT

Primer	Powder Type	Wad	Powder Charge (grains) / Velocity (fps) Minimum	Maximum	Maximum Pressure	Load Notes
ACTIV: ALL PLASTIC (SHORTENED BY CUTTING)				⁷/₈-OUNCE LEAD SHOT		
Win. 209	International	BP Compact		17.0/1180	7,500 psi	Note 1
REMINGTON: PREMIER & NITRO 27 & STS (SHORTENED BY CUTTING)				⁷/₈-OUNCE LEAD SHOT		
Win. 209	International	BP Compact		16.0/1180	8,400 psi	Note 1
WINCHESTER: COMPRESSION-FORMED AA TYPE (SHORTENED BY CUTTING) ⁷/₈-OUNCE LEAD SHOT						
Win. 209	International	BP Compact		16.0/1180	8,400 psi	Note 1

Load Notes: 1 = Ballistic Products Eurowad.

12-GAUGE 2″   1-OUNCE LEAD SHOT

Primer	Powder Type	Wad	Powder Charge (grains) / Velocity (fps) Minimum	Maximum	Maximum Pressure	Load Notes
ACTIV: ALL PLASTIC (SHORTENED BY CUTTING)				1-OUNCE LEAD SHOT		
Win. 209	International	BP Ultra Short		17.0/1180	8,600 psi	Note 1
REMINGTON: PREMIER & NITRO 27 & STS (SHORTENED BY CUTTING)				1-OUNCE LEAD SHOT		
Win. 209	Universal	BP Ultra Short		18.5/1180	9,200 psi	Note 1

Load Notes: 1 = Ballistic Products Eurowad

Caution: Follow load recipes exactly; do not substitute components, exceed listed maximums or load less than listed minimums.

1-OUNCE LEAD SHOT 12-GAUGE 2½"

Primer	Powder Type	Wad	Powder Charge (grains) / Velocity (fps) Minimum		Maximum	Maximum Pressure	Load Notes
ACTIV: ALL PLASTIC (SHORTENED BY CUTTING)					**1-OUNCE LEAD SHOT**		
Win. 209	Universal	WAA12			20.5/1200	8,400 psi	
FEDERAL: GOLD MEDAL PLASTIC (SHORTENED BY CUTTING)					**1-OUNCE LEAD SHOT**		
Win. 209	International	WAA12			20.0/1250	8,200 psi	
REMINGTON: PREMIER & NITRO 27 & STS (SHORTENED BY CUTTING)					**1-OUNCE LEAD SHOT**		
Win. 209	Universal	WAA12R			20.8/1180	7,300 psi	
WINCHESTER: COMPRESSION-FORMED AA TYPE (SHORTENED BY CUTTING)					**1-OUNCE LEAD SHOT**		
Win. 209	Universal	BP Compact			19.0/1130	8,900 psi	Note 1
Win. 209	Universal	WAA12R	20.0/1130	20.5/1190	22.0/1300	10,300 psi	

Load Notes: 1 = Ballistic Products Eurowad

Caution: Follow load recipes exactly; do not substitute components, exceed listed maximums or load less than listed minimums. 143

³⁄₄-OUNCE LEAD SHOT

Primer	Powder Type	Wad	Powder Charge (grains) / Velocity (fps) Minimum		Maximum		Maximum Pressure	Load Notes
WINCHESTER: COMPRESSION-FORMED AA TYPE						³⁄₄-OUNCE LEAD SHOT		
Fio. 615	IMR 700-X	BP DX12		18.9/1170	19.4/1225	19.8/1275	9,600 LUP	Note 1
Fio. 616	WSL	BP DX12				18.8/1290	7,900 LUP	Note 1
Win. 209	IMR 700-X	BP DX12				19.0/1255	9,500 LUP	Note 1

Load Notes: 1 = Disperser-X.

12-GAUGE 2³⁄₄″

24 GRAMS LEAD SHOT

Primer	Powder Type	Wad	Powder Charge (grains) / Velocity (fps) Minimum			Maximum	Maximum Pressure	Load Notes
FEDERAL: GOLD MEDAL PLASTIC						24 GRAMS LEAD SHOT		
Fed. 209A	IMR 700-X	Activ TG-30	15.5/1155	16.5/1200	17.5/1245	19.5/1335	8,800 psi	Note 1
Fed. 209A	IMR 700-X	CB 1100-12	15.5/1145	16.5/1195	17.5/1250	19.5/1335	7,400 psi	Note 1
Fed. 209A	IMR 700-X	CB 2100-12	16.0/1160	17.0/1210	18.0/1260	19.5/1330	7,500 psi	Note 1
Fed. 209A	IMR 700-X	Fed. 12S0	16.0/1160	17.0/1205	18.0/1255	19.5/1325	7,800 psi	Note 1
Fed. 209A	IMR 700-X	Rem. TGT12	15.5/1145	16.5/1195	17.5/1245	19.5/1325	7,100 psi	Note 1
Fed. 209A	IMR 700-X	WAA12SL	15.5/1155	16.5/1205	17.5/1255	19.0/1325	7,800 psi	Note 1
Fed. 209A	IMR PB	Activ TG-30	20.0/1145	21.5/1205	22.5/1250	24.5/1330	7,000 psi	Note 1
Fed. 209A	IMR PB	CB 2118-12	20.0/1150	21.0/1190	22.5/1250	24.5/1330	6,900 psi	Note 1
Fed. 209A	IMR PB	Fed. 12S3	20.0/1155	21.0/1195	22.5/1260	24.0/1320	7,000 psi	Note 1
Fed. 209A	IMR PB	Rem. TGT12	20.0/1145	21.5/1205	23.0/1265	24.5/1325	6,700 psi	Note 1
Fed. 209A	IMR PB	WAA12SL	20.0/1155	21.0/1195	22.5/1250	24.5/1325	6,600 psi	Note 1
Fed. 209A	SR-7625	Activ TG-30	23.5/1155	24.5/1200	26.0/1260	28.0/1335	5,900 psi	Note 1
Fed. 209A	SR-7625	CB 2100-12	24.0/1145	25.5/1205	26.5/1250	28.5/1325	5,000 psi	Note 1
Fed. 209A	SR-7625	Fed. 12S0	23.5/1145	25.0/1205	26.5/1265	28.0/1320	5,400 psi	Note 1
Fed. 209A	SR-7625	Rem. TGT12	24.0/1155	25.0/1195	26.5/1255	28.5/1335	5,400 psi	Note 1
Fed. 209A	SR-7625	WAA12SL	23.5/1150	24.5/1190	25.5/1255	27.0/1320	5,600 psi	Note 1
Rem. 209P	IMR 700-X	Activ TG-30	16.0/1145	17.5/1210	18.5/1250	20.0/1320	7,000 psi	Note 1
Rem. 209P	IMR 700-X	CB 1100-12	16.0/1140	17.5/1205	19.0/1250	21.0/1320	5,800 psi	Note 1
Rem. 209P	IMR 700-X	CB 2100-12	16.5/1140	18.0/1195	19.5/1265	21.0/1330	6,300 psi	Note 1
Rem. 209P	IMR 700-X	Fed. 12S0	16.5/1160	17.5/1205	18.5/1250	20.5/1340	7,300 psi	Note 1
Rem. 209P	IMR 700-X	Rem. TGT12	16.0/1150	17.0/1195	18.5/1250	21.0/1330	6,500 psi	Note 1
Rem. 209P	IMR 700-X	WAA12SL	16.0/1150	17.0/1205	18.0/1250	20.5/1325	6,600 psi	Note 1
Rem. 209P	IMR PB	Activ TG-30	20.0/1140	22.0/1205	23.5/1260	25.0/1325	6,400 psi	Note 1
Rem. 209P	IMR PB	CB 2118-12	21.0/1150	22.5/1205	24.0/1265	25.5/1330	6,100 psi	Note 1
Rem. 209P	IMR PB	Fed. 12S3	21.0/1160	22.0/1205	23.0/1250	25.0/1330	6,600 psi	Note 1
Rem. 209P	IMR PB	Rem. TGT12	21.0/1145	22.5/1200	24.0/1265	25.5/1330	6,000 psi	Note 1
Rem. 209P	IMR PB	WAA12SL	21.0/1140	22.5/1195	24.0/1255	25.5/1320	5,700 psi	Note 1
Win. 209	IMR 700-X	Activ TG-30	15.5/1145	16.5/1195	17.5/1245	19.5/1335	8,400 psi	Note 1
Win. 209	IMR 700-X	CB 1100-12	16.0/1155	17.0/1210	18.0/1260	19.5/1335	7,300 psi	Note 1
Win. 209	IMR 700-X	CB 2100-12	16.0/1160	17.0/1210	18.0/1260	19.5/1335	7,400 psi	Note 1
Win. 209	IMR 700-X	Fed. 12S0	15.5/1145	16.5/1195	17.5/1250	19.5/1330	7,800 psi	Note 1

Load Notes: 1 = Add one 20-gauge, 0.135″ card inside bottom of shotcup.

Caution: Follow load recipes exactly; do not substitute components, exceed listed maximums or load less than listed minimums.

Primer	Powder Type	Wad	Powder Charge (grains) / Velocity (fps) Minimum			Maximum	Maximum Pressure	Load Notes
FEDERAL: GOLD MEDAL PLASTIC (CONT.)						24 GRAMS LEAD SHOT		
Win. 209	IMR 700-X	Rem. TGT12	15.5/1150	16.5/1195	17.5/1245	19.5/1335	7,800 psi	Note 1
Win. 209	IMR 700-X	WAA12SL	15.5/1150	16.5/1200	17.5/1250	19.0/1320	7,500 psi	Note 1
Win. 209	IMR PB	Activ TG-30	20.5/1160	21.5/1200	22.5/1250	24.5/1325	6,900 psi	Note 1
Win. 209	IMR PB	CB 2118-12	20.5/1150	21.5/1195	23.0/1260	24.5/1320	6,600 psi	Note 1
Win. 209	IMR PB	Fed. 12S3	20.5/1145	22.0/1205	23.0/1250	24.5/1320	6,900 psi	Note 1
Win. 209	IMR PB	Rem. TGT12	20.5/1140	22.0/1200	23.5/1265	25.0/1325	6,300 psi	Note 1
Win. 209	IMR PB	WAA12SL	20.5/1145	21.5/1190	23.0/1255	25.0/1335	6,200 psi	Note 1
Win. 209	SR-7625	Activ TG-30	23.5/1140	25.0/1200	26.5/1260	28.0/1320	5,600 psi	Note 1
Win. 209	SR-7625	CB 2100-12	25.0/1155	26.0/1195	27.5/1250	29.5/1320	4,600 psi	Note 1
Win. 209	SR-7625	Fed. 12S0	24.5/1155	25.5/1200	27.0/1255	29.0/1330	5,200 psi	Note 1
Win. 209	SR-7625	Rem. TGT12	24.5/1150	25.5/1195	27.0/1250	29.0/1330	4,900 psi	Note 1
Win. 209	SR-7625	WAA12SL	24.5/1145	25.5/1195	27.0/1265	28.5/1335	5,400 psi	Note 1
REMINGTON: PREMIER & NITRO 27 & STS						24 GRAMS LEAD SHOT		
Fed. 209A	IMR 700-X	Activ TG-30	14.5/1155	15.5/1200	16.5/1250	18.0/1320	9,600 psi	Note 1
Fed. 209A	IMR 700-X	CB 1100-12	15.0/1155	16.0/1205	17.0/1255	18.5/1330	8,900 psi	Note 1
Fed. 209A	IMR 700-X	CB 2100-12	15.0/1155	16.0/1210	17.0/1260	18.5/1325	8,600 psi	Note 1
Fed. 209A	IMR 700-X	Fed. 12S0	15.0/1160	16.0/1210	17.0/1260	18.5/1325	9,200 psi	Note 1
Fed. 209A	IMR 700-X	Rem. TGT12	15.0/1160	16.0/1210	17.0/1265	18.5/1335	9,600 psi	Note 1
Fed. 209A	IMR 700-X	WAA12SL	14.5/1140	15.5/1195	16.5/1245	18.5/1335	10,000 psi	Note 1
Fed. 209A	IMR PB	Activ TG-30	18.5/1150	19.5/1190	21.0/1255	22.5/1320	8,000 psi	Note 1
Fed. 209A	IMR PB	CB 1100-12	18.0/1140	19.5/1205	20.5/1250	22.5/1330	7,800 psi	Note 1
Fed. 209A	IMR PB	Fed. 12S0	18.0/1155	19.0/1195	20.5/1255	22.0/1320	8,700 psi	Note 1
Fed. 209A	IMR PB	Rem. TGT12	18.0/1145	19.5/1205	20.5/1250	22.5/1330	7,800 psi	Note 1
Fed. 209A	IMR PB	WAA12SL	17.5/1155	18.5/1200	20.0/1265	21.5/1330	9,000 psi	Note 1
Fed. 209A	SR-7625	Activ TG-30	21.0/1140	22.5/1200	23.5/1245	25.5/1325	7,200 psi	Note 1
Fed. 209A	SR-7625	CB 1100-12	21.5/1150	23.0/1210	24.0/1250	26.0/1330	6,500 psi	Note 1
Fed. 209A	SR-7625	Fed. 12S0	21.5/1155	22.5/1200	24.0/1260	25.0/1325	7,300 psi	Note 1
Fed. 209A	SR-7625	Rem. Fig.-8	22.0/1150	23.0/1195	24.5/1260	26.0/1320	6,800 psi	Note 1
Fed. 209A	SR-7625	WAA12SL	20.5/1155	21.5/1195	23.0/1250	25.0/1320	7,500 psi	Notes
Rem. 209P	IMR 700-X	Activ TG-30	15.0/1155	16.0/1210	17.0/1260	18.5/1330	9,300 psi	Note 1
Rem. 209P	IMR 700-X	CB 1100-12	15.5/1155	16.5/1210	17.5/1260	19.0/1335	8,400 psi	Note 1
Rem. 209P	IMR 700-X	CB 2100-12	15.0/1150	16.0/1200	17.0/1250	18.5/1330	8,600 psi	Note 1
Rem. 209P	IMR 700-X	Fed. 12S0	15.0/1150	16.0/1205	17.0/1260	18.5/1340	9,800 psi	Note 1
Rem. 209P	IMR 700-X	Rem. TGT12	15.0/1150	16.0/1200	17.0/1250	19.0/1335	8,700 psi	Note 1
Rem. 209P	IMR 700-X	WAA12SL	15.0/1155	16.0/1210	17.0/1255	18.5/1320	8,900 psi	Note 1
Rem. 209P	IMR PB	Activ TG-30	19.0/1140	20.5/1210	21.5/1255	23.5/1335	7,500 psi	Note 1
Rem. 209P	IMR PB	CB 1100-12	19.5/1140	21.0/1205	22.0/1250	24.0/1330	6,400 psi	Note 1
Rem. 209P	IMR PB	Fed. 12S0	19.0/1145	20.5/1210	21.5/1255	23.5/1335	7,700 psi	Note 1
Rem. 209P	IMR PB	Rem. TGT12	19.5/1155	20.5/1195	22.0/1260	23.5/1325	6,900 psi	Note 1
Rem. 209P	IMR PB	WAA12SL	18.5/1145	19.5/1195	21.0/1265	22.5/1325	8,000 psi	Note 1
Rem. 209P	SR-7625	Activ TG-30	21.5/1155	23.0/1210	24.5/1260	26.0/1320	6,300 psi	Note 1
Rem. 209P	SR-7625	CB 1100-12	23.5/1145	25.0/1205	26.0/1250	27.5/1320	5,300 psi	Note 1

Load Notes: 1 = Add one 20-gauge, 0.135" card inside bottom of shotcup.

Caution: Follow load recipes exactly; do not substitute components, exceed listed maximums or load less than listed minimums.

Primer	Powder Type	Wad	Powder Charge (grains) / Velocity (fps) Minimum			Maximum	Maximum Pressure	Load Notes
REMINGTON: PREMIER & NITRO 27 & STS (CONT.)						24 GRAMS LEAD SHOT		
Rem. 209P	SR-7625	Fed. 12S0	21.5/1155	23.0/1210	24.0/1250	26.0/1335	6,900 psi	Note 1
Rem. 209P	SR-7625	Rem. Fig.-8	22.0/1140	23.5/1205	24.5/1245	26.5/1325	6,200 psi	Note 1
Rem. 209P	SR-7625	WAA12SL	21.5/1155	23.0/1205	24.5/1255	26.0/1325	6,800 psi	Note 1
Win. 209	IMR 700-X	Activ TG-30	14.5/1135	15.5/1190	17.0/1265	18.5/1335	9,700 psi	Note 1
Win. 209	IMR 700-X	CB 1100-12	15.0/1140	16.0/1200	17.0/1250	18.5/1325	8,500 psi	Note 1
Win. 209	IMR 700-X	CB 2100-12	15.0/1145	16.0/1200	17.0/1255	18.5/1335	8,500 psi	Note 1
Win. 209	IMR 700-X	Fed. 12S0	15.0/1160	16.0/1215	17.0/1265	18.5/1335	9,400 psi	Note 1
Win. 209	IMR 700-X	Rem. TGT12	15.0/1155	16.0/1205	17.0/1260	18.5/1335	9,200 psi	Note 1
Win. 209	IMR 700-X	WAA12SL	15.0/1160	16.0/1210	17.0/1260	18.5/1335	9,700 psi	Note 1
Win. 209	IMR PB	Activ TG-30	19.0/1155	20.0/1190	21.5/1255	23.0/1325	7,800 psi	Note 1
Win. 209	IMR PB	CB 1100-12	19.0/1145	20.5/1205	21.5/1245	23.5/1330	6,400 psi	Note 1
Win. 209	IMR PB	Fed. 12S0	19.0/1145	20.5/1210	21.5/1250	23.5/1335	7,700 psi	Note 1
Win. 209	IMR PB	Rem. TGT12	19.0/1155	20.0/1200	21.0/1245	23.0/1330	7,300 psi	Note 1
Win. 209	IMR PB	WAA12SL	18.0/1140	19.5/1200	20.5/1245	22.5/1330	8,100 psi	Note 1
Win. 209	SR-7625	Activ TG-30	21.5/1145	23.0/1205	24.0/1250	25.5/1320	7,000 psi	Note 1
Win. 209	SR-7625	CB 1100-12	23.0/1145	24.5/1210	25.5/1255	27.0/1325	5,700 psi	Note 1
Win. 209	SR-7625	Fed. 12S0	22.5/1160	23.5/1210	24.5/1255	26.0/1325	6,900 psi	Note 1
Win. 209	SR-7625	Rem. Fig.-8	22.5/1160	23.5/1205	24.5/1245	26.5/1325	6,500 psi	Note 1
Win. 209	SR-7625	WAA12SL	21.0/1160	22.0/1205	23.0/1250	24.5/1320	7,300 psi	Note 1
WINCHESTER: COMPRESSION-FORMED AA TYPE						24 GRAMS LEAD SHOT		
Fed. 209A	IMR 700-X	Activ TG-30	15.0/1145	16.0/1205	17.0/1255	18.5/1320	9,100 psi	Note 1
Fed. 209A	IMR 700-X	CB 1100-12	14.5/1140	15.5/1190	17.0/1260	18.5/1325	8,300 psi	Note 1
Fed. 209A	IMR 700-X	CB 2100-12	15.0/1160	16.0/1210	17.0/1260	18.5/1325	8,600 psi	Note 1
Fed. 209A	IMR 700-X	Fed. 12S0	15.0/1150	16.0/1200	17.0/1250	18.5/1325	9,000 psi	Note 1
Fed. 209A	IMR 700-X	Rem. TGT12	14.5/1140	16.0/1210	17.0/1255	18.5/1320	8,600 psi	Note 1
Fed. 209A	IMR 700-X	WAA12SL	14.5/1145	15.5/1195	17.0/1260	18.5/1320	9,100 psi	Note 1
Fed. 209A	IMR PB	Activ TG-30	18.5/1140	20.0/1205	21.0/1255	23.0/1330	7,700 psi	Note 1
Fed. 209A	IMR PB	CB 1100-12	18.5/1155	20.0/1205	21.0/1245	23.0/1320	6,600 psi	Note 1
Fed. 209A	IMR PB	Fed. 12S0	18.5/1150	19.5/1190	21.0/1250	23.0/1330	7,900 psi	Note 1
Fed. 209A	IMR PB	Rem. Fig.-8	18.0/1145	19.5/1200	21.0/1255	23.0/1325	7,200 psi	Note 1
Fed. 209A	IMR PB	WAA12SL	18.0/1160	19.0/1195	20.5/1255	22.5/1330	7,800 psi	Note 1
Fed. 209A	SR-7625	Activ TG-30	21.5/1145	23.0/1205	24.0/1250	26.0/1325	6,400 psi	Note 1
Fed. 209A	SR-7625	CB 1100-12	22.5/1155	23.5/1195	25.0/1250	27.0/1335	5,500 psi	Note 1
Fed. 209A	SR-7625	Fed. 12S0	22.0/1150	23.0/1195	24.5/1255	26.0/1320	6,400 psi	Note 1
Fed. 209A	SR-7625	Rem. Fig.-8	22.0/1150	23.0/1195	24.5/1255	26.5/1330	6,200 psi	Note 1
Fed. 209A	SR-7625	WAA12SL	21.0/1150	22.5/1200	24.0/1250	26.0/1330	6,400 psi	Note 1
Rem. 209P	IMR 700-X	Activ TG-30	15.5/1145	16.5/1200	18.0/1255	20.0/1330	7,500 psi	Note 1
Rem. 209P	IMR 700-X	CB 1100-12	16.0/1145	17.5/1200	19.0/1265	20.5/1335	6,400 psi	Note 1
Rem. 209P	IMR 700-X	CB 2100-12	15.0/1140	16.5/1200	18.0/1255	20.0/1325	6,300 psi	Note 1
Rem. 209P	IMR 700-X	Fed. 12S0	15.0/1150	16.5/1190	18.0/1250	19.5/1320	7,600 psi	Note 1
Rem. 209P	IMR 700-X	Rem. TGT12	15.5/1150	16.5/1190	18.0/1250	20.5/1325	6,800 psi	Note 1
Rem. 209P	IMR 700-X	WAA12SL	15.0/1140	16.5/1200	18.0/1265	19.5/1330	7,600 psi	Note 1

Load Notes: 1 = Add one 20-gauge, 0.135" card inside bottom of shotcup.

Caution: Follow load recipes exactly; do not substitute components, exceed listed maximums or load less than listed minimums.

Primer	Powder Type	Wad	Powder Charge (grains) / Velocity (fps)				Maximum Pressure	Load Notes
			Minimum			Maximum		
WINCHESTER: COMPRESSION-FORMED AA TYPE (CONT.)						24 GRAMS LEAD SHOT		
Rem. 209P	IMR PB	Activ TG-30	19.5/1150	20.5/1190	22.0/1255	23.5/1320	6,500 psi	Note 1
Rem. 209P	IMR PB	CB 1100-12	19.5/1155	20.5/1195	22.0/1250	24.5/1330	5,700 psi	Note 1
Rem. 209P	IMR PB	Fed. 12S0	19.5/1155	20.5/1200	22.0/1255	24.0/1325	6,800 psi	Note 1
Rem. 209P	IMR PB	Rem. Fig.-8	19.5/1150	20.5/1190	22.0/1255	23.5/1320	6,700 psi	Note 1
Rem. 209P	IMR PB	WAA12SL	18.5/1140	20.0/1195	21.5/1255	23.5/1335	7,200 psi	Note 1
Rem. 209P	SR-7625	Activ TG-30	22.5/1150	23.5/1195	25.0/1250	27.5/1325	5,600 psi	Note 1
Rem. 209P	SR-7625	CB 1100-12	23.5/1145	25.0/1205	26.5/1265	28.0/1330	4,700 psi	Note 1
Rem. 209P	SR-7625	Fed. 12S0	22.5/1140	24.0/1190	25.5/1250	27.0/1320	6,000 psi	Note 1
Rem. 209P	SR-7625	Rem. Fig.-8	23.0/1150	24.0/1195	25.5/1255	27.5/1335	5,700 psi	Note 1
Rem. 209P	SR-7625	WAA12SL	22.5/1150	24.0/1210	25.0/1250	27.0/1320	5,500 psi	Note 1
Win. 209	IMR 700-X	Activ TG-30	15.0/1150	16.0/1205	17.0/1255	18.5/1320	8,900 psi	Note 1
Win. 209	IMR 700-X	CB 1100-12	14.5/1135	15.5/1190	17.0/1260	18.5/1325	8,400 psi	Note 1
Win. 209	IMR 700-X	CB 2100-12	15.0/1140	16.0/1195	17.0/1255	18.5/1320	8,600 psi	Note 1
Win. 209	IMR 700-X	Fed. 12S0	14.5/1145	15.5/1195	17.0/1265	18.5/1325	9,300 psi	Note 1
Win. 209	IMR 700-X	Rem. TGT12	14.5/1140	16.0/1205	17.0/1250	18.5/1320	8,700 psi	Note 1
Win. 209	IMR 700-X	WAA12SL	14.5/1140	15.5/1190	17.0/1260	18.5/1325	9,100 psi	Note 1
Win. 209	IMR PB	Activ TG-30	19.0/1135	20.5/1205	21.5/1250	23.5/1330	7,300 psi	Note 1
Win. 209	IMR PB	CB 1100-12	19.0/1155	20.5/1205	22.0/1260	23.5/1325	6,300 psi	Note 1
Win. 209	IMR PB	Fed. 12S0	19.0/1155	20.0/1195	21.5/1260	23.0/1325	7,500 psi	Note 1
Win. 209	IMR PB	Rem. Fig.-8	19.0/1145	20.5/1200	22.0/1255	23.5/1320	6,800 psi	Note 1
Win. 209	IMR PB	WAA12SL	18.0/1145	19.5/1200	21.0/1260	22.5/1325	7,500 psi	Note 1
Win. 209	SR-7625	Activ TG-30	22.0/1140	23.5/1200	25.0/1255	27.0/1335	6,300 psi	Note 1
Win. 209	SR-7625	CB 1100-12	23.5/1150	24.5/1190	26.0/1250	28.0/1330	5,000 psi	Note 1
Win. 209	SR-7625	Fed. 12S0	22.0/1140	23.5/1195	25.0/1255	27.0/1335	6,200 psi	Note 1
Win. 209	SR-7625	Rem. Fig.-8	22.0/1155	23.0/1190	24.5/1245	26.5/1320	5,900 psi	Note 1
Win. 209	SR-7625	WAA12SL	22.5/1150	23.5/1195	25.0/1255	27.0/1330	6,000 psi	Note 1

Load Notes: 1 = Add one 20-gauge, 0.135″ card inside bottom of shotcup.

Primer	Powder Type	Wad	Powder Charge (grains) / Velocity (fps)				Maximum Pressure	Load Notes
			Minimum			Maximum		
ACTIV: ALL PLASTIC						⁷/₈-OUNCE LEAD SHOT		
CCI 209	American Select	BP DX12		20.5/1200	20.6/1210	20.7/1225	9,700 psi	Note 1
CCI 209	American Select	BP Pisk		20.2/1200	20.3/1210	20.5/1225	9,900 psi	Note 2
CCI 209	R. Scot D	Activ TG-30				22.0/1325	8,900 LUP	Note 7
CCI 209	Solo 1000	Activ TG-30				22.0/1325	9,000 LUP	Notes 6&7
CCI 209M	R. Scot D	Activ TG-30				21.5/1325	10,800 LUP	Note 7
CCI 209SC	Nitro-100	BP SPK				18.5/1325	7,500 psi	Notes 6&7
CCI 209SC	Solo 1000	BP SPK				21.5/1325	9,400 LUP	Notes 6&7

Load Notes: 1 = Disperser-X. 2 = Piston Skeet. 6 = Minimum overall length = 2¹⁰/₃₂″, maximum crimp depth = ²/₃₂″. 7 = Special Instructions: To prevent concave or open crimps in these ⁷/₈-ounce loads: lower press's pre-crimp die to gather more plastic (shortens final overall length); adjust pre-crimp to achieve OAL of 2⁸/₃₂″ (2⁹/₃₂″ for paper); where possible, lower final crimp tamp rod to achieve ³/₃₂″ crimp depth.

Caution: Follow load recipes exactly; do not substitute components, exceed listed maximums or load less than listed minimums.

Primer	Powder Type	Wad	Powder Charge (grains) / Velocity (fps) Minimum			Maximum	Maximum Pressure	Load Notes
ACTIV: ALL PLASTIC (CONT.)						**⁷/₈-OUNCE LEAD SHOT**		
Fed. 209	R. Scot D	Activ TG-30				22.0/1325	8,500 LUP	Note 7
Fed. 209	Solo 1000	Activ TG-30				22.0/1325	8,200 LUP	Note 7
Fed. 209A	Solo 1000	Activ TG-30				21.5/1325	8,200 LUP	Notes 6&7
Fio. 616	R. Scot D	Activ TG-30				21.5/1325	9,200 LUP	Note 7
Fio. 616	Solo 1000	Activ TG-30				21.5/1325	9,800 LUP	Notes 6&7
Rem. 209P	R. Scot D	Activ TG-30				22.0/1325	8,300 LUP	Note 7
Rem. 209P	Solo 1000	Activ TG-30				22.0/1325	8,600 LUP	Notes 6&7
Win. 209	R. Scot D	Activ TG-30				21.5/1325	8,700 LUP	Note 7
Win. 209	Solo 1000	Activ TG-30				21.5/1325	9,700 LUP	Notes 6&7
FEDERAL: GOLD MEDAL PLASTIC						**⁷/₈-OUNCE LEAD SHOT**		
CCI 209	Nitro-100	Fed. 12S0				19.5/1325	6,000 psi	Notes 6&7
CCI 209	R. Scot D	Fed. 12S0				22.5/1325	8,700 LUP	Note 7
CCI 209	Solo 1000	Fed. 12S0				22.0/1325	8,600 LUP	Notes 6&7
CCI 209M	Clays	Activ TG-30	17.2/1200	18.0/1250		19.3/1300	7,900 psi	
CCI 209M	Nitro-100	Fed. 12S0				19.0/1325	7,100 psi	Notes 6&7
CCI 209M	R. Scot D	Fed. 12S0				21.0/1325	8,500 LUP	Note 7
CCI 209M	Solo 1000	Fed. 12S0				20.5/1325	8,300 LUP	Notes 6&7
CCI 209SC	Clays	WAA12L		21.7/1350	22.1/1375	22.5/1400	11,300 psi	
CCI 209SC	Clays	WAA12SL	18.5/1200	19.0/1250		20.5/1300	8,000 psi	
CCI 209SC	International	WAA12L	22.7/1300	24.0/1350	25.0/1400	27.0/1500	10,300 psi	
Fed. 209	Bullseye	Fed. 12S0				17.0/1200	6,300 psi	Note 3
Fed. 209	Bullseye	Rem. PT12				17.5/1200	5,500 psi	Note 4
Fed. 209	Bullseye	WAA12F1				17.0/1200	5,800 psi	Note 4
Fed. 209	R. Scot D	Fed. 12S0				22.5/1325	7,000 LUP	Note 7
Fed. 209	Red Dot	Fed. 12S0				18.0/1200	6,200 psi	
Fed. 209	Red Dot	Rem. PT12				18.0/1200	6,400 psi	Note 4
Fed. 209	Red Dot	WAA12F1				18.0/1200	5,700 psi	
Fed. 209	Solo 1000	Fed. 12S0				22.0/1325	7,600 LUP	Note 7
Fed. 209A	American Select	Claybuster				21.5/1300	6,900 psi	
Fed. 209A	American Select	Fed. 12S0				21.0/1300	7,300 psi	
Fed. 209A	American Select	Pat. Ctrl. Prpl				21.5/1300	6,900 psi	
Fed. 209A	American Select	Rem. TGT12				21.0/1300	7,400 psi	
Fed. 209A	Clays	Fed. 12S0		17.0/1200	18.3/1250	19.5/1300	8,100 psi	
Fed. 209A	Clays	WAA12L	18.5/1200	20.0/1300	21.5/1350	22.5/1400	11,500 psi	
Fed. 209A	Green Dot	Fed. 12S0				22.0/1300	7,500 psi	
Fed. 209A	Green Dot	Pat. Ctrl. Prpl				22.5/1300	7,000 psi	Note 3
Fed. 209A	Green Dot	Rem. TGT12				22.0/1300	7,200 psi	Note 3
Fed. 209A	Green Dot	WAA12SL				21.5/1300	7,600 psi	Note 3
Fed. 209A	International	WAA12L	22.3/1300	23.2/1350	24.5/1400	25.7/1450	10,000 psi	
Fed. 209A	Nitro-100	Fed. 12S0				18.5/1325	7,600 psi	Notes 6&7

Load Notes: 3 = Add one 20-gauge, 0.135″ card inside bottom of shotcup. 4 = Add two 20-gauge, 0.135″ cards inside bottom of shotcup. 6 = Minimum overall length = 2¹⁰/₃₂″, maximum crimp depth = ²/₃₂″. 7 = Special Instructions: To prevent concave or open crimps in these ⁷/₈-ounce loads: lower press's pre-crimp die to gather more plastic (shortens final overall length); adjust pre-crimp to achieve OAL of 2⁸/₃₂″ (2⁹/₃₂″ for paper); where possible, lower final crimp tamp rod to achieve ³/₃₂ crimp depth.

Caution: Follow load recipes exactly; do not substitute components, exceed listed maximums or load less than listed minimums.

Primer	Powder Type	Wad	Powder Charge (grains) / Velocity (fps) Minimum			Maximum	Maximum Pressure	Load Notes
FEDERAL: GOLD MEDAL PLASTIC (CONT.)						**⁷/₈-OUNCE LEAD SHOT**		
Fed. 209A	Red Dot	Fed. 12S0	**17.5/1200**	**19.0/1250**	**19.5/1300**		8,400 psi	
Fed. 209A	Red Dot	Pat. Ctrl. Prpl	**17.0/1200**	**18.5/1250**	**19.5/1300**		7,900 psi	Note 3
Fed. 209A	Red Dot	Rem. TGT12	**17.5/1200**	**18.5/1250**	**19.5/1300**		8,500 psi	Note 3
Fed. 209A	Red Dot	WAA12SL	**17.0/1200**	**18.0/1250**	**19.0/1300**		8,400 psi	Note 3
Fed. 209A	Solo 1000	Fed. 12S0			**21.5/1325**		7,600 LUP	Notes 6&7
Fio. 616	Nitro-100	Fed. 12S0			**19.0/1325**		7,300 psi	Notes 6&7
Fio. 616	R. Scot D	Fed. 12S0			**22.0/1325**		8,500 LUP	Note 7
Fio. 616	Solo 1000	Fed. 12S0			**21.0/1325**		8,700 LUP	Notes 6&7
Rem. 209P	Nitro-100	Fed. 12S0			**19.5/1325**		7,000 psi	Notes 6&7
Rem. 209P	R. Scot D	Fed. 12S0			**22.0/1325**		8,400 LUP	Note 7
Rem. 209P	Solo 1000	Fed. 12S0			**21.5/1325**		7,500 LUP	Notes 6&7
Win. 209	Clays	Rem. TGT12	**17.6/1200**	**18.4/1250**	**19.2/1300**		6,900 psi	
Win. 209	Clays	WAA12L	**18.2/1200**	**20.3/1300**	**22.0/1350**	**23.0/1400**	10,500 psi	
Win. 209	International	WAA12L	**23.5/1300**	**24.3/1350**	**25.5/1400**	**27.0/1450**	9,600 psi	
Win. 209	R. Scot D	Fed. 12S0			**22.0/1325**		8,400 LUP	Note 7
Win. 209	Solo 1000	Fed. 12S0			**21.0/1325**		8,400 LUP	Notes 6&7
FEDERAL: PAPER						**⁷/₈-OUNCE LEAD SHOT**		
CCI 209	Nitro-100	Fed. 12S0			**20.5/1325**		6,300 psi	Notes 6&7
CCI 209	R. Scot D	Fed. 12S0			**24.0/1325**		8,000 LUP	Note 7
CCI 209	Solo 1000	Fed. 12S0			**22.5/1325**		5,800 psi	Notes 6&7
CCI 209M	Nitro-100	Fed. 12S0			**20.0/1325**		6,400 psi	Notes 6&7
CCI 209M	R. Scot D	Fed. 12S0			**23.0/1325**		8,200 LUP	Note 7
CCI 209M	Solo 1000	Fed. 12S0			**21.0/1325**		7,200 psi	Notes 6&7
Fed. 209	Bullseye	Fed. 12S0			**17.5/1200**		4,500 psi	
Fed. 209	Bullseye	Rem. PT12			**17.5/1200**		5,100 psi	Note 3
Fed. 209	Bullseye	WAA12F1			**17.5/1200**		4,600 psi	Note 3
Fed. 209	R. Scot D	Fed. 12S0			**24.0/1325**		7,500 LUP	Note 7
Fed. 209	Red Dot	Fed. 12S0			**17.5/1200**		5,700 psi	
Fed. 209	Red Dot	Rem. PT12			**17.5/1200**		5,000 psi	
Fed. 209	Red Dot	WAA12F1			**17.5/1200**		4,800 psi	
Fed. 209	Solo 1000	Fed. 12S0			**22.5/1325**		8,600 psi	Note 7
Fed. 209A	Nitro-100	Fed. 12S0			**19.5/1325**		6,800 psi	Notes 6&7
Fed. 209A	Solo 1000	Fed. 12S0			**22.0/1325**		6,700 psi	Notes 6&7
Fio. 616	Nitro-100	Fed. 12S0			**20.0/1325**		6,400 psi	Notes 6&7
Fio. 616	R. Scot D	Fed. 12S0			**23.0/1325**		8,500 LUP	Note 7
Fio. 616	Solo 1000	Fed. 12S0			**21.0/1325**		7,400 psi	Notes 6&7
Rem. 209P	Nitro-100	Fed. 12S0			**20.5/1325**		6,600 psi	Notes 6&7
Rem. 209P	R. Scot D	Fed. 12S0			**23.5/1325**		8,500 LUP	Note 7
Rem. 209P	Solo 1000	Fed. 12S0			**22.5/1325**		6,900 psi	Notes 6&7
Win. 209	Nitro-100	Fed. 12S0			**19.5/1325**		6,400 psi	Notes 6&7

Load Notes: 3 = Add one 20-gauge, 0.135″ card inside bottom of shotcup. 6 = Minimum overall length = 2¹⁰/₃₂″, maximum crimp depth = ²/₃₂″. 7 = Special Instructions: To prevent concave or open crimps in these ⁷/₈-ounce loads: lower press's pre-crimp die to gather more plastic (shortens final overall length); adjust pre-crimp to achieve OAL of 2⁸/₃₂″ (2⁹/₃₂″ for paper); where possible, lower final crimp tamp rod to achieve ³/₃₂″ crimp depth.

Caution: Follow load recipes exactly; do not substitute components, exceed listed maximums or load less than listed minimums.

Primer	Powder Type	Wad	Powder Charge (grains) / Velocity (fps) Minimum			Maximum	Maximum Pressure	Load Notes
FEDERAL: PAPER (CONT.)						**⁷/₈-OUNCE LEAD SHOT**		
Win. 209	R. Scot D	Fed. 12S0				23.0/1325	8,600 LUP	Note 7
Win. 209	Solo 1000	Fed. 12S0				21.0/1325	7,200 psi	Notes 6&7
FIOCCHI: PURPLE TARGET (HIGH BASE WAD)						**⁷/₈-OUNCE LEAD SHOT**		
CCI 209	R. Scot D	Fiocchi TL1				22.5/1325	8,200 LUP	Note 7
CCI 209	Solo 1000	Fiocchi TL1				22.0/1325	8,600 LUP	Notes 5&7
CCI 209M	Clays	Pat. Ctrl. Prpl		17.3/1200	18.1/1250	19.2/1300	7,700 psi	
CCI 209M	R. Scot D	Fiocchi TL1				21.5/1325	9,500 LUP	Note 7
CCI 209M	Solo 1000	Fiocchi TL1				21.0/1325	9,600 LUP	Notes 5&7
CCI 209SC	Clays	WAA12SL	17.7/1200	18.5/1250	19.5/1300	21.0/1350	9,900 psi	
CCI 209SC	International	WAA12SL		21.0/1250	22.0/1300	22.5/1350	8,500 psi	
Fed. 209	R. Scot D	Fiocchi TL1				22.5/1325	9,600 LUP	Note 7
Fed. 209	Solo 1000	Fiocchi TL1				22.0/1325	8,800 LUP	Note 7
Fed. 209A	Clays	Rem. TGT12		16.5/1200	17.7/1250	18.7/1300	7,400 psi	
Fed. 209A	Solo 1000	Fiocchi TL1				21.5/1325	8,800 LUP	Notes 5&7
Fio. 616	American Select	BP DX12		20.0/1150	20.2/1170	20.5/1200	9,300 psi	Note 1
Fio. 616	American Select	Fisk		19.8/1150	20.0/1175	20.2/1200	9,400 psi	Note 2
Fio. 616	Clays	Fed. 12S0		16.6/1200	17.8/1250	19.2/1300	8,500 psi	
Fio. 616	Green Dot	Pat. Ctrl. Prpl				22.5/1300	7,700 psi	
Fio. 616	Green Dot	Rein. TGT12				22.0/1300	7,600 psi	
Fio. 616	Green Dot	WAA12SL				22.0/1300	7,900 psi	
Fio. 616	IMR 700-X	BP DX12		15.2/1200	16.2/1225	17.2/1250	7,700 psi	Note 1
Fio. 616	R. Scot D	Fiocchi TL1				21.5/1325	10,300 LUP	Note 7
Fio. 616	Red Dot	BP DX12		17.5/1220	17.7/1245	18.2/1290	8,300 psi	Note 1
Fio. 616	Red Dot	Fed. 12S0		17.5/1200	19.0/1250	19.5/1300	8,800 psi	
Fio. 616	Red Dot	Pat. Ctrl. Prpl		17.5/1200	19.0/1250	20.0/1300	8,600 psi	Note 3
Fio. 616	Red Dot	Rem. TGT12		17.0/1200	18.5/1250	20.0/1300	7,900 psi	Note 3
Fio. 616	Red Dot	WAA12SL		17.0/1200	18.5/1250	20.0/1300	8,100 psi	Note 3
Fio. 616	Solo 1000	BP DX12		18.8/1200	19.2/1230	19.7/1260	8,600 psi	Note 1
Fio. 616	Solo 1000	Fiocchi TL1				21.0/1325	9,200 LUP	Notes 5&7
Rem. 209P	R. Scot D	Fiocchi TL1				22.0/1325	8,800 LUP	Note 7
Rem. 209P	Solo 1000	Fiocchi TL1				22.0/1325	8,000 LUP	Notes 5&7
Win. 209	Clays	WAA12SL		16.8/1200	18.0/1250	19.0/1300	8,000 psi	
Win. 209	R. Scot D	Fiocchi TL1				21.5/1325	10,000 LUP	Note 7
Win. 209	Solo 1000	Fiocchi TL1				21.0/1325	9,500 LUP	Notes 5&7
REMINGTON: PREMIER & NITRO 27 & STS						**⁷/₈-OUNCE LEAD SHOT**		
CCI 209	Nitro-100	Rem. TGT12				18.5/1325	8,000 psi	Notes 5&7
CCI 209	R. Scot D	Rem. TGT12				21.5/1325	8,600 LUP	Note 7
CCI 209	Solo 1000	Rem. TGT12				21.0/1325	8,600 LUP	Notes 5&7
CCI 209	WSL	WAA12SL	20.0/1325	20.7/1360		21.5/1400	9,700 psi	
CCI 209	WST	WAA12SL	21.5/1325	22.2/1360		23.0/1400	9,000 psi	

Load Notes: 1 = Disperser-X. 2 = Piston Skeet. 3 = Add one 20-gauge, 0.135" card inside bottom of shotcup. 5 = Minimum overall length = 2⁹/₃₂", maximum crimp depth = ²/₃₂". 7 = Special Instructions: To prevent concave or open crimps in these ⁷/₈-ounce loads: lower press's pre-crimp die to gather more plastic (shortens final overall length); adjust pre-crimp to achieve OAL of 2⁸/₃₂" (2⁹/₃₂" for paper); where possible, lower final crimp tamp rod to achieve ³/₃₂" crimp depth.

Primer	Powder Type	Wad	Powder Charge (grains) / Velocity (fps) Minimum			Maximum	Maximum Pressure	Load Notes
REMINGTON: PREMIER & NITRO 27 & STS (CONT.)						7/8-OUNCE LEAD SHOT		
CCI 209M	Nitro-100	Rem. TGT12				18.0/1325	8,000 psi	Notes 5&7
CCI 209M	R. Scot D	Rem. TGT12				20.5/1325	9,000 LUP	Note 7
CCI 209M	Solo 1000	Rem. TGT12				20.0/1325	9,400 LUP	Notes 5&7
CCI 209SC	Clays	Rem. TGT12	18.0/1200	18.8/1250	19.5/1300	20.5/1350	9,900 psi	
CCI 209SC	International	Rem. TGT12	20.0/1200	21.0/1300	22.2/1350	23.2/1400	9,200 psi	
Fed. 209	Clays	Activ TG-30		16.5/1200	17.5/1250	19.0/1300	9,200 psi	
Fed. 209	R. Scot D	Rem. TGT12				21.5/1325	8,900 LUP	Note 7
Fed. 209	Solo 1000	Rem. TGT12				21.0/1325	8,500 LUP	Note 7
Fed. 209A	Clays	Activ TG-30		16.2/1200	17.5/1250	18.5/1300	10,300 psi	
Fed. 209A	Nitro-100	Rem. TGT12				15.0/1325	9,000 psi	Notes 5&7
Fed. 209A	Solo 1000	Rem. TGT12				20.5/1325	8,500 LUP	Notes 5&7
Fed. 209A	WSL	WAA12SL		20.0/1325	20.7/1360	21.5/1400	9,400 psi	
Fed. 209A	WST	WAA12SL		21.0/1325	21.9/1360	23.0/1400	9,700 psi	
Fio. 616	Nitro-100	Rem. TGT12				18.0/1325	8,100 psi	Notes 5&7
Fio. 616	R. Scot D	Rem. TGT12				21.0/1325	9,200 LUP	Note 7
Fio. 616	Solo 1000	Rem. TGT12				20.5/1325	9,700 LUP	Notes 5&7
Rem. 209P	American Select	Claybuster				20.5/1300	6,900 psi	
Rem. 209P	American Select	BP DX12		20.0/1200	20.2/1210	20.5/1220	10,500 psi	Note 1
Rem. 209P	American Select	Fed. 12S0				20.5/1300	7,700 psi	
Rem. 209P	American Select	Fisk		19.6/1200	20.2/1220	20.7/1250	11,000 psi	Note 2
Rem. 209P	American Select	Rem. TGT12				20.5/1300	7,000 psi	
Rem. 209P	American Select	WAA12SL				20.5/1300	7,900 psi	
Rem. 209P	Clays	Fed. 12S0		16.0/1200	17.2/1250	18.8/1300	9,100 psi	
Rem. 209P	Clays	Rem. TGT12		16.4/1200	17.5/1250	18.9/1300	7,400 psi	
Rem. 209P	Clays	WAA12SL		18.0/1250	18.7/1270	19.5/1300	10,200 psi	
Rem. 209P	Green Dot	Fed. 12S0				22.0/1300	8,000 psi	
Rem. 209P	Green Dot	Rem. TGT12				22.0/1300	7,100 psi	
Rem. 209P	Green Dot	WAA12SL				21.5/1300	7,900 psi	
Rem. 209P	International	WAA12SL	20.0/1250	21.5/1300	23.5/1350	24.5/1400	10,200 psi	
Rem. 209P	Nitro-100	Rem. TGT12				18.0/1325	8,100 psi	Notes 5&7
Rem. 209P	R. Scot D	Rem. TGT12				21.5/1325	9,100 LUP	Note 7
Rem. 209P	Red Dot	Fed. 12S0		17.0/1200	18.0/1250	20.0/1300	8,100 psi	
Rem. 209P	Red Dot	Pat. Ctrl. Prpl		17.5*/1200	18.5/1250	20.0/1300	7,500 psi	*Note 3
Rem. 209P	Red Dot	Rem. TGT12		17.0*/1200	18.5*/1250	20.5/1300	8,200 psi	*Note 3
Rem. 209P	Red Dot	WAA12SL		17.0*/1200	18.5*/1250	20.5/1300	8,000 psi	*Note 3
Rem. 209P	Solo 1000	Rem. TGT12				25.5/1325	9,200 LUP	Notes 5&7
Win. 209	Clays	WAA12SL		15.9/1200	17.1/1250	18.2/1300	10,000 psi	
Win. 209	Nitro-100	Rem. TGT12				18.0/1325	7,600 psi	Notes 5&7
Win. 209	R. Scot D	Rem. TGT12				21.0/1325	9,700 LUP	Note 7
Win. 209	Solo 1000	Rem. TGT12				20.5/1325	10,000 LUP	Notes 5&7
Win. 209	WSL	WAA12SL		20.0/1325	20.7/1360	21.5/1400	9,300 psi	

Load Notes: 1 = Disperser-X. 2 = Piston Skeet. 3 = Add one 20-gauge, 0.135" card inside bottom of shotcup. 5 = Minimum overall length = 2⁹/₃₂", maximum crimp depth = ²/₃₂". 7 = Special Instructions: To prevent concave or open crimps in these 7/8-ounce loads: lower press's pre-crimp die to gather more plastic (shortens final overall length); adjust pre-crimp to achieve OAL of 2⁸/₃₂" (2⁹/₃₂" for paper); where possible, lower final crimp tamp rod to achieve ³/₃₂" crimp depth.

Caution: Follow load recipes exactly; do not substitute components, exceed listed maximums or load less than listed minimums.

Primer	Powder Type	Wad	Powder Charge (grains) / Velocity (fps) Minimum		Maximum	Maximum Pressure	Load Notes
REMINGTON: PREMIER & NITRO 27 & STS (CONT.)					**⁷/₈-OUNCE LEAD SHOT**		
Win. 209	WST	WAA12SL	21.0/1325	21.9/1360	23.0/1400	10,300 psi	
Win. AATP	Clays	WAA12SL	16.5/1200	17.8/1250	18.8/1300	9,500 psi	
VICTORY: PLASTIC					**⁷/₈-OUNCE LEAD SHOT**		
CCI 209M	Clays	Pat. Ctrl. Prpl	17.3/1200	18.1/1250	19.2/1300	7,700 psi	
CCI 209SC	Clays	WAA12SL	17.7/1200	18.5/1250	19.5/1300	21.0/1350	9,900 psi	
CCI 209SC	International	WAA12SL	21.0/1250	22.0/1300	22.5/1350	8,500 psi	
Fed. 209A	Clays	Rem. TGT12	16.5/1200	17.7/1250	18.7/1300	7,400 psi	
Fio. 616	Clays	Fed. 12S0	16.6/1200	17.8/1250	19.2/1300	8,500 psi	
Win. 209	Clays	WAA12SL	16.8/1200	18.0/1250	19.0/1300	8,000 psi	
WINCHESTER: COMPRESSION-FORMED AA TYPE					**⁷/₈-OUNCE LEAD SHOT**		
CCI 209	American Select	BP DX12	19.5/1200	19.7/1210	20.0/1230	9,900 psi	Note 1
CCI 209	American Select	BP Pisk	19.3/1200	19.5/1210	19.7/1225	9,800 psi	Note 2
CCI 209	Nitro-100	WAA12SL			18.5/1325	7,500 psi	Notes 5&7
CCI 209	R. Scot D	WAA12SL			21.5/1325	8,300 LUP	Note 7
CCI 209	Solo 1000	WAA12SL			20.5/1325	7,300 psi	Notes 5&7
CCI 209	WSL	WAA12SL			22.0/1400	10,000 psi	
CCI 209	WST	WAA12SL			23.5/1355	7,200 psi	
CCI 209M	Clays	Rem. TGT12	16.5/1200	17.5/1250	18.5/1300	8,900 psi	
CCI 209M	Nitro-100	WAA12SL			18.5/1325	7,300 psi	Notes 5&7
CCI 209M	R. Scot D	WAA12SL			20.5/1325	9,400 LUP	Note 7
CCI 209M	Solo 1000	WAA12SL			19.5/1325	8,400 psi	Notes 5&7
CCI 209SC	Clays	Rem. TGT12	16.3/1200	17.6/1250	18.7/1300	7,800 psi	
Fed. 209	American Select	Claybuster			21.0/1300	7,200 psi	
Fed. 209	American Select	Fed. 12S0			21.0/1300	8,300 psi	
Fed. 209	American Select	Pat. Ctrl. Prpl			20.5/1300	7,200 psi	
Fed. 209	American Select	Rem. TGT12			20.5/1300	7,600 psi	
Fed. 209	American Select	WAA12SL			20.5/1300	8,400 psi	
Fed. 209	American Select	WAAL Gray	18.5/1250	19.5/1300	22.0/1400	10,200 psi	
Fed. 209	Bullseye	Fed. 12S0			16.5/1200	7,400 psi	
Fed. 209	Bullseye	Rem. PT12			16.5/1200	7,100 psi	Note 3
Fed. 209	Bullseye	WAA12F1			16.5/1200	6,700 psi	Note 3
Fed. 209	Clays	Activ TG-30	17.6/1200	18.7/1250	20.5/1300	7,900 LUP	
Fed. 209	Green Dot	Fed. 12S0			21.0/1300	8,900 psi	
Fed. 209	Green Dot	Pat. Ctrl. Prpl			21.5/1300	7,900 psi	Note 3
Fed. 209	Green Dot	Rem. TGT12			21.0/1300	8,400 psi	
Fed. 209	Green Dot	WAA12SL			20.5/1300	8,800 psi	
Fed. 209	Green Dot	WAAL Gray			20.0/1300	8,300 psi	
Fed. 209	R. Scot D	WAA12SL			21.5/1325	8,600 LUP	Note 7
Fed. 209	Red Dot	Fed. 12S0			16.0/1200	8,000 psi	Note 3
Fed. 209	Red Dot	Rem. PT12			16.5/1200	7,300 psi	Note 3

Load Notes: 1 = Disperser-X. 2 = Piston Skeet. 3 = Add one 20-gauge, 0.135" card inside bottom of shotcup. 5 = Minimum overall length = 2⁹/₃₂", maximum crimp depth = ²/₃₂". 7 = Special Instructions: To prevent concave or open crimps in these ⁷/₈-ounce loads: lower press's pre-crimp die to gather more plastic (shortens final overall length); adjust pre-crimp to achieve OAL of 2⁸/₃₂" (2⁹/₃₂" for paper); where possible, lower final crimp tamp rod to achieve ³/₃₂" crimp depth.

152   Caution: Follow load recipes exactly; do not substitute components, exceed listed maximums or load less than listed minimums.

Primer	Powder Type	Wad	Powder Charge (grains) / Velocity (fps) Minimum		Maximum	Maximum Pressure	Load Notes
WINCHESTER: COMPRESSION-FORMED AA TYPE (CONT.)					**⁷/₈-OUNCE LEAD SHOT**		
Fed. 209	Red Dot	WAA12F1			16.5/1200	7,300 psi	
Fed. 209	Solo 1000	WAA12SL			21.5/1325	8,000 psi	Note 7
Fed. 209A	# 2 Improved	WAA12SL			20.5/1325	8,700 psi	Notes 5&7
Fed. 209A	Clays	Activ TG-30	16.0/1200	17.5/1250	18.5/1300	10,600 psi	
Fed. 209A	Clays	WAA12L	18.0/1250	18.5/1270	19.1/1300	9,300 psi	
Fed. 209A	Clays	WAA12SL	18.0/1250	19.0/1300	20.5/1350	10,800 psi	
Fed. 209A	International	WAA12SL	20.0/1250	21.0/1300	22.0/1350	9,500 psi	
Fed. 209A	Nitro-100	WAA12SL			18.0/1325	8,000 psi	Notes 5&7
Fed. 209A	Solo 1000	WAA12SL			19.5/1325	8,600 psi	Notes 5&7
Fed. 209A	WST	WAA12SL			23.5/1355	7,400 psi	
Fio. 615	WST	BP DX12			22.2/1240	9,600 LUP	Note 1
Fio. 616	R. Scot D	WAA12SL			20.5/1325	9,900 LUP	Note 7
Fio. 616	Green Dot	BP DX12			21.0/1250	9,200 LUP	Note 1
Fio. 616	Nitro-100	WAA12SL			18.5/1325	8,100 psi	Notes 5&7
Fio. 616	Solo 1000	WAA12SL			20.0/1325	8,400 psi	Notes 5&7
Fio. 616	WSL	BP DX12			18.5/1225	7,900 LUP	Note 1
Rem. 209P	Clays	Rem. TGT12	18.2/1200	18.5/1220	18.9/1250	6,800 LUP	
Rem. 209P	Nitro-100	WAA12SL			18.5/1325	7,900 psi	Notes 5&7
Rem. 209P	R. Scot D	WAA12SL			22.0/1325	9,300 LUP	Note 7
Rem. 209P	Solo 1000	WAA12SL			20.5/1325	8,800 psi	Notes 5&7
Win. 209	Clays	BP DX12	17.0/1200	17.7/1245	18.5/1290	7,700 LUP	Note 1
Win. 209	Clays	Fed. 12S0	17.1/1200	18.0/1250	20.0/1300	10,700 psi	
Win. 209	Clays	WAA12L	18.3/1250	19.2/1300	20.5/1350	10,000 psi	
Win. 209	Clays	WAA12SL	16.9/1200	18.1/1250	19.7/1300	8,400 LUP	
Win. 209	Green Dot	BP DX12	19.5/1220	20.0/1260	20.5/1300	8,800 psi	Note 1
Win. 209	IMR 700-X	BP DX12	18.5/1225	18.7/1230	19.0/1235	9,800 LUP	Note 1
Win. 209	International	WAA12SL	20.5/1250	21.0/1300	21.5/1350	22.5/1400	10,200 psi	
Win. 209	Nitro-100	BP DX12	18.5/1240	18.7/1265	19.0/1290	8,600 psi	Note 1
Win. 209	Nitro-100	WAA12SL			18.0/1325	8,000 psi	Notes 5&7
Win. 209	R. Scot D	WAA12SL			20.5/1325	9,900 LUP	Note 7
Win. 209	Red Dot	BP DX12	17.0/1220	17.7/1260	18.5/1280	9,700 psi	Note 1
Win. 209	Red Dot	Fed. 12S0	16.0*/1200	17.5/1250	19.0/1300	9,400 psi	*Note 3
Win. 209	Red Dot	Pat. Ctrl. Prpl	17.0/1200	18.0/1250	19.5/1300	9,000 psi	Note 3
Win. 209	Red Dot	Rem. TGT12	16.5/1200	18.0/1250	19.0/1300	9,300 psi	Note 3
Win. 209	Red Dot	WAA12SL	16.5*/1200	18.0*/1250	19.0/1300	10,300 psi	*Note 3
Win. 209	Red Dot	WAAL Gray	16.5/1200	17.5/1250	18.5/1300	9,300 psi	
Win. 209	Solo 1000	BP DX12	19.5/1250	19.7/1275	20.0/1300	9,000 psi	Note 1
Win. 209	Solo 1000	WAA12SL			20.0/1325	8,200 psi	Notes 5&7
Win. 209	W 452AA	WAA12SL			19.0*/1210	7,100 LUP	*Note 8
Win. 209	WAAP	WAA12SL	21.0*/1325	21.9/1360	23.0/1400	8,600 psi	*Note 9
Win. 209	WSL	WAA12SL			22.0/1400	9,500 psi	
Win. 209	WST	WAA12SL	22.0*/1325	22.7/1360	23.5/1400	8,200 psi	*Note 9
Win. AATP	Clays	WAA12SL	16.5/1200	17.8/1250	19.0/1300	9,600 psi	

Load Notes: 1 = Disperser-X. 3 = Add one 20-gauge, 0.135″ card inside bottom of shotcup. 5 = Minimum overall length = 2⁹/₃₂″, maximum crimp depth = ²/₃₂″. 7 = Special Instructions: To prevent concave or open crimps in these ⁷/₈-ounce loads: lower press's pre-crimp die to gather more plastic (shortens final overall length); adjust pre-crimp to achieve OAL of 2⁸/₃₂″ (2⁹/₃₂″ for paper); where possible, lower final crimp tamp rod to achieve ³/₃₂″ crimp depth. 8 = This load requires zero wad pressure. 9 = This load duplicates Winchester's AA International loading.

Caution: Follow load recipes exactly; do not substitute components, exceed listed maximums or load less than listed minimums.

12-GAUGE 2³/₄"   28 GRAMS LEAD SHOT

Primer	Powder Type	Wad	Powder Charge (grains) / Velocity (fps) Minimum	Maximum	Maximum Pressure	Load Notes
FEDERAL: GOLD MEDAL				28 GRAMS LEAD SHOT		
Fed. 209A	Green Dot	Fed. 12S0		24.5/1345	9,100 psi	
Fed. 209A	Green Dot	Pat. Ctrl. Prpl		25.0/1345	8,200 psi	
Fed. 209A	Green Dot	Rem. Fig.-8		25.0/1345	8,400 psi	
Fed. 209A	Green Dot	WAA12SL		24.5/1345	8,400 psi	
Fed. 209A	Red Dot	Fed. 12S0		23.0/1345	9,900 psi	
Fed. 209A	Red Dot	Pat. Ctrl. Prpl		23.0/1345	8,800 psi	
Fed. 209A	Red Dot	Rem. Fig.-8		22.5/1345	9,500 psi	
Fed. 209A	Red Dot	WAA12SL		22.5/1345	9,600 psi	
Fed. 209A	Unique	Fed. 12S0		27.5/1345	7,400 psi	
FIOCCHI: PURPLE TARGET (HIGH BASE WAD)				28 GRAMS LEAD SHOT		
Fio. 616	Green Dot	Fed. 12S3		24.0/1345	8,800 psi	
Fio. 616	Green Dot	Pat. Ctrl. Prpl		24.0/1345	8,800 psi	
Fio. 616	Green Dot	Rem. Fig.-8		24.0/1345	8,800 psi	
Fio. 616	Green Dot	WAA12SL		24.0/1345	8,800 psi	
Fio. 616	Red Dot	Fed. 12S3		22.0/1345	9,600 psi	
Fio. 616	Red Dot	Pat. Ctrl. Prpl		22.5/1345	9,500 psi	
Fio. 616	Red Dot	Rem. Fig.-8		21.5/1345	9,700 psi	
Fio. 616	Red Dot	WAA12SL		21.5/1345	10,400 psi	
Fio. 616	Unique	Rem. Fig.-8		26.5/1345	7,500 psi	
Fio. 616	Unique	WAA12SL		27.0/1345	7,700 psi	
REMINGTON: PREMIER & NITRO 27 & STS				28 GRAMS LEAD SHOT		
Rem. 209P	Green Dot	Fed. 12S3		23.0/1345	10,300 psi	
Rem. 209P	Green Dot	Pat. Ctrl. Prpl		24.0/1345	9,900 psi	
Rem. 209P	Green Dot	Rem. Fig.-8		23.0/1345	9,700 psi	
Rem. 209P	Green Dot	WAA12SL		23.0/1345	10,100 psi	
Rem. 209P	Red Dot	Pat. Ctrl. Prpl		21.5/1345	10,600 psi	
Rem. 209P	Red Dot	Rem. Fig.-8		21.5/1345	10,600 psi	
Rem. 209P	Unique	Pat. Ctrl. Prpl		27.0/1345	7,800 psi	
Rem. 209P	Unique	Rem. Fig.-8		26.0/1345	8,300 psi	
Rem. 209P	Unique	WAA12SL		27.0/1345	8,500 psi	
WINCHESTER: COMPRESSION-FORMED AA TYPE				28 GRAMS LEAD SHOT		
Win. 209	Green Dot	Pat. Ctrl. Prpl		23.0/1345	9,500 psi	
Win. 209	Green Dot	Rem. Fig.-8		22.5/1345	10,600 psi	
Win. 209	Unique	Fed. 12S3		25.5/1345	9,500 psi	
Win. 209	Unique	Pat. Ctrl. Prpl		26.5/1345	8,700 psi	
Win. 209	Unique	Rem. Fig.-8		25.0/1345	9,600 psi	
Win. 209	Unique	WAA12SL		25.5/1345	10,200 psi	

154   **Caution:** Follow load recipes exactly; do not substitute components, exceed listed maximums or load less than listed minimums.

Primer	Powder Type	Wad	Powder Charge (grains) / Velocity (fps) Minimum			Maximum	Maximum Pressure	Load Notes
ACTIV: ALL PLASTIC						1-OUNCE LEAD SHOT		
CCI 209	American Select	CS12S	20.0/1220	20.1/1230	20.3/1240	20.5/1255	10,800 psi	
CCI 209	American Select	BP DX12	20.0/1200	20.5/1240	21.0/1280	21.5/1310	11,200 psi	Note 1
CCI 209	American Select	BP Pisk	19.8/1200	20.3/1240	20.5/1255	20.7/1270	10,500 psi	Note 2
CCI 209	American Select	BP HCD24	20.6/1230	20.8/1245	20.9/1255	21.0/1265	9,400 psi	Note 3
CCI 209	American Select	BP SRC	20.5/1230	21.0/1300	21.2/1320	21.5/1345	11,200 psi	Note 4
CCI 209	American Select	BP Z21	20.6/1230	20.8/1245	20.9/1255	21.0/1265	9,600 psi	Note 5
CCI 209	Nitro-100	Activ TG-30	17.0/1200	17.8/1230	18.7/1260	19.5/1290	8,000 psi	Note 6
CCI 209	Nitro-100	Fed. 12S0	17.5/1200	18.2/1230	18.8/1260	19.5/1290	8,100 psi	Note 6
CCI 209	R. Scot D	Activ T-28	20.5/1200	21.3/1230	22.2/1260	23.0/1290	9,100 psi	
CCI 209	R. Scot D	Activ TG-30	20.0/1200	20.7/1230	21.3/1260	22.0/1290	10,800 psi	
CCI 209	R. Scot D	Fed. 12S0	20.5/1200	21.2/1230	21.8/1260	22.5/1290	9,700 psi	
CCI 209	Red Diamond	Activ TG-30	17.0/1180	17.6/1215	18.3/1250	19.0/1290	9,400 psi	Note 7
CCI 209	Red Diamond	Fed. 12S0	17.0/1180	17.8/1215	18.6/1250	19.5/1290	9,700 psi	Note 7
CCI 209	Red Diamond	L-29	17.5/1180	18.3/1215	19.1/1250	20.0/1290	8,300 psi	Note 7
CCI 209	Solo 1000	Activ T-28	20.0/1200	20.8/1230	21.7/1260	22.5/1290	8,100 LUP	Note 6
CCI 209	Solo 1000	Activ TG-30	19.5/1200	20.2/1230	20.8/1260	21.5/1290	10,000 LUP	Note 6
CCI 209	Solo 1000	Fed. 12S0	20.0/1200	20.7/1230	21.3/1260	22.0/1290	9,000 LUP	Note 6
CCI 209M	International	Activ TG-30	19.0/1180	19.6/1210	20.0/1235	21.5/1290	9,600 psi	
CCI 209M	R. Scot D	Activ T-28	20.0/1200	20.8/1230	21.7/1260	22.5/1290	9,800 psi	
CCI 209M	R. Scot D	Activ TG-30	19.5/1200	20.3/1230	21.2/1260	22.0/1290	10,600 psi	
CCI 209M	R. Scot D	Fed. 12S0	20.0/1200	20.7/1230	21.3/1260	22.0/1290	10,800 psi	
CCI 209M	Red Diamond	Activ TG-30	17.0/1180	17.6/1215	18.3/1250	19.0/1290	9,400 psi	Note 7
CCI 209M	Red Diamond	Fed. 12S0	17.0/1180	17.8/1215	18.6/1250	19.5/1290	8,300 psi	Note 7
CCI 209M	Red Diamond	L-29	17.5/1180	18.1/1215	18.8/1250	19.5/1290	8,400 psi	Note 7
CCI 209M	Solo 1000	Activ T-28	19.5/1200	20.3/1230	21.2/1260	22.0/1290		
CCI 209M	Solo 1000	Activ TG-30	19.0/1200	19.8/1230	20.7/1260	21.5/1290		
CCI 209M	Solo 1000	Fed. 12S0	19.5/1200	20.2/1230	20.8/1260	21.5/1290		
CCI 209SC	International	Activ TG-30	20.0/1180	20.4/1210	20.7/1235	22.0/1290	7,700 psi	
CCI 209SC	Nitro-100	Activ TG-30	17.0/1200	17.7/1230	18.3/1260	19.0/1290	9,500 psi	Note 6
CCI 209SC	Nitro-100	BP CS12	17.0/1200	17.7/1230	18.3/1260	19.0/1290	8,800 psi	Note 6
CCI 209SC	Nitro-100	Fed. 12S0	17.0/1200	17.7/1230	18.3/1260	19.0/1290	9,400 psi	Note 6
Fed. 209	R. Scot D	Activ T-28	20.5/1200	21.3/1230	22.2/1260	23.0/1290	8,900 psi	
Fed. 209	R. Scot D	Fed. 12S0	20.5/1200	21.3/1230	22.2/1260	23.0/1290	10,000 psi	
Fed. 209	Solo 1000	Activ T-28	20.0/1200	20.8/1230	21.7/1260	22.5/1290	8,300 LUP	Note 6
Fed. 209	Solo 1000	Fed. 12S0	20.0/1200	20.8/1230	21.7/1260	22.5/1290		
Fed. 209A	Clays	Fed. 12S0	18.0/1180	18.2/1200	18.5/1220	18.7/1235	9,200 psi	
Fed. 209A	International	Fed. 12S0	19.5/1180	20.3/1210	21.0/1235	22.0/1290	9,900 psi	
Fed. 209A	Nitro-100	Fed. 12S0	17.0/1200	17.7/1230	18.3/1260	19.0/1290	9,100 psi	Note 6
Fed. 209A	Red Diamond	Activ TG-30	17.0/1180	17.6/1215	18.3/1250	19.0/1290	10,000 psi	Note 7
Fed. 209A	Red Diamond	Fed. 12S0	17.0/1180	17.8/1215	18.6/1250	19.5/1290	8,700 psi	Note 7
Fed. 209A	Red Diamond	L-29	17.5/1180	18.1/1215	18.8/1250	19.5/1290	8,500 psi	Note 7

Load Notes: 1 = Disperser-X. 2 = Piston Skeet. 3 = Hex Cushion DR-24. 4 = Short Range Crusher. 5 = Trap Commander. 6 = Minimum overall length = 2¹⁰/₃₂″, maximum crimp depth = ²/₃₂″. 7 = Use 50-60 pounds wad pressure to ensure wad is firmly seated against powder.

Caution: Follow load recipes exactly; do not substitute components, exceed listed maximums or load less than listed minimums.

Primer	Powder Type	Wad	Powder Charge (grains) / Velocity (fps) Minimum			Maximum	Maximum Pressure	Load Notes
ACTIV: ALL PLASTIC (CONT.)						1-OUNCE LEAD SHOT		
Fio. 616	Clays	Rem. TGT12	18.0/1180	18.8/1210	19.5/1235	20.5/1290	9,100 psi	
Fio. 616	International	Rem. TGT12	19.0/1180	20.1/1210	21.0/1235	22.5/1290	8,000 psi	
Fio. 616	Nitro-100	Fed. 12S0	17.0/1200	17.7/1230	18.3/1260	19.0/1290	8,500 psi	Note 6
Fio. 616	R. Scot D	Activ T-28	20.5/1200	21.3/1230	22.2/1260	23.0/1290	9,000 psi	
Fio. 616	R. Scot D	Fed. 12S0	20.5/1200	21.2/1230	21.8/1260	22.5/1290	10,500 psi	
Fio. 616	Red Diamond	Activ TG-30	17.0/1180	17.6/1215	18.3/1250	19.0/1290	9,500 psi	Note 7
Fio. 616	Red Diamond	Fed. 12S0	17.0/1180	17.8/1215	18.6/1250	19.5/1290	8,500 psi	Note 7
Fio. 616	Red Diamond	L-29	17.5/1180	18.1/1215	18.8/1250	19.5/1290	8,500 psi	Note 7
Fio. 616	Solo 1000	Activ T-28	20.0/1200	20.8/1230	21.7/1260	22.5/1290	7,700 LUP	Note 6
Fio. 616	Solo 1000	Fed. 12S0	20.0/1200	20.7/1230	21.3/1260	22.0/1290	9,500 LUP	Note 6
Rem. 209	Red Diamond	Activ TG-30	17.0/1180	17.6/1215	18.3/1250	19.0/1290	9,000 psi	Note 7
Rem. 209	Red Diamond	Fed. 12S0	17.0/1180	17.8/1215	18.6/1250	19.5/1290	7,700 psi	Note 7
Rem. 209	Red Diamond	L-29	17.5/1180	18.3/1215	19.1/1250	20.0/1290	8,500 psi	Note 7
Win. 209	#2 Improved	Activ T-28	19.5/1200	20.2/1230	20.8/1260	21.5/1290	10,000 psi	Note 6
Win. 209	Clays	BP DX12	17.5/1180	18.0/1200	18.5/1235	18.8/1240	9,400 LUP	Note 1
Win. 209	Clays	WAA12SL	17.5/1180	18.1/1210	18.5/1235	19.5/1290	10,400 psi	
Win. 209	Green Dot	BP DX12	20.5/1200	20.7/1215	21.0/1230	21.5/1255	8,000 psi	Note 1
Win. 209	IMR 700-X	BP DX12	18.5/1200	18.8/1215	19.2/1230	19.5/1240	9,900 LUP	Note 1
Win. 209	International	WAA12SL	18.5/1180	19.6/1210	20.5/1235	22.0/1290	8,900 psi	
Win. 209	Nitro-100	Fed. 12S0	17.0/1200	17.7/1230	18.3/1260	19.0/1290	8,300 psi	Note 6
Win. 209	R. Scot D	Activ T-28	21.0/1200	21.7/1230	22.3/1260	23.0/1290	9,400 psi	
Win. 209	R. Scot D	Fed. 12S0	20.5/1200	21.2/1230	21.8/1260	22.5/1290	9,500 psi	
Win. 209	Red Diamond	Activ TG-30	17.0/1180	17.6/1215	18.3/1250	19.0/1290	9,600 psi	Note 7
Win. 209	Red Diamond	Fed. 12S0	17.0/1180	17.8/1215	18.6/1250	19.5/1290	8,700 psi	Note 7
Win. 209	Red Diamond	L-29	17.5/1180	18.1/1215	18.8/1250	19.5/1290	8,100 psi	Note 7
Win. 209	Red Dot	BP DX12				20.0/1250	9,600 LUP	Note 1
Win. 209	Scot 453	Activ T-28	19.5/1200	20.2/1230	20.8/1260	21.5/1290	10,000 psi	
Win. 209	Solo 1000	Activ T-28	20.5/1200	21.2/1230	21.8/1260	22.5/1290	8,000 LUP	Note 6
Win. 209	Solo 1000	BP DX12	20.0/1160	20.2/1180	20.5/1200	21.0/1220	7,300 psi	Note 1
Win. 209	Solo 1000	Fed. 12S0	20.0/1200	20.7/1230	21.3/1260	22.0/1290	8,800 LUP	Note 6
Win. 209	WSL	BP DX12				22.0/1300	9,900 LUP	Note 1
FEDERAL: GOLD MEDAL PLASTIC						1-OUNCE LEAD SHOT		
CCI 209	American Select	CS12S	19.5/1200	20.0/1220	20.2/1235	20.5/1255	10,600 psi	
CCI 209	American Select	BP Pisk	19.7/1200	20.3/1220	20.6/1280	21.3/1320	10,500 psi	Note 2
CCI 209	American Select	BP HCD24	20.5/1225	20.7/1245	20.8/1260	21.0/1270	9,200 psi	Note 3
CCI 209	American Select	SCAT	20.5/1220	21.0/1250	21.5/1270	22.0/1290	10,330 psi	Note 8
CCI 209	American Select	BP SRC	21.0/1245	21.5/1300	21.7/1320	22.0/1345	10,700 psi	Note 4
CCI 209	American Select	BP Z21	20.5/1225	20.7/1245	20.8/1255	21.0/1270	9,100 psi	Note 5
CCI 209	Bullseye	Fed. 12S0				19.0/1200	8,400 psi	
CCI 209	Clays	BP DX12	18.0/1200	18.5/1220	18.7/1235	19.0/1250	8,700 psi	Note 1

Load Notes: 1 = Disperser-X. 2 = Piston Skeet. 3 = Hex Cushion DR-24. 4 = Short Range Crusher. 5 = Trap Commander. 6 = Minimum overall length = 2¹⁰/₃₂″, maximum crimp depth = ²/₃₂″. 7 = Use 50-60 pounds wad pressure to ensure wad is firmly seated against powder. 8 = Scatter Master.

Caution: Follow load recipes exactly; do not substitute components, exceed listed maximums or load less than listed minimums.

Primer	Powder Type	Wad	Powder Charge (grains) / Velocity (fps) Minimum			Maximum	Maximum Pressure	Load Notes
FEDERAL: GOLD MEDAL PLASTIC (CONT.)						1-OUNCE LEAD SHOT		
CCI 209	Clays	Pat. Ctrl. Prpl	18.4/1125	19.6/1180	20.7/1235	21.8/1290	7,000 LUP	
CCI 209	IMR 700-X	BP DX12				18.0/1150	7,200 LUP	Note 1
CCI 209	International	BP DX12	19.0/1180	19.2/1195	19.5/1210	20.0/1235	8,600 psi	Note 1
CCI 209	Nitro-100	Fed. 12S0	18.5/1200	19.0/1230	19.5/1260	20.0/1290	8,900 psi	Note 6
CCI 209	R. Scot D	Fed. 12S0	19.5/1200	20.2/1230	20.8/1260	21.5/1290		
CCI 209	Red Diamond	Activ T-28	17.5/1180	18.3/1215	19.1/1250	20.0/1290	8,500 psi	Note 7
CCI 209	Red Diamond	Claybuster	17.5/1180	18.1/1215	18.8/1250	19.5/1290	8,000 psi	Note 7
CCI 209	Red Diamond	Fed. 12S0	17.5/1180	18.1/1215	18.8/1250	19.5/1290	8,300 psi	Note 7
CCI 209	Red Diamond	Fed. 12S0	17.5/1180	18.1/1215	18.8/1250	19.5/1290	8,000 psi	Note 7
CCI 209	Red Diamond	L-29	17.5/1180	18.3/1215	19.1/1250	20.0/1290	7,600 psi	Note 7
CCI 209	Red Diamond	Rem. TGT12	17.0/1180	17.6/1215	18.3/1250	19.0/1290	7,600 psi	Note 7
CCI 209	Red Dot	Fed. 12S0				19.0/1200	7,600 psi	
CCI 209	Solo 1000	BP DX12	20.0/1220	20.2/1235	20.5/1250	21.0/1270	8,900 psi	Note 1
CCI 209	Solo 1000	Fed. 12S0	20.0/1200	20.7/1230	21.3/1260	22.0/1290	8,500 LUP	Note 6
CCI 209	WST	Fed. 12S0	21.0/1235	21.5/1255	21.9/1275	22.5/1290	9,500 psi	
CCI 209	American Select	BP DX12	20.0/1200	20.5/1240	21.0/1290	21.5/1320	10,600 psi	Note 1
CCI 209M	Nitro-100	Fed. 12S0	17.0/1200	17.7/1230	18.3/1260	19.0/1290	9,200 psi	Note 6
CCI 209M	R. Scot D	Fed. 12S0	19.5/1200	20.3/1230	21.2/1260	22.0/1290	10,100 psi	
CCI 209M	Red Diamond	Activ T-28	17.0/1180	17.8/1215	18.6/1250	19.5/1290	8,300 psi	Note 7
CCI 209M	Red Diamond	Claybuster	17.5/1180	18.1/1215	18.8/1250	19.5/1290	8,200 psi	Note 7
CCI 209M	Red Diamond	Fed. 12S0	17.5/1180	18.1/1215	18.8/1250	19.5/1290	8,600 psi	Note 7
CCI 209M	Red Diamond	Fed. 12S0	17.5/1180	18.1/1215	18.8/1250	19.5/1290	8,200 psi	Note 7
CCI 209M	Red Diamond	L-29	17.0/1180	17.8/1215	18.6/1250	19.5/1290	8,300 psi	Note 7
CCI 209M	Red Diamond	Rem. TGT12	17.0/1180	17.6/1215	18.3/1250	19.0/1290	7,700 psi	Note 7
CCI 209M	Red Dot	Pat. Ctrl. Prpl				18.0/1200	6,900 psi	
CCI 209M	Solo 1000	Fed. 12S0	19.0/1200	19.8/1230	20.7/1260	21.5/1290	9,100 LUP	Note 6
CCI 209SC	Clays	Pat. Ctrl. Prpl	18.0/1180	18.6/1210	19.0/1235	20.0/1290	9,300 psi	
Fed. 209	Clays	Fed. 12S0	17.9/1125	18.9/1180	19.9/1235	20.9/1290	8,400 LUP	
Fed. 209	R. Scot D	Activ T-28	20.5/1200	21.2/1230	21.8/1260	22.5/1290	9,200 psi	
Fed. 209	R. Scot D	Claybuster	20.0/1200	20.8/1230	21.7/1260	22.5/1290	8,600 psi	
Fed. 209	R. Scot D	Fed. 12S0	20.5/1200	21.2/1230	21.8/1260	22.5/1290	9,600 psi	
Fed. 209	R. Scot D	Fed. 12S3	20.0/1200	20.7/1230	21.3/1260	22.0/1290	10,200 psi	
Fed. 209	R. Scot D	Rem. Fig.-8	20.0/1200	20.8/1230	21.7/1260	22.5/1290	9,400 psi	
Fed. 209	R. Scot D	Rem. TGT12	20.0/1200	20.8/1230	21.7/1260	22.5/1290	9,900 psi	
Fed. 209	R. Scot D	WAA12	19.5/1200	20.3/1230	21.2/1260	22.0/1290	9,600 psi	
Fed. 209	R. Scot D	WAA12F1	20.5/1200	21.2/1230	21.8/1260	22.5/1290	9,200 psi	
Fed. 209	Scot 453	Fed. 12S0	20.0/1200	20.3/1230	20.7/1260	21.0/1290	9,900 psi	
Fed. 209	Solo 1000	Activ T-28	20.0/1200	20.7/1230	21.3/1260	22.0/1290	8,100 LUP	Note 6
Fed. 209	Solo 1000	Claybuster	19.5/1200	20.3/1230	21.2/1260	22.0/1290		
Fed. 209	Solo 1000	Fed. 12S0	20.0/1200	20.7/1230	21.3/1260	22.0/1290		
Fed. 209	Solo 1000	Fed. 12S3	19.5/1200	20.2/1230	20.8/1260	21.5/1290		

Load Notes: 1 = Disperser-X. 6 = Minimum overall length = 2¹⁰/₃₂″, maximum crimp depth = ²/₃₂″. 7 = Use 50-60 pounds wad pressure to ensure wad is firmly seated against powder.

Caution: Follow load recipes exactly; do not substitute components, exceed listed maximums or load less than listed minimums.

Primer	Powder Type	Wad	Powder Charge (grains) / Velocity (fps) Minimum			Maximum	Maximum Pressure	Load Notes
FEDERAL: GOLD MEDAL PLASTIC (CONT.)						1-OUNCE LEAD SHOT		
Fed. 209	Solo 1000	Rem. Fig.-8	19.5/1200	20.3/1230	21.2/1260	22.0/1290		
Fed. 209	Solo 1000	Rem. TGT12	19.5/1200	20.3/1230	21.2/1260	22.0/1290		
Fed. 209	Solo 1000	WAA12	19.0/1200	19.8/1230	20.7/1260	21.5/1290	8,800 LUP	Note 6
Fed. 209	Solo 1000	WAA12F1	20.0/1200	20.7/1230	21.3/1260	22.0/1290		
Fed. 209	WST	Fed. 12S0				23.0/1290	8,400 psi	
Fed. 209A	#2 Improved	Fed. 12S0	20.0/1200	20.7/1230	21.3/1260	22.0/1290	9,900 psi	Note 6
Fed. 209A	American Select	Claybuster	20.0/1200	20.5/1230	21.0/1260	21.5/1290	8,000 psi	
Fed. 209A	American Select	Fed. 12S0	19.5/1200	20.3/1230	21.2/1260	22.0/1290	8,500 psi	
Fed. 209A	American Select	Rem. TGT12	19.5/1200	20.2/1230	20.8/1260	21.5/1290	8,800 psi	
Fed. 209A	American Select	WAA12SL	19.5/1200	20.2/1230	20.8/1260	21.5/1290	8,800 psi	
Fed. 209A	Bullseye	Fed. 12S0				18.0/1200	7,600 psi	
Fed. 209A	Bullseye	Pat. Ctrl. Prpl				19.0/1200	5,700 psi	
Fed. 209A	Bullseye	Rem. RXP12				17.5/1200	9,000 psi	Note 9
Fed. 209A	Bullseye	WAA12				17.5/1200	9,500 psi	Note 10
Fed. 209A	Bullseye	WAA12F1				18.5/1200	7,600 psi	Note 9
Fed. 209A	Clays	Fed. 12S0	16.8/1125	17.9/1180	19.3/1235	20.3/1290	10,800 psi	
Fed. 209A	Green Dot	BP DX12	20.0/1200	21.0/1225	21.2/1240	21.5/1255	8,500 psi	Note 1
Fed. 209A	Green Dot	Fed. 12S0				21.0/1200	7,100 psi	
Fed. 209A	Green Dot	Pat. Ctrl. Prpl	20.5*/1200	21.2*/1230	21.9/1260	22.5/1290	8,300 psi	*Note 9
Fed. 209A	Green Dot	Rem. PT12				21.0/1200	6,100 psi	
Fed. 209A	Green Dot	Rem. RXP12				20.0/1200	7,600 psi	
Fed. 209A	Green Dot	Rem. TGT12	20.0/1200	20.8/1230	21.7/1260	22.5/1290	8,500 psi	
Fed. 209A	Green Dot	WAA12				20.0/1200	8,200 psi	Note 9
Fed. 209A	Green Dot	WAA12F1				21.0/1200	7,200 psi	
Fed. 209A	Green Dot	WAA12SL	20.0/1200	20.8/1230	21.7/1260	22.5/1290	9,000 psi	
Fed. 209A	IMR 700-X	CB 2100-12	15.0/1110	16.0/1155	17.0/1200	18.0/1245	7,900 psi	
Fed. 209A	IMR 700-X	Fed. 12S0	15.0/1110	16.0/1155	17.0/1195	18.5/1250	8,200 psi	
Fed. 209A	IMR 700-X	Rem. TGT12	15.0/1100	16.0/1145	17.0/1190	18.5/1255	8,100 psi	
Fed. 209A	IMR 700-X	WAA12SL	15.0/1100	16.0/1150	17.0/1195	18.5/1250	8,500 psi	
Fed. 209A	IMR PB	CB 1100-12	20.0/1100	21.5/1150	23.0/1205	24.0/1255	6,300 psi	
Fed. 209A	IMR PB	Fed. 12S3	19.5/1105	20.5/1145	22.0/1210	23.0/1260	7,100 psi	
Fed. 209A	IMR PB	Rem. TGT12	19.5/1105	20.5/1140	22.0/1195	24.0/1260	6,800 psi	
Fed. 209A	IMR PB	WAA12SL	18.0/1110	19.5/1155	21.0/1205	22.5/1255	7,600 psi	
Fed. 209A	Nitro-100	BP ITD	17.5/1200	18.0/1230	18.5/1260	19.0/1290	8,100 psi	Note 6
Fed. 209A	Nitro-100	Fed. 12S0	17.5/1200	17.8/1230	18.2/1260	18.5/1290	9,000 psi	Note 6
Fed. 209A	Nitro-100	Fed. 12S3	17.0/1200	17.7/1230	18.3/1260	19.0/1290	9,100 psi	Note 6
Fed. 209A	Nitro-100	Rem. TGT12	17.0/1200	17.5/1230	18.0/1260	18.5/1290	8,700 psi	Note 6
Fed. 209A	Nitro-100	WAA12SL	17.0/1200	17.7/1230	18.3/1260	19.0/1290	9,000 psi	Note 6
Fed. 209A	Red Diamond	Activ T-28	17.0/1180	17.8/1215	18.6/1250	19.5/1290	8,700 psi	Note 7
Fed. 209A	Red Diamond	Claybuster	17.5/1180	18.1/1215	18.8/1250	19.5/1290	8,800 psi	Note 7
Fed. 209A	Red Diamond	Fed. 12S0	17.5/1180	18.1/1215	18.8/1250	19.5/1290	9,500 psi	Note 7

Load Notes: 1 = Disperser-X. 6 = Minimum overall length = 2¹⁰/₃₂", maximum crimp depth = ²/₃₂". 7 = Use 50-60 pounds wad pressure to ensure wad is firmly seated against powder. 9 = Add one 20-gauge, 0.135" card inside bottom of shotcup. 10 = Add two 20-gauge, 0.135" cards inside bottom of shotcup.

Caution: Follow load recipes exactly; do not substitute components, exceed listed maximums or load less than listed minimums.

Primer	Powder Type	Wad	Powder Charge (grains) / Velocity (fps) Minimum			Maximum	Maximum Pressure	Load Notes
FEDERAL: GOLD MEDAL PLASTIC (CONT.)						1-OUNCE LEAD SHOT		
Fed. 209A	Red Diamond	L-29	17.0/1180	17.8/1215	18.6/1250	19.5/1290	8,500 psi	Note 7
Fed. 209A	Red Diamond	Rem. TGT12	17.0/1180	17.6/1215	18.3/1250	19.0/1290	8,200 psi	Note 7
Fed. 209A	Red Dot	BP DX12				19.5/1290	10,000 psi	Note 1
Fed. 209A	Red Dot	Fed. 12S0	18.0/1200	18.8/1230	19.7/1260	20.5/1290	10,300 psi	
Fed. 209A	Red Dot	Fed. 12S0				18.0/1200	7,900 psi	
Fed. 209A	Red Dot	Pat. Ctrl. Prpl	18.0*/1200	19.5*/1255	20.1/1275	20.5/1290	9,300 psi	*Note 9
Fed. 209A	Red Dot	Pat. Ctrl. Prpl				18.5/1200	6,900 psi	
Fed. 209A	Red Dot	Rem. PT12				18.5/1200	7,500 psi	
Fed. 209A	Red Dot	Rem. RXP12				18.0/1200	8,700 psi	Note 9
Fed. 209A	Red Dot	Rem. TGT12	18.0/1200	18.7/1230	19.3/1260	20.0/1290	9,100 psi	
Fed. 209A	Red Dot	WAA12				18.0/1200	8,500 psi	Note 9
Fed. 209A	Red Dot	WAA12F1				18.0/1200	8,400 psi	Note 9
Fed. 209A	Red Dot	WAA12SL	18.0/1200	18.7/1230	19.3/1260	20.0/1290	10,300 psi	
Fed. 209A	Solo 1000	BP ITD	19.0/1200	19.7/1230	20.3/1260	21.0/1290	8,500 LUP	Note 6
Fed. 209A	Solo 1000	Fed. 12S0	19.0/1200	19.7/1230	20.3/1260	21.0/1290	9,500 LUP	Note 6
Fed. 209A	Solo 1000	Fed. 12S3	19.0/1200	19.7/1230	20.3/1260	21.0/1290	9,200 LUP	Note 6
Fed. 209A	Solo 1000	Rem. Fig.-8	19.0/1200	19.7/1230	20.3/1260	21.0/1290	8,500 LUP	Note 6
Fed. 209A	Solo 1000	Rem. TGT12	18.5/1200	19.3/1230	20.2/1260	21.0/1290	8,700 LUP	Note 6
Fed. 209A	Solo 1000	WAA12SL	18.5/1200	19.3/1230	20.2/1260	21.0/1290	9,500 LUP	Note 6
Fed. 209A	SR-7625	CB 2100-12	22.5/1090	23.5/1140	25.0/1200	26.0/1250	5,800 psi	
Fed. 209A	SR-7625	Fed. 12S3	22.0/1090	23.5/1160	24.5/1210	25.5/1255	6,600 psi	
Fed. 209A	SR-7625	Rem. TGT12	22.0/1100	23.0/1145	24.0/1190	25.5/1250	6,200 psi	
Fed. 209A	SR-7625	WAA12SL	22.5/1105	23.5/1160	24.5/1210	25.5/1265	6,600 psi	
Fio. 616	IMR 700-X	BP DX12				19.5/1250	9,600 LUP	Note 1
Fio. 616	Nitro-100	Fed. 12S0	17.0/1200	17.7/1230	18.3/1260	19.0/1290	9,300 psi	Note 6
Fio. 616	R. Scot D	Fed. 12S0	20.0/1200	20.8/1230	21.7/1260	22.5/1290	9,500 psi	
Fio. 616	Red Diamond	Activ T-28	17.0/1180	17.8/1215	18.6/1250	19.5/1290	8,500 psi	Note 7
Fio. 616	Red Diamond	Claybuster	17.5/1180	18.1/1215	18.8/1250	19.5/1290	8,700 psi	Note 7
Fio. 616	Red Diamond	Fed. 12S0	17.5/1180	18.1/1215	18.8/1250	19.5/1290	9,700 psi	Note 7
Fio. 616	Red Diamond	Fed. 12S0	17.5/1180	18.1/1215	18.8/1250	19.5/1290	8,700 psi	Note 7
Fio. 616	Red Diamond	L-29	17.0/1180	17.8/1215	18.6/1250	19.5/1290	8,600 psi	Note 7
Fio. 616	Red Diamond	Rem. TGT12	17.0/1180	17.6/1215	18.3/1250	19.0/1290	8,200 psi	Note 7
Fio. 616	Red Dot	BP DX12				20.0/1260	9,800 LUP	Note 1
Fio. 616	Solo 1000	Fed. 12S0	19.5/1200	20.3/1230	21.2/1260	22.0/1290	9,500 LUP	Note 6
Rem. 209	Bullseye	Pat. Ctrl. Prpl				18.5/1200	5,600 psi	
Rem. 209	Green Dot	Pat. Ctrl. Prpl				20.5/1200	6,100 psi	
Rem. 209	Red Diamond	Activ T-28	17.5/1180	18.3/1215	19.1/1250	20.0/1290	7,100 psi	Note 7
Rem. 209	Red Diamond	Claybuster	17.5/1180	18.1/1215	18.8/1250	19.5/1290	7,300 psi	Note 7
Rem. 209	Red Diamond	Fed. 12S0	17.5/1180	18.1/1215	18.8/1250	19.5/1290	9,000 psi	Note 7
Rem. 209	Red Diamond	Fed. 12S0	17.5/1180	18.1/1215	18.8/1250	19.5/1290	7,300 psi	Note 7
Rem. 209	Red Diamond	L-29	18.0/1180	18.6/1215	19.3/1250	20.0/1290	7,500 psi	Note 7

Load Notes: 1 = Disperser-X. 6 = Minimum overall length = 2¹⁰/₃₂″, maximum crimp depth = ²/₃₂″. 7 = Use 50-60 pounds wad pressure to ensure wad is firmly seated against powder. 9 = Add one 20-gauge, 0.135″ card inside bottom of shotcup.

Caution: Follow load recipes exactly; do not substitute components, exceed listed maximums or load less than listed minimums.

Primer	Powder Type	Wad	Powder Charge (grains) / Velocity (fps) Minimum			Maximum	Maximum Pressure	Load Notes
FEDERAL: GOLD MEDAL PLASTIC (CONT.)						1-OUNCE LEAD SHOT		
Rem. 209	Red Diamond	Rem. TGT12	18.0/1180	18.6/1215	19.3/1250	20.0/1290	7,400 psi	Note 7
Rem. 209	Red Dot	Pat. Ctrl. Prpl				18.5/1200	7,200 psi	
Rem. 209P	Clays	Rem. TGT12	18.2/1125	19.2/1180	20.2/1235	21.2/1290	7,300 LUP	
Rem. 209P	IMR 700-X	CB 2100-12	15.5/1095	16.5/1145	18.0/1200	19.5/1255	7,400 psi	
Rem. 209P	IMR 700-X	Fed. 12S0	15.0/1110	16.0/1145	18.0/1210	19.5/1250	8,000 psi	
Rem. 209P	IMR 700-X	Rem. TGT12	16.0/1110	17.0/1155	18.0/1195	19.5/1255	7,300 psi	
Rem. 209P	IMR 700-X	WAA12SL	15.5/1090	16.5/1150	17.5/1195	19.0/1260	8,400 psi	
Rem. 209P	IMR PB	CB 1100-12	21.0/1095	22.0/1140	23.5/1200	25.0/1255	5,600 psi	
Rem. 209P	IMR PB	Fed. 12S3	20.0/1105	21.0/1150	22.5/1210	23.5/1250	7,200 psi	
Rem. 209P	IMR PB	Rem. TGT12	20.5/1090	22.0/1160	23.0/1205	24.0/1250	6,300 psi	
Rem. 209P	IMR PB	WAA12SL	20.0/1095	21.5/1155	22.5/1195	24.0/1260	6,600 psi	
Rem. 209P	Nitro-100	Fed. 12S0	18.5/1200	19.0/1230	19.5/1260	20.0/1290	8,900 psi	Note 6
Rem. 209P	R. Scot D	Fed. 12S0	20.0/1200	20.8/1230	21.7/1260	22.5/1290	10,000 psi	
Rem. 209P	Solo 1000	Fed. 12S0	19.5/1200	20.3/1230	21.2/1260	22.0/1290	8,200 LUP	Note 6
Win. 209	Clays	WAA12SL	17.2/1125	18.2/1180	19.1/1235	20.0/1290	8,300 LUP	
Win. 209	IMR 700-X	BP DX12				20.0/1290	10,000 LUP	Note 1
Win. 209	IMR 700-X	CB 2100-12	15.5/1110	16.5/1160	17.5/1200	19.0/1260	8,100 psi	
Win. 209	IMR 700-X	Fed. 12S0	15.5/1105	16.5/1155	17.5/1200	18.5/1245	7,800 psi	
Win. 209	IMR 700-X	Rem. TGT12	15.5/1100	16.5/1145	17.5/1195	18.5/1245	7,800 psi	
Win. 209	IMR 700-X	WAA12SL	15.5/1105	16.5/1150	17.5/1200	18.5/1250	8,500 psi	
Win. 209	IMR PB	CB 1100-12	20.5/1100	21.5/1145	23.0/1205	24.5/1260	6,100 psi	
Win. 209	IMR PB	Fed. 12S3	19.5/1105	21.0/1155	22.5/1210	23.5/1250	6,900 psi	
Win. 209	IMR PB	Rem. TGT12	20.0/1110	21.0/1155	22.0/1205	23.5/1255	7,000 psi	
Win. 209	IMR PB	WAA12SL	19.5/1090	21.0/1150	22.5/1205	24.0/1265	6,700 psi	
Win. 209	Nitro-100	Fed. 12S0	17.5/1200	18.0/1230	18.5/1260	19.0/1290	9,100 psi	Note 6
Win. 209	R. Scot D	Fed. 12S0	20.0/1200	20.7/1230	21.3/1260	22.0/1290	10,100 psi	
Win. 209	Red Diamond	Activ T-28	17.0/1180	17.8/1215	18.6/1250	19.5/1290	8,200 psi	Note 7
Win. 209	Red Diamond	Claybuster	17.5/1180	18.1/1215	18.8/1250	19.5/1290	7,900 psi	Note 7
Win. 209	Red Diamond	Fed. 12S0	17.5/1180	18.1/1215	18.8/1250	19.5/1290	9,700 psi	Note 7
Win. 209	Red Diamond	L-29	17.0/1180	17.8/1215	18.6/1250	19.5/1290	8,200 psi	Note 7
Win. 209	Red Diamond	Rem. TGT12	17.0/1180	17.6/1215	18.3/1250	19.0/1290	7,600 psi	Note 7
Win. 209	Red Dot	Pat. Ctrl. Prpl				18.5/1200	6,700 psi	
Win. 209	Solo 1000	Fed. 12S0	19.5/1200	20.2/1230	20.8/1260	21.5/1290	9,200 LUP	Note 6
Win. 209	SR-7625	CB 2100-12	22.0/1095	23.5/1145	25.0/1195	26.5/1245	5,200 psi	
Win. 209	SR-7625	Fed. 12S3	21.5/1110	22.5/1150	24.0/1210	25.5/1255	6,600 psi	
Win. 209	SR-7625	Rem. TGT12	22.5/1105	23.5/1145	25.0/1205	26.0/1245	5,900 psi	
Win. 209	SR-7625	WAA12SL	22.5/1105	23.5/1150	25.0/1210	26.0/1250	5,600 psi	
Win. 209	WST	BP DX12	22.0/1235	22.4/1255	22.8/1275	23.0/1290	9,300 psi	Note 1
Win. 209	WST	Fed. 12S0	20.5/1180	22.0/1235	22.6/1265	23.0/1290	9,300 psi	
Win. AATP	Clays	WAA12SL	16.8/1125	17.8/1180	19.0/1235	20.0/1290	9,800 psi	

Load Notes: 1 = Disperser-X. 6 = Minimum overall length = 2¹⁰/₃₂″, maximum crimp depth = ²/₃₂″. 7 = Use 50-60 pounds wad pressure to ensure wad is firmly seated against powder.

    Caution: Follow load recipes exactly; do not substitute components, exceed listed maximums or load less than listed minimums.

Primer	Powder Type	Wad	Powder Charge (grains) / Velocity (fps) Minimum			Maximum	Maximum Pressure	Load Notes
						1-OUNCE LEAD SHOT		
CCI 209	Bullseye	Fed. 12S0				18.5/1200	7,600 psi	
CCI 209	Red Diamond	Fed. 12S3	17.5/1180	18.1/1215	18.8/1250	19.5/1290	8,200 psi	Note 7
CCI 209	Red Diamond	Fiocchi TL1	18.0/1180	18.6/1215	19.3/1250	20.0/1290	8,200 psi	Note 7
CCI 209	Red Diamond	H. Versalite	17.5/1180	18.3/1215	19.1/1250	20.0/1290	8,500 psi	Note 7
CCI 209	Red Diamond	Hawk II	17.0/1180	18.0/1215	18.9/1250	20.0/1290	9,000 psi	Note 7
CCI 209	Red Diamond	WAA12	16.5/1180	17.6/1215	18.7/1250	20.0/1290	8,900 psi	Note 7
CCI 209	Red Dot	Fed. 12S0				19.0/1200	7,600 psi	
CCI 209M	Bullseye	Pat. Ctrl. Prpl				18.0/1200	6,900 psi	
CCI 209M	Clays	Pat. Ctrl. Prpl	18.0/1180	18.8/1210	19.5/1235	20.5/1290	9,800 psi	
CCI 209M	Green Dot	Fed. 12S3				23.0/1290	7,800 psi	
CCI 209M	Nitro-100	Fed. 12S3	17.5/1200	18.0/1230	18.5/1260	19.0/1290	7,900 psi	Note 6
CCI 209M	R. Scot D	Fed. 12S3	19.5/1200	20.3/1230	21.2/1260	22.0/1290	10,700 psi	
CCI 209M	Red Diamond	Fed. 12S3	17.5/1180	18.0/1215	18.5/1250	19.0/1290	8,800 psi	Note 7
CCI 209M	Red Diamond	Fiocchi TL1	17.5/1180	18.1/1215	18.8/1250	19.5/1290	8,600 psi	Note 7
CCI 209M	Red Diamond	H. Versalite	17.0/1180	17.8/1215	18.6/1250	19.5/1290	8,500 psi	Note 7
CCI 209M	Red Diamond	Hawk II	17.0/1180	18.0/1215	18.9/1250	20.0/1290	9,500 psi	Note 7
CCI 209M	Red Diamond	WAA12	16.5/1180	17.6/1215	18.7/1250	20.0/1290	8,900 psi	Note 7
CCI 209M	Red Dot	Fed. 12S3				21.0/1290	8,700 psi	
CCI 209M	Red Dot	Pat. Ctrl. Prpl				18.5/1200	6,600 psi	
CCI 209M	Solo 1000	Fed. 12S3	19.0/1200	19.7/1230	20.3/1260	21.0/1290	9,000 psi	Note 6
CCI 209SC	Clays	Fed. 12S3	18.6/1180	19.4/1210	20.0/1235	21.8/1290	10,700 psi	
CCI 209SC	Clays	Windjam. II	18.3/1180	18.8/1210	19.2/1235	21.0/1290	9,700 psi	
Fed. 209	R. Scot D	Fed. 12S3	20.5/1200	21.3/1230	22.2/1260	23.0/1290	9,800 psi	
Fed. 209	R. Scot D	WAA12	21.0/1200	21.7/1230	22.3/1260	23.0/1290	9,500 psi	
Fed. 209	Scot 453	Fed. 12S0	21.0/1200	21.7/1230	22.3/1260	23.0/1290	10,100 psi	
Fed. 209	Solo 1000	Fed. 12S3	20.0/1200	20.8/1230	21.7/1260	22.5/1290		
Fed. 209	Solo 1000	WAA12	20.5/1200	21.2/1230	21.8/1260	22.5/1290		
Fed. 209A	Bullseye	Fed. 12S0				18.5/1200	7,800 psi	
Fed. 209A	Bullseye	Fed. 12S3				18.5/1200	8,500 psi	Note 9
Fed. 209A	Bullseye	H. Versalite				18.5/1200	8,500 psi	Note 9
Fed. 209A	Bullseye	Lage Uniwad				19.0/1200	8,600 psi	Note 9
Fed. 209A	Bullseye	Pat. Ctrl. Prpl				19.0/1200	6,400 psi	
Fed. 209A	Bullseye	Rein. PT12				18.0/1200	6,200 psi	
Fed. 209A	Bullseye	Rein. RXP12				18.5/1200	7,600 psi	Note 9
Fed. 209A	Bullseye	Rem. R12L				18.5/1200	7,800 psi	Note 9
Fed. 209A	Bullseye	WAA12				18.5/1200	8,700 psi	Note 9
Fed. 209A	Bullseye	WAA12F1				18.0/1200	7,500 psi	Note 9
Fed. 209A	Bullseye	Windjammer				19.0/1200	7,300 psi	Note 9
Fed. 209A	Clays	Fed. 12S0	18.0/1180	18.8/1210	19.5/1235	21.0/1290	10,900 psi	
Fed. 209A	Green Dot	Fed. 12S0				22.5/1290	9,200 psi	
Fed. 209A	Green Dot	Fed. 12S3				23.5/1290	9,400 psi	
Fed. 209A	Green Dot	Rem. R12L				21.5/1290	8,800 psi	

Load Notes: 6 = Minimum overall length = 2¹⁰/₃₂″, maximum crimp depth = ²/₃₂″. 7 = Use 50-60 pounds wad pressure to ensure wad is firmly seated against powder. 9 = Add one 20-gauge, 0.135″ card inside bottom of shotcup.

Caution: Follow load recipes exactly; do not substitute components, exceed listed maximums or load less than listed minimums.

Primer	Powder Type	Wad	Powder Charge (grains) / Velocity (fps) Minimum			Maximum	Maximum Pressure	Load Notes
FEDERAL: PAPER (CONT.)						**1-OUNCE LEAD SHOT**		
Fed. 209A	Nitro-100	Fed. 12S3	17.5/1200	18.2/1230	18.8/1260	19.5/1290	8,600 psi	Note 6
Fed. 209A	Nitro-100	WAA12	17.5/1200	18.0/1230	18.5/1260	19.0/1290	8,400 psi	Note 6
Fed. 209A	Red Diamond	Fed. 12S3	17.5/1180	18.0/1215	18.5/1250	19.0/1290	9,200 psi	Note 7
Fed. 209A	Red Diamond	Fiocchi TL1	17.0/1180	17.8/1215	18.6/1250	19.5/1290	9,100 psi	Note 7
Fed. 209A	Red Diamond	H. Versalite	17.0/1180	17.8/1215	18.6/1250	19.5/1290	8,900 psi	Note 7
Fed. 209A	Red Diamond	Hawk II	17.0/1180	18.0/1215	18.9/1250	20.0/1290	10,400 psi	Note 7
Fed. 209A	Red Diamond	WAA12	16.5/1180	17.6/1215	18.7/1250	20.0/1290	9,600 psi	Note 7
Fed. 209A	Red Dot	Fed. 12S0				20.5/1290	10,400 psi	
Fed. 209A	Red Dot	Fed. 12S0				19.0/1200	8,000 psi	
Fed. 209A	Red Dot	Fed. 12S3				20.5/1290	9,000 psi	
Fed. 209A	Red Dot	Fed. 12S3				18.5/1200	7,400 psi	
Fed. 209A	Red Dot	H. Versalite				18.0/1200	7,300 psi	
Fed. 209A	Red Dot	Lage Uniwad				19.0/1200	7,100 psi	
Fed. 209A	Red Dot	Pat. Ctrl. Prpl				19.0/1200	7,100 psi	
Fed. 209A	Red Dot	Rein. PT12				18.0/1200	7,500 psi	
Fed. 209A	Red Dot	Rein. RXP12				19.0/1200	7,200 psi	
Fed. 209A	Red Dot	Rem. R12L				20.0/1290	9,300 psi	
Fed. 209A	Red Dot	Rem. R12L				18.5/1200	7,100 psi	
Fed. 209A	Red Dot	WAA12				18.5/1200	7,800 psi	
Fed. 209A	Red Dot	WAA12F1				18.5/1200	8,100 psi	Note 9
Fed. 209A	Red Dot	Windjammer				19.0/1200	7,400 psi	Note 9
Fed. 209A	Solo 1000	Fed. 12S3	19.0/1200	19.7/1230	20.3/1260	21.0/1290	9,000 psi	Note 6
Fed. 209A	Solo 1000	WAA12	19.0/1200	19.5/1230	20.0/1260	20.5/1290	7,500 psi	Note 6
Fio. 616	Nitro-100	Fed. 12S3	17.5/1200	18.0/1230	18.5/1260	19.0/1290	8,100 psi	Note 6
Fio. 616	R. Scot D	Fed. 12S3	20.5/1200	21.2/1230	21.8/1260	22.5/1290	9,700 psi	
Fio. 616	Red Diamond	Fed. 12S3″	17.5/1180	18.0/1215	18.5/1250	19.0/1290	9,100 psi	Note 7
Fio. 616	Red Diamond	Fiocchi TL1	17.5/1180	18.1/1215	18.8/1250	19.5/1290	9,100 psi	Note 7
Fio. 616	Red Diamond	H. Versalite	17.0/1180	17.8/1215	18.6/1250	19.5/1290	8,900 psi	Note 7
Fio. 616	Red Diamond	Hawk II	17.0/1180	18.0/1215	18.9/1250	20.0/1290	9,400 psi	Note 7
Fio. 616	Red Diamond	WAA12	16.5/1180	17.6/1215	18.7/1250	20.0/1290	9,300 psi	Note 7
Fio. 616	Solo 1000	Fed. 12S3	19.0/1200	19.7/1230	20.3/1260	21.0/1290	8,600 psi	Note 6
Rem. 209	Bullseye	Pat. Ctrl. Prpl				18.5/1200	6,200 psi	
Rem. 209	Red Diamond	Fed. 12S3	17.5/1180	18.1/1215	18.8/1250	19.5/1290	7,900 psi	Note 7
Rem. 209	Red Diamond	Fiocchi TL1	18.0/1180	18.6/1215	19.3/1250	20.0/1290	8,500 psi	Note 7
Rem. 209	Red Diamond	H. Versalite	17.5/1180	18.3/1215	19.1/1250	20.0/1290	7,900 psi	Note 7
Rem. 209	Red Diamond	Hawk II	17.0/1180	18.0/1215	18.9/1250	20.0/1290	8,700 psi	Note 7
Rem. 209	Red Diamond	WAA12	16.5/1180	17.6/1215	18.7/1250	20.0/1290	8,900 psi	Note 7
Rem. 209	Red Dot	Pat. Ctrl. Prpl				18.0/1200	7,800 psi	
Rem. 209P	Clays	Rem. TGT12	18.5/1180	19.3/1210	20.0/1235	22.0/1290	7,700 psi	
Win. 209	Bullseye	Pat. Ctrl. Prpl				19.0/1200	7,100 psi	
Win. 209	Clays	WAA12SL	17.5/1180	18.3/1210	19.0/1235	21.0/1290	10,800 psi	
Win. 209	Clays	Windjammer	18.0/1180	18.8/1210	19.5/1235	20.5/1290	8,800 psi	

Load Notes: 6 = Minimum overall length = 2¹⁰/₃₂″, maximum crimp depth = ²/₃₂″. 7 = Use 50-60 pounds wad pressure to ensure wad is firmly seated against powder. 9 = Add one 20-gauge, 0.135″ card inside bottom of shotcup.

Caution: Follow load recipes exactly; do not substitute components, exceed listed maximums or load less than listed minimums.

Primer	Powder Type	Wad	Powder Charge (grains) / Velocity (fps) Minimum			Maximum	Maximum Pressure	Load Notes
FEDERAL: PAPER (CONT.)						**1-OUNCE LEAD SHOT**		
Win. 209	Nitro-100	Fed. 12S3	17.5/1200	18.0/1230	18.5/1260	19.0/1290	8,600 psi	Note 6
Win. 209	R. Scot D	Fed. 12S3	20.5/1200	21.3/1230	22.2/1260	23.0/1290	9,500 psi	
Win. 209	Red Diamond	Fed. 12S3	17.5/1180	18.0/1215	18.5/1250	19.0/1290	8,600 psi	Note 7
Win. 209	Red Diamond	Fiocchi TL1	17.5/1180	18.1/1215	18.8/1250	19.5/1290	8,500 psi	Note 7
Win. 209	Red Diamond	H. Versalite	17.0/1180	17.8/1215	18.6/1250	19.5/1290	9,100 psi	Note 7
Win. 209	Red Diamond	Hawk II	17.0/1180	18.0/1215	18.9/1250	20.0/1290	9,800 psi	Note 7
Win. 209	Red Diamond	WAA12	16.5/1180	17.6/1215	18.7/1250	20.0/1290	9,100 psi	Note 7
Win. 209	Red Dot	Pat. Ctrl. Prpl				19.0/1200	7,200 psi	
Win. 209	Solo 1000	Fed. 12S3	19.0/1200	19.7/1230	20.3/1260	21.0/1290	8,300 psi	Note 6
FEDERAL: PLASTIC (PAPER BASE WAD)						**1-OUNCE LEAD SHOT**		
Fed. 209A	Green Dot	Fed. 12S3				23.0/1290	7,500 psi	
Fed. 209A	Green Dot	Rem. R12L				22.5/1290	7,400 psi	
Fed. 209A	Red Dot	Fed. 12S3				21.0/1290	9,400 psi	
Fed. 209A	Red Dot	Rem. R12L				20.5/1290	8,500 psi	
FIOCCHI: PLASTIC (LOW BASE WAD)						**1-OUNCE LEAD SHOT**		
Fio. 616	American Select	BP DX12	20.0/1200	20.5/1230	20.7/1245	21.0/1270	10,300 psi	Note 1
Fio. 616	American Select	BP Pisk	19.8/1200	20.1/1220	20.4/1240	20.7/1260	10,400 psi	Note 2
Fio. 616	American Select	BP HCD24	20.5/1230	20.7/1245	20.8/1255	21.0/1270	9,300 psi	Note 3
Fio. 616	American Select	SCAT	21.5/1245	21.7/1265	21.8/1275	22.0/1290	10,400 psi	Note 8
Fio. 616	American Select	BP Z21	20.5/1230	20.7/1245	20.8/1255	21.0/1270	9,400 psi	Note 5
Fio. 616	Clays	BP DX12	18.0/1200	18.6/1220	19.0/1250	19.5/1290	9,300 psi	Note 1
Fio. 616	Green Dot	BP DX12	20.2/1200	21.2/1235	22.2/1270	22.6/1300	9,300 psi	Note 1
Fio. 616	IMR 700-X	BP DX12	18.5/1210	18.8/1235	19.1/1260	19.5/1290	9,900 LUP	Note 1
Fio. 616	International	BP DX12	19.6/1200	20.0/1220	20.5/1250	21.0/1290	9,800 psi	Note 1
Fio. 616	Red Dot	BP DX12				19.2/1285	9,900 psi	Note 1
Fio. 616	Solo 1000	BP DX12	19.5/1200	20.5/1240	21.5/1270	22.0/1290	7,800 psi	Note 1
Fio. 616	WSL	BP DX12	20.5/1260	20.8/1270	21.2/1285	21.5/1300	9,600 LUP	Note 1
Fio. 616	WST	BP DX12	21.1/1200	21.6/1215	22.0/1230	22.4/1255	9,200 psi	Note 1
FIOCCHI: PURPLE TARGET (HIGH BASE WAD)						**1-OUNCE LEAD SHOT**		
CCI 209	Red Diamond	Activ TG-30	17.5/1180	18.5/1215	19.4/1250	20.5/1290	8,300 psi	Note 7
CCI 209	Red Diamond	BP ITD	17.5/1180	18.5/1215	19.4/1250	20.5/1290	8,500 psi	Note 7
CCI 209	Red Diamond	Fed. 12S0	18.0/1180	19.0/1215	19.9/1250	21.0/1290	8,000 psi	Note 7
CCI 209	Red Diamond	Fiocchi TL1	17.0/1180	17.6/1215	18.3/1250	19.0/1290	7,300 psi	Note 7
CCI 209	Red Diamond	Pat. Ctrl. Prpl	17.5/1180	18.5/1215	19.4/1250	20.5/1290	7,700 psi	Note 7
CCI 209M	Clays	Pat. Ctrl. Prpl	18.0/1180	18.6/1210	19.1/1235	19.9/1290	9,400 psi	
CCI 209M	International	Pat. Ctrl. Prpl	19.6/1180	20.1/1210	20.5/1235	21.6/1290	8,200 psi	
CCI 209M	Nitro-100	Fed. 12S0	17.0/1200	17.5/1230	18.0/1260	18.5/1290	8,900 psi	Note 11
CCI 209M	R. Scot D	Fed. 12S0	19.5/1200	20.2/1230	20.8/1260	21.5/1290	10,700 psi	
CCI 209M	Red Diamond	Activ TG-30	17.0/1180	18.1/1215	19.2/1250	20.5/1290	9,200 psi	Note 7
CCI 209M	Red Diamond	BP ITD	17.0/1180	18.0/1215	18.9/1250	20.0/1290	8,700 psi	Note 7
CCI 209M	Red Diamond	Fed. 12S0	17.5/1180	18.5/1215	19.4/1250	20.5/1290	8,600 psi	Note 7

Load Notes: 1 = Disperser-X. 2 = Piston Skeet. 3 = Hex Cushion DR-24. 5 = Trap Commander. 6 = Minimum overall length = 2¹⁰/₃₂″, maximum crimp depth = ²/₃₂″. 7 = Use 50-60 pounds wad pressure to ensure wad is firmly seated against powder. 8 = Scatter Master. 11 = Minimum overall length = 2⁹/₃₂″, maximum crimp depth = ²/₃₂″.

Caution: Follow load recipes exactly; do not substitute components, exceed listed maximums or load less than listed minimums.

Primer	Powder Type	Wad	Powder Charge (grains) / Velocity (fps) Minimum			Maximum	Maximum Pressure	Load Notes
FIOCCHI: PURPLE TARGET (HIGH BASE WAD) (CONT.)						1-OUNCE LEAD SHOT		
CCI 209M	Red Diamond	Fiocchi TL1	17.0/1180	17.6/1215	18.3/1250	19.0/1290	8,600 psi	Note 7
CCI 209M	Red Diamond	Pat. Ctrl. Prpl	17.0/1180	18.1/1215	19.2/1250	20.5/1290	7,100 psi	Note 7
CCI 209M	Solo 1000	Fed. 12S0	19.0/1200	19.7/1230	20.3/1260	21.0/1290	9,500 LUP	Note 11
CCI 209SC	Clays	WAA12SL	18.0/1180	18.1/1195	18.3/1210	18.5/1235	9,500 psi	
CCI 209SC	International	WAA12SL	19.5/1180	20.6/1210	21.5/1235	22.5/1290	9,400 psi	
Fed. 209	R. Scot D	Fed. 12S0	20.0/1200	20.8/1230	21.7/1260	22.5/1290	8,900 psi	
Fed. 209	Solo 1000	Fed. 12S0	19.5/1200	20.3/1230	21.2/1260	22.0/1290		
Fed. 209A	Clays	Rem. TGT12	17.5/1180	18.1/1210	18.5/1235	19.7/1290	9,700 psi	
Fed. 209A	International	Rem. TGT12	19.3/1180	19.9/1210	20.3/1235	20.9/1290	8,800 psi	
Fed. 209A	Nitro-100	Fed. 12S0	17.0/1200	17.5/1230	18.0/1260	18.5/1290	10,300 psi	Note 11
Fed. 209A	Red Diamond	Activ TG-30	16.5/1180	17.5/1215	18.4/1250	19.5/1290	9,900 psi	Note 7
Fed. 209A	Red Diamond	BP ITD	17.0/1180	17.8/1215	18.6/1250	19.5/1290	8,900 psi	Note 7
Fed. 209A	Red Diamond	Fed. 12S0	17.0/1180	18.0/1215	18.9/1250	20.0/1290	9,400 psi	Note 7
Fed. 209A	Red Diamond	Fiocchi TL1	17.0/1180	17.6/1215	18.3/1250	19.0/1290	9,600 psi	Note 7
Fed. 209A	Red Diamond	Pat. Ctrl. Prpl	17.0/1180	18.0/1215	18.9/1250	20.0/1290	9,200 psi	Note 7
Fio. 616	#2 Improved	Fed. 12S0	19.0/1200	19.5/1230	20.0/1260	20.5/1290	10,900 psi	Note 11
Fio. 616	American Select	CS12S	20.0/1220	20.3/1225	20.7/1235	21.0/1240	10,800 psi	
Fio. 616	American Select	BP HCDP	20.2/1200	20.5/1220	20.7/1235	21.0/1260	9,100 psi	Note 12
Fio. 616	American Select	BP SRC	21.0/1270	21.5/1310	21.7/1325	22.0/1350	10,700 psi	Note 4
Fio. 616	American Select	BP Zero	19.3/1210	20.3/1255	20.8/1275	21.3/1295	8,800 psi	
Fio. 616	Clays	BP DX12	17.7/1200	18.4/1220	18.5/1235	18.6/1250	8,900 psi	Note 1
Fio. 616	Green Dot	BP DX12	20.0/1200	20.8/1225	21.5/1250	22.0/1270	9,000 psi	Note 1
Fio. 616	Green Dot	Fed. 12S0				20.0/1200	8,100 psi	
Fio. 616	Green Dot	Pat. Ctrl. Prpl	20.0/1200	21.0/1230	22.0/1260	23.0/1290	8,400 psi	
Fio. 616	Green Dot	Rem. TGT12	20.0/1200	20.8/1230	21.7/1260	22.5/1290	8,600 psi	
Fio. 616	Green Dot	WAA12SL	20.0/1200	20.8/1230	21.7/1260	22.5/1290	9,400 psi	
Fio. 616	IMR 700-X	BP DX12	18.2/1210	18.6/1235	18.9/1260	19.2/1290	9,900 LUP	Note 1
Fio. 616	International	BP DX12	19.1/1200	19.7/1220	19.9/1235	20.2/1250	9,300 psi	Note 1
Fio. 616	Nitro-100	Fed. 12S0	17.0/1200	17.5/1230	18.0/1260	18.5/1290	9,900 psi	Note 11
Fio. 616	R. Scot D	Fed. 12S0	19.5/1200	20.3/1230	21.2/1260	22.0/1290	9,500 psi	
Fio. 616	Red Diamond	Activ TG-30	16.5/1180	17.5/1215	18.4/1250	19.5/1290	9,600 psi	Note 7
Fio. 616	Red Diamond	BP ITD	17.0/1180	17.8/1215	18.6/1250	19.5/1290	8,700 psi	Note 7
Fio. 616	Red Diamond	Fed. 12S0	17.0/1180	18.1/1215	19.2/1250	20.5/1290	10,000 psi	Note 7
Fio. 616	Red Diamond	Fiocchi TL1	17.0/1180	17.6/1215	18.3/1250	19.0/1290	9,300 psi	Note 7
Fio. 616	Red Diamond	Pat. Ctrl. Prpl	17.0/1180	18.0/1215	18.9/1250	20.0/1290	7,600 psi	Note 7
Fio. 616	Red Dot	BP DX12				19.0/1285	9,900 psi	Note 1
Fio. 616	Red Dot	Fed. 12S0				18.0/1200	9,100 psi	
Fio. 616	Red Dot	Pat. Ctrl. Prpl	18.0/1200	19.0/1230	20.0/1260	21.0/1290	9,800 psi	
Fio. 616	Red Dot	Rem. TGT12	18.0/1200	18.8/1230	19.7/1260	20.5/1290	10,100 psi	
Fio. 616	Red Dot	WAA12SL	18.0/1200	18.8/1230	19.7/1260	20.5/1290	10,300 psi	
Fio. 616	Scot 453	Fiocchi TL1	19.0/1200	19.5/1230	20.0/1260	20.5/1290	10,900 psi	
Fio. 616	Solo 1000	BP DX12	19.2/1200	19.7/1220	20.7/1250	21.8/1290	7,800 psi	Note 1

Load Notes: 1 = Disperser-X. 4 = Short Range Crusher. 7 = Use 50-60 pounds wad pressure to ensure wad is firmly seated against powder. 11 = Minimum overall length = 2⁹/₃₂″, maximum crimp depth = ²/₃₂″. 12 = Helix Cushion Platform.

    Caution: Follow load recipes exactly; do not substitute components, exceed listed maximums or load less than listed minimums.

Primer	Powder Type	Wad	Powder Charge (grains) / Velocity (fps) Minimum			Maximum	Maximum Pressure	Load Notes
FIOCCHI: PURPLE TARGET (HIGH BASE WAD) (CONT.)						**1-OUNCE LEAD SHOT**		
Fio. 616	Solo 1000	Fed. 12S0	19.0/1200	19.8/1230	20.7/1260	21.5/1290	9,000 LUP	Note 11
Fio. 616	WSL	BP DX12				20.2/1260	9,200 LUP	Note 1
Fio. 616	WST	BP DX12	21.0/1200	21.4/1215	21.8/1230	22.1/1255	9,200 psi	Note 1
Rem. 209	Red Diamond	Activ TG-30	18.0/1180	19.0/1215	19.9/1250	21.0/1290	7,600 psi	Note 7
Rem. 209	Red Diamond	BP ITD	17.5/1180	18.3/1215	19.1/1250	20.0/1290	8,100 psi	Note 7
Rem. 209	Red Diamond	Fed. 12S0	18.0/1180	19.0/1215	19.9/1250	21.0/1290	7,800 psi	Note 7
Rem. 209	Red Diamond	Fiocchi TL1	17.0/1180	17.6/1215	18.3/1250	19.0/1290	7,600 psi	Note 7
Rem. 209P	Nitro-100	Fed. 12S0	17.0/1200	17.5/1230	18.0/1260	18.5/1290	8,800 psi	Note 11
Rem. 209P	R. Scot D	Fed. 12S0	20.5/1200	21.2/1230	21.8/1260	22.5/1290	8,400 psi	
Rem. 209P	Solo 1000	Fed. 12S0	20.0/1200	20.7/1230	21.3/1260	22.0/1290	7,600 LUP	Note 11
Win. 209	Clays	WAA12SL	17.1/1180	17.9/1210	18.5/1235	19.3/1290	10,600 psi	
Win. 209	International	WAA12SL	19.0/1180	19.6/1210	20.0/1235	21.1/1290	9,600 psi	
Win. 209	Nitro-100	Fed. 12S0	17.0/1200	17.5/1230	18.0/1260	18.5/1290	8,800 psi	Note 11
Win. 209	R. Scot D	Fed. 12S0	20.0/1200	20.8/1230	21.7/1260	22.5/1290	9,400 psi	
Win. 209	Red Diamond	Activ TG-30	16.5/1180	17.5/1215	18.4/1250	19.5/1290	10,000 psi	Note 7
Win. 209	Red Diamond	BP ITD	17.0/1180	17.8/1215	18.6/1250	19.5/1290	8,700 psi	Note 7
Win. 209	Red Diamond	Fed. 12S0	17.0/1180	18.0/1215	18.9/1250	20.0/1290	9,300 psi	Note 7
Win. 209	Red Diamond	Fiocchi TL1	17.0/1180	17.6/1215	18.3/1250	19.0/1290	9,400 psi	Note 7
Win. 209	Red Diamond	Pat. Ctrl. Prpl	17.0/1180	18.0/1215	18.9/1250	20.0/1290	8,900 psi	Note 7
Win. 209	Solo 1000	Fed. 12S0	19.5/1200	20.3/1230	21.2/1260	22.0/1290	7,800 LUP	Note 11
PETERS: BLUE MAGIC						**1-OUNCE LEAD SHOT**		
CCI 209	R. Scot D	Rem. Fig.-8	19.0/1200	19.8/1230	20.7/1260	21.5/1290	10,300 psi	
CCI 209	Solo 1000	Rem. Fig.-8	18.5/1200	19.3/1230	20.2/1260	21.0/1290		
CCI 209M	Bullseye	Pat. Ctrl. Prpl				17.0/1200	7,400 psi	
CCI 209M	Bullseye	Rem. R12L				17.5/1200	9,000 psi	
CCI 209M	Green Dot	Pat. Ctrl. Prpl				19.5/1200	7,000 psi	
CCI 209M	R. Scot D	Rem. Fig.-8				18.5/1200		
CCI 209M	Red Dot	Pat. Ctrl. Prpl				17.5/1200	8,000 psi	
CCI 209M	Red Dot	Rem. R12L				18.0/1200	8,800 psi	
CCI 209M	Solo 1000	Rem. Fig.-8				18.0/1200		
Fed. 209	Bullseye	Pat. Ctrl. Prpl				18.0/1200	6,300 psi	
Fed. 209	Green Dot	Pat. Ctrl. Prpl				20.0/1200	6,400 psi	
Fed. 209	R. Scot D	Rem. Fig.-8	19.0/1200	19.7/1230	20.3/1260	21.0/1290	10,900 psi	
Fed. 209	Red Dot	Pat. Ctrl. Prpl				18.5/1200	8,400 psi	
Fed. 209	Solo 1000	Rem. Fig.-8	18.5/1200	19.2/1230	19.8/1260	20.5/1290		
Fed. 209	W 452AA	WAA12SL	20.5/1180	21.5/1235	22.3/1265	23.0/1290	8,100 LUP	
Fio. 615	WSL	BP HCDP				21.0/1300	8,900 LUP	Note 12
Rem. 209	Bullseye	Pat. Ctrl. Prpl				17.5/1200	7,200 psi	
Rem. 209	Green Dot	Pat. Ctrl. Prpl				19.0/1200	7,300 psi	
Rem. 209	Red Dot	Pat. Ctrl. Prpl				17.5/1200	8,300 psi	
Rem. 209P	R. Scot D	Claybuster	19.0/1200	19.7/1230	20.3/1260	21.0/1290	9,400 psi	

Load Notes: 7 = Use 50-60 pounds wad pressure to ensure wad is firmly seated against powder. 11 = Minimum overall length = 2⁹/₃₂", maximum crimp depth = ²/₃₂". 12 = Helix Cushion Platform.

Caution: Follow load recipes exactly; do not substitute components, exceed listed maximums or load less than listed minimums.

Primer	Powder Type	Wad	Powder Charge (grains) / Velocity (fps) Minimum			Maximum	Maximum Pressure	Load Notes
PETERS: BLUE MAGIC (CONT.)						**1-OUNCE LEAD SHOT**		
Rem. 209P	R. Scot D	Rem. Fig.-8	19.0/1200	19.7/1230	20.3/1260	21.0/1290	9,500 psi	
Rem. 209P	R. Scot D	WAA12	18.5/1200	19.0/1230	19.5/1260	20.0/1290	10,600 psi	
Rem. 209P	Solo 1000	Claybuster	18.5/1200	19.2/1230	19.8/1260	20.5/1290		
Rem. 209P	Solo 1000	Rem. Fig.-8	18.5/1200	19.2/1230	19.8/1260	20.5/1290		
Rem. 209P	Solo 1000	WAA12	18.0/1200	18.5/1230	19.0/1260	19.5/1290		
Rem. 97*	Bullseye	Fed. 12S0				18.0/1200	10,300 psi	
Rem. 97*	Bullseye	Fed. 12S3				18.5/1200	8,500 psi	Note 9
Rem. 97*	Bullseye	Lage Uniwad				18.0/1200	9,600 psi	Note 9
Rem. 97*	Bullseye	Rem. R12L				17.5/1200	8,300 psi	Note 9
Rem. 97*	Bullseye	Rem. RXP12				17.5/1200	8,800 psi	Note 9
Rem. 97*	Bullseye	WAA12				17.5/1200	9,900 psi	Note 9
Rem. 97*	Bullseye	WAA12F1				18.0/1200	8,700 psi	
Rem. 97*	Bullseye	Windjammer				18.0/1200	8,700 psi	Note 9
Rem. 97*	Green Dot	Fed. 12S3				19.5/1200	7,300 psi	
Rem. 97*	Green Dot	Lage Uniwad				20.5/1200	6,700 psi	
Rem. 97*	Green Dot	Rem. R12L				20.0/1200	7,100 psi	
Rem. 97*	Green Dot	Rem. RXP12				20.0/1200	7,500 psi	
Rem. 97*	Green Dot	WAA12				19.5/1200	7,500 psi	
Rem. 97*	Green Dot	WAA12F1				21.0/1200	7,500 psi	
Rem. 97*	Red Dot	Fed. 12S0				18.0/1200	9,400 psi	
Rem. 97*	Red Dot	Fed. 12S3				18.0/1200	8,600 psi	Note 9
Rem. 97*	Red Dot	Lage Uniwad				18.0/1200	8,600 psi	Note 9
Rem. 97*	Red Dot	Rem. R12L				18.0/1200	8,000 psi	Note 9
Rem. 97*	Red Dot	Rem. RXP12				18.0/1200	8,400 psi	Note 9
Rem. 97*	Red Dot	WAA12				18.0/1200	9,100 psi	Note 9
Rem. 97*	Red Dot	WAA12F1				18.0/1200	8,500 psi	
Rem. 97*	Red Dot	Windjammer				19.0/1200	8,300 psi	Note 9
Win. 209	Bullseye	Pat. Ctrl. Prpl				18.0/1200	6,800 psi	
Win. 209	R. Scot D	Rem. Fig.-8	19.0/1200	19.8/1230	20.7/1260	21.5/1290	10,500 psi	
Win. 209	Red Dot	Pat. Ctrl. Prpl				18.0/1200	7,700 psi	
Win. 209	Solo 1000	Rem. Fig.-8	18.5/1200	19.3/1230	20.2/1260	21.0/1290		
Win. 209	W 452AA	WAA12SL	20.5/1180	21.5/1235	22.3/1265	23.0/1290	8,400 LUP	
Win. 209	WSL	BP HCDP				21.5/1280	9,400 LUP	Note 12
REMINGTON: PREMIER & NITRO 27 & STS						**1-OUNCE LEAD SHOT**		
CCI 209	Clays	Pat. Ctrl. Prpl	17.1/1125	18.3/1180	19.5/1235	20.7/1290	8,400 LUP	
CCI 209	International	Pat. Ctrl. Prpl	20.6/1180	21.2/1215	21.8/1250	22.7/1290	8,300 LUP	
CCI 209	Nitro-100	Rem. Fig.-8	16.5/1200	17.0/1230	17.5/1260	18.0/1290	6,700 psi	Note 11
CCI 209	Nitro-100	Rem. TGT12	16.5/1200	17.0/1230	17.5/1260	18.0/1290	10,200 psi	Note 11
CCI 209	R. Scot D	Rem. Fig.-8	19.5/1200	20.2/1230	20.8/1260	21.5/1290	9,500 psi	
CCI 209	R. Scot D	Rem. TGT12	19.5/1200	20.2/1230	20.8/1260	21.5/1290	10,300 psi	
CCI 209	Red Diamond	Hawk II	16.5/1180	17.1/1215	17.8/1250	18.5/1290	10,300 psi	Note 7

Load Notes: 7 = Use 50-60 pounds wad pressure to ensure wad is firmly seated against powder. 9 = Add one 20-gauge, 0.135″ card inside bottom of shotcup. 11 = Minimum overall length = 2⁹/₃₂″, maximum crimp depth = ²/₃₂″. 12 = Helix Cushion Platform.

    Caution: Follow load recipes exactly; do not substitute components, exceed listed maximums or load less than listed minimums.

Primer	Powder Type	Wad	Powder Charge (grains) / Velocity (fps) Minimum			Maximum	Maximum Pressure	Load Notes
REMINGTON: PREMIER & NITRO 27 & STS (CONT.)						1-OUNCE LEAD SHOT		
CCI 209	Red Diamond	Pat. Ctrl. Red	16.5/1180	17.3/1215	18.1/1250	19.0/1290	8,600 psi	Note 7
CCI 209	Red Diamond	Rem. Fig.-8	16.5/1180	17.1/1215	17.8/1250	18.5/1290	9,200 psi	Note 7
CCI 209	Red Diamond	Rem. TGT12	16.5/1180	17.1/1215	17.8/1250	18.5/1290	8,800 psi	Note 7
CCI 209	Red Diamond	WAA12SL	16.5/1180	17.3/1215	18.1/1250	19.0/1290	10,000 psi	Note 7
CCI 209	Solo 1000	Rem. Fig.-8	19.0/1200	19.7/1230	20.3/1260	21.0/1290	9,000 LUP	Note 11
CCI 209	Solo 1000	Rem. Fig.-8	19.0/1200	19.7/1230	20.3/1260	21.0/1290		
CCI 209	Solo 1000	Rem. TGT12	19.0/1200	19.7/1230	20.3/1260	21.0/1290	9,000 LUP	Note 11
CCI 209	WSL	Fed. 12S0				21.0/1290	10,300 psi	
CCI 209	WSL	WAA12SL				20.5/1290	10,800 psi	
CCI 209	WST	Fed. 12S0	18.5/1180	19.5/1235	20.1/1265	20.5/1290	10,800 psi	
CCI 209	WST	WAA12SL	19.0/1180	20.0/1235	20.6/1265	21.0/1290	10,100 psi	
CCI 209M	Bullseye	Rem. Fig.-8				17.0/1200	8,300 psi	
CCI 209M	Green Dot	Rem. Fig.-8				18.5/1200	7,700 psi	
CCI 209M	Green Dot	Rem. R12L				22.0/1290	9,100 psi	
CCI 209M	R. Scot D	Rem. Fig.-8				21.0/1290	10,400 LUP	
CCI 209M	R. Scot D	Rem. TGT12				21.0/1290	10,700 LUP	
CCI 209M	Red Diamond	Hawk II	16.5/1180	17.1/1215	17.8/1250	18.5/1290	10,500 psi	Note 7
CCI 209M	Red Diamond	Pat. Ctrl. Red	16.5/1180	17.1/1215	17.8/1250	18.5/1290	9,100 psi	Note 7
CCI 209M	Red Diamond	Rem. Fig.-8	16.5/1180	17.1/1215	17.8/1250	18.5/1290	9,600 psi	Note 7
CCI 209M	Red Diamond	Rem. TGT12	16.5/1180	17.1/1215	17.8/1250	18.5/1290	8,700 psi	Note 7
CCI 209M	Red Diamond	WAA12SL	16.5/1180	17.1/1215	17.8/1250	18.5/1290	9,700 psi	Note 7
CCI 209M	Red Dot	Rem. Fig.-8				17.5/1200	8,900 psi	
CCI 209M	Red Dot	Rem. R12L				20.0/1290	10,300 psi	
CCI 209M	Solo 1000	Rem. Fig.-8				20.5/1290	9,700 LUP	Note 11
CCI 209M	Solo 1000	Rem. TGT12				20.5/1290	10,500 LUP	Note 11
CCI 209SC	Clays	Rem. TGT12	15.7/1125	17.8/1180	18.8/1235	20.5/1290	11,100 psi	
CCI 209SC	International	Rem. TGT12	19.5/1180	20.8/1235	22.2/1290	22.8/1345	10,300 psi	
Fed. 209	Bullseye	Rem. Fig.-8				17.5/1200	7,500 psi	
Fed. 209	Clays	Fed. 12S0	16.5/1125	17.7/1180	18.9/1235	20.0/1290	10,100 LUP	
Fed. 209	Green Dot	Rem. Fig.-8				20.0/1200	7,200 psi	
Fed. 209	Green Dot	Rem. R12L				22.5/1290	9,200 psi	
Fed. 209	International	Fed. 12S0	19.6/1180	20.2/1210	20.6/1235	22.3/1290	9,300 LUP	
Fed. 209	R. Scot D	Rem. Fig.-8	19.0/1200	19.8/1230	20.7/1260	21.5/1290	10,300 psi	
Fed. 209	R. Scot D	Rem. TGT12	19.0/1200	19.8/1230	20.7/1260	21.5/1290	10,600 psi	
Fed. 209	Red Dot	Rem. Fig.-8				18.0/1200	8,400 psi	
Fed. 209	Red Dot	Rem. R12L				20.5/1290	10,500 psi	
Fed. 209	Solo 1000	Rem. Fig.-8	18.5/1200	19.3/1230	20.2/1260	21.0/1290		
Fed. 209	Solo 1000	Rem. TGT12	18.5/1200	19.3/1230	20.2/1260	21.0/1290		
Fed. 209	WSL	Fed. 12S0				21.0/1290	9,700 psi	
Fed. 209	WSL	WAA12SL				20.5/1290	10,100 psi	
Fed. 209	WST	Fed. 12S0	19.0/1180	20.0/1235	20.6/1265	21.0/1290	10,900 psi	
Fed. 209	WST	WAA12SL	19.0/1180	20.5/1235	21.1/1265	21.5/1290	9,700 psi	

Load Notes: 7 = Use 50-60 pounds wad pressure to ensure wad is firmly seated against powder. 11 = Minimum overall length = 2⁹/₃₂″, maximum crimp depth = ²/₃₂″.

Caution: Follow load recipes exactly; do not substitute components, exceed listed maximums or load less than listed minimums.

Primer	Powder Type	Wad	Powder Charge (grains) / Velocity (fps) Minimum			Maximum	Maximum Pressure	Load Notes
REMINGTON: PREMIER & NITRO 27 & STS (CONT.)						1-OUNCE LEAD SHOT		
Fed. 209A	IMR 700-X	CB 1100-12	14.5/1090	16.0/1160	17.0/1205	18.0/1250	9,600 psi	
Fed. 209A	IMR 700-X	Fed. 12S3	14.5/1095	15.5/1140	17.0/1210	18.0/1250	11,200 psi	
Fed. 209A	IMR 700-X	BP HCDP				18.0/1260	10,200 psi	Note 12
Fed. 209A	IMR 700-X	Rem. TGT12	14.5/1100	15.5/1150	16.5/1205	17.5/1245	10,000 psi	
Fed. 209A	IMR 700-X	WAA12SL	14.5/1105	15.5/1150	16.5/1200	18.0/1260	10,800 psi	
Fed. 209A	IMR PB	CB 1100-12	18.5/1095	20.0/1155	21.0/1195	22.5/1255	8,000 psi	
Fed. 209A	IMR PB	Fed. 12S3	18.0/1100	19.0/1140	20.5/1200	22.0/1260	9,300 psi	
Fed. 209A	IMR PB	BP HCDP				22.0/1250	9,200 psi	Note 12
Fed. 209A	IMR PB	Rem. TGT12	18.5/1105	19.5/1145	21.0/1200	22.5/1255	8,200 psi	
Fed. 209A	IMR PB	WAA12SL	18.0/1115	19.0/1150	20.5/1200	22.0/1255	8,900 psi	
Fed. 209A	International	Fed. 12S0	18.0/1180	18.7/1210	19.3/1235	21.0/1290	11,300 psi	
Fed. 209A	Nitro-100	Rem. Fig.-8	16.0/1200	16.7/1230	17.3/1260	18.0/1290	10,200 psi	Note 11
Fed. 209A	Nitro-100	Rem. TGT12	16.0/1200	16.7/1230	17.3/1260	18.0/1290	10,900 psi	Note 11
Fed. 209A	Red Diamond	Hawk II	16.5/1180	17.1/1215	17.8/1250	18.5/1290	10,800 psi	Note 7
Fed. 209A	Red Diamond	Pat. Ctrl. Red	16.5/1180	17.1/1215	17.8/1250	18.5/1290	9,600 psi	Note 7
Fed. 209A	Red Diamond	Rem. Fig.-8	16.5/1180	17.1/1215	17.8/1250	18.5/1290	10,100 psi	Note 7
Fed. 209A	Red Diamond	Rem. TGT12	16.5/1180	17.1/1215	17.8/1250	18.5/1290	9,600 psi	Note 7
Fed. 209A	Red Diamond	WAA12SL	16.5/1180	17.1/1215	17.8/1250	18.5/1290	10,100 psi	Note 7
Fed. 209A	SR-7625	CB 1100-12	20.5/1090	22.0/1150	23.0/1195	24.5/1255	7,400 psi	
Fed. 209A	SR-7625	Fed. 12S3	20.0/1095	21.0/1140	22.5/1205	23.5/1250	8,300 psi	
Fed. 209A	SR-7625	BP HCDP				23.5/1245	8,200 psi	Note 12
Fed. 209A	SR-7625	Rem. TGT12	20.5/1095	22.0/1160	23.0/1200	24.0/1245	7,400 psi	
Fed. 209A	SR-7625	WAA12SL	19.0/1095	20.5/1150	22.0/1205	23.5/1260	8,500 psi	
Fio. 615	IMR 700-X	BP HCDP	18.4/1245	19.1/1260	19.4/1270	19.8/1280	10,200 LUP	Note 12
Fio. 616	Red Diamond	Hawk II	16.5/1180	17.1/1215	17.8/1250	18.5/1290	10,600 psi	Note 7
Fio. 616	Red Diamond	Pat. Ctrl. Red	16.5/1180	17.3/1215	18.1/1250	19.0/1290	9,400 psi	Note 7
Fio. 616	Red Diamond	Rem. Fig.-8	16.5/1180	17.1/1215	17.8/1250	18.5/1290	9,900 psi	Note 7
Fio. 616	Red Diamond	Rem. TGT12	16.5/1180	17.1/1215	17.8/1250	18.5/1290	9,200 psi	Note 7
Fio. 616	Red Diamond	WAA12SL	16.5/1180	17.1/1215	17.8/1250	18.5/1290	9,600 psi	Note 7
Rem. 209	American Select	BP Zero	18.3/1200	19.8/1255	20.3/1275	20.9/1300	9,200 psi	
Rem. 209	Red Diamond	Hawk II	16.5/1180	17.1/1215	17.8/1250	18.5/1290	9,900 psi	Note 7
Rem. 209	Red Diamond	Pat. Ctrl. Red	16.5/1180	17.1/1215	17.8/1250	18.5/1290	8,700 psi	Note 7
Rem. 209	Red Diamond	Rem. Fig.-8	16.5/1180	17.1/1215	17.8/1250	18.5/1290	9,100 psi	Note 7
Rem. 209	Red Diamond	Rem. TGT12	16.5/1180	17.1/1215	17.8/1250	18.5/1290	9,000 psi	Note 7
Rem. 209	Red Diamond	WAA12SL	16.5/1180	17.3/1215	18.1/1250	19.0/1290	9,900 psi	Note 7
Rem. 209	Scot 453	Rem. TGT12	20.0/1200	20.5/1230	21.0/1260	21.5/1290	10,900 psi	
Rem. 209	WSL	BP HCDP				20.5/1290	10,100 psi	Note 12
Rem. 209P	#2 Improved	Rem. TGT12	19.0/1200	19.5/1230	20.0/1260	20.5/1290	10,900 psi	Note 11
Rem. 209P	American Select	Claybuster	19.5/1200	20.5/1230	21.5/1260	22.5/1290	8,500 psi	
Rem. 209P	American Select	CS12S		19.0/1220	19.2/1230	19.5/1245	10,600 psi	
Rem. 209P	American Select	BP DX12		19.5/1200	19.7/1210	20.0/1220	10,700 psi	Note 1
Rem. 209P	American Select	BP DX12		19.5/1200	19.8/1210	20.0/1220	10,700 psi	Note 1

Load Notes: 1 = Disperser-X. 7 = Use 50-60 pounds wad pressure to ensure wad is firmly seated against powder. 11 = Minimum overall length = 2⁹/₃₂″, maximum crimp depth = ²/₃₂″. 12 = Helix Cushion Platform.

Caution: Follow load recipes exactly; do not substitute components, exceed listed maximums or load less than listed minimums.

Primer	Powder Type	Wad	Powder Charge (grains) / Velocity (fps) Minimum			Maximum	Maximum Pressure	Load Notes
REMINGTON: PREMIER & NITRO 27 & STS (CONT.)					1-OUNCE LEAD SHOT			
Rem. 209P	American Select	Fed. 12S0	19.5/1200	20.2/1230	20.8/1260	21.5/1290	9,900 psi	
Rem. 209P	American Select	Fisk		19.5/1200	19.7/1220	20.3/1245	11,200 psi	Note 2
Rem. 209P	American Select	Rem. TGT12	19.0/1200	20.2/1230	21.3/1260	22.5/1290	8,700 psi	
Rem. 209P	American Select	WAA12SL	19.0/1200	19.8/1230	20.7/1260	21.5/1290	9,200 psi	
Rem. 209P	Bullseye	Fed. 12S0				17.5/1200	7,800 psi	
Rem. 209P	Bullseye	H. Versalite				17.0/1200	7,500 psi	
Rem. 209P	Bullseye	Pat. Ctrl. Prpl				18.0/1200	6,900 psi	
Rem. 209P	Bullseye	Rem. Fig.-8				17.0/1200	7,100 psi	
Rem. 209P	Bullseye	WAA12F1				17.5/1200	6,900 psi	
Rem. 209P	Clays	Rem. TGT12	16.8/1125	17.9/1180	18.9/1235	19.9/1290	8,800 LUP	
Rem. 209P	Green Dot	Fed. 12S0	19.5/1200	20.3/1230	21.2/1260	22.0/1290	8,700 psi	
Rem. 209P	Green Dot	Fed. 12S0				19.5/1200	7,200 psi	
Rem. 209P	Green Dot	H. Versalite				20.0/1200	6,600 psi	
Rem. 209P	Green Dot	Pat. Ctrl. Prpl	20.5/1200	21.2/1230	21.8/1260	22.5/1290	8,200 psi	
Rem. 209P	Green Dot	Pat. Ctrl. Prpl				20.5/1200	6,200 psi	
Rem. 209P	Green Dot	Rem. Fig.-8				22.0/1290	8,100 psi	
Rem. 209P	Green Dot	Rem. Fig.-8				20.0/1200	6,500 psi	
Rem. 209P	Green Dot	Rem. TGT12	20.0/1200	20.8/1230	21.7/1260	22.5/1290	8,400 psi	
Rem. 209P	Green Dot	WAA12F1				23.0/1290	7,200 psi	
Rem. 209P	Green Dot	WAA12F1				19.0/1200	6,200 psi	
Rem. 209P	Green Dot	WAA12SL	19.5/1200	20.5/1230	21.5/1260	22.5/1290	9,000 psi	
Rem. 209P	IMR 700-X	CB 1100-12	15.0/1105	16.0/1150	17.0/1195	18.5/1260	9,400 psi	
Rem. 209P	IMR 700-X	Fed. 12S3	14.5/1090	15.5/1140	17.0/1205	18.0/1250	10,600 psi	
Rem. 209P	IMR 700-X	BP HCDP				18.0/1205	9,600 psi	Note 12
Rem. 209P	IMR 700-X	Rem. TGT12	14.5/1090	15.5/1140	16.5/1190	18.0/1250	9,500 psi	
Rem. 209P	IMR 700-X	WAA12SL	14.5/1100	15.5/1145	16.5/1195	18.0/1255	10,500 psi	
Rem. 209P	IMR PB	CB 1100-12	19.5/1100	20.5/1150	21.5/1190	23.0/1250	7,200 psi	
Rem. 209P	IMR PB	Fed. 12S3	18.5/1095	20.0/1155	21.0/1200	22.5/1260	8,500 psi	
Rem. 209P	IMR PB	BP HCDP				22.5/1260	8,600 psi	Note 12
Rem. 209P	IMR PB	Rem. TGT12	19.0/1110	20.0/1150	21.5/1210	22.5/1250	7,600 psi	
Rem. 209P	IMR PB	WAA12SL	18.0/1095	19.5/1150	20.5/1190	22.5/1265	8,700 psi	
Rem. 209P	International	Rem. TGT12	20.2/1180	20.6/1210	20.9/1235	21.4/1290	8,900 LUP	
Rem. 209P	Nitro-100	Claybuster	16.0/1200	16.7/1230	17.3/1260	18.0/1290	10,100 psi	Note 11
Rem. 209P	Nitro-100	Rem. Fig.-8	16.5/1200	17.0/1230	17.5/1260	18.0/1290	9,300 psi	Note 11
Rem. 209P	Nitro-100	Rem. TGT12	16.5/1200	17.0/1230	17.5/1260	18.0/1290	10,100 psi	Note 11
Rem. 209P	Nitro-100	WAA12SL	16.0/1200	16.5/1230	17.0/1260	17.5/1290	10,200 psi	Note 11
Rem. 209P	R. Scot D	Claybuster	19.0/1200	19.7/1230	20.3/1260	21.0/1290	10,900 psi	
Rem. 209P	R. Scot D	Rem. Fig.-8	19.5/1200	20.2/1230	20.8/1260	21.5/1290	9,600 psi	
Rem. 209P	R. Scot D	Rem. TGT12	19.5/1200	20.2/1230	20.8/1260	21.5/1290	9,800 psi	
Rem. 209P	R. Scot D	WAA12	18.5/1200	19.3/1230	20.2/1260	21.0/1290	10,900 psi	
Rem. 209P	R. Scot D	WAA12F1	19.5/1200	20.2/1230	20.8/1260	21.5/1290	10,200 psi	
Rem. 209P	Red Dot	Fed. 12S0	18.0/1200	18.7/1230	19.3/1260	20.0/1290	10,500 psi	

Load Notes: 11 = Minimum overall length = 2⁹/₃₂″, maximum crimp depth = ²/₃₂″. 12 = Helix Cushion Platform.

Caution: Follow load recipes exactly; do not substitute components, exceed listed maximums or load less than listed minimums.

Primer	Powder Type	Wad	Powder Charge (grains) / Velocity (fps) Minimum			Maximum	Maximum Pressure	Load Notes
REMINGTON: PREMIER & NITRO 27 & STS (CONT.)						**1-OUNCE LEAD SHOT**		
Rem. 209P	Red Dot	Fed. 12S0				18.0/1200	8,800 psi	
Rem. 209P	Red Dot	H. Versalite				17.5/1200	8,600 psi	
Rem. 209P	Red Dot	Pat. Ctrl. Prpl	18.5/1200	19.2/1230	19.8/1260	20.5/1290	9,100 psi	
Rem. 209P	Red Dot	Pat. Ctrl. Prpl				18.5/1200	7,700 psi	
Rem. 209P	Red Dot	Rem. Fig.-8				21.5/1290	9,100 psi	
Rem. 209P	Red Dot	Rem. Fig.-8				18.0/1200	8,400 psi	
Rem. 209P	Red Dot	Rem. R12L				20.5/1290	9,900 psi	
Rem. 209P	Red Dot	Rem. TGT12	18.0/1200	19.0/1230	20.0/1260	21.0/1290	10,700 psi	
Rem. 209P	Red Dot	WAA12F1				20.5/1290	9,100 psi	
Rem. 209P	Red Dot	WAA12F1				18.0/1200	7,800 psi	
Rem. 209P	Red Dot	WAA12SL	18.0/1200	18.8/1230	19.7/1260	20.5/1290	10,400 psi	
Rem. 209P	Solo 1000	Claybuster	18.5/1200	19.2/1230	19.8/1260	20.5/1290	10,300 LUP	Note 11
Rem. 209P	Solo 1000	Rem. Fig.-8	19.0/1200	19.7/1230	20.3/1260	21.0/1290	9,300 LUP	Note 11
Rem. 209P	Solo 1000	Rem. TGT12	19.0/1200	19.7/1230	20.3/1260	21.0/1290	9,500 LUP	Note 11
Rem. 209P	Solo 1000	WAA12	18.0/1200	18.8/1230	19.7/1260	20.5/1290	10,500 LUP	Note 11
Rem. 209P	Solo 1000	WAA12F1	19.0/1200	19.7/1230	20.3/1260	21.0/1290		
Rem. 209P	Solo 1250	Rem. TGT12				16.5/1200	8,400 LUP	Note 11
Rem. 209P	SR-7625	CB 1100-12	22.0/1110	23.0/1155	24.0/1200	25.0/1250	5,900 psi	
Rem. 209P	SR-7625	Fed. 12S3	20.0/1105	21.0/1140	22.5/1190	24.0/1260	7,800 psi	
Rem. 209P	SR-7625	BP HCDP				24.0/1260	7,800 psi	Note 12
Rem. 209P	SR-7625	Rem. TGT12	21.5/1110	22.5/1155	23.5/1195	25.0/1255	7,000 psi	
Rem. 209P	SR-7625	WAA12SL	21.0/1100	22.0/1150	23.0/1195	24.5/1260	8,100 psi	
Win. 209	Bullseye	Rem. Fig.-8				17.5/1200	7,900 psi	
Win. 209	Clays	BP HCDP	16.5/1160	17.5/1200	18.5/1235	19.0/1255	10,000 LUP	Note 12
Win. 209	Clays	WAA12SL	15.7/1125	17.0/1180	18.4/1235	19.8/1290	10,700 LUP	
Win. 209	Clays	Windjam. II	15.4/1125	16.0/1180	17.8/1235	19.5/1290	11,300 psi	
Win. 209	Green Dot	Rem. Fig.-8				20.0/1200	7,100 psi	
Win. 209	Green Dot	Rem. R12L				22.0/1290	8,700 psi	
Win. 209	IMR 700-X	CB 1100-12	15.0/1095	16.0/1150	17.0/1195	18.0/1240	9,200 psi	
Win. 209	IMR 700-X	Fed. 12S3	14.5/1090	15.5/1135	17.0/1210	18.0/1255	11,100 psi	
Win. 209	IMR 700-X	BP HCDP				17.5/1250	10,400 psi	Note 12
Win. 209	IMR 700-X	Rem. TGT12	15.0/1110	15.5/1140	16.5/1195	18.0/1255	9,800 psi	
Win. 209	IMR 700-X	WAA12SL	15.0/1110	16.0/1160	17.0/1205	18.0/1250	10,300 psi	
Win. 209	IMR PB	CB 1100-12	19.5/1105	20.5/1150	21.5/1195	23.0/1250	7,100 psi	
Win. 209	IMR PB	Fed. 12S3	19.0/1110	20.0/1150	21.0/1195	22.5/1255	8,700 psi	
Win. 209	IMR PB	BP HCDP				22.5/1260	8,600 psi	Note 12
Win. 209	IMR PB	Rem. TGT12	19.0/1100	20.0/1145	21.0/1190	22.5/1255	7,700 psi	
Win. 209	IMR PB	WAA12	18.5/1100	19.5/1140	21.0/1195	22.5/1255	8,100 psi	
Win. 209	International	BP HCDP	19.0/1200	19.3/1210	19.6/1220	20.0/1235	8,000 LUP	Note 12
Win. 209	International	WAA12SL	18.4/1180	19.2/1210	20.1/1235	21.0/1290	10,000 LUP	
Win. 209	Nitro-100	Rem. Fig.-8	16.0/1200	16.7/1230	17.3/1260	18.0/1290	9,200 psi	Note 11
Win. 209	Nitro-100	Rem. TGT12	16.0/1200	16.7/1230	17.3/1260	18.0/1290	9,900 psi	Note 11

Load Notes: 11 = Minimum overall length = 2⁹/₃₂″, maximum crimp depth = ²/₃₂″. 12 = Helix Cushion Platform.

Caution: Follow load recipes exactly; do not substitute components, exceed listed maximums or load less than listed minimums.

Primer	Powder Type	Wad	Powder Charge (grains) / Velocity (fps) Minimum			Maximum	Maximum Pressure	Load Notes
REMINGTON: PREMIER & NITRO 27 & STS (CONT.)						**1-OUNCE LEAD SHOT**		
Win. 209	R. Scot D	Rem. Fig.-8	19.0/1200	19.8/1230	20.7/1260	21.5/1290	9,500 psi	
Win. 209	R. Scot D	Rem. TGT12	19.5/1200	20.2/1230	20.8/1260	21.5/1290	10,300 psi	
Win. 209	Red Diamond	Hawk II	16.5/1180	17.1/1215	17.8/1250	18.5/1290	10,400 psi	Note 7
Win. 209	Red Diamond	Pat. Ctrl. Red	16.5/1180	17.3/1215	18.1/1250	19.0/1290	9,400 psi	Note 7
Win. 209	Red Diamond	Rem. Fig.-8	16.5/1180	17.1/1215	17.8/1250	18.5/1290	9,700 psi	Note 7
Win. 209	Red Diamond	Rem. TGT12	16.5/1180	17.1/1215	17.8/1250	18.5/1290	9,200 psi	Note 7
Win. 209	Red Diamond	WAA12SL	16.5/1180	17.1/1215	17.8/1250	18.5/1290	9,800 psi	Note 7
Win. 209	Red Dot	Rem. Fig.-8				18.0/1200	7,100 psi	
Win. 209	Red Dot	Rem. R12L				20.0/1290	10,100 psi	
Win. 209	Solo 1000	Rem. Fig.-8	18.5/1200	19.3/1230	20.2/1260	21.0/1290	9,600 LUP	Note 11
Win. 209	Solo 1000	Rem. TGT12	19.0/1200	19.7/1230	20.3/1260	21.0/1290	9,300 LUP	Note 11
Win. 209	SR-7625	CB 1100-12	21.0/1090	22.5/1150	24.0/1195	25.5/1250	5,900 psi	
Win. 209	SR-7625	Fed. 12S3	21.0/1100	22.0/1145	23.0/1195	24.0/1250	7,900 psi	
Win. 209	SR-7625	BP HCDP				24.0/1250	7,800 psi	Note 12
Win. 209	SR-7625	Rem. TGT12	21.0/1105	22.0/1145	23.0/1190	24.5/1260	7,100 psi	
Win. 209	SR-7625	WAA12SL	20.0/1105	21.5/1150	23.0/1200	24.0/1250	7,200 psi	
Win. 209	WSL	Fed. 12S0				21.0/1290	9,800 psi	
Win. 209	WSL	WAA12SL				20.5/1290	10,100 psi	
Win. 209	WST	Fed. 12S0	19.0/1180	20.0/1235	20.6/1265	21.0/1290	9,700 psi	
Win. 209	WST	BP HCDP	19.0/1180	19.5/1230	20.0/1250	20.5/1290	9,900 psi	Note 12
Win. 209	WST	WAA12SL	19.5/1235	20.3/1260	20.6/1275	21.0/1290	10,000 psi	
Win. AATP	Clays	WAA12SL	15.5/1125	16.5/1180	17.3/1210	18.2/1235	11,000 psi	
Win. AATP	International	WAA12SL	18.5/1180	19.2/1210	19.7/1235	21.0/1290	10,500 psi	
REMINGTON: UNIBODY (INTEGRAL PLASTIC BASE WAD)						**1-OUNCE LEAD SHOT**		
CCI 157	W 452AA	Fed. 12S1				23.5/1290	10,200 LUP	
CCI 157	W 452AA	Rem. R12L				23.5/1290	9,700 LUP	
CCI 157	W 452AA	WAA12				23.5/1290	9,800 LUP	
CCI 209	Green Dot	Rem. R12L				23.5/1290	8,100 psi	
CCI 209	Red Dot	Rem. R12L				21.0/1290	9,700 psi	
CCI 209M	Green Dot	Rem. R12L				22.5/1290	8,100 psi	
CCI 209M	Red Dot	Rem. R12L				20.0/1290	10,600 psi	
Fed. 209	Green Dot	Rem. R12L				22.0/1290	9,600 psi	
Fed. 209	Red Dot	Rem. R12L				19.5/1290	10,400 psi	
Rem. 209	Green Dot	Rem. R12L				22.0/1290	9,200 psi	
Rem. 209	Green Dot	Rem. RXP12				21.5/1290	9,900 psi	
Rem. 209	Green Dot	WAA12F1				21.0/1290	9,900 psi	
Win. 209	Green Dot	Rem. R12L				21.5/1290	8,800 psi	
Win. 209	Red Dot	Rem. R12L				20.0/1290	10,700 psi	
REMINGTON: RXP						**1-OUNCE LEAD SHOT**		
Rem. 209	IMR 700-X	BP HCDP	16.5/1200	16.7/1210	16.8/1220	17.0/1230	8,200 LUP	Note 12
Win. 209	W 452AA	Fed. 12S1				22.5/1290	10,300 LUP	

Load Notes: 7 = Use 50-60 pounds wad pressure to ensure wad is firmly seated against powder. 11 = Minimum overall length = 2⁹/₃₂", maximum crimp depth = ²/₃₂". 12 = Helix Cushion Platform.

Caution: Follow load recipes exactly; do not substitute components, exceed listed maximums or load less than listed minimums.

Primer	Powder Type	Wad	Powder Charge (grains) / Velocity (fps) Minimum			Maximum	Maximum Pressure	Load Notes
REMINGTON: RXP (CONT.)						**1-OUNCE LEAD SHOT**		
Win. 209	W 452AA	Rem. R12L				22.5/1290	10,100 LUP	
Win. 209	W 452AA	WAA12				22.5/1290	10,300 LUP	
VICTORY: PLASTIC						**1-OUNCE LEAD SHOT**		
CCI 209M	Clays	Pat. Ctrl. Prpl	18.0/1180	18.6/1210	19.1/1235	19.9/1290	9,400 psi	
CCI 209M	International	Pat. Ctrl. Prpl	19.6/1180	20.1/1210	20.5/1235	21.6/1290	8,200 psi	
CCI 209SC	Clays	WAA12SL	18.0/1180	18.2/1200	18.4/1225	18.5/1235	9,500 psi	
CCI 209SC	International	WAA12SL	19.5/1180	20.6/1210	21.5/1235	22.5/1290	9,400 psi	
Fed. 209A	Clays	Rem. TGT12	17.5/1180	18.1/1210	18.5/1235	19.7/1290	9,700 psi	
Fed. 209A	International	Rem. TGT12	19.3/1180	19.9/1210	20.3/1235	20.9/1290	8,800 psi	
Win. 209	Clays	WAA12SL	17.1/1180	17.9/1210	18.5/1235	19.3/1290	10,600 psi	
Win. 209	International	WAA12SL	19.0/1180	19.6/1210	20.0/1235	21.1/1290	9,600 psi	
WINCHESTER: COMPRESSION-FORMED AA TYPE						**1-OUNCE LEAD SHOT**		
CCI 209	American Select	BP DX12				19.5/1225	9,700 psi	Note 1
CCI 209	American Select	BP Pisk	19.1/1220	19.3/1230	19.4/1235	19.6/1240	10,100 psi	Note 2
CCI 209	American Select	BP HCDP	20.5/1210	20.7/1230	20.8/1240	21.0/1260	10,200 psi	Note 12
CCI 209	Bullseye	Pat. Ctrl. Prpl				18.0/1200	7,300 psi	
CCI 209	Clays	Rem. TGT12	16.6/1125	17.7/1180	18.7/1235	19.8/1290	9,500 LUP	
CCI 209	Green Dot	Pat. Ctrl. Prpl				21.0/1200	6,300 psi	
CCI 209	International	WAA12SL	19.2/1180	20.0/1210	20.6/1235	22.3/1290	8,800 LUP	
CCI 209	Nitro-100	H. Versalite				19.0/1275		
CCI 209	Nitro-100	WAA12	16.5/1200	17.2/1230	17.8/1260	18.5/1290	10,300 psi	Note 11
CCI 209	R. Scot D	WAA12	19.0/1200	19.8/1230	20.7/1260	21.5/1290	10,800 psi	
CCI 209	Red Diamond	Activ T-32	17.0/1180	17.8/1215	18.6/1250	19.5/1290	8,200 psi	Note 7
CCI 209	Red Diamond	Claybuster	17.0/1180	17.8/1215	18.6/1250	19.5/1290	7,600 psi	Note 7
CCI 209	Red Diamond	H. Versalite	16.5/1180	17.5/1215	18.4/1250	19.5/1290	8,800 psi	Note 7
CCI 209	Red Diamond	Hawk II	17.5/1180	18.1/1215	18.8/1250	19.5/1290	10,000 psi	Note 7
CCI 209	Red Diamond	WAA12	17.0/1180	17.8/1215	18.6/1250	19.5/1290	7,600 psi	Note 7
CCI 209	Red Diamond	WAA12SL				19.5/1290	7,600 psi	Note 7
CCI 209	Red Dot	Pat. Ctrl. Prpl				18.5/1200	7,800 psi	
CCI 209	Solo 1000	WAA12	18.5/1200	19.2/1230	19.8/1260	20.5/1290	9,400 psi	Note 11
CCI 209	W 452AA	WAA12SL	20.0/1180	21.5/1235	22.3/1265	23.0/1290	7,800 LUP	
CCI 209	WSL	Fed. 12S0				21.0/1290	10,400 psi	
CCI 209	WSL	WAA12L				21.5/1325	10,700 psi	
CCI 209	WSL	WAA12SL				21.0/1290	9,400 psi	
CCI 209	WST	Fed. 12S0	19.0/1180	20.5/1235	21.1/1265	21.5/1290	9,500 psi	
CCI 209	WST	WAA12L	21.0/1255	21.5/1270	22.0/1300	22.5/1325	10,200 psi	
CCI 209	WST	WAA12SL	21.5/1235	21.8/1250	22.1/1265	22.5/1290	7,900 psi	
CCI 209M	Bullseye	Pat. Ctrl. Prpl				17.5/1200	7,900 psi	
CCI 209M	Green Dot	Pat. Ctrl. Prpl				19.0/1200	6,600 psi	
CCI 209M	Green Dot	WAA12				21.5/1290	9,900 psi	
CCI 209M	Nitro-100	WAA12	16.0/1200	16.7/1230	17.3/1260	18.0/1290	10,700 psi	Note 11

Load Notes: 1 = Disperser-X. 2 = Piston Skeet. 7 = Use 50-60 pounds wad pressure to ensure wad is firmly seated against powder. 11 = Minimum overall length = 2⁹/₃₂", maximum crimp depth = ²/₃₂". 12 = Helix Cushion Platform.

Caution: Follow load recipes exactly; do not substitute components, exceed listed maximums or load less than listed minimums.

Primer	Powder Type	Wad	Powder Charge (grains) / Velocity (fps) Minimum			Maximum	Maximum Pressure	Load Notes
WINCHESTER: COMPRESSION-FORMED AA TYPE (CONT.)						1-OUNCE LEAD SHOT		
CCI 209M	R. Scot D	WAA12	18.5/1200	19.2/1230	19.8/1260	20.5/1290	10,500 psi	
CCI 209M	Red Diamond	Activ T-32	17.0/1180	17.5/1215	18.0/1250	18.5/1290	9,000 psi	Note 7
CCI 209M	Red Diamond	Claybuster	16.5/1180	17.1/1215	17.8/1250	18.5/1290	8,700 psi	Note 7
CCI 209M	Red Diamond	H. Versalite	16.5/1180	17.3/1215	18.1/1250	19.0/1290	9,700 psi	Note 7
CCI 209M	Red Diamond	Hawk II	17.0/1180	17.6/1215	18.3/1250	19.0/1290	10,400 psi	Note 7
CCI 209M	Red Diamond	WAA12	16.5/1180	17.1/1215	17.8/1250	18.5/1290	8,700 psi	Note 7
CCI 209M	Red Diamond	WAA12SL	17.0/1180	17.6/1215	18.3/1250	19.0/1290	9,200 psi	Note 7
CCI 209M	Red Dot	Pat. Ctrl. Prpl				17.5/1200	8,500 psi	
CCI 209M	Red Dot	WAA12				18.5/1290	10,400 psi	
CCI 209M	Red Dot	WAA12				17.5/1200	9,900 psi	
CCI 209M	Solo 1000	WAA12	18.0/1200	18.5/1230	19.0/1260	19.5/1290	9,900 psi	Note 11
CCI 209SC	Clays	Rem. TGT12	15.2/1125	16.6/1180	17.5/1235	19.2/1290	11,000 psi	
CCI 209SC	International	WAA12SL	19.0/1180	19.6/1210	20.0/1235	21.0/1290	10,000 psi	
Fed. 209	Bullseye	Pat. Ctrl. Prpl				17.5/1200	7,600 psi	
Fed. 209	Green Dot	Pat. Ctrl. Prpl				19.0/1200	7,200 psi	
Fed. 209	International	Pat. Ctrl. Prpl	20.6/1180	21.5/1210	22.2/1235	23.2/1290	7,400 LUP	
Fed. 209	Nitro-100	H. Versalite	17.0/1200	17.7/1225	18.3/1250	19.0/1275		
Fed. 209	Nitro-100	WAA12	17.0/1200	17.5/1225	18.0/1250	18.5/1275		
Fed. 209	R. Scot D	WAA12	19.0/1200	19.7/1230	20.3/1260	21.0/1290	10,200 psi	
Fed. 209	Red Dot	Pat. Ctrl. Prpl				17.5/1200	8,900 psi	
Fed. 209	Solo 1000	WAA12	18.5/1200	19.2/1230	19.8/1260	20.5/1290		
Fed. 209	W 452AA	WAA12SL	20.0/1180	21.5/1235	22.3/1265	23.0/1290	7,800 LUP	
Fed. 209	WSL	Fed. 12S0				21.5/1290	9,600 psi	
Fed. 209	WSL	WAA12SL				21.0/1290	9,300 psi	
Fed. 209	WST	Fed. 12S0	19.5/1180	21.0/1235	21.8/1265	22.5/1290	9,300 psi	
Fed. 209	WST	WAA12SL	21.0/1235	21.4/1250	21.8/1265	22.5/1290	7,400 psi	
Fed. 209A	IMR 700-X	CB 1100-12	15.0/1100	16.0/1145	17.5/1205	18.5/1250	8,700 psi	
Fed. 209A	IMR 700-X	Fed. 12S3	14.5/1090	15.5/1140	17.0/1210	18.0/1250	10,700 psi	
Fed. 209A	IMR 700-X	BP HCDP				17.0/1210	9,800 psi	Note 12
Fed. 209A	IMR 700-X	Rem. TGT12	15.0/1110	16.0/1155	17.0/1195	18.5/1260	9,400 psi	
Fed. 209A	IMR 700-X	WAA12SL	15.0/1110	16.0/1155	17.0/1195	18.5/1255	9,700 psi	
Fed. 209A	IMR PB	CB 1100-12	18.5/1095	20.0/1145	21.5/1200	23.0/1260	7,200 psi	
Fed. 209A	IMR PB	Fed. 12S3	18.0/1095	19.5/1155	20.5/1195	22.0/1255	8,900 psi	
Fed. 209A	IMR PB	BP HCDP				20.5/1200	7,900 psi	Note 12
Fed. 209A	IMR PB	Rem. Fig.-8	18.5/1095	20.0/1150	21.0/1190	22.5/1250	7,400 psi	
Fed. 209A	IMR PB	WAA12	18.5/1110	19.5/1150	21.0/1210	22.5/1260	8,600 psi	
Fed. 209A	International	Pat. Ctrl. Prpl	19.2/1180	20.0/1210	20.6/1235	21.7/1290	9,600 psi	
Fed. 209A	Nitro-100	WAA12	16.0/1200	16.8/1230	17.7/1260	18.5/1290	10,300 psi	Note 11
Fed. 209A	Red Diamond	Activ T-32	16.5/1180	17.1/1215	17.8/1250	18.5/1290	9,900 psi	Note 7
Fed. 209A	Red Diamond	Claybuster	16.5/1180	17.1/1215	17.8/1250	18.5/1290	9,600 psi	Note 7
Fed. 209A	Red Diamond	H. Versalite	16.5/1180	17.1/1215	17.8/1250	18.5/1290	10,500 psi	Note 7

Load Notes: 7 = Use 50-60 pounds wad pressure to ensure wad is firmly seated against powder. 11 = Minimum overall length = 2⁹/₃₂″, maximum crimp depth = ²/₃₂″. 12 = Helix Cushion Platform.

Caution: Follow load recipes exactly; do not substitute components, exceed listed maximums or load less than listed minimums.

Primer	Powder Type	Wad	Powder Charge (grains) / Velocity (fps) Minimum			Maximum	Maximum Pressure	Load Notes
WINCHESTER: COMPRESSION-FORMED AA TYPE (CONT.)						1-OUNCE LEAD SHOT		
Fed. 209A	Red Diamond	Hawk II	16.5/1180	17.1/1215	17.8/1250	18.5/1290	10,300 psi	Note 7
Fed. 209A	Red Diamond	WAA12	16.5/1180	17.1/1215	17.8/1250	18.5/1290	9,600 psi	Note 7
Fed. 209A	Red Diamond	WAA12SL	16.5/1180	17.0/1215	17.5/1250	18.0/1290	9,800 psi	Note 7
Fed. 209A	Solo 1000	WAA12	17.5/1200	18.2/1230	18.8/1260	19.5/1290	10,600 psi	Note 11
Fed. 209A	SR-7625	CB 1118-12	21.0/1100	22.0/1145	23.5/1210	24.5/1250	6,700 psi	
Fed. 209A	SR-7625	Fed. 12S3	20.5/1110	21.5/1145	23.0/1200	24.5/1255	7,300 psi	
Fed. 209A	SR-7625	BP HCDP				24.5/1255	7,400 psi	Note 12
Fed. 209A	SR-7625	Rem. RXP12	21.5/1110	22.5/1150	23.5/1190	25.0/1250	6,700 psi	
Fed. 209A	SR-7625	WAA12	20.0/1095	21.5/1145	23.5/1205	25.0/1260	7,400 psi	
Fed. 209A	WSL	WAA12L				21.0/1325	10,400 psi	
Fed. 209A	WST	WAA12L				21.5/1255	8,800 psi	
Fio. 615	IMR 700-X	BP DX12	18.9/1200	19.0/1235	19.2/1265	19.3/1300	10,000 LUP	Note 1
Fio. 615	IMR 700-X	BP HCDP	18.9/1200	19.1/1250	19.2/1275	19.3/1300	10,000 LUP	Note 1
Fio. 615	WSL	BP DX12				21.2/1290	10,000 LUP	Note 1
Fio. 615	WSL	BP HCDP				21.2/1290	10,000 LUP	Note 12
Fio. 616	Nitro-100	WAA12	16.0/1200	16.7/1230	17.3/1260	18.0/1290	10,600 psi	Note 11
Fio. 616	R. Scot D	WAA12	19.0/1200	19.5/1230	20.0/1260	20.5/1290	10,900 psi	
Fio. 616	Red Diamond	Activ T-32	16.5/1180	17.1/1215	17.8/1250	18.5/1290	9,700 psi	Note 7
Fio. 616	Red Diamond	Claybuster	16.5/1180	17.1/1215	17.8/1250	18.5/1290	9,300 psi	Note 7
Fio. 616	Red Diamond	H. Versalite	16.5/1180	17.1/1215	17.8/1250	18.5/1290	10,100 psi	Note 7
Fio. 616	Red Diamond	Hawk II	16.5/1180	17.1/1215	17.8/1250	18.5/1290	10,500 psi	Note 7
Fio. 616	Red Diamond	WAA12	16.5/1180	17.1/1215	17.8/1250	18.5/1290	9,300 psi	Note 7
Fio. 616	Red Diamond	WAA12SL	16.5/1180	17.0/1215	17.5/1250	18.0/1290	8,800 psi	Note 7
Fio. 616	Solo 1000	WAA12	18.0/1200	18.5/1230	19.0/1260	19.5/1290	9,600 psi	Note 7
Rem. 209	Green Dot	Pat. Ctrl. Prpl				19.0/1200	7,700 psi	
Rem. 209	Nitro-100	H. Versalite	17.0/1200	17.7/1225	18.3/1250	19.0/1275		
Rem. 209	Nitro-100	WAA12	17.5/1200	18.0/1225	18.5/1250	19.0/1275		
Rem. 209	Red Diamond	Activ T-32	17.5/1180	18.1/1215	18.8/1250	19.5/1290	8,900 psi	Note 7
Rem. 209	Red Diamond	Claybuster	17.0/1180	18.0/1215	18.9/1250	20.0/1290	8,300 psi	Note 7
Rem. 209	Red Diamond	H. Versalite	17.0/1180	17.8/1215	18.6/1250	19.5/1290	8,600 psi	Note 7
Rem. 209	Red Diamond	Hawk II	17.5/1180	18.1/1215	18.8/1250	19.5/1290	9,800 psi	Note 7
Rem. 209	Red Diamond	WAA12	17.0/1180	18.0/1215	18.9/1250	20.0/1290	8,300 psi	Note 7
Rem. 209	Red Diamond	WAA12SL				19.5/1290	7,400 psi	Note 7
Rem. 209	Red Dot	Pat. Ctrl. Prpl				17.5/1200	8,600 psi	
Rem. 209P	Clays	Pat. Ctrl. Prpl	17.6/1125	18.6/1180	19.5/1235	20.5/1290	7,600 LUP	
Rem. 209P	IMR 700-X	CB 1100-12	16.0/1110	17.0/1150	18.0/1190	19.5/1250	7,000 psi	
Rem. 209P	IMR 700-X	Fed. 12S3	15.0/1105	16.5/1160	17.5/1200	18.5/1250	9,300 psi	
Rem. 209P	IMR 700-X	BP HCDP				17.0/1200	8,600 psi	Note 12
Rem. 209P	IMR 700-X	Rem. TGT12	15.5/1105	16.5/1140	18.0/1205	19.0/1250	7,700 psi	
Rem. 209P	IMR 700-X	WAA12SL	15.0/1095	16.5/1155	18.0/1210	19.0/1245	8,000 psi	
Rem. 209P	IMR PB	CB 1100-12	19.0/1100	20.5/1150	22.0/1200	23.5/1260	6,500 psi	
Rem. 209P	IMR PB	Fed. 12S3	19.0/1095	20.5/1150	22.0/1205	23.5/1260	7,600 psi	

Load Notes: 1 = Disperser-X. 7 = Use 50-60 pounds wad pressure to ensure wad is firmly seated against powder. 11 = Minimum overall length = 2⁹/₃₂″, maximum crimp depth = ²/₃₂″. 12 = Helix Cushion Platform.

    Caution: Follow load recipes exactly; do not substitute components, exceed listed maximums or load less than listed minimums.

Primer	Powder Type	Wad	Powder Charge (grains) / Velocity (fps) Minimum		Maximum	Maximum Pressure	Load Notes
WINCHESTER: COMPRESSION-FORMED AA TYPE (CONT.)					**1-OUNCE LEAD SHOT**		
Rem. 209P	IMR PB	BP HCDP			20.5/1165	6,700 psi	Note 12
Rem. 209P	IMR PB	Rem. Fig.-8	19.0/1085	21.0/1150	22.0/1190	23.5/1255	6,700 psi	
Rem. 209P	IMR PB	WAA12	19.0/1110	20.0/1145	21.5/1205	22.5/1250	7,700 psi	
Rem. 209P	International	Rem. TGT12	20.8/1180	21.2/1210	21.5/1235	22.3/1290	7,800 LUP	
Rem. 209P	Nitro-100	WAA12	16.5/1200	17.2/1230	17.8/1260	18.5/1290	10,200 psi	Note 11
Rem. 209P	R. Scot D	WAA12	19.5/1200	20.2/1230	20.8/1260	21.5/1290	9,700 psi	
Rem. 209P	Solo 1000	WAA12	18.5/1200	19.0/1230	19.5/1260	20.0/1290	9,600 psi	Note 11
Rem. 209P	SR-7625	CB 1118-12	22.5/1110	23.5/1145	24.5/1190	26.0/1265	6,300 psi	
Rem. 209P	SR-7625	Fed. 12S3	22.0/1095	23.5/1160	24.5/1210	25.5/1265	6,900 psi	
Rem. 209P	SR-7625	BP HCDP			25.5/1255	7,400 psi	Note 12	
Rem. 209P	SR-7625	Rem. RXP12	22.5/1100	23.5/1145	24.5/1190	25.5/1245	6,000 psi	
Rem. 209P	SR-7625	WAA12	21.5/1105	22.5/1150	23.5/1195	25.0/1255	7,100 psi	
Win. 209	#2 Improved	WAA12SL	18.5/1200	19.2/1230	19.8/1260	20.5/1290	10,900 psi	Note 11
Win. 209	American Select	Claybuster	19.0/1200	19.8/1230	20.7/1260	21.5/1290	9,200 psi	
Win. 209	American Select	CS12S		18.3/1210	18.4/1220	18.5/1225	10,600 psi	
Win. 209	American Select	Fed. 12S0	19.0/1200	19.5/1230	20.0/1260	20.5/1290	10,200 psi	
Win. 209	American Select	Rem. TGT12	19.0/1200	19.7/1230	20.3/1260	21.0/1290	9,500 psi	
Win. 209	American Select	WAA12SL	19.0/1200	19.8/1230	20.7/1260	21.5/1290	10,300 psi	
Win. 209	American Select	BP Zero	18.3/1200	18.8/1225	19.3/1250	19.8/1300	9,400 psi	
Win. 209	Bullseye	Fed. 12S0				18.0/1200	9,600 psi	
Win. 209	Bullseye	Fed. 12S3				17.5/1200	8,700 psi	Note 9
Win. 209	Bullseye	Lage Uniwad				17.5/1200	8,900 psi	Note 9
Win. 209	Bullseye	Pat. Ctrl. prpl				17.5/1200	7,300 psi	
Win. 209	Bullseye	Rem. R12L				18.0/1200	8,800 psi	Note 9
Win. 209	Bullseye	Rem. RXP12				17.5/1200	8,800 psi	
Win. 209	Bullseye	WAA12				17.5/1200	9,900 psi	Note 9
Win. 209	Bullseye	WAA12F1				18.0/1200	9,500 psi	Note 9
Win. 209	Bullseye	Windjammer				18.0/1200	9,500 psi	Note 10
Win. 209	Clays	BP DX12	16.5/1160	17.5/1200	18.5/1240	19.5/1280	9,700 LUP	Note 1
Win. 209	Clays	BP HCDP	16.5/1160	17.5/1180	18.0/1200	19.0/1255	9,500 LUP	Note 12
Win. 209	Clays	Trapper	15.0/1125	15.6/1155	16.0/1180	18.0/1235	9,800 LUP	
Win. 209	Clays	WAA12SL	16.0/1125	17.2/1180	18.5/1235	19.8/1290	10,200 LUP	
Win. 209	Clays	Windjam. II	15.3/1125	16.0/1180	17.8/1235	19.0/1290	11,200 psi	
Win. 209	Clays	Windjammer	15.3/1125	16.5/1180	18.0/1235	19.6/1290	10,700 psi	
Win. 209	Green Dot	BP DX12	19.5/1200	20.0/1220	20.6/1240	21.0/1255	8,800 psi	Note 12
Win. 209	Green Dot	Fed. 12C1				21.0/1290	8,800 psi	
Win. 209	Green Dot	Fed. 12S0				19.5/1200	8,400 psi	
Win. 209	Green Dot	Fed. 12S0				19.5/1200	8,400 psi	
Win. 209	Green Dot	Fed. 12S3				22.5/1290	9,700 psi	
Win. 209	Green Dot	BP HCDP	19.5/1200	20.0/1220	21.0/1255	21.5/1290	9,700 psi	Note 12
Win. 209	Green Dot	Lage Uniwad				20.5/1200	7,400 psi	
Win. 209	Green Dot	Pat. Ctrl. Prpl	19.5/1200	20.3/1230	21.2/1260	22.0/1290	9,000 psi	

Load Notes: 1 = Disperser-X. 9 = Add one 20-gauge, 0.135″ card inside bottom of shotcup. 10 = Add two 20-gauge, 0.135″ cards inside bottom of shotcup. 11 = Minimum overall length = 2⁹/₃₂″, maximum crimp depth = ²/₃₂″. 12 = Helix Cushion Platform.

Caution: Follow load recipes exactly; do not substitute components, exceed listed maximums or load less than listed minimums.

Primer	Powder Type	Wad	Powder Charge (grains) / Velocity (fps) Minimum		Maximum	Maximum Pressure	Load Notes
WINCHESTER: COMPRESSION-FORMED AA TYPE (CONT.)					**1-OUNCE LEAD SHOT**		
Win. 209	Green Dot	Pat. Ctrl. Prpl			**19.5/1200**	6,900 psi	
Win. 209	Green Dot	Rem. R12L			**20.0/1200**	7,100 psi	
Win. 209	Green Dot	Rem. RXP12			**21.0/1290**	8,800 psi	
Win. 209	Green Dot	Rem. RXP12			**20.0/1200**	7,100 psi	
Win. 209	Green Dot	Rem. TGT12	**19.5/1200**	20.3/1230 21.2/1260	**22.0/1290**	9,700 psi	
Win. 209	Green Dot	WAA12			**20.0/1290**	8,700 psi	
Win. 209	Green Dot	WAA12			**19.5/1200**	7,500 psi	
Win. 209	Green Dot	WAA12F1			**20.0/1200**	7,600 psi	
Win. 209	Green Dot	WAA12SL	**19.5/1200**	20.2/1230 20.8/1260	**21.5/1290**	9,500 psi	
Win. 209	Green Dot	Windjammer			**20.0/1200**	7,600 psi	
Win. 209	IMR 700-X	BP DX12	**18.5/1245**	18.7/1255 18.8/1265	**19.0/1275**	9,700 LUP	Note 1
Win. 209	IMR 700-X	CB 1100-12	**14.5/1090**	15.5/1140 17.0/1205	**18.0/1245**	9,300 psi	
Win. 209	IMR 700-X	Fed. 12S3	**14.5/1100**	15.5/1140 17.0/1205	**18.0/1250**	10,500 psi	
Win. 209	IMR 700-X	BP HCDP			**17.0/1200**	9,600 psi	Note 12
Win. 209	IMR 700-X	BP HCDP	**18.5/1245**	18.7/1260 18.8/1265	**19.0/1275**	9,700 LUP	Note 12
Win. 209	IMR 700-X	Rem. TGT12	**14.5/1095**	15.5/1140 16.5/1190	**18.0/1250**	9,400 psi	
Win. 209	IMR 700-X	WAA12SL	**14.5/1105**	15.5/1145 16.5/1195	**18.0/1250**	10,100 psi	
Win. 209	IMR PB	CB 1100-12	**19.0/1110**	20.5/1140 22.0/1190	**23.5/1255**	6,600 psi	
Win. 209	IMR PB	Fed. 12S3	**19.0/1105**	20.5/1160 21.5/1200	**23.0/1250**	8,100 psi	
Win. 209	IMR PB	BP HCDP	**20.5/1165**	20.9/1180 21.2/1190	**21.5/1200**	7,000 psi	Note 12
Win. 209	IMR PB	Rem. Fig.-8	**19.0/1100**	20.0/1140 21.5/1195	**23.0/1255**	7,200 psi	
Win. 209	IMR PB	Rem. TGT12	**18.0/1095**	19.5/1140 21.5/1200	**23.0/1260**	7,500 psi	
Win. 209	IMR PB	WAA12	**18.5/1105**	20.0/1150 21.5/1200	**23.0/1260**	7,900 psi	
Win. 209	International	WAA12SL	**18.9/1180**	19.7/1210 20.4/1235	**21.3/1290**	8,900 LUP	
Win. 209	Nitro-100	BP 21			**18.5/1290**	8,500 psi	Note 11
Win. 209	Nitro-100	BP DX12	**17.0/1200**	17.5/1220 18.0/1240	**18.5/1275**	9,300 psi	Note 1
Win. 209	Nitro-100	BP TC			**17.0/1200**	6,800 psi	Note 11
Win. 209	Nitro-100	CB 1118-12	**18.5/1200**	18.5/1230 18.5/1260	**18.5/1290**	9,800 psi	Note 11
Win. 209	Nitro-100	Fed. 12S0	**16.5/1200**	17.0/1230 17.5/1260	**18.0/1290**	9,700 psi	Note 11
Win. 209	Nitro-100	H. Versalite	**17.0/1200**	17.7/1225 18.3/1250	**19.0/1275**		
Win. 209	Nitro-100	BP HCDP	**17.0/1200**	17.5/1220 18.5/1275	**19.0/1320**	10,000 psi	Note 12
Win. 209	Nitro-100	Rem. Fig.-8	**16.5/1200**	17.0/1230 17.5/1260	**18.0/1290**	8,400 psi	Note 11
Win. 209	Nitro-100	Rem. TGT12	**16.5/1200**	17.0/1230 17.5/1260	**18.0/1290**	8,700 psi	Note 11
Win. 209	Nitro-100	WAA12	**17.0/1200**	17.5/1225 18.0/1250	**18.5/1275**		
Win. 209	Nitro-100	WAA12SL	**17.0/1200**	17.3/1230 17.7/1260	**18.0/1290**	9,000 psi	Note 11
Win. 209	R. Scot D	Claybuster	**19.5/1200**	20.2/1230 20.8/1260	**21.5/1290**	8,600 psi	
Win. 209	R. Scot D	Fed. 12S0	**19.0/1200**	19.8/1230 20.7/1260	**21.5/1290**	10,400 psi	
Win. 209	R. Scot D	Rem. Fig.-8	**19.5/1200**	20.2/1230 20.8/1260	**21.5/1290**	10,100 psi	
Win. 209	R. Scot D	Rem. TGT12	**19.0/1200**	19.8/1230 20.7/1260	**21.5/1290**	9,800 psi	
Win. 209	R. Scot D	WAA12	**19.0/1200**	19.7/1230 20.3/1260	**21.0/1290**	10,300 psi	
Win. 209	R. Scot D	WAA12F1	**19.5/1200**	20.2/1230 20.8/1260	**21.5/1290**	9,300 psi	
Win. 209	Red Diamond	Activ T-32			**16.5/1180**	8,200 psi	Note 7

Load Notes: 1 = Disperser-X. 7 = Use 50-60 pounds wad pressure to ensure wad is firmly seated against powder. 11 = Minimum overall length = 2⁹/₃₂″, maximum crimp depth = ²/₃₂″. 12 = Helix Cushion Platform.

Caution: Follow load recipes exactly; do not substitute components, exceed listed maximums or load less than listed minimums.

Primer	Powder Type	Wad	Powder Charge (grains) / Velocity (fps) Minimum			Maximum	Maximum Pressure	Load Notes
WINCHESTER: COMPRESSION-FORMED AA TYPE (CONT.)					**1-OUNCE LEAD SHOT**			
Win. 209	Red Diamond	Claybuster	16.5/1180	17.1/1215	17.8/1250	18.5/1290	9,800 psi	Note 7
Win. 209	Red Diamond	H. Versalite	16.5/1180	17.1/1215	17.8/1250	18.5/1290	9,900 psi	Note 7
Win. 209	Red Diamond	Hawk II	16.5/1180	17.1/1215	17.8/1250	18.5/1290	10,100 psi	Note 7
Win. 209	Red Diamond	WAA12	16.5/1180	17.1/1215	17.8/1250	18.5/1290	9,800 psi	Note 7
Win. 209	Red Diamond	WAA12SL	16.5/1180	17.0/1215	17.5/1250	18.0/1290	9,900 psi	Note 7
Win. 209	Red Dot	BP DX12				17.5/1250	10,000 psi	Note 1
Win. 209	Red Dot	Fed. 12C1				20.0/1290	10,200 psi	
Win. 209	Red Dot	Fed. 12S0				18.0/1200	9,600 psi	
Win. 209	Red Dot	Fed. 12S0				18.0/1200	9,600 psi	
Win. 209	Red Dot	Fed. 12S3				20.0/1290	9,900 psi	
Win. 209	Red Dot	Fed. 12S3				18.0/1200	8,400 psi	
Win. 209	Red Dot	Lage Uniwad				18.0/1200	8,000 psi	
Win. 209	Red Dot	Pat. Ctrl. Prpl	18.0/1200	18.7/1230	19.3/1260	20.0/1290	10,400 psi	
Win. 209	Red Dot	Pat. Ctrl. Prpl				17.5/1200	8,800 psi	
Win. 209	Red Dot	Rem. R12L				18.0/1200	7,600 psi	
Win. 209	Red Dot	Rem. RXP12				20.0/1290	10,100 psi	
Win. 209	Red Dot	Rem. RXP12				18.0/1200	8,300 psi	
Win. 209	Red Dot	Rem. TGT12	18.0/1200	18.4/1215	18.8/1230	19.5/1255	9,800 psi	
Win. 209	Red Dot	WAA12				19.0/1290	10,500 psi	
Win. 209	Red Dot	WAA12				18.0/1200	8,800 psi	
Win. 209	Red Dot	WAA12F1				18.0/1200	9,000 psi	
Win. 209	Red Dot	WAA12SL	18.0/1200	18.3/1215	18.5/1230	19.0/1255	10,500 psi	
Win. 209	Red Dot	Windjammer				18.0/1200	9,100 psi	Note 9
Win. 209	Red Dot	WT12 Orange				17.5/1200	10,600 psi	
Win. 209	Scot 453	WAA12SL	17.5/1200	18.2/1230	18.8/1260	19.5/1290		
Win. 209	Solo 1000	BP DX12	18.5/1200	19.5/1240	20.0/1260	20.5/1290	8,900 psi	Note 1
Win. 209	Solo 1000	BP TC	18.0/1200	18.5/1230	19.0/1260	19.5/1290	9,000 psi	Note 11
Win. 209	Solo 1000	CB 1118-12	18.0/1200	18.5/1230	19.0/1260	19.5/1290	9,500 psi	Note 11
Win. 209	Solo 1000	Claybuster	19.0/1200	19.7/1230	20.3/1260	21.0/1290		
Win. 209	Solo 1000	Fed. 12S0	18.0/1200	18.5/1230	19.0/1260	19.5/1290	9,900 psi	Note 11
Win. 209	Solo 1000	BP HCDP	18.5/1200	19.0/1220	20.0/1260	21.0/1330	9,500 psi	Note 12
Win. 209	Solo 1000	Rem. Fig.-8	18.0/1200	18.5/1230	19.0/1260	19.5/1290	9,300 psi	Note 11
Win. 209	Solo 1000	Rem. TGT12	18.0/1200	18.5/1230	19.0/1260	19.5/1290	9,000 psi	Note 11
Win. 209	Solo 1000	WAA12	18.5/1200	19.2/1230	19.8/1260	20.5/1290		
Win. 209	Solo 1000	WAA12F1	19.0/1200	19.7/1230	20.3/1260	21.0/1290		
Win. 209	Solo 1000	WAA12SL	18.0/1200	18.5/1230	19.0/1260	19.5/1290	10,300 psi	Note 11
Win. 209	SR-7625	CB 1118-12	22.0/1095	23.5/1150	25.0/1210	26.0/1250	6,200 psi	
Win. 209	SR-7625	Fed. 12S3	22.0/1105	23.0/1155	24.0/1205	25.0/1250	7,100 psi	
Win. 209	SR-7625	BP HCDP				24.5/1200	6,000 psi	Note 12
Win. 209	SR-7625	Rem. RXP12	22.0/1095	23.5/1140	25.0/1200	26.0/1245	6,200 psi	
Win. 209	SR-7625	WAA12	21.5/1095	23.0/1150	24.0/1190	25.5/1255	6,600 psi	
Win. 209	W 452AA	BP HCDP				23.0/1290	9,000 LUP	Note 12

Load Notes: 1 = Disperser-X. 7 = Use 50-60 pounds wad pressure to ensure wad is firmly seated against powder. 9 = Add one 20-gauge, 0.135″ card inside bottom of shotcup. 11 = Minimum overall length = 2⁹/₃₂″, maximum crimp depth = ²/₃₂″. 12 = Helix Cushion Platform.

Caution: Follow load recipes exactly; do not substitute components, exceed listed maximums or load less than listed minimums.

Primer	Powder Type	Wad	Powder Charge (grains) / Velocity (fps) Minimum			Maximum	Maximum Pressure	Load Notes
WINCHESTER: COMPRESSION-FORMED AA TYPE (CONT.)						1-OUNCE LEAD SHOT		
Win. 209	W 452AA	WAA12SL	20.0/1180	21.5/1235	22.3/1265	23.0/1290	7,900 LUP	
Win. 209	WAAP	WAA12SL	18.0*/1180	19.0/1235	19.7/1265	20.5/1290	9,700 psi	*Note 13
Win. 209	WSL	BP DX12				21.0/1290	9,600 psi	Note 1
Win. 209	WSL	Fed. 12S0				21.5/1290	10,100 psi	
Win. 209	WSL	WAA12SL				21.0/1290	9,500 psi	
Win. 209	WST	BP DX12	19.5/1180	20.3/1215	20.6/1230	21.0/1250	9,700 psi	Note 1
Win. 209	WST	Fed. 12S0	19.0/1180	20.5/1235	21.3/1265	22.0/1290	9,500 psi	
Win. 209	WST	BP HCDP	19.5/1180	20.0/1215	20.5/1255	21.0/1290	9,600 psi	Note 12
Win. 209	WST	WAA12L	19.5/1200	21.0/1255	21.7/1285	22.5/1325	11,100 psi	
Win. 209	WST	WAA12SL	19.5*/1180	21.0/1235	21.6/1265	22.0/1290	8,100 psi	*Note 13
Win. AATP	Clays	WAA12SL	15.6/1125	16.3/1155	16.9/1180	18.2/1235	10,900 psi	
Win. AATP	International	WAA12SL	18.2/1180	18.8/1200	19.4/1220	20.0/1235	9,000 psi	
Win. AATP	WST	WAA12SL	19.5/1180	20.5/1235	21.3/1265	22.0/1290	9,600 psi	
WINCHESTER: POLYFORMED (SEPARATE PLASTIC BASE WAD)						1-OUNCE LEAD SHOT		
CCI 209M	Green Dot	WAA12F1				23.0/1290	7,500 psi	
CCI 209M	Red Dot	WAA12F1				21.0/1290	8,400 psi	
Fed. 209	Red Dot	WAA12F1				21.0/1290	8,200 psi	
Fio. 616	Green Dot	WAA12F1				23.0/1290	7,400 psi	
Fio. 616	Red Dot	WAA12F1				21.5/1290	7,900 psi	
Rem. 209P	Red Dot	WAA12F1				21.5/1290	7,800 psi	
Win. 209	Green Dot	Pat. Ctrl. Prpl				24.0/1290	6,800 psi	
Win. 209	Green Dot	Rem. Fig.-8				23.0/1290	7,800 psi	
Win. 209	Green Dot	WAA12F1				23.5/1290	7,000 psi	
Win. 209	Red Dot	Fed. 12S0				21.0/1290	9,600 psi	
Win. 209	Red Dot	Pat. Ctrl. Prpl				21.5/1290	7,900 psi	
Win. 209	Red Dot	Rem. Fig.-8				21.5/1290	8,500 psi	
Win. 209	Red Dot	WAA12F1				22.0/1290	7,600 psi	
Win. 209	W 452AA	Fed. 12S3				23.0/1290	8,400 LUP	

Load Notes: 1 = Disperser-X. 12 = Helix Cushion Platform. 13 = This load duplicates Winchester's AA-Xtra-Lite target loading.

Primer	Powder Type	Wad	Powder Charge (grains) / Velocity (fps) Minimum			Maximum	Maximum Pressure	Load Notes
WINCHESTER: COMPRESSION-FORMED AA TYPE						1¹/₁₆ OUNCES LEAD SHOT		
Win. 209	Nitro-100	BP HCDP	17.0/1200	17.5/1220	18.0/1255	18.5/1300	10,000 psi	Note 1
Win. 209	Solo 1000	BP HCDP	18.0/1160	18.5/1200	19.0/1230	20.0/1270	9,900 psi	Note 1

1 = Helix Cushion Platform.

    Caution: Follow load recipes exactly; do not substitute components, exceed listed maximums or load less than listed minimums.

Primer	Powder Type	Wad	Powder Charge (grains) / Velocity (fps) Minimum			Maximum	Maximum Pressure	Load Notes
ACTIV: ALL PLASTIC						**1 1/8 OUNCES LEAD SHOT**		
CCI 209	#2 Improved	Activ TG-30				18.5/1145	10,200 psi	Note 1
CCI 209	American Select	CS12S	19.5/1200	19.7/1210	19.8/1215	20.0/1220	11,500 psi	
CCI 209	American Select	BP HCD24	19.6/1200	19.8/1210	20.0/1220	20.2/1230	11,200 psi	Note 2
CCI 209	American Select	BP HCDP	19.6/1200	19.8/1210	20.0/1220	20.2/1225	11,000 psi	Note 3
CCI 209	American Select	BP Z21	19.5/1200	19.7/1210	19.9/1220	20.1/1230	11,200 psi	Note 4
CCI 209	Clays	Activ TG-30	18.4/1090	19.0/1120	19.5/1145	20.6/1200	7,700 LUP	
CCI 209	Nitro-100	Activ TG-30	16.5/1145	17.0/1175	17.5/1200	19.0/1255	10,100 psi	Note 1
CCI 209	R. Scot D	Activ TG-30	19.5/1125	20.3/1145	21.0/1200	22.5/1255	10,800 LUP	
CCI 209	Red Diamond	Activ T-28	17.0/1145	17.5/1175	18.0/1200	19.5/1255	9,400 psi	Note 1
CCI 209	Red Diamond	Activ TG-30	16.5/1145	17.3/1175	18.0/1200	19.5/1255	10,400 psi	Note 1
CCI 209	Red Diamond	Claybuster	17.0/1145	17.8/1175	18.5/1200	19.5/1255	9,200 psi	Note 5
CCI 209	Red Diamond	Fed. 12S0	17.0/1145	17.8/1175	18.5/1200	19.5/1255	9,200 psi	Note 5
CCI 209	Red Diamond	Fed. 12S3	16.5/1145	17.5/1175	18.5/1200	19.5/1255	9,600 psi	Note 5
CCI 209	Red Dot	Fed. 12S3	18.5/1145	18.9/1160	19.3/1175	20.0/1200	8,200 psi	
CCI 209	Solo 1000	Activ TG-30	19.0/1125	19.6/1145	20.5/1200	22.0/1255	10,000 LUP	Note 1
CCI 209	Solo 1250	Activ TG-30	25.5/1200	26.3/1230	27.0/1255	28.5/1310	9,400 LUP	Note 1
CCI 209	Solo 1250	Lage Uniwad	27.5/1200	28.0/1230	28.5/1255	28.5/1310	9,400 LUP	
CCI 209M	Green Dot	Fed. 12S3	21.5/1200	21.7/1225	21.8/1240	22.0/1255	9,400 psi	
CCI 209M	Green Dot	WAA12				23.0/1255	8,800 psi	
CCI 209M	International	Activ TG-30	19.8/1090	20.5/1145	21.5/1200	22.7/1255	9,300 LUP	
CCI 209M	R. Scot D	Activ TG-30	19.0/1125	19.5/1145	20.5/1200	21.5/1255	10,800 LUP	
CCI 209M	Red Diamond	Activ T-28	17.0/1145	17.5/1175	18.0/1200	19.5/1255	9,500 psi	Note 5
CCI 209M	Red Diamond	Activ TG-30	16.5/1145	16.9/1160	17.3/1175	18.0/1200	9,600 psi	Note 5
CCI 209M	Red Diamond	Claybuster	17.0/1145	17.8/1175	18.5/1200	19.5/1255	9,300 psi	Note 5
CCI 209M	Red Diamond	Fed. 12S0	17.0/1145	17.8/1175	18.5/1200	19.5/1255	9,300 psi	Note 5
CCI 209M	Red Diamond	Fed. 12S3	16.5/1145	17.5/1175	18.5/1200	19.5/1255	9,800 psi	Note 5
CCI 209M	Red Dot	Fed. 12S3	17.5/1145	18.0/1160	18.6/1175	19.5/1200	10,000 psi	
CCI 209M	Solo 1000	Activ TG-30				18.5/1125	7,800 LUP	Note 1
CCI 209M	Solo 1250	Activ TG-30	24.5/1200	24.9/1215	25.3/1230	26.0/1255	9,500 LUP	
CCI 209M	Universal	Fed. 12S0	24.0/1200	25.0/1230	26.0/1255	27.0/1310	10,200 psi	
CCI 209SC	American Select	Activ T-G30	19.5/1145	20.3/1175	21.0/1200	22.5/1250	10,600 psi	
CCI 209SC	American Select	Claybuster	19.0/1145	19.8/1175	20.5/1200	22.0/1250	10,500 psi	
CCI 209SC	Clays	Activ TG-30	16.1/1090	16.6/1120	17.0/1145	19.0/1200	10,400 psi	
CCI 209SC	International	Activ TG-30	17.7/1090	18.3/1145	20.5/1200	22.0/1255	9,900 psi	
CCI 209SC	Nitro-100	Activ TG-30	16.5/1145	17.0/1175	17.5/1200	19.0/1255	10,900 psi	Note 1
CCI 209SC	Nitro-100	Fed. 12S3	17.5/1200	17.7/1215	18.0/1230	18.5/1255	11,100 psi	Note 1
CCI 209SC	Solo 1000	Activ TG-30				21.0/1255	10,500 LUP	Note 1
CCI 209SC	Solo 1250	Activ TG-30	24.5/1200	24.9/1215	25.3/1230	26.0/1255	9,500 LUP	Note 1
CCI 209SC	Solo 1250	Fed. 12S3	25.0/1200	25.4/1215	25.8/1230	26.5/1255	8,900 LUP	Note 1
CCI 209SC	Universal	Fed. 12S0	24.8/1200	25.0/1230	25.2/1255	27.0/1310	9,400 psi	
Fed. 209	Clays	Fed. 12S0	18.3/1090	18.7/1120	19.1/1145	19.9/1200	8,400 LUP	
Fed. 209	Green Dot	Fed. 12S3				21.5/1200	7,500 psi	

Load Notes: 1 = Minimum overall length = 2 10/32", maximum crimp depth = 2/32". 2 = Hex Cushion DR-24. 3 = Helix Cushion Platform. 4 = Trap Commander. 5 = Use 50-60 pounds wad pressure to ensure wad is firmly seated against powder.

Caution: Follow load recipes exactly; do not substitute components, exceed listed maximums or load less than listed minimums.

Primer	Powder Type	Wad	Powder Charge (grains) / Velocity (fps) Minimum			Maximum	Maximum Pressure	Load Notes
ACTIV: ALL PLASTIC (CONT.)						1¹/₈ OUNCES LEAD SHOT		
Fed. 209	International	Fed. 12S0	21.2/1090	21.8/1145	23.2/1200	24.0/1255	8,200 LUP	
Fed. 209	Nitro-100	Fed. 12S3				16.5/1145	8,400 psi	Note 1
Fed. 209	R. Scot D	Activ TG-30	19.0/1125	19.5/1145	21.0/1200	22.0/1255	10,900 LUP	
Fed. 209	Red Dot	Fed. 12S3	18.0/1145	18.4/1160	18.8/1175	19.5/1200	9,600 psi	
Fed. 209	Solo 1000	Activ TG-30				18.5/1125	7,900 LUP	Note 1
Fed. 209	Solo 1000	Fed. 12S3				19.0/1145	8,500 LUP	Note 1
Fed. 209	Solo 1250	Activ TG-30				28.0/1310	10,000 LUP	Note 1
Fed. 209A	American Select	Activ T-G30	19.5/1145	20.1/1175	20.5/1200	21.0/1250	9,000 psi	
Fed. 209A	American Select	Claybuster	19.0/1145	19.8/1175	20.5/1200	21.5/1250	10,800 psi	
Fed. 209A	Red Diamond	Activ T-28	17.0/1145	17.5/1175	18.0/1200	19.5/1255	9,800 psi	Note 5
Fed. 209A	Red Diamond	Activ TG-30	16.5/1145	16.9/1160	17.3/1175	18.0/1200	10,000 psi	Note 5
Fed. 209A	Red Diamond	Claybuster	17.0/1145	17.8/1175	18.5/1200	19.5/1255	9,700 psi	Note 5
Fed. 209A	Red Diamond	Fed. 12S0	17.0/1145	17.8/1175	18.5/1200	19.5/1255	9,700 psi	Note 5
Fed. 209A	Red Diamond	Fed. 12S3	16.5/1145	17.5/1175	18.5/1200	19.5/1255	10,100 psi	Note 5
Fed. 209A	Universal	Rem. TGT12	24.0/1200	24.8/1230	25.5/1255	26.7/1310	9,700 psi	
Fio. 616	#2 Improved	Activ TG-30				17.5/1125	9,300 psi	Note 1
Fio. 616	Nitro-100	Activ TG-30	16.5/1145	16.5/1175	16.5/1200	19.0/1255	10,700 psi	Note 1
Fio. 616	R. Scot D	Activ TG-30	19.0/1125	19.5/1145	21.0/1200	22.0/1255	10,900 LUP	
Fio. 616	Red Diamond	Activ T-28	17.0/1145	17.5/1175	18.0/1200	19.5/1255	9,500 psi	Note 5
Fio. 616	Red Diamond	Activ TG-30	16.5/1145	16.9/1160	17.3/1175	18.0/1200	9,700 psi	Note 5
Fio. 616	Red Diamond	Claybuster	17.0/1145	17.8/1175	18.5/1200	19.5/1255	9,900 psi	Note 5
Fio. 616	Red Diamond	Fed. 12S0	17.0/1145	17.8/1175	18.5/1200	19.5/1255	9,900 psi	Note 5
Fio. 616	Red Diamond	Fed. 12S3	16.5/1145	17.5/1175	18.5/1200	19.5/1255	10,500 psi	Note 5
Fio. 616	Solo 1000	Activ TG-30	18.5/1125	19.0/1145	20.5/1200	21.5/1255	10,300 LUP	Note 1
Fio. 616	Solo 1250	Activ TG-30	24.5/1200	24.9/1215	25.3/1230	26.0/1255	9,500 LUP	Note 1
Rem. 209	Red Diamond	Activ T-28	17.0/1145	17.8/1175	18.5/1200	19.5/1255	9,000 psi	Note 5
Rem. 209	Red Diamond	Activ TG-30	16.5/1145	17.3/1175	18.0/1200	19.5/1255	10,100 psi	Note 5
Rem. 209	Red Diamond	Claybuster	17.0/1145	17.8/1175	18.5/1200	19.5/1255	9,200 psi	Note 5
Rem. 209	Red Diamond	Fed. 12S0	17.0/1145	17.8/1175	18.5/1200	19.5/1255	9,200 psi	Note 5
Rem. 209	Red Diamond	Fed. 12S3	16.5/1145	17.5/1175	18.5/1200	19.5/1255	9,500 psi	Note 5
Rem. 209P	American Select	Activ T-G30	20.0/1145	20.6/1175	21.0/1200	22.5/1250	8,900 psi	
Rem. 209P	American Select	Claybuster	20.0/1145	20.6/1175	21.0/1200	22.5/1250	10,000 psi	
Rem. 209P	Clays	Rem. TGT12	18.0/1090	18.6/1120	19.1/1145	20.2/1200	7,600 LUP	
Rem. 209P	International	Rem. TGT12	21.1/1090	21.7/1145	23.4/1200	24.3/1255	7,500 LUP	
Rem. 209P	Solo 1250	Activ TG-30				28.0/1310	10,000 LUP	Note 1
Win. 209	#2 Improved	Activ TG-30				19.5/1255	10,900 psi	Note 1
Win. 209	American Select	Activ T-G30	19.5/1145	20.1/1175	21.0/1200	22.0/1250	10,100 psi	
Win. 209	American Select	Claybuster	19.0/1145	19.8/1175	20.5/1200	22.0/1250	9,700 psi	
Win. 209	American Select	BP Zero	17.8/1160	18.3/1185	18.8/1210	19.8/1230	10,400 psi	
Win. 209	Clays	BP SCAT	19.0/1145	19.6/1175	20.0/1200	20.5/1240	8,800 LUP	Note 6
Win. 209	Clays	BP HCDP	18.0/1090	19.0/1145	20.0/1200	21.0/1270	9,900 LUP	Note 3
Win. 209	Clays	Pat. Ctrl. Prpl	18.5/1090	19.0/1120	19.5/1145	20.5/1200	7,500 LUP	

Load Notes: 1 = Minimum overall length = 2¹⁰/₃₂″, maximum crimp depth = ²/₃₂″. 3 = Helix Cushion Platform. 5 = Use 50-60 pounds wad pressure to ensure wad is firmly seated against powder. 6 = Scatter Master.

    Caution: Follow load recipes exactly; do not substitute components, exceed listed maximums or load less than listed minimums.

Primer	Powder Type	Wad	Powder Charge (grains) / Velocity (fps) Minimum			Maximum	Maximum Pressure	Load Notes
ACTIV: ALL PLASTIC (CONT.)					1 1/8 OUNCES LEAD SHOT			
Win. 209	Green Dot	BP SCAT	20.0/1160	20.5/1180	21.0/1200	21.5/1230	9,400 psi	Note 6
Win. 209	Green Dot	Fed. 12S3				21.5/1200	7,400 psi	
Win. 209	Green Dot	BP HCDP	19.5/1145	20.5/1180	21.5/1230	22.0/1255	9,900 psi	Note 3
Win. 209	Green Dot	Pat. Ctrl. Prpl				23.0/1200	7,000 psi	
Win. 209	Green Dot	Rem. PT12				22.0/1200	8,000 psi	
Win. 209	Green Dot	WAA12F1				22.5/1200	6,500 psi	
Win. 209	IMR 700-X	BP SCAT				19.0/1180	7,700 LUP	Note 6
Win. 209	IMR 700-X	BP HCDP	18.5/1140	19.0/1180	19.5/1200	20.0/1230	9,000 LUP	Note 3
Win. 209	IMR 800-X	BP SCAT			24.5/1230	25.0/1250	6,900 LUP	Note 6
Win. 209	IMR 800-X	BP HCDP	24.0/1210	24.5/1230	25.0/1250	25.5/1280	7,400 LUP	Note 3
Win. 209	International	BP SCAT	20.5/1145	21.0/1170	22.0/1230	22.6/1255	8,800 LUP	Note 6
Win. 209	International	BP HCDP	20.5/1145	21.5/1200	22.0/1230	23.0/1270	9,300 LUP	Note 3
Win. 209	International	WAA12SL	20.0/1090	20.6/1145	21.5/1200	22.6/1255	8,700 LUP	
Win. 209	Nitro-100	Activ TG-30	16.5/1200	17.1/1215	17.8/1230	19.0/1255	10,500 psi	Note 1
Win. 209	Nitro-100	BP SCAT	18.0/1145	18.3/1175	18.6/1205	19.0/1240	8,900 LUP	Note 6
Win. 209	Nitro-100	Fed. 12S3				16.5/1145	8,600 psi	Note 1
Win. 209	Nitro-100	BP HCDP	18.5/1200	18.8/1215	19.1/1230	19.5/1255	9,400 LUP	Note 3
Win. 209	R. Scot D	Activ TG-30	19.5/1125	20.0/1145	21.0/1200	22.5/1255	10,900 LUP	
Win. 209	Red Diamond	Activ T-28	17.0/1145	17.5/1175	18.0/1200	19.5/1255	9,400 psi	Note 5
Win. 209	Red Diamond	Activ TG-30	16.5/1145	16.9/1160	17.3/1175	18.0/1200	9,600 psi	Note 5
Win. 209	Red Diamond	Claybuster	17.0/1145	17.8/1175	18.5/1200	19.5/1255	9,800 psi	Note 5
Win. 209	Red Diamond	Fed. 12S0	17.0/1145	17.8/1175	18.5/1200	19.5/1255	9,800 psi	Note 5
Win. 209	Red Diamond	Fed. 12S3	16.5/1145	17.5/1175	18.5/1200	19.5/1255	9,600 psi	Note 5
Win. 209	Red Dot	Fed. 12S3	18.0/1145	18.4/1160	18.8/1175	19.5/1200	10,300 psi	
Win. 209	Red Dot	Pat. Ctrl. Prpl	18.5/1145	18.9/1160	19.3/1175	20.0/1200	8,400 psi	
Win. 209	Red Dot	Rem. PT12	17.5/1145	17.8/1160	18.1/1175	19.5/1200	9,400 psi	
Win. 209	Red Dot	WAA12F1	18.5/1145	18.8/1160	19.1/1175	19.5/1200	8,700 psi	
Win. 209	Scot 453	Activ TG-30	18.0/1125	18.5/1145	19.0/1175	19.5/1200	10,900 psi	
Win. 209	Solo 1000	Activ TG-30	18.0/1125	19.5/1145	20.5/1200	22.0/1255		
Win. 209	Solo 1000	Activ TG-30	19.0/1125	19.8/1165	20.5/1200	22.0/1255	9,300 LUP	Note 1
Win. 209	Solo 1000	BP SCAT		20.0/1180	20.2/1190	20.5/1200	8,300 psi	Note 6
Win. 209	Solo 1000	Fed. 12S3				19.5/1145	7,900 LUP	Note 1
Win. 209	Solo 1000	BP HCDP	20.5/1200	20.7/1210	20.8/1215	21.0/1220	9,000 psi	Note 3
Win. 209	Solo 1250	Activ TG-30	25.0/1200	25.8/1230	26.5/1255	28.0/1310	10,400 LUP	Note 1
Win. 209	Solo 1250	BP SCAT	25.5/1200	26.1/1230	26.5/1255	27.0/1265	8,600 psi	Note 6
Win. 209	Solo 1250	Claybuster				28.5/1310	9,000 LUP	Note 1
Win. 209	Solo 1250	Fed. 12S3				28.5/1310	9,500 LUP	Note 1
Win. 209	Solo 1250	BP HCDP	25.5/1200	26.5/1255	27.5/1285	28.0/1300	9,600 psi	Note 3
Win. 209	Solo 1250	WAA12	25.5/1200	26.0/1230	26.5/1255	28.5/1310	9,900 LUP	Note 1
Win. 209	Universal	Activ TG-30	24.0/1200	24.8/1230	25.5/1255	27.0/1310	10,100 psi	

Load Notes: 1 = Minimum overall length = 2¹⁰/₃₂″, maximum crimp depth = ²/₃₂″. 3 = Helix Cushion Platform. 5 = Use 50-60 pounds wad pressure to ensure wad is firmly seated against powder. 6 = Scatter Master.

Caution: Follow load recipes exactly; do not substitute components, exceed listed maximums or load less than listed minimums.

Primer	Powder Type	Wad	Powder Charge (grains) / Velocity (fps) Minimum			Maximum	Maximum Pressure	Load Notes

ESTATE: CHEDITE (LOW BASE WAD) — 1¹/₈ OUNCES LEAD SHOT

Primer	Powder Type	Wad	Minimum			Maximum	Maximum Pressure	Load Notes
Fed. 209A	Clays	Fed. 12S3	16.0/1090	16.3/1120	16.5/1145	18.5/1200	10,400 psi	
Fed. 209A	Clays	Fiocchi TL1	16.5/1090	16.8/1120	17.0/1145	19.0/1200	10,300 psi	
Fed. 209A	International	Fed. 12S3	19.0/1090	19.4/1115	20.0/1145	21.8/1200	10,700 psi	
Fed. 209A	International	Fiocchi TL1	18.0/1090	18.5/1145	20.0/1200	21.0/1255	10,500 psi	
Fio. 616	Clays	Activ TG-30	16.5/1090	16.8/1120	17.0/1145	18.5/1200	9,500 psi	
Fio. 616	Clays	Fiocchi TL1	16.0/1090	16.5/1120	17.0/1145	19.0/1200	11,300 psi	
Fio. 616	International	Activ TG-30	19.5/1145	20.5/1175	21.5/1200	22.5/1255	9,500 psi	
Fio. 616	International	Fiocchi TL1	19.0/1145	19.8/1175	20.5/1200	22.0/1255	10,000 psi	
Win. 209	Clays	Fed. 12S3	16.5/1090	16.8/1120	17.0/1145	19.0/1200	10,300 psi	
Win. 209	International	Fed. 12S3	19.5/1145	20.3/1175	21.0/1200	22.0/1255	9,900 psi	

FEDERAL: GOLD MEDAL PLASTIC — 1¹/₈ OUNCES LEAD SHOT

Primer	Powder Type	Wad	Minimum			Maximum	Maximum Pressure	Load Notes
CCI 209	American Select	CS12S	20.0/1200	20.2/1215	20.3/1225	20.5/1240	11,400 psi	
CCI 209	American Select	BP HCD24		19.8/1200	19.9/1210	20.0/1220	10,800 psi	Note 2
CCI 209	American Select	BP HCDP		20.0/1210	20.2/1215	20.5/1225	11,100 psi	Note 3
CCI 209	American Select	SCAT				21.0/1190	11,200 psi	Note 6
CCI 209	American Select	SF12 STR-8				20.0/1225	10,700 psi	
CCI 209	American Select	BP Z21		19.8/1200	19.9/1210	20.0/1220	10,900 psi	Note 4
CCI 209	Clays	BP SCAT	19.5/1200	20.0/1220	20.2/1235	20.5/1250	9,500 psi	Note 6
CCI 209	Clays	H. Versalite	17.3/1090	17.9/1120	18.5/1145	19.7/1200	8,100 LUP	
CCI 209	Clays	BP HCDP	19.5/1200	20.0/1220	20.2/1230	20.5/1250	9,500 psi	Note 3
CCI 209	Green Dot	Fed. 12S3	19.0/1145	19.6/1160	21.2/1175	22.0/1200	9,200 psi	
CCI 209	IMR 800-X	CB 2118-12	21.5/1095	23.0/1145	24.5/1205	26.0/1265	6,800 psi	
CCI 209	IMR 800-X	Fed. 12S3	21.0/1095	22.5/1155	24.0/1200	26.0/1260	7,300 psi	
CCI 209	IMR 800-X	Rem. Fig.-8	21.0/1105	22.5/1150	24.0/1200	26.0/1260	6,900 psi	
CCI 209	IMR 800-X	WAA12	21.5/1105	22.5/1145	24.0/1200	25.5/1265	7,100 psi	
CCI 209	IMR 800-X	Windjammer	22.5/1100	23.5/1145	25.0/1205	26.0/1250	6,300 psi	
CCI 209	International	BP SCAT	19.5/1120	20.3/1160	21.0/1200	21.5/1220	8,300 psi	Note 6
CCI 209	International	H. Versalite	20.4/1145	21.5/1175	22.5/1200	24.2/1255	8,700 LUP	
CCI 209	International	BP HCDP	20.5/1145	21.0/1200	21.5/1220	22.0/1250	8,500 psi	Note 3
CCI 209	Nitro-100	BP SCAT	18.5/1180	19.0/1200	19.5/1220	20.0/1255	9,700 psi	Note 6
CCI 209	Nitro-100	Fed. 12S3	17.5/1145	18.0/1175	18.5/1200	19.5/1255	9,700 psi	Note 1
CCI 209	Nitro-100	H. Versalite				20.5/1255		
CCI 209	Nitro-100	BP HCDP	18.5/1180	19.0/1200	19.5/1220	20.0/1255	9,700 psi	Note 3
CCI 209	Nitro-100	WAA12	18.0/1145	18.3/1175	18.5/1200	20.0/1255		
CCI 209	R. Scot D	Fed. 12S3	19.0/1125	19.5/1145	20.5/1200	22.0/1255	10,500 LUP	
CCI 209	Red Diamond	Activ TG-30	17.0/1145	17.8/1175	18.5/1200	20.0/1255	9,600 psi	Note 5
CCI 209	Red Diamond	BP CS12	18.5/1200	19.1/1220	19.7/1240	20.0/1255	9,200 psi	Note 5
CCI 209	Red Diamond	BP ITD	17.0/1145	17.8/1175	18.5/1200	19.5/1255	8,500 psi	Note 5
CCI 209	Red Diamond	Claybuster	17.0/1145	17.8/1175	18.5/1200	19.5/1255	8,800 psi	Note 5
CCI 209	Red Diamond	Fed. 12S0	17.0/1145	17.8/1175	18.5/1200	19.5/1255	8,800 psi	Note 5
CCI 209	Red Diamond	Fed. 12S3	16.5/1145	17.3/1175	18.0/1200	19.5/1255	9,700 psi	Note 5
CCI 209	Red Diamond	H. Versalite	17.0/1145	17.5/1175	18.0/1200	19.5/1255	8,900 psi	Note 5

Load Notes: 1 = Minimum overall length = 2¹⁰/₃₂″, maximum crimp depth = ²/₃₂″. 2 = Hex Cushion DR-24. 3 = Helix Cushion Platform. 4 = Trap Commander. 6 = Scatter Master.

Caution: Follow load recipes exactly; do not substitute components, exceed listed maximums or load less than listed minimums.

Primer	Powder Type	Wad	Powder Charge (grains) / Velocity (fps) Minimum			Maximum	Maximum Pressure	Load Notes
FEDERAL: GOLD MEDAL PLASTIC (CONT.)						1 1/8 OUNCES LEAD SHOT		
CCI 209	Red Diamond	Rem. Fig.-8				20.0/1255	8,200 psi	Note 5
CCI 209	Red Diamond	Rem. TGT12	17.0/1145	17.8/1175	18.5/1200	19.5/1255	8,300 psi	Note 5
CCI 209	Red Diamond	WAA12				19.5/1255	9,300 psi	Note 5
CCI 209	Red Dot	Fed. 12S3	18.0/1145	18.6/1160	19.2/1175	20.0/1200	9,800 psi	
CCI 209	Solo 1000	BP SCAT	19.0/1145	20.0/1200	20.5/1220	21.0/1240	9,200 psi	Note 6
CCI 209	Solo 1000	Fed. 12S3	18.5/1125	19.0/1145	20.0/1200	21.5/1255	10,200 LUP	Note 1
CCI 209	Solo 1000	BP HCDP		20.5/1220	20.7/1230	21.0/1240	9,200 psi	Note 3
CCI 209	Solo 1250	BP SCAT	26.5/1220	27.0/1250	27.2/1275	27.5/1300	9,700 psi	Note 6
CCI 209	Solo 1250	Fed. 12S3	25.5/1200	26.3/1230	27.0/1255	28.5/1310	10,000 LUP	Note 1
CCI 209	Solo 1250	BP HCDP	26.0/1200	26.5/1220	27.0/1250	27.5/1300	9,700 psi	Note 3
CCI 209	Unique	Fed. 12S3				24.0/1200	8,300 psi	
CCI 209	Universal	Windjammer	25.2/1200	25.9/1230	26.5/1255	28.0/1310	8,800 psi	
CCI 209	WST	Fed. 12S3	19.5/1145	20.0/1165	20.5/1180	21.0/1200	10,300 psi	
CCI 209M	Green Dot	Fed. 12S3	19.5/1145	20.3/1175	21.0/1200	22.5/1250	9,800 psi	
CCI 209M	International	Rem. TGT12	19.5/1090	20.0/1145	20.6/1200	22.5/1255	8,600 LUP	
CCI 209M	Nitro-100	Fed. 12S3	17.5/1145	18.0/1175	18.5/1200	19.5/1255	10,900 psi	Note 1
CCI 209M	R. Scot D	Fed. 12S3	18.5/1125	19.0/1145	20.0/1200	21.5/1255	10,900 LUP	
CCI 209M	Red Diamond	Activ TG-30	17.0/1145	17.5/1175	18.0/1200	19.5/1255	9,600 psi	Note 5
CCI 209M	Red Diamond	BP CS12	17.0/1200	17.8/1215	18.5/1230	20.0/1255	9,500 psi	Note 5
CCI 209M	Red Diamond	BP ITD	16.5/1145	17.3/1175	18.0/1200	19.5/1255	8,900 psi	Note 5
CCI 209M	Red Diamond	Claybuster	17.0/1145	17.5/1175	18.0/1200	19.5/1255	9,000 psi	Note 5
CCI 209M	Red Diamond	Fed. 12S0	17.0/1145	17.5/1175	18.0/1200	19.5/1255	9,000 psi	Note 5
CCI 209M	Red Diamond	Fed. 12S3	16.5/1145	17.3/1175	18.0/1200	19.5/1255	10,100 psi	Note 5
CCI 209M	Red Diamond	H. Versalite	16.5/1145	17.3/1175	18.0/1200	19.5/1255	9,000 psi	Note 5
CCI 209M	Red Diamond	Rem. Fig.-8				20.0/1255	9,200 psi	Note 5
CCI 209M	Red Diamond	Rem. TGT12	17.0/1145	17.5/1175	18.0/1200	19.5/1255	8,900 psi	Note 5
CCI 209M	Red Diamond	WAA12				19.5/1255	9,500 psi	Note 5
CCI 209M	Red Dot	Fed. 12S3	17.0/1090	18.0/1145	18.6/1175	19.0/1200	8,900 psi	
CCI 209M	Solo 1000	Fed. 12S3	18.0/1125	18.5/1145	19.5/1200	21.0/1255	10,700 LUP	Note 1
CCI 209M	Solo 1250	Fed. 12S3	24.5/1200	25.3/1230	26.0/1255	27.0/1310	10,400 LUP	Note 1
CCI 209M	Unique	Fed. 12S3	23.5/1200	23.7/1225	23.8/1235	24.0/1250	9,100 psi	
CCI 209M	Universal	H. Versalite	23.0/1200	23.6/1230	24.2/1255	25.3/1310	10,300 psi	
CCI 209SC	American Select	Fed. 12S3	18.5/1145	19.1/1160	19.7/1175	20.5/1200	10,000 psi	
CCI 209SC	Clays	H. Versalite	16.0/1090	16.5/1120	17.0/1145	18.2/1200	10,400 psi	
CCI 209SC	Green Dot	Fed. 12S3	20.5/1145	21.1/1160	21.7/1175	22.5/1200	8,900 psi	
CCI 209SC	Green Dot	Rem. Fig.-8	21.0/1145	21.6/1160	22.2/1175	23.0/1200	9,200 psi	
CCI 209SC	Green Dot	WAA12	20.5/1145	20.9/1160	21.3/1175	22.0/1200	10,200 psi	
CCI 209SC	International	H. Versalite	19.0/1145	19.8/1175	20.5/1200	21.5/1255	10,300 psi	
CCI 209SC	International	Rem. TGT12	19.0/1090	19.2/1145	20.0/1200	21.5/1255	9,500 psi	
CCI 209SC	Red Dot	Fed. 12S3	19.0/1145	19.4/1160	19.9/1175	20.5/1200	10,700 psi	
CCI 209SC	Red Dot	Rem. Fig.-8	19.5/1145	19.9/1160	20.3/1175	21.0/1200	9,800 psi	

Load Notes: 1 = Minimum overall length = 2 10/32", maximum crimp depth = 2/32". 3 = Helix Cushion Platform. 5 = Use 50-60 pounds wad pressure to ensure wad is firmly seated against powder. 6 = Scatter Master.

Caution: Follow load recipes exactly; do not substitute components, exceed listed maximums or load less than listed minimums.

12-GAUGE 2¾" — 1⅛ OUNCES LEAD SHOT (CONT.)

Primer	Powder Type	Wad	Minimum			Maximum	Maximum Pressure	Load Notes
			FEDERAL: GOLD MEDAL PLASTIC (CONT.)			**1⅛ OUNCES LEAD SHOT**		
CCI 209SC	Red Dot	WAA12	18.5/1145	18.9/1160	19.3/1175	20.0/1200	10,500 psi	
CCI 209SC	Universal	H. Versalite	23.2/1200	23.9/1230	24.5/1255	25.5/1310	9,600 psi	
CCI 209SC	Universal	Windjammer	24.5/1200	25.3/1230	26.0/1255	26.7/1310	8,900 psi	
Fed. 209	#2 Improved	Fed. 12S0				18.5/1125	8,100 psi	Note 1
Fed. 209	#2 Improved	Fed. 12S3				19.0/1145	8,700 psi	Note 1
Fed. 209	Clays	Fed. 12S3	17.7/1090	18.2/1120	18.7/1145	19.8/1200	8,100 LUP	
Fed. 209	Clays	Rem. Fig.-8	17.6/1090	18.2/1120	18.7/1145	19.8/1200	7,800 LUP	
Fed. 209	Clays	WAA12	17.2/1090	17.9/1120	18.5/1145	19.8/1200	8,000 LUP	
Fed. 209	International	Fed. 12S3	21.3/1145	21.9/1175	22.5/1200	23.7/1255	8,100 LUP	
Fed. 209	International	Pat. Ctrl. Red	20.5/1090	21.5/1145	22.9/1200	24.2/1255	8,100 LUP	
Fed. 209	International	Windjammer	22.0/1090	22.3/1145	23.1/1200	24.4/1255	7,500 LUP	
Fed. 209	Nitro-100	Fed. 12S0	18.0/1145	18.5/1175	19.0/1200	20.5/1255		
Fed. 209	Nitro-100	H. Versalite				18.0/1145		
Fed. 209	Nitro-100	WAA12	17.5/1145	18.0/1175	18.5/1200	20.0/1255		
Fed. 209	R. Scot D	Activ TG-30	19.0/1125	19.5/1145	20.5/1200	22.0/1255	10,900 LUP	
Fed. 209	R. Scot D	Claybuster	19.0/1125	19.5/1145	20.5/1200	22.0/1255	9,500 LUP	
Fed. 209	R. Scot D	Fed. 12C1	19.0/1125	19.5/1145	20.5/1200	22.5/1255	10,300 LUP	
Fed. 209	R. Scot D	Fed. 12S0	18.0*/1125	19.5/1145	20.1/1175	20.5/1200	10,400 LUP	Note 7
Fed. 209	R. Scot D	Fed. 12S3	18.5/1125	19.0/1145	20.5/1200	22.0/1255	10,900 LUP	
Fed. 209	R. Scot D	H. Versalite	19.0/1125	19.5/1145	20.5/1200	22.0/1255	10,900 LUP	
Fed. 209	R. Scot D	Lage Uniwad	19.0/1125	19.5/1145	21.0/1200	22.5/1255	9,900 LUP	
Fed. 209	R. Scot D	Pat. Ctrl. Red	19.0/1125	19.5/1145	20.5/1200	22.0/1255	10,700 LUP	
Fed. 209	R. Scot D	Rem. Fig.-8	19.0/1125	19.5/1145	20.5/1200	22.5/1255	10,900 LUP	
Fed. 209	R. Scot D	WAA12	19.0/1125	19.5/1145	20.5/1200	22.0/1255	10,000 LUP	
Fed. 209	R. Scot D	Windjammer	19.0/1125	19.5/1145	21.0/1200	22.5/1255	9,500 LUP	
Fed. 209	Scot 453	Fed. 12S3	18.5/1125	19.0/1145	19.8/1175	20.5/1200	9,800 psi	
Fed. 209	Solo 1000	Activ TG-30	18.5/1125	19.0/1145	20.0/1200	21.5/1255	10,700 LUP	Note 1
Fed. 209	Solo 1000	Claybuster	18.5/1125	19.0/1145	20.0/1200	21.5/1255		
Fed. 209	Solo 1000	Fed. 12C1				18.5/1125	7,100 LUP	Note 1
Fed. 209	Solo 1000	Fed. 12S0				17.5*/1125	6,900 LUP	Note 1&7
Fed. 209	Solo 1000	Fed. 12S3	18.0/1125	18.2/1135	18.3/1140	18.5/1145	8,000 LUP	Note 1
Fed. 209	Solo 1000	H. Versalite				18.5/1125	7,600 LUP	Note 1
Fed. 209	Solo 1000	Lage Uniwad				18.5/1125	7,100 LUP	Note 1
Fed. 209	Solo 1000	Pat. Ctrl. Red				18.5/1125	7,600 LUP	Note 1
Fed. 209	Solo 1000	Rem. Fig.-8	18.5/1125	19.0/1145	20.0/1200	22.0/1255		
Fed. 209	Solo 1000	WAA12				18.5/1125	7,200 LUP	Note 1
Fed. 209	Solo 1000	Windjammer	18.5/1125	19.0/1145	20.5/1200	22.0/1255	8,700 LUP	Note 1
Fed. 209	Solo 1250	Activ TG-30	25.5/1200	26.3/1230	27.0/1255	28.0/1310	10,900 LUP	Note 1
Fed. 209	Solo 1250	Claybuster	28.5/1255	28.8/1275	29.2/1290	29.5/1310	9,100 LUP	Note 1
Fed. 209	Solo 1250	Fed. 12C1				29.0/1310	10,300 LUP	Note 1
Fed. 209	Solo 1250	Fed. 12S3				28.5/1310	10,700 LUP	Note 1
Fed. 209	Solo 1250	H. Versalite				29.0/1310	10,200 LUP	Note 1

Load Notes: 1 = Minimum overall length = 2¹⁰/₃₂", maximum crimp depth = ²/₃₂". 7 = This load is a close match to Federal's Extra-Lite factory loading.

Caution: Follow load recipes exactly; do not substitute components, exceed listed maximums or load less than listed minimums.

Primer	Powder Type	Wad	Powder Charge (grains) / Velocity (fps) Minimum			Maximum	Maximum Pressure	Load Notes
FEDERAL: GOLD MEDAL PLASTIC (CONT.)					1¹/₈ OUNCES LEAD SHOT			
Fed. 209	Solo 1250	Rem. RXP12	26.5/1200	27.3/1235	28.3/1275	29.0/1310	10,100 LUP	Note 1
Fed. 209	Solo 1250	WAA12				28.5/1310	10,200 LUP	Note 1
Fed. 209	Solo 1250	Windjammer	28.0/1255	28.3/1275	28.7/1290	29.0/1310	9,900 LUP	Note 1
Fed. 209	Universal	Fed. 12S3	23.5/1200	24.2/1230	24.8/1255	26.0/1310	9,500 psi	
Fed. 209	WST	Fed. 12S3	20.0/1145	20.5/1165	21.0/1180	21.5/1200	9,000 psi	
Fed. 209A	#2 Improved	Fed. 12S3				20.5/1200	9,800 psi	Note 1
Fed. 209A	American Select	Claybuster	17.5/1090	19.0/1145	20.5/1200	22.0/1250	10,600 psi	
Fed. 209A	American Select	Fed. 12S3	17.5/1090	19.0/1145	20.5/1200	22.0/1250	10,100 psi	
Fed. 209A	American Select	H. Versalite	17.0*/1090	18.5*/1145	20.0*/1200	21.0/1250	10,900 psi	*Note 8
Fed. 209A	American Select	Rem. Fig.-8	17.5/1090	19.0/1145	19.6/1175	20.0/1200	10,300 psi	Note 8
Fed. 209A	American Select	WAA12	17.5/1090	19.0/1145	19.8/1175	20.5/1200	9,400 psi	Note 8
Fed. 209A	American Select	Windjammer	19.0/1145	19.8/1175	20.5/1200	21.5/1250	10,700 psi	Note 8
Fed. 209A	American Select	WT12 Orange	18.0/1090	19.0/1145	19.8/1175	20.5/1200	10,400 psi	Note 8
Fed. 209A	American Select	BP Zero	18.3/1150	18.5/1170	18.8/1200	19.8/1245	10,800 psi	
Fed. 209A	Clays	Fed. 12S3	16.8/1090	17.6/1160	18.1/1175	19.0/1200	10,400 psi	
Fed. 209A	Clays	Rem. Fig.-8	17.0/1090	17.3/1120	17.5/1145	19.0/1200	9,600 psi	
Fed. 209A	Clays	WAA12	16.5/1090	16.8/1120	17.0/1145	18.5/1200	10,300 psi	
Fed. 209A	Clays	Windjam. II	16.2/1090	16.9/1120	17.5/1145	18.5/1200	9,900 psi	
Fed. 209A	Green Dot	BP SCAT	18.0/1090	19.0/1145	20.0/1200	21.5/1250	9,500 psi	Note 6
Fed. 209A	Green Dot	Fed. 12S3	18.5/1090	19.5/1145	20.0/1200	21.5/1250	9,500 psi	
Fed. 209A	Green Dot	Fiocchi FTW1	18.0*/1090	19.5/1145	20.1/1175	20.5/1200	9,300 psi	*Note 8
Fed. 209A	Green Dot	H. Versalite	18.0/1090	19.0/1145	20.5/1200	21.5/1250	9,000 psi	
Fed. 209A	Green Dot	BP HCDP	19.0/1145	19.5/1175	20.0/1200	21.5/1250	9,500 psi	Note 3
Fed. 209A	Green Dot	Rem. Fig.-8	18.0/1090	19.0/1145	20.0/1200	22.0/1250	9,200 psi	
Fed. 209A	Green Dot	Rem. RXP12	19.0/1145	20.0/1200	21.5/1250	24.0/1310	10,400 psi	
Fed. 209A	Green Dot	WAA12	18.0*/1090	20.0/1200	21.9/1265	23.0/1310	10,400 psi	*Note 8
Fed. 209A	Green Dot	WAA12SL	18.0/1090	19.0/1145	19.6/1175	20.0/1200	8,800 psi	
Fed. 209A	Green Dot	Windjammer	18.5/1090	21.0/1200	22.9/1275	24.0/1310	8,800 psi	
Fed. 209A	Green Dot	WT12 Orange	20.0/1145	20.4/1160	20.9/1175	21.5/1200	8,800 psi	Note 8
Fed. 209A	Herco	Fed. 12S3				26.0/1250	8,000 psi	
Fed. 209A	Herco	H. Versalite				26.0/1250	8,200 psi	
Fed. 209A	Herco	Rem. Fig.-8				26.0/1250	7,700 psi	
Fed. 209A	Herco	Rem. RXP12				26.0/1250	8,000 psi	
Fed. 209A	Herco	WAA12				26.0/1250	8,300 psi	
Fed. 209A	Herco	Windjammer				26.0/1250	7,400 psi	
Fed. 209A	IMR 700-X	BP SCAT	17.0/1150	17.5/1175	17.9/1185	18.5/1200	9,500 psi	Note 6
Fed. 209A	IMR 700-X	CB 2118-12	16.0/1110	17.0/1155	18.0/1195	19.5/1260	10,800 psi	
Fed. 209A	IMR 700-X	Fed. 12S3	16.0/1105	17.0/1145	18.5/1205	20.0/1260	10,400 psi	
Fed. 209A	IMR 700-X	BP HCDP	18.5/1200	19.0/1225	19.2/1235	19.5/1250	10,000 psi	Note 3
Fed. 209A	IMR 700-X	Rem. TGT12	16.0/1100	17.0/1145	18.0/1190	19.5/1250	10,500 psi	
Fed. 209A	IMR 700-X	WAA12SL	16.0/1110	17.0/1150	18.0/1190	19.5/1250	10,600 psi	

Load Notes: 1 = Minimum overall length = 2¹⁰/₃₂″, maximum crimp depth = ²/₃₂″. 3 = Helix Cushion Platform. 6 = Scatter Master. 8 = Add one 20-gauge, 0.135″ card inside bottom of shotcup.

Caution: Follow load recipes exactly; do not substitute components, exceed listed maximums or load less than listed minimums.

Primer	Powder Type	Wad	Powder Charge (grains) / Velocity (fps) Minimum			Maximum	Maximum Pressure	Load Notes
FEDERAL: GOLD MEDAL PLASTIC (CONT.)						**1¹/₈ OUNCES LEAD SHOT**		
Fed. 209A	IMR 800-X	BP SCAT	20.5/1100	21.3/1150	23.0/1200	25.0/1260	7,700 psi	Note 6
Fed. 209A	IMR 800-X	CB 2118-12	20.5/1090	22.5/1150	23.0/1195	24.5/1250	7,400 psi	
Fed. 209A	IMR 800-X	Fed. 12S3	20.5/1090	22.0/1155	23.0/1195	25.0/1265	7,700 psi	
Fed. 209A	IMR 800-X	BP HCDP				25.0/1260	7,700 psi	Note 3
Fed. 209A	IMR 800-X	Rem. Fig.-8	21.0/1100	22.5/1155	24.0/1205	25.5/1255	7,100 psi	
Fed. 209A	IMR 800-X	WAA12	20.5/1100	21.5/1140	23.0/1195	24.5/1255	7,700 psi	
Fed. 209A	IMR 800-X	Windjammer	22.0/1100	23.0/1145	24.0/1190	25.5/1260	6,700 psi	
Fed. 209A	IMR PB	BP SCAT	19.5/1100	21.0/1150	22.5/1200	24.0/1255	8,700 psi	Note 6
Fed. 209A	IMR PB	CB 1118-12	20.0/1105	21.0/1140	22.5/1195	24.0/1250	8,000 psi	
Fed. 209A	IMR PB	Fed. 12S3	19.5/1095	21.0/1140	22.5/1190	24.0/1255	8,700 psi	
Fed. 209A	IMR PB	BP HCDP				24.0/1255	8,700 psi	Note 3
Fed. 209A	IMR PB	Rem. Fig.-8	20.0/1095	21.5/1145	23.0/1200	24.5/1255	8,000 psi	
Fed. 209A	IMR PB	WAA12	19.5/1095	21.0/1150	22.5/1205	24.0/1260	8,800 psi	
Fed. 209A	IMR PB	Windjammer	20.5/1105	21.5/1145	23.0/1205	24.0/1250	7,800 psi	
Fed. 209A	International	Fed. 12S3	18.5/1090	19.0/1145	20.5/1200	22.2/1255	10,600 psi	
Fed. 209A	International	Pat. Ctrl. Red	19.0/1090	19.7/1145	21.0/1200	22.3/1255	9,600 psi	
Fed. 209A	International	Windjam. II	19.0/1145	19.2/1160	19.5/1175	20.0/1200	8,500 psi	
Fed. 209A	International	Windjammer	19.0/1090	19.5/1145	20.8/1200	22.5/1255	9,200 psi	
Fed. 209A	Nitro-100	BP ITD	16.5/1145	17.0/1175	17.5/1200	19.0/1255	10,200 psi	Note 1
Fed. 209A	Nitro-100	Claybuster	16.0/1125	16.5/1145	17.5/1200	18.5/1255	10,100 psi	Note 1
Fed. 209A	Nitro-100	Fed. 12C1	17.0/1145	17.3/1175	17.5/1200	18.5/1255	10,000 psi	Note 1
Fed. 209A	Nitro-100	Fed. 12S0	16.5/1145	16.7/1160	17.0/1175	17.5/1200	9,500 psi	Note 1
Fed. 209A	Nitro-100	Fed. 12S3	17.5/1200	17.7/1215	18.0/1230	18.5/1255		Note 1
Fed. 209A	Nitro-100	H. Versalite	16.0/1145	16.5/1175	17.0/1200	20.5/1255	8,900 psi	Note 1
Fed. 209A	Nitro-100	Pat. Ctrl. Red	16.5/1145	17.3/1175	18.0/1200	19.0/1255	9,400 psi	Note 1
Fed. 209A	Nitro-100	Rem. Fig.-8	16.5/1125	17.0/1145	17.5/1200	19.0/1255	9,600 psi	Note 1
Fed. 209A	Nitro-100	WAA12	16.0/1145	17.0/1175	18.0/1200	18.5/1255	9,700 psi	Note 1
Fed. 209A	Red Diamond	Activ TG-30	16.5/1145	17.3/1175	18.0/1200	19.5/1255	10,100 psi	Note 5
Fed. 209A	Red Diamond	BP CS12	18.0/1200	18.5/1215	19.0/1230	20.0/1255	9,900 psi	Note 5
Fed. 209A	Red Diamond	BP ITD	16.5/1145	17.3/1175	18.0/1200	19.5/1255	9,600 psi	Note 5
Fed. 209A	Red Diamond	Claybuster	16.5/1145	17.3/1175	18.0/1200	19.5/1255	9,400 psi	Note 5
Fed. 209A	Red Diamond	Fed. 12S0	16.5/1145	17.3/1175	18.0/1200	19.5/1255	9,400 psi	Note 5
Fed. 209A	Red Diamond	Fed. 12S3	16.5/1145	17.3/1175	18.0/1200	19.5/1255	10,900 psi	Note 5
Fed. 209A	Red Diamond	H. Versalite	16.5/1145	17.3/1175	18.0/1200	19.5/1255	9,800 psi	Note 5
Fed. 209A	Red Diamond	Rem. Fig.-8				20.0/1255	9,400 psi	Note 5
Fed. 209A	Red Diamond	Rem. TGT12	16.5/1145	17.3/1175	18.0/1200	19.5/1255	9,600 psi	Note 5
Fed. 209A	Red Diamond	WAA12				19.5/1255	9,900 psi	Note 5
Fed. 209A	Red Dot	BP SCAT	17.0/1090	18.0/1145	18.6/1175	19.0/1200	10,000 psi	Note 6
Fed. 209A	Red Dot	Fed. 12S3	17.0/1090	18.0/1145	18.9/1175	19.5/1200	10,000 psi	
Fed. 209A	Red Dot	Fiocchi FTW1	16.5*/1090	18.0*/1145	18.6/1175	19.0/1200	10,500 psi	*Note 8
Fed. 209A	Red Dot	H. Versalite	17.0*/1090	18.0*/1145	19.0/1200	20.0/1250	10,700 psi	*Note 8

Load Notes: 1 = Minimum overall length = 2¹⁰/₃₂″, maximum crimp depth = ²/₃₂″. 3 = Helix Cushion Platform. 5 = Use 50-60 pounds wad pressure to ensure wad is firmly seated against powder. 6 = Scatter Master. 8 = Add one 20-gauge, 0.135″ card inside bottom of shotcup.

Caution: Follow load recipes exactly; do not substitute components, exceed listed maximums or load less than listed minimums.

Primer	Powder Type	Wad	Powder Charge (grains) / Velocity (fps) Minimum		Maximum		Maximum Pressure	Load Notes
FEDERAL: GOLD MEDAL PLASTIC (CONT.)					**1 1/8 OUNCES LEAD SHOT**			
Fed. 209A	Red Dot	Rem. Fig.-8	17.0/1090	18.0/1145	19.0/1200	20.0/1250	9,500 psi	
Fed. 209A	Red Dot	Rem. RXP12	18.0/1145	18.6/1175	19.0/1200	20.0/1250	10,100 psi	
Fed. 209A	Red Dot	WAA12	16.5/1090	17.5/1145	18.4/1175	19.0/1200	10,400 psi	Note 8
Fed. 209A	Red Dot	WAA12SL	17.0/1090	18.0/1145	18.6/1175	19.0/1200	10,000 psi	
Fed. 209A	Red Dot	Windjammer	17.5/1090	18.5/1145	19.5/1200	20.5/1250	9,500 psi	
Fed. 209A	Red Dot	WT12 Orange	18.5/1145	18.9/1160	19.4/1175	20.0/1200	10,400 psi	Note 8
Fed. 209A	Solo 1000	BP ITD	18.0/1145	18.8/1175	19.5/1200	20.5/1255	9,700 LUP	Note 1
Fed. 209A	Solo 1000	Claybuster	17.0/1125	17.5/1145	19.0/1200	20.0/1255	10,700 psi	Note 1
Fed. 209A	Solo 1000	Fed. 12C1	18.0/1145	18.8/1175	19.5/1200	20.5/1255	10,500 LUP	Note 1
Fed. 209A	Solo 1000	Fed. 12S0	18.0/1145	18.2/1160	18.5/1175	19.0/1200	9,200 LUP	Note 1
Fed. 209A	Solo 1000	Fed. 12S3	19.5/1200	19.7/1215	20.0/1230	20.5/1255	10,200 psi	Note 1
Fed. 209A	Solo 1000	H. Versalite	18.0/1145	18.5/1175	19.0/1200	20.0/1255	10,200 LUP	Note 1
Fed. 209A	Solo 1000	Pat. Ctrl. Red	18.5/1145	19.0/1175	19.5/1200	20.5/1255	9,600 LUP	Note 1
Fed. 209A	Solo 1000	Rem. Fig.-8	17.0/1125	17.5/1145	19.0/1200	20.0/1255	10,300 psi	Note 1
Fed. 209A	Solo 1000	WAA12	18.0/1145	18.5/1175	19.0/1200	20.0/1255	10,500 LUP	Note 1
Fed. 209A	Solo 1250	Claybuster				27.0/1200	8,100 LUP	Note 1
Fed. 209A	Solo 1250	Fed. 12C1	26.0/1200	26.4/1215	26.8/1230	27.5/1255	9,100 LUP	Note 1
Fed. 209A	Solo 1250	Fed. 12S3	25.5/1200	25.9/1215	26.3/1230	27.0/1255	9,600 LUP	Note 1
Fed. 209A	Solo 1250	H. Versalite				26.0/1200	9,000 LUP	Note 1
Fed. 209A	SR-7625	BP SCAT	23.5/1150	24.0/1170	24.2/1180	24.5/1190	6,900 psi	Note 6
Fed. 209A	SR-7625	CB 2118-12	22.0/1095	23.5/1150	24.5/1195	26.0/1250	7,700 psi	
Fed. 209A	SR-7625	Fed. 12S3	22.0/1090	23.5/1150	24.5/1190	26.5/1260	7,700 psi	
Fed. 209A	SR-7625	BP HCDP				26.5/1265	7,700 psi	Note 3
Fed. 209A	SR-7625	Rem. Fig.-8	22.5/1090	24.0/1140	25.5/1205	26.5/1245	7,100 psi	
Fed. 209A	SR-7625	WAA12	21.5/1100	23.0/1155	24.5/1200	26.0/1265	8,200 psi	
Fed. 209A	SR-7625	Windjammer	23.0/1105	24.0/1140	25.5/1200	27.0/1265	7,400 psi	
Fed. 209A	Unique	Fed. 12S3	22.5/1200	23.1/1225	23.3/1235	23.5/1250	8,100 psi	
Fed. 209A	Unique	Fiocchi FTW1				22.5/1200	8,100 psi	
Fed. 209A	Unique	H. Versalite	22.0/1200	24.0/1250	24.0/1280	25.0/1310	10,000 psi	
Fed. 209A	Unique	BP HCDP				25.0/1310	9,700 psi	Note 3
Fed. 209A	Unique	Rem. Fig.-8	22.5/1200	23.1/1225	23.3/1235	23.5/1250	7,800 psi	
Fed. 209A	Unique	Rem. RXP12	22.5/1200	23.5/1250	24.8/1280	26.0/1310	10,300 psi	
Fed. 209A	Unique	WAA12	22.5/1200	23.0/1250	24.0/1280	25.0/1310	9,200 psi	
Fed. 209A	Unique	Windjammer	22.5/1200	24.0/1250	24.0/1280	25.0/1310	9,700 psi	
Fed. 209A	Unique	WT12 Orange				23.5/1200	8,300 psi	Note 8
Fed. 209A	Universal	Fed. 12S3	23.0/1200	23.7/1230	24.4/1255	25.7/1310	10,500 psi	
Fio. 616	Clays	Fiocchi TL1	16.5/1090	17.2/1120	17.9/1145	19.3/1200	9,400 LUP	
Fio. 616	International	Fiocchi TL1	19.2/1090	19.7/1145	21.1/1200	22.5/1255	9,200 LUP	
Fio. 616	Nitro-100	Fed. 12S3	17.5/1145	18.0/1175	18.5/1200	19.5/1255	10,200 psi	Note 1
Fio. 616	R. Scot D	Fed. 12S3	18.5/1125	19.0/1145	20.5/1200	22.0/1255	10,200 LUP	
Fio. 616	Red Diamond	Activ TG-30	16.5/1145	17.3/1175	18.0/1200	19.5/1255	9,400 psi	Note 1

Load Notes: 1 = Minimum overall length = 2¹⁰/₃₂″, maximum crimp depth = ²/₃₂″. 3 = Helix Cushion Platform. 6 = Scatter Master. 8 = Add one 20-gauge, 0.135″ card inside bottom of shotcup.

Caution: Follow load recipes exactly; do not substitute components, exceed listed maximums or load less than listed minimums.

Primer	Powder Type	Wad	Powder Charge (grains) / Velocity (fps) Minimum		Maximum		Maximum Pressure	Load Notes
FEDERAL: GOLD MEDAL PLASTIC (CONT.)						**1¹/₈ OUNCES LEAD SHOT**		
Fio. 616	Red Diamond	BP CS12	18.0/1200	18.5/1215	19.0/1230	20.0/1255	9,600 psi	Note 5
Fio. 616	Red Diamond	BP ITD	16.5/1145	17.3/1175	18.0/1200	19.5/1255	9,200 psi	Note 5
Fio. 616	Red Diamond	Claybuster	16.5/1145	17.3/1175	18.0/1200	19.5/1255	9,100 psi	Note 5
Fio. 616	Red Diamond	Fed. 12S0	16.5/1145	17.3/1175	18.0/1200	19.5/1255	9,100 psi	Note 5
Fio. 616	Red Diamond	Fed. 12S3	16.5/1145	17.3/1175	18.0/1200	19.5/1255	10,800 psi	Note 5
Fio. 616	Red Diamond	H. Versalite	16.5/1145	17.3/1175	18.0/1200	19.5/1255	9,700 psi	Note 5
Fio. 616	Red Diamond	Rem. Fig.-8				20.0/1255	9,300 psi	Note 5
Fio. 616	Red Diamond	Rem. TGT12	16.5/1145	17.3/1175	18.0/1200	19.5/1255	8,900 psi	Note 5
Fio. 616	Red Diamond	WAA12				19.5/1255	10,000 psi	Note 5
Fio. 616	Red Dot	Fed. 12S3				17.5/1090	8,200 psi	
Fio. 616	Solo 1000	Fed. 12S3	18.0/1125	18.5/1145	20.0/1200	21.5/1255	9,500 LUP	Note 1
Fio. 616	Universal	Fiocchi TL1	23.3/1200	23.8/1230	24.2/1255	26.0/1310	10,100 psi	
Rem. 209	Nitro-100	Fed. 12S0	18.0/1145	18.5/1175	19.0/1200	20.5/1255		
Rem. 209	Nitro-100	H. Versalite				20.5/1255		
Rem. 209	Nitro-100	WAA12	18.0/1145	18.3/1175	18.5/1200	20.0/1255		
Rem. 209	Red Diamond	Activ TG-30	17.0/1145	17.8/1175	18.5/1200	20.0/1255	9,100 psi	Note 5
Rem. 209	Red Diamond	BP CS12	18.5/1200	18.9/1215	19.3/1230	20.0/1255	9,300 psi	Note 5
Rem. 209	Red Diamond	BP ITD	17.0/1145	17.8/1175	18.5/1200	19.5/1255	9,000 psi	Note 5
Rem. 209	Red Diamond	Claybuster	17.5/1145	18.0/1175	18.5/1200	19.5/1255	8,300 psi	Note 5
Rem. 209	Red Diamond	Fed. 12S0	17.5/1145	18.0/1175	18.5/1200	19.5/1255	8,300 psi	Note 5
Rem. 209	Red Diamond	Fed. 12S3	16.5/1145	17.3/1175	18.0/1200	19.5/1255	9,500 psi	Note 5
Rem. 209	Red Diamond	H. Versalite	17.0/1145	17.5/1175	18.0/1200	19.5/1255	8,800 psi	Note 5
Rem. 209	Red Diamond	Rem. Fig.-8				20.0/1255	7,700 psi	Note 5
Rem. 209	Red Diamond	Rem. TGT12	17.5/1145	18.0/1175	18.5/1200	19.5/1255	8,300 psi	Note 5
Rem. 209	Red Diamond	WAA12				19.5/1255	9,000 psi	Note 5
Rem. 209P	American Select	Fed. 12S3	19.5/1145	20.1/1160	20.7/1175	21.5/1200	9,000 psi	
Rem. 209P	Clays	Pat. Ctrl. Red	17.5/1090	18.0/1120	18.5/1145	19.4/1200	8,300 LUP	
Rem. 209P	Green Dot	Fed. 12S3	20.5/1145	21.0/1160	21.5/1200	23.0/1250	8,800 psi	
Rem. 209P	IMR 700-X	CB 2118-12	16.0/1095	17.0/1140	18.5/1195	20.0/1250	9,600 psi	
Rem. 209P	IMR 700-X	Fed. 12S3	16.0/1095	17.5/1155	18.5/1190	20.0/1250	9,800 psi	
Rem. 209P	IMR 700-X	Rem. TGT12	16.0/1090	17.5/1150	18.5/1190	20.0/1250	9,500 psi	
Rem. 209P	IMR 700-X	WAA12SL	16.5/1110	17.5/1155	18.5/1195	20.0/1255	9,500 psi	
Rem. 209P	IMR PB	CB 1118-12	21.0/1105	22.5/1150	23.5/1200	25.0/1265	8,000 psi	
Rem. 209P	IMR PB	Fed. 12S3	20.5/1100	22.0/1155	23.0/1190	25.0/1265	8,400 psi	
Rem. 209P	IMR PB	Rem. Fig.-8	21.0/1100	22.5/1155	23.5/1190	25.0/1245	7,500 psi	
Rem. 209P	IMR PB	WAA12SL	20.5/1095	21.5/1140	23.0/1195	25.0/1260	8,000 psi	
Rem. 209P	IMR PB	Windjammer	21.0/1095	22.5/1155	24.0/1205	25.5/1250	6,900 psi	
Rem. 209P	Nitro-100	Fed. 12S3	17.5/1145	18.0/1175	18.5/1200	19.0/1255	10,000 psi	Note 1
Rem. 209P	R. Scot D	Fed. 12S3	19.0/1125	19.5/1145	20.5/1200	22.0/1255	10,100 LUP	
Rem. 209P	Red Dot	Fed. 12S3	18.5/1145	18.8/1160	19.1/1175	19.5/1200	9,300 psi	
Rem. 209P	Solo 1000	Fed. 12S3	18.5/1125	19.0/1145	20.0/1200	21.5/1255	9,600 LUP	Note 1

Load Notes: 1 = Minimum overall length = 2¹⁰/₃₂", maximum crimp depth = ²/₃₂". 5 = Use 50-60 pounds wad pressure to ensure wad is firmly seated against powder.

Caution: Follow load recipes exactly; do not substitute components, exceed listed maximums or load less than listed minimums.

Primer	Powder Type	Wad	Powder Charge (grains) / Velocity (fps) Minimum			Maximum	Maximum Pressure	Load Notes
Federal: Gold Medal Plastic (cont.)						**1 1/8 Ounces Lead Shot**		
Rem. 209P	Solo 1250	Fed. 12S3	25.5/1200	26.3/1230	27.0/1255	28.5/1310	10,300 LUP	Note 1
Rem. 209P	SR-7625	CB 2118-12	22.5/1105	24.5/1150	26.0/1205	27.0/1250	7,300 psi	
Rem. 209P	SR-7625	Fed. 12S3	23.0/1095	24.5/1155	25.5/1195	27.0/1255	7,400 psi	
Rem. 209P	SR-7625	Rem. Fig.-8	24.0/1100	25.5/1155	27.0/1205	28.5/1260	6,300 psi	
Rem. 209P	SR-7625	WAA12	22.0/1100	23.5/1145	25.5/1205	27.5/1255	7,200 psi	
Rem. 209P	SR-7625	Windjammer	24.0/1095	25.5/1140	27.0/1200	28.5/1265	6,100 psi	
Rem. 209P	Unique	Fed. 12S3	24.0/1200	24.5/1225	24.7/1235	25.0/1250	7,600 psi	
Win. 209	American Select	Fed. 12S3	19.5/1145	19.8/1160	20.1/1175	20.5/1200	9,900 psi	
Win. 209	Clays	Windjammer	17.3/1090	17.8/1120	18.3/1145	19.4/1200	8,100 LUP	
Win. 209	Green Dot	Fed. 12S3	19.5/1145	20.0/1160	20.5/1200	22.5/1250	10,500 psi	
Win. 209	IMR 700-X	CB 2118-12	16.0/1100	17.0/1145	18.5/1205	19.5/1245	10,000 psi	
Win. 209	IMR 700-X	Fed. 12S3	16.0/1105	17.0/1150	18.0/1190	19.5/1255	10,700 psi	
Win. 209	IMR 700-X	Rem. TGT12	16.0/1095	17.0/1140	18.5/1195	20.0/1255	9,600 psi	
Win. 209	IMR 700-X	WAA12SL	16.0/1100	17.0/1145	18.5/1205	19.5/1245	9,900 psi	
Win. 209	IMR 800-X	BP SCAT	24.0/1205	24.5/1225	24.7/1235	25.0/1245	6,800 LUP	Note 6
Win. 209	IMR 800-X	CB 2118-12	20.5/1095	22.0/1145	23.5/1200	25.0/1260	7,400 psi	
Win. 209	IMR 800-X	Fed. 12S3	20.5/1095	22.0/1155	23.0/1195	24.5/1250	7,500 psi	
Win. 209	IMR 800-X	BP HCDP	24.0/1205	24.5/1220	25.0/1245	25.5/1280	7,400 LUP	Note 3
Win. 209	IMR 800-X	Rem. Fig.-8	21.0/1100	22.0/1140	23.5/1200	25.0/1255	7,100 psi	
Win. 209	IMR 800-X	WAA12	20.5/1100	21.5/1140	23.0/1195	25.0/1265	7,700 psi	
Win. 209	IMR 800-X	Windjammer	22.0/1105	23.0/1150	24.0/1190	25.5/1255	6,700 psi	
Win. 209	IMR PB	CB 1118-12	20.5/1100	22.0/1150	23.5/1200	25.0/1245	7,600 psi	
Win. 209	IMR PB	Fed. 12S3	20.5/1090	22.0/1150	23.0/1190	24.5/1250	8,400 psi	
Win. 209	IMR PB	Rem. Fig.-8	21.0/1105	22.0/1140	23.5/1200	25.0/1255	7,800 psi	
Win. 209	IMR PB	WAA12SL	21.0/1100	22.0/1140	23.5/1200	25.0/1255	8,200 psi	
Win. 209	IMR PB	Windjammer	21.0/1105	22.0/1145	23.5/1205	24.5/1250	7,700 psi	
Win. 209	International	BP HCDP				22.4/1255	8,800 LUP	Note 3
Win. 209	International	WAA12SL	19.1/1090	20.1/1145	21.0/1200	22.4/1255	8,900 LUP	
Win. 209	Nitro-100	Fed. 12S3	17.5/1145	18.0/1175	18.5/1200	19.5/1255	10,200 psi	Note 1
Win. 209	Nitro-100	H. Versalite	17.5/1145	17.7/1165	17.8/1175	18.0/1200		
Win. 209	Nitro-100	WAA12	18.0/1145	18.3/1175	18.5/1200	20.0/1255		
Win. 209	R. Scot D	Fed. 12S3	19.0/1125	19.5/1145	20.5/1200	22.0/1255	10,200 LUP	
Win. 209	Red Diamond	Activ TG-30	16.5/1145	17.3/1175	18.0/1200	19.5/1255	9,900 psi	Note 5
Win. 209	Red Diamond	BP CS12	18.0/1200	18.5/1215	19.0/1230	20.0/1255	9,600 psi	Note 5
Win. 209	Red Diamond	BP ITD	16.5/1145	17.3/1175	18.0/1200	19.5/1255	9,100 psi	Note 5
Win. 209	Red Diamond	Claybuster	16.5/1145	17.3/1175	18.0/1200	19.5/1255	9,200 psi	Note 5
Win. 209	Red Diamond	Fed. 12S0	16.5/1145	17.3/1175	18.0/1200	19.5/1255	9,200 psi	Note 5
Win. 209	Red Diamond	Fed. 12S3	16.5/1145	17.3/1175	18.0/1200	19.5/1255	10,400 psi	Note 5
Win. 209	Red Diamond	H. Versalite	16.5/1145	17.3/1175	18.0/1200	19.5/1255	9,400 psi	Note 5
Win. 209	Red Diamond	Rem. Fig.-8				20.0/1255	9,100 psi	Note 5
Win. 209	Red Diamond	Rem. TGT12	16.5/1145	17.3/1175	18.0/1200	19.5/1255	9,000 psi	Note 5
Win. 209	Red Diamond	WAA12				19.5/1255	9,400 psi	Note 5

Load Notes: 1 = Minimum overall length = 2¹⁰/₃₂", maximum crimp depth = ²/₃₂". 3 = Helix Cushion Platform. 5 = Use 50-60 pounds wad pressure to ensure wad is firmly seated against powder. 6 = Scatter Master.

Caution: Follow load recipes exactly; do not substitute components, exceed listed maximums or load less than listed minimums.

Primer	Powder Type	Wad	Powder Charge (grains) / Velocity (fps) Minimum			Maximum	Maximum Pressure	Load Notes
FEDERAL: GOLD MEDAL PLASTIC (CONT.)					**1¹/₈ OUNCES LEAD SHOT**			
Win. 209	Red Dot	Fed. 12S3	17.0/1090	17.5/1145	18.4/1175	19.0/1200	10,500 psi	
Win. 209	Solo 1000	Fed. 12S3	18.5/1125	19.0/1145	20.0/1200	21.5/1255	9,700 LUP	Note 1
Win. 209	Solo 1250	Fed. 12S3	25.0/1200	25.8/1230	26.5/1255	28.0/1310	10,100 LUP	Note 1
Win. 209	SR-7625	CB 2118-12	22.5/1095	24.0/1150	25.5/1200	27.0/1250	7,300 psi	
Win. 209	SR-7625	Fed. 12S3	23.0/1100	24.5/1155	25.5/1195	27.0/1255	7,500 psi	
Win. 209	SR-7625	Rem. Fig.-8	23.0/1095	24.5/1150	25.5/1190	27.0/1250	7,100 psi	
Win. 209	SR-7625	WAA12	22.5/1100	24.0/1155	25.0/1190	26.5/1250	7,400 psi	
Win. 209	SR-7625	Windjammer	23.0/1095	24.5/1140	26.0/1200	27.0/1245	6,900 psi	
Win. 209	Unique	Fed. 12S3	23.0/1200	23.5/1225	23.7/1235	24.0/1250	9,800 psi	
Win. 209	Universal	Rem. Fig.-8	24.0/1200	24.5/1230	25.0/1255	26.8/1310	9,500 psi	
Win. 209	Universal	WAA12	23.2/1200	23.9/1230	24.5/1255	25.0/1310	10,400 psi	
Win. 209	WST	BP SCAT	20.0/1165	20.5/1185	21.0/1200	21.5/1220	10,000 psi	Note 6
Win. 209	WST	Fed. 12S3				21.0/1200	9,500 psi	
Win. 209	WST	BP HCDP	20.5/1185	20.7/1190	21.0/1200	21.5/1220	10,000 psi	Note 3
Win. AATP	Clays	Windjammer	17.0/1090	17.3/1120	17.5/1145	19.0/1200	8,500 psi	
Win. AATP	International	WAA12SL	18.5/1090	19.3/1145	20.8/1200	22.0/1255	10,300 psi	
FEDERAL: PAPER					**1¹/₈ OUNCES LEAD SHOT**			
CCI 109	Green Dot	Fed. 12C1	19.0/1145	19.4/1160	19.8/1175	20.5/1200	8,200 psi	
CCI 109	Red Dot	Fed. 12C1	18.5/1145	18.6/1160	18.7/1175	19.0/1200	9,200 psi	
CCI 109	Unique	Fed. 12C1				22.0/1200	7,500 psi	
CCI 209	Red Diamond	Activ TG-30	17.5/1145	18.3/1175	19.0/1200	20.5/1255	9,800 psi	Note 5
CCI 209	Red Diamond	Fed. 12C1	17.5/1145	18.0/1175	18.5/1200	20.0/1255	10,200 psi	Note 5
CCI 209	Red Diamond	Fed. 12S4	17.0/1145	17.8/1175	18.5/1200	19.5/1255	10,000 psi	Note 5
CCI 209	Red Diamond	Pat. Ctrl. Red	17.5/1145	18.3/1175	19.0/1200	20.5/1255	9,200 psi	Note 5
CCI 209	Red Diamond	WAA12	17.0/1145	17.8/1175	18.5/1200	20.5/1255	10,000 psi	Note 5
CCI 209	Solo 1250	Fed. 12C1	27.0/1200	27.5/1230	28.0/1255	29.5/1310	9,400 psi	
CCI 209M	Green Dot	Fed. 12C1	20.0/1145	20.0/1145	21.5/1200	22.5/1255	8,500 psi	
CCI 209M	International	Pat. Ctrl. Red	21.2/1090	21.6/1120	21.9/1145	22.8/1200	8,800 LUP	
CCI 209M	International	Rem. Fig.-8	19.4/1090	20.3/1145	21.8/1200	22.6/1255	8,900 LUP	
CCI 209M	Nitro-100	Fed. 12C1	17.5/1145	17.8/1175	18.0/1200	19.0/1255	8,700 psi	Note 1
CCI 209M	R. Scot D	Fed. 12C1	19.5/1125	20.0/1145	21.0/1200	22.5/1255	10,900 LUP	
CCI 209M	Red Diamond	Activ TG-30	17.0/1145	17.8/1175	18.5/1200	20.0/1255	9,900 psi	Note 5
CCI 209M	Red Diamond	Fed. 12C1	17.5/1145	18.0/1175	18.5/1200	20.0/1255	9,800 psi	Note 5
CCI 209M	Red Diamond	Fed. 12S4	17.0/1145	17.8/1175	18.5/1200	19.5/1255	10,200 psi	Note 5
CCI 209M	Red Diamond	Pat. Ctrl. Red	17.0/1145	17.8/1175	18.5/1200	20.0/1255	9,400 psi	Note 5
CCI 209M	Red Diamond	WAA12	17.0/1145	17.8/1175	18.5/1200	20.5/1255	10,000 psi	Note 5
CCI 209M	Red Dot	Fed. 12C1	18.5/1145	19.3/1175	20.0/1200	21.0/1255	10,500 psi	
CCI 209M	Solo 1000	Fed. 12C1	18.5/1145	19.0/1175	19.5/1200	21.0/1255	9,600 psi	Note 1
CCI 209M	Solo 1250	Fed. 12C1				26.0/1310	7,700 psi	Note 1
CCI 209M	Unique	Fed. 12C1	24.0/1200	24.5/1255	25.7/1285	26.5/1310	9,400 psi	
CCI 209SC	American Select	Fed. 12S3	19.0/1145	19.4/1160	19.8/1175	20.5/1200	9,800 psi	

Load Notes: 1 = Minimum overall length = 2¹⁰/₃₂″, maximum crimp depth = ²/₃₂″. 3 = Helix Cushion Platform. 5 = Use 50-60 pounds wad pressure to ensure wad is firmly seated against powder. 6 = Scatter Master.

Caution: Follow load recipes exactly; do not substitute components, exceed listed maximums or load less than listed minimums.

Primer	Powder Type	Wad	Powder Charge (grains) / Velocity (fps) Minimum			Maximum	Maximum Pressure	Load Notes
FEDERAL: PAPER (CONT.)						1¹/₈ OUNCES LEAD SHOT		
CCI 209SC	Clays	Fed. 12S4	17.5/1090	17.7/1110	17.8/1125	18.0/1145		
CCI 209SC	Clays	Windjam. II	17.0/1090	17.5/1120	18.0/1145	19.5/1200	10,800 psi	
CCI 209SC	International	Fed. 12S4	19.5/1090	20.0/1120	20.5/1145	21.5/1200	8,600 psi	
Fed. 209	International	Fed. 12S4	20.2/1090	20.8/1145	22.4/1200	23.6/1255	8,700 LUP	
Fed. 209	International	H. Versalite	21.1/1090	21.7/1145	23.2/1200	23.9/1255	8,200 LUP	
Fed. 209	International	Windjammer	21.2/1090	21.8/1145	23.2/1200	24.4/1255	7,400 LUP	
Fed. 209	R. Scot D	Claybuster	19.5/1125	20.5/1145	21.5/1200	23.0/1255	10,900 LUP	
Fed. 209	R. Scot D	Fed. 12C1	20.0/1125	20.5/1145	21.5/1200	23.0/1255	10,900 LUP	
Fed. 209	R. Scot D	Fed. 12S4	19.5/1125	20.0/1145	21.0/1200	22.5/1255	10,900 LUP	
Fed. 209	R. Scot D	WAA12	19.5/1125	20.5/1145	21.5/1200	23.0/1255	10,900 LUP	
Fed. 209	R. Scot D	Windjammer	20.0/1125	20.5/1145	21.5/1200	23.0/1255	10,900 LUP	
Fed. 209	Scot 453	Fed. 12C1	19.0/1125	20.0/1145	20.5/1175	21.0/1200	10,400 psi	
Fed. 209	Solo 1000	Claybuster	19.0/1125	20.0/1145	21.0/1200	22.5/1255		
Fed. 209	Solo 1000	Fed. 12C1	19.5/1125	20.0/1145	21.0/1200	22.5/1255		
Fed. 209	Solo 1000	Fed. 12S4	19.0/1125	19.5/1145	20.5/1200	22.0/1255		
Fed. 209	Solo 1000	WAA12	19.0/1125	20.0/1145	21.0/1200	22.5/1255		
Fed. 209	Solo 1000	Windjammer	19.5/1125	20.0/1145	21.0/1200	22.5/1255		
Fed. 209	Solo 1250	Fed. 12C1	26.5/1200	27.0/1230	27.5/1255	29.0/1310	9,900 psi	
Fed. 209	Solo 1250	H. Versalite	27.0/1200	27.5/1230	28.0/1255	30.0/1310	9,500 psi	
Fed. 209	Solo 1250	WAA12F114	27.0/1200	27.5/1230	28.0/1255	30.5/1310	9,500 psi	
Fed. 209	W 452AA	Fed. 12C1	21.0/1145	21.5/1165	22.0/1180	22.5/1200	9,300 LUP	
Fed. 209	W 452AA	Fed. 12S3	20.5/1145	21.0/1165	21.5/1180	22.0/1200	8,200 LUP	
Fed. 209	W 452AA	Fed. 12S3				22.0/1200	9,200 LUP	
Fed. 209A	#2 Improved	Fed. 12C1				20.0/1145	9,200 psi	Note 1
Fed. 209A	#2 Improved	Fed. 12S4	19.0/1145	19.3/1175	19.5/1200	20.5/1255	9,800 psi	Note 1
Fed. 209A	American Select	Claybuster	19.0/1145	19.4/1160	19.8/1175	20.5/1200	9,300 psi	
Fed. 209A	American Select	Fed. 12S3	19.0/1145	19.5/1160	20.1/1175	20.5/1200	10,400 psi	
Fed. 209A	American Select	H. Versalite	19.0/1145	19.3/1160	19.6/1175	20.0/1200	10,100 psi	
Fed. 209A	American Select	Rem. Fig.-8	19.0/1145	19.3/1160	19.6/1175	20.0/1200	9,800 psi	
Fed. 209A	American Select	WAA12	19.0/1145	19.5/1160	20.1/1175	20.5/1200	10,400 psi	
Fed. 209A	American Select	Windjammer	19.5/1145	19.6/1160	19.8/1175	20.0/1200	9,100 psi	
Fed. 209A	American Select	WT12 Orange	19.0/1145	19.4/1160	19.8/1175	20.5/1200	10,200 psi	
Fed. 209A	Clays	Fed. 12S3	17.0/1090	17.5/1120	18.0/1145	19.5/1200	10,500 psi	
Fed. 209A	Green Dot	Fed. 12C1	19.0/1145	20.0/1200	21.5/1255	24.5/1310	9,900 psi	
Fed. 209A	Green Dot	Fed. 12S3	19.5/1145	19.5/1145	21.0/1200	23.0/1255	9,100 psi	
Fed. 209A	Green Dot	Fiocchi FTW1	20.0/1145	20.3/1160	20.6/1175	21.0/1200	8,200 psi	
Fed. 209A	Green Dot	H. Versalite	19.5/1145	19.5/1145	21.0/1200	22.5/1255	8,500 psi	
Fed. 209A	Green Dot	Lage Uniwad	19.0/1145	19.3/1160	19.6/1175	20.0/1200	8,800 psi	
Fed. 209A	Green Dot	Pat. Ctrl. Red	20.0/1145	20.0/1145	21.0/1200	22.5/1255	9,600 psi	
Fed. 209A	Green Dot	Rem. R12H	19.5/1200	19.5/1200	19.5/1200	21.5/1255	9,900 psi	
Fed. 209A	Green Dot	Rem. R12L	19.0/1145	19.3/1160	19.6/1175	20.0/1200	8,600 psi	
Fed. 209A	Green Dot	Rem. RXP12	18.5/1145	20.0/1200	21.5/1255	24.5/1310	9,800 psi	

Load Notes: 1 = Minimum overall length = 2¹⁰/₃₂″, maximum crimp depth = ²/₃₂″.

Caution: Follow load recipes exactly; do not substitute components, exceed listed maximums or load less than listed minimums.

Primer	Powder Type	Wad	Powder Charge (grains) / Velocity (fps) Minimum			Maximum	Maximum Pressure	Load Notes
FEDERAL: PAPER (CONT.)						**1¹/₈ OUNCES LEAD SHOT**		
Fed. 209A	Green Dot	WAA12	18.5/1145	19.5/1200	21.5/1255	24.5/1310	9,700 psi	
Fed. 209A	Green Dot	Windjammer	20.5/1145	20.9/1160	21.3/1175	22.0/1200	7,700 psi	
Fed. 209A	International	Fed. 12S4	18.8/1090	19.5/1145	21.0/1200	22.0/1255	11,200 psi	
Fed. 209A	Nitro-100	BP Trap C	17.0/1145	17.5/1175	18.0/1200	19.0/1255	9,900 psi	Note 1
Fed. 209A	Nitro-100	Fed. 12C1	17.0/1145	17.8/1175	18.5/1200	20.0/1255	10,500 psi	Note 1
Fed. 209A	Nitro-100	Fed. 12S4	16.5/1145	17.0/1175	17.5/1200	19.0/1255	11,300 psi	Note 1
Fed. 209A	Nitro-100	Hawk II	17.0/1145	17.5/1175	18.0/1200	19.0/1255	9,500 psi	Note 1
Fed. 209A	Nitro-100	WAA12	16.5/1145	17.3/1175	18.0/1200	19.0/1255	10,000 psi	Note 1
Fed. 209A	Red Diamond	Activ TG-30	17.0/1145	18.0/1175	19.0/1200	20.0/1255	10,600 psi	Note 5
Fed. 209A	Red Diamond	Fed. 12C1	17.5/1145	18.0/1175	18.5/1200	20.0/1255	10,600 psi	Note 5
Fed. 209A	Red Diamond	Fed. 12S4	17.0/1145	17.8/1175	18.5/1200	19.5/1255	10,700 psi	Note 5
Fed. 209A	Red Diamond	Pat. Ctrl. Red	17.0/1145	17.8/1175	18.5/1200	20.0/1255	9,900 psi	Note 5
Fed. 209A	Red Diamond	WAA12	17.0/1145	17.8/1175	18.5/1200	20.5/1255	10,200 psi	Note 5
Fed. 209A	Red Dot	Fed. 12C1	18.0/1145	18.6/1175	19.0/1200	21.0/1255	10,200 psi	
Fed. 209A	Red Dot	Fed. 12S3	18.0/1145	18.6/1175	19.0/1200	21.0/1255	9,400 psi	
Fed. 209A	Red Dot	Fiocchi FTW1	18.5/1145	18.7/1160	19.0/1175	19.5/1200	9,500 psi	
Fed. 209A	Red Dot	H. Versalite	18.0/1145	18.6/1175	19.0/1200	20.5/1255	9,900 psi	
Fed. 209A	Red Dot	Lage Uniwad	18.0/1145	18.1/1160	18.3/1175	18.5/1200	9,400 psi	
Fed. 209A	Red Dot	Pat. Ctrl. Red	18.0/1145	18.6/1175	19.0/1200	20.5/1255	10,700 psi	
Fed. 209A	Red Dot	Rem. R12H				19.0/1200	9,200 psi	
Fed. 209A	Red Dot	Rem. R12L	18.5/1145	18.8/1160	19.2/1175	19.5/1200	9,500 psi	
Fed. 209A	Red Dot	Rem. RXP12	18.0/1145	18.6/1175	19.0/1200	21.0/1255	10,000 psi	
Fed. 209A	Red Dot	WAA12	18.0/1145	18.2/1160	18.5/1175	19.0/1200	10,500 psi	
Fed. 209A	Red Dot	Windjammer	18.5/1145	18.6/1160	18.8/1175	19.0/1200	8,700 psi	
Fed. 209A	Solo 1000	BP Trap C	18.5/1145	19.0/1175	19.5/1200	20.5/1255	10,900 psi	Note 1
Fed. 209A	Solo 1000	Fed. 12C1	19.0/1145	19.5/1175	20.0/1200	22.0/1255	10,100 psi	Note 1
Fed. 209A	Solo 1000	Fed. 12S4	18.0/1145	18.5/1175	19.0/1200	20.5/1255	10,800 psi	Note 1
Fed. 209A	Solo 1000	Hawk II	18.0/1145	18.2/1160	18.5/1175	19.0/1200	10,200 psi	Note 1
Fed. 209A	Solo 1000	WAA12	18.0/1145	18.8/1175	19.5/1200	20.5/1255	10,500 psi	Note 1
Fed. 209A	Solo 1250	Fed. 12C1				26.0/1310	8,000 psi	Note 1
Fed. 209A	Solo 1250	H. Versalite				25.0/1310	8,500 psi	Note 1
Fed. 209A	Solo 1250	Hawk II	25.0/1255	25.2/1270	25.5/1285	26.0/1310	8,100 psi	Note 1
Fed. 209A	Solo 1250	WAA12F114				26.0/1310	9,200 psi	Note 1
Fed. 209A	Unique	Fed. 12C1	22.0/1200	22.0/1200	22.5/1255	26.5/1310	9,000 psi	
Fed. 209A	Unique	Fed. 12S3	22.0/1200	22.0/1200	23.0/1255	26.5/1310	9,700 psi	
Fed. 209A	Unique	H. Versalite	22.0/1200	22.3/1215	22.6/1230	23.0/1255	8,700 psi	
Fed. 209A	Unique	Lage Uniwad				22.0/1200	8,000 psi	
Fed. 209A	Unique	Pat. Ctrl. Red	22.5/1200	23.1/1215	23.7/1230	24.5/1255	8,500 psi	
Fed. 209A	Unique	Rem. R12H				22.5/1255	9,000 psi	
Fed. 209A	Unique	Rem. R12L				22.0/1200	7,800 psi	
Fed. 209A	Unique	Rem. RXP12	21.0/1200	22.0/1255	24.5/1285	26.5/1310	8,600 psi	
Fed. 209A	Unique	WAA12	21.0/1200	22.0/1255	24.5/1285	26.5/1310	9,100 psi	

Load Notes: 1 = Minimum overall length = 2¹⁰/₃₂″, maximum crimp depth = ²/₃₂″. 5 = Use 50-60 pounds wad pressure to ensure wad is firmly seated against powder.

Caution: Follow load recipes exactly; do not substitute components, exceed listed maximums or load less than listed minimums.

Primer	Powder Type	Wad	Powder Charge (grains) / Velocity (fps) Minimum			Maximum	Maximum Pressure	Load Notes
Federal: Paper (cont.)						**1 1/8 Ounces Lead Shot**		
Fed. 209A	Unique	Windjammer				23.5/1200	7,600 psi	
Fed. 399	W 452AA	Fed. 12C1	21.0/1145	21.5/1165	22.0/1180	22.5/1200	9,200 LUP	
Fio. 616	Clays	H. Versalite	16.8/1090	17.2/1120	17.5/1145	19.0/1200	10,300 psi	
Fio. 616	International	Fiocchi TL1	19.9/1090	20.6/1145	22.5/1200	23.7/1255	9,200 LUP	
Fio. 616	Nitro-100	Fed. 12C1	17.5/1145	17.7/1160	18.0/1175	18.5/1200	8,000 psi	Note 1
Fio. 616	R. Scot D	Fed. 12C1	20.0/1125	20.5/1145	21.0/1175	21.5/1200	10,600 LUP	
Fio. 616	Red Diamond	Activ TG-30	17.0/1145	18.0/1175	19.0/1200	20.0/1255	10,700 psi	Note 5
Fio. 616	Red Diamond	Fed. 12C1	17.5/1145	18.0/1175	18.5/1200	20.0/1255	10,400 psi	Note 5
Fio. 616	Red Diamond	Fed. 12S4	17.0/1145	17.8/1175	18.5/1200	19.5/1255	10,600 psi	Note 5
Fio. 616	Red Diamond	Pat. Ctrl. Red	17.0/1145	17.8/1175	18.5/1200	20.0/1255	9,400 psi	Note 5
Fio. 616	Red Diamond	WAA12	17.0/1145	17.8/1175	18.5/1200	20.5/1255	9,900 psi	Note 5
Fio. 616	Solo 1000	Fed. 12C1	19.0/1145	19.2/1160	19.5/1175	20.0/1200	8,200 psi	Note 1
Fio. 616	Solo 1250	Fed. 12C1				26.0/1310	7,300 psi	Note 1
Rem. 209	Red Diamond	Activ TG-30	17.5/1145	18.3/1175	19.0/1200	20.5/1255	10,500 psi	Note 5
Rem. 209	Red Diamond	Fed. 12C1	17.5/1145	18.0/1175	18.5/1200	20.0/1255	9,800 psi	Note 5
Rem. 209	Red Diamond	Fed. 12S4	17.0/1145	17.8/1175	18.5/1200	19.5/1255	10,100 psi	Note 5
Rem. 209	Red Diamond	Pat. Ctrl. Red	17.5/1145	18.3/1175	19.0/1200	20.5/1255	9,400 psi	Note 5
Rem. 209	Red Diamond	WAA12	17.0/1145	17.8/1175	18.5/1200	20.5/1255	9,200 psi	Note 5
Rem. 209P	American Select	Fed. 12S3	19.0/1145	19.6/1160	20.2/1175	21.0/1200	9,700 psi	
Rem. 209P	Clays	Rem. Fig.-8	18.0/1090	18.3/1120	18.5/1145	19.5/1200	9,200 psi	
Rem. 209P	Green Dot	Fed. 12C1	20.0/1145	22.0/1200	23.5/1255	25.5/1310	9,300 psi	
Rem. 209P	Red Dot	Fed. 12C1	18.5/1145	19.3/1175	20.0/1200	21.5/1255	10,700 psi	
Rem. 209P	Solo 1250	Fed. 12C1	27.0/1200	27.5/1230	28.0/1255	29.5/1310	9,400 psi	
Rem. 209P	Unique	Fed. 12C1	24.0/1200	26.0/1255	26.9/1285	27.5/1310	8,300 psi	
Win. 209	American Select	Fed. 12S3	19.0/1145	19.4/1160	19.8/1175	20.5/1200	9,700 psi	
Win. 209	Clays	WAA12	17.0/1090	18.0/1145	18.5/1175	19.0/1200	10,900 psi	
Win. 209	Green Dot	Fed. 12C1	19.5/1145	19.5/1145	21.0/1200	22.5/1255	9,000 psi	
Win. 209	International	WAA12	20.0/1090	20.6/1145	21.6/1200	23.2/1255	8,600 LUP	
Win. 209	Nitro-100	Fed. 12C1	17.0/1145	17.5/1175	18.0/1200	19.0/1255	9,200 psi	Note 1
Win. 209	R. Scot D	Fed. 12C1	20.5/1125	21.0/1145	22.0/1200	23.5/1255	10,800 LUP	
Win. 209	Red Diamond	Activ TG-30	17.0/1145	18.0/1175	19.0/1200	20.0/1255	10,600 psi	Note 5
Win. 209	Red Diamond	Fed. 12C1	17.5/1145	18.0/1175	18.5/1200	20.0/1255	10,300 psi	Note 5
Win. 209	Red Diamond	Fed. 12S4	17.0/1145	17.8/1175	18.5/1200	19.5/1255	10,500 psi	Note 5
Win. 209	Red Diamond	Pat. Ctrl. Red	17.0/1145	17.8/1175	18.5/1200	20.0/1255	9,300 psi	Note 5
Win. 209	Red Diamond	WAA12	17.0/1145	17.8/1175	18.5/1200	20.5/1255	10,500 psi	Note 5
Win. 209	Red Dot	Fed. 12C1	18.5/1145	19.1/1175	19.5/1200	21.0/1255	10,300 psi	
Win. 209	Solo 1000	Fed. 12C1	19.0/1145	19.5/1175	20.0/1200	21.0/1255	10,000 psi	Note 1
Win. 209	Solo 1250	Fed. 12C1				26.0/1310	8,100 psi	Note 1
Win. 209	Unique	Fed. 12C1	23.0/1200	24.5/1255	25.7/1285	26.5/1310	9,200 psi	
Win. 209	W 452AA	Fed. 12C1	21.0/1145	21.5/1165	22.0/1180	22.5/1200	9,600 LUP	
Win. 209	W 452AA	WAA12	20.5/1145	21.0/1165	21.5/1180	22.0/1200	9,900 LUP	
Win. AATP	International	WAA12	19.5/1090	19.9/1145	21.5/1200	23.0/1255	9,900 psi	

Load Notes: 1 = Minimum overall length = 2¹⁰/₃₂″, maximum crimp depth = ²/₃₂″. 5 = Use 50-60 pounds wad pressure to ensure wad is firmly seated against powder.

Caution: Follow load recipes exactly; do not substitute components, exceed listed maximums or load less than listed minimums.

Primer	Powder Type	Wad	Powder Charge (grains) / Velocity (fps) Minimum			Maximum	Maximum Pressure	Load Notes
FEDERAL: PLASTIC (PAPER BASE WAD)						**1 ¹/₈ OUNCES LEAD SHOT**		
CCI 209M	Green Dot	Fed. 12S3	20.0/1145	20.8/1175	21.2/1200	22.0/1255	9,600 psi	
CCI 209M	Red Dot	Fed. 12S3	18.5/1145	19.3/1175	20.0/1200	21.5/1255	10,100 psi	
CCI 209M	Unique	Fed. 12S3	24.0/1200	24.5/1220	25.0/1240	25.5/1255	8,400 psi	
Fed. 209	IMR 700-X	Fed. 12S3	18.0/1140	18.5/1160	19.0/1180	19.5/1200	8,800 LUP	
Fed. 209	IMR 700-X	Fed. 12S4				21.0/1255	8,800 LUP	
Fed. 209	IMR PB	Fed. 12S4	22.0/1150	23.0/1195	23.8/1225	24.5/1250	8,800 LUP	
Fed. 209	SR-7625	Fed. 12S4	24.5/1145	25.5/1190	26.3/1225	27.0/1260	8,800 LUP	
Fed. 209A	Green Dot	Fed. 12C1	20.5/1200	21.0/1220	21.5/1240	22.0/1255	10,100 psi	
Fed. 209A	Green Dot	Fed. 12S3	20.0/1145	20.8/1175	21.2/1200	22.0/1255	9,000 psi	
Fed. 209A	Green Dot	H. Versalite	19.5/1145	20.3/1175	21.5/1200	23.5/1255	8,600 psi	
Fed. 209A	Green Dot	Rem. RXP12	19.0/1145	19.8/1175	20.8/1200	22.5/1255	10,000 psi	
Fed. 209A	Green Dot	WAA12	18.5/1145	19.3/1175	19.9/1200	22.0/1255	10,300 psi	
Fed. 209A	Red Dot	Fed. 12C1				21.0/1255	10,200 psi	
Fed. 209A	Red Dot	Fed. 12S3	18.5/1145	19.3/1175	19.7/1200	21.5/1255	10,100 psi	
Fed. 209A	Red Dot	H. Versalite	18.5/1145	19.3/1175	19.7/1200	20.5/1255	9,700 psi	
Fed. 209A	Red Dot	Rem. RXP12	18.5/1145	19.3/1175	19.5/1200	21.0/1255	9,800 psi	
Fed. 209A	Red Dot	WAA12	18.5/1145	18.7/1175	18.8/1185	19.0/1200	9,800 psi	
Fed. 209A	Unique	Fed. 12S3	23.0/1200	23.3/1220	23.6/1240	24.0/1255	8,100 psi	
Fed. 209A	Unique	H. Versalite	22.5/1200	22.8/1220	23.1/1240	23.5/1255	8,200 psi	
Fed. 209A	Unique	Rem. RXP12	22.0/1200	22.3/1220	22.6/1240	23.0/1255	8,100 psi	
Fed. 209A	Unique	WAA12	21.0/1200	21.6/1220	22.3/1240	23.0/1255	8,600 psi	
Fed. 209A	Universal	Fed. 12S3	24.0/1200	24.5/1230	25.0/1255	26.5/1310	9,400 psi	
Rem. 209P	Green Dot	Fed. 12S3	21.0/1145	21.8/1175	22.2/1200	23.0/1255	8,500 psi	
Rem. 209P	Red Dot	Fed. 12S3	18.5/1145	19.3/1175	20.5/1200	22.0/1255	10,300 psi	
Win. 209	Green Dot	Fed. 12S3	20.0/1145	20.8/1175	21.6/1200	23.0/1255	9,400 psi	
Win. 209	Red Dot	Fed. 12S3	18.5/1145	19.3/1175	20.0/1200	21.5/1255	10,700 psi	
Win. 209	Unique	Fed. 12S3	23.5/1200	24.0/1220	24.5/1240	25.0/1255	9,100 psi	
Win. 209	Universal	WAA12	24.0/1200	24.5/1230	25.0/1255	26.5/1310	9,700 psi	
FIOCCHI: PLASTIC (LOW BASE WAD)						**1 ¹/₈ OUNCES LEAD SHOT**		
Fio. 616	American Select	BP HCD24	19.5/1200	19.7/1210	19.8/1215	20.0/1225	11,000 psi	Note 2
Fio. 616	American Select	BP Z21	19.5/1200	19.7/1210	19.8/1215	20.0/1225	11,100 psi	Note 4
Fio. 616	American Select	BP Zero	17.3/1150	18.0/1170	18.8/1200	20.3/1225	9,800 psi	
Fio. 616	Clays	BP HCDP	19.6/1200	20.0/1225	20.2/1235	20.4/1245	9,700 psi	Note 3
Fio. 616	IMR 800-X	BP HCDP	24.5/1220	24.7/1230	24.8/1235	25.0/1245	7,200 LUP	Note 3
Fio. 616	IMR PB	BP HCDP				24.0/1255	8,900 psi	Note 3
Fio. 616	Nitro-100	BP HCDP	19.1/1200	19.6/1220	19.9/1235	20.2/1255	9,700 psi	Note 3
Fio. 616	Red Dot	BP HCDP	18.0/1145	18.2/1155	18.5/1175	18.8/1200	10,000 psi	Note 3
Fio. 616	Solo 1000	BP SCAT			20.0/1200	20.5/1225	8,700 psi	Note 6
Fio. 616	Solo 1000	BP HCDP	20.5/1225	20.7/1235	20.8/1245	21.0/1255	9,100 psi	Note 3
Fio. 616	Solo 1250	BP SCAT	27.0/1220	27.5/1240	27.7/1250	28.0/1260	8,200 psi	Note 6
Fio. 616	Solo 1250	BP HCDP	26.5/1200	27.5/1240	28.5/1255	29.5/1310	9,900 psi	Note 3

Load Notes: 2 = Hex Cushion DR-24. 3 = Helix Cushion Platform. 4 = Trap Commander. 6 = Scatter Master.

    Caution: Follow load recipes exactly; do not substitute components, exceed listed maximums or load less than listed minimums.

Primer	Powder Type	Wad	Powder Charge (grains) / Velocity (fps) Minimum			Maximum	Maximum Pressure	Load Notes
Fiocchi: Plastic (low base wad) (cont.)						**1 1/8 Ounces Lead Shot**		
Fio. 616	SR-7625	BP HCDP	26.0/1250	26.5/1275	26.7/1285	27.0/1300	8,100 psi	Note 3
Win. 209	International	BP SCAT	19.7/1145	20.4/1175	21.0/1200	22.0/1255	8,800 LUP	Note 6
Win. 209	International	BP HCDP	21.0/1200	21.4/1225	21.7/1240	22.0/1255	8,800 LUP	Note 3
Fiocchi: Purple Target (high base wad)						**1 1/8 Ounces Lead Shot**		
CCI 209	Clays	H. Versalite	17.9/1090	18.4/1120	18.9/1145	20.0/1200	7,700 LUP	
CCI 209	Red Diamond	Fed. 12S3	17.5/1145	18.3/1175	19.0/1200	20.5/1255	9,000 psi	Note 5
CCI 209	Red Diamond	Fiocchi TL1	17.5/1145	18.0/1175	18.5/1200	20.5/1255	8,800 psi	Note 5
CCI 209	Red Diamond	H. Versalite	17.5/1145	18.3/1175	19.0/1200	20.0/1255	9,300 psi	Note 5
CCI 209	Red Diamond	Hawk II	17.5/1145	18.3/1175	19.0/1200	20.0/1255	9,000 psi	Note 5
CCI 209	Red Diamond	Pat. Ctrl. white	17.5/1145	18.5/1175	19.5/1200	20.5/1255	8,700 psi	Note 5
CCI 209M	Green Dot	Rem. RXP12				24.0/1310	10,000 psi	
CCI 209M	International	H. Versalite	18.5/1090	19.5/1145	20.9/1200	22.0/1255	7,300 LUP	
CCI 209M	Nitro-100	Activ TG-30	16.5/1145	16.8/1160	17.2/1180	17.5/1200	10,000 psi	Note 9
CCI 209M	Nitro-100	Fed. 12S3	16.5/1145	16.7/1160	17.0/1175	17.5/1200	10,300 psi	Note 9
CCI 209M	R. Scot D	Activ TG-30	18.0/1125	18.0/1145	19.0/1175	20.0/1200	10,500 LUP	
CCI 209M	R. Scot D	Fed. 12S3	18.0/1125	18.0/1145	19.2/1175	20.0/1200	9,900 LUP	
CCI 209M	Red Diamond	Fed. 12S3	17.0/1145	17.8/1175	18.5/1200	20.0/1255	9,600 psi	Note 5
CCI 209M	Red Diamond	Fiocchi TL1	16.5/1145	17.3/1175	18.0/1200	19.0/1255	9,800 psi	Note 5
CCI 209M	Red Diamond	H. Versalite	17.5/1145	18.0/1175	18.5/1200	19.5/1255	9,700 psi	Note 5
CCI 209M	Red Diamond	Hawk II	17.0/1145	17.8/1175	18.5/1200	20.0/1255	10,100 psi	Note 5
CCI 209M	Red Diamond	Pat. Ctrl. White	17.5/1145	18.3/1175	19.0/1200	20.0/1255	9,000 psi	Note 5
CCI 209M	Solo 1000	Activ TG-30	17.5/1125	17.5/1145	18.4/1170	19.5/1200	9,500 LUP	Note 9
CCI 209M	Solo 1000	Fed. 12S3	17.5/1125	17.5/1145	18.5/1175	19.5/1200	8,800 LUP	Note 9
CCI 209M	Solo 1250	Activ TG-30	26.0/1200	26.9/1235	28.1/1280	29.0/1310	10,400 LUP	Note 9
CCI 209M	Solo 1250	Fed. 12S3				25.5/1200	7,900 LUP	Note 9
CCI 209M	Unique	Rem. RXP12				26.5/1310	8,400 psi	
CCI 209SC	Clays	Fiocchi TL1	16.8/1090	17.1/1105	17.4/1120	18.0/1145	8,900 psi	
CCI 209SC	International	Fiocchi TL1	19.0/1090	19.5/1120	20.0/1145	21.0/1200	9,400 psi	
Fed. 209	Clays	Fed. 1283	17.1/1090	17.7/1120	18.3/1145	19.5/1200	8,500 LUP	
Fed. 209	Green Dot	Fed. 12S3				24.5/1310	10,300 psi	
Fed. 209	International	Fed. 12S3	20.0/1090	20.3/1120	20.5/1145	21.6/1200	8,100 LUP	
Fed. 209	R. Scot D	Activ TG-30	18.5/1125	19.0/1145	19.5/1175	20.0/1200	8,600 LUP	
Fed. 209	R. Scot D	Fed. 12S3	18.5/1125	19.0/1145	20.0/1200	21.5/1255	10,400 LUP	
Fed. 209	Solo 1000	Activ TG-30				18.0/1125	6,900 LUP	Note 9
Fed. 209	Solo 1000	Fed. 12S3	18.0/1125	18.7/1155	19.5/1190	21.0/1255	9,400 LUP	Note 9
Fed. 209	Solo 1250	Activ TG-30	27.0/1200	27.8/1230	28.5/1255	30.0/1310	9,500 LUP	Note 9
Fed. 209	Solo 1250	Fed. 12S3	26.5/1200	27.3/1230	28.0/1255	29.5/1310	10,000 LUP	Note 9
Fed. 209	Unique	Fed. 12S3				27.0/1310	9,200 psi	
Fed. 209A	Clays	Fed. 1233	16.5/1090	16.6/1105	16.8/1120	17.0/1145	10,000 psi	
Fed. 209A	International	Fiocchi TL1	18.0/1090	18.3/1120	18.5/1145	20.0/1200	10,400 psi	
Fed. 209A	Nitro-100	Activ TG-30	16.5/1145	16.7/1160	17.0/1175	17.5/1200	11,000 psi	Note 9

Load Notes: 3 = Helix Cushion Platform. 5 = Use 50-60 pounds wad pressure to ensure wad is firmly seated against powder. 6 = Scatter Master. 9 = Minimum overall length = 2⁹/₃₂", maximum crimp depth = ²/₃₂".

Caution: Follow load recipes exactly; do not substitute components, exceed listed maximums or load less than listed minimums.

Primer	Powder Type	Wad	Powder Charge (grains) / Velocity (fps)				Maximum Pressure	Load Notes
			Minimum			Maximum		
FIOCCHI: PURPLE TARGET (HIGH BASE WAD) (CONT.)						**1¹/₈ OUNCES LEAD SHOT**		
Fed. 209A	Nitro-100	Fed. 12S3	16.5/1145	16.7/1160	17.0/1175	17.5/1200	10,500 psi	Note 9
Fed. 209A	Red Diamond	Fed. 12S3	17.0/1145	17.8/1175	18.5/1200	19.5/1255	10,300 psi	Note 5
Fed. 209A	Red Diamond	Fiocchi TL1	16.5/1145	17.3/1175	18.0/1200	19.0/1255	10,400 psi	Note 5
Fed. 209A	Red Diamond	H. Versalite	17.0/1145	17.5/1175	18.0/1200	19.0/1255	10,400 psi	Note 5
Fed. 209A	Red Diamond	Hawk II	17.0/1145	17.5/1175	18.0/1200	19.5/1255	10,600 psi	Note 5
Fed. 209A	Red Diamond	Pat. Ctrl. White	17.0/1145	17.5/1175	18.0/1200	19.5/1255	10,000 psi	Note 5
Fed. 209A	Solo 1250	Activ TG-30				27.0/1200	7,800 LUP	Note 9
Fed. 209A	Solo 1250	Fed. 12S3				26.5/1200	6,900 LUP	Note 9
Fio. 616	#2 Improved	Fed. 12S3	17.5/1125	18.0/1145	18.5/1175	19.0/1200	10,700 psi	Note 9
Fio. 616	American Select	Claybuster Red	18.0/1090	19.5/1145	21.0/1200	22.5/1250	10,700 psi	
Fio. 616	American Select	CS12S	20.0/1200	20.2/1220	20.3/1230	20.5/1245	11,400 psi	
Fio. 616	American Select	Fed. 12S3	17.5/1090	19.0/1145	20.5/1200	22.0/1250	10,300 psi	
Fio. 616	American Select	Fiocchi TL1	18.0/1090	19.5/1145	20.5/1200	22.0/1250	10,200 psi	
Fio. 616	American Select	BP HCDP	20.5/1200	20.7/1205	20.8/1210	21.0/1220	10,800 psi	Note 3
Fio. 616	American Select	SF12 STR-8				19.8/1200	10,200 psi	
Fio. 616	Clays	Fiocchi TL1	16.5/1090	17.9/1145	18.7/1175	19.4/1200	9,100 LUP	
Fio. 616	Clays	BP HCDP	19.2/1200	19.7/1225	19.8/1235	19.9/1245	9,700 psi	Note 3
Fio. 616	Green Dot	Fed. 12C1	18.5/1090	19.5/1145	21.0/1200	22.5/1250	9,300 psi	
Fio. 616	Green Dot	Fed. 12S3	18.5/1090	19.3/1120	20.0/1145	25.0/1310	9,600 psi	
Fio. 616	Green Dot	Fiocchi FTW1	18.5/1090	20.0/1145	21.0/1200	23.0/1250	9,200 psi	
Fio. 616	Green Dot	H. Versalite	18.5/1090	19.5/1145	21.0/1200	22.5/1250	9,300 psi	
Fio. 616	Green Dot	Rem. Fig.-8	18.5/1090	20.0/1145	21.5/1200	23.0/1250	8,800 psi	
Fio. 616	Green Dot	Rem. RXP12	18.5/1090	20.0/1145	21.5/1200	23.0/1250	9,200 psi	
Fio. 616	Green Dot	WAA12	18.5/1090	20.0/1145	21.5/1200	23.0/1250	8,900 psi	
Fio. 616	Green Dot	Windjammer	19.5/1145	21.0/1200	21.8/1225	22.5/1250	9,000 psi	
Fio. 616	Herco	Fed. 12C1				26.0/1250	7,500 psi	
Fio. 616	Herco	Fiocchi FTW1				26.0/1250	8,300 psi	
Fio. 616	Herco	H. Versalite				25.5/1250	7,700 psi	
Fio. 616	Herco	Rem. Fig.-8				26.0/1250	7,300 psi	
Fio. 616	Herco	Rem. RXP12				26.0/1250	7,500 psi	
Fio. 616	Herco	WAA12				26.0/1250	7,900 psi	
Fio. 616	Herco	Windjammer				26.5/1250	7,700 psi	
Fio. 616	IMR 800-X	BP HCDP	23.8/1220	24.1/1230	24.3/1235	24.6/1245	7,200 LUP	Note 3
Fio. 616	IMR PB	BP HCDP				23.8/1255	8,900 psi	Note 3
Fio. 616	International	Fiocchi TL1	19.3/1090	20.3/1145	21.0/1200	22.6/1255	9,900 LUP	
Fio. 616	Nitro-100	Activ TG-30	16.5/1145	17.0/1175	17.5/1200	18.5/1255	10,800 psi	Note 9
Fio. 616	Nitro-100	Fed. 12S3	16.5/1145	17.0/1175	17.5/1200	18.5/1255	10,900 psi	Note 9
Fio. 616	Nitro-100	BP HCDP	18.9/1200	19.2/1220	19.5/1235	20.0/1255	9,700 psi	Note 3
Fio. 616	R. Scot D	Activ TG-30	18.5/1125	19.0/1145	20.0/1200	21.5/1255	9,600 LUP	
Fio. 616	R. Scot D	Fed. 12S3	18.5/1125	19.0/1145	20.0/1200	21.5/1255	9,900 LUP	
Fio. 616	Red Diamond	Fed. 12S3	17.0/1145	17.8/1175	18.5/1200	19.5/1255	10,300 psi	Note 5

Load Notes: 3 = Helix Cushion Platform. 5 = Use 50-60 pounds wad pressure to ensure wad is firmly seated against powder. 9 = Minimum overall length = 2⁹/₃₂″, maximum crimp depth = ²/₃₂″.

Caution: Follow load recipes exactly; do not substitute components, exceed listed maximums or load less than listed minimums.

Primer	Powder Type	Wad	Powder Charge (grains) / Velocity (fps) Minimum			Maximum	Maximum Pressure	Load Notes
Fiocchi: Purple Target (high base wad) (cont.)					1 1/8 Ounces Lead Shot			
Fio. 616	Red Diamond	Fiocchi TL1	16.5/1145	17.3/1175	18.0/1200	19.0/1255	10,700 psi	Note 5
Fio. 616	Red Diamond	H. Versalite	17.0/1145	17.5/1175	18.0/1200	19.0/1255	10,000 psi	Note 5
Fio. 616	Red Diamond	Hawk II	11.0/1145	14.5/1175	18.0/1200	19.5/1255	10,400 psi	Note 5
Fio. 616	Red Diamond	Pat. Ctrl. White	17.0/1145	17.5/1175	18.0/1200	19.5/1255	9,300 psi	Note 5
Fio. 616	Red Dot	Fed. 12C1	18.0/1145	19.0/1200	19.7/1225	20.5/1250	10,700 psi	
Fio. 616	Red Dot	Fed. 12S3	16.0/1090	18.0/1145	18.6/1175	19.0/1200	9,700 psi	
Fio. 616	Red Dot	Fiocchi FTW1	16.5/1090	17.5/1145	19.0/1200	21.0/1250	10,500 psi	
Fio. 616	Red Dot	H. Versalite	16.5/1090	17.1/1120	17.5/1145	18.5/1200	9,500 psi	
Fio. 616	Red Dot	BP HCDP				18.5/1200	10,000 psi	Note 3
Fio. 616	Red Dot	Rem. Fig.-8	16.0/1090	18.0/1145	19.5/1200	20.5/1250	10,200 psi	
Fio. 616	Red Dot	Rem. RXP12	16.5/1090	17.3/1120	18.0/1145	19.5/1200	9,700 psi	
Fio. 616	Red Dot	WAA12	17.0/1090	17.6/1120	18.0/1145	19.5/1200	9,400 psi	
Fio. 616	Red Dot	WAA12SL	17.0/1090	17.3/1105	17.6/1120	18.0/1145	8,300 psi	
Fio. 616	Red Dot	Windjammer	18.5/1145	20.0/1200	20.5/1225	21.0/1250	9,400 psi	
Fio. 616	Scot 453	Fiocchi TL1	17.5/1125	18.0/1145	18.5/1175	19.0/1200	10,700 psi	
Fio. 616	Solo 1000	Activ TG-30	18.0/1125	18.5/1145	19.5/1200	21.0/1255	9,000 LUP	Note 9
Fio. 616	Solo 1000	Fed. 12S3	18.0/1125	18.5/1145	19.5/1200	21.0/1255	9,100 LUP	Note 9
Fio. 616	Solo 1000	BP HCDP				20.7/1255	9,100 psi	Note 3
Fio. 616	Solo 1250	Activ TG-30	26.5/1200	27.0/1230	27.5/1255	29.5/1310	9,700 LUP	Note 9
Fio. 616	Solo 1250	Fed. 12S3	26.0/1200	26.8/1230	27.5/1255	29.5/1310	10,200 LUP	Note 9
Fio. 616	Solo 1250	BP HCDP	26.2/1200	27.2/1240	28.2/1255	29.0/1310	9,900 psi	Note 3
Fio. 616	SR-7625	BP HCDP	25.7/1250	26.3/1280	26.5/1290	26.8/1300	8,100 psi	Note 3
Fio. 616	Unique	Fed. 12C1	23.5/1200	24.0/1225	24.2/1235	24.5/1250	8,000 psi	
Fio. 616	Unique	Fed. 12S3				27.0/1310	8,600 psi	
Fio. 616	Unique	Fiocchi FTW1		23.5/1200	24.0/1225	24.5/1250	8,200 psi	
Fio. 616	Unique	H. Versalite	24.0/1200	24.5/1225	24.7/1235	25.0/1250	7,800 psi	
Fio. 616	Unique	Rem. Fig.-8	23.5/1200	24.0/1225	24.2/1235	24.5/1250	7,600 psi	
Fio. 616	Unique	Rem. RXP12	22.5/1200	23.0/1225	23.2/1235	23.5/1250	8,200 psi	
Fio. 616	Unique	WAA12	23.5/1200	23.8/1210	24.2/1225	25.0/1250	7,800 psi	
Fio. 616	Unique	Windjammer	24.0/1200	24.7/1225	25.1/1235	25.5/1250	6,900 psi	
Fio. 616	Universal	Fiocchi TL1	23.4/1200	24.2/1230	25.0/1255	26.5/1310	10,600 psi	
Rem. 209	Red Diamond	Fed. 12S3	17.5/1145	18.3/1175	19.0/1200	21.0/1255	8,900 psi	Note 5
Rem. 209	Red Diamond	Fiocchi TL1	17.5/1145	18.3/1175	19.0/1200	20.5/1255	8,600 psi	Note 5
Rem. 209	Red Diamond	H. Versalite	18.0/1145	18.5/1175	19.0/1200	20.5/1255	9,100 psi	Note 5
Rem. 209	Red Diamond	Hawk II	17.5/1145	18.3/1175	19.0/1200	21.0/1255	9,300 psi	Note 5
Rem. 209	Red Diamond	Pat. Ctrl. White	18.0/1145	18.8/1175	19.5/1200	21.0/1255	8,500 psi	Note 5
Rem. 209P	Clays	Rem. Fig.-8	17.6/1090	18.8/1145	19.4/1175	19.9/1200	7,500 LUP	
Rem. 209P	Nitro-100	Activ TG-30	16.5/1145	16.7/1160	17.0/1175	17.5/1200	8,700 psi	Note 9
Rem. 209P	Nitro-100	Fed. 12S3	16.5/1145	16.7/1160	17.0/1175	17.5/1200	9,100 psi	Note 9
Rem. 209P	R. Scot D	Activ TG-30	19.0/1125	19.5/1145	20.0/1175	20.5/1200	9,000 LUP	
Rem. 209P	R. Scot D	Fed. 12S3	19.0/1125	19.5/1145	20.0/1175	20.5/1200	9,000 LUP	

Load Notes: 3 = Helix Cushion Platform. 5 = Use 50-60 pounds wad pressure to ensure wad is firmly seated against powder. 9 = Minimum overall length = 2⁹/₃₂″, maximum crimp depth = ²/₃₂″.

Caution: Follow load recipes exactly; do not substitute components, exceed listed maximums or load less than listed minimums.

Primer	Powder Type	Wad	Powder Charge (grains) / Velocity (fps)				Maximum Pressure	Load Notes
			Minimum			Maximum		
FIOCCHI: PURPLE TARGET (HIGH BASE WAD) (CONT.)					1¹/₈ OUNCES LEAD SHOT			
Rem. 209P	Solo 1000	Activ TG-30	18.5/1125	19.0/1145	19.5/1175	20.0/1200	8,000 LUP	Note 9
Rem. 209P	Solo 1000	Fed. 12S3	18.5/1125	19.0/1145	19.5/1175	20.0/1200	8,000 LUP	Note 9
Rem. 209P	Solo 1250	Activ TG-30	27.0/1200	27.8/1235	28.7/1280	29.5/1310	9,000 LUP	Note 9
Rem. 209P	Solo 1250	Fed. 12S3	26.5/1200	27.0/1235	27.6/1280	28.5/1310	10,100 LUP	Note 9
Win. 209	Clays	WAA12	16.3/1090	17.0/1120	17.6/1145	18.9/1200	9,200 LUP	
Win. 209	Green Dot	WAA12				25.0/1310	8,700 psi	
Win. 209	International	BP HCDP	20.7/1200	21.1/1225	21.4/1240	21.7/1255	8,800 LUP	Note 3
Win. 209	International	WAA12	19.2/1090	19.7/1145	21.0/1200	22.0/1255	9,800 LUP	
Win. 209	Nitro-100	Activ TG-30	16.5/1145	16.7/1160	17.0/1175	17.5/1200	10,200 psi	Note 9
Win. 209	Nitro-100	Fed. 12S3	16.5/1145	17.0/1175	17.5/1200	18.5/1255	10,700 psi	Note 9
Win. 209	R. Scot D	Activ TG-30	18.5/1125	19.5/1145	20.0/1175	20.5/1200	8,500 LUP	
Win. 209	R. Scot D	Fed. 12S3	18.5/1125	19.5/1145	20.5/1200	21.5/1255	10,000 LUP	
Win. 209	Red Diamond	Fed. 12S3	17.0/1145	17.8/1175	18.5/1200	19.5/1255	10,100 psi	Note 5
Win. 209	Red Diamond	Fiocchi TL1	16.5/1145	17.3/1175	18.0/1200	19.0/1255	10,400 psi	Note 5
Win. 209	Red Diamond	H. Versalite	17.0/1145	17.5/1175	18.0/1200	19.0/1255	10,200 psi	Note 5
Win. 209	Red Diamond	Hawk II	17.0/1145	17.5/1175	18.0/1200	19.5/1255	11,000 psi	Note 5
Win. 209	Red Diamond	Pat. Ctrl. White	17.0/1145	17.5/1175	18.0/1200	19.0/1255	9,900 psi	Note 5
Win. 209	Solo 1000	Activ TG-30	18.0/1125	19.0/1145	19.5/1175	20.0/1200	8,200 LUP	Note 9
Win. 209	Solo 1000	Fed. 12S3	18.0/1125	19.0/1145	20.0/1200	21.0/1255	9,100 LUP	Note 9
Win. 209	Solo 1250	Activ TG-30	26.5/1200	27.6/1235	28.7/1280	29.5/1310	9,200 LUP	Note 9
Win. 209	Solo 1250	Fed. 12S3	26.5/1200	27.3/1230	28.0/1255	29.5/1310	9,900 LUP	Note 9
Win. 209	Unique	WAA12				26.5/1310	8,300 psi	
Win. 209	Universal	WAA12	23.3/1200	24.0/1255	24.5/1285	25.0/1310	10,800 psi	
Win. AATP	Clays	WAA12	16.2/1090	16.4/1105	16.6/1120	17.0/1145	9,300 psi	
Win. AATP	International	WAA12	17.8/1090	18.5/1145	20.2/1200	21.0/1255	10,900 psi	
PETERS: BLUE MAGIC					1¹/₈ OUNCES LEAD SHOT			
CCI 209	R. Scot D	Rem. RXP12	18.0/1125	18.5/1145	19.3/1175	20.0/1200	10,500 LUP	
CCI 209	Solo 1000	Rem. RXP12	17.5/1125	18.0/1145	18.8/1175	19.5/1200		
CCI 209	W 452AA	Fed. 12S1	19.5/1145	20.0/1165	20.5/1180	21.0/1200	9,200 LUP	
CCI 209	W 452AA	Rem. RXP12	19.5/1145	19.8/1165	20.2/1180	20.5/1200	9,800 LUP	
CCI 209	W 452AA	WAA12	18.5/1145	19.0/1165	19.5/1180	20.0/1200	10,400 LUP	
CCI 209M	R. Scot D	Rem. RXP12	18.0/1125	18.5/1145	19.1/1175	19.5/1200	10,900 LUP	
CCI 209M	Solo 1000	Rem. RXP12	17.5/1125	18.0/1145	18.6/1175	19.0/1200		
Fed. 209	R. Scot D	Rem. RXP12	18.0/1125	18.0/1145	19.1/1175	20.0/1200	10,900 LUP	
Fed. 209	Solo 1000	Rem. RXP12	17.0/1125	17.5/1145	18.6/1175	19.5/1200		
Rem. 209P	R. Scot D	Claybuster	18.0/1125	18.5/1145	19.1/1175	19.5/1200	10,900 LUP	
Rem. 209P	R. Scot D	H. Versalite	18.0/1125	18.5/1145	19.1/1175	19.5/1200	10,800 LUP	
Rem. 209P	R. Scot D	Pat. Ctrl. Red	18.0/1145	18.4/1160	18.8/1175	19.5/1200	10,500 LUP	
Rem. 209P	R. Scot D	Rem. RXP12	18.0/1125	18.5/1145	19.5/1200	20.5/1255	10,900 LUP	
Rem. 209P	R. Scot D	WAA12	18.0/1125	18.5/1145	18.8/1175	19.0/1200	10,900 LUP	
Rem. 209P	R. Scot D	Windjammer	18.5/1125	19.5/1145	20.0/1200	21.5/1255	10,700 LUP	

Load Notes: 3 = Helix Cushion Platform. 5 = Use 50-60 pounds wad pressure to ensure wad is firmly seated against powder. 9 = Minimum overall length = 2⁹/₃₂", maximum crimp depth = ²/₃₂".

Caution: Follow load recipes exactly; do not substitute components, exceed listed maximums or load less than listed minimums.

Primer	Powder Type	Wad	Powder Charge (grains) / Velocity (fps) Minimum			Maximum	Maximum Pressure	Load Notes
PETERS: BLUE MAGIC (CONT.)						**1¹/₈ OUNCES LEAD SHOT**		
Rem. 209P	Solo 1000	Claybuster	17.5/1125	18.0/1145	18.6/1175	19.0/1200		
Rem. 209P	Solo 1000	H. Versalite	17.5/1125	18.0/1145	18.6/1175	19.0/1200		
Rem. 209P	Solo 1000	Pat. Ctrl. Red	17.5/1145	18.3/1175	18.7/1175	19.0/1200		
Rem. 209P	Solo 1000	Rem. RXP12	17.5/1125	18.0/1145	19.0/1200	20.0/1255		
Rem. 209P	Solo 1000	WAA12	17.5/1125	18.0/1145	18.3/1175	18.5/1200		
Rem. 209P	Solo 1000	Windjammer	18.0/1125	19.0/1145	19.5/1200	21.0/1255		
Win. 209	R. Scot D	Rem. RXP12	18.0/1125	18.5/1145	19.3/1175	20.0/1200	10,500 LUP	
Win. 209	Solo 1000	Rem. RXP12	17.5/1125	18.0/1145	18.8/1175	19.5/1200		
Win. 209	W 452AA	Fed. 12S1	20.5/1145	20.8/1165	21.2/1180	21.5/1200	9,800 LUP	
Win. 209	W 452AA	Rem. RXP12	20.0/1145	20.5/1165	21.0/1180	21.5/1200	10,400 LUP	
Win. 209	W 452AA	WAA12				19.5/1145	10,100 LUP	
Win. 209	W 473AA	Rem. RXP12	24.0/1200	25.5/1255	26.0/1280	26.5/1300	9,500 LUP	
Win. 209	W 473AA	WAA12	24.0/1200	24.3/1220	24.7/1235	25.0/1255	9,400 LUP	
REMINGTON: PREMIER & NITRO 27 & STS						**1¹/₈ OUNCES LEAD SHOT**		
CCI 209	Clays	Windjammer	16.6/1090	17.3/1120	18.0/1145	19.4/1200	8,600 LUP	
CCI 209	Green Dot	Rem. Fig.-8	19.5/1145	19.9/1160	20.3/1175	21.0/1200	8,700 psi	
CCI 209	IMR 800-X	CB 1118-12	19.5/1095	21.0/1155	22.0/1195	23.5/1255	8,400 psi	
CCI 209	IMR 800-X	Fed. 12S3	19.5/1100	20.5/1140	22.0/1200	23.5/1260	9,400 psi	
CCI 209	IMR 800-X	BP HCDP				23.5/1260	9,300 psi	Note 3
CCI 209	IMR 800-X	Rem. Fig.-8	19.5/1095	21.0/1155	22.0/1190	24.0/1265	8,700 psi	
CCI 209	IMR 800-X	WAA12	19.5/1105	20.5/1150	21.5/1190	23.0/1255	9,100 psi	
CCI 209	IMR 800-X	Windjammer	20.0/1095	21.0/1145	22.0/1195	23.5/1250	8,200 psi	
CCI 209	International	Windjammer	19.2/1090	19.8/1145	21.2/1200	22.3/1255	8,300 LUP	
CCI 209	Nitro-100	Rem. Fig.-8				16.0/1145	8,600 psi	Note 9
CCI 209	Nitro-100	Rem. RXP12	15.5/1145	15.9/1160	16.3/1175	17.0/1200	10,300 psi	Note 9
CCI 209	Nitro-100	Rem. TGT12	16.0/1145	16.2/1160	16.5/1175	17.0/1200	10,300 psi	Note 9
CCI 209	R. Scot D	Rem. Fig.-8	18.5/1125	19.0/1145	19.8/1175	20.5/1200	10,400 LUP	
CCI 209	R. Scot D	Rem. RXP12	18.5/1125	19.0/1145	19.8/1175	20.5/1200	9,900 LUP	
CCI 209	R. Scot D	Rem. TGT12	18.5/1125	19.0/1145	19.8/1175	20.5/1200	10,400 LUP	
CCI 209	Red Diamond	H. Versalite	16.0/1145	16.5/1175	17.0/1200	18.5/1255	9,900 psi	Note 5
CCI 209	Red Diamond	Pat. Ctrl. Red	16.5/1145	17.0/1175	17.5/1200	19.0/1255	9,600 psi	Note 5
CCI 209	Red Diamond	Rem. Fig.-8	16.0/1145	16.8/1175	17.5/1200	19.0/1255	9,600 psi	Note 5
CCI 209	Red Diamond	Rem. RXP12	16.0/1145	16.8/1175	17.5/1200	19.0/1255	10,200 psi	Note 5
CCI 209	Red Diamond	Rem. TGT12	16.0/1145	16.8/1175	17.5/1200	19.0/1255	9,300 psi	Note 5
CCI 209	Red Dot	Rem. Fig.-8	17.5/1145	18.0/1160	18.6/1175	19.5/1200	9,900 psi	
CCI 209	Solo 1000	Rem. Fig.-8	18.0/1125	18.5/1145	19.3/1175	20.0/1200	9,200 LUP	Note 9
CCI 209	Solo 1000	Rem. RXP12	18.0/1125	18.5/1145	19.3/1175	20.0/1200	9,500 LUP	Note 9
CCI 209	Solo 1000	Rem. TGT12	18.0/1125	18.5/1145	19.3/1175	20.0/1200	9,600 LUP	Note 9
CCI 209	Solo 1250	Rem. Fig.-8	25.0/1200	25.8/1235	26.8/1280	27.5/1310	10,500 LUP	Note 9
CCI 209	Unique	Rem. Fig.-8				22.5/1200	8,500 psi	
CCI 209	Universal	Windjammer	23.2/1200	23.8/1230	24.4/1255	25.7/1310	10,200 psi	

Load Notes: 3 = Helix Cushion Platform. 5 = Use 50-60 pounds wad pressure to ensure wad is firmly seated against powder. 9 = Minimum overall length = 2⁹/₃₂, maximum crimp depth = ²/₃₂.

Caution: Follow load recipes exactly; do not substitute components, exceed listed maximums or load less than listed minimums.

Primer	Powder Type	Wad	Powder Charge (grains) / Velocity (fps) Minimum			Maximum	Maximum Pressure	Load Notes
REMINGTON: PREMIER & NITRO 27 & STS (CONT.)						1¹/₈ OUNCES LEAD SHOT		
CCI 209	WSL	Fed. 12S3				18.0/1145	8,600 psi	
CCI 209	WSL	Rem. Fig.-8	19.0/1200	19.3/1220	19.7/1235	20.0/1255	10,600 psi	
CCI 209	WSL	Rem. RXP12	19.0/1200	19.3/1220	19.7/1235	20.0/1255	10,900 psi	
CCI 209	WSL	WAA12	18.0/1145	18.3/1165	18.7/1180	19.0/1200	10,800 psi	
CCI 209	WSL	WAA12SL	19.0/1200	19.3/1220	19.7/1235	20.0/1255	10,900 psi	
CCI 209	WST	Rem. Fig.-8				18.5/1145	10,200 psi	
CCI 209	WST	Rem. RXP12				18.5/1145	10,800 psi	
CCI 209	WST	WAA12				18.0/1145	10,800 psi	
CCI 209M	Green Dot	Fed. 12S3	17.5/1090	19.0/1145	20.5/1200	21.5/1250	10,600 psi	
CCI 209M	Green Dot	Fiocchi FTW1	17.5/1090	19.5/1145	20.1/1175	20.5/1200	9,700 psi	
CCI 209M	Green Dot	H. Versalite	19.0/1145	19.6/1175	20.0/1200	21.5/1250	10,200 psi	
CCI 209M	Green Dot	Pat. Ctrl. Red	18.0/1090	19.0/1145	20.5/1200	22.0/1250	9,600 psi	
CCI 209M	Green Dot	Rem. Fig.-8	18.0/1090	19.0/1145	19.6/1175	20.0/1200	9,300 psi	
CCI 209M	Green Dot	Rem. RXP12	17.5/1090	19.0/1145	20.5/1200	22.0/1250	9,600 psi	
CCI 209M	Green Dot	WAA12	17.0/1090	19.0/1145	21.0/1200	22.5/1250	10,700 psi	
CCI 209M	Green Dot	Windjammer	18.0/1090	19.5/1145	20.5/1200	22.0/1250	9,400 psi	
CCI 209M	Herco	Fed. 12S3				24.5/1250	9,900 psi	
CCI 209M	Herco	H. Versalite				24.5/1250	9,900 psi	
CCI 209M	Herco	Pat. Ctrl. Red				25.0/1250	9,500 psi	
CCI 209M	Herco	Rem. RXP12	24.5/1250	24.5/1250	24.5/1250	26.5/1310	9,700 psi	
CCI 209M	Herco	WAA12				24.5/1250	10,400 psi	
CCI 209M	Herco	Windjammer				25.0/1250	9,400 psi	
CCI 209M	R. Scot D	Rem. Fig.-8	17.5/1125	18.0/1145	18.8/1175	19.5/1200	10,900 LUP	
CCI 209M	R. Scot D	Rem. RXP12				17.5/1125	9,800 LUP	
CCI 209M	R. Scot D	Rem. TGT12				17.5/1125	10,400 LUP	
CCI 209M	Red Diamond	H. Versalite	15.5/1145	16.3/1175	17.0/1200	18.5/1255	10,000 psi	Note 5
CCI 209M	Red Diamond	Pat. Ctrl. Red	16.0/1145	16.8/1175	17.5/1200	19.0/1255	9,700 psi	Note 5
CCI 209M	Red Diamond	Rem. Fig.-8	16.0/1145	16.8/1175	17.5/1200	19.0/1255	10,000 psi	Note 5
CCI 209M	Red Diamond	Rem. RXP12	16.0/1145	16.8/1175	17.5/1200	19.0/1255	10,200 psi	Note 5
CCI 209M	Red Diamond	Rem. TGT12	16.0/1145	16.8/1175	17.5/1200	19.0/1255	9,300 psi	Note 5
CCI 209M	Red Dot	Fed. 12S3	16.0/1090	16.7/1115	17.1/1130	17.5/1145	10,600 psi	
CCI 209M	Red Dot	Fiocchi FTW1	16.5/1090	17.0/1145	17.8/1175	18.5/1200	10,600 psi	
CCI 209M	Red Dot	H. Versalite	17.0/1145	17.5/1160	18.1/1175	19.0/1200	10,400 psi	
CCI 209M	Red Dot	Pat. Ctrl. Red	16.5/1090	17.0/1145	18.2/1175	19.0/1200	10,400 psi	
CCI 209M	Red Dot	Rem. Fig.-8	16.5/1090	17.5/1145	18.1/1175	18.5/1200	10,400 psi	
CCI 209M	Red Dot	Rem. RXP12	16.0/1090	17.0/1145	17.8/1175	18.5/1200	10,500 psi	
CCI 209M	Red Dot	WAA12	16.0/1090	16.2/1115	16.3/1130	16.5/1145	10,200 psi	
CCI 209M	Red Dot	Windjammer	16.5/1090	17.0/1145	17.8/1175	18.5/1200	9,700 psi	
CCI 209M	Solo 1000	Rem. Fig.-8	17.0/1125	17.5/1145	18.3/1175	19.0/1200	10,800 LUP	Note 9
CCI 209M	Solo 1000	Rem. RXP12				17.0/1125	9,600 LUP	Note 9
CCI 209M	Solo 1000	Rem. TGT12				17.0/1125	9,900 LUP	Note 9
CCI 209M	Solo 1250	Rem. Fig.-8				23.5/1200	8,600 LUP	Note 9

Load Notes: 5 = Use 50-60 pounds wad pressure to ensure wad is firmly seated against powder. 9 = Minimum overall length = 2⁹/₃₂", maximum crimp depth = ²/₃₂".

Caution: Follow load recipes exactly; do not substitute components, exceed listed maximums or load less than listed minimums.

Primer	Powder Type	Wad	Powder Charge (grains) / Velocity (fps) Minimum			Maximum	Maximum Pressure	Load Notes
REMINGTON: PREMIER & NITRO 27 & STS (CONT.)						1 1/8 OUNCES LEAD SHOT		
CCI 209M	Unique	Fed. 12S3	22.0/1200	22.7/1225	23.0/1235	23.5/1250	10,200 psi	
CCI 209M	Unique	H. Versalite	22.0/1200	22.8/1225	23.1/1235	23.5/1250	9,900 psi	
CCI 209M	Unique	Pat. Ctrl. Red	22.5/1200	23.3/1225	23.6/1235	24.0/1250	9,400 psi	
CCI 209M	Unique	Rem. Fig.-8				22.5/1200	9,500 psi	
CCI 209M	Unique	Rem. RXP12	22.5/1200	24.0/1250	24.5/1280	25.0/1310	10,000 psi	
CCI 209M	Unique	WAA12	22.0/1200	23.0/1225	23.4/1235	24.0/1250	10,300 psi	
CCI 209M	Unique	Windjammer	23.5/1200	24.3/1225	24.6/1235	25.0/1250	9,300 psi	
CCI 209M	Universal	H. Versalite	21.1/1200	21.8/1230	22.5/1255	24.3/1310	11,400 psi	
CCI 209SC	American Select	Rem. Fig.-8	18.5/1145	18.8/1160	19.2/1175	20.0/1200	10,300 psi	
CCI 209SC	Clays	Rem. Fig.-8	16.0/1090	16.5/1120	17.0/1145	18.0/1200	8,800 psi	
CCI 209SC	Green Dot	Fed. 12S3	19.5/1145	19.6/1160	19.8/1175	20.0/1200	10,600 psi	
CCI 209SC	Green Dot	Rem. Fig.-8	20.5/1145	20.6/1160	20.8/1175	21.0/1200	10,600 psi	
CCI 209SC	Green Dot	WAA12				20.0/1145	10,600 psi	
CCI 209SC	Green Dot	Windjammer				22.0/1200	10,400 psi	
CCI 209SC	International	Rem. Fig.-8	18.0/1090	19.0/1145	20.3/1200	22.0/1255	10,300 psi	
CCI 209SC	Red Dot	Fed. 12S3				18.5/1145	10,400 psi	
CCI 209SC	Red Dot	Rem. Fig.-8				18.0/1145	10,400 psi	
CCI 209SC	Red Dot	Windjammer				18.5/1145	9,800 psi	
Fed. 209	Clays	Pat. Ctrl. Red	16.3/1090	17.8/1145	18.6/1175	19.3/1200	9,200 LUP	
Fed. 209	Green Dot	Rem. RXP12				22.0/1250	10,500 psi	
Fed. 209	Herco	Rem. RXP12				27.0/1310	9,200 psi	
Fed. 209	International	Pat. Ctrl. Red	19.2/1090	19.7/1145	21.2/1200	22.0/1255	9,200 LUP	
Fed. 209	Nitro-100	Rem. Fig.-8				18.5/1200		
Fed. 209	Nitro-100	Rem. RXP12	17.0/1145	17.8/1180	18.4/1215	19.5/1255		
Fed. 209	R. Scot D	Rem. Fig.-8	18.0/1125	18.5/1145	19.3/1175	20.0/1200	10,300 LUP	
Fed. 209	R. Scot D	Rem. RXP12	18.0/1125	18.7/1150	19.4/1175	20.0/1200	10,900 LUP	
Fed. 209	R. Scot D	Rem. TGT12	18.0/1125	18.5/1145	19.3/1175	20.0/1200	10,900 LUP	
Fed. 209	Red Dot	Rem. Fig.-8				16.0/1090	9,800 psi	
Fed. 209	Solo 1000	Rem. Fig.-8	17.5/1125	18.2/1150	18.8/1175	19.5/1200	10,100 LUP	Note 9
Fed. 209	Solo 1000	Rem. RXP12				17.5/1125	8,900 LUP	Note 9
Fed. 209	Solo 1000	Rem. TGT12				17.5/1125	9,200 LUP	Note 9
Fed. 209	Solo 1250	Rem. Fig.-8				24.5/1200	8,600 LUP	Note 9
Fed. 209	Unique	Rem. RXP12				24.0/1250	10,100 psi	
Fed. 209	Universal	Fed. 12S3	22.5/1200	23.0/1230	23.5/1255	24.0/1310	11,500 psi	
Fed. 209	WSL	Fed. 12S3		18.5/1145	19.0/1200	20.5/1255	10,400 psi	
Fed. 209	WSL	Rem. Fig.-8	20.0/1200	20.3/1220	20.7/1235	21.0/1255	9,180 psi	
Fed. 209	WSL	Rem. RXP12	19.5/1200	20.0/1220	20.5/1235	21.0/1255	9,900 psi	
Fed. 209	WSL	WAA12	18.0/1145	18.5/1175	19.0/1200	20.5/1255	9,900 psi	
Fed. 209	WSL	WAA12SL	18.5/1145	19.3/1175	20.0/1200	21.0/1255	10,400 psi	
Fed. 209	WST	Rem. Fig.-8				18.5/1145	10,000 psi	
Fed. 209	WST	Rem. RXP12				18.5/1145	10,000 psi	
Fed. 209A	American Select	Rem. Fig.-8	18.5/1145	18.8/1160	19.2/1175	20.0/1200	10,700 psi	

Load Notes: 9 = Minimum overall length = 2⁹/₃₂″, maximum crimp depth = ²/₃₂″.

Caution: Follow load recipes exactly; do not substitute components, exceed listed maximums or load less than listed minimums.

Primer	Powder Type	Wad	Powder Charge (grains) / Velocity (fps) Minimum			Maximum	Maximum Pressure	Load Notes
REMINGTON: PREMIER & NITRO 27 & STS (CONT.)						1¹/₈ OUNCES LEAD SHOT		
Fed. 209A	Clays	Pat. Ctrl. Red	15.8/1090	16.2/1120	16.6/1145	18.0/1200	11,300 psi	
Fed. 209A	Green Dot	Fed. S3				19.0/1145	9,900 psi	
Fed. 209A	Green Dot	Pat. Ctrl. Red				19.5/1145	10,000 psi	
Fed. 209A	Green Dot	Rem. Fig.-8	19.5/1145	19.8/1160	20.1/1175	20.5/1200	10,500 psi	
Fed. 209A	Green Dot	Rem. RXP12	19.5/1145	19.9/1160	20.3/1175	21.0/1200	10,400 psi	
Fed. 209A	Green Dot	Windjammer				20.0/1145	9,600 psi	
Fed. 209A	IMR 700-X	CB 1118-12	15.5/1110	16.0/1135	16.5/1160	17.5/1200	10,800 psi	
Fed. 209A	IMR 700-X	Fed. 12S3	15.0/1095	16.0/1135	16.8/1170	17.5/1200	11,500 psi	
Fed. 209A	IMR 700-X	BP HCDP				17.0/1200	10,200 psi	Note 3
Fed. 209A	IMR 700-X	Rem. Fig.-8	15.5/1105	16.0/1130	16.5/1150	17.5/1195	11,000 psi	
Fed. 209A	IMR 700-X	WAA12	15.0/1100	15.4/1115	15.8/1130	16.5/1160	10,900 psi	
Fed. 209A	IMR 700-X	Windjammer	15.5/1110	16.5/1155	17.5/1200	18.5/1240	11,100 psi	
Fed. 209A	IMR 800-X	CB 1118-12	19.5/1105	20.5/1150	21.5/1200	23.0/1250	9,000 psi	
Fed. 209A	IMR 800-X	Fed. 12S3	19.0/1100	20.0/1140	21.5/1205	23.0/1260	9,900 psi	
Fed. 209A	IMR 800-X	BP HCDP				23.5/1260	9,900 psi	Note 3
Fed. 209A	IMR 800-X	Rem. Fig.-8	19.5/1100	20.5/1140	22.0/1200	23.5/1260	9,200 psi	
Fed. 209A	IMR 800-X	WAA12	19.0/1095	20.0/1145	21.0/1190	22.5/1250	9,700 psi	
Fed. 209A	IMR 800-X	Windjammer	20.0/1110	21.0/1160	22.0/1205	23.0/1250	8,800 psi	
Fed. 209A	IMR PB	CB 1118-12	19.0/1100	20.5/1150	22.0/1205	23.5/1260	9,500 psi	
Fed. 209A	IMR PB	Fed. 12S4	18.5/1105	19.5/1140	21.0/1190	23.0/1265	10,900 psi	
Fed. 209A	IMR PB	BP HCDP				23.0/1270	10,800 psi	Note 3
Fed. 209A	IMR PB	Rem. Fig.-8	19.5/1110	20.5/1150	22.0/1200	23.5/1255	9,600 psi	
Fed. 209A	IMR PB	WAA12	18.5/1100	20.0/1155	21.0/1190	23.0/1260	11,000 psi	
Fed. 209A	IMR PB	Windjammer	19.5/1100	20.5/1145	22.0/1200	23.5/1260	9,500 psi	
Fed. 209A	Nitro-100	Rem. RXP12	15.5/1145	15.7/1160	16.0/1175	16.5/1200	10,800 psi	Note 9
Fed. 209A	Nitro-100	Rem. TGT12	15.5/1145	15.7/1160	16.0/1175	16.5/1200	10,700 psi	Note 9
Fed. 209A	Red Diamond	H. Versalite	15.5/1145	16.3/1175	17.0/1200	18.5/1255	10,500 psi	Note 5
Fed. 209A	Red Diamond	Pat. Ctrl. Red	16.0/1145	16.8/1175	17.5/1200	19.0/1255	10,400 psi	Note 5
Fed. 209A	Red Diamond	Rem. Fig.-8	16.0/1145	16.8/1175	17.5/1200	19.0/1255	10,200 psi	Note 5
Fed. 209A	Red Diamond	Rem. RXP12	16.0/1145	16.8/1175	17.5/1200	19.0/1255	10,800 psi	Note 5
Fed. 209A	Red Diamond	Rem. TGT12	16.0/1145	16.8/1175	17.5/1200	19.0/1255	10,000 psi	Note 5
Fed. 209A	Red Dot	Fed. S3				16.5/1145	10,100 psi	
Fed. 209A	Red Dot	Pat. Ctrl. Red				17.0/1145	10,700 psi	
Fed. 209A	Red Dot	Rem. Fig.-8	16.5/1145	16.6/1160	16.8/1175	17.0/1200	10,400 psi	
Fed. 209A	Red Dot	Rem. RXP12	16.0/1145	16.3/1160	16.6/1175	17.0/1200	10,100 psi	
Fed. 209A	Red Dot	Windjammer				17.5/1145	10,500 psi	
Fed. 209A	Solo 1250	Rem. Fig.-8				27.0/1310	10,900 LUP	Note 9
Fed. 209A	SR-7625	CB 1118-12	20.0/1090	21.5/1150	22.5/1190	24.0/1250	9,200 psi	
Fed. 209A	SR-7625	Fed. 12S3	20.0/1095	21.0/1140	22.5/1195	24.0/1250	10,000 psi	
Fed. 209A	SR-7625	BP HCDP				23.0/1240	10,500 psi	Note 3
Fed. 209A	SR-7625	Rem. RXP12	20.5/1095	22.0/1155	23.0/1190	24.5/1250	9,400 psi	

Load Notes: 3 = Helix Cushion Platform. 5 = Use 50-60 pounds wad pressure to ensure wad is firmly seated against powder. 9 = Minimum overall length = 2⁹/₃₂, maximum crimp depth = ²/₃₂.

   Caution: Follow load recipes exactly; do not substitute components, exceed listed maximums or load less than listed minimums.

Primer	Powder Type	Wad	Powder Charge (grains) / Velocity (fps) Minimum			Maximum	Maximum Pressure	Load Notes
REMINGTON: PREMIER & NITRO 27 & STS (CONT.)						1 1/8 OUNCES LEAD SHOT		
Fed. 209A	SR-7625	WAA12	19.5/1100	20.5/1140	22.0/1205	23.0/1245	10,500 psi	
Fed. 209A	SR-7625	Windjammer	21.0/1105	22.0/1150	23.5/1205	25.0/1255	8,400 psi	
Fed. 209A	Unique	Rem. Fig.-8				23.0/1200	9,200 psi	
Fed. 209A	Unique	Rem. RXP12				22.0/1200	9,100 psi	
Fed. 209A	Universal	Fed. 12S3	21.7/1200	21.9/1215	22.2/1230	22.7/1255	11,000 psi	
Fio. 616	Clays	Fiocchi TL1	15.5/1090	16.2/1120	16.9/1145	18.4/1200	10,900 LUP	
Fio. 616	Green Dot	Rem. Fig.-8	19.0/1145	19.3/1160	19.6/1175	20.0/1200	8,700 psi	
Fio. 616	Green Dot	Rem. RXP12				22.0/1250	9,100 psi	
Fio. 616	Herco	Rem. RXP12				27.5/1310	9,300 psi	
Fio. 616	International	Fiocchi TL1	18.1/1090	18.4/1120	18.7/1145	19.9/1200	10,000 LUP	
Fio. 616	R. Scot D	Rem. Fig.-8	18.5/1145	18.9/1160	19.3/1175	20.0/1200	10,900 LUP	
Fio. 616	Red Diamond	H. Versalite	15.5/1145	16.3/1175	17.0/1200	18.5/1255	10,400 psi	Note 5
Fio. 616	Red Diamond	Pat. Ctrl. Red	16.0/1145	16.8/1175	17.5/1200	19.0/1255	9,700 psi	Note 5
Fio. 616	Red Diamond	Rem. Fig.-8	16.0/1145	16.8/1175	17.5/1200	19.0/1255	10,100 psi	Note 5
Fio. 616	Red Diamond	Rem. RXP12	16.0/1145	16.8/1175	17.5/1200	19.0/1255	10,500 psi	Note 5
Fio. 616	Red Diamond	Rem. TGT12	16.0/1145	16.8/1175	17.5/1200	19.0/1255	9,600 psi	Note 5
Fio. 616	Red Dot	Rem. Fig.-8	16.5/1090	17.5/1145	18.7/1175	19.5/1200	10,600 psi	
Fio. 616	Solo 1000	Rem. Fig.-8	18.0/1145	18.4/1160	18.8/1175	19.5/1200		
Fio. 616	Solo 1000	Rem. Fig.-8	18.0/1145	18.4/1160	18.8/1175	19.5/1200	10,700 LUP	Note 9
Fio. 616	Unique	Rem. Fig.-8				23.0/1200	8,500 psi	
Fio. 616	Unique	Rem. RXP12	23.5/1250	24.6/1270	25.3/1290	26.0/1310	9,900 psi	
Fio. 616	Universal	Fiocchi TL1	22.5/1200	22.7/1215	23.0/1230	23.5/1255	10,600 psi	
Rem. 209	International	BP HCDP	18.5/1145	19.3/1200	19.7/1225	21.2/1255	10,700 LUP	Note 3
Rem. 209	Nitro-100	Fed. 12C1				18.5/1200		
Rem. 209	Nitro-100	Fed. 12S0				18.5/1200		
Rem. 209	Nitro-100	Fed. 12S3				18.5/1200		
Rem. 209	Nitro-100	H. Versalite				18.5/1200		
Rem. 209	Nitro-100	BP HCDP	17.0/1145	17.5/1160	18.0/1175	18.5/1200	9,800 psi	Note 3
Rem. 209	Nitro-100	Lage Uniwad				18.5/1200		
Rem. 209	Nitro-100	Rem. Fig.-8		18.5/1200	19.3/1230	20.0/1255		
Rem. 209	Nitro-100	Rem. RXP12	17.0/1145	17.8/1180	18.6/1220	19.5/1255		
Rem. 209	Red Diamond	H. Versalite	16.0/1145	16.5/1175	17.0/1200	18.5/1255	9,900 psi	Note 5
Rem. 209	Red Diamond	Pat. Ctrl. Red	16.5/1145	17.0/1175	17.5/1200	19.0/1255	9,100 psi	Note 5
Rem. 209	Red Diamond	Rem. Fig.-8	16.0/1145	16.8/1175	17.5/1200	19.0/1255	9,500 psi	Note 5
Rem. 209	Red Diamond	Rem. RXP12	16.0/1145	16.8/1175	17.5/1200	19.0/1255	9,800 psi	Note 5
Rem. 209	Red Diamond	Rem. TGT12	16.0/1145	16.8/1175	17.5/1200	19.0/1255	9,000 psi	Note 5
Rem. 209	Red Dot	BP HCDP	16.0/1090	16.5/1120	17.0/1145	17.5/1200	10,300 psi	Note 3
Rem. 209	Scot 453	Rem. Fig.-8	17.5/1125	18.0/1145	18.5/1175	19.0/1200	10,900 psi	
Rem. 209	Solo 1250	BP HCDP	24.0/1200	24.5/1220	25.0/1255	25.5/1270	9,900 psi	Note 3
Rem. 209	WSL	BP HCDP	18.5/1150	19.0/1180	19.5/1200	20.0/1230	9,700 psi	Note 3
Rem. 209P	#2 Improved	Rem. Fig.-8	17.5/1125	18.0/1145	18.5/1175	19.0/1200	10,900 psi	Note 9

Load Notes: 3 = Helix Cushion Platform. 5 = Use 50-60 pounds wad pressure to ensure wad is firmly seated against powder. 9 = Minimum overall length = 2⁹/₃₂″, maximum crimp depth = ²/₃₂″.

Caution: Follow load recipes exactly; do not substitute components, exceed listed maximums or load less than listed minimums.

Primer	Powder Type	Wad	Powder Charge (grains) / Velocity (fps) Minimum			Maximum	Maximum Pressure	Load Notes
REMINGTON: PREMIER & NITRO 27 & STS (CONT.)						**1¹/₈ OUNCES LEAD SHOT**		
Rem. 209P	American Select	Claybuster	17.5/1090	19.0/1145	20.0/1200	21.5/1250	10,600 psi	
Rem. 209P	American Select	CS12S	18.0/1200	18.2/1215	18.6/1225	18.8/1235	11,300 psi	
Rem. 209P	American Select	Fed. 12S3	17.5/1090	18.5/1145	19.2/1175	20.0/1200	10,600 psi	
Rem. 209P	American Select	Pat. Ctrl. Red	17.5/1090	19.0/1145	19.8/1175	20.5/1200	9,700 psi	
Rem. 209P	American Select	Rem. Fig.-8	17.5/1090	19.0/1145	20.5/1200	21.5/1250	9,900 psi	
Rem. 209P	American Select	Rem. RXP12	17.0/1090	18.5/1145	20.5/1200	21.0/1250	10,500 psi	
Rem. 209P	American Select	Windjammer	18.0/1090	19.0/1145	19.8/1175	20.5/1200	9,100 psi	
Rem. 209P	American Select	WT12 Orange	17.0/1090	18.5/1145	19.2/1175	20.0/1200	10,600 psi	Note 8
Rem. 209P	Clays	CB 3118-12-A	15.4/1090	16.0/1145	16.6/1175	17.2/1200	11,200 psi	
Rem. 209P	Clays	CB 3118-12-AR	15.0/1090	16.2/1145	16.5/1175	16.8/1200	11,200 psi	
Rem. 209P	Clays	Fed. 12S3	16.4/1090	17.6/1145	18.2/1175	18.8/1200	9,600 LUP	
Rem. 209P	Clays	Rem. Fig.-8	16.9/1090	18.0/1145	18.6/1175	19.2/1200	9,000 LUP	
Rem. 209P	Clays	WAA12	16.6/1090	17.7/1145	18.3/1175	18.8/1200	10,300 LUP	
Rem. 209P	Green Dot	Fed. 12S3	19.0/1145	19.4/1160	19.8/1175	20.5/1200	9,700 psi	
Rem. 209P	Green Dot	Fiocchi FTW1	19.5/1145	20.0/1160	20.1/1175	20.5/1200	9,900 psi	
Rem. 209P	Green Dot	H. Versalite	19.0/1145	19.3/1160	19.6/1175	20.0/1200	8,700 psi	
Rem. 209P	Green Dot	Lage Uniwad				19.0/1145	8,000 psi	
Rem. 209P	Green Dot	Pat. Ctrl. Red	19.0/1145	19.6/1160	20.2/1175	21.0/1200	8,500 psi	
Rem. 209P	Green Dot	Rem. Fig.-8	19.0/1145	19.5/1160	20.1/1175	21.0/1200	8,800 psi	
Rem. 209P	Green Dot	Rem. RXP12	19.0/1145	19.4/1160	19.8/1175	20.5/1200	8,700 psi	
Rem. 209P	Green Dot	WAA12	19.0/1145	19.5/1160	20.1/1175	21.0/1200	8,900 psi	
Rem. 209P	Green Dot	Windjammer	19.5/1145	20.0/1160	20.1/1175	20.5/1200	8,200 psi	
Rem. 209P	Green Dot	WT12 Orange	19.5/1145	20.0/1160	20.6/1175	21.5/1200	8,700 psi	Note 8
Rem. 209P	Herco	Activ T-32				27.0/1310	9,600 psi	
Rem. 209P	Herco	H. Versalite				27.0/1310	8,800 psi	
Rem. 209P	Herco	Rem. RXP12				27.5/1310	8,400 psi	
Rem. 209P	Herco	WAA12				27.0/1310	8,800 psi	
Rem. 209P	Herco	Windjammer				28.5/1310	8,600 psi	
Rem. 209P	IMR 700-X	CB 1118-12	15.5/1110	16.5/1155	17.5/1195	19.0/1250	11,100 psi	
Rem. 209P	IMR 700-X	Fed. 12S3	15.0/1095	15.8/1125	16.5/1150	17.5/1195	11,100 psi	
Rem. 209P	IMR 700-X	BP HCDP				17.0/1190	9,800 psi	Note 3
Rem. 209P	IMR 700-X	Rem. Fig.-8	15.5/1095	16.5/1140	18.0/1205	19.0/1250	11,300 psi	
Rem. 209P	IMR 700-X	WAA12	15.0/1090	16.0/1140	16.8/1175	17.5/1205	11,200 psi	
Rem. 209P	IMR 700-X	Windjammer	15.5/1090	16.5/1135	18.0/1200	19.0/1245	10,500 psi	
Rem. 209P	IMR PB	CB 1118-12	19.5/1090	21.0/1150	22.5/1200	24.0/1250	8,600 psi	
Rem. 209P	IMR PB	Fed. 12S4	19.0/1100	20.0/1140	21.5/1195	23.0/1245	10,000 psi	
Rem. 209P	IMR PB	BP HCDP				23.0/1240	9,900 psi	Note 3
Rem. 209P	IMR PB	Rem. Fig.-8	20.0/1100	21.5/1150	23.0/1205	24.5/1260	9,300 psi	
Rem. 209P	IMR PB	WAA12	19.5/1105	20.5/1145	22.0/1200	23.5/1255	9,500 psi	
Rem. 209P	IMR PB	Windjammer	20.0/1100	21.0/1140	22.5/1205	24.0/1265	8,900 psi	
Rem. 209P	International	CB 3118-12-A	16.8/1090	18.0/1145	19.0/1200	21.0/1255	10,200 psi	
Rem. 209P	International	CB 3118-12-AR	18.0/1090	18.2/1145	19.0/1200	21.0/1255	10,400 psi	

Load Notes: 3 = Helix Cushion Platform. 8 = Add one 20-gauge, 0.135" card inside bottom of shotcup.

Caution: Follow load recipes exactly; do not substitute components, exceed listed maximums or load less than listed minimums.

Primer	Powder Type	Wad	Powder Charge (grains) / Velocity (fps) Minimum			Maximum	Maximum Pressure	Load Notes
REMINGTON: PREMIER & NITRO 27 & STS (CONT.)						**1 1/8 OUNCES LEAD SHOT**		
Rem. 209P	International	Fed. 12S3	17.6/1090	18.3/1145	19.4/1200	20.6/1255	10,200 LUP	
Rem. 209P	International	Rem. Fig.-8	18.6/1090	19.6/1145	20.9/1200	21.7/1255	9,100 LUP	
Rem. 209P	International	WAA12	18.3/1090	18.8/1145	19.7/1200	20.9/1255	10,400 LUP	
Rem. 209P	Nitro-100	H. Versalite				17.0/1200	9,800 psi	Note 9
Rem. 209P	Nitro-100	Rem. Fig.-8	16.0/1145	16.2/1160	16.5/1175	17.0/1200	8,600 psi	Note 9
Rem. 209P	Nitro-100	Rem. RXP12	15.5/1145	15.7/1160	16.0/1175	16.5/1200	10,100 psi	Note 9
Rem. 209P	Nitro-100	Rem. TGT12	16.0/1145	16.2/1160	16.5/1175	17.0/1200	10,400 psi	Note 9
Rem. 209P	Nitro-100	Windjammer				17.0/1200	8,800 psi	Note 9
Rem. 209P	R. Scot D	Claybuster	17.5/1125	18.5/1145	19.3/1175	20.0/1200	9,600 LUP	
Rem. 209P	R. Scot D	H. Versalite	17.5/1125	18.0/1145	19.2/1175	20.0/1200	10,900 LUP	
Rem. 209P	R. Scot D	Lage Uniwad	18.0/1125	18.5/1130	18.8/1140	19.0/1145	10,200 LUP	
Rem. 209P	R. Scot D	Pat. Ctrl. Red	18.0/1125	18.5/1145	20.5/1200	21.0/1255	10,900 LUP	
Rem. 209P	R. Scot D	Rem. Fig.-8	18.0/1125	18.5/1145	19.3/1175	20.0/1200	10,600 LUP	
Rem. 209P	R. Scot D	Rem. RXP12	18.0/1125	18.5/1145	20.5/1200	21.0/1255	10,900 LUP	
Rem. 209P	R. Scot D	Rem. TGT12	17.0*/1125	18.5/1145	19.3/1175	20.0/1200	10,400 LUP	Note 10
Rem. 209P	R. Scot D	WAA12	18.0/1125	18.5/1145	19.3/1175	20.0/1200	10,800 LUP	
Rem. 209P	R. Scot D	Windjammer	18.0/1125	18.5/1145	20.0/1200	21.0/1255	10,900 LUP	
Rem. 209P	Red Dot	Fed. 12S3	16.0/1090	16.8/1115	17.4/1130	18.0/1145	10,100 psi	
Rem. 209P	Red Dot	Fiocchi FTW1	16.5/1090	17.5/1145	18.1/1175	18.5/1200	10,700 psi	
Rem. 209P	Red Dot	H. Versalite				17.5/1145	9,000 psi	
Rem. 209P	Red Dot	Lage Uniwad				17.5/1145	9,900 psi	
Rem. 209P	Red Dot	Pat. Ctrl. Red	16.5/1090	17.5/1145	18.1/1175	19.5/1200	10,100 psi	
Rem. 209P	Red Dot	Rem. Fig.-8	16.5/1090	18.0/1145	18.6/1175	19.0/1200	10,100 psi	
Rem. 209P	Red Dot	Rem. RXP12	16.0/1090	17.5/1145	18.3/1175	19.0/1200	10,000 psi	
Rem. 209P	Red Dot	WAA12	16.0/1090	16.4/1115	16.7/1130	17.0/1145	10,100 psi	
Rem. 209P	Red Dot	Windjammer	16.5/1090	17.5/1145	18.1/1175	18.5/1200	9,400 psi	
Rem. 209P	Red Dot	WT12 Orange	18.5/1145	18.8/1160	19.1/1175	19.5/1200	10,700 psi	Note 8
Rem. 209P	Solo 1000	Claybuster	17.5/1125	18.0/1145	18.8/1175	19.5/1200	9,500 LUP	Note 9
Rem. 209P	Solo 1000	H. Versalite	17.0/1125	17.5/1145	18.7/1175	19.5/1200	10,200 LUP	Notes 9
Rem. 209P	Solo 1000	Lage Uniwad				17.5/1125	7,500 LUP	Note 9
Rem. 209P	Solo 1000	Pat. Ctrl. Red	17.5/1125	18.0/1145	20.0/1200	20.5/1255	10,400 LUP	Note 9
Rem. 209P	Solo 1000	Rem. Fig.-8	17.5/1125	18.0/1145	18.8/1175	19.5/1200	9,600 LUP	Note 9
Rem. 209P	Solo 1000	Rem. RXP12	17.5/1125	18.0/1145	20.0/1200	20.5/1255	10,700 LUP	Note 9
Rem. 209P	Solo 1000	Rem. TGT12	16.5*/1125	18.0/1145	18.8/1175	19.5/1200	9,200 LUP	Note 9&10
Rem. 209P	Solo 1000	WAA12	17.5/1125	18.0/1145	18.8/1175	19.5/1200	10,200 LUP	Note 9
Rem. 209P	Solo 1000	Windjammer	17.5/1125	18.0/1145	19.5/1200	20.5/1255	10,400 LUP	Note 9
Rem. 209P	Solo 1250	Claybuster	24.5/1200	25.5/1235	26.6/1280	27.5/1310	10,500 LUP	Note 9
Rem. 209P	Solo 1250	H. Versalite				24.0/1200	8,800 LUP	Note 9
Rem. 209P	Solo 1250	Rem. Fig.-8	24.5/1200	25.5/1235	26.6/1280	27.5/1310	10,900 LUP	Note 9
Rem. 209P	Solo 1250	Rem. RXP12	24.5/1200	25.0/1230	25.5/1255	27.5/1310	10,800 LUP	Note 9
Rem. 209P	Solo 1250	WAA12	24.0/1200	24.6/1230	25.0/1255	27.5/1310	10,600 LUP	
Rem. 209P	Solo 1250	WAA12F114				27.5/1310	10,600 LUP	Note 9

Load Notes: 8 = Add one 20-gauge, 0.135″ card inside bottom of shotcup. 9 = Minimum overall length = 2⁹/₃₂″, maximum crimp depth = ²/₃₂″. 10 = This load is a close match to Remington's REM-LITE factory loading.

Caution: Follow load recipes exactly; do not substitute components, exceed listed maximums or load less than listed minimums.

Primer	Powder Type	Wad	Powder Charge (grains) / Velocity (fps) Minimum			Maximum	Maximum Pressure	Load Notes

REMINGTON: PREMIER & NITRO 27 & STS (CONT.)						1¹/₈ OUNCES LEAD SHOT		
Rem. 209P	Solo 1250	Windjammer	24.5/1200	25.3/1230	26.0/1255	27.5/1310	10,400 LUP	Note 9
Rem. 209P	SR-7625	CB 1118-12	20.5/1095	22.0/1155	23.0/1195	24.5/1250	8,800 psi	
Rem. 209P	SR-7625	Fed. 12S3	21.0/1110	22.0/1150	23.5/1210	24.5/1250	9,500 psi	
Rem. 209P	SR-7625	BP HCDP				24.5/1250	9,500 psi	Note 3
Rem. 209P	SR-7625	Rem. RXP12	21.0/1095	22.5/1150	24.0/1205	25.5/1250	9,000 psi	
Rem. 209P	SR-7625	WAA12	20.0/1090	21.5/1150	23.0/1200	24.5/1255	9,400 psi	
Rem. 209P	SR-7625	Windjammer	21.5/1095	23.0/1150	24.0/1195	25.5/1250	8,400 psi	
Rem. 209P	Unique	Activ T-32				25.0/1310	9,900 psi	
Rem. 209P	Unique	Fed. 12S3				22.0/1200	9,100 psi	
Rem. 209P	Unique	H. Versalite	22.0/1200	22.0/1200	22.0/1200	25.5/1310	9,900 psi	
Rem. 209P	Unique	Pat. Ctrl. Red				22.5/1200	7,800 psi	
Rem. 209P	Unique	Rem. Fig.-8				22.5/1200	8,200 psi	
Rem. 209P	Unique	Rem. RXP12	22.5/1200	22.5/1200	22.5/1200	24.5/1310	9,700 psi	
Rem. 209P	Unique	WAA12	22.0/1200	22.0/1200	22.0/1200	25.0/1310	10,500 psi	
Rem. 209P	Unique	Windjammer	23.5/1200	23.5/1200	23.5/1200	26.5/1310	8,600 psi	
Rem. 209P	Unique	WT12 Orange				23.5/1200	8,300 psi	Note 8
Win. 209	American Select	Rem. Fig.-8	18.5/1145	18.8/1160	19.2/1175	20.0/1200	10,200 psi	
Win. 209	Clays	H. Versalite	15.8/1090	17.2/1145	17.9/1175	18.6/1200	10,500 LUP	
Win. 209	Clays	BP HCDP	16.5/1090	17.0/1125	17.5/1145	18.0/1180	9,600 LUP	Note 3
Win. 209	Clays	Windjam. II	15.5/1090	16.3/1145	16.9/1175	17.5/1200	11,200 psi	
Win. 209	Green Dot	Rem. Fig.-8	19.0/1145	19.3/1160	19.6/1175	20.0/1200	8,600 psi	
Win. 209	Green Dot	Rem. RXP12				22.0/1250	9,400 psi	
Win. 209	Herco	Rem. RXP12				27.0/1310	9,500 psi	
Win. 209	IMR 700-X	CB 1118-12	15.5/1095	16.5/1145	17.5/1190	19.0/1250	11,400 psi	
Win. 209	IMR 700-X	Fed. 12S3	15.5/1100	16.0/1125	16.5/1145	17.5/1190	10,900 psi	
Win. 209	IMR 700-X	BP HCDP				17.0/1190	10,800 psi	Note 3
Win. 209	IMR 700-X	Rem. Fig.-8	15.5/1095	16.5/1140	17.3/1175	18.0/1205	10,800 psi	
Win. 209	IMR 700-X	WAA12	15.5/1105	16.5/1145	17.0/1170	17.5/1190	11,200 psi	
Win. 209	IMR 700-X	Windjammer	15.5/1100	16.5/1150	17.5/1190	19.0/1255	11,100 psi	
Win. 209	IMR 800-X	CB 1118-12	19.5/1100	20.5/1145	21.5/1190	23.0/1250	8,700 psi	
Win. 209	IMR 800-X	Fed. 12S3	19.0/1090	20.0/1135	21.5/1205	23.0/1260	9,600 psi	
Win. 209	IMR 800-X	BP HCDP	22.0/1200	22.2/1210	22.2/1215	22.5/1225	8,800 psi	Note 3
Win. 209	IMR 800-X	Rem. Fig.-8	19.5/1095	20.5/1140	22.0/1205	23.5/1265	8,900 psi	
Win. 209	IMR 800-X	WAA12	19.0/1090	20.0/1140	21.0/1190	22.5/1250	9,600 psi	
Win. 209	IMR 800-X	Windjammer	20.0/1095	21.0/1145	22.0/1190	23.5/1250	8,400 psi	
Win. 209	IMR PB	CB 1118-12	20.0/1100	21.0/1140	22.5/1200	24.0/1255	8,800 psi	
Win. 209	IMR PB	Fed. 12S4	19.0/1095	20.5/1155	21.5/1190	23.5/1260	10,400 psi	
Win. 209	IMR PB	BP HCDP				23.5/1260	10,500 psi	Note 3
Win. 209	IMR PB	Rem. Fig.-8	19.5/1095	21.0/1155	22.0/1190	23.5/1250	9,300 psi	
Win. 209	IMR PB	WAA12	19.0/1100	20.0/1140	22.0/1205	23.5/1255	10,200 psi	
Win. 209	IMR PB	Windjammer	20.0/1105	21.0/1145	22.5/1205	24.0/1260	9,100 psi	
Win. 209	International	H. Versalite	17.8/1090	18.4/1145	19.5/1200	20.6/1255	10,400 LUP	

Load Notes: 3 = Helix Cushion Platform. 8 = Add one 20-gauge, 0.135″ card inside bottom of shotcup. 9 = Minimum overall length = 2⁹/₃₂, maximum crimp depth = ²/₃₂.

Caution: Follow load recipes exactly; do not substitute components, exceed listed maximums or load less than listed minimums.

Primer	Powder Type	Wad	Powder Charge (grains) / Velocity (fps) Minimum			Maximum	Maximum Pressure	Load Notes
Remington: Premier & Nitro 27 & STS (cont.)						**1 1/8 Ounces Lead Shot**		
Win. 209	International	BP HCDP	18.5/1120	19.0/1160	19.5/1200	20.0/1220	9,200 LUP	Note 3
Win. 209	International	Windjam. II	17.5/1090	18.0/1145	18.8/1175	19.5/1200	9,500 psi	
Win. 209	Nitro-100	Rem. Fig.-8				15.5/1145	8,500 psi	Note 9
Win. 209	Nitro-100	Rem. RXP12	15.5/1145	15.7/1160	16.0/1175	16.5/1200	10,000 psi	Note 9
Win. 209	Nitro-100	Rem. TGT12	16.0/1145	16.1/1160	16.3/1175	16.5/1200	10,200 psi	Note 9
Win. 209	R. Scot D	Rem. Fig.-8	18.5/1125	19.0/1145	19.8/1175	20.5/1200	10,200 LUP	
Win. 209	R. Scot D	Rem. RXP12	18.5/1125	18.5/1145	19.3/1175	20.0/1200	10,700 LUP	
Win. 209	R. Scot D	Rem. TGT12	18.5/1125	19.0/1145	19.5/1175	20.0/1200	10,800 LUP	
Win. 209	Red Diamond	H. Versalite	15.5/1145	17.0/1200	17.8/1230	18.5/1255	10,300 psi	Note 5
Win. 209	Red Diamond	Pat. Ctrl. Red	16.0/1145	17.5/1200	18.3/1230	19.0/1255	9,800 psi	Note 5
Win. 209	Red Diamond	Rem. Fig.-8	16.0/1145	16.8/1175	17.5/1200	19.0/1255	9,700 psi	Note 5
Win. 209	Red Diamond	Rem. RXP12	16.0/1145	16.8/1175	17.5/1200	19.0/1255	10,400 psi	Note 5
Win. 209	Red Diamond	Rem. TGT12	16.0/1145	16.8/1175	17.5/1200	19.0/1255	9,500 psi	Note 5
Win. 209	Red Dot	Rem. Fig.-8	16.5/1090	18.0/1145	18.6/1175	19.0/1200	10,400 psi	
Win. 209	Solo 1000	BP HCDP	18.5/1145	19.0/1160	19.5/1180	20.0/1200	9,400 psi	Note 3
Win. 209	Solo 1000	Rem. Fig.-8	18.0/1125	18.5/1145	19.3/1175	20.0/1200	9,400 LUP	Note 9
Win. 209	Solo 1000	Rem. RXP12	18.0/1125	18.5/1145	19.0/1175	19.5/1200	9,500 LUP	Note 9
Win. 209	Solo 1000	Rem. TGT12	18.0/1125	18.5/1145	19.0/1175	19.5/1200	10,300 LUP	Note 9
Win. 209	Solo 1250	Rem. Fig.-8	24.5/1200	25.3/1235	26.2/1280	27.0/1310	10,900 LUP	Note 9
Win. 209	SR-7625	CB 1118-12	21.0/1090	22.5/1155	23.0/1200	24.5/1245	8,600 psi	
Win. 209	SR-7625	Fed. 12S3	20.5/1090	22.0/1145	23.5/1205	24.5/1255	9,600 psi	
Win. 209	SR-7625	Rem. RXP12	21.0/1090	22.5/1155	23.5/1195	25.0/1250	8,800 psi	
Win. 209	SR-7625	WAA12	20.5/1090	22.0/1155	23.0/1195	24.5/1250	9,500 psi	
Win. 209	SR-7625	Windjammer	21.5/1095	22.5/1140	24.0/1205	25.0/1250	8,500 psi	
Win. 209	Unique	Rem. Fig.-8				22.5/1200	8,400 psi	
Win. 209	Unique	Rem. RXP12	24.5/1250	24.5/1250	24.5/1250	26.0/1310	9,800 psi	
Win. 209	Universal	Rem. Fig.-8	22.5/1200	23.1/1230	23.7/1255	25.0/1310	10,800 psi	
Win. 209	Universal	WAA12	21.5/1200	21.9/1215	22.3/1230	23.0/1255	10,700 psi	
Win. 209	WSF	Fed. 12S3	28.0/1365	28.3/1375	28.7/1390	29.0/1400	9,500 psi	
Win. 209	WSF	BP HCDP	27.0/1310	27.5/1325	28.0/1345	28.5/1365	10,700 psi	Note 3
Win. 209	WSF	WAA12	27.0/1300	27.5/1320	28.0/1345	28.5/1365	10,700 psi	
Win. 209	WSL	Fed. 12S3				19.5/1200	10,200 psi	
Win. 209	WSL	Rem. Fig.-8	19.5/1200	19.8/1220	20.2/1235	20.5/1255	10,700 psi	
Win. 209	WSL	Rem. RXP12	19.5/1200	19.8/1220	20.2/1235	20.5/1255	10,500 psi	
Win. 209	WSL	WAA12	18.5/1145	18.8/1165	19.2/1180	19.5/1200	9,700 psi	
Win. 209	WSL	WAA12				20.5/1255	10,900 psi	
Win. 209	WSL	WAA12SL	19.5/1200	19.8/1220	20.2/1235	20.5/1255	10,600 psi	
Win. 209	WST	Rem. Fig.-8				19.0/1145	10,400 psi	
Win. 209	WST	Rem. RXP12				19.0/1145	10,500 psi	
Win. AATP	Clays	H. Versalite	15.5/1090	15.7/1100	16.0/1120	16.4/1145	10,400 psi	
Win. AATP	International	H. Versalite	17.2/1090	17.8/1145	18.4/1175	19.0/1200	10,200 psi	

Load Notes: 3 = Helix Cushion Platform. 5 = Use 50-60 pounds wad pressure to ensure wad is firmly seated against powder. 9 = Minimum overall length = 2⁹/₃₂″, maximum crimp depth = ²/₃₂″.

Caution: Follow load recipes exactly; do not substitute components, exceed listed maximums or load less than listed minimums.

Primer	Powder Type	Wad	Powder Charge (grains) / Velocity (fps) Minimum			Maximum	Maximum Pressure	Load Notes
REMINGTON: RXP						1¹/₈ OUNCES LEAD SHOT		
CCI 109	W 473AA	Fed. 12S1				23.0/1200	8,700 LUP	
CCI 109	W 473AA	Rem. RXP12				23.5/1200	8,300 LUP	
CCI 109	W 473AA	WAA12				23.0/1200	9,000 LUP	
CCI 109	W 473AA	WAA12XW				23.0/1200	9,600 LUP	
Rem. 209	IMR 700-X	BP HCDP	17.0/1140	17.5/1170	17.7/1185	18.0/1200	9,900 psi	Note 3
Rem. 209	International	BP HCDP	18.5/1200	19.0/1230	19.4/1255	20.1/1290	8,600 LUP	Note 3
Rem. 209	Solo 1250	BP HCDP	24.5/1200	25.5/1250	26.5/1280	27.0/1300	10,200 psi	Note 3
Rem. 209P	IMR 800-X	BP HCDP	21.5/1160	22.5/1200	23.5/1230	24.0/1250	7,700 LUP	Note 3
Win. 209	W 452AA	Fed. 12S1				19.5/1145	9,900 LUP	
Win. 209	W 452AA	Rem. RXP12	19.5/1145	20.0/1165	20.5/1180	21.0/1200	10,400 LUP	
Win. 209	W 452AA	WAA12	19.5/1145	20.0/1165	20.5/1180	21.0/1200	10,800 LUP	
Win. 209	W 452AA	WAA12XW				19.5/1145	10,000 LUP	
Win. 209	W 473AA	Fed. 12S1				23.5/1200	8,500 LUP	
Win. 209	W 473AA	Rem. RXP12	24.0/1200	24.5/1220	25.0/1235	25.5/1255	9,700 LUP	
Win. 209	W 473AA	Rem. RXP12				27.5/1330	10,500 LUP	
Win. 209	W 473AA	WAA12	23.5/1200	24.8/1245	26.2/1285	27.5/1330	9,900 LUP	
Win. 209	W 473AA	WAA12				25.0/1255	9,600 LUP	
Win. 209	W 473AA	WAA12XW				23.5/1200	8,600 LUP	
Win. 209	W 540	Rem. RXP12				33.0/1255	8,500 LUP	
REMINGTON: UNIBODY (INTEGRAL PLASTIC BASE WAD)						1¹/₈ OUNCES LEAD SHOT		
CCI 157	W 452AA	Fed. 12S1	19.5/1145	20.0/1165	20.5/1180	21.0/1200	10,400 LUP	
CCI 157	W 452AA	Rem. R12H	19.5/1145	20.2/1165	20.8/1180	21.5/1200	10,300 LUP	
CCI 157	W 452AA	WAA12	19.5/1145	20.2/1165	20.8/1180	21.5/1200	10,200 LUP	
CCI 157	W 473AA	Rem. R12H	24.5/1200	26.0/1255	27.3/1295	28.5/1330	9,400 LUP	
CCI 209	Green Dot	Rem. RXP12	18.5/1145	19.9/1175	21.0/1200	22.5/1255	10,500 psi	
CCI 209	Herco	Rem. R12H				27.0/1310	9,300 psi	
CCI 209	IMR PB	Fed. 12S4				23.0/1240	9,000 psi	
CCI 209	IMR PB	Rem. R12H				24.5/1260	8,100 psi	
CCI 209	IMR PB	Rem. RXP12	21.0/1145	21.5/1160	21.8/1170	22.5/1195	7,500 psi	
CCI 209	Red Dot	Rem. RXP12				18.0/1145	10,100 psi	
CCI 209	Unique	Rem. R12H				25.5/1310	9,600 psi	
CCI 209	Unique	Rem. RXP12				23.0/1200	8,300 psi	
CCI 209M	Green Dot	Rem. RXP12	18.5/1145	19.3/1175	20.0/1200	21.0/1255	10,100 psi	
CCI 209M	Herco	Rem. R12H				26.5/1310	10,300 psi	
CCI 209M	IMR 800-X	Lage Uniwad	24.0/1250	24.8/1280	25.5/1305	28.5/1405	10,400 psi	
CCI 209M	Red Dot	Rem. RXP12				17.0/1145	10,200 psi	
CCI 209M	Unique	Rem. R12H				25.0/1310	10,700 psi	
CCI 209M	Unique	Rem. RXP12				22.0/1200	8,800 psi	
Fed. 209	Green Dot	Rem. RXP12	18.0/1145	18.6/1175	20.0/1200	20.5/1255	10,200 psi	
Fed. 209	Herco	Rem. R12H				25.5/1310	10,700 psi	
Fed. 209	Red Dot	Rem. RXP12				18.0/1200	10,100 psi	
Fed. 209	Red Dot	Rem. RXP12				17.5/1145	10,500 psi	

Load Notes: 3 = Helix Cushion Platform.

   Caution: Follow load recipes exactly; do not substitute components, exceed listed maximums or load less than listed minimums.

Primer	Powder Type	Wad	Powder Charge (grains) / Velocity (fps) Minimum			Maximum	Maximum Pressure	Load Notes
Remington: Unibody (integral plastic base wad) (cont.)						**1 1/8 Ounces Lead Shot**		
Fed. 209	SR-7625	Fed. 12S4				22.5/1195	8,200 psi	
Fed. 209	SR-7625	Rem. R12H				25.5/1250	7,900 psi	
Fed. 209	SR-7625	WAA12				23.5/1205	8,000 psi	
Fed. 209	Unique	Rem. RXP12	22.0/1200	22.3/1215	22.6/1230	23.0/1255	10,000 psi	
Rem. 209	Green Dot	Fed. 12S3				19.0/1145	9,200 psi	
Rem. 209	Green Dot	H. Versalite	18.0/1145	18.3/1160	18.6/1175	19.0/1200	9,900 psi	
Rem. 209	Green Dot	Rem. R12H	19.0/1145	19.3/1175	19.5/1200	21.0/1255	10,400 psi	
Rem. 209	Green Dot	Rem. RXP12	19.0/1145	19.6/1175	20.0/1200	20.5/1255	10,300 psi	
Rem. 209	Green Dot	WAA12	17.5/1145	18.0/1160	18.6/1175	19.5/1200	10,000 psi	
Rem. 209	Green Dot	Windjammer				20.5/1200	8,300 psi	
Rem. 209	Herco	Rem. R12H				25.5/1310	10,100 psi	
Rem. 209	Herco	Rem. RXP12				25.5/1310	10,200 psi	
Rem. 209	Herco	WAA12				24.5/1310	10,200 psi	
Rem. 209	Red Dot	Fed. 12S3				17.0/1145	10,100 psi	
Rem. 209	Red Dot	H. Versalite	17.0/1145	17.3/1160	17.6/1175	18.0/1200	10,000 psi	
Rem. 209	Red Dot	Rem. R12H	17.5/1145	17.7/1165	17.8/1175	18.0/1200	10,000 psi	
Rem. 209	Red Dot	Rem. RXP12				18.0/1200	10,500 psi	
Rem. 209	Red Dot	WAA12				17.0/1145	10,200 psi	
Rem. 209	Red Dot	Windjammer				18.5/1200	9,600 psi	
Rem. 209	Unique	Fed. 12S3	21.5/1200	21.8/1215	22.1/1230	22.5/1255	9,800 psi	
Rem. 209	Unique	H. Versalite	21.0/1200	21.6/1215	22.2/1230	23.0/1255	8,800 psi	
Rem. 209	Unique	Rem. R12H	21.5/1200	22.5/1255	23.6/1285	24.5/1310	10,100 psi	
Rem. 209	Unique	Rem. RXP12	22.0/1200	22.5/1255	23.3/1285	24.0/1310	10,000 psi	
Rem. 209	Unique	WAA12	21.5/1200	21.8/1215	22.1/1230	22.5/1255	9,200 psi	
Rem. 209	Unique	WAA12				24.0/1310	10,300 psi	
Rem. 209	Unique	Windjammer	21.0/1200	21.6/1215	22.2/1230	23.0/1255	9,700 psi	
Rem. 209P	IMR 700-X	Activ T-32				17.0/1155	8,900 psi	
Rem. 209P	IMR 700-X	Rem. Fig.-8				16.0/1145	10,000 psi	
Rem. 209P	IMR 700-X	Rem. RXP12				17.5/1140	10,000 psi	
Rem. 209P	IMR 800-X	Activ T-35	24.0/1200	26.5/1290	28.0/1350	29.5/1410	10,800 psi	
Rem. 209P	IMR 800-X	Rem. Fig.-8	24.5/1200	25.8/1250	27.0/1300	30.0/1400	10,400 psi	
Rem. 97*	Green Dot	Rem. R12H				21.0/1255	10,100 psi	
Rem. 97*	Green Dot	Rem. RXP12				21.0/1255	10,600 psi	
Win. 209	Green Dot	Rem. RXP12	18.5/1145	19.7/1175	20.5/1200	21.5/1255	10,700 psi	
Win. 209	Herco	Rem. R12H				26.5/1310	10,700 psi	
Win. 209	Red Dot	Rem. RXP12				17.0/1145	10,500 psi	
Win. 209	Unique	Rem. R12H				25.0/1310	10,700 psi	
Win. 209	Unique	Rem. RXP12	22.0/1200	22.4/1215	22.8/1230	23.5/1255	9,800 psi	
Victory: Plastic						**1 1/8 Ounces Lead Shot**		
CCI 209	Clays	H. Versalite	17.9/1090	18.9/1145	19.5/1175	20.0/1200	7,700 LUP	
CCI 209M	International	H. Versalite	18.5/1090	19.5/1145	20.9/1200	22.0/1255	7,300 LUP	
CCI 209SC	Clays	Fiocchi TL1	16.8/1090	17.1/1105	17.4/1120	18.0/1145	8,900 psi	
CCI 209SC	International	Fiocchi TL1	19.0/1090	19.5/1120	20.0/1145	21.0/1200	9,400 psi	

Caution: Follow load recipes exactly; do not substitute components, exceed listed maximums or load less than listed minimums.

Primer	Powder Type	Wad	Powder Charge (grains) / Velocity (fps) Minimum			Maximum	Maximum Pressure	Load Notes
VICTORY: PLASTIC (CONT.)						1 ¹/₈ OUNCES LEAD SHOT		
Fed. 209	Clays	Fed. 1283	17.1/1090	17.7/1120	18.3/1145	19.5/1200	8,500 LUP	
Fed. 209	International	Fed. 12S3	20.0/1090	20.3/1120	20.5/1145	21.6/1200	8,100 LUP	
Fed. 209A	Clays	Fed. 1233	16.5/1090	16.6/1105	16.8/1120	17.0/1145	10,000 psi	
Fed. 209A	International	Fiocchi TL1	18.0/1090	18.3/1120	18.5/1145	20.0/1200	10,400 psi	
Fio. 616	Clays	Fiocchi TL1	16.5/1090	17.2/1120	17.9/1145	19.4/1200	9,100 LUP	
Fio. 616	International	Fiocchi TL1	19.3/1090	20.3/1145	21.0/1200	22.6/1255	9,900 LUP	
Fio. 616	Universal	Fiocchi TL1	23.4/1200	24.2/1230	25.0/1255	26.5/1310	10,600 psi	
Rem. 209P	Clays	Rem. Fig.-8	17.6/1090	18.2/1120	18.8/1145	19.9/1200	7,500 LUP	
Win. 209	Clays	WAA12	16.3/1090	17.0/1120	17.6/1145	18.9/1200	9,200 LUP	
Win. 209	International	WAA12	19.2/1090	19.7/1145	21.0/1200	22.0/1255	9,800 LUP	
Win. 209	Universal	WAA12	23.3/1200	24.0/1255	24.5/1285	25.0/1310	10,800 psi	
Win. AATP	Clays	WAA12	16.2/1090	16.4/1105	16.6/1120	17.0/1145	9,300 psi	
Win. AATP	International	WAA12	17.8/1090	18.5/1145	20.2/1200	21.0/1255	10,900 psi	
WINCHESTER: COMPRESSION-FORMED AA TYPE						1 ¹/₈ OUNCES LEAD SHOT		
CCI 109	Green Dot	WAA12	18.0/1145	18.0/1145	18.6/1175	19.0/1200	9,300 psi	
CCI 109	Red Dot	WAA12	17.0/1145	17.3/1160	17.6/1175	18.0/1200	10,400 psi	
CCI 109	W 452AA	Fed. 12C1	19.5/1145	19.8/1165	20.2/1180	20.5/1200	10,400 LUP	
CCI 109	W 452AA	Fed. 12S1	19.5/1145	19.8/1165	20.2/1180	20.5/1200	10,400 LUP	
CCI 109	W 452AA	Rem. RXP12				19.0/1145	9,600 LUP	
CCI 109	W 452AA	Rem. RXP12				20.5/1200	10,400 LUP	
CCI 109	W 452AA	WAA12				19.0/1145	9,600 LUP	
CCI 109	W 452AA	WAA12				20.5/1200	10,500 LUP	
CCI 109	W 473AA	Fed. 12C1				24.0/1200	8,500 LUP	
CCI 109	W 473AA	Fed. 12S1	23.5/1200	25.0/1255	26.0/1295	27.0/1330	10,500 LUP	
CCI 109	W 473AA	Rem. RXP12	23.5/1200	25.0/1255	26.0/1295	27.0/1330	10,100 LUP	
CCI 109	W 473AA	WAA12	23.5/1200	24.5/1255	25.8/1295	27.0/1330	10,400 LUP	
CCI 209	Clays	Fed. 12S3	16.2/1090	17.6/1145	18.3/1175	19.0/1200	10,100 LUP	
CCI 209	IMR 800-X	CB 1118-12	21.0/1095	22.5/1150	24.0/1200	25.5/1250	6,700 psi	
CCI 209	IMR 800-X	CS12S				22.3/1200	6,800 psi	
CCI 209	IMR 800-X	Fed. 12S3	20.5/1090	22.0/1150	23.0/1190	24.5/1255	7,800 psi	
CCI 209	IMR 800-X	BP HCDP				23.0/1200	6,800 psi	Note 3
CCI 209	IMR 800-X	Rem. Fig.-8	21.0/1095	22.0/1135	23.5/1195	25.5/1260	6,900 psi	
CCI 209	IMR 800-X	WAA12	20.5/1095	22.0/1155	23.0/1195	24.5/1250	7,700 psi	
CCI 209	IMR 800-X	Windjammer	21.5/1100	22.5/1150	24.0/1195	26.0/1260	6,200 psi	
CCI 209	International	Fed. 12S3	19.2/1145	19.6/1175	20.0/1200	21.6/1255	10,200 LUP	
CCI 209	Nitro-100	CB 1118-12	15.5/1125	16.0/1145	16.5/1175	17.0/1200	9,600 psi	Note 9
CCI 209	Nitro-100	H. Versalite				17.0/1145		
CCI 209	Nitro-100	WAA12	15.5/1125	16.0/1145	16.5/1175	17.0/1200	10,000 psi	Note 9
CCI 209	R. Scot D	Claybuster	18.5/1125	19.0/1145	20.5/1200	21.5/1255	10,600 LUP	
CCI 209	R. Scot D	WAA12	18.5/1125	19.0/1145	19.8/1175	20.5/1200	10,300 LUP	
CCI 209	Red Diamond	BP CS12	17.0/1145	17.5/1175	18.0/1200	19.5/1255	10,600 psi	Note 5
CCI 209	Red Diamond	H. Versalite	17.0/1145	18.5/1200	18.8/1230	19.0/1255	10,300 psi	Note 5

Load Notes: 3 = Helix Cushion Platform. 5 = Use 50-60 pounds wad pressure to ensure wad is firmly seated against powder. 9 = Minimum overall length = 2⁹/₃₂″, maximum crimp depth = ²/₃₂″.

     Caution: Follow load recipes exactly; do not substitute components, exceed listed maximums or load less than listed minimums.

Primer	Powder Type	Wad	Powder Charge (grains) / Velocity (fps) Minimum			Maximum	Maximum Pressure	Load Notes
WINCHESTER: COMPRESSION-FORMED AA TYPE (CONT.)					1 1/8 OUNCES LEAD SHOT			
CCI 209	Red Diamond	Hawk Original	17.0/1145	17.5/1175	18.0/1200	19.0/1255	9,000 psi	Note 5
CCI 209	Red Diamond	WAA12	17.0/1145	17.1/1160	17.3/1175	17.5/1200	8,300 psi	Note 5
CCI 209	Solo 1000	CB 1118-12	17.0/1125	17.5/1145	18.5/1200	20.0/1255	10,300 psi	Note 5
CCI 209	Solo 1000	Claybuster	18.0/1125	18.5/1145	20.0/1200	21.0/1255		
CCI 209	Solo 1000	WAA12	16.5/1125	17.0/1145	17.5/1175	18.0/1200	10,500 psi	Note 9
CCI 209	Solo 1250	WAA12	24.0/1200	25.1/1235	26.2/1280	27.0/1310	10,200 LUP	Note 9
CCI 209	Universal	Windjammer	23.3/1200	23.5/1215	23.8/1230	24.3/1255	9,300 psi	
CCI 209	WSL	Fed. 12S3				19.5/1200	10,400 psi	
CCI 209	WSL	Rem. Fig.-8				18.5/1145	8,500 psi	
CCI 209	WSL	Rem. Fig.-8				21.0/1255	10,900 psi	
CCI 209	WSL	Rem. Fig.-8				19.5/1200	9,700 psi	
CCI 209	WSL	Rem. R12L	19.5/1200	20.0/1220	20.5/1235	21.0/1255	10,600 psi	
CCI 209	WSL	Rem. RXP12				21.0/1255	10,700 psi	
CCI 209	WSL	WAA12				19.5/1200	10,800 psi	
CCI 209	WSL	WAA12SL	18.5/1145	18.9/1170	19.5/1200	21.0/1255	10,900 psi	
CCI 209	WST	Fed. 12S3	19.0/1145	19.5/1165	20.0/1180	20.5/1200	10,800 psi	
CCI 209	WST	Rem. Fig.-8	19.0/1145	19.5/1165	20.0/1180	20.5/1200	10,000 psi	
CCI 209	WST	Rem. RXP12	19.5/1145	19.8/1165	20.2/1180	20.5/1200	10,300 psi	
CCI 209	WST	WAA12	19.0/1145	19.5/1165	20.0/1180	20.5/1200	10,300 psi	
CCI 209M	Green Dot	WAA12	18.5/1145	18.5/1145	19.3/1175	20.0/1200	10,400 psi	
CCI 209M	Nitro-100	WAA12	15.5/1125	16.0/1145	16.5/1175	17.0/1200	10,800 psi	Note 9
CCI 209M	R. Scot D	WAA12	17.5/1125	18.0/1145	18.5/1175	19.0/1200	10,000 LUP	
CCI 209M	Red Diamond	BP CS12	16.5/1145	17.0/1175	17.5/1200	18.5/1255	10,300 psi	Note 5
CCI 209M	Red Diamond	H. Versalite	16.5/1145	17.3/1175	18.0/1200	19.0/1255	10,600 psi	Note 5
CCI 209M	Red Diamond	Hawk Original	16.5/1145	17.0/1175	17.5/1200	19.0/1255	10,000 psi	Note 5
CCI 209M	Red Diamond	Lage Uniwad				19.0/1255	9,600 psi	Note 5
CCI 209M	Red Diamond	WAA12	16.0/1145	16.4/1160	16.8/1175	17.5/1200	8,800 psi	Note 5
CCI 209M	Red Dot	WAA12	17.0/1090	17.5/1145	18.1/1175	18.5/1200	10,500 psi	
CCI 209M	Solo 1000	WAA12	16.0/1125	17.0/1145	17.5/1175	18.0/1200	9,800 psi	Note 9
CCI 209M	Solo 1000	WAA12	17.0/1125	17.5/1145	18.0/1175	18.5/1200		
CCI 209M	Solo 1250	WAA12				23.0/1200	8,700 LUP	Note 9
CCI 209M	Unique	WAA12	21.5/1200	21.5/1200	21.5/1200	25.5/1310	9,700 psi	
CCI 209M	Universal	H. Versalite	22.0/1200	22.2/1215	22.5/1230	23.0/1255	10,700 psi	
CCI 209SC	American Select	WAA12	17.0/1090	18.5/1145	19.1/1175	19.5/1200	10,100 psi	
CCI 209SC	Green Dot	Rem. Fig.-8	20.5/1145	21.0/1165	21.6/1185	22.0/1200	10,400 psi	
CCI 209SC	Green Dot	WAA12	19.5/1145	19.5/1145	20.1/1175	20.5/1200	10,700 psi	
CCI 209SC	Green Dot	Windjammer	20.5/1145	21.0/1165	21.6/1185	22.0/1200	10,200 psi	
CCI 209SC	International	Fed. 12S3	18.5/1145	19.5/1200	20.0/1230	20.3/1255	11,200 psi	
CCI 209SC	Red Dot	Rem. Fig.-8	18.0/1145	18.1/1160	18.3/1175	18.5/1200	10,400 psi	
CCI 209SC	Red Dot	WAA12				17.5/1145	10,600 psi	
CCI 209SC	Red Dot	Windjammer				18.0/1145	9,900 psi	
CCI 209SC	Universal	H. Versalite	22.3/1200	22.6/1215	22.9/1230	23.5/1255	9,400 psi	

Load Notes: 5 = Use 50-60 pounds wad pressure to ensure wad is firmly seated against powder. 9 = Minimum overall length = 2 9/32", maximum crimp depth = 2/32".

Caution: Follow load recipes exactly; do not substitute components, exceed listed maximums or load less than listed minimums.

Primer	Powder Type	Wad	Powder Charge (grains) / Velocity (fps) Minimum			Maximum	Maximum Pressure	Load Notes
WINCHESTER: COMPRESSION-FORMED AA TYPE (CONT.)					1¹/₈ OUNCES LEAD SHOT			
CCI 209SC	Universal	Windjammer	22.4/1200	23.2/1230	24.0/1255	24.4/1310	9,800 psi	
Fed. 209	Clays	Windjammer	17.2/1090	18.4/1145	19.0/1175	19.6/1200	8,200 LUP	
Fed. 209	International	Windjammer	18.6/1090	19.7/1145	21.1/1200	22.1/1255	8,200 LUP	
Fed. 209	Nitro-100	H. Versalite				16.5/1145		
Fed. 209	Nitro-100	WAA12	17.0/1145	17.3/1160	17.6/1175	18.0/1200		
Fed. 209	R. Scot D	WAA12	18.0/1125	18.5/1145	19.0/1175	19.5/1200	10,800 LUP	
Fed. 209	Red Dot	WAA12				16.0/1090	9,900 psi	
Fed. 209	Solo 1000	WAA12	17.5/1125	18.0/1145	18.5/1175	19.0/1200		
Fed. 209	Solo 1250	WAA12	24.0/1200	24.2/1215	24.5/1230	25.0/1255	9,800 LUP	
Fed. 209	Solo 1250	WAA12F114				25.5/1255	9,400 LUP	
Fed. 209	Unique	WAA12	24.0/1250	24.0/1250	24.0/1250	24.5/1310	10,600 psi	
Fed. 209	Universal	Fed. 12S3	22.7/1200	23.0/1215	23.3/1230	23.8/1255	10,000 psi	
Fed. 209	W 452AA	Fed. 12C1	20.0/1145	20.3/1165	20.7/1180	21.0/1200	9,900 LUP	
Fed. 209	W 452AA	Fed. 12S1	19.5/1145	19.8/1165	20.2/1180	20.5/1200	9,900 LUP	
Fed. 209	W 452AA	Rem. RXP12				19.5/1145	8,700 LUP	
Fed. 209	W 452AA	WAA12	19.5/1145	19.8/1165	20.2/1180	20.5/1200	10,000 LUP	
Fed. 209	W 473AA	Fed. 12C1				23.5/1200	8,700 LUP	
Fed. 209	W 473AA	Fed. 12S1	23.5/1200	24.0/1220	24.5/1235	25.0/1255	9,600 LUP	
Fed. 209	W 473AA	Rem. RXP12	23.5/1200	24.0/1220	24.5/1235	25.0/1255	9,300 LUP	
Fed. 209	W 473AA	WAA12	23.5/1200	23.8/1220	24.2/1235	24.5/1255	9,900 LUP	
Fed. 209	WSL	Fed. 12S3	19.0/1145	19.3/1165	19.7/1180	20.0/1200	10,500 psi	
Fed. 209	WSL	Rem. Fig.-8	19.0/1145	19.5/1175	20.0/1200	21.5/1255	10,900 psi	
Fed. 209	WSL	Rem. R12L				21.5/1255	10,500 psi	
Fed. 209	WSL	Rem. RXP12	19.0/1145	19.5/1175	20.0/1200	21.0/1255	10,700 psi	
Fed. 209	WSL	WAA12				20.0/1200	10,700 psi	
Fed. 209	WSL	WAA12SL	18.5/1145	19.3/1175	20.0/1200	21.5/1255	10,300 psi	
Fed. 209	WST	Fed. 12S3	19.5/1145	20.0/1165	20.5/1180	21.0/1200	10,900 psi	
Fed. 209	WST	Rem. Fig.-8	19.5/1145	20.0/1165	20.5/1180	21.0/1200	9,200 psi	
Fed. 209	WST	Rem. RXP12				21.0/1200	10,000 psi	
Fed. 209	WST	WAA12	19.0/1145	19.5/1165	20.0/1180	20.5/1200	10,000 psi	
Fed. 209A	American Select	WAA12	17.0/1090	18.5/1145	19.1/1175	19.5/1200	10,800 psi	
Fed. 209A	Clays	WAA12	15.0/1090	15.2/1105	15.5/1120	16.0/1145	10,800 psi	
Fed. 209A	Green Dot	Claybuster	18.5/1145	18.5/1145	19.1/1175	19.5/1200	9,300 psi	
Fed. 209A	Green Dot	H. Versalite	18.5/1145	18.5/1145	19.1/1175	19.5/1200	10,400 psi	
Fed. 209A	Green Dot	Pat. Ctrl. Red	18.5/1145	18.5/1145	19.1/1175	19.5/1200	10,500 psi	
Fed. 209A	Green Dot	Rem. Fig.-8	18.5/1145	18.5/1145	19.1/1175	19.5/1200	9,400 psi	
Fed. 209A	Green Dot	WAA12	18.0/1145	18.0/1145	18.6/1175	19.0/1200	10,200 psi	
Fed. 209A	Green Dot	Windjammer	18.5/1145	18.5/1145	19.8/1175	20.0/1200	9,200 psi	
Fed. 209A	IMR 700-X	CB 1118-12	15.0/1095	16.0/1140	17.5/1200	18.5/1245	11,500 psi	
Fed. 209A	IMR 700-X	CS12S				16.3/1200	10,600 psi	
Fed. 209A	IMR 700-X	Fed. 12S3	15.5/1100	16.5/1145	17.3/1175	18.0/1205	11,200 psi	
Fed. 209A	IMR 700-X	BP HCDP				17.0/1200	10,600 psi	Note 3
Fed. 209A	IMR 700-X	Rem. Fig.-8	15.5/1100	16.5/1145	18.0/1205	19.0/1240	11,200 psi	

Load Notes: 3 = Helix Cushion Platform.

    Caution: Follow load recipes exactly; do not substitute components, exceed listed maximums or load less than listed minimums.

Primer	Powder Type	Wad	Powder Charge (grains) / Velocity (fps) Minimum			Maximum	Maximum Pressure	Load Notes
WINCHESTER: COMPRESSION-FORMED AA TYPE (CONT.)					**1⅛ OUNCES LEAD SHOT**			
Fed. 209A	IMR 700-X	WAA12	15.0/1090	16.0/1135	16.8/1170	17.5/1200	11,300 psi	
Fed. 209A	IMR 700-X	Windjammer	15.0/1095	16.0/1140	17.5/1200	19.0/1255	11,000 psi	
Fed. 209A	IMR 800-X	CB 1118-12	20.5/1095	22.0/1155	23.0/1195	24.5/1250	7,500 psi	
Fed. 209A	IMR 800-X	CS12S				22.3/1200	6,700 psi	
Fed. 209A	IMR 800-X	Fed. 12S3	19.5/1095	21.0/1150	22.5/1200	24.0/1255	8,500 psi	
Fed. 209A	IMR 800-X	BP HCDP				23.0/1200	6,700 psi	Note 3
Fed. 209A	IMR 800-X	Rem. Fig.-8	20.5/1090	21.5/1135	23.0/1200	24.5/1260	7,700 psi	
Fed. 209A	IMR 800-X	WAA12	20.0/1105	21.0/1140	22.5/1200	24.0/1260	8,600 psi	
Fed. 209A	IMR 800-X	Windjammer	21.0/1105	22.0/1150	23.0/1195	24.5/1265	7,600 psi	
Fed. 209A	IMR PB	CB 1118-12	19.5/1105	21.0/1155	22.5/1205	24.0/1255	8,600 psi	
Fed. 209A	IMR PB	CS12S				21.3/1200	9,200 psi	
Fed. 209A	IMR PB	Fed. 12S4	19.0/1100	20.5/1150	22.0/1200	23.5/1255	10,100 psi	
Fed. 209A	IMR PB	BP HCDP				22.0/1200	9,200 psi	Note 3
Fed. 209A	IMR PB	Rem. RXP12	19.5/1105	20.5/1140	22.0/1195	23.5/1250	9,300 psi	
Fed. 209A	IMR PB	WAA12	19.0/1100	20.5/1150	22.0/1205	23.5/1260	9,700 psi	
Fed. 209A	IMR PB	Windjammer	19.5/1100	21.0/1155	22.5/1205	24.0/1260	8,700 psi	
Fed. 209A	International	Windjammer	17.4/1090	18.0/1145	19.5/1200	21.3/1255	11,200 psi	
Fed. 209A	Nitro-100	WAA12	15.5/1125	15.5/1145	16.1/1175	16.5/1200	10,900 psi	Note 9
Fed. 209A	Red Diamond	BP CS12	16.5/1145	17.0/1175	17.5/1200	18.5/1255	10,600 psi	Note 5
Fed. 209A	Red Diamond	H. Versalite	16.5/1145	17.3/1175	18.0/1200	18.5/1255	11,100 psi	Note 5
Fed. 209A	Red Diamond	Hawk Original	16.5/1145	17.0/1175	17.5/1200	18.5/1255	10,700 psi	Note 5
Fed. 209A	Red Diamond	Lage Uniwad				19.0/1255	10,400 psi	Note 5
Fed. 209A	Red Diamond	WAA12	16.0/1145	16.4/1160	16.8/1175	17.5/1200	10,700 psi	Note 5
Fed. 209A	Red Dot	Claybuster	17.0/1145	17.4/1160	17.8/1175	18.5/1200	10,500 psi	
Fed. 209A	Red Dot	H. Versalite	17.0/1145	17.3/1160	17.6/1175	18.0/1200	10,700 psi	
Fed. 209A	Red Dot	Pat. Ctrl. Red	17.0/1145	17.3/1160	17.6/1175	18.0/1200	10,000 psi	
Fed. 209A	Red Dot	Rem. Fig.-8	17.0/1145	17.4/1160	17.8/1175	18.5/1200	10,200 psi	
Fed. 209A	Red Dot	WAA12				17.0/1145	10,600 psi	
Fed. 209A	Red Dot	Windjammer	17.0/1145	17.3/1160	17.6/1175	18.0/1200	10,000 psi	
Fed. 209A	Solo 1000	WAA12	16.0/1125	16.5/1145	17.5/1175	18.5/1200	11,200 psi	Note 9
Fed. 209A	Solo 1250	WAA12				24.0/1200	8,600 LUP	Note 9
Fed. 209A	SR-7625	CB 1118-12	21.5/1105	22.5/1145	24.0/1195	25.5/1250	8,400 psi	
Fed. 209A	SR-7625	CS12S				24.3/1255	9,200 psi	
Fed. 209A	SR-7625	Fed. 12S4	21.0/1100	22.5/1155	23.5/1195	25.0/1255	9,300 psi	
Fed. 209A	SR-7625	BP HCDP				25.0/1255	9,200 psi	Note 3
Fed. 209A	SR-7625	Rem. RXP12	21.5/1095	22.5/1140	24.0/1195	25.5/1250	8,600 psi	
Fed. 209A	SR-7625	WAA12	21.0/1100	22.5/1155	23.5/1190	25.5/1260	9,100 psi	
Fed. 209A	SR-7625	Windjammer	22.0/1095	23.5/1155	24.5/1200	25.5/1245	7,900 psi	
Fed. 209A	Universal	WAA12	21.5/1200	22.2/1230	22.8/1255	23.6/1310	11,300 psi	
Fed. 209A	WAAP	WAA12	18.0/1145	18.6/1165	19.0/1180	19.5/1200	10,600 psi	
Fed. 399	W 452AA	Fed. 12C1	20.0/1145	20.3/1165	20.7/1180	21.0/1200	10,100 LUP	
Fed. 399	W 452AA	Fed. 12S1				21.0/1200	10,200 LUP	

Load Notes: 3 = Helix Cushion Platform. 5 = Use 50-60 pounds wad pressure to ensure wad is firmly seated against powder. 9 = Minimum overall length = 2⁹⁄₃₂″, maximum crimp depth = ²⁄₃₂″.

Caution: Follow load recipes exactly; do not substitute components, exceed listed maximums or load less than listed minimums.

Primer	Powder Type	Wad	Powder Charge (grains) / Velocity (fps) Minimum			Maximum	Maximum Pressure	Load Notes
WINCHESTER: COMPRESSION-FORMED AA TYPE (CONT.)						1¹/₈ OUNCES LEAD SHOT		
Fed. 399	W 452AA	Rem. RXP12	20.0/1145	20.5/1165	21.0/1180	21.5/1200	9,900 LUP	
Fed. 399	W 452AA	WAA12	20.0/1145	20.2/1165	20.3/1180	20.5/1200	10,000 LUP	
Fio. 616	Clays	Fiocchi FTWI	16.5/1090	17.6/1145	18.2/1175	18.8/1200	10,600 LUP	
Fio. 616	Green Dot	WAA12	18.5/1145	20.0/1200	21.7/1225	23.5/1250	10,100 psi	
Fio. 616	International	Fiocchi TL-1	18.2/1090	18.8/1145	20.0/1200	21.5/1255	10,600 LUP	
Fio. 616	Nitro-100	WAA12	15.5/1125	16.0/1145	16.5/1175	17.0/1200	10,700 psi	Note 9
Fio. 616	R. Scot D	WAA12	18.0/1125	18.5/1145	19.0/1175	19.5/1200	10,900 LUP	
Fio. 616	Red Diamond	BP CS12	16.5/1145	17.5/1200	18.0/1230	18.5/1255	10,400 psi	Note 5
Fio. 616	Red Diamond	H. Versalite	16.5/1145	18.0/1200	18.3/1230	18.5/1255	11,100 psi	Note 5
Fio. 616	Red Diamond	Hawk Original	16.5/1145	17.5/1200	18.0/1230	18.5/1255	10,900 psi	Note 5
Fio. 616	Red Diamond	Lage Uniwad				19.0/1255	10,200 psi	Note 5
Fio. 616	Red Diamond	WAA12	16.0/1145	16.4/1160	16.8/1175	17.5/1200	9,900 psi	Note 5
Fio. 616	Red Dot	WAA12	16.0/1090	17.0/1145	18.0/1200	22.0/1250	10,500 psi	
Fio. 616	Solo 1000	WAA12	16.0/1125	16.5/1145	17.5/1175	18.5/1200	10,000 psi	Note 9
Fio. 616	Unique	WAA12				21.5/1200	9,100 psi	
Fio. 616	Universal	Fiocchi TL1	22.5/1200	22.7/1215	22.9/1230	23.3/1255	10,900 psi	
Rem. 209	Nitro-100	H. Versalite				16.5/1145		
Rem. 209	Nitro-100	WAA12	17.0/1145	17.2/1160	17.5/1175	18.0/1200		
Rem. 209	Red Diamond	BP CS12	17.0/1145	17.5/1175	18.0/1200	19.5/1255	10,500 psi	Note 5
Rem. 209	Red Diamond	H. Versalite	17.0/1145	17.8/1175	18.5/1200	19.0/1255	9,900 psi	Note 5
Rem. 209	Red Diamond	Hawk Original	17.0/1145	17.5/1175	18.0/1200	19.5/1255	9,200 psi	Note 5
Rem. 209	Red Diamond	WAA12	17.0/1145	17.1/1160	17.3/1175	17.5/1200	8,200 psi	Note 5
Rem. 209P	American Select	Rem. Fig.-8				22.5/1250	9,400 psi	
Rem. 209P	American Select	WAA12	17.0/1090	19.0/1145	20.1/1175	21.0/1200	9,600 psi	
Rem. 209P	Clays	Pat. Ctrl. Red	17.1/1090	18.4/1145	19.0/1175	19.6/1200	8,400 LUP	
Rem. 209P	Green Dot	WAA12				20.0/1200	9,800 psi	
Rem. 209P	Herco	WAA12				27.0/1310	8,100 psi	
Rem. 209P	IMR 700-X	CB 1118-12	15.5/1090	17.0/1150	18.0/1195	19.5/1255	10,400 psi	
Rem. 209P	IMR 700-X	CS12S				16.3/1190	8,500 psi	
Rem. 209P	IMR 700-X	Fed. 12S3	15.5/1090	16.5/1135	18.0/1190	19.5/1250	10,900 psi	
Rem. 209P	IMR 700-X	BP HCDP				17.0/1190	8,500 psi	Note 3
Rem. 209P	IMR 700-X	Rem. Fig.-8	16.0/1100	17.0/1145	18.5/1205	19.5/1250	10,200 psi	
Rem. 209P	IMR 700-X	WAA12	15.5/1095	17.0/1150	18.5/1205	20.0/1260	10,800 psi	
Rem. 209P	IMR 700-X	Windjammer	16.0/1090	17.5/1145	19.0/1195	20.5/1245	9,300 psi	
Rem. 209P	IMR PB	CB 1118-12	20.5/1100	21.5/1140	23.0/1200	24.5/1250	7,700 psi	
Rem. 209P	IMR PB	CS12S				23.3/1200	8,500 psi	
Rem. 209P	IMR PB	Fed. 12S4	19.5/1095	20.5/1140	22.0/1195	24.0/1260	9,600 psi	
Rem. 209P	IMR PB	BP HCDP				24.0/1200	8,500 psi	Note 3
Rem. 209P	IMR PB	Rem. RXP12	20.0/1100	21.0/1140	22.5/1200	24.0/1255	8,900 psi	
Rem. 209P	IMR PB	WAA12	20.0/1100	21.0/1140	23.0/1200	24.5/1260	8,600 psi	
Rem. 209P	IMR PB	Windjammer	20.0/1095	21.5/1145	23.0/1205	24.5/1255	7,900 psi	
Rem. 209P	International	Rem. Fig.-8	20.1/1145	20.6/1175	21.1/1200	22.1/1255	8,000 LUP	

Load Notes: 3 = Helix Cushion Platform. 5 = Use 50-60 pounds wad pressure to ensure wad is firmly seated against powder. 9 = Minimum overall length = 2⁹/₃₂″, maximum crimp depth = ²/₃₂″.

Caution: Follow load recipes exactly; do not substitute components, exceed listed maximums or load less than listed minimums.

Primer	Powder Type	Wad	Powder Charge (grains) / Velocity (fps) Minimum			Maximum	Maximum Pressure	Load Notes
WINCHESTER: COMPRESSION-FORMED AA TYPE (CONT.)					1 1/8 OUNCES LEAD SHOT			
Rem. 209P	Nitro-100	WAA12	15.5/1125	15.5/1145	16.3/1175	17.0/1200	10,100 psi	Note 9
Rem. 209P	R. Scot D	WAA12	18.5/1125	19.0/1145	19.5/1175	20.0/1200	10,800 LUP	
Rem. 209P	Red Dot	WAA12	17.0/1090	17.5/1145	18.3/1175	19.0/1200	9,500 psi	
Rem. 209P	Solo 1000	WAA12	17.0/1125	17.0/1145	17.5/1175	18.0/1200	11,500 psi	Note 9
Rem. 209P	Solo 1250	WAA12	24.0/1200	24.6/1235	25.3/1280	26.0/1310	10,300 LUP	Note 9
Rem. 209P	Solo 1250	WAA12F114				25.5/1255	9,200 LUP	
Rem. 209P	SR-7625	CB 1118-12	22.0/1105	23.0/1145	24.5/1205	25.5/1250	8,000 psi	
Rem. 209P	SR-7625	CS12S				24.8/1265	9,200 psi	
Rem. 209P	SR-7625	Fed. 12S4	21.5/1100	22.5/1145	24.0/1205	25.5/1255	9,100 psi	
Rem. 209P	SR-7625	BP HCDP				25.5/1265	9,200 psi	Note 3
Rem. 209P	SR-7625	Rem. RXP12	22.0/1105	23.0/1145	24.5/1205	25.5/1250	8,200 psi	
Rem. 209P	SR-7625	WAA12	22.0/1110	23.0/1145	24.5/1195	26.0/1255	8,000 psi	
Rem. 209P	SR-7625	Windjammer	22.0/1095	23.5/1150	24.5/1190	26.0/1250	7,200 psi	
Rem. 209P	Unique	WAA12	23.0/1200	23.5/1225	24.0/1250	26.0/1310	9,700 psi	
Win. 209	#2 Improved	WAA12	17.5/1145	17.7/1160	18.0/1175	18.5/1200	11,200 psi	Note 9
Win. 209	#2 Improved	WAA12SL				17.0/1125	9,800 psi	Note 9
Win. 209	American Select	Claybuster	17.0/1090	18.5/1145	19.5/1200	20.5/1250	10,700 psi	
Win. 209	American Select	CS12S				18.0/1200	11,200 psi	
Win. 209	American Select	Pat. Ctrl. Red	17.0/1090	18.5/1145	20.0/1200	21.5/1250	10,800 psi	
Win. 209	American Select	Rem. Fig.-8	17.5/1090	19.0/1145	19.6/1175	20.0/1200	9,800 psi	
Win. 209	American Select	Rem. RXP12	17.0/1090	19.0/1145	20.5/1200	21.0/1250	10,800 psi	
Win. 209	American Select	WAA12	17.0/1090	18.0/1145	18.8/1175	19.5/1200	10,300 psi	
Win. 209	American Select	WT12 Orange	18.5/1145	18.8/1160	19.2/1175	19.5/1200	10,700 psi	
Win. 209	Clays	CB 3118-12-A	15.0/1090	15.3/1105	15.6/1120	16.0/1145	10,500 psi	
Win. 209	Clays	CB 3118-12-AR	15.0/1090	15.2/1120	15.3/1130	15.4/1145	10,600 psi	
Win. 209	Clays	CS12S	16.8/1145	17.0/1170	17.1/1180	17.3/1200	9,700 LUP	
Win. 209	Clays	H. Versalite	16.4/1090	17.6/1145	18.2/1175	18.8/1200	10,600 LUP	
Win. 209	Clays	BP HCDP	17.5/1145	17.7/1170	17.8/1180	18.0/1200	9,700 LUP	Note 3
Win. 209	Clays	Rem. Fig.-8	16.0/1090	17.0/1145	17.6/1175	18.1/1200	9,400 LUP	
Win. 209	Clays	Trapper	15.5/1090	15.6/1115	15.7/1130	16.5/1145	10,700 LUP	
Win. 209	Clays	WAA12	16.1/1090	17.3/1145	17.8/1175	18.2/1200	9,800 LUP	
Win. 209	Clays	Windjam. II	15.5/1090	16.3/1145	17.0/1175	17.5/1200	11,100 psi	
Win. 209	Green Dot	Activ T-32				23.0/1250	8,800 psi	
Win. 209	Green Dot	BP SCAT				19.0/1175	8,800 psi	Note 6
Win. 209	Green Dot	CS12S	18.3/1175	18.8/1200	19.3/1215	19.8/1230	10,000 psi	
Win. 209	Green Dot	Fed. 12C1	18.5/1145	19.3/1175	19.5/1200	21.0/1250	10,200 psi	
Win. 209	Green Dot	Fed. 12S3				18.0/1090	9,700 psi	
Win. 209	Green Dot	Fiocchi FTW1	19.5/1145	19.6/1160	19.8/1175	20.0/1200	9,900 psi	
Win. 209	Green Dot	H. Versalite	17.5/1090	19.5/1145	21.0/1200	22.0/1250	9,900 psi	
Win. 209	Green Dot	BP HCDP	19.0/1175	19.5/1200	20.0/1215	20.5/1230	10,000 psi	Note 3
Win. 209	Green Dot	Pat. Ctrl. Red	18.0/1090	20.5/1200	22.2/1275	23.0/1310	10,200 psi	
Win. 209	Green Dot	Rem. Fig.-8	18.0/1090	19.0/1145	20.5/1200	22.0/1250	10,300 psi	

Load Notes: 3 = Helix Cushion Platform. 6 = Scatter Master. 9 = Minimum overall length = 2⁹/₃₂″, maximum crimp depth = ²/₃₂″.

Caution: Follow load recipes exactly; do not substitute components, exceed listed maximums or load less than listed minimums.

12-GAUGE 2³/₄″ — 1¹/₈ OUNCES LEAD SHOT (CONT.)

Primer	Powder Type	Wad	Powder Charge (grains) / Velocity (fps) Minimum			Maximum	Maximum Pressure	Load Notes
WINCHESTER: COMPRESSION-FORMED AA TYPE (CONT.)					1¹/₈ OUNCES LEAD SHOT			
Win. 209	Green Dot	Rem. RXP12	17.5/1090	18.0/1145	19.5/1200	21.0/1250	9,500 psi	
Win. 209	Green Dot	WAA12	17.5/1090	18.0/1145	19.5/1200	21.5/1250	10,500 psi	
Win. 209	Green Dot	WAA12SL	18.0/1090	19.0/1145	19.8/1175	20.5/1200	10,700 psi	
Win. 209	Green Dot	Windjammer	18.0/1145	18.9/1160	19.8/1175	21.0/1200	9,000 psi	
Win. 209	Green Dot	WT12 Orange	16.5/1090	18.0/1145	19.0/1200	19.0/1250	9,900 psi	
Win. 209	Herco	Fed. 12C1				25.0/1250	9,400 psi	
Win. 209	Herco	H. Versalite	24.5/1250	24.5/1250	24.5/1250	26.5/1310	9,900 psi	
Win. 209	Herco	Pat. Ctrl. Red				25.0/1250	9,100 psi	
Win. 209	Herco	Rem. RXP12	25.0/1250	25.0/1250	25.0/1250	26.5/1310	9,100 psi	
Win. 209	Herco	WAA12	25.0/1250	25.0/1250	25.0/1250	26.5/1310	9,300 psi	
Win. 209	IMR 700-X	BP SCAT	16.2/1180	16.6/1185	17.1/1190	18.0/1200	8,600 psi	Note 6
Win. 209	IMR 700-X	CB 1118-12	15.5/1105	16.5/1150	17.5/1195	19.0/1255	11,200 psi	
Win. 209	IMR 700-X	CS12S				16.3/1190	10,500 psi	
Win. 209	IMR 700-X	Fed. 12S3	15.5/1100	16.2/1130	16.9/1160	17.5/1190	11,100 psi	
Win. 209	IMR 700-X	BP HCDP				17.0/1190	10,500 psi	Note 3
Win. 209	IMR 700-X	Rem. Fig.-8	15.5/1090	16.5/1135	18.0/1200	19.5/1255	11,400 psi	
Win. 209	IMR 700-X	WAA12	15.5/1105	16.0/1130	16.5/1150	17.5/1190	10,800 psi	
Win. 209	IMR 700-X	Windjammer	15.5/1110	16.5/1150	17.5/1195	19.0/1250	11,000 psi	
Win. 209	IMR 800-X	CB 1118-12	20.0/1095	21.5/1150	23.0/1205	24.5/1260	7,800 psi	
Win. 209	IMR 800-X	CS12S				22.3/1220	8,000 psi	
Win. 209	IMR 800-X	CS12S	21.3/1145	22.3/1185	23.3/1220	24.3/1255	7,800 LUP	
Win. 209	IMR 800-X	Fed. 12S3	20.0/1100	21.5/1155	22.5/1195	24.0/1250	8,400 psi	
Win. 209	IMR 800-X	Rem. Fig.-8	20.0/1105	21.0/1150	22.5/1195	24.5/1255	7,700 psi	
Win. 209	IMR 800-X	WAA12	20.0/1100	21.0/1145	22.0/1190	24.0/1265	8,800 psi	
Win. 209	IMR 800-X	Windjammer	20.5/1095	21.5/1145	22.5/1190	24.0/1260	7,700 psi	
Win. 209	IMR PB	CB 1118-12	20.0/1100	21.5/1155	23.0/1210	24.0/1250	8,500 psi	
Win. 209	IMR PB	CS12S				23.3/1200	7,700 psi	
Win. 209	IMR PB	Fed. 12S4	19.5/1105	20.5/1145	22.0/1200	23.5/1255	9,900 psi	
Win. 209	IMR PB	BP HCDP				24.0/1200	7,700 psi	Note 3
Win. 209	IMR PB	Rem. RXP12	20.0/1110	21.0/1155	22.5/1205	24.0/1265	9,500 psi	
Win. 209	IMR PB	WAA12	19.5/1095	21.0/1150	22.5/1205	24.0/1265	9,400 psi	
Win. 209	IMR PB	Windjammer	20.0/1100	21.5/1155	23.0/1205	24.5/1260	8,400 psi	
Win. 209	International	CB 3118-12-A	16.5/1090	17.4/1145	19.0/1200	20.0/1255	11,600 psi	
Win. 209	International	CB 3118-12-AR	16.8/1090	17.5/1145	19.6/1200	20.5/1255	10,600 psi	
Win. 209	International	CS12S	16.9/1090	17.4/1145	18.5/1200	20.5/1255	10,800 LUP	
Win. 209	International	H. Versalite	17.4/1090	18.1/1145	18.7/1175	19.2/1200	9,800 LUP	
Win. 209	International	BP HCDP	17.6/1090	18.1/1145	19.2/1200	21.2/1255	10,800 LUP	Note 3
Win. 209	International	Pat. Ctrl. Red	18.3/1090	18.9/1145	20.2/1200	21.3/1255	9,700 LUP	
Win. 209	International	WAA12	17.6/1090	18.1/1145	19.2/1200	21.3/1255	10,800 LUP	
Win. 209	International	Windjam. II	17.5/1090	18.0/1145	18.9/1175	19.7/1200	9,400 psi	
Win. 209	Nitro-100	BP 18	15.5/1125	16.0/1145	17.0/1200	18.0/1255	10,800 psi	Note 9
Win. 209	Nitro-100	CB 1118-12	15.5/1125	16.5/1145	16.8/1175	17.0/1200	9,300 psi	Note 9

Load Notes: 3 = Helix Cushion Platform. 6 = Scatter Master. 9 = Minimum overall length = 2⁹/₃₂″, maximum crimp depth = ²/₃₂″.

Caution: Follow load recipes exactly; do not substitute components, exceed listed maximums or load less than listed minimums.

Primer	Powder Type	Wad	Powder Charge (grains) / Velocity (fps) Minimum			Maximum	Maximum Pressure	Load Notes
Winchester: Compression-Formed AA Type (cont.)					**1 1/8 Ounces Lead Shot**			
Win. 209	Nitro-100	CS12S	16.3/1145	16.8/1175	17.3/1200	17.8/1255	10,000 psi	
Win. 209	Nitro-100	Fed. 12C1	15.5/1125	16.0/1145	17.0/1200	18.0/1255	11,400 psi	Note 9
Win. 209	Nitro-100	Fed. 12S3	15.5/1125	15.5/1145	16.3/1175	17.0/1200	11,100 psi	Note 9
Win. 209	Nitro-100	H. Versalite	15.5/1125	15.5/1145	16.3/1175	17.0/1200	11,200 psi	Note 9
Win. 209	Nitro-100	Hawk II	16.0/1145	16.2/1160	16.5/1175	17.0/1200	10,400 psi	Note 9
Win. 209	Nitro-100	BP HCDP	17.0/1145	17.2/1155	17.3/1160	17.5/1175	8,500 psi	Note 3
Win. 209	Nitro-100	BP HCDP	18.0/1200	18.2/1225	18.3/1235	18.5/1255	10,000 psi	Note 3
Win. 209	Nitro-100	Lage Uniwad				18.5/1200		
Win. 209	Nitro-100	Pat. Ctrl. Red	15.5/1125	15.5/1145	17.5/1200	18.5/1255	11,100 psi	Note 9
Win. 209	Nitro-100	Rem. Fig.-8	15.5/1125	17.0/1145	17.0/1175	17.0/1200	9,600 psi	Note 9
Win. 209	Nitro-100	Rem. RXP12	16.0/1145	17.0/1200	18.0/1230	19.0/1255	10,500 psi	Note 9
Win. 209	Nitro-100	Rem. TGT12	15.5/1125	16.3/1170	17.2/1210	18.0/1255	11,500 psi	Note 9
Win. 209	Nitro-100	Trapper	15.5/1145	15.7/1160	16.0/1175	16.5/1200	10,800 psi	Note 9
Win. 209	Nitro-100	WAA12	15.5/1125	16.0/1145	16.5/1175	17.0/1200	9,400 psi	Note 9
Win. 209	Nitro-100	WAA12SL	15.5/1125	15.5/1145	16.3/1175	17.0/1200	9,900 psi	Note 9
Win. 209	R. Scot D	Claybuster	18.0/1125	18.5/1145	20.0/1200	21.5/1255	10,500 LUP	
Win. 209	R. Scot D	Fed. 12C1	18.5/1125	19.0/1145	20.5/1200	21.5/1255	10,900 LUP	
Win. 209	R. Scot D	Fed. 12S3	18.0/1125	18.5/1145	19.0/1175	19.5/1200	10,400 LUP	
Win. 209	R. Scot D	H. Versalite	18.0/1125	19.3/1175	20.0/1200	21.0/1255	10,900 LUP	
Win. 209	R. Scot D	Lage Uniwad	18.5/1125	19.0/1145	19.8/1175	20.5/1200		
Win. 209	R. Scot D	Pat. Ctrl. Red	18.5/1125	19.0/1145	20.0/1200	21.0/1255	10,800 LUP	
Win. 209	R. Scot D	Rem. Fig.-8	19.0/1125	19.5/1145	20.0/1175	20.5/1200	10,100 LUP	
Win. 209	R. Scot D	Rem. RXP12	18.5/1125	19.0/1145	20.5/1200	21.5/1255	10,900 LUP	
Win. 209	R. Scot D	WAA12	18.5/1125	19.0/1145	19.5/1175	20.0/1200	10,800 LUP	
Win. 209	R. Scot D	WAA12F1	18.5/1125	19.0/1145	19.6/1175	20.0/1200	10,000 LUP	
Win. 209	R. Scot D	WAA12F114	20.0/1200	20.4/1215	20.9/1230	21.5/1255	10,900 LUP	
Win. 209	R. Scot D	WAA12SL	18.0*/1125	18.3/1130	18.6/1135	19.0/1145	9,100 LUP	Note 11
Win. 209	R. Scot D	Windjammer	18.5/1125	19.0/1145	20.5/1200	21.5/1255	10,700 LUP	
Win. 209	Red Diamond	BP CS12	16.5/1145	17.0/1175	17.5/1200	18.5/1255	10,800 psi	Note 5
Win. 209	Red Diamond	H. Versalite	16.5/1145	17.3/1175	18.0/1200	18.5/1255	10,500 psi	Note 5
Win. 209	Red Diamond	Hawk Original	16.5/1145	17.0/1175	17.5/1200	18.5/1255	10,700 psi	Note 5
Win. 209	Red Diamond	Lage Uniwad				19.0/1255	10,000 psi	Note 5
Win. 209	Red Diamond	WAA12	16.0/1145	16.4/1160	16.8/1175	17.5/1200	11,000 psi	Note 5
Win. 209	Red Dot	Activ T-32				21.5/1250	9,600 psi	
Win. 209	Red Dot	BP SCAT	16.5/1100	16.7/1120	16.8/1130	17.0/1145	10,000 psi	Note 6
Win. 209	Red Dot	CS12S	15.3/1060	15.5/1075	15.8/1100	16.3/1145	10,000 psi	
Win. 209	Red Dot	Fed. 12C1	17.5/1145	17.8/1160	18.1/1175	18.5/1200	9,700 psi	
Win. 209	Red Dot	Fed. 12S3				17.0/1090	10,400 psi	
Win. 209	Red Dot	Fiocchi FTW1	17.5/1145	17.8/1160	18.1/1175	18.5/1200	10,700 psi	
Win. 209	Red Dot	H. Versalite	16.5/1090	18.0/1145	18.6/1175	19.0/1200	9,700 psi	
Win. 209	Red Dot	BP HCDP	16.0/1060	16.5/1100	16.7/1120	17.0/1145	10,000 psi	Note 3
Win. 209	Red Dot	Pat. Ctrl. Red	16.0/1090	17.5/1145	18.1/1175	18.5/1200	10,500 psi	

Load Notes: 3 = Helix Cushion Platform. 5 = Use 50-60 pounds wad pressure to ensure wad is firmly seated against powder. 6 = Scatter Master. 9 = Minimum overall length = 2⁹/₃₂, maximum crimp depth = ²/₃₂. 11 = This load is a close match to the Winchester Super-Lite factory loading.

Caution: Follow load recipes exactly; do not substitute components, exceed listed maximums or load less than listed minimums.

Primer	Powder Type	Wad	Powder Charge (grains) / Velocity (fps) Minimum			Maximum	Maximum Pressure	Load Notes
WINCHESTER: COMPRESSION-FORMED AA TYPE (CONT.)						1¹/₈ OUNCES LEAD SHOT		
Win. 209	Red Dot	Rem. Fig.-8	16.0/1090	17.5/1145	18.1/1175	18.5/1200	10,700 psi	
Win. 209	Red Dot	Rem. RXP12	16.5/1090	17.0/1145	17.8/1175	18.5/1200	9,800 psi	
Win. 209	Red Dot	WAA12	16.0/1090	17.0/1145	17.6/1175	18.0/1200	10,400 psi	
Win. 209	Red Dot	WAA12SL				16.0/1090	9,300 psi	
Win. 209	Red Dot	Windjammer	17.5/1145	17.8/1160	18.1/1175	18.5/1200	9,900 psi	
Win. 209	Red Dot	WT12 Orange	16.5/1145	16.6/1160	16.8/1175	17.0/1200	10,700 psi	
Win. 209	Scot 453	WAA12SL	16.0/1125	17.5/1145	18.1/1175	18.5/1200	11,200 psi	
Win. 209	Solo 1000	BP 18	17.0/1125	17.5/1145	18.0/1175	18.5/1200	9,700 psi	Note 9
Win. 209	Solo 1000	CB 1118-12	16.5/1125	17.0/1145	18.0/1200	19.5/1255	11,500 psi	Note 9
Win. 209	Solo 1000	Claybuster	17.5/1125	18.0/1145	19.5/1200	21.0/1255		
Win. 209	Solo 1000	CS12S	17.3/1145	17.8/1170	18.3/1190	19.3/1255	10,600 psi	
Win. 209	Solo 1000	Fed. 12C1	16.5/1125	17.0/1145	17.5/1175	18.0/1200	11,400 psi	Note 9
Win. 209	Solo 1000	Fed. 12S3	16.0/1125	16.5/1145	17.3/1175	18.0/1200	10,700 psi	Note 9
Win. 209	Solo 1000	H. Versalite	16.5/1125	17.0/1145	17.5/1175	18.0/1200	10,300 psi	Note 9
Win. 209	Solo 1000	Hawk II	17.0/1145	17.2/1160	17.5/1175	18.0/1200	11,500 psi	Note 9
Win. 209	Solo 1000	BP HCDP	18.0/1145	18.5/1170	19.0/1190	20.0/1255	10,600 psi	Note 3
Win. 209	Solo 1000	Lage Uniwad	18.0/1125	18.5/1145	19.2/1170	20.0/1200		
Win. 209	Solo 1000	Pat. Ctrl. Red	17.0/1125	17.5/1145	18.5/1200	19.5/1255	11,000 psi	Note 9
Win. 209	Solo 1000	Rem. Fig.-8	16.5/1125	17.0/1145	17.5/1175	18.0/1200	9,800 psi	Note 9
Win. 209	Solo 1000	Rem. RXP12	17.0/1145	17.2/1160	17.5/1175	18.0/1200	10,700 psi	Note 9
Win. 209	Solo 1000	Rem. TGT12				16.5/1125	8,800 psi	Note 9
Win. 209	Solo 1000	Trapper	17.0/1145	17.2/1160	17.5/1175	18.0/1200	10,800 psi	Note 9
Win. 209	Solo 1000	WAA12	17.0/1125	17.5/1145	18.0/1175	18.5/1200	10,800 psi	Note 9
Win. 209	Solo 1000	WAA12F1	18.0/1125	18.5/1145	19.1/1175	19.5/1200		
Win. 209	Solo 1000	WAA12F114	18.5/1145	19.1/1175	19.5/1200	21.0/1255		
Win. 209	Solo 1000	WAA12SL				16.5/1125	9,500 psi	Note 9
Win. 209	Solo 1000	Windjammer	18.0/1125	18.5/1145	20.0/1200	21.0/1255	9,700 psi	
Win. 209	Solo 1250	BP 18	24.5/1200	24.9/1215	25.3/1230	26.0/1255	8,400 LUP	Note 9
Win. 209	Solo 1250	BP SCAT	23.5/1200	24.0/1220	24.2/1230	24.5/1240	9,000 psi	Note 6
Win. 209	Solo 1250	CB 1118-12	24.5/1200	26.0/1255	26.5/1285	27.0/1310	10,500 LUP	Note 9
Win. 209	Solo 1250	Claybuster	24.5/1200	26.0/1255	26.5/1285	27.0/1310	10,500 LUP	
Win. 209	Solo 1250	CS12S	22.8/1200	23.3/1220	23.8/1240	24.3/1280	9,700 psi	
Win. 209	Solo 1250	H. Versalite	23.5/1200	23.9/1215	24.3/1230	25.0/1255	9,000 LUP	Note 9
Win. 209	Solo 1250	Hawk II				24.5/1200	8,300 LUP	Note 9
Win. 209	Solo 1250	BP HCDP	23.5/1200	24.0/1220	24.5/1240	25.0/1280	9,700 psi	Note 3
Win. 209	Solo 1250	Lage Uniwad				27.0/1310	10,400 LUP	Note 9
Win. 209	Solo 1250	Pat. Ctrl. Red	24.5/1200	26.0/1255	26.3/1285	26.5/1310	10,400 LUP	Note 9
Win. 209	Solo 1250	Rem. Fig.-8	24.0/1200	24.8/1235	25.7/1280	26.5/1310	10,400 LUP	Note 9
Win. 209	Solo 1250	Trapper				24.0/1200	8,700 LUP	Note 9
Win. 209	Solo 1250	WAA12	23.5/1200	24.6/1235	25.7/1280	26.5/1310	10,500 LUP	Note 9
Win. 209	Solo 1250	WAA12F114				25.5/1255	9,500 LUP	Note 9
Win. 209	Solo 1250	Windjammer				27.0/1310	10,400 LUP	Note 9

Load Notes: 3 = Helix Cushion Platform. 6 = Scatter Master. 9 = Minimum overall length = 2⁹/₃₂", maximum crimp depth = ²/₃₂".

Caution: Follow load recipes exactly; do not substitute components, exceed listed maximums or load less than listed minimums.

Primer	Powder Type	Wad	Powder Charge (grains) / Velocity (fps) Minimum			Maximum	Maximum Pressure	Load Notes
WINCHESTER: COMPRESSION-FORMED AA TYPE (CONT.)					**1 ⅛ OUNCES LEAD SHOT**			
Win. 209	SR-7625	CB 1118-12	21.5/1100	22.5/1145	24.0/1195	26.0/1265	8,200 psi	
Win. 209	SR-7625	CS12S				24.8/1260	9,200 psi	
Win. 209	SR-7625	Fed. 12S4	21.0/1095	22.5/1145	24.0/1200	25.5/1260	9,200 psi	
Win. 209	SR-7625	BP HCDP				25.5/1260	9,200 psi	Note 3
Win. 209	SR-7625	Rem. RXP12	22.0/1105	23.0/1145	24.5/1200	26.0/1255	8,300 psi	
Win. 209	SR-7625	WAA12	21.0/1090	22.5/1150	23.5/1190	25.5/1295	9,600 psi	
Win. 209	SR-7625	Windjammer	22.0/1105	23.0/1140	24.5/1200	26.0/1255	7,900 psi	
Win. 209	Unique	Fed. 12C1	22.0/1200	22.5/1225	22.7/1235	23.0/1250	9,500 psi	
Win. 209	Unique	Fiocchi FTW1				22.5/1200	8,800 psi	
Win. 209	Unique	H. Versalite	21.0/1200	24.0/1250	24.5/1280	25.0/1310	10,300 psi	
Win. 209	Unique	Pat. Ctrl. Red	23.5/1200	24.5/1250	24.8/1280	25.0/1310	9,100 psi	
Win. 209	Unique	Rem. Fig.-8	22.5/1200	23.0/1210	23.7/1225	24.0/1250	9,000 psi	
Win. 209	Unique	Rem. RXP12	22.0/1200	23.0/1250	23.5/1280	24.0/1310	9,800 psi	
Win. 209	Unique	WAA12	21.0/1200	23.5/1250	24.5/1280	25.5/1310	10,000 psi	
Win. 209	Unique	WAA12SL	22.5/1200	23.7/1225	23.8/1235	24.0/1250	9,900 psi	
Win. 209	Unique	Windjammer				22.5/1200	8,200 psi	
Win. 209	Unique	WT12 Orange	21.5/1200	22.0/1225	22.2/1235	22.5/1250	9,500 psi	
Win. 209	Universal	Rem. Fig.-8	22.5/1200	23.5/1255	24.0/1285	24.5/1310	10,700 psi	
Win. 209	Universal	WAA12	22.0/1200	22.2/1215	22.4/1230	22.7/1255	10,600 psi	
Win. 209	W 452AA	Fed. 12C1	19.5/1145	20.0/1165	20.5/1180	21.0/1200	10,000 LUP	
Win. 209	W 452AA	Fed. 12S1	19.5/1145	19.8/1165	20.2/1180	20.5/1200	10,200 LUP	
Win. 209	W 452AA	Rem. RXP12	19.5/1145	20.0/1165	20.5/1180	21.0/1200	9,900 LUP	
Win. 209	W 452AA	WAA12	19.5/1145	19.8/1165	20.2/1180	20.5/1200	10,100 LUP	
Win. 209	W 473AA	Fed. 12C1				24.0/1200	8,300 LUP	
Win. 209	W 473AA	Fed. 12S1	24.0/1200	25.0/1255	26.5/1295	28.0/1330	10,400 LUP	
Win. 209	W 473AA	Rem. RXP12	24.0/1200	25.0/1255	26.5/1295	28.0/1330	10,100 LUP	
Win. 209	W 473AA	WAA12	23.5/1200	25.0*/1255	27.0*/1300	28.0/1330	10,100 LUP	*Note 12&13
Win. 209	W 540	WAA12	32.5/1300	33.2/1335	34.2/1370	35.0/1400	10,000 LUP	
Win. 209	WSF	CS12S	26.8/1315	27.5/1340	28.3/1370	28.6/1400	10,600 psi	
Win. 209	WSF	Fed. 12S3	27.5/1310	28.0/1340	28.5/1365	29.5/1400	10,800 psi	
Win. 209	WSF	BP HCDP	27.5/1315	28.3/1345	29.0/1370	30.0/1400	10,600 psi	Note 3
Win. 209	WSF	WAA12	27.5/1310	28.3/1340	29.2/1370	30.0/1400	10,600 psi	
Win. 209	WSL	Fed. 12S3				20.0/1200	10,200 psi	
Win. 209	WSL	Rem. Fig.-8	19.0/1145	19.5/1175	20.0/1200	21.0/1255	10,800 psi	
Win. 209	WSL	Rem. R12L				21.5/1255	10,800 psi	
Win. 209	WSL	Rem. RXP12	19.5/1200	20.0/1220	20.5/1235	21.0/1255	10,900 psi	
Win. 209	WSL	WAA12	20.0/1200	20.3/1220	20.7/1235	21.0/1255	10,900 psi	
Win. 209	WSL	WAA12SL	18.5/1145	19.3/1175	20.0/1200	21.5/1255	10,800 psi	
Win. 209	WST	Fed. 12S3	19.0/1145	19.3/1165	19.7/1180	20.0/1200	10,900 psi	
Win. 209	WST	Rem. Fig.-8	19.0/1145	19.5/1165	20.0/1180	20.5/1200	10,000 psi	
Win. 209	WST	Rem. RXP12	19.0/1145	19.3/1165	19.7/1180	20.0/1200	9,700 psi	
Win. 209	WST	WAA12	18.5*/1145	19.0/1165	19.5/1180	20.0*/1200	9,800 psi	*Note 14&15

Load Notes: 3 = Helix Cushion Platform. 12 = This load duplicates ballistics of Winchester's 3¼ dram equivalent Xpert loading. 13 = This load duplicates ballistics of Winchester's 3½ dram equivalent AA International Skeet loading. 14 = This load duplicates ballistics of Winchester's 2 dram equivalent Lite AA target loading. 15 = This load duplicates ballistics of Winchester's 3 dram equivalent Heavy AA target loading.

Caution: Follow load recipes exactly; do not substitute components, exceed listed maximums or load less than listed minimums.

Primer	Powder Type	Wad	Powder Charge (grains) / Velocity (fps) Minimum			Maximum	Maximum Pressure	Load Notes
WINCHESTER: COMPRESSION-FORMED AA TYPE (CONT.)						**1¹/₈ OUNCES LEAD SHOT**		
Win. AATP	International	Pat. Ctrl. Red	17.3/1090	17.7/1145	20.0/1200	20.9/1255	10,700 psi	
Win. AATP	International	WAA12	17.0/1090	17.5/1145	18.1/1175	18.5/1200	11,000 psi	
Win. AATP	WSL	WAA12SL	18.0*/1125	18.5/1150	19.0/1175	19.5/1200	10,100 psi	*Note 16
Win. AATP	WST	WAA12	19.0*/1145	19.5/1165	20.0/1180	20.5*/1200	10,400 psi	*Notes 14&15
WINCHESTER: POLYFORMED (SEPARATE PLASTIC BASE WAD)						**1¹/₈ OUNCES LEAD SHOT**		
CCI 209M	Green Dot	WAA12	18.5/1090	20.0/1145	23.0/1255	25.0/1310	9,000 psi	
CCI 209M	Red Dot	WAA12	17.0/1090	18.0/1145	21.5/1255	22.0/1310	9,400 psi	
CCI 209M	Unique	WAA12	25.0/1255	25.0/1255	25.0/1255	26.0/1310	8,500 psi	
CCI 209M	Universal	Windjammer	24.5/1200	25.1/1225	25.8/1255	26.2/1310	9,600 psi	
CCI 209SC	Universal	Windjammer	25.0/1200	25.7/1225	26.5/1255	27.5/1310	7,900 psi	
Fed. 209	Green Dot	WAA12	18.5/1090	20.0/1145	23.5/1255	24.5/1310	9,400 psi	
Fed. 209	Red Dot	WAA12	16.5/1090	18.0/1145	19.0/1200	20.5/1255	10,200 psi	
Fed. 209	Unique	WAA12	23.5/1200	25.0/1255	25.8/1285	27.0/1310	8,500 psi	
Fed. 209A	Universal	Rem. Fig.-8	24.0/1200	24.3/1225	24.8/1255	26.0/1310	9,400 psi	
Fio. 616	Green Dot	WAA12	18.5/1090	20.7/1170	23.0/1255	24.5/1310	8,900 psi	
Fio. 616	Red Dot	WAA12	17.0/1090	19.5/1200	21.5/1255	22.5/1310	10,600 psi	
Fio. 616	Unique	WAA12	23.5/1200	25.0/1255	26.6/1285	27.5/1310	9,200 psi	
Rem. 209P	Green Dot	WAA12				25.0/1310	8,800 psi	
Rem. 209P	Red Dot	WAA12	16.5/1090	19.5/1200	21.5/1255	22.5/1310	10,200 psi	
Rem. 209P	Unique	WAA12	23.5/1200	25.5/1255	26.4/1285	27.0/1310	9,000 psi	
Win. 209	Green Dot	Activ T-32	23.5/1255	23.5/1255	23.5/1255	24.5/1310	9,500 psi	
Win. 209	Green Dot	Fed. 12S3	21.5/1200	23.5/1255	24.1/1285	24.5/1310	9,900 psi	
Win. 209	Green Dot	H. Versalite	18.5/1090	21.5/1200	24.0/1255	25.0/1310	8,900 psi	
Win. 209	Green Dot	Pat. Ctrl. Red	20.5/1145	22.0/1200	23.5/1255	25.5/1310	8,700 psi	
Win. 209	Green Dot	Rem. Fig.-8	18.5/1090	18.9/1115	19.5/1145	21.5/1200	8,200 psi	
Win. 209	Green Dot	WAA12	20.5/1145	22.0/1200	23.5/1255	25.5/1310	8,900 psi	
Win. 209	Red Dot	Activ T-32				21.0/1255	10,100 psi	
Win. 209	Red Dot	Fed. 12S3	17.5/1090	17.6/1105	17.8/1125	18.0/1145	8,900 psi	
Win. 209	Red Dot	H. Versalite	16.5/1090	18.0/1145	21.5/1255	22.5/1310	10,300 psi	
Win. 209	Red Dot	Pat. Ctrl. Red	17.0/1090	19.5/1200	21.0/1255	22.5/1310	10,200 psi	
Win. 209	Red Dot	Rem. Fig.-8	17.0/1090	17.3/1105	17.7/1125	18.0/1145	8,000 psi	
Win. 209	Red Dot	WAA12	16.5/1090	18.0/1145	19.5/1200	21.0/1255	9,400 psi	
Win. 209	Unique	Activ T-32	25.0/1255	25.0/1255	25.0/1255	26.5/1310	9,000 psi	
Win. 209	Unique	Fed. 12S3	23.5/1200	25.0/1255	25.7/1285	26.0/1310	9,400 psi	
Win. 209	Unique	H. Versalite	23.0/1200	25.0/1255	25.9/1285	26.5/1310	9,000 psi	
Win. 209	Unique	Pat. Ctrl. Red	23.5/1200	25.0/1255	25.9/1285	26.5/1310	8,600 psi	
Win. 209	Unique	Rem. Fig.-8				23.0/1200	7,400 psi	
Win. 209	Unique	WAA12	23.0/1200	25.0/1255	25.9/1285	26.5/1310	8,600 psi	
Win. 209	Universal	WAA12	24.0/1200	24.5/1225	25.3/1255	26.0/1310	10,100 psi	
Win. 209	W 452AA	Fed. 12S3				20.5/1145	7,500 LUP	

Load Notes: 14 = This load duplicates ballistics of Winchester's 2 dram equivalent Lite AA target loading. 15 = This load duplicates ballistics of Winchester's 3 dram equivalent Heavy AA target loading. 16 = This load duplicates ballistics of Winchester's 2 dram equivalent. AA Super-Lite target loading.

Caution: Follow load recipes exactly; do not substitute components, exceed listed maximums or load less than listed minimums.

Primer	Powder Type	Wad	Powder Charge (grains) / Velocity (fps) Minimum			Maximum	Maximum Pressure	Load Notes
ACTIV: ALL PLASTIC						**1 ¼ OUNCES LEAD SHOT**		
CCI 209	Blue Dot	Fed. 12S4				39.5/1330	9,300 psi	
CCI 209	Green Dot	Activ T-32				23.0/1220	9,300 psi	
CCI 209	Green Dot	WAA12				23.5/1220	9,000 psi	
CCI 209	Herco	Fed. 12S4				30.5/1330	9,800 psi	
CCI 209	Solo 1250	Activ T-35	27.0/1220	27.3/1240	27.6/1255	28.0/1275	9,700 LUP	
CCI 209	Unique	Activ T-32				25.5/1220	8,100 psi	
CCI 209	Unique	WAA12				25.5/1220	8,400 psi	
CCI 209M	Green Dot	Activ T-32				22.0/1220	9,600 psi	
CCI 209M	Green Dot	WAA12				22.5/1220	10,000 psi	
CCI 209M	Herco	Activ T-32				29.0/1330	10,200 psi	
CCI 209M	Solo 1250	Activ T-35				25.5/1220	9,600 LUP	
CCI 209M	Unique	Activ T-32				24.5/1220	9,000 psi	
CCI 209M	Unique	WAA12				24.5/1220	9,000 psi	
CCI 209M	Universal	Activ TG-32				25.0/1220	9,100 psi	
CCI 209SC	Universal	Activ TG-30				24.3/1220	8,600 psi	
Fed. 209	Blue Dot	Fed. 12S4				37.0/1330	10,100 psi	
Fed. 209	Green Dot	Activ T-32				22.5/1220	10,000 psi	
Fed. 209	Green Dot	WAA12				22.5/1220	9,800 psi	
Fed. 209	Herco	Activ T-32				29.5/1330	10,300 psi	
Fed. 209	IMR 800-X	Activ T-32				29.0/1320	10,000 LUP	
Fed. 209	IMR PB	Activ T-35				28.0/1330	10,600 LUP	
Fed. 209	Solo 1250	Activ T-35	26.5/1220	27.0/1240	27.5/1255	28.0/1275	10,000 LUP	
Fed. 209	SR-4756	Activ T-35				34.5/1320	8,200 LUP	
Fed. 209	SR-7625	Activ T-35				30.5/1330	8,900 LUP	
Fed. 209	Unique	Activ T-32	24.5/1220	25.5/1255	26.5/1295	27.5/1330	10,500 psi	
Fed. 209	Unique	WAA12				24.5/1220	9,500 psi	
Fed. 209	Universal	H. Versalite				27.0/1220	10,200 psi	
Fed. 209A	Universal	Activ TG-32				23.7/1220	10,600 psi	
Rem. 209P	IMR 800-X	Activ T-32				28.0/1290	10,000 LUP	
Rem. 209P	IMR PB	Activ T-35				27.0/1315	10,600 LUP	
Rem. 209P	Solo 1250	Activ T-35	27.0/1220	27.3/1240	27.6/1255	28.0/1275	10,400 LUP	
Win. 209	Blue Dot	Fed. 12S4				39.5/1330	9,000 psi	
Win. 209	Blue Dot	Rem. SP12				39.0/1330	8,700 psi	
Win. 209	Blue Dot	WAA12F114				40.0/1330	8,800 psi	
Win. 209	Green Dot	Activ T-32				23.0/1220	9,700 psi	
Win. 209	Green Dot	Rem. RXP12				22.0/1220	9,900 psi	
Win. 209	Green Dot	WAA12				22.0/1220	10,200 psi	
Win. 209	Herco	Activ T-32				29.0/1330	9,700 psi	
Win. 209	Herco	Rem. SP12				28.5/1330	9,800 psi	
Win. 209	Herco	WAA12F114				28.5/1330	10,300 psi	
Win. 209	HS-6	Activ TG-32	34.0/1220	34.7/1255	35.4/1295	36.0/1330	10,200 LUP	
Win. 209	HS-7	WAA12				38.0/1330	9,200 LUP	
Win. 209	IMR 800-X	Activ T-32				28.5/1320	10,200 LUP	

Caution: Follow load recipes exactly; do not substitute components, exceed listed maximums or load less than listed minimums.

Primer	Powder Type	Wad	Powder Charge (grains) / Velocity (fps) Minimum			Maximum	Maximum Pressure	Load Notes
ACTIV: ALL PLASTIC (CONT.)						**1¹/₄ OUNCES LEAD SHOT**		
Win. 209	IMR PB	Activ T-35				28.5/1330	10,600 LUP	
Win. 209	Solo 1250	Activ T-35	26.0/1220	27.0/1255	27.5/1275	29.0/1330	10,900 LUP	Note 1
Win. 209	Solo 1250	Rem. RXP12				26.5/1220	9,600 LUP	
Win. 209	Solo 1500	Activ T-35				37.5/1330	9,000 LUP	
Win. 209	SR-4756	Activ T-35				34.0/1320	7,800 LUP	
Win. 209	SR-7625	Activ T-35				31.0/1340	8,800 LUP	
Win. 209	Unique	Activ T-32	24.5/1220	25.5/1255	26.5/1295	27.5/1330	10,200 psi	
Win. 209	Unique	Fed. 12C1				24.5/1220	8,900 psi	
Win. 209	Unique	Rem. RXP12				24.5/1220	9,200 psi	
Win. 209	Unique	WAA12				24.0/1220	9,200 psi	
Win. 209	Universal	WAA12				24.0/1220	9,800 psi	
ESTATE: CHEDITE (LOW BASE WAD)						**1¹/₄ OUNCES LEAD SHOT**		
Fed. 209A	HS-6	Fiocchi TL1				34.5/1330	10,500 psi	
Fio. 616	Universal	WAA12F114	24.5/1220	24.8/1240	25.1/1255	25.5/1275	10,300 psi	
Win. 209	HS-6	Rem. Fig.-8				35.0/1330	9,400 psi	
Win. 209	Universal	Fed. 12S4	24.5/1220	24.8/1240	25.1/1255	25.5/1275	10,500 psi	
FEDERAL: GOLD MEDAL PLASTIC						**1¹/₄ OUNCES LEAD SHOT**		
CCI 209	Solo 1250	Fed. 12S4				26.5/1220	9,900 LUP	
CCI 209	Universal	Fed. 12S4				25.0/1220	10,100 psi	
CCI 209	WSF	Fed. 12S4	27.0/1255	27.8/1280	28.7/1305	29.5/1330	10,600 psi	
CCI 209M	Blue Dot	Fed. 12S4	35.0/1275	35.8/1295	36.6/1310	37.5/1330	8,300 psi	
CCI 209M	Herco	Fed. 12S4				25.5/1220	8,700 psi	
CCI 209M	Solo 1250	Fed. 12S4				25.5/1220	10,400 LUP	
CCI 209M	SR-4756	Rem. SP12				31.0/1215	6,300 LUP	
CCI 209M	SR-7625	Rem. SP12	28.0/1225	28.8/1255	29.6/1290	30.5/1320	7,600 LUP	
CCI 209M	Unique	Fed. 12S4				24.5/1220	9,500 psi	
CCI 209SC	Universal	Fed. 12S4				24.0/1220	9,500 psi	
Fed. 209	HS-6	Fed. 12S4	32.0/1220	33.0/1255	34.0/1295	35.0/1330	10,400 LUP	
Fed. 209	IMR 700-X	Fed. 12S4				20.5/1220	10,900 LUP	
Fed. 209	IMR 700-X	Rem. R12H				21.0/1225	10,300 LUP	
Fed. 209	IMR 800-X	Fed. 12S3				25.0/1235	8,300 LUP	
Fed. 209	IMR 800-X	Fed. 12S4				27.5/1325	9,700 LUP	
Fed. 209	IMR 800-X	Lage Uniwad	25.5/1235	26.3/1265	27.1/1290	28.0/1320	8,900 LUP	
Fed. 209	IMR 800-X	Rem. R12H	25.0/1220	26.0/1255	27.0/1290	28.0/1325	8,900 LUP	
Fed. 209	IMR 800-X	WAA12F114	25.0/1225	26.0/1260	27.0/1295	28.0/1330	8,900 LUP	
Fed. 209	IMR PB	Rem. SP12	26.0/1235	27.0/1270	28.0/1300	29.0/1335	10,200 LUP	
Fed. 209	Solo 1250	Activ T-35				27.0/1220	10,400 LUP	
Fed. 209	Solo 1250	Fed. 12S4	26.0/1220	26.5/1240	27.0/1255	27.5/1275	10,900 LUP	
Fed. 209	Solo 1250	Rem. SP12				26.5/1220	10,100 LUP	
Fed. 209	SR-4756	Rem. RP12				34.0/1325	7,500 LUP	
Fed. 209	SR-4756	Rem. SP12				30.5/1215	6,300 LUP	

Load Notes: 1 = Minimum overall length = 2¹⁰/₃₂″, maximum crimp depth = ²/₃₂″.

    Caution: Follow load recipes exactly; do not substitute components, exceed listed maximums or load less than listed minimums.

Primer	Powder Type	Wad	Powder Charge (grains) / Velocity (fps) Minimum			Maximum	Maximum Pressure	Load Notes
FEDERAL: GOLD MEDAL PLASTIC (CONT.)						**1¼ OUNCES LEAD SHOT**		
Fed. 209	SR-4756	WAA12R				34.5/1325	7,300 LUP	
Fed. 209	SR-7625	Rem. SP12	28.5/1230	29.3/1260	30.1/1295	31.0/1325	7,700 LUP	
Fed. 209	Universal	Fed. 12S4				25.0/1220	9,300 psi	
Fed. 209A	Blue Dot	Fed. 12S4				34.0/1275	8,900 psi	
Fed. 209A	Herco	Fed. 12S4				25.0/1220	10,200 psi	
Fed. 209A	Herco	Rem. SP12	26.0/1220	26.3/1240	26.6/1255	27.0/1275	10,100 psi	
Fed. 209A	Herco	WAA12F114	25.0/1220	25.7/1240	26.4/1255	27.0/1275	10,500 psi	
Fed. 209A	Unique	Fed. 12S4				24.0/1220	10,500 psi	
Fed. 209A	Unique	Rem. SP12				24.0/1220	10,400 psi	
Fed. 209A	Unique	WAA12F114				24.0/1220	10,600 psi	
Fed. 209A	Universal	Fed. 12S4				23.3/1220	10,400 psi	
Fio. 616	Universal	Rem. SP12				24.7/1220	9,200 psi	
Rem. 209P	Blue Dot	Fed. 12S4				35.0/1330	10,500 psi	
Rem. 209P	Herco	Fed. 12S4	25.5/1220	26.2/1240	26.9/1255	27.5/1275	9,200 psi	
Rem. 209P	Unique	Fed. 12S4				25.0/1220	9,800 psi	
Win. 209	Blue Dot	Fed. 12S4	35.0/1275	35.7/1295	36.4/1310	37.0/1330	9,000 psi	
Win. 209	Herco	Fed. 12S4				25.5/1220	9,400 psi	
Win. 209	HS-6	WAA12F114	32.0/1220	32.8/1255	33.6/1295	34.5/1330	10,100 LUP	
Win. 209	IMR 700-X	Fed. 12S4				20.5/1215	10,500 LUP	
Win. 209	IMR 700-X	Rem. R12H				21.0/1225	9,900 LUP	
Win. 209	IMR PB	Rem. SP12	26.0/1235	27.0/1270	28.0/1310	29.0/1345	10,400 LUP	
Win. 209	Solo 1250	Fed. 12S4				26.0/1220	10,100 LUP	
Win. 209	Solo 1500	WAA12R				34.5/1330	10,500 LUP	
Win. 209	Unique	Fed. 12S4				24.0/1220	9,500 psi	
Win. 209	Universal	WAA12F114				24.5/1220	10,300 psi	
Win. 209	WSF	Fed. 12S4				31.5/1330	9,500 psi	
FEDERAL: ONE-PIECE PLASTIC HUNTING (HI-POWER)						**1¼ OUNCES LEAD SHOT**		
CCI 209M	Blue Dot	Fed. 12S4				37.5/1330	9,000 psi	
CCI 209M	Herco	Fed. 12S4	26.0/1220	26.5/1240	27.0/1255	27.5/1275	9,500 psi	
CCI 209M	Unique	Fed. 12S4				25.5/1220	9,200 psi	
Fed. 209A	Blue Dot	Fed. 12S4				38.5/1330	8,500 psi	
Fed. 209A	Blue Dot	WAA12F114				39.0/1330	7,700 psi	
Fed. 209A	Herco	Fed. 12S4	26.0/1220	26.7/1240	27.4/1255	28.0/1275	9,500 psi	
Fed. 209A	Herco	Rem. SP12	26.5/1220	26.8/1240	27.1/1255	27.5/1275	8,200 psi	
Fed. 209A	Herco	WAA12F114	26.0/1220	26.5/1240	27.0/1255	27.5/1275	8,700 psi	
Fed. 209A	Unique	Fed. 12S4				25.0/1220	9,100 psi	
Fed. 209A	Unique	Rem. SP12				25.5/1220	8,700 psi	
Fed. 209A	Unique	WAA12F114				25.0/1220	8,700 psi	
Rem. 209	Herco	Fed. 12S4	26.5/1220	27.2/1240	27.9/1255	28.5/1275	9,400 psi	
Rem. 209	Unique	Fed. 12S4				25.5/1220	8,800 psi	
Win. 209	Blue Dot	Fed. 12S4				39.0/1330	8,400 psi	
Win. 209	Herco	Fed. 12S4	26.0/1220	26.5/1240	27.0/1255	27.5/1275	9,000 psi	
Win. 209	Unique	Fed. 12S4				25.0/1220	9,200 psi	

Caution: Follow load recipes exactly; do not substitute components, exceed listed maximums or load less than listed minimums.

Primer	Powder Type	Wad	Powder Charge (grains) / Velocity (fps) Minimum			Maximum	Maximum Pressure	Load Notes
FEDERAL: PLASTIC (PAPER BASE WAD)						**1¹/₄ OUNCES LEAD SHOT**		
CCI 209M	Blue Dot	Fed. 12S4				38.0/1330	9,800 psi	
CCI 209M	Herco	Fed. 12S4				30.0/1330	9,500 psi	
CCI 209M	Unique	Fed. 12S4				25.0/1220	10,000 psi	
CCI 209M	Universal	Rem. SP12				25.5/1220	7,900 psi	
Fed. 209	IMR PB	Rem. RP12	25.5/1230	26.7/1265	27.9/1300	29.0/1335	10,900 LUP	
Fed. 209	IMR PB	WAA12R	25.5/1215	26.7/1255	27.9/1290	29.0/1330	10,200 LUP	
Fed. 209	Solo 1500	Fed. 12S4				36.0/1330	10,900 LUP	
Fed. 209	SR-4756	Rem. RP12				36.0/1330	8,200 LUP	
Fed. 209	SR-4756	Rem. SP12				32.5/1225	7,000 LUP	
Fed. 209	SR-4756	WAA12R	33.0/1225	34.2/1260	35.4/1295	36.5/1330	7,800 LUP	
Fed. 209	SR-7625	Rem. RP12				30.0/1320	9,200 LUP	
Fed. 209	SR-7625	Rem. SP12				27.5/1225	7,500 LUP	
Fed. 209	SR-7625	WAA12R	27.5/1215	28.7/1250	29.9/1290	31.0/1325	8,600 LUP	
Fed. 209A	Green Dot	Fed. 12S4				23.0/1220	9,800 psi	
Fed. 209A	Green Dot	H. Versalite				23.0/1220	9,700 psi	
Fed. 209A	Green Dot	Rem. R12H				22.0/1220	10,500 psi	
Fed. 209A	Green Dot	Rem. RXP12				22.0/1220	9,600 psi	
Fed. 209A	Green Dot	WAA12				21.5/1220	9,500 psi	
Fed. 209A	Green Dot	WAA12F114				23.0/1220	9,900 psi	
Fed. 209A	Herco	Fed. 12C1				28.5/1330	9,800 psi	
Fed. 209A	Herco	Fed. 12S4				29.0/1330	10,200 psi	
Fed. 209A	Herco	Rem. SP12				28.5/1330	9,900 psi	
Fed. 209A	Herco	WAA12				29.0/1330	10,500 psi	
Fed. 209A	Herco	WAA12F114				29.5/1330	9,400 psi	
Fed. 209A	Unique	Fed. 12C1	23.0/1220	23.8/1255	24.6/1295	25.5/1330	10,200 psi	
Fed. 209A	Unique	Fed. 12S4				23.0/1220	9,500 psi	
Fed. 209A	Unique	H. Versalite				23.5/1220	8,800 psi	
Fed. 209A	Unique	Rem. RXP12				23.0/1220	8,300 psi	
Fed. 209A	Unique	Rem. SP12				25.5/1330	10,200 psi	
Fed. 209A	Unique	WAA12				23.0/1220	9,600 psi	
Fed. 209A	Unique	WAA12F114				23.0/1220	9,400 psi	
Fed. 209A	Universal	Fed. 12S4				24.0/1220	10,300 psi	
Fio. 616	Universal	Fed. 12S4				26.0/1220	8,900 psi	
Rem. 209P	Unique	Fed. 12S4				25.5/1220	9,000 psi	
Win. 209	Blue Dot	Fed. 12S4				38.0/1330	8,600 psi	
Win. 209	Herco	Fed. 12S4				30.0/1330	10,200 psi	
Win. 209	Unique	Fed. 12S4				25.0/1220	9,500 psi	
Win. 209	Universal	Fed. 12S4				25.2/1220	8,800 psi	
Win. 209	Universal	WAA12F114				25.5/1220	9,400 psi	
FIOCCHI: PURPLE TARGET (HIGH BASE WAD)						**1¹/₄ OUNCES LEAD SHOT**		
CCI 209	Solo 1250	Activ T-35				30.0/1275	9,100 LUP	
CCI 209	Solo 1250	Rem. SP12				33.0/1330	10,400 LUP	Note 1

Load Notes: 1 = Minimum overall length = 2¹⁰/₃₂", maximum crimp depth = ²/₃₂".

*Caution: Follow load recipes exactly; do not substitute components, exceed listed maximums or load less than listed minimums.

Primer	Powder Type	Wad	Powder Charge (grains) / Velocity (fps) Minimum			Maximum	Maximum Pressure	Load Notes
Fiocchi: Purple Target (high base wad) (cont.)						**1¼ Ounces Lead Shot**		
CCI 209M	Green Dot	Rem. R12H				24.5/1220	8,000 psi	
CCI 209M	Herco	Rem. SP12	28.0/1275	28.7/1285	29.4/1290	30.0/1300	9,200 psi	
Fed. 209	Blue Dot	Fed. 12S4				37.0/1300	8,800 psi	
Fed. 209	Green Dot	Fed. 12S4				23.0/1220	10,000 psi	
Fed. 209	Herco	Fed. 12S4	27.5/1275	28.3/1285	29.1/1290	30.0/1300	10,300 psi	
Fed. 209	Solo 1250	Activ T-35	27.5/1220	28.2/1240	28.9/1255	29.5/1275	9,500 LUP	
Fed. 209	Solo 1250	Rem. SP12				32.5/1330	10,400 LUP	Note 2
Fed. 209	Solo 1250	Rem. SP12				32.5/1330	10,400 LUP	
Fed. 209	Unique	Fed. 12S4	24.5/1220	24.9/1235	25.3/1250	26.0/1275	10,100 psi	
Fed. 209	Universal	Rem. SP12				24.0/1220	10,200 psi	
Fio. 616	Blue Dot	Fed. 12S4				40.0/1300	8,300 psi	
Fio. 616	Blue Dot	Rem. SP12				41.0/1300	7,700 psi	
Fio. 616	Blue Dot	WAA12F114				39.5/1300	7,500 psi	
Fio. 616	Green Dot	Fed. 12S4				23.0/1220	9,700 psi	
Fio. 616	Herco	Fed. 12S4	28.0/1275	28.7/1285	29.4/1290	30.0/1300	9,500 psi	
Fio. 616	Herco	Rem. SP12				30.5/1300	8,600 psi	
Fio. 616	Herco	WAA12F114				30.0/1300	9,200 psi	
Fio. 616	Solo 1250	Activ T-35	27.5/1220	28.0/1240	28.5/1255	29.0/1275	9,700 LUP	
Fio. 616	Solo 1250	Fed. 12S4	26.5/1220	27.2/1240	27.9/1255	28.5/1275	10,500 LUP	
Fio. 616	Solo 1250	Rem. SP12	29.5/1275	30.5/1295	31.5/1310	32.5/1330	10,400 LUP	Note 2
Fio. 616	Solo 1250	WAA12	26.5/1220	27.2/1240	27.9/1255	28.5/1275	10,500 LUP	
Fio. 616	Unique	Fed. 12S4	25.0/1220	25.5/1235	26.0/1250	27.0/1275	10,300 psi	
Fio. 616	Universal	WAA12F114				24.0/1220	10,900 psi	
Win. 209	Blue Dot	WAA12F114				38.5/1300	8,300 psi	
Win. 209	Green Dot	WAA12F114				23.0/1220	10,000 psi	
Win. 209	Herco	WAA12F114	28.0/1275	28.7/1285	29.4/1290	30.0/1300	10,100 psi	
Win. 209	HS-6	Rem. 12H				35.0/1330	9,200 LUP	
Win. 209	Solo 1250	Activ T-35	27.0/1220	27.8/1240	28.6/1255	29.5/1275	10,100 LUP	
Win. 209	Solo 1250	Fed. 12S4				26.5/1220	9,900 LUP	
Win. 209	Solo 1250	Rem. SP12				32.5/1330	10,400 LUP	Note 2
Win. 209	Solo 1250	Rem. SP12				32.5/1330	10,400 LUP	
Win. 209	Unique	WAA12F114	25.0/1220	25.5/1235	26.0/1250	27.0/1275	10,000 psi	
Win. 209	Universal	Rem. SP12				24.0/1220	10,900 psi	
Peters: Blue Magic						**1¼ Ounces Lead Shot**		
CCI 209	SR-4756	Rem. RP12				31.5/1320	10,200 LUP	
CCI 209	SR-4756	WAA12R				31.5/1325	10,600 LUP	
CCI 209M	IMR 800-X	Fed. 12S4				24.0/1235	10,500 LUP	
CCI 209M	IMR 800-X	H. Versalite				24.0/1235	9,900 LUP	
CCI 209M	IMR 800-X	Lage Uniwad				24.0/1215	9,300 LUP	
CCI 209M	IMR 800-X	Rem. SP12				24.0/1225	9,600 LUP	
CCI 209M	IMR 800-X	WAA12F114				24.0/1235	9,700 LUP	
CCI 209M	IMR 800-X	Windjammer				24.0/1230	9,000 LUP	

Load Notes: 2 = Minimum overall length = 2⁹⁄₃₂″, maximum crimp depth = ²⁄₃₂″.

Caution: Follow load recipes exactly; do not substitute components, exceed listed maximums or load less than listed minimums.

Primer	Powder Type	Wad	Powder Charge (grains) / Velocity (fps) Minimum			Maximum	Maximum Pressure	Load Notes
PETERS: BLUE MAGIC (CONT.)						**1¹/₄ OUNCES LEAD SHOT**		
Fed. 209	IMR PB	Rem. SP12				23.0/1220	10,700 LUP	
Fed. 209	SR-4756	H. Versalite				27.0/1215	10,000 LUP	
Fed. 209	SR-4756	Lage Uniwad				28.0/1230	10,100 LUP	
Fed. 209	SR-4756	Rem. RP12				27.5/1220	9,800 LUP	
Fed. 209	SR-4756	WAA12R				28.5/1230	9,000 LUP	
Fed. 209	SR-7625	Lage Uniwad				24.5/1215	10,100 LUP	
Fed. 209	SR-7625	Rem. SP12				25.0/1230	9,700 LUP	
Fed. 209	SR-7625	WAA12F114				24.5/1225	10,600 LUP	
Rem. 209P	IMR 800-X	Activ T-32				24.0/1230	9,100 LUP	
Rem. 209P	IMR 800-X	Activ T-35				26.5/1325	10,400 LUP	
Rem. 209P	IMR 800-X	Fed. 12S4				24.0/1230	9,500 LUP	
Rem. 209P	IMR 800-X	H. Versalite				24.0/1225	8,900 LUP	
Rem. 209P	IMR 800-X	Lage Uniwad	24.5/1220	25.3/1255	26.1/1285	27.0/1320	10,600 LUP	
Rem. 209P	IMR 800-X	Rem. Fig.-8				24.5/1220	8,500 LUP	
Rem. 209P	IMR 800-X	Rem. SP12	24.0/1225	25.0/1260	26.0/1290	27.0/1325	10,300 LUP	
Rem. 209P	IMR 800-X	WAA12F114	23.5/1220	24.7/1255	25.9/1290	27.0/1325	10,900 LUP	
Rem. 209P	IMR 800-X	Windjammer	24.0/1220	25.2/1255	26.4/1295	27.5/1330	9,600 LUP	
Rem. 209P	Solo 1500	Rem. SP12				34.5/1330	10,600 LUP	
Win. 209	IMR PB	Rem. SP12				23.5/1215	10,100 LUP	
Win. 209	SR-4756	Rem. RP12	28.5/1210	29.5/1250	30.5/1285	31.5/1325	10,100 LUP	
Win. 209	SR-4756	WAA12R	29.5/1225	30.3/1260	31.1/1295	32.0/1330	10,100 LUP	
Win. 209	SR-7625	WAA12R				28.5/1325	10,800 LUP	
Win. 209	W 473AA	Rem. RXP12				26.0/1220	10,300 LUP	
Win. 209	W 473AA	WAA12				25.5/1220	10,500 LUP	
Win. 209	W 540	Rem. RXP12				36.0/1330	10,400 LUP	
REMINGTON: PREMIER & NITRO 27 & STS						**1¹/₄ OUNCES LEAD SHOT**		
CCI 209	Solo 1250	Rem. SP12				25.0/1220	9,900 LUP	
CCI 209	Universal	Rem. SP12				23.7/1220	9,200 psi	
CCI 209	WSF	WAA12F114	25.5/1220	27.0/1255	27.8/1295	28.5/1330	10,900 psi	
CCI 209M	Blue Dot	Rem. SP12	34.5/1275	34.8/1295	35.1/1310	35.5/1330	10,300 psi	
CCI 209M	Herco	Rem. SP12				24.5/1220	10,000 psi	
CCI 209M	Unique	Rem. SP12				23.5/1220	10,300 psi	
Fed. 209	Blue Dot	Rem. SP12	35.0/1275	35.5/1295	36.0/1310	36.5/1330	9,700 psi	
Fed. 209	Herco	Rem. SP12				25.0/1220	9,800 psi	
Fed. 209	Unique	Rem. SP12				23.0/1220	9,900 psi	
Fed. 209	Universal	Fed. 12S4				23.5/1220	10,000 psi	
Fed. 209	WSF	Rem. RXP12	28.0/1255	28.5/1280	29.0/1305	29.5/1330	10,700 psi	
Fed. 209	WSF	WAA12F114	26.5/1220	28.0/1255	28.8/1295	29.5/1330	10,200 psi	
Fed. 209A	Universal	Rem. SP12				22.5/1220	11,300 psi	
Fio. 616	Blue Dot	Rem. SP12	35.5/1275	35.5/1295	35.5/1310	35.5/1330	9,900 psi	
Fio. 616	Herco	Rem. SP12				24.5/1220	9,300 psi	
Fio. 616	Unique	Rem. SP12				23.0/1220	9,600 psi	

1¼ Ounces Lead Shot (cont.)

12-Gauge 2³/₄″

Primer	Powder Type	Wad	Powder Charge (grains) / Velocity (fps) Minimum			Maximum	Maximum Pressure	Load Notes
Remington: Premier & Nitro 27 & STS (cont.)						**1¼ Ounces Lead Shot**		
Rem. 209P	Blue Dot	Activ T-35				35.0/1275	8,500 psi	
Rem. 209P	Blue Dot	Fed. 12S4				34.0/1275	10,100 psi	
Rem. 209P	Blue Dot	Rem. SP12	34.5/1275	35.5/1295	36.5/1310	37.5/1330	9,700 psi	
Rem. 209P	Herco	Activ T-32				25.0/1220	8,800 psi	
Rem. 209P	Herco	Activ T-35				27.0/1275	9,900 psi	
Rem. 209P	Herco	Fed. 12S4				25.0/1220	10,400 psi	
Rem. 209P	Herco	H. Versalite				25.0/1220	8,400 psi	
Rem. 209P	Herco	Rem. SP12				25.0/1220	9,600 psi	
Rem. 209P	Herco	WAA12F114	24.5/1220	25.2/1240	25.9/1255	26.5/1275	10,500 psi	
Rem. 209P	Solo 1250	Rem. RP12				25.0/1220	9,700 LUP	
Rem. 209P	Solo 1250	Rem. SP12	25.0/1220	25.5/1240	26.0/1255	26.5/1275	10,900 LUP	
Rem. 209P	Solo 1250	Windjammer				25.0/1220	9,600 LUP	
Rem. 209P	Solo 1500	Rem. SP12				33.5/1330	10,600 LUP	
Rem. 209P	Unique	Activ T-32				23.5/1220	9,400 psi	
Rem. 209P	Unique	Fed. 12S4				23.0/1220	10,700 psi	
Rem. 209P	Unique	H. Versalite				23.5/1220	9,400 psi	
Rem. 209P	Unique	Rem. SP12				23.5/1220	9,300 psi	
Rem. 209P	Unique	WAA12F114				24.0/1220	10,100 psi	
Rem. 209P	Universal	Rem. SP12				24.0/1220	9,600 psi	
Win. 209	Blue Dot	Rem. SP12	35.5/1275	35.8/1295	36.1/1310	36.5/1330	9,900 psi	
Win. 209	Herco	Rem. SP12	24.5/1220	25.0/1240	25.5/1255	26.0/1275	10,600 psi	
Win. 209	HS-6	Rem. R12H	32.0/1220	32.7/1255	33.4/1295	34.0/1330	10,200 LUP	
Win. 209	HS-6	WAA12F114	32.0/1220	32.7/1255	33.4/1295	34.0/1330	10,400 LUP	
Win. 209	Solo 1250	Rem. SP12				25.0/1220	10,100 LUP	
Win. 209	Unique	Rem. SP12				23.5/1220	10,000 psi	
Win. 209	Universal	WAA12F114				23.5/1220	10,900 psi	
Win. 209	WSF	WAA12F114	27.5/1255	28.2/1280	28.8/1305	29.5/1330	10,400 psi	
Remington: RXP						**1¼ Ounces Lead Shot**		
Win. 209	W 473AA	Fed. 12C1				25.0/1220	10,300 LUP	
Win. 209	W 473AA	Rem. RXP12				25.0/1220	10,400 LUP	
Win. 209	W 473AA	WAA12				25.0/1220	10,300 LUP	
Win. 209	W 540	Fed. 12S1				33.5/1330	10,000 LUP	
Win. 209	W 540	Rem. RXP12				34.5/1330	9,700 LUP	
Win. 209	W 540	WAA12				33.5/1330	10,300 LUP	
Win. 209	W 540	WAA12F114	29.0/1220	30.0/1255	30.5/1295	31.0/1330	10,300 LUP	
Remington: Unibody (integral plastic base wad)						**1¼ Ounces Lead Shot**		
CCI 209	Blue Dot	Rem. RP12				37.5/1330	9,700 psi	
CCI 209	Blue Dot	Rem. SP12				35.5/1275	8,900 psi	
CCI 209	Herco	Rem. SP12				25.5/1220	9,100 psi	
CCI 209	IMR PB	Rem. RP12				24.0/1220	9,900 LUP	
CCI 209	IMR PB	WAA12R				24.5/1230	9,600 LUP	
CCI 209	SR-7625	Rem. RP12	26.0/1220	26.7/1250	27.4/1285	28.0/1315	10,500 LUP	

Caution: Follow load recipes exactly; do not substitute components, exceed listed maximums or load less than listed minimums.

Primer	Powder Type	Wad	Powder Charge (grains) / Velocity (fps) Minimum			Maximum	Maximum Pressure	Load Notes
REMINGTON: UNIBODY (INTEGRAL PLASTIC BASE WAD) (CONT.)						1¹/₄ OUNCES LEAD SHOT		
CCI 209	SR-7625	WAA12R	26.5/1225	27.5/1265	28.5/1305	29.5/1345	10,600 LUP	
CCI 209	Unique	Rem. SP12				24.5/1220	9,600 psi	
CCI 209M	Blue Dot	Rem. RP12				35.5/1330	10,400 psi	
CCI 209M	Blue Dot	Rem. SP12	32.0/1220	32.5/1240	33.0/1255	33.5/1275	9,800 psi	
CCI 209M	IMR 800-X	Lage Uniwad	24.0/1225	25.2/1260	26.4/1295	27.5/1330	10,900 LUP	
CCI 209M	IMR 800-X	Rem. SP12				27.0/1325	10,600 LUP	
CCI 209M	Unique	Rem. SP12				23.0/1220	10,100 psi	
Fed. 209	Blue Dot	Rem. SP12	31.5/1220	31.8/1240	32.1/1255	32.5/1275	10,600 psi	
Fed. 209	Herco	Rem. SP12				23.5/1220	10,400 psi	
Fed. 209	IMR PB	Rem. RP12				23.0/1210	10,800 LUP	
Fed. 209	IMR PB	WAA12R				23.0/1210	10,600 LUP	
Fed. 209	SR-4756	Rem. RP12	28.5/1220	29.5/1255	30.5/1295	31.5/1330	10,900 LUP	
Fed. 209	SR-4756	WAA12R	29.0/1215	30.0/1250	31.0/1290	32.0/1325	10,500 LUP	
Fed. 209	SR-7625	Rem. RP12				25.0/1215	8,900 LUP	
Fed. 209	SR-7625	WAA12R				25.5/1225	8,900 LUP	
Fed. 209	Unique	Rem. SP12				22.5/1220	10,700 psi	
Rem. 209	Blue Dot	Rem. SP12				32.0/1275	10,200 psi	
Rem. 209	Blue Dot	WAA12F114	30.0/1220	30.7/1240	31.4/1255	32.0/1275	10,000 psi	
Rem. 209	Herco	Rem. SP12				23.5/1220	9,400 psi	
Rem. 209	Herco	WAA12F114				23.0/1220	10,100 psi	
Rem. 209	Unique	Rem. SP12				22.5/1220	9,700 psi	
Rem. 209P	IMR 800-X	Rem. SP12				25.0/1220	9,300 LUP	
Win. 209	Blue Dot	Rem. SP12	33.0/1220	33.7/1240	34.4/1255	35.0/1275	10,300 psi	
Win. 209	Herco	Rem. SP12				24.5/1220	10,500 psi	
Win. 209	SR-4756	Rem. RP12	29.5/1215	30.7/1255	31.9/1300	33.0/1340	10,300 LUP	
Win. 209	SR-4756	WAA12R	30.5/1215	31.5/1250	32.5/1290	33.5/1325	9,800 LUP	
Win. 209	Unique	Rem. SP12				23.0/1220	10,600 psi	
VICTORY: PLASTIC						1¹/₄ OUNCES LEAD SHOT		
Fed. 209	Universal	Rem. SP12				24.0/1220	10,200 psi	
Fio. 616	Universal	WAA12F114				24.0/1220	10,900 psi	
Win. 209	HS-6	Rem. 12H				35.0/1330	9,200 LUP	
Win. 209	Universal	Rem. SP12				24.0/1220	10,900 psi	
WINCHESTER: COMPRESSION-FORMED AA TYPE						1¹/₄ OUNCES LEAD SHOT		
CCI 109	W 473AA	WAA12				24.5/1220	9,800 LUP	
CCI 109	W 540	WAA12				34.5/1330	10,800 LUP	
CCI 209	Solo 1250	WAA12R				26.0/1220	10,100 LUP	
CCI 209	Universal	WAA12F114				23.5/1220	10,000 psi	
CCI 209	WSF	Rem. RXP12				29.0/1275	10,400 psi	
CCI 209	WSF	Rem. SP12				28.0/1330	9,800 psi	
CCI 209M	Blue Dot	WAA12F114	35.0/1275	35.5/1295	36.0/1310	36.5/1330	9,500 psi	
CCI 209M	Herco	WAA12F114	24.0/1220	25.0/1240	26.0/1255	27.0/1275	10,700 psi	
CCI 209M	Unique	WAA12F114				23.5/1220	9,900 psi	

Caution: Follow load recipes exactly; do not substitute components, exceed listed maximums or load less than listed minimums.

Primer	Powder Type	Wad	Powder Charge (grains) / Velocity (fps) Minimum		Maximum	Maximum Pressure	Load Notes
WINCHESTER: COMPRESSION-FORMED AA TYPE (CONT.)					1¼ OUNCES LEAD SHOT		
CCI 209SC	Universal	WAA12F114			22.0/1220	10,700 psi	
Fed. 209	Blue Dot	WAA12F114	32.0/1275	32.5/1295	33.0/1310	33.5/1330	10,500 psi
Fed. 209	Herco	WAA12F114	24.0/1220	24.7/1240	25.4/1255	26.0/1275	10,700 psi
Fed. 209	IMR 800-X	Fed. 12S4			24.5/1225	9,900 LUP	
Fed. 209	IMR 800-X	H. Versalite			27.5/1325	10,900 LUP	
Fed. 209	IMR 800-X	H. Versalite			24.5/1230	9,400 LUP	
Fed. 209	IMR 800-X	Lage Uniwad	25.0/1230	26.0/1265	27.0/1295	28.0/1330	10,900 LUP
Fed. 209	IMR 800-X	Rem. SP12	24.5/1220	25.7/1260	26.9/1295	28.0/1335	10,800 LUP
Fed. 209	IMR 800-X	WAA12F114	24.5/1220	25.5/1255	26.5/1295	27.5/1330	10,900 LUP
Fed. 209	IMR 800-X	Windjammer	24.5/1210	25.7/1250	26.9/1295	28.0/1335	9,700 LUP
Fed. 209	IMR PB	Rem. RP12			23.5/1210	10,000 LUP	
Fed. 209	IMR PB	WAA12R			24.5/1220	9,500 LUP	
Fed. 209	Solo 1250	WAA12R			25.5/1220	10,200 LUP	
Fed. 209	SR-4756	Rem. RP12	30.0/1220	31.0/1255	32.0/1295	33.0/1330	10,000 LUP
Fed. 209	SR-4756	WAA12R	31.0/1225	31.8/1255	32.6/1290	33.5/1320	9,300 LUP
Fed. 209	SR-7625	Rem. RP12			28.5/1320	10,800 LUP	
Fed. 209	SR-7625	Rem. SP12			26.0/1215	8,600 LUP	
Fed. 209	SR-7625	WAA12R	26.5/1225	27.5/1260	28.5/1295	29.5/1330	10,300 LUP
Fed. 209	Unique	WAA12F114			23.0/1220	10,000 psi	
Fed. 209	Universal	Fed. 12S4			23.5/1220	10,200 psi	
Fed. 209	W 473AA	WAA12			25.0/1220	10,500 LUP	
Fed. 209A	Solo 1250	WAA12R			25.5/1220	10,200 LUP	
Fio. 616	Blue Dot	WAA12F114			34.0/1275	8,600 psi	
Fio. 616	Herco	WAA12F114	25.0/1220	25.3/1240	25.6/1255	26.0/1275	10,100 psi
Fio. 616	Unique	WAA12F114			23.0/1220	10,300 psi	
Fio. 616	Universal	Rem. SP12			24.5/1220	9,600 psi	
Rem. 209P	Herco	WAA12F114	25.5/1220	26.0/1240	26.5/1255	27.0/1275	9,400 psi
Rem. 209P	Solo 1250	WAA12R			25.5/1220	10,300 LUP	
Rem. 209P	Unique	WAA12F114			24.0/1220	10,000 psi	
Win. 209	Blue Dot	Activ T-35	34.5/1275	35.2/1295	35.9/1310	36.5/1330	9,700 psi
Win. 209	Blue Dot	Fed. 12S4			34.0/1275	10,500 psi	
Win. 209	Blue Dot	Rem. RP12			38.0/1330	10,200 psi	
Win. 209	Blue Dot	Rem. SP12	35.0/1275	35.7/1295	36.4/1310	37.0/1330	10,300 psi
Win. 209	Blue Dot	WAA12F114			34.5/1275	9,900 psi	
Win. 209	Blue Dot	WAA12F114			37.0/1330	10,600 psi	
Win. 209	Herco	Activ T-35	24.5/1220	25.0/1240	25.5/1255	26.0/1275	10,700 psi
Win. 209	Herco	Fed. 12S4	25.0/1220	25.3/1240	25.6/1255	26.0/1275	10,700 psi
Win. 209	Herco	H. Versalite			25.5/1220	8,500 psi	
Win. 209	Herco	WAA12F114	25.0/1220	25.5/1240	26.0/1255	26.5/1275	10,700 psi
Win. 209	HS-6	Fed. 12C1	32.0/1220	33.0/1255	34.0/1295	35.0/1330	10,400 LUP
Win. 209	HS-6	Rem. R12H	31.5/1220	32.7/1255	33.9/1295	35.0/1330	10,600 LUP
Win. 209	HS-6	WAA12F114	30.0/1220	31.0/1255	32.0/1295	33.0/1330	10,500 LUP
Win. 209	IMR 800-X	Fed. 12S4			24.5/1215	9,200 LUP	

Caution: Follow load recipes exactly; do not substitute components, exceed listed maximums or load less than listed minimums.

Primer	Powder Type	Wad	Powder Charge (grains) / Velocity (fps) Minimum			Maximum	Maximum Pressure	Load Notes
WINCHESTER: COMPRESSION-FORMED AA TYPE (CONT.)						**1¹/₄ OUNCES LEAD SHOT**		
Win. 209	IMR 800-X	H. Versalite	24.5/1215	25.5/1250	26.5/1290	27.5/1325	10,400 LUP	
Win. 209	IMR 800-X	Lage Uniwad	25.0/1220	26.0/1260	27.0/1300	28.0/1340	10,500 LUP	
Win. 209	IMR 800-X	Rem. SP12	25.0/1230	26.0/1265	27.0/1295	28.0/1330	10,200 LUP	
Win. 209	IMR 800-X	WAA12F114	25.0/1225	25.8/1255	26.6/1290	27.5/1320	10,300 LUP	
Win. 209	IMR 800-X	Windjammer	25.0/1215	26.2/1255	27.4/1295	28.5/1335	9,600 LUP	
Win. 209	IMR PB	Rem. RP12				24.0/1215	9,800 LUP	
Win. 209	IMR PB	WAA12R				25.0/1220	8,900 LUP	
Win. 209	Solo 1250	Activ T-35				25.0/1220	10,200 LUP	
Win. 209	Solo 1250	WAA12R	25.5/1220	26.0/1240	26.5/1255	27.0/1275	10,900 LUP	
Win. 209	Solo 1500	WAA12R				34.5/1330	10,600 LUP	
Win. 209	SR-4756	Rem. RP12	30.5/1215	31.5/1255	32.5/1295	33.5/1335	9,900 LUP	
Win. 209	SR-4756	WAA12R	31.0/1210	32.0/1250	33.0/1290	34.0/1330	9,200 LUP	
Win. 209	SR-7625	Rem. RP12				29.0/1330	10,700 LUP	
Win. 209	SR-7625	Rem. SP12				26.5/1215	8,200 LUP	
Win. 209	SR-7625	WAA12R	27.0/1215	28.0/1255	29.0/1295	30.0/1335	10,200 LUP	
Win. 209	Unique	Activ T-35				22.5/1220	10,700 psi	
Win. 209	Unique	Fed. 12S4				23.5/1220	10,400 psi	
Win. 209	Unique	H. Versalite				24.0/1220	9,800 psi	
Win. 209	Unique	Rem. RP12				22.5/1220	9,500 psi	
Win. 209	Unique	WAA12F114				23.5/1220	9,900 psi	
Win. 209	Universal	WAA12F114				23.0/1220	10,900 psi	
Win. 209	W 473AA	Rem. RXP12	23.5/1150	24.0/1175	24.5/1195	25.0/1220	10,100 LUP	
Win. 209	W 473AA	WAA12	23.5/1150	24.0/1175	24.5/1195	25.0/1220	10,300 LUP	
Win. 209	W 473AA	WAA12F114	23.5/1150	24.0/1175	24.5/1195	25.0*/1220	10,100 LUP	*Note 3
Win. 209	W 540	Fed. 12C1	32.0/1220	33.0/1255	34.0/1295	35.0/1330	10,200 LUP	
Win. 209	W 540	Rem. R12H	31.5/1220	33.0/1255	34.0/1295	35.0/1330	10,300 LUP	
Win. 209	W 540	WAA12	31.5/1220	33.0/1255	33.8/1295	34.5/1330	10,100 LUP	
Win. 209	W 540	WAA12F114	30.0/1220	31.0/1255	32.0/1295	33.0/1330	10,400 LUP	
Win. 209	WSF	Fed. 12S4				26.0/1220	27.5/1275	10,900 psi	
Win. 209	WSF	WAA12F114	28.0/1275	28.5/1295	29.0/1310	29.5*/1330	10,600 psi	*Note 4
WINCHESTER: POLYFORMED (PLASTIC BASE WAD)						**1¹/₄ OUNCES LEAD SHOT**		
Win. 209	W 540	Rem. R12H				35.0/1330	8,400 LUP	

Load Notes: 3 = This load duplicates ballistics of Winchester's 3¹/₄ dram equivalent Xpert loading. 4 = This load duplicates ballistics of Winchester's 3³/₄ dram equivalent. Super-X loading.

Caution: Follow load recipes exactly; do not substitute components, exceed listed maximums or load less than listed minimums.

Primer	Powder Type	Wad	Powder Charge (grains) / Velocity (fps) Minimum		Maximum	Maximum Pressure	Load Notes
ACTIV: ALL PLASTIC					**1³/₈ OUNCES LEAD SHOT**		
CCI 209	Blue Dot	Rem. RP12			40.0/1295	8,500 psi	
CCI 209	Herco	Activ T-35			30.5/1295	10,300 psi	
CCI 209M	Blue Dot	Activ T-35			38.5/1295	8,700 psi	
CCI 209M	Blue Dot	Rem. RP12			38.0/1295	9,400 psi	
CCI 209M	Herco	Activ T-35			29.5/1295	10,500 psi	
Fed. 209	Blue Dot	Activ T-35	38.0/1295	38.7/1315	39.4/1330 40.0/1350	10,100 psi	
Fed. 209	Blue Dot	Rem. RP12			37.0/1295	10,200 psi	
Fed. 209	IMR 800-X	Activ T-35			28.0/1295	9,300 LUP	
Rem. 209P	IMR 800-X	Activ T-35			28.0/1290	9,600 LUP	
Win. 209	Blue Dot	Activ T-35	39.0/1295	39.2/1315	39.4/1330 39.5/1350	10,100 psi	
Win. 209	Blue Dot	Rem. RP12			38.0/1295	9,500 psi	
Win. 209	IMR 800-X	Activ T-35			28.0/1295	9,200 LUP	
Win. 209	Solo 1500	Activ T-35			36.0/1295	10,500 LUP	
FEDERAL: GOLD MEDAL PLASTIC					**1³/₈ OUNCES LEAD SHOT**		
CCI 209M	Blue Dot	Rem. RP12	35.0/1240	35.5/1260	36.0/1275 36.5/1295	9,000 psi	
CCI 209M	IMR 800-X	Fed. 12S4			26.5/1290	10,600 LUP	
CCI 209M	IMR 800-X	Rem. SP12			28.0/1305	10,000 LUP	
CCI 209M	IMR 800-X	WAA12F114			27.5/1310	10,200 LUP	
Fed. 209	HS-7	Fed. 12S4			37.0/1285	10,100 LUP	
Fed. 209	IMR 800-X	Fed. 12S4			26.5/1280	10,900 LUP	
Fed. 209	IMR 800-X	Rem. SP12			28.0/1310	10,300 LUP	
Fed. 209	IMR 800-X	WAA12F114			27.5/1310	10,300 LUP	
Fed. 209	Solo 1500	Fed. 12S4			34.5/1295	10,700 LUP	
Fed. 209	SR-4756	Rem. RP12			34.0/1340	9,900 LUP	
Fed. 209	SR-4756	WAA12R			34.0/1315	8,600 LUP	
Fed. 209	SR-7625	Rem. RP12			31.5/1325	9,800 LUP	
Fed. 209	SR-7625	WAA12R			31.5/1305	9,300 LUP	
Fed. 209A	Blue Dot	Rem. RP12	34.0/1240	34.5/1260	35.0/1275 35.5/1295	10,700 psi	
Fed. 209A	Blue Dot	WAA12F114			33.0/1240	10,100 psi	
Rem. 209P	Blue Dot	Rem. RP12	36.0/1240	37.0/1260	38.0/1275 39.0/1295	8,600 psi	
Win. 209	Blue Dot	Rem. RP12	34.5/1240	35.0/1260	35.5/1275 36.0/1295	9,200 psi	
Win. 209	HS-7	Fed. 12S4			37.0/1285	11,200 psi	
Win. 209	HS-7	WAA12R			36.5/1285	10,100 LUP	
FEDERAL: ONE-PIECE PLASTIC HUNTING					**1³/₈ OUNCES LEAD SHOT**		
CCI 209M	Blue Dot	Rem. RP12			38.0/1295	9,200 psi	
CCI 209M	Blue Dot	Rem. SP12			37.5/1240	8,300 psi	
Fed. 209A	Blue Dot	Rem. RP12			38.5/1295	8,700 psi	
Fed. 209A	Blue Dot	Rem. SP12			37.0/1240	8,100 psi	
Fed. 209A	Blue Dot	WAA12F114			38.0/1240	7,900 psi	
Rem. 209	Blue Dot	Rem. RP12			38.5/1295	9,500 psi	
Win. 209	Blue Dot	Rem. RP12			38.5/1295	9,300 psi	
Win. 209	Blue Dot	Rem. SP12			37.5/1240	7,700 psi	

Caution: Follow load recipes exactly; do not substitute components, exceed listed maximums or load less than listed minimums.

Primer	Powder Type	Wad	Powder Charge (grains) / Velocity (fps) Minimum			Maximum	Maximum Pressure	Load Notes
FEDERAL: PLASTIC (PAPER BASE WAD)						**1³/₈ OUNCES LEAD SHOT**		
CCI 209M	Blue Dot	Rem. RP12	39.0/1295	39.2/1315	39.4/1330	39.5/1350	9,600 psi	
Fed. 209	Solo 1500	Fed. 12S4				35.0/1295	10,900 LUP	
Fed. 209	Solo 1500	Rem. RP12				37.0/1295	9,500 LUP	
Fed. 209	SR-4756	Rem. RP12				33.0/1255	8,400 LUP	
Fed. 209	SR-4756	WAA12R				34.0/1285	8,600 LUP	
Fed. 209	SR-7625	Rem. RP12				30.5/1305	10,300 LUP	
Fed. 209	SR-7625	WAA12R				32.0/1340	10,900 LUP	
Fed. 209A	Blue Dot	Rem. RP12	38.5/1295	38.8/1315	39.1/1330	39.5/1350	9,700 psi	
Fed. 209A	Blue Dot	Rem. SP12				38.0/1295	9,000 psi	
Fed. 209A	Blue Dot	WAA12				37.5/1295	8,500 psi	
Fed. 209A	Blue Dot	WAA12F114				37.5/1295	9,100 psi	
Rem. 209P	Blue Dot	Rem. RP12				39.0/1295	8,400 psi	
Win. 209	Blue Dot	Rem. RP12	39.0/1295	39.3/1315	39.6/1330	40.0/1350	9,600 psi	
FIOCCHI: PURPLE TARGET (HIGH BASE WAD)						**1³/₈ OUNCES LEAD SHOT**		
CCI 209M	Blue Dot	Rem. RP12	37.0/1295	38.0/1315	39.0/1330	40.0/1350	10,100 psi	
Fed. 209	Blue Dot	Rem. RP12	36.0/1295	37.0/1315	38.0/1330	39.0/1350	10,200 psi	
Fio. 616	Blue Dot	Rem. RP12	38.0/1295	39.2/1315	40.4/1330	41.5/1350	9,400 psi	
Win. 209	Blue Dot	Rem. RP12	38.0/1295	38.7/1315	39.4/1330	40.0/1350	9,900 psi	
PETER BLUE MAGIC						**1³/₈ OUNCES LEAD SHOT**		
CCI 209	IMR 800-X	Rem. SP12				24.5/1220	10,600 LUP	
CCI 209	IMR 800-X	WAA12R				24.5/1220	10,300 LUP	
Rem. 209P	Solo 1500	Rem. RP12				32.5/1240	10,700 LUP	
Win. 209	SR-4756	WAA12R				30.0/1245	10,800 LUP	
Win. 209	W 571	Rem. SP12				38.0/1330	10,400 LUP	
Win. 209	W 571	WAA12R				38.5/1330	10,000 LUP	
REMINGTON: PREMIER & NITRO 27 & STS						**1³/₈ OUNCES LEAD SHOT**		
CCI 209M	Blue Dot	Rem. RP12				35.5/1295	10,400 psi	
CCI 209M	Blue Dot	Rem. SP12				34.0/1240	9,400 psi	
Fed. 209	Blue Dot	Rem. RP12				35.5/1295	10,500 psi	
Fed. 209	Blue Dot	Rem. SP12				35.0/1240	9,100 psi	
Fio. 616	Blue Dot	Rem. RP12				35.5/1295	10,000 psi	
Fio. 616	Blue Dot	Rem. SP12				34.0/1240	9,100 psi	
Rem. 209P	Blue Dot	Activ T-35	34.0/1240	34.8/1260	35.6/1275	36.5/1295	9,900 psi	
Rem. 209P	Blue Dot	Rem. SP12	35.0/1240	35.8/1260	36.6/1275	37.5/1295	10,300 psi	
Rem. 209P	Solo 1500	Rem. RP12				32.5/1240	10,900 LUP	
Win. 209	Blue Dot	Rem. RP12				35.5/1295	10,500 psi	
Win. 209	Blue Dot	Rem. SP12				35.0/1240	9,100 psi	
Win. 209	HS-7	Rem. R12H				38.0/1220	10,100 LUP	
Win. 209	HS-7	WAA12R				38.5/1220	9,900 LUP	
REMINGTON: RXP						**1³/₈ OUNCES LEAD SHOT**		
Win. 209	W 571	Rem. RP12				37.5/1295	10,000 LUP	
Win. 209	W 571	WAA12F114				34.0/1250	10,500 LUP	

Caution: Follow load recipes exactly; do not substitute components, exceed listed maximums or load less than listed minimums.

Primer	Powder Type	Wad	Powder Charge (grains) / Velocity (fps) Minimum	Maximum	Maximum Pressure	Load Notes
REMINGTON: RXP (CONT.)				1³/₈ OUNCES LEAD SHOT		
Win. 209	W 571	WAA12R		37.5/1295	10,100 LUP	
REMINGTON: UNIBODY (INTEGRAL PLASTIC BASE WAD)				1³/₈ OUNCES LEAD SHOT		
CCI 209	Blue Dot	Rem. RP12		36.0/1240	10,100 psi	
CCI 209M	Blue Dot	Rem. RP12		32.5/1240	10,500 psi	
CCI 209M	IMR 800-X	Lage Uniwad		24.0/1200	10,800 LUP	
Rem. 209P	IMR 800-X	Activ T-35		25.5/1210	10,600 LUP	
Rem. 209P	IMR 800-X	Rem. RP12		25.5/1215	10,800 LUP	
Rem. 209P	IMR 800-X	WAA12R		25.5/1220	10,100 LUP	
WINCHESTER: COMPRESSION-FORMED AA TYPE				1³/₈ OUNCES LEAD SHOT		
CCI 209M	Blue Dot	WAA12F114		33.5/1240	8,300 psi	
Fed. 209	Blue Dot	WAA12F114		32.0/1240	10,100 psi	
Fed. 209	HS-7	Rem. RP12		35.5/1285	10,200 LUP	
Fed. 209	HS-7	WAA12R		35.5/1285	10,400 LUP	
Fed. 209	IMR 800-X	Rem. SP12		25.5/1205	10,700 LUP	
Fed. 209	IMR 800-X	WAA12R		25.5/1225	10,300 LUP	
Fed. 209	SR-4756	Rem. RP12		32.0/1270	10,700 LUP	
Fed. 209	SR-4756	WAA12R		32.5/1280	10,400 LUP	
Fed. 209	W 571	Rem. RP12		35.5/1285	10,100 LUP	
Fed. 209	W 571	WAA12R		35.5/1285	10,500 LUP	
Win. 209	Blue Dot	Fed. 12S4		33.0/1240	10,400 psi	
Win. 209	Blue Dot	Rem. SP12		33.0/1240	10,600 psi	
Win. 209	Blue Dot	WAA12F114		34.0/1240	10,500 psi	
Win. 209	HS-7	WAA12R		35.5/1285	10,300 LUP	
Win. 209	IMR 800-X	Rem. SP12		26.0/1235	10,300 LUP	
Win. 209	IMR 800-X	WAA12R		26.0/1250	10,500 LUP	
Win. 209	Solo 1500	WAA12R		32.0/1240	10,800 LUP	
Win. 209	SR-4756	Rem. RP12		32.0/1260	10,300 LUP	
Win. 209	SR-4756	WAA12R		32.5/1265	10,000 LUP	
Win. 209	W 540	WAA12F114		32.0/1275	10,300 LUP	
Win. 209	W 571	WAA12F114		36.0/1285	10,300 LUP	

Caution: Follow load recipes exactly; do not substitute components, exceed listed maximums or load less than listed minimums.

12-GAUGE 2³/₄"   1½ OUNCES LEAD SHOT

Primer	Powder Type	Wad	Powder Charge (grains) / Velocity (fps) Minimum		Maximum	Maximum Pressure	Load Notes
ACTIV: ALL PLASTIC					**1½ OUNCES LEAD SHOT**		
CCI 209	Blue Dot	Activ T-42			38.5/1260	9,600 psi	
CCI 209M	Blue Dot	Activ T-42	34.0/1150	34.8/1185	35.6/1225 36.5/1260	10,200 psi	
CCI 209M	Blue Dot	Rem. RP12	34.5/1150	34.8/1185	35.1/1225 35.5/1260	10,000 psi	
Fed. 209	Blue Dot	Activ T-42			32.5/1150	8,600 psi	
Fed. 209	IMR 800-X	Activ T-35			28.0/1250	11,000 LUP	
Fed. 209	SR-4756	Activ T-42			31.0/1240	11,000 LUP	
Fio. 616	Blue Dot	Activ T-42			33.5/1150	9,100 psi	
Rem. 209P	Blue Dot	Activ T-42			34.0/1150	8,200 psi	
Rem. 209P	IMR 800-X	Activ T-35			28.0/1245	9,600 LUP	
Rem. 209P	SR-4756	Activ T-42			32.0/1250	11,000 LUP	
Win. 209	Blue Dot	Activ T-42	33.0/1150	34.0/1185	35.0/1225 36.0/1260	10,400 psi	
Win. 209	Blue Dot	Rem. RP12			35.5/1260	9,900 psi	
Win. 209	HS-7	Activ T-35			38.0/1260	10,900 LUP	
Win. 209	IMR 800-X	Activ T-35			27.5/1245	10,900 LUP	
Win. 209	SR-4756	Activ T-42			32.0/1245	11,000 LUP	
ESTATE: CHEDITE (LOW BASE WAD)					**1½ OUNCES LEAD SHOT**		
Fio. 616	HS-7	WAA12R			36.0/1260	10,600 psi	
Win. 209	HS-7	WAA12R			36.0/1260	10,600 psi	
FEDERAL: GOLD MEDAL PLASTIC					**1½ OUNCES LEAD SHOT**		
CCI 209M	Blue Dot	Activ T-42			32.5/1150	9,400 psi	
CCI 209M	Blue Dot	Rem. RP12			34.0/1205	9,400 psi	
CCI 209M	IMR 800-X	Rem. RP12			27.5/1245	10,800 LUP	
CCI 209M	IMR 800-X	WAA12R			27.0/1265	10,600 LUP	
Fed. 209	HS-7	Fed. 12S4			37.0/1260	10,900 LUP	
Fed. 209	IMR 800-X	Rem. RP12			27.5/1255	10,900 LUP	
Fed. 209	IMR 800-X	WAA12R			27.0/1270	10,800 LUP	
Fed. 209	SR-4756	BP BPGS			32.0/1245	9,900 LUP	Note 1
Fed. 209A	Blue Dot	Rem. RP12	33.5/1150	33.7/1170	33.9/1185 34.0/1205	9,700 psi	
Fed. 209A	Herco	Rem. RP12			25.5/1150	10,100 psi	
Fio. 616	Blue Dot	Activ T-42			32.0/1150	9,700 psi	
Rem. 209P	Blue Dot	Activ T-42			32.5/1150	9,300 psi	
Rem. 209P	Blue Dot	Rem. RP12			35.5/1205	8,100 psi	
Win. 209	Blue Dot	Activ T-42			32.5/1150	9,200 psi	
Win. 209	Blue Dot	Rem. RP12			34.5/1205	9,900 psi	
Win. 209	HS-7	WAA12R			37.0/1260	10,900 LUP	
FEDERAL: ONE-PIECE PLASTIC HUNTING					**1½ OUNCES LEAD SHOT**		
CCI 209M	Blue Dot	Rem. RP12	36.0/1205	36.7/1225	37.4/1240 38.0/1260	10,000 psi	
CCI 209M	Herco	Fed. 12S4			26.5/1150	10,000 psi	
Fed. 209A	Blue Dot	Rem. RP12			36.0/1205	8,800 psi	
Fed. 209A	Blue Dot	Rem. RP12			38.0/1205		
Fed. 209A	Herco	Activ T-35			26.5/1150	8,500 psi	

Load Notes: 1 = Ballistic Products Filler.

Caution: Follow load recipes exactly; do not substitute components, exceed listed maximums or load less than listed minimums.

Primer	Powder Type	Wad	Powder Charge (grains) / Velocity (fps) Minimum			Maximum	Maximum Pressure	Load Notes
FEDERAL: ONE-PIECE PLASTIC HUNTING (CONT.)						**1½ OUNCES LEAD SHOT**		
Fed. 209A	Herco	Fed. 12S4				27.0/1150	9,200 psi	
Fed. 209A	Herco	Rem. SP12				27.0/1150	8,600 psi	
Fed. 209A	Herco	WAA12F114				26.5/1150	8,700 psi	
Fio. 616	Herco	Fed. 12S4				26.0/1150	10,100 psi	
Rem. 209	Blue Dot	Rem. RP12	36.0/1205	36.7/1225	37.4/1240	38.0/1260	8,700 psi	
Rem. 209P	Herco	Fed. 12S4				26.5/1150	9,900 psi	
Win. 209	Blue Dot	Rem. RP12	37.0/1205	37.3/1225	37.6/1240	38.0/1260	9,100 psi	
Win. 209	Herco	Fed. 12S4				26.5/1150	10,100 psi	
FEDERAL: PLASTIC (PAPER BASE WAD)						**1½ OUNCES LEAD SHOT**		
CCI 209M	Blue Dot	Activ T-42				33.5/1150	7,900 psi	
CCI 209M	Blue Dot	Rem. RP12	35.0/1205	35.7/1225	36.4/1240	37.0/1260	9,500 psi	
Fed. 209	SR-4756	WAA12R				30.0/1160	8,500 LUP	
Fed. 209	SR-7625	WAA12R				27.0/1150	8,900 LUP	
Fed. 209A	Blue Dot	Activ T-42				32.5/1150	9,100 psi	
Fed. 209A	Blue Dot	Rem. RP12	33.5/1150	34.0/1180	34.5/1205	36.0/1260	9,500 psi	
Fed. 209A	Blue Dot	Rem. SP12				37.0/1260	9,600 psi	
Fed. 209A	Herco	Rem. SP12				26.5/1150	8,900 psi	
Fio. 616	Blue Dot	Activ T-42				32.5/1150	9,500 psi	
Rem. 209P	Blue Dot	Activ T-42				33.0/1150	8,800 psi	
Win. 209	Blue Dot	Activ T-42				32.5/1150	9,500 psi	
Win. 209	Blue Dot	Rem. RP12	34.5/1205	35.3/1225	36.1/1240	37.0/1260	9,900 psi	
FIOCCHI: PURPLE TARGET (HIGH BASE WAD)						**1½ OUNCES LEAD SHOT**		
CCI 209M	Blue Dot	Activ T-42				34.0/1150	8,500 psi	
CCI 209M	Blue Dot	Rem. RP12				33.0/1205	9,500 psi	
CCI 209M	Blue Dot	Rem. RP12				36.5/1260	10,600 psi	
Fed. 209	Blue Dot	Activ T-42				32.5/1150	8,100 psi	
Fed. 209	Blue Dot	Rem. RP12				34.5/1205	8,500 psi	
Fio. 616	Blue Dot	Activ T-42				32.5/1150	9,000 psi	
Fio. 616	Blue Dot	Rem. RP12	32.5/1150	33.8/1170	35.1/1185	36.5/1205	9,000 psi	
Fio. 616	Blue Dot	Rem. RP12				37.5/1260	9,600 psi	
Fio. 616	HS-7	WAA12R				39.0/1260	10,800 LUP	
Rem. 209P	Blue Dot	Activ T-42				33.5/1150	8,300 psi	
Win. 209	Blue Dot	Activ T-42				33.5/1150	8,700 psi	
Win. 209	Blue Dot	Rem. RP12				35.5/1205	8,600 psi	
Win. 209	Blue Dot	Rem. RP12				36.5/1260	10,300 psi	
PETERS: BLUE MAGIC						**1½ OUNCES LEAD SHOT**		
Win. 209	W 571	Rem. RP12				36.0/1230	10,400 LUP	
Win. 209	W 571	WAA12R				35.5/1230	10,400 LUP	
REMINGTON: PREMIER & NITRO 27 & STS						**1½ OUNCES LEAD SHOT**		
CCI 209M	Blue Dot	Rem. RP12	31.0/1150	31.7/1170	32.4/1185	33.0/1205	10,100 psi	
Fed. 209	Blue Dot	Rem. RP12	31.0/1150	31.7/1170	32.4/1185	33.0/1205	10,300 psi	
Fed. 209	HS-7	Rem. R12H				36.0/1220	10,600 LUP	

Caution: Follow load recipes exactly; do not substitute components, exceed listed maximums or load less than listed minimums.

Primer	Powder Type	Wad	Powder Charge (grains) / Velocity (fps) Minimum			Maximum	Maximum Pressure	Load Notes
REMINGTON: PREMIER & NITRO 27 & STS (CONT.)						**1½ OUNCES LEAD SHOT**		
Fio. 616	Blue Dot	Rem. RP12	31.0/1150	31.7/1170	32.4/1185	33.0/1205	10,100 psi	
Rem. 209P	Blue Dot	Activ T-42	30.5/1150	30.8/1170	31.1/1185	31.5/1205	10,600 psi	
Rem. 209P	Blue Dot	Rem. RP12	31.0/1150	31.7/1170	32.4/1185	33.0/1205	10,200 psi	
Win. 209	Blue Dot	Rem. RP12	31.5/1150	32.0/1170	32.5/1185	33.0/1205	10,200 psi	
Win. 209	HS-7	WAA12R				35.5/1220	10,300 LUP	
REMINGTON: RXP						**1½ OUNCES LEAD SHOT**		
Win. 209	W 571	Rem. RP12				36.5/1240	10,400 LUP	
REMINGTON: UNIBODY (INTEGRAL PLASTIC BASE WAD)						**1½ OUNCES LEAD SHOT**		
CCI 209M	Blue Dot	Rem. RP12				32.0/1150	8,400 psi	
CCI 209M	IMR 800-X	WAA12R				22.0/1130	10,800 LUP	
Fed. 209	Blue Dot	Rem. RP12				31.5/1150	9,100 psi	
Fio. 616	Blue Dot	Rem. RP12				31.5/1150	9,200 psi	
Rem. 209P	Blue Dot	Activ T-42				31.5/1150	9,600 psi	
Rem. 209P	Blue Dot	Rem. RP12				32.5/1150	8,000 psi	
Rem. 209P	IMR 800-X	Activ T-35				22.5/1090	9,700 LUP	
Rem. 209P	IMR 800-X	Rem. RP12				24.0/1120	10,700 LUP	
Win. 209	Blue Dot	Rem. RP12				32.0/1150	8,300 psi	
WINCHESTER: COMPRESSION-FORMED AA TYPE						**1½ OUNCES LEAD SHOT**		
CCI 109	W 571	Win. WAA12R				35.5/1260	10,500 LUP	
CCI 209M	Blue Dot	Activ T-42				30.0/1150	10,400 psi	
Rem. 209P	Blue Dot	Activ T-42				30.0/1150	10,400 psi	
Win. 209	Blue Dot	Activ T-42				30.0/1150	10,000 psi	
Win. 209	Blue Dot	Rem. RP12				31.0/1150	9,400 psi	
Win. 209	HS-7	Rem. RP12				36.5/1260	9,900 LUP	
Win. 209	HS-7	WAA12R				36.5/1260	10,400 LUP	
Win. 209	W 540	Rem. RP12				27.5/1095	8,700 LUP	
Win. 209	W 540	WAA12R				27.5/1095	8,500 LUP	
Win. 209	W 571	Rem. RP12				36.5/1260	9,800 LUP	
Win. 209	W 571	WAA12R				36.5/1260	10,300 LUP	
WINCHESTER: POLYFORMED (PLASTIC BASE WAD)						**1½ OUNCES LEAD SHOT**		
Win. 209	W 540	WAA12R				33.5/1260	8,900 LUP	

Caution: Follow load recipes exactly; do not substitute components, exceed listed maximums or load less than listed minimums.

Primer	Powder Type	Wad	Powder Charge (grains) / Velocity (fps) Minimum	Maximum	Maximum Pressure	Load Notes
ACTIV: ALL PLASTIC				**1⅝ OUNCES LEAD SHOT**		
CCI 209M	Blue Dot	Activ T-42		31.5/1115	9,600 psi	
Fed. 209	Blue Dot	Activ T-42		31.0/1115	9,100 psi	
Fio. 616	Blue Dot	Activ T-42		31.0/1115	9,200 psi	
Rem. 209P	Blue Dot	Activ T-42		31.5/1115	9,400 psi	
Win. 209	Blue Dot	Activ T-42		31.5/1115	9,500 psi	
FIOCCHI: PURPLE TARGET (HIGH BASE WAD)				**1⅝ OUNCES LEAD SHOT**		
CCI 209M	Blue Dot	Activ T-42		31.5/1115	8,900 psi	
Fed. 209	Blue Dot	Activ T-42		31.0/1115	9,300 psi	
Fio. 616	Blue Dot	Activ T-42		31.0/1115	9,600 psi	
Rem. 209P	Blue Dot	Activ T-42		31.5/1115	8,600 psi	
Win. 209	Blue Dot	Activ T-42		31.0/1115	9,000 psi	
REMINGTON: UNIBODY (INTEGRAL PLASTIC BASE WAD)				**1⅝ OUNCES LEAD SHOT**		
CCI 209M	Blue Dot	Activ T-42		29.5/1115	10,300 psi	
Fed. 209A	Blue Dot	Activ T-42		29.0/1115	10,400 psi	
Fio. 616	Blue Dot	Activ T-42		29.5/1115	10,400 psi	
Rem. 209P	Blue Dot	Activ T-42		29.5/1115	10,500 psi	
Win. 209	Blue Dot	Activ T-42		29.5/1115	10,400 psi	

Caution: Follow load recipes exactly; do not substitute components, exceed listed maximums or load less than listed minimums.

12-GAUGE 3″ — 1¼ OUNCES LEAD SHOT

Primer	Powder Type	Wad	Powder Charge (grains) / Velocity (fps) Minimum		Maximum	Maximum Pressure	Load Notes
FEDERAL: PLASTIC (PAPER BASE WAD)					1¼ OUNCES LEAD SHOT		
Fed. 209	IMR 800-X	Fed. 12S3			33.0/1420	9,700 LUP	Note 1
Fed. 209	IMR PB	Fed. 12S4			31.0/1365	10,300 LUP	
Fed. 209	SR-7625	WAA12			37.0/1440	9,400 LUP	
Win. 209	IMR PB	WAA12			33.0/1400	10,400 LUP	
Win. 209	SR-7625	Fed. 12S4			37.0/1470	10,900 LUP	
WINCHESTER: COMPRESSION-FORMED AA TYPE					1¼ OUNCES LEAD SHOT		
Fed. 209	SR-7625	Rem. RXP12			32.0/1375	10,300 LUP	
Fed. 209	SR-7625	WAA12			33.0/1400	10,400 LUP	
Win. 209	IMR PB	Rem. RXP12			28.0/1310	10,100 LUP	
Win. 209	IMR PB	WAA12			29.0/1325	9,800 LUP	

Load Notes: 1 = Add one 20-gauge, 0.135″ card inside bottom of shotcup.

12-GAUGE 3″ — 1³⁄₈ OUNCES LEAD SHOT

Primer	Powder Type	Wad	Powder Charge (grains) / Velocity (fps) Minimum		Maximum	Maximum Pressure	Load Notes
ACTIV: ALL PLASTIC					1³⁄₈ OUNCES LEAD SHOT		
CCI 209M	Blue Dot	Activ T32			43.0/1350	8,300 psi	
CCI 209M	Blue Dot	Fed. 12S3			41.5/1350	8,600 psi	
CCI 209M	Blue Dot	Rem. RXP12			42.5/1350	7,900 psi	
CCI 209M	Blue Dot	WAA12			40.5/1350	8,700 psi	
CCI 209M	Herco	Activ T32			33.5/1350	10,700 psi	
CCI 209M	Herco	Fed. 12S3			31.5/1295	10,400 psi	
CCI 209M	Herco	Rem. RXP12	31.5/1295	32.3/1325	33.0/1350	10,400 psi	
CCI 209M	Herco	WAA12			31.5/1295	10,100 psi	
Win. 209	Solo 1500	Activ T-35			39.0/1350	9,400 LUP	
FEDERAL: ONE-PIECE PLASTIC HUNTING					1³⁄₈ OUNCES LEAD SHOT		
Fed. 209A	Blue Dot	Fed. 12S3			40.5/1295	7,900 psi	
Fed. 209A	Blue Dot	Rem. RXP12			42.0/1350	8,000 psi	
Fed. 209A	Blue Dot	WAA12	38.0/1295	41.0/1325	44.0/1350	9,900 psi	
Fed. 209A	Herco	Fed. 12S3			31.0/1295	10,500 psi	
Fed. 209A	Herco	Rem. RXP12			32.0/1295	10,100 psi	
FEDERAL: PLASTIC (PAPER BASE WAD)					1³⁄₈ OUNCES LEAD SHOT		
Fed. 209	IMR 800-X	Fed. 12S3	29.5/1295	30.8/1325	32.0/1355	10,000 LUP	
Fed. 209	IMR 800-X	Fed. 12S3			26.5/1200	7,000 LUP	Note 1
Fed. 209	SR-4756	Rem. SP12			42.0/1460	10,400 LUP	
Fed. 209	SR-4756	WAA12R			43.0/1480	10,800 LUP	
Fed. 209	SR-7625	Fed. 12S4			35.0/1375	10,600 LUP	
Fed. 209	SR-7625	Rem. R12H			35.0/1370	10,000 LUP	
Fed. 209A	Blue Dot	Fed. 12S4			40.0/1350	9,400 psi	

Load Notes: 1 = Add one 20-gauge, 0.135″ card inside bottom of shotcup.

Caution: Follow load recipes exactly; do not substitute components, exceed listed maximums or load less than listed minimums.

Primer	Powder Type	Wad	Powder Charge (grains) / Velocity (fps) Minimum		Maximum	Maximum Pressure	Load Notes
Federal: Plastic (paper base wad) (cont.)					**1³/₈ Ounces Lead Shot**		
Fed. 209A	Blue Dot	Rem. RXP12			38.0/1295	9,000 psi	
Fed. 209A	Blue Dot	Rem. SP12			40.0/1350	8,900 psi	
Fed. 209A	Blue Dot	WAA12F114			40.0/1350	9,800 psi	
Fed. 209A	Blue Dot	WAA12			38.0/1295	8,800 psi	
Fed. 209A	Herco	Fed. 12S3			30.5/1295	10,000 psi	
Fed. 209A	Herco	Rem. RXP12			30.5/1295	9,300 psi	
Fed. 209A	Herco	WAA12			30.5/1295	9,700 psi	
Win. 209	IMR PB	Fed. 12S4			29.0/1265	10,500 LUP	
Win. 209	IMR PB	WAA12			30.0/1275	10,500 LUP	
Fiocchi: Plastic (low base wad)					**1³/₈ Ounces Lead Shot**		
CCI 209M	Blue Dot	Fed. 12S3			37.0/1295	9,000 psi	
CCI 209M	Blue Dot	Fed. 12S4			38.0/1350	10,400 psi	
CCI 209M	Herco	Fed. 12S3			30.0/1295	10,000 psi	
Fio. 616	Herco	Activ T32			32.5/1350	10,300 psi	
Fio. 616	Herco	Fed. 12S3			31.5/1295	9,100 psi	
Fio. 616	Herco	Fed. 12S4			32.0/1350	10,700 psi	
Fio. 616	Herco	Fiocchi FTW1			31.0/1295	9,200 psi	
Fio. 616	Herco	Rem. RXP12			32.5/1295	8,600 psi	
Fio. 616	Herco	Rem. SP12			32.5/1350	10,100 psi	
Fio. 616	Herco	WAA12	31.5/1295	32.0/1325	32.5/1350	10,700 psi	
Win. 209	Blue Dot	Fed. 12S3			37.5/1295	8,800 psi	
Win. 209	Blue Dot	Fed. 12S4			38.5/1350	10,100 psi	
Win. 209	Herco	Fed. 12S3			29.5/1295	10,600 psi	
Remington: SP (separate black plastic base wad)					**1³/₈ Ounces Lead Shot**		
CCI 209M	Blue Dot	Fed. 12S3			42.0/1350	8,400 psi	
CCI 209M	Blue Dot	Rem. RXP12			42.5/1350	8,000 psi	
CCI 209M	Blue Dot	WAA12			42.0/1350	8,500 psi	
CCI 209M	Herco	Fed. 12S3			29.5/1295	10,000 psi	
CCI 209M	Herco	Rem. RXP12			30.0/1295	9,200 psi	Note 1
CCI 209M	Herco	WAA12			30.0/1295	10,000 psi	Note 1
Rem. 209P	HS-6	Rem. R12L			37.0/1295	9,400 LUP	
Rem. 209P	HS-6	WAA12			36.0/1295	9,900 LUP	
Rem. 209P	Solo 1500	Rem. SP12			39.0/1350	9,300 LUP	
Remington: Unibody (integral plastic base wad)					**1³/₈ Ounces Lead Shot**		
Win. 209	Alliant 2400	Activ T32			38.5/1350	9,800 psi	
Win. 209	Alliant 2400	Activ TG30			36.5/1295	9,200 psi	
Win. 209	Alliant 2400	Fed. 12S3			37.0/1295	9,300 psi	
Win. 209	Alliant 2400	Fed. 12S4			38.0/1350	10,200 psi	
Win. 209	Alliant 2400	Rem. RXP12	37.5/1295	38.0/1325	38.5/1350	9,900 psi	
Win. 209	Alliant 2400	WAA12F114			38.0/1350	10,500 psi	
Win. 209	Alliant 2400	WAA12			36.5/1295	9,400 psi	

Load Notes: 1 = Add one 20-gauge, 0.135″ card inside bottom of shotcup.

Caution: Follow load recipes exactly; do not substitute components, exceed listed maximums or load less than listed minimums.

Primer	Powder Type	Wad	Powder Charge (grains) / Velocity (fps) Minimum	Maximum	Maximum Pressure	Load Notes
REMINGTON: UNIBODY (INTEGRAL PLASTIC BASE WAD) (CONT.)				1³/₈ OUNCES LEAD SHOT		
Win. 209	Alliant 2400	Win. WAA12SL		35.5/1295	10,100 psi	
WINCHESTER: COMPRESSION-FORMED AA TYPE				1³/₈ OUNCES LEAD SHOT		
Fed. 209	HS-6	Rem R12L		35.0/1295	9,400 LUP	
Fed. 209	SR-4756	Rem. SP12		36.0/1365	10,600 LUP	
Fed. 209	SR-4756	WAA12F114		36.0/1380	10,800 LUP	
Fed. 209	SR-7625	Fed. 12S4		29.0/1260	10,800 LUP	
Fed. 209	SR-7625	Rem. RXP12		31.0/1310	10,700 LUP	
Win. 209	Blue Dot	Fed. 12S3		37.5/1295	10,300 psi	
Win. 209	Blue Dot	Fed. 12S4		40.0/1350	10,500 psi	
Win. 209	Blue Dot	Rem. RXP12		38.0/1295	9,400 psi	
Win. 209	Blue Dot	Rem. SP12		40.5/1350	9,300 psi	
Win. 209	Blue Dot	WAA12F114		39.0/1350	9,900 psi	
Win. 209	Blue Dot	WAA12		37.5/1295	10,000 psi	
Win. 209	HS-6	WAA12		35.5/1295	9,400 LUP	
Win. 209	SR-7625	WAA12		31.0/1290	10,000 LUP	
Win. 209	W 540	Rem. R12L		35.5/1295	9,500 LUP	
Win. 209	W 540	WAA12		35.0/1295	9,500 LUP	

12-GAUGE 3″ — 1¹/₂ OUNCES LEAD SHOT

Primer	Powder Type	Wad	Powder Charge (grains) / Velocity (fps) Minimum	Maximum	Maximum Pressure	Load Notes
ACTIV: ALL PLASTIC				1¹/₂ OUNCES LEAD SHOT		
CCI 209M	Blue Dot	Activ T35		41.0/1315	9,600 psi	
CCI 209M	Blue Dot	Fed. 12S4		40.5/1315	9,200 psi	
CCI 209M	Blue Dot	Rem. R12H		41.5/1315	8,500 psi	
CCI 209M	Blue Dot	WAA12F114		40.0/1315	9,800 psi	
FEDERAL: ONE-PIECE PLASTIC HUNTING				1¹/₂ OUNCES LEAD SHOT		
Fed. 209A	Blue Dot	Fed. 1234		40.0/1315	9,700 psi	
Fed. 209A	Blue Dot	Rem. SP12		40.0/1315	9,000 psi	
Fed. 209A	Blue Dot	WAA12F114		42.0/1315	9,800 psi	
FEDERAL: PLASTIC (PAPER BASE WAD)				1¹/₂ OUNCES LEAD SHOT		
CCI 209M	IMR 800-X	WAA12		30.0/1285	10,600 LUP	
Fed. 209	IMR 800-X	Fed. 12S3	27.5/1215 · 28.8/1250	30.0/1285	10,700 LUP	
Fed. 209	SR-4756	Rem. SP12		38.0/1350	10,600 LUP	
Fed. 209	SR-4756	WAA12R		39.0/1365	10,700 LUP	
Fed. 209	SR-7625	Fed. 12S4		31.0/1235	10,100 LUP	
Fed. 209A	Blue Dot	Activ TG30		38.0/1315	9,400 psi	
Fed. 209A	Blue Dot	Fed. 12S3		38.0/1315	9,700 psi	
Fed. 209A	Blue Dot	Rem. RXP12		38.5/1315	9,600 psi	
Fed. 209A	Blue Dot	WAA12		37.5/1315	9,800 psi	

Caution: Follow load recipes exactly; do not substitute components, exceed listed maximums or load less than listed minimums.

Primer	Powder Type	Wad	Powder Charge (grains) / Velocity (fps) Minimum	Maximum	Maximum Pressure	Load Notes
FEDERAL: PLASTIC (PAPER BASE WAD) (CONT.)				**1½ OUNCES LEAD SHOT**		
Win. 209	SR-7625	WAA12F114		33.0/1275	10,400 LUP	
FIOCCHI: PLASTIC (LOW BASE WAD)				**1½ OUNCES LEAD SHOT**		
CCI 209M	Blue Dot	Fed. 12S4		38.0/1315	10,400 psi	
Fio. 616	Blue Dot	Activ T35		39.0/1315	9,000 psi	
Fio. 616	Blue Dot	Fed. 12S4		39.0/1315	10,300 psi	
Fio. 616	Blue Dot	Rem. SP12		39.0/1315	9,700 psi	
Fio. 616	Blue Dot	WAA12F114		39.0/1315	9,400 psi	
Win. 209	Blue Dot	Fed. 12S4		39.0/1315	10,600 psi	
REMINGTON: UNIBODY (INTEGRAL PLASTIC BASE WAD)				**1½ OUNCES LEAD SHOT**		
CCI 209M	Blue Dot	Fed. 12S4		39.5/1315	9,800 psi	Note 1
CCI 209M	Blue Dot	Rem. SP12		40.0/1315	9,400 psi	Note 1
CCI 209M	Blue Dot	WAA12F114		39.5/1315	9,800 psi	Note 1
CCI 209M	Alliant 2400	Rem. SP12		37.5/1315	10,700 psi	
WINCHESTER: COMPRESSION-FORMED AA TYPE				**1½ OUNCES LEAD SHOT**		
Fed. 209	SR-4756	Rem. SP12		34.0/1290	10,900 LUP	
Fed. 209	SR-4756	WAA12R		33.0/1255	10,700 LUP	
Win. 209	Blue Dot	Rem. SP12		38.5/1315	10,300 psi	
Win. 209	SR-7625	Rem. SP12		29.0/1210	10,000 LUP	
Win. 209	SR-7625	WAA12F114		29.0/1205	10,200 LUP	

Load Notes: 1 = Add one 20-gauge, 0.135″ card inside bottom of shotcup.

1⅝ OUNCES LEAD SHOT   12-GAUGE 3″

Primer	Powder Type	Wad	Powder Charge (grains) / Velocity (fps) Minimum	Maximum	Maximum Pressure	Load Notes
ACTIV: ALL PLASTIC				**1⅝ OUNCES LEAD SHOT**		
CCI 209M	Blue Dot	Activ T35		39.0/1280	10,000 psi	
CCI 209M	Blue Dot	Fed. 12S4		39.5/1280	10,600 psi	
CCI 209M	Blue Dot	Rem. SP12		41.5/1280	10,100 psi	
CCI 209M	Blue Dot	WAA12F114		40.0/1280	9,900 psi	
Win. 209	Solo 1500	Activ T-42		36.0/1280	10,900 LUP	
FEDERAL: ONE-PIECE PLASTIC HUNTING				**1⅝ OUNCES LEAD SHOT**		
Fed. 209A	Blue Dot	Fed. 1234		40.0/1280	10,100 psi	
Fed. 209A	Blue Dot	Rem. SP12		40.0/1280	9,400 psi	
Fed. 209A	Blue Dot	WAA12F114		40.0/1280	10,000 psi	
FEDERAL: PLASTIC (PAPER BASE WAD)				**1⅝ OUNCES LEAD SHOT**		
CCI 209M	IMR 800-X	Lage Uniwad		28.5/1205	10,000 LUP	
Fed. 209	IMR 800-X	Fed. 12S4		28.0/1200	10,700 LUP	
Fed. 209	SR-4756	Rem. RP12		36.0/1280	10,900 LUP	
Fed. 209	SR-4756	WAA12R		36.0/1275	10,400 LUP	
Fed. 209	SR-7625	REM RP12		32.0/1215	10,500 LUP	

Caution: Follow load recipes exactly; do not substitute components, exceed listed maximums or load less than listed minimums.

12-GAUGE 3" — 1⅝ OUNCES LEAD SHOT (CONT.)

Primer	Powder Type	Wad	Powder Charge (grains) / Velocity (fps) Minimum	Maximum	Maximum Pressure	Load Notes
FEDERAL: PLASTIC (PAPER BASE WAD) (CONT.)				**1⅝ OUNCES LEAD SHOT**		
Fed. 209A	Blue Dot	Rem. SP12		39.0/1280	10,400 psi	
Fed. 209A	HS-7	Fed. 12S0		39.0/1250	10,800 psi	
Win. 209	HS-7	Activ TG-30		38.0/1250	10,400 psi	
Win. 209	HS-7	Fiocchi TL1		38.0/1250	10,400 psi	
Win. 209	SR-7625	WAA12R		32.0/1220	10,500 LUP	
FIOCCHI: PLASTIC (LOW BASE WAD)				**1⅝ OUNCES LEAD SHOT**		
Fio. 616	Blue Dot	Activ T32		39.0/1280	10,500 psi	
Fio. 616	Blue Dot	Fed. 12S4		39.0/1280	10,700 psi	
Fio. 616	Blue Dot	Rem. SP12		39.5/1280	9,700 psi	
Fio. 616	Blue Dot	WAA12F114		38.5/1280	10,500 psi	
REMINGTON: SP (SEPARATE BLACK PLASTIC BASE WAD)				**1⅝ OUNCES LEAD SHOT**		
CCI 209M	Blue Dot	Fed. 12S4		38.5/1280	10,200 psi	
CCI 209M	Blue Dot	Rem. SP12		39.0/1280	9,800 psi	
CCI 209M	Blue Dot	WAA12F114		38.5/1280	10,500 psi	
Rem. 209P	Solo 1500	Rem. RP12		37.5/1280	10,900 LUP	
WINCHESTER: COMPRESSION-FORMED AA TYPE				**1⅝ OUNCES LEAD SHOT**		
Fed. 209	SR-4756	WAA12R		32.0/1200	10,400 LUP	
Win. 209	Alliant 2400	Rem. RP12		50.0/1335	10,000 psi	
Win. 209	HS-7	Rem. 12H		36.0/1205	10,200 LUP	
Win. 209	HS-7	WAA12		36.0/1205	10,400 LUP	
Win. 209	SR-4756	Rem. RP12		32.0/1200	10,300 LUP	
Win. 209	W 571	Rem. R12H		36.0/1205	10,100 LUP	
Win. 209	W 571	WAA12		36.0/1205	10,500 LUP	

12-GAUGE 3" — 1¾ OUNCES LEAD SHOT

Primer	Powder Type	Wad	Powder Charge (grains) / Velocity (fps) Minimum	Maximum	Maximum Pressure	Load Notes
ACTIV: ALL PLASTIC				**1¾ OUNCES LEAD SHOT**		
CCI 209M	Blue Dot	Activ T32		40.0/1245	10,400 psi	
CCI 209M	Blue Dot	Rem. SP12		40.0/1245	10,700 psi	
FEDERAL: ONE-PIECE PLASTIC HUNTING				**1¾ OUNCES LEAD SHOT**		
Fed. 209A	Blue Dot	Rem. RP12		39.0/1245	10,500 psi	
FEDERAL: PLASTIC (PAPER BASE WAD)				**1¾ OUNCES LEAD SHOT**		
CCI 209M	IMR 800-X	Lage Uniwad		26.5/1120	10,600 LUP	
Fed. 209	IMR 800-X	Fed. 12S4		25.5/1105	10,500 LUP	
Fed. 209	SR-4756	Rem. RP12		33.0/1180	10,800 LUP	
Fed. 209	SR-4756	WAA12R		33.0/1175	10,600 LUP	
Fed. 209A	Blue Dot	Rem. RP12		39.0/1245	10,500 psi	
FIOCCHI: PLASTIC (LOW BASE WAD)				**1¾ OUNCES LEAD SHOT**		
Fio. 616	Blue Dot	Activ T32		37.5/1245	10,300 psi	

242 **Caution:** Follow load recipes exactly; do not substitute components, exceed listed maximums or load less than listed minimums.

1³/₄ Ounces Lead Shot (cont.)   12-Gauge 3″

Primer	Powder Type	Wad	Powder Charge (grains) / Velocity (fps) Minimum	Maximum	Maximum Pressure	Load Notes
REMINGTON: SP (SEPARATE BLACK PLASTIC BASE WAD)				1³/₄ OUNCES LEAD SHOT		
CCI 209M	Blue Dot	Activ T35		37.5/1245	10,400 psi	
CCI 209M	Blue Dot	Rem. RP12		38.5/1245	10,700 psi	
WINCHESTER: COMPRESSION-FORMED AA TYPE				1³/₄ OUNCES LEAD SHOT		
CCI 209	SR-4756	Rem. RP12		31.0/1135	10,000 LUP	
CCI 209	SR-4756	WAA12R		31.0/1140	10,300 LUP	
Win. 209	Alliant 2400	Rem. RP12		45.0/1245	9,900 psi	

1⁷/₈ Ounces Lead Shot   12-Gauge 3″

Primer	Powder Type	Wad	Powder Charge (grains) / Velocity (fps) Minimum	Maximum	Maximum Pressure	Load Notes
ACTIV: ALL PLASTIC				1⁷/₈ OUNCES LEAD SHOT		
CCI 209M	Blue Dot	Activ T35		36.5/1155	10,000 psi	
CCI 209M	Blue Dot	Rem. SP12		37.0/1155	10,200 psi	
FEDERAL: ONE-PIECE PLASTIC				1⁷/₈ OUNCES LEAD SHOT		
Fed. 209A	Blue Dot	Activ T35		35.5/1155	9,300 psi	
Fed. 209A	Blue Dot	Rem. SP12		36.5/1155	9,900 psi	
FEDERAL: PLASTIC (PAPER BASE WAD)				1⁷/₈ OUNCES LEAD SHOT		
Fed. 209	SR-4756	WAA12R	31.0/1110	33.0/1140	10,600 LUP	
Fed. 209A	Blue Dot	Activ T35		34.5/1155	10,100 psi	
Fed. 209A	Blue Dot	Rem. RP12		34.0/1155	10,500 psi	
Fed. 209A	Blue Dot	Rem. SP12		36.0/1155	10,300 psi	
Fed. 209A	HS-7	Fed. 12S3		33.0/1155	11,400 psi	
Fed. 209A	HS-7	WAA12		34.0/1155	10,600 psi	
Win. 209	HS-7	Activ TG-30		32.0/1155	10,200 psi	
Win. 209	HS-7	Fed. 12S3		33.0/1155	9,400 psi	
Win. 209	HS-7	Fiocchi TL1		33.0/1155	10,600 psi	
FIOCCHI: PLASTIC (LOW BASE WAD)				1⁷/₈ OUNCES LEAD SHOT		
CCI 209M	HS-7	Rem. R12H		30.5/1100	10,400 psi	
Fio. 616	Blue Dot	Activ T35		34.5/1155	10,300 psi	
Fio. 616	Blue Dot	Rem. RP12		34.5/1155	10,700 psi	
Fio. 616	HS-7	Rem. Fig.-8		34.0/1155	10,400 LUP	
Win. 209	HS-7	Rem. R12H		31.0/1100	10,600 psi	
REMINGTON: SP (SEPARATE BLACK PLASTIC BASE WAD)				1⁷/₈ OUNCES LEAD SHOT		
CCI 157	W 571	Rem. RP12		36.0/1140	10,500 LUP	
CCI 157	W 571	WAA12R		36.0/1140	10,500 LUP	
CCI 209M	Blue Dot	Activ T35		34.0/1155	10,100 psi	
CCI 209M	Blue Dot	Rem. RP12		34.0/1155	10,300 psi	
Rem. 209P	HS-7	Rem. RP12		36.0/1140	10,700 LUP	

Caution: Follow load recipes exactly; do not substitute components, exceed listed maximums or load less than listed minimums.

12-GAUGE 3″ — 1⁷/₈ OUNCES LEAD SHOT (CONT.)

Primer	Powder Type	Wad	Powder Charge (grains) / Velocity (fps) Minimum	Maximum	Maximum Pressure	Load Notes
REMINGTON: SP (SEPARATE BLACK PLASTIC BASE WAD) (CONT.)				1⁷/₈ OUNCES LEAD SHOT		
Rem. 209P	HS-7	WAA12R		36.0/1140	10,800 LUP	
WINCHESTER: COMPRESSION-FORMED AA TYPE				1⁷/₈ OUNCES LEAD SHOT		
Fed. 209	HS-7	Rem. RP12		34.0/1100	10,400 LUP	
Win. 209	HS-7	WAA12R		33.5/1100	10,600 LUP	
Win. 209	W 571	Rem. RP12		34.0/1100	10,100 LUP	
Win. 209	W 571	WAA12R		33.0/1100	10,500 LUP	

12-GAUGE 3″ — 2 OUNCES LEAD SHOT

Primer	Powder Type	Wad	Powder Charge (grains) / Velocity (fps) Minimum	Maximum	Maximum Pressure	Load Notes
ACTIV: ALL PLASTIC				2 OUNCES LEAD SHOT		
CCI 209M	Blue Dot	Rem. RP12		35.0/1120	10,600 psi	

Caution: Follow load recipes exactly; do not substitute components, exceed listed maximums or load less than listed minimums.

1⅞ OUNCES LEAD SHOT — 12-GAUGE 3½"

Primer	Powder Type	Wad	Powder Charge (grains) / Velocity (fps) Minimum	Maximum	Maximum Pressure	Load Notes
FEDERAL: ONE-PIECE PLASTIC HUNTING				**1⅞ OUNCES LEAD SHOT**		
CCI 209M	Blue Dot	Fed. 12S0		41.0/1200	9,100 psi	Note 1
CCI 209M	Blue Dot	Fed. 12S0		43.0/1255	9,800 psi	
CCI 209M	Blue Dot	Rem. R12L		40.5/1200	9,600 psi	Note 2
CCI 209M	Blue Dot	Rem. R12L		42.5/1255	10,100 psi	Note 1
CCI 209M	Blue Dot	Win. WAA12SL		41.0/1200	8,900 psi	Note 1
CCI 209M	Blue Dot	Win. WAA12SL		43.0/1255	9,500 psi	
CCI 209M	HS-7	Fed. 12S0		42.0/1250	10,700 psi	Note 3
CCI 209M	HS-7	WAA12SL		42.5/1250	11,200 psi	Note 3
Fed. 209A	HS-7	Fed. 12S0		42.0/1250	11,600 psi	Note 3
Win. 209	Blue Dot	Fed. 12S0		40.0/1200	9,000 psi	Note 1
Win. 209	Blue Dot	Fed. 12S0		42.5/1255	10,100 psi	
Win. 209	HS-7	Fed. 12S0		42.5/1250	10,500 psi	Note 3
Win. 209	HS-7	WAA12SL		42.0/1250	10,500 psi	Note 3
REMINGTON: PLASTIC				**1⅞ OUNCES LEAD SHOT**		
CCI 209M	Blue Dot	Fed. 12S0		38.0/1200	10,100 psi	Note 1
CCI 209M	Blue Dot	Fed. 12S0		39.0/1255	10,600 psi	Note 1
CCI 209M	Blue Dot	Rem. R12L		38.0/1200	10,300 psi	Note 1
CCI 209M	Blue Dot	Rem. R12L		39.0/1255	10,900 psi	Note 1
CCI 209M	Blue Dot	Win. WAA12SL		38.0/1200	10,000 psi	Note 1
CCI 209M	Blue Dot	Win. WAA12SL		39.0/1255	10,400 psi	Note 1
CCI 209M	HS-7	Fed. 12S0		42.0/1250	11,700 psi	
Fed. 209	HS-7	Fed. 12S0		41.0/1250	12,400 psi	
Win. 209	Blue Dot	Rem. R12L		37.5/1200	10,500 psi	Note 1
Win. 209	Blue Dot	Rem. R12L		38.5/1255	11,000 psi	Note 1
Win. 209	HS-7	Fed. 12S0		41.5/1250	11,600 psi	
WINCHESTER: POLYFORMED (SEPARATE PLASTIC BASE WAD)				**1⅞ OUNCES LEAD SHOT**		
CCI 209M	Blue Dot	Win. WAA12SL		38.0/1200	10,100 psi	
CCI 209M	Blue Dot	Win. WAA12SL		39.5/1255	10,500 psi	
CCI 209M	HS-7	Fed. 12S0		42.0/1250	11,000 psi	
Fed. 209A	HS-7	Fed. 12S0		41.0/1250	11,900 psi	
Win. 209	Blue Dot	Fed. 12S0		38.5/1200	10,600 psi	
Win. 209	Blue Dot	Fed. 12S0		40.5/1255	10,700 psi	
Win. 209	Blue Dot	Rem. R12L		38.5/1200	10,300 psi	Note 1
Win. 209	Blue Dot	Rem. R12L		40.0/1255	10,700 psi	Note 1
Win. 209	Blue Dot	Win. WAA12SL		38.5/1200	10,000 psi	
Win. 209	Blue Dot	Win. WAA12SL		40.0/1255	10,800 psi	
Win. 209	HS-7	Fed. 12S0		41.5/1250	10,500 psi	

Load Notes: 1 = Add one 20-gauge, 0.135" card inside bottom of shotcup. 2 = Add two 20-gauge, 0.135" cards inside bottom of shotcup. 3 = Add one 20-gauge, 0.135" card inside bottom of shotcup.

Caution: Follow load recipes exactly; do not substitute components, exceed listed maximums or load less than listed minimums.

Primer	Powder Type	Wad	Powder Charge (grains) / Velocity (fps) Minimum	Maximum	Maximum Pressure	Load Notes
FEDERAL: ONE-PIECE PLASTIC HUNTING				**2 OUNCES LEAD SHOT**		
CCI 209M	Blue Dot	Fed. 12S0		42.5/1220	10,000 psi	
CCI 209M	Blue Dot	Rem. R12L		42.0/1220	10,000 psi	
CCI 209M	Blue Dot	Win. WAA12SL		42.5/1220	9,800 psi	
CCI 209M	HS-7	Fed. 12S0		41.5/1200	10,600 psi	Note 1
CCI 209M	HS-7	WAA12SL		42.0/1200	11,500 psi	Note 1
Fed. 209A	HS-7	Fed. 12S0		41.0/1200	11,600 psi	Note 1
Fed. 209A	HS-7	WAA12SL		40.0/1200	11,500 psi	Note 1
Win. 209	Blue Dot	Fed. 12S0		41.0/1220	9,900 psi	
Win. 209	HS-7	Fed. 12S0		42.0/1200	10,600 psi	Note 1
Win. 209	HS-7	WAA12SL		42.5/1200	10,700 psi	Note 1
REMINGTON: PLASTIC				**2 OUNCES LEAD SHOT**		
CCI 209M	Blue Dot	Fed. 12S0		39.5/1220	10,800 psi	
CCI 209M	Blue Dot	Rem. R12L		39.5/1220	11,100 psi	
CCI 209M	Blue Dot	Win. WAA12SL		39.0/1220	10,700 psi	
CCI 209M	HS-7	Rem. RXP12		40.0/1200	11,500 psi	Note 1
CCI 209M	HS-7	WAA12SL		39.5/1200	10,900 psi	
Fed. 209A	HS-7	WAA12SL		39.0/1200	12,100 psi	
Win. 209	Blue Dot	Rem. R12L		39.0/1220	11,200 psi	
Win. 209	HS-7	WAA12SL		38.5/1200	12,100 psi	
WINCHESTER: POLYFORMED (SEPARATE PLASTIC BASE WAD)				**2 OUNCES LEAD SHOT**		
CCI 209M	Blue Dot	Win. WAA12SL		39.0/1220	11,200 psi	
CCI 209M	HS-7	Fed. 12S0		39.0/1200	11,000 psi	
Fed. 209A	HS-7	Fed. 12S0		39.0/1200	11,200 psi	
Fed. 209A	HS-7	WAA12SL		39.0/1200	12,200 psi	
Win. 209	Blue Dot	Fed. 12S0		40.5/1220	11,000 psi	
Win. 209	Blue Dot	Rem. R12L		39.0/1220	10,600 psi	
Win. 209	Blue Dot	Win. WAA12SL		40.0/1220	11,200 psi	
Win. 209	HS-7	Fed. 12S0		39.0/1200	10,700 psi	
Win. 209	HS-7	WAA12SL		39.0/1200	10,700 psi	Note 2

Load Notes: 1 = Add one 20-gauge, 0.135″ card inside bottom of shotcup. 2 = Add one 28-gauge, 0.040″ card inside bottom of shotcup.

     Caution: Follow load recipes exactly; do not substitute components, exceed listed maximums or load less than listed minimums.

Primer	Powder Type	Wad	Powder Charge (grains) / Velocity (fps) Minimum	Maximum	Maximum Pressure	Load Notes
FEDERAL: ONE-PIECE PLASTIC HUNTING			**2¼ OUNCES LEAD SHOT**			
CCI 209M	Blue Dot	Fed. 12S4		38.5/1150	11,100 psi	
CCI 209M	Blue Dot	Rem. SP12		39.5/1150	11,200 psi	
CCI 209M	Blue Dot	WAA12F114		38.5/1150	11,100 psi	
CCI 209M	HS-7	Fed. 12S4		38.5/1150	11,800 psi	Note 1
CCI 209M	HS-7	Pat. Ctrl. Prpl		41.5/1150	9,200 psi	
Fed. 209A	H5-7	Fed. 12S4		39.0/1150	12,500 psi	Note 1
Fed. 209A	HS-7	Activ TG30		38.5/1150	10,400 psi	
Win. 209	Blue Dot	Fed. 12S4		38.0/1150	10,900 psi	
Win. 209	HS-7	Fed. 12S4		40.0/1150	12,600 psi	Note 1
Win. 209	HS-7	Pat. Ctrl. Prpl		41.0/1150	9,100 psi	
REMINGTON: PLASTIC			**2¼ OUNCES LEAD SHOT**			
CCI 209M	Blue Dot	Fed. 12S4		37.0/1150	11,100 psi	
CCI 209M	Blue Dot	Rem. SP12		38.0/1150	11,100 psi	
Fed. 209A	HS-7	Rem. SP12		36.5/1150	11,900 psi	Note 1
Win. 209	Blue Dot	Rem. SP12		38.0/1150	11,500 psi	
Win. 209	HS-7	Rem. SP12		38.5/1150	11,000 psi	Note 1
WINCHESTER: POLYFORMED (SEPARATE PLASTIC BASE WAD)			**2¼ OUNCES LEAD SHOT**			
CCI 209M	HS-7	Rem. SP12		39.0/1150	12,000 psi	Note 1
Win. 209	Blue Dot	Rem. SP12		37.0/1150	11,200 psi	
Win. 209	HS-7	WAA12F114		38.0/1150	12,900 psi	

Load Notes: 1 = Add one 20-gauge, 0.135″ card inside bottom of shotcup.

END OF 12-GAUGE LEAD SHOT LOAD DATA

16-GAUGE 2½" — 11/16-OUNCE LEAD SHOT

Primer	Powder Type	Wad	Powder Charge (grains) / Velocity (fps) Minimum	Maximum	Maximum Pressure	Load Notes
ACTIV: ENGLISH STYLE				11/16-OUNCE LEAD SHOT		
Win. 209	Unique	BP DX16		20.0/1160	8,000 psi	Note 1
FIOCCHI: ENGLISH STYLE				11/16-OUNCE LEAD SHOT		
Fio. 616	Herco	BP DX16		21.0/1160	8,100 psi	Note 1

Load Notes: 1 = Spreader.

16-GAUGE 2½" — 7/8-OUNCE LEAD SHOT

Primer	Powder Type	Wad	Powder Charge (grains) / Velocity (fps) Minimum	Maximum	Maximum Pressure	Load Notes
ACTIV: ALL PLASTIC (SHORTENED BY CUTTING)				7/8-OUNCE LEAD SHOT		
Fio. 615	SR-7625	BP DX16		21.5/1200	7,000 LUP	Note 1

Load Notes: 1 = Spreader.

Caution: Follow load recipes exactly; do not substitute components, exceed listed maximums or load less than listed minimums.

³/₄-OUNCE LEAD SHOT

Primer	Powder Type	Wad	Powder Charge (grains) / Velocity (fps) Minimum		Maximum	Maximum Pressure	Load Notes
ACTIV: ALL PLASTIC					³/₄-OUNCE LEAD SHOT		
Rem. 209P	Unique	BP DX16			21.5/1400	9,800 psi	Note 1
Rem. 209P	Unique	BP SG16			21.0/1400	9,900 psi	Note 2
Win. 209	Unique	BP SG16			21.0/1400	10,000 psi	Note 2
FIOCCHI: PLASTIC					³/₄-OUNCE LEAD SHOT		
Fio. 616	Unique	BP DX16	19.5/1290	20.0/1340	21.0/1400	9,500 psi	Note 1
Fio. 616	Unique	BP SG16	20.2/1165	21.2/1220	21.7/1235	8,200 psi	Note 2
REMINGTON: SP (SEPARATE PLASTIC BASE WAD)					³/₄-OUNCE LEAD SHOT		
Fio. 615	Unique	BP SG16			21.0/1400	9,900 psi	Note 3
WINCHESTER: COMPRESSION FORMED (AA-TYPE)					³/₄-OUNCE LEAD SHOT		
Win. 209	Green Dot	BP DX16			17.5/1200	9,700 psi	Note 1

Load Notes: 1 = Spreader. 2 = Sporting. 3 = Sporting (Add 20-gauge cork over powder.)

⁷/₈-OUNCE LEAD SHOT

Primer	Powder Type	Wad	Powder Charge (grains) / Velocity (fps) Minimum		Maximum	Maximum Pressure	Load Notes
ACTIV: ALL PLASTIC					⁷/₈-OUNCE LEAD SHOT		
Rem. 209P	Unique	BP SG16	22.0/1340	22.5/1365	23.0/1390	9,900 psi	Note 1
Win. 209	Herco	BP DX16			23.0/1280	9,500 psi	Note 2
Win. 209	SR-7625	BP DX16			23.0/1275	9,400 psi	Note 2
Win. 209	Unique	BP DX16			22.0/1220	10,200 psi	Note 2
Win. 209	WSF	BP DX16			21.0/1210	8,100 psi	Note 1
Win. 209	WSF	BP SG16	21.0/1210	22.0/1265	22.5/1290	9,500 psi	Note 1
FEDERAL: PLASTIC (PAPER BASE WAD)					⁷/₈-OUNCE LEAD SHOT		
CCI 209	Herco	BP DX16			23.1/1290	9,600 psi	Note 2
CCI 209	SR-7625	BP DX16	22.2/1175	22.7/1225	23.2/1280	9,600 psi	Note 2
CCI 209	Unique	BP DX16			22.2/1225	10,100 psi	Note 2
CCI 209	WSF	BP DX16			21.2/1210	8,300 psi	Note 2
FIOCCHI: PLASTIC					⁷/₈-OUNCE LEAD SHOT		
Fio. 616	Herco	BP DX16	22.0/1290	22.3/1340	22.6/1390	10,400 psi	Note 2
Fio. 616	Herco	BP SG16			23.0/1390	10,300 psi	Note 1
Fio. 616	SR-7625	BP DX16			22.0/1260	9,500 psi	Note 2
Fio. 616	Unique	BP DX16			21.0/1290	9,300 psi	Note 2
Fio. 616	Unique	BP SG16	22.0/1340	22.5/1370	23.0/1400	9,800 psi	Note 1
Fio. 616	WSF	BP DX16			21.0/1200	8,000 psi	Note 2
REMINGTON: SP (SEPARATE PLASTIC BASE WAD)					⁷/₈-OUNCE LEAD SHOT		
Rem. 209	Unique	BP DX16			21.0/1220	8,300 psi	Note 2
Rem. 209	Unique	BP SG16			21.0/1220	8,300 psi	Note 1

Load Notes: 1 = Sporting. 2 = Spreader.

Caution: Follow load recipes exactly; do not substitute components, exceed listed maximums or load less than listed minimums.

Primer	Powder Type	Wad	Powder Charge (grains) / Velocity (fps) Minimum			Maximum	Maximum Pressure	Load Notes
REMINGTON: SP (SEPARATE PLASTIC BASE WAD) (CONT.)						**⁷/₈-OUNCE LEAD SHOT**		
Rem. 209	WSF	BP DX16				21.0/1220	8,300 psi	Note 2
Rem. 209	WSF	BP SG16	21.0/1220	21.5/1250		22.0/1280	9,300 psi	Note 1
Win. 209	WSF	BP DX16				21.2/1210	8,400 psi	Note 2
WINCHESTER: COMPRESSION-FORMED AA TYPE						**⁷/₈-OUNCE LEAD SHOT**		
Win. 209	Herco	BP DX16				20.0/1230	10,000 psi	Note 2
Win. 209	Unique	BP DX16				19.0/1200	9,200 psi	Note 2
Win. 209	W 540	BP DX16				23.5/1200	9,300 psi	Note 2
Win. 209	WSF	BP DX16				20.0/1165	8,400 psi	Note 2

Load Notes: 1 = Sporting. 2 = Spreader.

Primer	Powder Type	Wad	Powder Charge (grains) / Velocity (fps) Minimum			Maximum	Maximum Pressure	Load Notes
ACTIV: ALL PLASTIC						**1-OUNCE LEAD SHOT**		
CCI 209	Green Dot	BP DX16	18.0/1165	18.4/1180	18.8/1195	19.5/1220	9,800 psi	Note 1
CCI 209	Herco	BP DX16	23.0/1220	23.7/1245	24.1/1260	24.5/1275	8,700 psi	Note 1
CCI 209	Herco	BP SG16	23.0/1220	23.2/1240	23.4/1260	23.5/1275	8,700 psi	Note 2
CCI 209	Herco	BP SG16				23.5/1365	10,900 psi	Note 2
CCI 209	Unique	BP DX16	20.0/1165	21.5/1220	22.3/1250	23.0/1275	9,100 psi	Note 1
CCI 209	Unique	BP SG16	20.0/1165	21.5/1220	22.3/1250	23.0/1275	9,100 psi	Note 2
Rem. 209P	Blue Dot	BP SG16	30.0/1350	30.7/1370	31.4/1390	32.0/1415	9,400 psi	Note 2
Rem. 209P	Unique	BP SG16	22.0/1320	22.3/1335	22.6/1345	23.0/1360	10,500 psi	Note 2
Win. 209	Herco	BP SG16				23.0/1330	10,200 psi	Note 2
Win. 209	SR-7625	BP SG16				23.0/1275	9,400 psi	Note 2
Win. 209	Unique	BP SG16				22.0/1220	10,200 psi	Note 2
Win. 209	WSF	BP SG16				21.0/1230	9,000 psi	Note 2
FEDERAL: PLASTIC (PAPER BASE WAD)						**1-OUNCE LEAD SHOT**		
CCI 209	Herco	BP SG16	21.5/1220	22.5/1245	23.0/1260	23.5/1275	8,500 psi	Note 2
CCI 209	SR-7625	BP SG16				23.5/1270	9,500 LUP	Note 2
CCI 209	Unique	BP SG16	21.5/1220	22.0/1245	22.2/1260	22.5/1275	9,000 psi	Note 2
CCI 209	W 540	BP DX16				23.0/1220	9,800 psi	Note 1
CCI 209	WSF	BP SG16				22.5/1235	8,800 LUP	Note 2
Fed. 209A	Green Dot	BP DX16				18.5/1220	9,300 psi	Note 1
Fed. 209A	Herco	BP DX16	21.5/1220	22.4/1245	22.9/1260	23.5/1275	8,500 psi	Note 1
Fed. 209A	Unique	BP DX16	21.5/1220	21.9/1245	22.2/1260	22.5/1275	9,000 psi	Note 1
FIOCCHI: PLASTIC 1260						**1-OUNCE LEAD SHOT**		
CCI 209	Unique	BP DX16				23.0/1275	9,100 psi	Note 1
Fio. 616	Blue Dot	BP SG16	30.0/1350	30.7/1365	31.4/1380	32.0/1400	9,400 psi	Note 2
Fio. 616	Green Dot	BP DX16				18.0/1165	8,200 psi	Note 1

Load Notes: 1 = Spreader. 2 = Sporting.

Caution: Follow load recipes exactly; do not substitute components, exceed listed maximums or load less than listed minimums.

Primer	Powder Type	Wad	Powder Charge (grains) / Velocity (fps) Minimum			Maximum	Maximum Pressure	Load Notes
FIOCCHI: PLASTIC 1260 (CONT.)						**1-OUNCE LEAD SHOT**		
Fio. 616	Herco	BP DX16	21.0/1220	21.4/1245	21.7/1260	22.0/1275	9,000 psi	Note 1
Fio. 616	Herco	BP SG16	21.0/1220	21.5/1245	21.7/1260	22.0/1275	9,000 psi	Note 2
Fio. 616	Unique	BP DX16	18.0/1165	20.0/1220	20.8/1250	21.5/1275	9,600 psi	Note 1
Fio. 616	Unique	BP SG16	18.0/1165	20.0/1220	21.2/1250	22.0/1275	10,400 psi	Note 2
Fio. 616	Universal	BP SG16				23.0/1280	9,600 LUP	Note 2
Fio. 616	WSF	BP SG16				21.3/1230	8,900 psi	Note 2
REMINGTON: SP (SEPARATE PLASTIC BASE WAD)						**1-OUNCE LEAD SHOT**		
Rem. 209P	Green Dot	Activ G-28				17.5/1165	9,700 psi	
Rem. 209P	Green Dot	BP DX16				17.5/1165	9,700 psi	Note 1
Rem. 209P	Green Dot	WAA16				16.5/1165	10,200 psi	
Rem. 209P	Herco	Activ G-28	21.0/1220	21.3/1240	21.7/1260	22.0/1275	9,800 psi	
Rem. 209P	Herco	BP DX16	21.0/1220	21.4/1245	21.7/1260	22.0/1275	9,800 psi	Note 1
Rem. 209P	Herco	BP SG16	21.0/1220	21.4/1245	21.7/1260	22.0/1275	9,800 psi	Note 2
Rem. 209P	Herco	WAA16	21.0/1220	21.3/1240	21.7/1260	22.0/1275	9,600 psi	
Rem. 209P	Unique	Activ G-28	19.5/1165	20.0/1195	20.5/1220	21.0/1275	10,200 psi	
Rem. 209P	Unique	BP DX16	19.5/1165	20.5/1220	20.8/1250	21.0/1275	10,200 psi	Note 1
Rem. 209P	Unique	BP SG16	19.5/1165	20.5/1220	20.8/1250	21.0/1275	10,200 psi	Note 2
Rem. 209P	Unique	WAA16	19.0/1165	19.5/1195	20.0/1220	21.0/1275	10,200 psi	
Win. 209	WSF	BP DX16				20.6/1200	8,800 psi	Note 1
WINCHESTER: COMPRESSION-FORMED AA TYPE						**1-OUNCE LEAD SHOT**		
CCI 109	W 452AA	Rem. SP16				17.5/1165	10,500 LUP	
CCI 109	W 473AA	Rem. SP16	20.0/1165	20.3/1185	20.7/1200	21.0/1220	9,000 LUP	
CCI 209	HS-6	WAA16	23.5/1165	23.8/1185	24.1/1200	24.5/1220	8,800 LUP	
CCI 209	HS-7	WAA16	25.0/1165	25.5/1185	26.0/1200	26.5/1220	9,100 LUP	
CCI 209	HS-7	WAA16	25.0/1165	25.5/1185	26.0/1200	26.5/1220	9,100 LUP	
CCI 209	W 540	BP SG16				22.5/1180	8,800 psi	Note 2
CCI 209	W 540	WAA16	23.5/1165	23.8/1185	24.2/1200	24.5/1220	9,000 psi	
CCI 209	W 571	WAA16	25.0/1165	25.5/1185	26.0/1200	26.5/1220	9,100 psi	
CCI 209	WSF	WAA16				21.0/1220	8,800 psi	
Fed. 209	HS-6	WAA16	22.5/1165	23.0/1185	23.5/1200	24.0/1220	9,400 LUP	
Fed. 209	HS-7	WAA16	25.0/1165	25.3/1185	25.6/1200	26.0/1220	9,200 LUP	
Fed. 209	W 540	WAA16	22.5/1165	23.0/1185	23.5/1200	24.0/1220	9,500 psi	
Fed. 209	W 571	WAA16	25.0/1165	25.3/1185	25.7/1200	26.0/1220	9,400 psi	
Fed. 209	WSF	WAA16				21.5/1220	8,600 psi	
Win. 209	Blue Dot	Rem. SP16				29.0/1275	9,300 psi	
Win. 209	Herco	Activ G-28				20.0/1220	10,100 psi	
Win. 209	Herco	BP SG16				20.0/1220	10,100 psi	Note 2
Win. 209	Herco	WAA16				20.0/1220	10,200 psi	
Win. 209	HS-6	WAA16	23.0/1165	23.3/1185	23.6/1200	24.0/1220	9,300 LUP	
Win. 209	Unique	Activ G-28				19.0/1165	9,100 psi	
Win. 209	Unique	BP SG16				19.0/1165	9,200 psi	Note 2
Win. 209	Unique	WAA16	19.0/1165	19.2/1185	19.4/1200	19.5/1220	10,500 psi	

Load Notes: 1 = Spreader. 2 = Sporting.

Caution: Follow load recipes exactly; do not substitute components, exceed listed maximums or load less than listed minimums.

Primer	Powder Type	Wad	Powder Charge (grains) / Velocity (fps) Minimum			Maximum	Maximum Pressure	Load Notes
WINCHESTER: COMPRESSION-FORMED AA TYPE (CONT.)						1-OUNCE LEAD SHOT		
Win. 209	Universal	Activ G-28	19.0/1165	19.7/1195	20.3/1220	21.5/1275	10,600 psi	
Win. 209	Universal	BP G/BP	19.5/1165	19.8/1195	20.0/1220	21.0/1275	10,700 psi	
Win. 209	Universal	WAA16	19.0/1165	19.5/1195	20.0/1220	20.7/1275	11,000 psi	
Win. 209	W 452AA	Rem. SP16				17.5/1165	10,300 LUP	
Win. 209	W 473AA	Rem. SP16	20.5/1165	20.8/1185	21.2/1200	21.5/1220	8,800 LUP	
Win. 209	W 540	WAA16	23.0/1165	23.3/1185	23.7/1200	24.0/1220	9,500 psi	
Win. 209	W 571	WAA16	25.0/1165	25.5/1185	26.0/1200	26.5/1220	9,300 psi	
Win. 209	WSF	WAA16	20.0*/1165	20.3/1185	20.7/1200	21.0/1220	9,000 psi	*Note 3

Load Notes: 3 = This load duplicates ballistics of Winchester's 2½ dram equivalent Promotional Field loading.

Primer	Powder Type	Wad	Powder Charge (grains) / Velocity (fps) Minimum	Maximum	Maximum Pressure	Load Notes
ACTIV: ALL PLASTIC				1¹/₁₆ OUNCES LEAD SHOT		
Win. 209	IMR 800-X	BP SG16		21.5/1240	9,600 LUP	Note 1
Win. 209	W 540	BP SG16		22.5/1220	9,100 psi	Note 1
FEDERAL: PLASTIC (PAPER BASE WAD)				1¹/₁₆ OUNCES LEAD SHOT		
CCI 209	W 540	BP SG16		22.6/1225	9,200 LUP	Note 1
FIOCCHI: PLASTIC				1¹/₁₆ OUNCES LEAD SHOT		
Fio. 616	W 540	BP SG16		22.3/1200	9,100 psi	Note 1
WINCHESTER: COMPRESSION-FORMED AA TYPE				1¹/₁₆ OUNCES LEAD SHOT		
CCI 209	W 540	BP SG16		22.0/1180	9,000 psi	Note 1
Win. 209	W 540	BP SG16		24.8/1200	10,800 psi	Note 1

Load Notes: 1 = Sporting.

Primer	Powder Type	Wad	Powder Charge (grains) / Velocity (fps) Minimum			Maximum	Maximum Pressure	Load Notes
ACTIV: ALL PLASTIC						1¹/₈ OUNCES LEAD SHOT		
CCI 209	Herco	Rem. SP16	22.0/1185	22.7/1205	23.4/1220	24.0/1240	9,400 psi	
CCI 209	Herco	WAA16	22.0/1185	22.3/1205	22.6/1220	23.0/1240	10,200 psi	
CCI 209	Unique	Rem. SP16	21.5/1185	21.8/1205	22.1/1220	22.5/1240	10,200 psi	
CCI 209	Unique	WAA16	20.5/1185	21.0/1205	21.5/1220	22.0/1240	10,000 psi	
CCI 209M	Blue Dot	Rem. SP16				31.0/1295	9,100 psi	
Win. 209	Solo 1500	Rem. SP16				29.5/1260	9,900 LUP	
FEDERAL: PLASTIC (PAPER BASE WAD)						1¹/₈ OUNCES LEAD SHOT		
CCI 209	SR-7625	Rem. SP16				24.5/1295	9,900 LUP	
CCI 209M	IMR 800-X	Rem. SP16	20.5/1190	21.3/1220	22.0/1245	23.5/1290	10,000 LUP	
Fed. 209	IMR 800-X	Rem. SP16	20.0/1185	20.8/1210	21.1/1225	21.5/1230	9,500 LUP	

Caution: Follow load recipes exactly; do not substitute components, exceed listed maximums or load less than listed minimums.

Primer	Powder Type	Wad	Powder Charge (grains) / Velocity (fps) Minimum			Maximum	Maximum Pressure	Load Notes
FEDERAL: PLASTIC (PAPER BASE WAD) (CONT.)						**1¹/₈ OUNCES LEAD SHOT**		
Fed. 209	Solo 1500	Rem. SP16				30.5/1260	9,500 LUP	
Fed. 209	SR-4756	Rem. SP16				23.5/1190	8,300 LUP	
Fed. 209	SR-7625	Rem. SP16				21.0/1190	8,900 LUP	
Fed. 209A	Blue Dot	Rem. SP16				32.0/1295	8,600 psi	
Fed. 209A	Green Dot	Rem. SP16				19.0/1185	10,600 psi	
Fed. 209A	Green Dot	WAA16				18.5/1185	10,200 psi	
Fed. 209A	Herco	Rem. SP16	22.0/1185	22.5/1205	23.0/1220	23.5/1240	10,100 psi	
Fed. 209A	Herco	Rem. SP16				24.5/1295	10,300 psi	
Fed. 209A	Herco	WAA16	22.0/1185	22.7/1205	23.4/1220	24.0/1240	10,200 psi	
Fed. 209A	Unique	Rem. SP16	21.5/1185	21.8/1205	22.1/1220	22.5/1240	9,600 psi	
Fed. 209A	Unique	WAA16	21.0/1185	21.3/1205	21.6/1220	22.0/1240	10,200 psi	
Win. 209	IMR 800-X	Rem. SP16				23.5/1305	10,100 LUP	
Win. 209	SR-4756	Rem. SP16				24.5/1190	7,800 LUP	
Win. 209	SR-7625	Rem. SP16				21.5/1185	8,100 LUP	
FIOCCHI: PLASTIC						**1¹/₈ OUNCES LEAD SHOT**		
Fio. 616	Blue Dot	Rem. SP16	31.0/1240	31.5/1260	32.0/1275	32.5/1295	9,200 psi	
Fio. 616	Herco	Rem. SP16	21.0/1185	21.8/1205	22.6/1220	23.5/1240	10,700 psi	
Fio. 616	Unique	Rem. SP16				20.5/1185	9,900 psi	
Fio. 616	Unique	WAA16				19.5/1185	10,600 psi	
REMINGTON: SP (SEPARATE PLASTIC BASE WAD)						**1¹/₈ OUNCES LEAD SHOT**		
Rem. 209P	Blue Dot	Rem. SP16				27.0/1240	9,900 psi	
Rem. 209P	Herco	Activ G-28				21.0/1185	10,500 psi	
Rem. 209P	Herco	WAA16				21.0/1185	10,600 psi	
Rem. 209P	Solo 1500	Rem. SP16				29.0/1260	10,500 LUP	
Rem. 209P	Unique	Activ G-28				20.5/1185	10,700 psi	
Rem. 209P	Unique	WAA16				20.0/1185	10,300 psi	
WINCHESTER: COMPRESSION-FORMED AA TYPE						**1¹/₈ OUNCES LEAD SHOT**		
CCI 109	W 540	Rem. SP16	26.5/1185	27.5/1240	28.0/1265	28.5/1290	9,600 LUP	
CCI 209	W 540	WAA16				24.5/1185	10,400 psi	
CCI 209	W 571	WAA16	26.0/1185	26.5/1205	27.0/1220	27.5/1240	10,800 psi	
CCI 209	WSF	WAA16				20.5/1185	10,800 psi	
CCI 209M	IMR 800-X	Rem. SP16				21.5/1240	9,600 LUP	
Fed. 209	HS-6	Rem. SP16	26.5/1185	26.7/1200	27.0/1215	27.5/1240	9,300 LUP	
Fed. 209	HS-6	WAA16				24.0/1185	10,400 LUP	
Fed. 209	HS-7	WAA16	25.5/1185	25.7/1200	26.0/1215	26.5/1240	10,600 LUP	
Fed. 209	IMR 800-X	Rem. SP16				20.0/1185	9,600 LUP	
Fed. 209	SR-4756	Rem. SP16				23.0/1185	9,400 LUP	
Fed. 209	SR-7625	Rem. SP16				20.5/1195	10,000 LUP	
Fed. 209	W 571	WAA16				25.5/1185	10,200 psi	
Fed. 209	W 571	WAA16				26.5/1240	10,900 psi	
Fed. 410	IMR 800-X	Rem. SP16				23.0/1285	10,300 LUP	
Rem. 209P	IMR 800-X	Rem. SP16				24.0/1290	8,500 LUP	

Caution: Follow load recipes exactly; do not substitute components, exceed listed maximums or load less than listed minimums.

16-GAUGE 2³/₄"   1¹/₈ OUNCES LEAD SHOT (CONT.)

Primer	Powder Type	Wad	Powder Charge (grains) / Velocity (fps) Minimum			Maximum	Maximum Pressure	Load Notes
WINCHESTER: COMPRESSION-FORMED AA TYPE (CONT.)						1¹/₈ OUNCES LEAD SHOT		
Win. 209	Blue Dot	Rem. SP16				27.0/1185	10,000 psi	
Win. 209	HS-6	Rem. SP16	26.5/1185	26.7/1200	27.0/1215	27.5/1240	9,400 LUP	
Win. 209	HS-6	WAA16				24.5/1185	10,600 LUP	
Win. 209	HS-7	WAA16	26.0/1185	26.2/1200	26.5/1215	27.0/1240	10,700 LUP	
Win. 209	IMR 800-X	Rem. SP16	20.0/1175	20.4/1190	20.8/1205	21.5/1235	9,800 LUP	
Win. 209	Solo 1500	Rem. SP16				29.0/1260	10,900 LUP	
Win. 209	SR-4756	Rem. SP16				24.0/1190	9,000 LUP	
Win. 209	SR-7625	Rem. SP16				21.0/1200	9,800 LUP	
Win. 209	W 571	WAA16	26.0/1185	26.3/1205	26.7/1220	27.0/1240	10,900 psi	

16-GAUGE 2³/₄"   1¹/₄ OUNCES LEAD SHOT

Primer	Powder Type	Wad	Powder Charge (grains) / Velocity (fps) Minimum	Maximum	Maximum Pressure	Load Notes
ACTIV: ALL PLASTIC				1¹/₄ OUNCES LEAD SHOT		
CCI 209M	Blue Dot	Rem. SP16		30.0/1260	10,000 psi	
Win. 209	Solo 1500	Rem. SP16		28.0/1220	10,800 LUP	
FEDERAL: PLASTIC (PAPER BASE WAD)				1¹/₄ OUNCES LEAD SHOT		
Fed. 209	Solo 1500	Rem. SP16		30.0/1265	10,000 LUP	
Fed. 209A	Blue Dot	Rem. SP16		30.5/1260	10,200 psi	
WINCHESTER: COMPRESSION FORMED AA TYPE				1¹/₄ OUNCES LEAD SHOT		
Win. 209	W 571	Rem. SP16		30.5/1230	10,500 LUP	

END OF 16-GAUGE LEAD SHOT LOAD DATA

Caution: Follow load recipes exactly; do not substitute components, exceed listed maximums or load less than listed minimums.

Primer	Powder Type	Wad	Powder Charge (grains) / Velocity (fps) Minimum		Maximum	Maximum Pressure	Load Notes
FIOCCHI: ENGLISH STYLE					³/₄-OUNCE LEAD SHOT		
Fio. 615	Unique	BP SG20L	15.0/1160	16.0/1210	17.0/1245	9,900 psi	Long wad

Primer	Powder Type	Wad	Powder Charge (grains) / Velocity (fps)		Maximum Pressure	Load Notes
			Minimum	Maximum		
ACTIV: ALL PLASTIC				³/₄-OUNCE LEAD SHOT		
Rem. 209P	American Select	BP Z20		**14.0/1210**	9,800 psi	
Rem. 209P	Unique	BP SG20L		**16.0/1120**	5,900 LUP	Note 5
ESTATE: CHEDDITE (LOW BASE WAD)				³/₄-OUNCE LEAD SHOT		
Fio. 615	WSF	BP SG20S		**18.0/1220**	9,700 LUP	Note 4
Fio. 615	WSF	BP SG20L		**18.0/1220**	9,700 LUP	Note 5
FEDERAL: PLASTIC (PAPER BASE WAD)				³/₄-OUNCE LEAD SHOT		
Fed. 209	Green Dot	Fed. 20S1		**15.0/1200**	9,000 psi	Note 2
Fed. 209	Green Dot	Rem. RXP20		**15.0/1200**	8,600 psi	Note 2
Fed. 209	Green Dot	WAA20		**15.0/1200**	8,900 psi	Note 2
Fed. 209	Green Dot	Windjammer		**15.5/1200**	8,700 psi	Note 2
Fed. 209	Red Dot	Fed. 20S1		**13.0/1200**	10,100 psi	Note 3
Fed. 209	Unique	Fed. 20S1		**15.0/1200**	9,000 psi	Note 1
Fed. 209	Unique	Rem. RXP20		**16.0/1200**	8,600 psi	Note 1
Fed. 209	Unique	WAA20		**16.0/1200**	8,200 psi	Note 1
Fed. 209	Unique	Windjammer		**17.0/1200**	7,500 psi	Note 2
FIOCCHI: PLASTIC				³/₄-OUNCE LEAD SHOT		
Fio. 616	Unique	BP SG20S		**16.0/1160**	5,900 LUP	Note 4
Fio. 616	Unique	BP SG20L		**16.0/1160**	6,100 LUP	Note 5
Fio. 616	WSF	BP SG20S		**18.0/1220**	9,700 LUP	Note 4
REMINGTON: PREMIER & NITRO 27 & STS				³/₄-OUNCE LEAD SHOT		
Rem. 209P	Green Dot	Fed. 20S1		**14.0/1200**	10,000 psi	Note 1
Rem. 209P	Green Dot	H. Versalite		**14.5/1200**	10,000 psi	Note 1
Rem. 209P	Green Dot	Lage Uniwad		**14.0/1200**	9,800 psi	Note 1
Rem. 209P	Green Dot	Rem. RXP20		**14.0/1200**	10,000 psi	Note 1
Rem. 209P	Green Dot	WAA20		**14.0/1200**	10,500 psi	Note 1
Rem. 209P	Green Dot	Windjammer		**14.0/1200**	10,300 psi	Note 1
Rem. 209P	Red Dot	Fed. 20S1		**13.0/1200**	10,600 psi	Note 1
Rem. 209P	Unique	BP SG20S		**15.9/1160**	5,600 LUP	Note 4
Rem. 209P	Unique	BP SG20L		**15.9/1160**	5,600 LUP	Note 5
Rem. 209P	Unique	Fed. 20S1		**15.5/1200**	8,400 psi	Note 1
Rem. 209P	Unique	H. Versalite		**16.0/1200**	8,900 psi	Note 1
Rem. 209P	Unique	Lage Uniwad		**15.5/1200**	8,600 psi	Note 1
Rem. 209P	Unique	Rem. RXP20		**15.5/1200**	8,700 psi	Note 1
Rem. 209P	Unique	WAA20		**15.5/1200**	8,900 psi	Note 1
Rem. 209P	Unique	Windjammer		**15.5/1200**	8,900 psi	Note 1
REMINGTON: RXP				³/₄-OUNCE LEAD SHOT		
Rem. 97*	Green Dot	Fed. 20S1		**13.5/1200**	11,100 psi	
Rem. 97*	Green Dot	Rem. RXP20		**13.5/1200**	10,400 psi	
Rem. 97*	Green Dot	WAA20		**13.5/1200**	10,400 psi	
Rem. 97*	Unique	Fed. 20S1		**15.5/1200**	9,900 psi	

Load Notes: 1 = Add two 28-gauge, 0.135" cards inside bottom of shotcup. 2 = Add one 28-gauge, 0.135" card inside bottom of shotcup. 3 = Add two 28-gauge, 0.135" cards inside bottom of shotcup. 4 = Add one 20-gauge, 0.100" nitro card over powder. 5 = Long wad.

Caution: Follow load recipes exactly; do not substitute components, exceed listed maximums or load less than listed minimums.

³/₄-OUNCE LEAD SHOT (CONT.)

20-GAUGE 2³/₄″

Primer	Powder Type	Wad	Powder Charge (grains) / Velocity (fps) Minimum	Maximum	Maximum Pressure	Load Notes
REMINGTON: RXP (CONT.)				**³/₄-OUNCE LEAD SHOT**		
Rem. 97*	Unique	Rem. RXP20		15.5/1200	9,900 psi	
Rem. 97*	Unique	WAA20		15.0/1200	9,400 psi	
WINCHESTER: COMPRESSION-FORMED AA TYPE				**³/₄-OUNCE LEAD SHOT**		
Fio. 615	Unique	BP SG20S		16.0/1160	5,600 LUP	Note 6
Fio. 615	Unique	BP SG20L		16.0/1160	5,400 LUP	Note 5
Win. 209	Green Dot	Fed. 20S1		14.0/1200	9,900 psi	Note 2
Win. 209	Green Dot	Rem. RXP20		14.0/1200	10,200 psi	Note 2
Win. 209	Green Dot	WAA20		14.0/1200	10,800 psi	Note 2
Win. 209	Solo 1250	BP SG20L		16.5/1200	10,600 LUP	Note 5
Win. 209	Unique	Fed. 20S1		15.5/1200	9,700 psi	
Win. 209	Unique	Rem. RXP20		15.5/1200	9,900 psi	Note 2
Win. 209	Unique	WAA20		15.5/1200	9,100 psi	Note 2
Win. 209	W 452AA	WAA20	14.0/1145	15.0/1200	10,600 LUP	Note 7
Win. 209	W 473AA	Rem. RXP20	16.0/1145	17.0/1200	9,300 LUP	Note 7

Load Notes: 2 = Add one 28-gauge, 0.135″ card inside bottom of shotcup. 5 = Long wad. 6 = Place one 20-gauge, 0.100″ nitro card over powder. 7 = Add one 410-bore, 0.135″ card inside bottom of shotcup.

⁷/₈-OUNCE LEAD SHOT

20-GAUGE 2³/₄″

Primer	Powder Type	Wad	Powder Charge (grains) / Velocity (fps) Minimum		Maximum	Maximum Pressure	Load Notes
ACTIV: ALL PLASTIC					**⁷/₈-OUNCE LEAD SHOT**		
CCI 209	International	Windjammer			16.0/1200	9,300 psi	
CCI 209	Solo 1250	Activ W-28	18.0/1155	18.5/1180	19.0/1200	10,400 psi	Note 1
CCI 209	Universal	Windjammer			19.5/1200	7,800 psi	
CCI 209M	Herco	Fed. 20S1			18.0/1200	9,500 psi	
CCI 209M	Herco	H. Versalite			18.0/1200	9,800 psi	
CCI 209M	Herco	Rem. RXP20			18.5/1200	9,500 psi	
CCI 209M	Herco	WAA20			18.0/1200	9,500 psi	
Fed. 209	Herco	H. Versalite			18.0/1200	9,300 psi	
Fed. 209	Solo 1250	Activ: W-28	17.5/1155	18.0/1180	18.5/1200	10,300 psi	Note 1
Fio. 616	International	Fed. 20S1			15.5/1200	9,700 psi	
Fio. 616	Universal	Fed. 20S1			18.5/1200	8,100 psi	
Rem. 209	Herco	H. Versalite			18.0/1200	9,500 psi	
Rem. 209P	Herco	BP SG20L	16.5/1130	17.3/1190	18.0/1245	9,500 psi	Note 2
Rem. 209P	Unique	BP SG20S			17.0/1200	9,800 LUP	Note 3
Rem. 209P	Unique	BP SG20L			16.0/1150	8,200 LUP	Note 2
Rem. 209P	Unique	BP Z20			16.2/1200	11,000 psi	Note 4
Rem. 209P	Unique	BP Z20			16.2/1200	11,000 psi	Note 4
Win. 209	Herco	H. Versalite			18.5/1200	9,300 psi	
Win. 209	International	WAA20			15.5/1200	10,000 psi	

Load Notes: 1 = 6-point crimp. 2 = Long wad. 3 = Short wad. 4 = Maximum Field.

Caution: Follow load recipes exactly; do not substitute components, exceed listed maximums or load less than listed minimums.

Primer	Powder Type	Wad	Powder Charge (grains) / Velocity (fps)		Maximum	Maximum Pressure	Load Notes
			Minimum		Maximum		
ACTIV: ALL PLASTIC (CONT.)					**⁷/₈-OUNCE LEAD SHOT**		
Win. 209	Solo 1250	Activ W-28	17.5/1155	18.0/1180	18.5/1200	10,600 psi	Note 1
Win. 209	Solo 1250	BP SG20S	17.8/1150	18.0/1175	18.2/1200	10,200 LUP	Note 3
Win. 209	Solo 1250	BP SG20L			18.5/1200	10,200 LUP	Note 2
Win. 209	Solo 1250	Pat. Ctrl. 20	18.0/1155	18.5/1180	19.0/1200	10,400 psi	Note 1
Win. 209	Solo 1250	Windjammer	17.5/1155	18.0/1180	18.5/1200	10,800 psi	Note 1
Win. 209	Universal	WAA20			18.5/1200	8,300 psi	
ESTATE: CHEDDITE (LOW BASE WAD)					**⁷/₈-OUNCE LEAD SHOT**		
Fio. 615	WSF	BP SG20L			17.0/1200	10,500 LUP	Note 2
FEDERAL: PAPER					**⁷/₈-OUNCE LEAD SHOT**		
CCI 109	Green Dot	Fed. 20S1	14.5/1155	14.8/1180	15.0/1200	9,000 psi	
CCI 109	Green Dot	Rem. RXP20	15.0/1155	15.5/1180	16.0/1200	9,900 psi	
CCI 109	Green Dot	WAA20	14.5/1155	15.0/1180	15.5/1200	8,800 psi	
CCI 109	Unique	Fed. 20S1			17.0/1200	8,400 psi	
CCI 109	Unique	Rem. RXP20	15.0/1155	16.0/1180	17.0/1200	8,500 psi	
CCI 109	Unique	WAA20			17.0/1200	8,500 psi	
CCI 209M	Green Dot	Fed. 20S1	14.5/1155	14.8/1180	15.0/1200	10,500 psi	
CCI 209M	Herco	Fed. 20S1			17.0/1200	9,600 psi	
CCI 209M	Unique	Fed. 20S1	16.0/1155	16.5/1180	17.0/1200	9,900 psi	
Fed. 209	Green Dot	Fed. 20S1	14.0/1155	14.5/1180	15.0/1200	9,600 psi	
Fed. 209	Green Dot	Rem. RXP20	14.5/1155	15.0/1180	15.5/1200	10,900 psi	
Fed. 209	Green Dot	WAA20	14.5/1155	14.8/1180	15.0/1200	9,700 psi	
Fed. 209	Unique	Fed. 20S1	14.5/1155	15.0/1180	15.5/1200	9,400 psi	
Fed. 209	Unique	Rem. RXP20	15.5/1155	16.0/1180	16.5/1200	9,800 psi	
Fed. 209	Unique	WAA20	15.0/1155	15.5/1180	16.0/1200	9,200 psi	
FEDERAL: PLASTIC (PAPER BASE WAD)					**⁷/₈-OUNCE LEAD SHOT**		
CCI 109	Green Dot	Fed. 20S1	14.5/1155	15.0/1180	15.5/1200	9,400 psi	
CCI 109	Green Dot	Lage Uniwad	15.5/1155	15.8/1180	16.0/1200	10,000 psi	
CCI 109	Green Dot	Rem. RXP20			16.0/1200	9,600 psi	
CCI 109	Green Dot	WAA20	14.5/1155	15.0/1180	15.5/1200	9,100 psi	
CCI 109	Herco	Fed. 20S1			17.0/1200	9,300 psi	
CCI 109	Herco	Rem. RXP20			18.0/1200	8,800 psi	
CCI 109	Herco	WAA20			17.0/1200	9,100 psi	
CCI 109	Unique	Fed. 20S1			17.0/1200	8,500 psi	
CCI 109	Unique	Lage Uniwad	17.0/1155	17.5/1180	18.0/1200	8,800 psi	
CCI 109	Unique	Rem. RXP20	16.0/1155	16.5/1180	17.0/1200	9,200 psi	
CCI 109	Unique	WAA20			17.0/1200	8,500 psi	
CCI 209	Green Dot	Fed. 20S1	14.5/1155	15.5/1180	16.5/1200	9,300 psi	
CCI 209	Herco	Fed. 20S1			17.5/1200	7,600 psi	
CCI 209	Solo 1250	BP SG20S	18.2/1150	18.5/1175	18.8/1200	10,000 LUP	Note 3
CCI 209	Solo 1250	Fed. 20S1	18.5/1155	19.0/1180	19.5/1200	10,400 psi	Note 1
CCI 209	Unique	Fed. 20S1	16.0/1155	16.5/1180	17.0/1200	9,100 psi	

Load Notes: 1 = 6-point crimp. 2 = Long wad. 3 = Short wad.

Caution: Follow load recipes exactly; do not substitute components, exceed listed maximums or load less than listed minimums.

Primer	Powder Type	Wad	Powder Charge (grains) / Velocity (fps) Minimum		Maximum	Maximum Pressure	Load Notes
FEDERAL: PLASTIC (PAPER BASE WAD) (CONT.)					⅞-OUNCE LEAD SHOT		
Fed. 209	Green Dot	Fed. 20S1			16.5/1200	10,600 psi	
Fed. 209	Green Dot	H. Versalite	15.5/1155	15.8/1180	16.0/1200	10,500 psi	
Fed. 209	Green Dot	Lage Uniwad	16.0/1155	16.3/1180	16.5/1200	11,000 psi	
Fed. 209	Green Dot	WAA20			14.5/1155	9,700 psi	
Fed. 209	Green Dot	Windjammer	15.0/1155	15.5/1180	16.0/1200	10,900 psi	
Fed. 209	Herco	Windjammer			18.5/1200	10,200 psi	
Fed. 209	International	H. Versalite			15.7/1200	9,100 psi	
Fed. 209	Solo 1250	Activ W-28			18.5/1155	8,400 psi	Note 1
Fed. 209	Solo 1250	Fed. 20S1	18.0/1155	18.5/1180	19.0/1200	9,900 psi	Note 1
Fed. 209	Solo 1250	Pat. Ctrl. 20	18.5/1155	19.0/1180	19.5/1200	10,100 psi	Note 1
Fed. 209	Solo 1250	Rem. RXP20	18.5/1155	19.0/1180	19.5/1200	10,400 psi	Note 1
Fed. 209	Solo 1250	Windjammer			18.0/1155	9,100 psi	Note 1
Fed. 209	Unique	Windjammer	16.5/1155	16.8/1180	17.0/1200	10,600 psi	
Fed. 209	Universal	H. Versalite			17.5/1200	7,900 psi	
Fed. 209A	Green Dot	Pat. Ctrl. 20			16.0/1200	11,200 psi	
Fed. 209A	Herco	Pat. Ctrl. 20			18.0/1200	9,200 psi	
Fed. 209A	IMR 800-X	CB 1078-20			17.0/1190	7,800 psi	
Fed. 209A	IMR 800-X	Fed. 20S1			17.0/1190	8,200 psi	
Fed. 209A	IMR 800-X	Rem. RXP20			17.5/1200	7,600 psi	
Fed. 209A	IMR 800-X	WAA20			17.5/1205	8,000 psi	
Fed. 209A	IMR 800-X	Windjammer			17.5/1205	8,000 psi	
Fed. 209A	IMR PB	CB 1078-20			17.0/1195	9,800 psi	
Fed. 209A	IMR PB	Fed. 20S1			17.5/1210	10,000 psi	
Fed. 209A	IMR PB	Rem. RXP20			17.5/1205	9,300 psi	
Fed. 209A	IMR PB	WAA20			17.5/1200	9,400 psi	
Fed. 209A	IMR PB	Windjammer			17.5/1200	9,500 psi	
Fed. 209A	International	H. Versalite			15.7/1200	10,900 psi	
Fed. 209A	SR-4756	Fed. 20S1			20.5/1210	8,700 psi	
Fed. 209A	SR-4756	Rem. RXP20			21.0/1200	7,800 psi	
Fed. 209A	SR-4756	WAA20F1			20.5/1205	8,500 psi	
Fed. 209A	SR-4756	Windjammer			20.5/1210	8,700 psi	
Fed. 209A	SR-7625	CB 1078-20			18.5/1210	9,500 psi	
Fed. 209A	SR-7625	Fed. 20S1			18.5/1195	8,700 psi	
Fed. 209A	SR-7625	Rem. RXP20			19.0/1210	8,700 psi	
Fed. 209A	SR-7625	WAA20			18.5/1210	9,200 psi	
Fed. 209A	SR-7625	Windjammer			18.5/1190	8,600 psi	
Fed. 209A	Unique	Pat. Ctrl. 20			18.0/1200	9,800 psi	
Fed. 209A	Universal	H. Versalite			17.5/1200	9,300 psi	
Fio. 616	International	BP SG20S			15.6/1200	10,600 psi	Note 3
Rem. 209P	IMR 800-X	CB 1078-20			17.5/1205	7,900 psi	
Rem. 209P	IMR 800-X	Fed. 20S1			17.5/1195	7,900 psi	
Rem. 209P	IMR 800-X	Rem. RXP20			18.0/1210	7,600 psi	

Load Notes: 1 = 6-point crimp. 3 = Short wad.

Caution: Follow load recipes exactly; do not substitute components, exceed listed maximums or load less than listed minimums.

Primer	Powder Type	Wad	Powder Charge (grains) / Velocity (fps) Minimum		Maximum	Maximum Pressure	Load Notes
FEDERAL: PLASTIC (PAPER BASE WAD) (CONT.)					⁷/₈-OUNCE LEAD SHOT		
Rem. 209P	IMR 800-X	WAA20			17.5/1200	7,600 psi	
Rem. 209P	IMR 800-X	Windjammer			17.0/1195	7,300 psi	
Rem. 209P	IMR PB	CB 1078-20			17.5/1200	9,300 psi	
Rem. 209P	IMR PB	Fed. 20S1			17.5/1200	9,400 psi	
Rem. 209P	IMR PB	Rem. RXP20			17.5/1200	8,900 psi	
Rem. 209P	IMR PB	WAA20			17.5/1200	9,300 psi	
Rem. 209P	IMR PB	Windjammer			18.0/1210	9,500 psi	
Rem. 209P	SR-4756	Fed. 20S1			21.5/1205	7,600 psi	
Rem. 209P	SR-4756	Rem. RXP20			21.5/1180	7,000 psi	
Rem. 209P	SR-4756	WAA20F1			21.5/1200	7,900 psi	
Rem. 209P	SR-4756	Windjammer			21.5/1200	7,900 psi	
Rem. 209P	SR-7625	CB 1078-20			18.5/1195	8,600 psi	
Rem. 209P	SR-7625	Fed. 20S1			19.0/1200	8,300 psi	
Rem. 209P	SR-7625	Rem. RXP20			19.5/1205	8,300 psi	
Rem. 209P	SR-7625	WAA20			18.5/1195	8,500 psi	
Rem. 209P	SR-7625	Windjammer			19.0/1200	8,300 psi	
Win. 209	Green Dot	BP SG20S			14.5/1150	10,000 LUP	Note 3
Win. 209	IMR 800-X	CB 1078-20			17.0/1195	8,100 psi	
Win. 209	IMR 800-X	Fed. 20S1			17.5/1200	8,300 psi	
Win. 209	IMR 800-X	Rem. RXP20			17.5/1210	8,000 psi	
Win. 209	IMR 800-X	WAA20			17.5/1210	8,100 psi	
Win. 209	IMR 800-X	Windjammer			17.5/1200	8,000 psi	
Win. 209	IMR PB	CB 1078-20			17.5/1200	9,500 psi	
Win. 209	IMR PB	Fed. 20S1			17.5/1210	10,100 psi	
Win. 209	IMR PB	Rem. RXP20			18.0/1195	9,000 psi	
Win. 209	IMR PB	WAA20			17.5/1200	9,400 psi	
Win. 209	IMR PB	Windjammer			17.5/1195	9,500 psi	
Win. 209	International	BP SG20L			16.0/1200	9,400 LUP	Note 2
Win. 209	International	WAA20			15.5/1200	9,400 psi	
Win. 209	Solo 1250	Fed. 20S1	18.0/1155	18.5/1180	19.0/1200	10,500 psi	Note 1
Win. 209	SR-4756	Fed. 20S1			20.5/1205	8,500 psi	
Win. 209	SR-4756	Rem. RXP20			21.0/1205	7,900 psi	
Win. 209	SR-4756	WAA20F1			20.5/1195	8,200 psi	
Win. 209	SR-4756	Windjammer			20.5/1195	8,300 psi	
Win. 209	SR-7625	CB 1078-20			18.5/1210	9,000 psi	
Win. 209	SR-7625	Fed. 20S1			18.5/1195	8,600 psi	
Win. 209	SR-7625	Rem. RXP20			18.5/1195	8,500 psi	
Win. 209	SR-7625	WAA20			18.5/1195	8,400 psi	
Win. 209	SR-7625	Windjammer			19.0/1200	9,100 psi	
Win. 209	Universal	WAA20			17.5/1200	8,000 psi	

Load Notes: 1 = 6-point crimp. 2 = Long wad. 3 = Short wad.

Caution: Follow load recipes exactly; do not substitute components, exceed listed maximums or load less than listed minimums.

Primer	Powder Type	Wad	Powder Charge (grains) / Velocity (fps) Minimum		Maximum	Maximum Pressure	Load Notes
FIOCCHI: PLASTIC					**7/8-OUNCE LEAD SHOT**		
CCI 209	International	Rem. RXP20			16.0/1200	9,400 psi	
CCI 209	Universal	Fed. 20S1			18.2/1200	8,200 psi	
CCI 209	Universal	Rem. RXP20			19.0/1200	7,000 psi	
CCI 209M	Green Dot	Fed. 20S1	14.5/1155	15.0/1180	15.5/1200	10,700 psi	
CCI 209M	Herco	Fed. 20S1			17.0/1200	9,900 psi	
CCI 209M	Unique	Fed. 20S1	16.0/1155	16.5/1180	17.0/1200	10,000 psi	
Fed. 209	Green Dot	Fed. 20S1	14.5/1155	15.0/1180	15.5/1200	11,100 psi	
Fed. 209	Herco	Fed. 20S1			17.5/1200	10,200 psi	
Fed. 209	Unique	Fed. 20S1	15.5/1155	16.3/1180	17.0/1200	10,800 psi	
Fio. 615	Green Dot	Fed. 20S1	15.0/1155	15.5/1180	16.0/1200	10,900 psi	
Fio. 615	Green Dot	H. Versalite	15.5/1155	15.8/1180	16.0/1200	10,000 psi	
Fio. 615	Green Dot	Lage Uniwad	15.5/1155	16.5/1180	17.5/1200	8,200 psi	
Fio. 615	Green Dot	Rem. RXP20			16.5/1200	10,300 psi	
Fio. 615	Green Dot	WAA20			16.0/1200	10,800 psi	
Fio. 615	Herco	Fed. 20S1			18.0/1200	9,200 psi	
Fio. 615	Herco	H. Versalite			19.0/1200	8,300 psi	
Fio. 615	Herco	Rem. RXP20			19.0/1200	8,500 psi	
Fio. 615	Herco	WAA20			18.5/1200	8,700 psi	
Fio. 615	Unique	Fed. 20S1	17.0/1155	17.5/1180	18.0/1200	9,700 psi	
Fio. 615	Unique	H. Versalite			18.0/1155	8,300 psi	
Fio. 615	Unique	Lage Uniwad	17.5/1155	18.3/1180	19.0/1200	8,000 psi	
Fio. 615	Unique	WAA20			17.5/1200	9,600 psi	
Fio. 616	Green Dot	Fed. 20S1	14.5/1155	15.0/1180	15.5/1200	10,600 psi	
Fio. 616	Herco	Fed. 20S1			18.0/1200	9,200 psi	
Fio. 616	International	BP SG20S			15.6/1200	10,600 psi	Note 3
Fio. 616	Solo 1250	BP SG20S	18.1/1170	18.4/1185	18.8/1200	10,000 LUP	Note 3
Fio. 616	Unique	BP Z20	16.0/1160	16.5/1190	17.0/1220	11,100 psi	Note 4
Fio. 616	Unique	BP Z20	16.0/1160	16.5/1190	17.0/1220	11,100 psi	Note 4
Fio. 616	Unique	Fed. 20S1	16.0/1155	16.8/1180	17.5/1200	10,000 psi	
Rem. 209	Green Dot	Fed. 20S1	14.5/1155	15.0/1180	15.5/1200	10,800 psi	
Rem. 209	Herco	Fed. 20S1			16.5/1200	9,900 psi	
Rem. 209	Unique	Fed. 20S1			16.0/1155	9,400 psi	
Rem. 209P	Unique	BP Z20			16.0/1190	11,300 psi	
Win. 209	Green Dot	Fed. 20S1	14.5/1155	15.3/1180	16.0/1200	10,400 psi	
Win. 209	Herco	Fed. 20S1			18.0/1200	9,900 psi	
Win. 209	International	WAA20			15.3/1200	11,100 psi	
Win. 209	International	Windjammer			14.8/1200	10,400 psi	
Win. 209	Unique	Fed. 20S1	16.5/1155	16.8/1180	17.0/1200	10,100 psi	
Win. 209	Universal	WAA20			18.5/1200	8,200 psi	
REMINGTON: PREMIER & NITRO 27 & STS					**7/8-OUNCE LEAD SHOT**		
CCI 209	Green Dot	Rem. RXP20			14.5/1155	10,900 psi	
CCI 209	Herco	Rem. RXP20	16.5/1155	17.0/1180	17.5/1200	9,400 psi	

Load Notes: 3 = Short wad. 4 = Maximum Field.

Caution: Follow load recipes exactly; do not substitute components, exceed listed maximums or load less than listed minimums.   **261**

Primer	Powder Type	Wad	Powder Charge (grains) / Velocity (fps) Minimum		Maximum	Maximum Pressure	Load Notes
REMINGTON: PREMIER & NITRO 27 & STS (CONT.)					⁷/₈-OUNCE LEAD SHOT		
CCI 209	Unique	Rem. RXP20	16.0/1155	16.3/1180	16.5/1200	9,900 psi	
CCI 209M	Herco	Rem. RXP20	16.5/1155	16.8/1180	17.0/1200	10,800 psi	
CCI 209M	Unique	Rem. RXP20	15.5/1155	15.8/1180	16.0/1200	11,300 psi	
Fed. 209	Herco	Rem. RXP20	16.5/1155	16.8/1180	17.0/1200	11,000 psi	
Fed. 209	Unique	Rem. RXP20	15.5/1155	16.0/1180	16.5/1200	11,300 psi	
Fed. 209A	IMR 800-X	CB 1078-20			16.0/1215	9,900 psi	
Fed. 209A	IMR 800-X	Fed. 20S1			16.0/1210	10,000 psi	
Fed. 209A	IMR 800-X	Rem. RXP20			16.0/1190	9,100 psi	
Fed. 209A	IMR 800-X	WAA20			16.0/1195	9,300 psi	
Fed. 209A	IMR 800-X	Windjammer			16.0/1200	9,500 psi	
Fed. 209A	IMR PB	Fed. 20S1			15.0/1160	11,900 psi	
Fed. 209A	IMR PB	Rem. RXP20			16.0/1195	11,600 psi	
Fed. 209A	IMR PB	WAA20F1			16.0/1210	11,900 psi	
Fed. 209A	IMR PB	Windjammer			15.5/1185	11,900 psi	
Fed. 209A	SR-4756	Rem. SP20			17.5/1195	10,600 psi	
Fed. 209A	SR-4756	WAA20F1			17.5/1190	10,200 psi	
Fed. 209A	SR-7625	CB 1078-20			16.5/1195	11,400 psi	
Fed. 209A	SR-7625	Fed. 20S1			16.5/1190	12,000 psi	
Fed. 209A	SR-7625	Rem. RXP20			17.0/1210	11,000 psi	
Fed. 209A	SR-7625	WAA20			16.5/1205	12,000 psi	
Fed. 209A	SR-7625	Windjammer			16.5/1200	11,400 psi	
Fio. 616	Herco	Rem. RXP20	16.5/1155	16.8/1180	17.0/1200	10,700 psi	
Fio. 616	Unique	Rem. RXP20	16.0/1155	16.3/1180	16.5/1200	11,200 psi	
Rem. 209	Solo 1250	BP SG20S			15.1/1150	10,100 LUP	Note 3
Rem. 209P	Green Dot	BP SG20S			13.9/1150	10,300 LUP	Note 3
Rem. 209P	Green Dot	H. Versalite			14.0/1155	11,500 psi	
Rem. 209P	Green Dot	Lage Uniwad			14.0/1155	11,400 psi	
Rem. 209P	Green Dot	Pat. Ctrl. 20			14.5/1200	11,200 psi	
Rem. 209P	Green Dot	Rem. RXP20			14.5/1155	11,500 psi	
Rem. 209P	Green Dot	WAA20			14.0/1155	11,100 psi	
Rem. 209P	Green Dot	Windjammer			14.0/1155	11,200 psi	
Rem. 209P	Herco	Fed. 20S1	16.0/1155	16.5/1180	17.0/1200	10,500 psi	
Rem. 209P	Herco	H. Versalite	16.0/1155	16.8/1180	17.5/1200	10,400 psi	
Rem. 209P	Herco	Lage Uniwad	16.0/1155	16.8/1180	17.5/1200	10,300 psi	
Rem. 209P	Herco	Pat. Ctrl. 20			17.5/1200	10,200 psi	
Rem. 209P	Herco	Rem. RXP20	16.5/1155	16.8/1180	17.0/1200	10,600 psi	
Rem. 209P	Herco	WAA20	16.0/1155	16.5/1180	17.0/1200	10,700 psi	
Rem. 209P	Herco	Windjammer	16.0/1155	16.5/1180	17.0/1200	10,100 psi	
Rem. 209P	IMR 800-X	CB 1078-20			16.0/1205	9,500 psi	
Rem. 209P	IMR 800-X	Fed. 20S1			16.0/1195	9,600 psi	
Rem. 209P	IMR 800-X	Rem. RXP20			16.5/1200	9,100 psi	
Rem. 209P	IMR 800-X	WAA20			16.5/1205	9,100 psi	

Load Notes: 3 = Short wad.

Caution: Follow load recipes exactly; do not substitute components, exceed listed maximums or load less than listed minimums.

Primer	Powder Type	Wad	Powder Charge (grains) / Velocity (fps) Minimum		Maximum	Maximum Pressure	Load Notes
REMINGTON: PREMIER & NITRO 27 & STS (CONT.)					⅞-OUNCE LEAD SHOT		
Rem. 209P	IMR 800-X	Windjammer			16.5/1210	9,500 psi	
Rem. 209P	IMR PB	CB 1078-20			16.0/1195	11,800 psi	
Rem. 209P	IMR PB	Fed. 20S1			15.5/1185	11,800 psi	
Rem. 209P	IMR PB	Rem. RXP20			16.0/1195	11,000 psi	
Rem. 209P	IMR PB	WAA20F1			16.0/1195	11,400 psi	
Rem. 209P	IMR PB	Windjammer			16.0/1210	11,700 psi	
Rem. 209P	Solo 1250	BP SG20S	15.1/1150	15.6/1175	16.1/1200	10,700 LUP	Note 3
Rem. 209P	SR-4756	Rem. SP20			18.5/1205	10,200 psi	
Rem. 209P	SR-4756	WAA20F1			18.5/1195	9,500 psi	
Rem. 209P	SR-7625	CB 1078-20			17.0/1205	11,000 psi	
Rem. 209P	SR-7625	Fed. 20S1			17.0/1195	11,100 psi	
Rem. 209P	SR-7625	Rem. RXP20			17.0/1190	10,100 psi	
Rem. 209P	SR-7625	WAA20			17.0/1205	11,000 psi	
Rem. 209P	SR-7625	Windjammer			17.0/1210	11,000 psi	
Rem. 209P	Unique	Fed. 20S1	15.5/1155	16.0/1180	16.5/1200	10,800 psi	
Rem. 209P	Unique	H. Versalite	15.5/1155	16.0/1180	16.5/1200	10,200 psi	
Rem. 209P	Unique	Lage Uniwad	15.5/1155	16.0/1180	16.5/1200	10,400 psi	
Rem. 209P	Unique	Pat. Ctrl. 20			17.0/1200	10,500 psi	
Rem. 209P	Unique	Rem. RXP20	15.5/1155	16.0/1180	16.5/1200	10,700 psi	
Rem. 209P	Unique	WAA20	15.5/1155	16.0/1180	16.5/1200	10,900 psi	
Rem. 209P	Unique	Windjammer	15.5/1155	15.8/1180	16.0/1200	10,400 psi	
Win. 209	Herco	Rem. RXP20	16.5/1155	16.8/1180	17.0/1200	10,600 psi	
Win. 209	IMR 800-X	CB 1078-20			16.0/1205	9,600 psi	
Win. 209	IMR 800-X	Fed. 20S1			16.0/1200	9,600 psi	
Win. 209	IMR 800-X	Rem. RXP20			16.5/1210	9,500 psi	
Win. 209	IMR 800-X	WAA20			16.0/1190	9,300 psi	
Win. 209	IMR 800-X	Windjammer			16.0/1190	9,500 psi	
Win. 209	IMR PB	CB 1078-20			16.0/1195	11,700 psi	
Win. 209	IMR PB	Rem. RXP20			16.0/1190	11,100 psi	
Win. 209	IMR PB	WAA20F1			16.0/1190	11,100 psi	
Win. 209	IMR PB	Windjammer			16.0/1200	11,700 psi	
Win. 209	Red Dot	BP SG20S			11.5/1155	11,000 LUP	Note 3
Win. 209	Solo 1250	BP SG20S			16.0/1200	10,600 LUP	Note 3
Win. 209	SR-4756	Rem. SP20			18.5/1205	10,300 psi	
Win. 209	SR-4756	WAA20F1			19.0/1205	9,600 psi	
Win. 209	SR-7625	CB 1078-20			17.0/1205	11,100 psi	
Win. 209	SR-7625	Fed. 20S1			17.0/1210	11,800 psi	
Win. 209	SR-7625	Rem. RXP20			17.0/1195	10,300 psi	
Win. 209	SR-7625	WAA20			17.0/1200	10,900 psi	
Win. 209	SR-7625	Windjammer			17.0/1200	10,800 psi	
Win. 209	Unique	BP SG20S			16.8/1220	10,100 LUP	Note 3
Win. 209	Unique	Rem. RXP20	15.5/1155	16.0/1180	16.5/1200	11,300 psi	

Load Notes: 3 = Short wad.

Caution: Follow load recipes exactly; do not substitute components, exceed listed maximums or load less than listed minimums.

Primer	Powder Type	Wad	Powder Charge (grains) / Velocity (fps) Minimum		Maximum	Maximum Pressure	Load Notes
REMINGTON: PREMIER & RXP					**⁷/₈-OUNCE LEAD SHOT**		
CCI 209	International	H. Versalite			14.0/1200	11,400 psi	
CCI 209	Universal	H. Versalite			15.8/1200	9,900 psi	
Fed. 209	International	Windjammer			14.0/1200	11,800 psi	
Fed. 209	Universal	Windjammer			15.8/1200	9,600 psi	
Fed. 209A	International	BP SG20S			15.5/1200	11,200 psi	Note 3
Fed. 209A	Universal	Windjammer			16.0/1200	10,600 psi	
Rem. 209P	International	Rem. RXP20			14.0/1200	10,700 psi	
Rem. 209P	Universal	Rem. RXP20			15.8/1200	9,000 psi	
Win. 209	International	Pat. Ctrl. 20			14.0/1200	11,000 psi	
Win. 209	International	WAA20			14.0/1200	11,900 psi	
Win. 209	Universal	Pat. Ctrl. 20			15.8/1200	9,200 psi	
Win. 209	Universal	WAA20			15.8/1200	9,600 psi	
Win. AATP	Universal	WAA20			16.2/1200	10,900 psi	
REMINGTON: RXP					**⁷/₈-OUNCE LEAD SHOT**		
CCI 109	Green Dot	Fed. 20S1			13.5/1155	11,100 psi	
CCI 109	Green Dot	Lage Uniwad	14.5/1155	15.0/1180	15.5/1200	11,400 psi	
CCI 109	Green Dot	Rem. RXP20	14.0/1155	14.3/1180	14.5/1200	10,900 psi	
CCI 109	Green Dot	WAA20			14.0/1155	10,700 psi	
CCI 109	Herco	Fed. 20S1			17.0/1200	11,300 psi	
CCI 109	Herco	Rem. RXP20			17.0/1200	9,900 psi	
CCI 109	Herco	WAA20			16.5/1200	10,400 psi	
CCI 109	Unique	Fed. 20S1			16.0/1200	10,500 psi	
CCI 109	Unique	Lage Uniwad	15.5/1155	16.0/1180	16.5/1200	10,400 psi	
CCI 109	Unique	WAA20			16.0/1200	10,800 psi	
CCI 209	WSF	Fed. 20S1			17.5/1200	11,100 psi	
CCI 209	WSF	Rem. RXP20			17.5/1200	9,700 psi	
CCI 209	WSF	WAA20			17.0/1200	10,500 psi	
CCI 209M	Herco	Rem. RXP20			16.5/1200	10,700 psi	
CCI 209M	Unique	Rem. RXP20			16.0/1200	10,500 psi	
Fed. 209	Solo 1250	Rem. RXP20			17.0/1200	11,400 psi	Note 5
Fed. 209	WSF	Fed. 20S1			17.0/1200	10,800 psi	
Fed. 209	WSF	Rem. RXP20			17.5/1200	10,300 psi	
Fed. 209	WSF	WAA20			17.0/1200	10,700 psi	
Rem. 209P	Solo 1250	Rem. RXP20	16.0/1155	16.5/1180	17.0/1200	11,200 psi	Note 5
Rem. 209P	Solo 1250	Rem. SP20			16.0/1155	10,000 psi	Note 5
Rem. 209P	Solo 1250	WAA20			16.0/1155	10,800 psi	Note 5
Rem. 209P	Solo 1250	Windjammer			16.0/1155	10,400 psi	Note 5
Rem. 209P	Unique	BP Z20			16.0/1190	11,270 psi	Note 4
Rem. 209P	Unique	BP Z20			16.0/1190	11,270 psi	Note 4
Rem. 97*	Green Dot	Fed. 20S1			13.0/1155	11,500 psi	
Rem. 97*	Green Dot	Rem. RXP20			14.0/1155	11,300 psi	
Rem. 97*	Green Dot	WAA20			13.5/1155	11,400 psi	

Load Notes: 3 = Short wad. 4 = Maximum Field. 5 = 8-point crimp.

Caution: Follow load recipes exactly; do not substitute components, exceed listed maximums or load less than listed minimums.

Primer	Powder Type	Wad	Powder Charge (grains) / Velocity (fps) Minimum		Maximum	Maximum Pressure	Load Notes
REMINGTON: RXP (CONT.)					**7/8-OUNCE LEAD SHOT**		
Rem. 97*	Herco	Rem. RXP20			17.0/1200	10,600 psi	
Rem. 97*	Herco	WAA20			17.0/1200	10,600 psi	
Rem. 97*	Unique	Fed. 20S1			16.0/1200	10,500 psi	
Rem. 97*	Unique	Lage Uniwad	15.5/1155	15.8/1180	16.0/1200	10,900 psi	
Rem. 97*	Unique	Rem. RXP20			16.0/1200	9,700 psi	
Rem. 97*	Unique	WAA20			16.0/1200	10,700 psi	
Win. 209	Solo 1250	Rem. RXP20			17.0/1200	11,400 psi	Note 5
Win. 209	W 473AA	Rem. RXP20			17.5/1200	10,800 LUP	
Win. 209	W 540	WAA20			20.5/1200	9,700 LUP	
Win. 209	WSF	Fed. 20S1			17.0/1200	11,300 psi	
Win. 209	WSF	Rem. RXP20			17.5/1200	10,600 psi	
Win. 209	WSF	WAA20			17.0/1200	10,500 psi	
REMINGTON: SP (SEPARATE PLASTIC BASE WAD)					**7/8-OUNCE LEAD SHOT**		
CCI 209M	IMR 800-X	WAA20			17.0/1205	9,000 LUP	
Rem. 209	Unique	Rem. RXP20			16.5/1200	9,100 psi	
Rem. 209	Unique	WAA20			16.5/1200	9,800 psi	
REMINGTON: UNIBODY (INTEGRAL PLASTIC BASE WAD)					**7/8-OUNCE LEAD SHOT**		
CCI 209M	Herco	Rem. RXP20			17.5/1200	11,300 psi	
CCI 209M	Unique	Rem. RXP20			16.5/1200	10,900 psi	
Fed. 209	Herco	Rem. RXP20			16.5/1200	10,700 psi	
Fed. 209	Unique	Rem. RXP20			16.0/1200	11,500 psi	
Rem. 209	Herco	H. Versalite			16.5/1200	10,900 psi	
Rem. 209	Herco	Rem. RXP20			16.5/1200	10,200 psi	
Rem. 209	Unique	Rem. RXP20			16.5/1200	10,800 psi	
Rem. 209	Unique	WAA20			16.5/1200	11,200 psi	
Win. 209	Herco	Rem. RXP20			17.5/1200	10,900 psi	
WINCHESTER: COMPRESSION-FORMED AA TYPE					**7/8-OUNCE LEAD SHOT**		
CCI 109	Green Dot	Fed. 20S1	14.0/1155	14.3/1180	14.5/1200	10,500 psi	
CCI 109	Green Dot	Rem. RXP20	14.5/1155	14.8/1180	15.0/1200	10,000 psi	
CCI 109	Green Dot	WAA20	14.0/1155	14.3/1180	14.5/1200	10,300 psi	
CCI 109	Herco	Fed. 20S1			16.5/1200	10,200 psi	
CCI 109	Herco	Rem. RXP20			16.5/1200	8,800 psi	
CCI 109	Herco	WAA20			16.5/1200	10,200 psi	
CCI 109	Unique	Fed. 20S1	15.5/1155	15.8/1180	16.0/1200	10,000 psi	
CCI 109	Unique	Lage Uniwad	16.0/1155	16.3/1180	16.5/1200	10,800 psi	
CCI 109	Unique	Rem. RXP20	15.5/1155	15.8/1180	16.0/1200	9,900 psi	
CCI 109	Unique	WAA20	15.5/1155	15.8/1180	16.0/1200	10,700 psi	
CCI 109	W 473AA	WAA20			17.5/1200	10,900 LUP	
CCI 209	International	H. Versalite			14.0/1200	11,000 psi	
CCI 209	Universal	H. Versalite			15.8/1200	10,400 psi	
CCI 209	WSF	Fed. 20S1			16.5/1200	11,400 psi	

Load Notes: 5 = 8-point crimp.

Caution: Follow load recipes exactly; do not substitute components, exceed listed maximums or load less than listed minimums.

Primer	Powder Type	Wad	Powder Charge (grains) / Velocity (fps) Minimum	Maximum	Maximum Pressure	Load Notes
WINCHESTER: COMPRESSION-FORMED AA TYPE (CONT.)				⁷/₈-OUNCE LEAD SHOT		
CCI 209	WSF	Rem. RXP20		17.5/1200	10,500 psi	
CCI 209	WSF	WAA20		16.5/1200	11,300 psi	
CCI 209M	Herco	WAA20		17.5/1200	10,000 psi	
CCI 209M	Unique	WAA20		15.0/1155	10,200 psi	
Fed. 209	International	Windjammer		14.0/1200	11,100 psi	
Fed. 209	Universal	Windjammer		15.8/1200	10,500 psi	
Fed. 209	WSF	Fed. 20S1		16.5/1200	11,400 psi	
Fed. 209	WSF	Rem. RXP20		17.0/1200	10,500 psi	
Fed. 209	WSF	WAA20		16.5/1200	11,400 psi	
Fed. 209A	IMR 800-X	CB 1078-20		16.0/1190	9,400 psi	
Fed. 209A	IMR 800-X	Fed. 20S1		16.0/1190	9,700 psi	
Fed. 209A	IMR 800-X	Rem. RXP20		16.5/1200	8,800 psi	
Fed. 209A	IMR 800-X	WAA20		16.5/1205	9,400 psi	
Fed. 209A	IMR 800-X	Windjammer		16.5/1215	10,100 psi	
Fed. 209A	IMR PB	Fed. 20S1		15.0/1160	11,900 psi	
Fed. 209A	IMR PB	WAA20		15.5/1180	11,700 psi	
Fed. 209A	SR-4756	CB 1078-20		18.0/1195	10,300 psi	
Fed. 209A	SR-4756	Fed. 20S1		18.0/1190	10,600 psi	
Fed. 209A	SR-4756	Rem. SP20		18.5/1215	10,700 psi	
Fed. 209A	SR-4756	WAA20F1		18.0/1190	10,000 psi	
Fed. 209A	SR-4756	Windjammer		18.5/1185	10,000 psi	
Fed. 209A	SR-7625	CB 1078-20		16.5/1195	11,700 psi	
Fed. 209A	SR-7625	Fed. 20S1		16.5/1190	11,700 psi	
Fed. 209A	SR-7625	Rem. RXP20		17.0/1200	10,800 psi	
Fed. 209A	SR-7625	WAA20		16.5/1205	11,700 psi	
Fed. 209A	SR-7625	Windjammer		16.5/1200	11,900 psi	
Fed. 209A	Universal	Windjammer		15.8/1200	11,700 psi	
Rem. 209P	IMR 800-X	CB 1078-20		16.5/1195	8,400 psi	
Rem. 209P	IMR 800-X	Fed. 20S1		16.5/1190	8,200 psi	
Rem. 209P	IMR 800-X	Rem. RXP20		16.5/1190	7,500 psi	
Rem. 209P	IMR 800-X	WAA20		16.5/1210	9,300 psi	
Rem. 209P	IMR 800-X	Windjammer		16.5/1190	8,400 psi	
Rem. 209P	IMR PB	WAA20		16.0/1200	11,600 psi	
Rem. 209P	IMR PB	Windjammer		16.0/1200	11,300 psi	
Rem. 209P	International	Rem. RXP20		14.0/1200	10,800 psi	
Rem. 209P	SR-4756	CB 1078-20		18.5/1200	10,000 psi	
Rem. 209P	SR-4756	Fed. 20S1		18.5/1190	10,100 psi	
Rem. 209P	SR-4756	Rem. SP20		19.0/1210	9,700 psi	
Rem. 209P	SR-4756	WAA20F1		18.5/1200	9,800 psi	
Rem. 209P	SR-7625	CB 1078-20		17.0/1210	11,300 psi	
Rem. 209P	SR-7625	Fed. 20S1		16.5/1185	11,100 psi	
Rem. 209P	SR-7625	Rem. RXP20		17.0/1190	10,100 psi	
Rem. 209P	SR-7625	WAA20		17.0/1200	10,900 psi	

   Caution: Follow load recipes exactly; do not substitute components, exceed listed maximums or load less than listed minimums.

Primer	Powder Type	Wad	Powder Charge (grains) / Velocity (fps) Minimum		Maximum	Maximum Pressure	Load Notes
WINCHESTER: COMPRESSION-FORMED AA TYPE (CONT.)					7/8-OUNCE LEAD SHOT		
Rem. 209P	SR-7625	Windjammer			17.5/1210	10,300 psi	
Rem. 209P	Universal	Rem. RXP20			15.8/1200	9,800 psi	
Win. 209	Blue Dot	BP Z20	19.5/1205	19.7/1215	20.0/1225	11,500 psi	Note 4
Win. 209	Blue Dot	BP Z20	19.5/1205	19.7/1215	20.0/1225	11,500 psi	Note 4
Win. 209	Green Dot	BP SG20S			14.0/1150	10,300 LUP	Note 3
Win. 209	Green Dot	Fed. 20S1	14.0/1155	14.3/1180	14.5/1200	10,300 psi	
Win. 209	Green Dot	Rem. RXP20	14.5/1155	14.8/1180	15.0/1200	10,000 psi	
Win. 209	Green Dot	WAA20	14.0/1155	14.3/1180	14.5/1200	10,600 psi	
Win. 209	Herco	Fed. 20S1			16.5/1200	10,700 psi	
Win. 209	Herco	Pat. Ctrl. 20			16.5/1200	11,300 psi	
Win. 209	Herco	Rem. RXP20			16.5/1200	9,000 psi	
Win. 209	Herco	WAA20			16.5/1200	9,600 psi	
Win. 209	IMR 800-X	CB 1078-20			16.0/1190	9,600 psi	
Win. 209	IMR 800-X	Fed. 20S1			16.0/1190	9,600 psi	
Win. 209	IMR 800-X	Rem. RXP20			16.5/1210	9,400 psi	
Win. 209	IMR 800-X	WAA20			16.5/1205	9,900 psi	
Win. 209	IMR 800-X	Windjammer			16.5/1200	10,300 psi	
Win. 209	IMR PB	BP SG20S	15.0/1200	15.2/1210	15.5/1225	11,000 LUP	Note 3
Win. 209	IMR PB	Fed. 20S1			15.5/1175	11,800 psi	
Win. 209	IMR PB	Rem. RXP20			16.0/1195	11,400 psi	
Win. 209	IMR PB	WAA20			16.0/1195	11,700 psi	
Win. 209	IMR PB	Windjammer			16.5/1200	11,800 psi	
Win. 209	International	BP SG20S			15.4/1200	11,000 psi	Note 3
Win. 209	International	Pat. Ctrl. 20			14.0/1200	11,200 psi	
Win. 209	International	WAA20			14.0/1200	11,800 psi	
Win. 209	Solo 1250	BP SG20S	15.2/1150	15.7/1175	16.2/1200	10,700 LUP	Note 3
Win. 209	Solo 1250	BP SG20L			16.2/1200	10,400 LUP	Note 2
Win. 209	Solo 1250	Pat. Ctrl. 20	14.5/1155	15.0/1180	15.5/1200	11,800 psi	Note 5
Win. 209	Solo 1250	Rem. RXP20	14.5/1155	15.0/1180	15.5/1200	11,500 psi	Note 5
Win. 209	Solo 1250	WAA20			14.0/1155	11,400 psi	Note 5
Win. 209	Solo 1250	WAA20F1			15.0/1200	12,000 psi	Note 5
Win. 209	SR-4756	CB 1078-20			18.0/1180	9,700 psi	
Win. 209	SR-4756	Fed. 20S1			18.0/1205	10,700 psi	
Win. 209	SR-4756	Rem. SP20			18.5/1200	9,900 psi	
Win. 209	SR-4756	WAA20F1			18.5/1200	9,900 psi	
Win. 209	SR-4756	Windjammer			18.5/1195	9,900 psi	
Win. 209	SR-7625	CB 1078-20			16.5/1190	10,800 psi	
Win. 209	SR-7625	Fed. 20S1			16.5/1195	11,700 psi	
Win. 209	SR-7625	Rem. RXP20			17.0/1210	10,600 psi	
Win. 209	SR-7625	WAA20			17.0/1205	10,600 psi	
Win. 209	SR-7625	Windjammer			17.0/1205	10,900 psi	
Win. 209	Unique	Fed. 20S1	15.0/1155	15.3/1180	15.5/1200	10,400 psi	

Load Notes: 2 = Long wad. 3 = Short wad. 4 = Maximum Field. 5 = 8-point crimp.

Caution: Follow load recipes exactly; do not substitute components, exceed listed maximums or load less than listed minimums.

Primer	Powder Type	Wad	Powder Charge (grains) / Velocity (fps) Minimum		Maximum	Maximum Pressure	Load Notes
WINCHESTER: COMPRESSION-FORMED AA TYPE (CONT.)					**⁷/₈-OUNCE LEAD SHOT**		
Win. 209	Unique	Lage Uniwad			15.5/1155	10,500 psi	
Win. 209	Unique	Pat. Ctrl. 20			16.0/1200	11,200 psi	
Win. 209	Unique	Rem. RXP20	15.0/1155	15.5/1180	16.0/1200	9,000 psi	
Win. 209	Unique	WAA20	15.0/1155	15.5/1180	16.0/1200	10,500 psi	
Win. 209	Universal	BP SG20S			15.7/1200	10,300 LUP	Note 3
Win. 209	Universal	Pat. Ctrl. 20			15.8/1200	10,800 psi	
Win. 209	Universal	WAA20			15.5/1200	10,200 psi	
Win. 209	WSF	BP SG20L			15.2/1200	11,000 LUP	Note 2
Win. 209	WSF	Rem. RXP20			17.0/1200	10,700 psi	
Win. 209	WSF	WAA20			16.5/1200	11,200 psi	
Win. AATP	Universal	WAA20			16.0/1200	11,200 psi	
Win. AATP	WSF	WAA20			16.5/1200	11,000 psi	Note 6
WINCHESTER: POLYFORMED (SEPARATE PLASTIC BASE WAD)					**⁷/₈-OUNCE LEAD SHOT**		
CCI 209	International	Rem. RXP20			15.0/1200	9,200 psi	
CCI 209	International	WAA20F1			14.5/1200	9,300 psi	
CCI 209	International	Windjammer			15.0/1200	10,400 psi	
CCI 209	Solo 1250	WAA20	16.5/1155	17.5/1180	18.5/1200	10,800 psi	Note 1
CCI 209	Universal	Rem. RXP20			18.5/1200	7,500 psi	
CCI 209	Universal	WAA20F1			18.0/1200	7,900 psi	
Fed. 209	Solo 1250	WAA20			16.0/1155	9,400 psi	Note 1
Fed. 209A	International	Rem. RXP20			14.7/1200	11,100 psi	
Fed. 209A	International	Windjammer			14.7/1200	11,000 psi	
Fed. 209A	Universal	Rem. RXP20			17.5/1200	8,500 psi	
Fed. 209A	Universal	WAA20F1			17.0/1200	8,500 psi	
Fed. 209A	Universal	Windjammer			17.0/1200	8,700 psi	
Rem. 209P	Solo 1250	WAA20	16.5/1155	17.5/1180	18.5/1200	10,400 psi	Note 1
Win. 209	International	Rem. RXP20			15.5/1200	10,600 psi	
Win. 209	International	WAA20F1			15.0/1200	10,700 psi	
Win. 209	International	Windjammer			15.0/1200	11,200 psi	
Win. 209	Solo 1250	Pat. Ctrl. 20			17.0/1155	9,300 psi	Note 1
Win. 209	Solo 1250	Rem. RXP20	17.5/1155	18.0/1180	18.5/1200	10,800 psi	Note 1
Win. 209	Solo 1250	WAA20	17.5/1155	18.0/1180	18.5/1200	10,700 psi	Note 1
Win. 209	Solo 1250	WAA20F1			17.5/1155	9,000 psi	Note 1
Win. 209	Solo 1250	Windjammer			16.5/1155	10,000 psi	Note 1
Win. 209	Unique	Fed. 20S1			14.5/1155	9,700 psi	
Win. 209	Unique	Fed. 20S1			15.5/1200	10,800 psi	
Win. 209	Unique	Rem. RXP20			15.5/1200	9,700 psi	
Win. 209	Unique	WAA20			14.5/1155	9,800 psi	
Win. 209	Unique	WAA20			15.5/1200	10,700 psi	
Win. 209	Universal	Rem. RXP20			18.0/1200	8,600 psi	
Win. 209	Universal	WAA20F1			17.5/1200	8,300 psi	
Win. 209	Universal	Windjammer			17.5/1200	8,500 psi	

Load Notes: 1 = 6-point crimp. 2 = Long wad. 3 = Short wad. 6 = This load duplicates ballistics of Winchester's 2½ dram equivalent AA Target loading.

Caution: Follow load recipes exactly; do not substitute components, exceed listed maximums or load less than listed minimums.

Primer	Powder Type	Wad	Powder Charge (grains) / Velocity (fps) Minimum		Maximum	Maximum Pressure	Load Notes
ACTIV: ALL PLASTIC					**1-OUNCE LEAD SHOT**		
CCI 209	HS-6	WAA20F1	21.0/1165	22.0/1195	23.0/1220	9,500 psi	
CCI 209	IMR 800-X	BP SG20S			16.0/1165	10,200 psi	Note 1
CCI 209	Universal	WAA20F1	18.5/1165	18.8/1195	19.0/1220	9,600 psi	
CCI 209M	Herco	Activ W-28			16.5/1165	10,000 psi	
CCI 209M	Herco	Fed. 20S1			17.5/1165	10,300 psi	
CCI 209M	Herco	H. Versalite			16.5/1165	10,800 psi	
CCI 209M	Herco	Rem. RXP20			18.5/1165	10,900 psi	
CCI 209M	Herco	WAA20			18.0/1165	11,300 psi	
Fed. 209	IMR 800-X	Activ W-28			17.5/1195	10,100 LUP	
Fed. 209	SR-4756	Fed. 20S1			20.0/1190	10,900 LUP	
Rem. 209	Herco	Activ W-28			17.0/1165	10,900 psi	
Rem. 209P	Blue Dot	BP Z20	24.0/1230	24.4/1245	25.0/1265	10,900 psi	Note 2
Rem. 209P	Blue Dot	BP Z20	24.0/1230	24.4/1245	25.0/1265	10,900 psi	Note 2
Rem. 209P	Herco	BP SG20S	16.5/1105	17.0/1165	18.0/1230	11,000 psi	Note 1
Rem. 209P	Herco	BP Z20	16.5/1115	16.7/1140	17.0/1165	10,800 psi	Note 2
Rem. 209P	Herco	BP Z20	16.5/1115	16.7/1140	17.0/1165	10,800 psi	Note 2
Rem. 209P	IMR 800-X	Activ W-28			18.0/1195	10,700 LUP	
Rem. 209P	SR-4756	Rem. SP20			21.5/1210	10,500 LUP	
Rem. 209P	Unique	BP SG20S			16.0/1200	10,000 LUP	Note 1
Win. 209	Herco	Activ W-28			18.0/1165	10,700 psi	
Win. 209	HS-6	BP SG20L			22.0/1165	10,200 psi	Note 3
Win. 209	HS-6	Rem. RXP20	21.0/1165	22.0/1195	23.0/1220	9,600 psi	
Win. 209	HS-7	H. Versalite			24.5/1165	10,000 psi	
Win. 209	IMR 800-X	Activ W-28			18.0/1210	10,200 LUP	
Win. 209	Solo 1500	Activ W-32			23.5/1165	9,600 LUP	
Win. 209	SR-4756	WAA20			21.5/1210	10,200 LUP	
Win. 209	SR-7625	WAA20			19.5/1205	10,800 LUP	
Win. 209	Universal	Rem. RXP20	18.0/1165	18.7/1195	19.3/1220	10,000 psi	
Win. 209	W 473AA	BP SG20L	17.2/1145	17.5/1165	17.8/1200	10,800 LUP	Note 3
Win. 209	W 571	BP SG20L			25.5/1250	11,000 LUP	Note 3
ESTATE: CHEDDITE					**1-OUNCE LEAD SHOT**		
Fio. 615	W 571	BP SG20L			22.0/1200	9,700 LUP	Note 3
FEDERAL: PAPER					**1-OUNCE LEAD SHOT**		
Fed. 209	Herco	Rem. RXP20			17.0/1165	11,500 psi	
Fed. 209	Herco	Rem. SP20			16.5/1165	11,500 psi	
Fed. 209	Herco	WAA20			16.0/1165	11,200 psi	
Fed. 209	Herco	WAA20F1			16.5/1165	11,300 psi	
FEDERAL: PLASTIC (PAPER BASE WAD)					**1-OUNCE LEAD SHOT**		
CCI 209	Herco	Fed. 20S1			18.5/1220	9,800 psi	
CCI 209	IMR PB	Rem. SP20			17.5/1155	10,600 LUP	
CCI 209	IMR PB	Trico No. 2			17.0/1150	10,500 LUP	

Load Notes: 1 = Short wad. 2 = Maximum Field. 3 = Long wad.

Caution: Follow load recipes exactly; do not substitute components, exceed listed maximums or load less than listed minimums.

Primer	Powder Type	Wad	Powder Charge (grains) / Velocity (fps) Minimum		Maximum	Maximum Pressure	Load Notes
FEDERAL: PLASTIC (PAPER BASE WAD) (CONT.)					**1-OUNCE LEAD SHOT**		
CCI 209	SR-7625	Rem. SP20			19.5/1205	10,000 LUP	
CCI 209	SR-7625	Trico No. 2			19.5/1225	10,500 LUP	
CCI 209M	HS-7	Rem. RXP20	24.0/1165	24.6/1195	25.2/1220	8,600 psi	
CCI 209M	IMR 800-X	Fed. 20S1			18.0/1175	9,600 LUP	
CCI 209M	IMR 800-X	H. Versalite			18.5/1180	9,200 LUP	
CCI 209M	IMR 800-X	Lage Uniwad			18.5/1170	8,500 LUP	
CCI 209M	IMR 800-X	Rem. SP20			18.0/1165	8,600 LUP	
CCI 209M	IMR 800-X	WAA20F1			18.0/1175	8,600 LUP	
Fed. 209	Blue Dot	Rem. SP20			24.0/1220	10,200 psi	
Fed. 209	Blue Dot	WAA20F1			24.0/1220	10,100 psi	
Fed. 209	Herco	Rem. RXP20			17.0/1165	11,300 psi	
Fed. 209	Herco	Rem. SP20			17.0/1165	9,600 psi	
Fed. 209	Herco	WAA20F1			16.5/1165	11,100 psi	
Fed. 209	IMR 800-X	Fed. 20S1	17.5/1160	18.0/1190	18.5/1215	10,500 LUP	
Fed. 209	IMR 800-X	H. Versalite	18.0/1165	18.5/1195	19.0/1220	9,900 LUP	
Fed. 209	IMR 800-X	Lage Uniwad	18.0/1165	18.5/1195	19.0/1225	10,200 LUP	
Fed. 209	IMR 800-X	Rem. SP20	17.5/1160	18.3/1190	19.0/1220	9,600 LUP	
Fed. 209	IMR 800-X	WAA20F1	17.5/1160	18.3/1195	19.0/1230	10,000 LUP	
Fed. 209	Solo 1500	Fed. 20S1	22.5/1165	23.0/1195	23.5/1220	10,600 LUP	
Fed. 209	SR-4756	Rem. SP20	20.5/1165	21.0/1195	21.5/1220	10,600 LUP	
Fed. 209	SR-4756	Trico No. 2	20.5/1170	21.3/1200	22.0/1230	10,300 LUP	
Fed. 209	SR-7625	Rem. SP20			17.5/1160	10,000 LUP	
Fed. 209	Unique	Rem. SP20			16.0/1165	10,800 psi	
Fed. 209	Unique	WAA20F1			15.5/1165	11,300 psi	
Fed. 209A	HS-6	Fed. 20S1	20.2/1165	21.4/1195	22.5/1220	10,100 psi	
Fed. 209A	HS-7	Fed. 20S1	23.0/1165	24.0/1195	25.0/1220	9,300 psi	
Fed. 410	IMR PB	Lage Uniwad			17.5/1170	10,900 LUP	
Fed. 410	IMR PB	Rem. SP20			17.5/1160	10,300 LUP	
Fed. 410	SR-7625	Lage Uniwad			20.0/1205	9,800 LUP	
Win. 209	HS-6	Rem. RXP20	21.5/1165	22.4/1195	23.2/1220	8,700 psi	
Win. 209	HS-7	Rem. RXP20	23.5/1165	24.5/1195	25.5/1220	8,900 psi	
Win. 209	SR-4756	Lage Uniwad			21.5/1210	9,900 LUP	
Win. 209	SR-7625	Rem. SP20	18.0/1160	18.5/1185	19.0/1205	10,500 LUP	
Win. 209	SR-7625	Trico No. 2	18.0/1165	18.3/1175	18.5/1180	10,600 LUP	
FIOCCHI: PLASTIC					**1-OUNCE LEAD SHOT**		
CCI 209	HS-6	Fed. 20S1	21.5/1165	21.8/1195	22.0/1220	10,200 psi	
CCI 209	HS-7	Fed. 20S1	23.0/1165	23.5/1195	24.0/1220	10,600 psi	
CCI 209	HS-7	Rem. RXP20	24.0/1165	24.5/1195	25.0/1220	8,800 psi	
CCI 209M	Blue Dot	Rem. SP20			24.0/1220	10,700 psi	
Fed. 209	Blue Dot	Rem. SP20	23.0/1220	24.0/1250	25.0/1275	10,300 psi	
Fed. 209A	HS-7	Rem. RXP20	22.5/1165	23.8/1195	25.0/1220	9,800 psi	
Fio. 615	Blue Dot	Rem. SP20			27.5/1220	9,200 psi	

Load Notes: 2 = Maximum Field.

Caution: Follow load recipes exactly; do not substitute components, exceed listed maximums or load less than listed minimums.

Primer	Powder Type	Wad	Powder Charge (grains) / Velocity (fps) Minimum		Maximum	Maximum Pressure	Load Notes
FIOCCHI: PLASTIC (CONT.)					**1-OUNCE LEAD SHOT**		
Fio. 616	Blue Dot	BP Z20	24.0/1235	24.7/1250	25.5/1265	11,400 psi	Note 2
Fio. 616	Blue Dot	BP Z20	24.0/1235	24.7/1250	25.5/1265	11,400 psi	Note 2
Fio. 616	Blue Dot	Rem. SP20	24.5/1220	25.3/1250	26.0/1275	10,800 psi	
Fio. 616	Herco	BP Z20	17.0/1200	17.1/1210	17.3/1225	11,300 psi	Note 2
Fio. 616	Herco	BP Z20	17.0/1200	17.1/1210	17.3/1225	11,300 psi	Note 2
Fio. 616	HS-6	BP SG20L			22.0/1175	10,300 psi	Note 3
Fio. 616	IMR 800-X	BP SG20S			16.0/1170	10,300 psi	Note 1
Fio. 616	Unique	BP SG20S	16.0/1100	16.5/1150	17.5/1225	10,800 psi	Note 1
Rem. 209	Blue Dot	Rem. SP20			22.5/1220	10,600 psi	
Win. 209	Blue Dot	Rem. SP20			26.0/1275	10,600 psi	
Win. 209	HS-6	WAA20	21.0/1165	21.5/1195	22.0/1220	10,200 psi	
Win. 209	HS-6	Windjammer	20.5/1165	21.0/1195	21.5/1220	10,200 psi	
Win. 209	HS-7	WAA20	23.0/1165	23.5/1195	24.0/1220	9,800 psi	
Win. 209	HS-7	Windjammer	23.0/1165	23.8/1195	24.5/1220	9,800 psi	
REMINGTON: PREMIER & NITRO 27 & STS					**1-OUNCE LEAD SHOT**		
CCI 209	Blue Dot	Rem. SP20	22.0/1155	22.5/1190	23.0/1220	10,300 psi	
CCI 209M	Blue Dot	Rem. SP20	21.5/1155	22.0/1190	22.5/1220	10,900 psi	
Fed. 209	Blue Dot	Rem. SP20			20.5/1155	11,300 psi	
Fio. 616	Blue Dot	Rem. SP20	22.5/1155	23.0/1190	23.5/1220	11,000 psi	
Rem. 209P	Blue Dot	Rem. SP20	21.5/1155	22.8/1190	24.0/1220	11,100 psi	
Rem. 209P	Blue Dot	WAA20F1	21.5/1155	22.5/1190	23.5/1220	10,900 psi	
Rem. 209P	Herco	WAA20F1			17.5/1155	11,500 psi	
Rem. 209P	SR-4756	BP SG20S			19.5/1200	10,300 LUP	Note 1
Win. 209	Blue Dot	Rem. SP20	21.5/1155	21.8/1190	22.0/1220	11,100 psi	
Win. 209	Unique	BP SG20S			16.0/1200	9,200 LUP	Note 1
Win. 209	WSF	BP SG20L			17.5/1200	10,600 LUP	Note 3
REMINGTON: PREMIER & RXP					**1-OUNCE LEAD SHOT**		
Fed. 209A	HS-6	Fed. 20S1	19.0/1165	19.7/1195	20.4/1220	11,800 psi	
Fed. 209A	HS-7	Fed. 20S1	20.5/1165	21.3/1195	22.0/1220	11,200 psi	
Rem. 209P	HS-7	Rem. SP20	23.0/1165	24.0/1195	25.0/1220	10,800 LUP	
Win. 209	HS-6	WAA20			19.0/1165	10,400 psi	
Win. 209	HS-7	WAA20			21.0/1165	10,500 psi	
Win. 209	HS-7	WAA20F1	21.0/1165	22.0/1195	23.0/1220	11,200 psi	
REMINGTON: RXP					**1-OUNCE LEAD SHOT**		
Rem. 209P	Solo 1500	Rem. SP20			21.5/1165	10,600 LUP	
Rem. 97*	Herco	Rem. RXP20			18.0/1220	11,000 psi	
Rem. 97*	Unique	Fed. 20S1			15.5/1165	10,800 psi	
Rem. 97*	Unique	Rem. RXP20			16.0/1165	10,600 psi	
Rem. 97*	Unique	WAA20			15.5/1165	11,200 psi	
Win. 209	W 540	WAA20F1			21.0/1165	10,100 LUP	
Win. 209	W 540	WAA20F1			22.0/1220	10,700 LUP	

Load Notes: 1 = Short wad. 2 = Maximum Field. 3 = Long wad.

Caution: Follow load recipes exactly; do not substitute components, exceed listed maximums or load less than listed minimums.

Primer	Powder Type	Wad	Powder Charge (grains) / Velocity (fps) Minimum	Maximum	Maximum Pressure	Load Notes
REMINGTON: RXP (CONT.)				**1-OUNCE LEAD SHOT**		
Win. 209	W 571	WAA20F1		23.0/1165	9,700 LUP	
Win. 209	W 571	WAA20F1		25.0/1240	10,900 LUP	
REMINGTON: SP (SEPARATE PLASTIC BASE WAD)				**1-OUNCE LEAD SHOT**		
CCI 209M	IMR 800-X	Lage Uniwad		18.0/1210	10,700 LUP	
Rem. 209	Blue Dot	Rem. SP20		23.0/1220	10,300 psi	
Rem. 209	Blue Dot	WAA20F1		24.0/1220	10,100 psi	
Rem. 209	Herco	Rem. SP20		17.5/1165	11,300 psi	
Rem. 209	Herco	WAA20F1		17.5/1165	10,700 psi	
Rem. 209P	Blue Dot	BP SG20S		23.5/1235	10,600 psi	Note 1
REMINGTON: UNIBODY (INTEGRAL PLASTIC BASE WAD)				**1-OUNCE LEAD SHOT**		
CCI 209M	Blue Dot	Rem. SP20		22.0/1165	10,500 psi	
Fed. 209	Blue Dot	Rem. SP20		21.5/1165	10,500 psi	
Fed. 209	Alliant 2400	Activ W-32		29.5/1220	10,500 psi	
Rem. 209	Blue Dot	Rem. SP20		21.0/1165	11,500 psi	
Rem. 209	Blue Dot	WAA20F1		21.5/1165	11,100 psi	
Win. 209	Blue Dot	Rem. SP20		22.0/1165	11,300 psi	
WINCHESTER: COMPRESSION-FORMED AA TYPE				**1-OUNCE LEAD SHOT**		
CCI 209	SR-4756	Trico No. 2		20.0/1145	10,100 LUP	
CCI 209M	IMR 800-X	Lage Uniwad		18.0/1210	10,700 LUP	
CCI 209M	IMR 800-X	WAA20F1		18.0/1215	10,900 LUP	
Fed. 209	IMR 800-X	H. Versalite		16.5/1155	10,600 LUP	
Fed. 209	IMR 800-X	Lage Uniwad		16.5/1155	10,700 LUP	
Fed. 209	IMR 800-X	Rem. RXP20		17.0/1175	10,600 LUP	
Fed. 209	IMR 800-X	WAA20F1		16.5/1165	10,600 LUP	
Fed. 410	SR-4756	Trico No. 2		20.5/1170	10,800 LUP	
Rem. 209P	IMR 800-X	H. Versalite		20.0/1220	10,900 LUP	
Win. 209	Blue Dot	Rem. RXP20		23.0/1220	11,300 psi	
Win. 209	Blue Dot	Rem. SP20		23.5/1220	11,400 psi	
Win. 209	Blue Dot	WAA20F1		23.0/1220	11,500 psi	
Win. 209	Herco	Rem. RXP20		16.5/1165	9,600 psi	
Win. 209	Herco	Rem. SP20		16.5/1165	10,000 psi	
Win. 209	Herco	WAA20		16.5/1165	10,400 psi	
Win. 209	HS-6	BP SG20S		22.5/1220	10,900 LUP	Note 1
Win. 209	HS-6	Rem. SP20	23.0/1165 23.5/1195	24.0/1220	10,800 LUP	
Win. 209	HS-6	WAA20F1	21.5/1165 22.0/1195	22.5/1220	10,900 LUP	
Win. 209	HS-7	BP SG20S		25.0/1250	10,700 LUP	Note 1
Win. 209	HS-7	Rem. SP20	23.5/1165 24.0/1195	24.5/1220	10,600 LUP	
Win. 209	HS-7	WAA20F1	23.5/1165 24.5/1220	25.5/1250	10,800 LUP	
Win. 209	IMR 800-X	H. Versalite		17.0/1170	10,300 LUP	
Win. 209	IMR 800-X	Lage Uniwad	17.0/1165 17.5/1185	18.0/1205	10,600 LUP	
Win. 209	IMR 800-X	Rem. RXP20		17.0/1165	10,300 LUP	

Load Notes: 1 = Short wad.

Caution: Follow load recipes exactly; do not substitute components, exceed listed maximums or load less than listed minimums.

Primer	Powder Type	Wad	Powder Charge (grains) / Velocity (fps) Minimum		Maximum	Maximum Pressure	Load Notes
WINCHESTER: COMPRESSION-FORMED AA TYPE (CONT.)					**1-OUNCE LEAD SHOT**		
Win. 209	IMR 800-X	WAA20F1	16.5/1160	17.0/1185	17.5/1205	10,700 LUP	
Win. 209	Solo 1500	Rem. SP20			21.5/1165	11,000 LUP	
Win. 209	W 540	Rem. SP20			23.0/1165	10,000 LUP	
Win. 209	W 540	Rem. SP20			24.0/1220	10,700 LUP	
Win. 209	W 540	WAA20F1			21.5/1165	9,900 LUP	Note 4
Win. 209	W 540	WAA20F1			22.5/1220	10,900 LUP	
Win. 209	W 571	Rem. SP20			23.5/1165	9,800 LUP	Note 5
Win. 209	W 571	Rem. SP20			24.5/1220	10,300 LUP	
Win. 209	W 571	WAA20F1			23.5/1165	9,300 LUP	
Win. 209	W 571	WAA20F1			25.5/1250	10,800 LUP	
WINCHESTER: POLYFORMED (SEPARATE PLASTIC BASE WAD)					**1-OUNCE LEAD SHOT**		
CCI 209	HS-6	Activ W32			20.5/1165	9,200 psi	
CCI 209	Universal	Activ W32			17.5/1165	9,200 psi	
Fed. 209A	HS-6	Rem. SP20	20.0/1165	20.8/1195	21.5/1220	10,300 psi	
Fed. 209A	Universal	Activ W32			16.0/1165	10,000 psi	
Fed. 209A	Universal	Rem. SP20			16.5/1165	9,400 psi	
Fed. 209A	Universal	WAA20F1	16.3/1165	16.8/1195	17.2/1220	11,200 psi	
Win. 209	HS-6	WAA20F1			20.0/1165	8,900 psi	
Win. 209	Solo 1500	WAA20F1	22.5/1165	23.3/1195	24.0/1220	10,100 LUP	
Win. 209	Universal	WAA20F1			16.5/1165	8,900 psi	

Load Notes: 4 = This load duplicates ballistics of Winchester's 2½ dram equivalent Xpert loading. 5 = This load duplicates ballistics of Winchester's 2¾ dram equivalent Super-X loading.

1¹/₈ OUNCES LEAD SHOT 20-GAUGE 2³/₄"

Primer	Powder Type	Wad	Powder Charge (grains) / Velocity (fps) Minimum		Maximum	Maximum Pressure	Load Notes
ACTIV: ALL PLASTIC					**1¹/₈ OUNCES LEAD SHOT**		
CCI 209M	HS-7	Activ W28			23.5/1175	10,300 psi	
CCI 209M	HS-7	Rem. RXP20			24.0/1175	9,600 psi	
Win. 209	HS-7	Activ W20			24.0/1175	10,100 psi	
Win. 209	HS-7	Rem. RXP20			24.0/1175	9,600 psi	
FEDERAL: PLASTIC (PAPER BASE WAD)					**1¹/₈ OUNCES LEAD SHOT**		
Fed. 209	Blue Dot	Rem. SP20			23.0/1175	10,900 psi	
Fed. 209	IMR 800-X	Rem. SP20			19.0/1170	10,700 LUP	
Win. 209	IMR 800-X	Lage Uniwad			19.0/1170	10,600 LUP	
Win. 209	IMR 800-X	WAA20F1			19.0/1180	10,700 LUP	
FIOCCHI: PLASTIC					**1¹/₈ OUNCES LEAD SHOT**		
Fed. 209	Blue Dot	Rem. SP20			23.5/1175	10,700 psi	
Fio. 616	Blue Dot	Rem. SP20			23.5/1175	10,000 psi	
Win. 209	Blue Dot	Rem. SP20			23.5/1175	11,400 psi	

Caution: Follow load recipes exactly; do not substitute components, exceed listed maximums or load less than listed minimums.

Primer	Powder Type	Wad	Powder Charge (grains) / Velocity (fps) Minimum	Maximum	Maximum Pressure	Load Notes
REMINGTON: RXP				**1¹/₈ OUNCES LEAD SHOT**		
Win. 209	W 571	WAA20F1		23.5/1150	11,100 LUP	
REMINGTON: UNIBODY & RXP & PREMIER				**1¹/₈ OUNCES LEAD SHOT**		
Rem. 209P	Blue Dot	Rem. SP20		22.0/1175	11,300 psi	
Rem. 209P	Blue Dot	WAA20F1		22.0/1175	11,500 psi	
Rem. 209P	HS-7	Rem. RP20		23.5/1150	11,000 LUP	
WINCHESTER: COMPRESSION-FORMED AA TYPE				**1¹/₈ OUNCES LEAD SHOT**		
CCI 109	W 571	Rem. RP20		24.5/1175	10,500 LUP	
Fed. 209	HS-7	Rem. RP20		24.0/1175	11,000 LUP	
Fed. 209	W 571	Rem. RP20		24.0/1175	11,000 LUP	
Rem. 209P	HS-7	Rem. RP20		24.5/1175	10,600 LUP	
Win. 209	HS-7	Rem. RP20		24.5/1175	10,300 LUP	
Win. 209	W 571	Rem. RP20		24.5/1175	10,200 LUP	
Win. 209	W 571	WAA20F1		24.0/1150	10,700 LUP	Note 1

Load Notes: 1 = This load requires 80 to 100 pounds wad pressure.

    Caution: Follow load recipes exactly; do not substitute components, exceed listed maximums or load less than listed minimums.

1 1/16 Ounces Lead Shot

Primer	Powder Type	Wad	Powder Charge (grains) / Velocity (fps) Minimum			Maximum	Maximum Pressure	Load Notes
FEDERAL: PLASTIC (PAPER BASE WAD)						**1 1/16 Ounces Lead Shot**		
Fed. 209	Blue Dot	Fed. 20S1				28.0/1310	10,300 psi	
Fed. 209	Blue Dot	Rem. RXP20	27.0/1255	27.3/1275	27.6/1290	28.0/1310	10,200 psi	
Fed. 209	Blue Dot	WAA20	26.5/1255	27.2/1275	27.9/1290	28.5/1310	10,600 psi	
WINCHESTER: COMPRESSION-FORMED AA TYPE						**1 1/16 Ounces Lead Shot**		
Win. 209	Blue Dot	Rem. SP20				26.0/1255	10,600 psi	

1 1/8 Ounces Lead Shot

Primer	Powder Type	Wad	Powder Charge (grains) / Velocity (fps) Minimum	Maximum	Maximum Pressure	Load Notes
ACTIV: ALL PLASTIC				**1 1/8 Ounces Lead Shot**		
CCI 209M	HS-7	WAA20		28.0/1250	10,900 psi	
Win. 209	HS-7	WAA20		28.0/1250	10,600 psi	
FEDERAL: PLASTIC (PAPER BASE WAD)				**1 1/8 Ounces Lead Shot**		
Fed. 209	Blue Dot	Rem. SP20		26.5/1230	10,300 psi	
Fed. 209	Blue Dot	WAA20F1		26.0/1230	10,100 psi	
Fed. 209	IMR 800-X	Fed. 20S1		20.5/1205	10,400 LUP	
Fed. 209	IMR 800-X	Lage Uniwad		20.5/1200	10,800 LUP	
Fed. 209	IMR 800-X	Rem. RXP20		21.0/1215	10,700 LUP	
Fed. 209	SR-4756	Rem. SP20		24.0/1215	10,900 LUP	
Fed. 209	SR-4756	Trico No. 2		24.0/1200	10,600 LUP	
Fed. 209	SR-4756	WAA20F1		24.0/1215	10,500 LUP	
Fed. 209A	HS-6	Fed. 20S1		23.5/1220	11,500 psi	
Fed. 209A	HS-7	Fed. 20S1		25.8/1220	11,600 psi	
Fed. 209A	HS-7	Fed. 20S1		27.3/1250	11,700 psi	
Fed. 410	SR-4756	Lage Uniwad		24.5/1220	10,500 LUP	
Win. 209	HS-6	WAA20F1		23.0/1220	10,600 psi	
Win. 209	HS-7	Fed. 20S1		28.0/1250	11,400 psi	
Win. 209	HS-7	WAA20F1		25.5/1220	10,100 psi	
Win. 209	SR-4756	Rem. SP20		26.0/1270	10,600 LUP	
Win. 209	SR-4756	WAA20F1		26.0/1265	10,600 LUP	
REMINGTON: NITRO STEEL (3-PIECE SEPARATE PLASTIC BASE WAD)				**1 1/8 Ounces Lead Shot**		
Win. 209	HS-7	WAA20		27.5/1250	10,900 psi	
REMINGTON: PREMIER & NITRO 27 & STS				**1 1/8 Ounces Lead Shot**		
CCI 209M	HS-7	Rem. RXP20		24.8/1250	11,500 psi	
Win. 209	HS-7	Rem. RXP20		25.0/1250	11,900 psi	
WINCHESTER: COMPRESSION-FORMED AA TYPE				**1 1/8 Ounces Lead Shot**		
CCI 109	W 571	WAA20		27.0/1220	11,100 LUP	
CCI 209M	HS-7	WAA20		26.5/1250	12,100 psi	
Fed. 410	SR-4756	Lage Uniwad		21.5/1190	10,900 LUP	

Caution: Follow load recipes exactly; do not substitute components, exceed listed maximums or load less than listed minimums.

20-GAUGE 3″ — 1 1/8 OUNCES LEAD SHOT (CONT.)

Primer	Powder Type	Wad	Powder Charge (grains) / Velocity (fps) Minimum — Maximum	Maximum Pressure	Load Notes
WINCHESTER: COMPRESSION-FORMED AA TYPE (CONT.)			1 1/8 OUNCES LEAD SHOT		
Fed. 410	SR-4756	Rem. SP20	25.0/1215	10,900 LUP	
Fed. 410	SR-4756	Trico No. 2	24.0/1190	10,600 LUP	
Fed. 410	SR-4756	WAA20F1	24.5/1200	10,400 LUP	
Rem. 209P	HS-7	WAA20	27.0/1220	11,200 LUP	
Win. 209	Blue Dot	Rem. SP20	25.5/1230	11,000 psi	
Win. 209	Blue Dot	WAA20F1	25.5/1230	11,100 psi	
Win. 209	HS-7	WAA20	27.0/1220	11,100 LUP	
Win. 209	HS-7	WAA20	27.0/1250	11,800 psi	
Win. 209	SR-4756	Rem. SP20	23.5/1200	10,900 LUP	
Win. 209	SR-4756	Trico No. 2	23.0/1170	10,800 LUP	
Win. 209	SR-4756	WAA20F1	23.5/1185	10,900 LUP	
Win. 209	W 571	WAA20	27.0/1220	11,000 LUP	

20-GAUGE 3″ — 1 3/16 OUNCES LEAD SHOT

Primer	Powder Type	Wad	Powder Charge (grains) / Velocity (fps) Minimum — Maximum	Maximum Pressure	Load Notes
WINCHESTER: COMPRESSION-FORMED AA TYPE			1 3/16 OUNCES LEAD SHOT		
Win. 209	W 571	Rem. R20	27.5/1195	10,600 LUP	

Caution: Follow load recipes exactly; do not substitute components, exceed listed maximums or load less than listed minimums.

Primer	Powder Type	Wad	Powder Charge (grains) / Velocity (fps) Minimum	Maximum	Maximum Pressure	Load Notes
Activ: all plastic				**1¼ Ounces Lead Shot**		
CCI 209M	HS-7	Activ: W28		25.5/1115	10,800 psi	
Federal: Plastic (paper base wad)				**1¼ Ounces Lead Shot**		
Fed. 209	Blue Dot	Rem. SP20		25.5/1185	10,600 psi	Note 1
Fed. 209	Blue Dot	WAA20F1		25.5/1185	10,400 psi	
Fed. 209	IMR 800-X	Lage Uniwad		19.0/1100	10,900 LUP	
Fed. 209	IMR 800-X	Rem. RXP20		19.5/1120	10,400 LUP	
Fed. 209A	HS-7	Rem. RXP20		25.5/1185	11,000 psi	
Remington: Nitro Steel (3-piece separate plastic base wad)				**1¼ Ounces Lead Shot**		
Win. 209	HS-7	Rem. RXP20		26.5/1185	10,600 psi	
Remington: Premier & Nitro 27 & STS				**1¼ Ounces Lead Shot**		
Win. 209	HS-7	H. Versalite		23.0/1185	11,600 psi	
Winchester: Compression-Formed AA Type				**1¼ Ounces Lead Shot**		
CCI 109	W 571	WAA20		24.0/1135	11,000 LUP	
Fed. 209	IMR 4227	Lage Uniwad		40.0/1180	8,900 LUP	Note 2
Rem. 209P	HS-7	WAA20		24.0/1135	11,000 LUP	
Win. 209	Blue Dot	Rem. SP20		24.0/1135	10,900 psi	
Win. 209	Blue Dot	Rem. SP20		25.0/1190	11,500 psi	
Win. 209	Blue Dot	WAA20F1		23.0/1135	10,200 psi	
Win. 209	Alliant 2400	Rem. SP20		34.5/1240	9,600 psi	
Win. 209	HS-7	WAA20		24.0/1135	10,900 LUP	
Win. 209	HS-7	WAA20F1		24.7/1185	11,800 psi	
Win. 209	W 571	WAA20		24.0/1135	10,800 LUP	

Load Notes: 1 = Add one 28-gauge, 0.135″ card inside bottom of shotcup. 2 = Remove insert from wad.

END OF 20-GAUGE LEAD SHOT LOAD DATA

Caution: Follow load recipes exactly; do not substitute components, exceed listed maximums or load less than listed minimums.

24-GAUGE 2½″ — 5/8-OUNCE LEAD SHOT

Primer	Powder Type	Wad	Powder Charge (grains) / Velocity (fps) Minimum	Maximum	Maximum Pressure	Load Notes
FIOCCHI: PLASTIC				5/8-OUNCE LEAD SHOT		
Fio. 615	Blue Dot	BP BW24		22.0/1205	9,400 psi	
Fio. 615	Herco	BP BW24		16.5/1200	9,900 psi	
Fio. 615	SR-4756	BP BW24		18.0/1210	10,100 psi	
Fio. 615	SR-7625	BP BW24		15.5/1210	10,100 psi	

24-GAUGE 2½″ — 3/4-OUNCE LEAD SHOT

Primer	Powder Type	Wad	Powder Charge (grains) / Velocity (fps) Minimum	Maximum	Maximum Pressure	Load Notes
FIOCCHI: PLASTIC				3/4-OUNCE LEAD SHOT		
Fio. 615	Blue Dot	BP SG24		23.5/1250	10,200 psi	
Fio. 615	Herco	BP SG24		16.0/1210	9,700 psi	
Fio. 615	SR-7625	BP SG24		16.5/1200	10,200 psi	

24-GAUGE 2½″ — 7/8-OUNCE LEAD SHOT

Primer	Powder Type	Wad	Powder Charge (grains) / Velocity (fps) Minimum	Maximum	Maximum Pressure	Load Notes
FIOCCHI: PLASTIC				7/8-OUNCE LEAD SHOT		
Fio. 615	Blue Dot	BP SG24		22.0/1215	10,000 psi	
Fio. 615	SR-4756	BP SG24		16.5/1200	10,000 psi	

END OF 24-GAUGE LEAD SHOT LOAD DATA

Caution: Follow load recipes exactly; do not substitute components, exceed listed maximums or load less than listed minimums.

Primer	Powder Type	Wad	Powder Charge (grains) / Velocity (fps) Minimum		Maximum	Maximum Pressure	Load Notes
Fiocchi: Purple Target (high base wad)					⅝-Ounce Lead Shot		
Fio. 615	Blue Dot	BP BW28	21.0/1330	21.5/1365	22.0/1410	8,500 psi	
Fio. 616	Blue Dot	BP SG28	21.5/1350	21.7/1370	22.0/1400	8,400 psi	
Fio. 616	Herco	BP BW28	17.0/1380	17.1/1395	17.2/1405	10,200 psi	
Fio. 616	Herco	BP SG28	16.0/1320	16.5/1350	17.0/1380	9,900 psi	

Caution: Follow load recipes exactly; do not substitute components, exceed listed maximums or load less than listed minimums.

28-GAUGE 2³/₄″ — ⁵/₈-OUNCE LEAD SHOT

Primer	Powder Type	Wad	Powder Charge (grains) / Velocity (fps) Minimum		Maximum	Maximum Pressure	Load Notes
FEDERAL: PLASTIC (PAPER BASE WAD)					⁵/₈-OUNCE LEAD SHOT		
CCI 209	Blue Dot	BP BW28			22.0/1400	8,500 psi	
CCI 209	Herco	BP BW28	16.0/1320	16.5/1350	17.0/1380	8,900 psi	
Rem. 209P	Blue Dot	BP SG28	21.0/1350	21.5/1375	22.0/1390	8,500 psi	
Rem. 209P	Herco	BP SG28	16.0/1320	16.5/1335	17.0/1350	9,200 psi	

28-GAUGE 2³/₄″ — ¹¹/₁₆-OUNCE LEAD SHOT

Primer	Powder Type	Wad	Powder Charge (grains) / Velocity (fps) Minimum		Maximum	Maximum Pressure	Load Notes
FEDERAL: PLASTIC (PAPER BASE WAD)					¹¹/₁₆-OUNCE LEAD SHOT		
CCI 209	Solo 1250	BP SG 28			13.0/1155	11,400 psi	Note 1
Rem. 209	Solo 1250	BP SG 28			13.5/1200	10,300 psi	Note 1
REMINGTON: PREMIER & NITRO 27 & STS & UNIBODY (INTEGRAL PLASTIC BASE WAD)							
Rem. 209	Solo 1250	BP SG 28	12.5/1155	12.8/1180	13.0/1200	10,400 psi	Note 1
WINCHESTER: COMPRESSION-FORMED AA TYPE					¹¹/₁₆-OUNCE LEAD SHOT		
CCI 209	IMR PB	Fed. 28S1			12.3/1165	11,200 LUP	
CCI 209	SR-4756	Fed. 28S1			16.5/1265	11,400 LUP	
CCI 209	SR-7625	Fed. 28S1			13.7/1210	11,300 LUP	
Fed. 209	SR-4756	WAA28			15.0/1215	10,600 LUP	
Win. 209	IMR PB	WAA28			12.6/1190	11,200 LUP	
Win. 209	Solo 1250	WAA28			11.0/1155	12,000 psi	
Win. 209	SR-4756	Fed. 28S1			15.6/1225	11,200 LUP	
Win. 209	SR-4756	WAA28			15.0/1175	9,000 LUP	
Win. 209	SR-7625	WAA28			14.0/1225	10,300 LUP	

Load Notes: 1 = #9 shot only.

28-GAUGE 2³/₄″ — ³/₄-OUNCE LEAD SHOT

Primer	Powder Type	Wad	Powder Charge (grains) / Velocity (fps) Minimum		Maximum	Maximum Pressure	Load Notes
FEDERAL: PLASTIC (PAPER BASE WAD)					³/₄-OUNCE LEAD SHOT		
CCI 109	Blue Dot	Rem. SP28			18.5/1200	9,800 psi	
CCI 109	Herco	Rem. SP28			14.5/1200	10,000 psi	
CCI 109	Herco	WAA28			15.0/1200	10,500 psi	
CCI 109	Unique	Rem. SP28			13.5/1200	9,400 psi	
CCI 109	Unique	WAA28			14.0/1200	10,400 psi	
CCI 209	Solo 1250	Fed. 28S1			13.0/1155	12,500 psi	
Fed. 209	Blue Dot	Fed. 28S1A			17.5/1200	9,600 psi	
Fed. 209	Blue Dot	Rem. SP28	18.0/1200	19.0/1250	20.0/1295	10,900 psi	
Fed. 209	Blue Dot	WAA28			17.5/1200	8,700 psi	
Fed. 209	Herco	Fed. 28S1A			14.0/1200	11,700 psi	

Caution: Follow load recipes exactly; do not substitute components, exceed listed maximums or load less than listed minimums.

Primer	Powder Type	Wad	Powder Charge (grains) / Velocity (fps) Minimum	Maximum	Maximum Pressure	Load Notes
FEDERAL: PLASTIC (PAPER BASE WAD) (CONT.)				³/₄-OUNCE LEAD SHOT		
Fed. 209	Herco	Rem. SP28		13.0/1200	10,100 psi	
Fed. 209	Herco	WAA28		14.0/1200	10,900 psi	
Fed. 209	Solo 1250	Fed. 28S1		14.5/1200	11,300 psi	
Fed. 209	Unique	Fed. 28S1A		13.5/1200	11,600 psi	
Fed. 209	Unique	Rem. SP28		13.0/1200	11,200 psi	
Fed. 209	Unique	WAA28		13.5/1200	10,500 psi	
Fed. 209	Universal	Rem. PT28		14.0/1200	10,800 psi	
Fed. 209A	IMR 800-X	CB 1034-28		13.5/1200	10,000 psi	
Fed. 209A	IMR 800-X	Fed. 28S1		13.5/1205	11,000 psi	
Fed. 209A	IMR 800-X	Pat. Ctrl. 28		13.5/1215	10,600 psi	
Fed. 209A	IMR 800-X	Rem. PT28		13.5/1205	10,700 psi	
Fed. 209A	IMR 800-X	WAA28		13.5/1195	10,100 psi	
Fed. 209A	IMR PB	CB 1034-28		13.0/1165	12,100 psi	
Fed. 209A	IMR PB	Rem. PT28		13.0/1160	12,300 psi	
Fed. 209A	IMR PB	WAA28		13.0/1165	12,400 psi	
Fed. 209A	SR-4756	Fed. 28S1		15.5/1205	11,900 psi	
Fed. 209A	SR-4756	Pat. Ctrl. 28		15.5/1210	11,400 psi	
Fed. 209A	SR-4756	Rem. PT28		15.5/1200	11,400 psi	
Fed. 209A	SR-7625	CB 1034-28		14.0/1195	12,000 psi	
Fed. 209A	SR-7625	Fed. 28S1		14.0/1185	12,000 psi	
Fed. 209A	SR-7625	Pat. Ctrl. 28		14.0/1195	11,900 psi	
Fed. 209A	SR-7625	Rem. PT28		15.5/1195	11,800 psi	
Fed. 209A	SR-7625	WAA28		14.5/1215	12,300 psi	
Fed. 209A	Universal	Rem. PT28		14.2/1200	11,400 psi	
Rem. 209P	IMR 800-X	CB 1034-28		14.0/1205	9,800 psi	
Rem. 209P	IMR 800-X	Fed. 28S1		14.0/1210	10,400 psi	
Rem. 209P	IMR 800-X	Pat. Ctrl. 28		14.0/1200	9,600 psi	
Rem. 209P	IMR 800-X	Rem. PT28		14.0/1195	9,900 psi	
Rem. 209P	IMR 800-X	WAA28		14.5/1210	9,500 psi	
Rem. 209P	IMR PB	Fed. 28S1		14.0/1190	12,200 psi	
Rem. 209P	IMR PB	Pat. Ctrl. 28		14.5/1200	11,500 psi	
Rem. 209P	IMR PB	Rem. PT28		14.5/1200	11,700 psi	
Rem. 209P	IMR PB	WAA28		14.5/1205	11,400 psi	
Rem. 209P	SR-4756	Fed. 28S1		16.5/1195	9,800 psi	
Rem. 209P	SR-4756	Pat. Ctrl. 28		16.0/1185	9,600 psi	
Rem. 209P	SR-4756	Rem. PT28		17.0/1170	10,300 psi	
Rem. 209P	SR-7625	Fed. 28S1		14.5/1190	10,800 psi	
Rem. 209P	SR-7625	Pat. Ctrl. 28		15.0/1190	10,200 psi	
Rem. 209P	SR-7625	Rem. PT28		15.0/1205	10,100 psi	
Rem. 209P	SR-7625	WAA28		14.5/1185	10,500 psi	
Win. 209	IMR 800-X	CB 1034-28		13.5/1190	9,800 psi	
Win. 209	IMR 800-X	Fed. 28S1		13.5/1200	10,500 psi	
Win. 209	IMR 800-X	Pat. Ctrl. 28		13.5/1190	9,900 psi	

Caution: Follow load recipes exactly; do not substitute components, exceed listed maximums or load less than listed minimums.

Primer	Powder Type	Wad	Powder Charge (grains) / Velocity (fps) Minimum		Maximum	Maximum Pressure	Load Notes
FEDERAL: PLASTIC (PAPER BASE WAD) (CONT.)					**³/₄-OUNCE LEAD SHOT**		
Win. 209	IMR 800-X	Rem. PT28			13.5/1190	10,100 psi	
Win. 209	IMR 800-X	WAA28			14.0/1210	10,000 psi	
Win. 209	IMR PB	Fed. 28S1			14.0/1185	12,500 psi	
Win. 209	IMR PB	Pat. Ctrl. 28			14.5/1210	12,000 psi	
Win. 209	IMR PB	Rem. PT28			14.5/1205	12,100 psi	
Win. 209	IMR PB	WAA28			14.5/1215	11,900 psi	
Win. 209	SR-4756	Fed. 28S1			16.0/1195	10,600 psi	
Win. 209	SR-4756	Pat. Ctrl. 28			16.0/1200	10,300 psi	
Win. 209	SR-4756	Rem. PT28			16.0/1190	10,500 psi	
Win. 209	SR-7625	Fed. 28S1			15.0/1205	11,200 psi	
Win. 209	SR-7625	Pat. Ctrl. 28			15.0/1205	10,900 psi	
Win. 209	SR-7625	Rem. PT28			15.0/1200	11,100 psi	
Win. 209	SR-7625	WAA28			14.5/1185	10,800 psi	
Win. 209	Universal	Pat. Ctrl. 28			13.8/1200	10,200 psi	
FIOCCHI: PURPLE TARGET (HIGH BASE WAD)					**³/₄-OUNCE LEAD SHOT**		
Fio. 616	Universal	Rem. PT28			14.2/1200	10,600 psi	
Win. 209	Universal	Pat. Ctrl. 28			14.2/1200	10,700 psi	
REMINGTON: 3-PIECE (SEPARATE BLACK PLASTIC BASE WAD)					**³/₄-OUNCE LEAD SHOT**		
CCI 109	Blue Dot	Fed. 28S1A			18.5/1200	10,100 psi	
CCI 109	Blue Dot	Rem. SP28			18.0/1200	7,500 psi	
CCI 109	Blue Dot	WAA28			18.0/1200	7,300 psi	
CCI 109	Herco	Fed. 28S1A			14.5/1200	10,700 psi	
CCI 109	Herco	Rem. SP28			14.0/1200	8,900 psi	
CCI 109	Herco	WAA28			14.0/1200	8,300 psi	
CCI 109	Unique	Fed. 28S1A			14.0/1200	10,900 psi	
CCI 109	Unique	Rem. SP28			13.0/1200	9,100 psi	
CCI 109	Unique	WAA28			13.0/1200	9,100 psi	
Rem. 209P	Blue Dot	Fed. 28S1A			18.0/1200	9,200 psi	
Rem. 209P	Blue Dot	Rem. SP28	18.0/1200	19.5/1250	21.0/1295	9,700 psi	
Rem. 209P	Blue Dot	WAA28			18.0/1200	7,700 psi	
Rem. 209P	Herco	Fed. 28S1A			14.5/1200	11,200 psi	
Rem. 209P	Herco	Rem. SP28	14.0/1200	15.3/1250	16.5/1295	10,300 psi	
Rem. 209P	Herco	WAA28			14.0/1200	8,800 psi	
Rem. 209P	Solo 1250	Activ T-28			14.5/1200	11,300 psi	
Rem. 209P	Unique	Fed. 28S1A			13.5/1200	11,300 psi	
Rem. 209P	Unique	Rem. SP28	13.0/1200	14.0/1250	15.0/1295	10,600 psi	
Rem. 209P	Unique	WAA28			13.0/1200	8,900 psi	
Rem. 209P	Universal	Rem. PT28			13.8/1200	11,600 psi	
Win. 209	Universal	Pat. Ctrl. 28			13.7/1200	10,900 psi	
REMINGTON: PREMIER & NITRO 27 & STS & UNIBODY (INTEGRAL PLASTIC BASE WAD)							
CCI 209	Universal	Pat. Ctrl. 28			14.0/1200	10,000 psi	
Fed. 209A	IMR 800-X	CB 1034-28			13.0/1200	10,800 psi	

Caution: Follow load recipes exactly; do not substitute components, exceed listed maximums or load less than listed minimums.

| Primer | Powder Type | Wad | Powder Charge (grains) / Velocity (fps) | | Maximum Pressure | Load Notes |
			Minimum	Maximum		
Fed. 209A	IMR 800-X	Fed. 28S1		13.0/1205	11,700 psi	
Fed. 209A	IMR 800-X	Pat. Ctrl. 28		13.0/1210	11,400 psi	
Fed. 209A	IMR 800-X	Rem. PT28		13.0/1205	11,400 psi	
Fed. 209A	IMR 800-X	WAA28		13.0/1195	11,000 psi	
Fed. 209A	SR-4756	Fed. 28S1		14.0/1175	12,300 psi	
Fed. 209A	SR-4756	Pat. Ctrl. 28		14.5/1200	12,200 psi	
Fed. 209A	SR-4756	Rem. PT28		14.0/1185	12,500 psi	
Rem. 209	Solo 1250	Activ T-28	13.0/1155 13.3/1180	13.5/1200	12,000 psi	
Rem. 209	Solo 1250	Pat. Ctrl. 28	12.5/1155 13.0/1180	13.5/1200	11,900 psi	
Rem. 209P	IMR 800-X	CB-1034-28		13.5/1205	10,300 psi	
Rem. 209P	IMR 800-X	Fed. 28S1		13.5/1215	11,600 psi	
Rem. 209P	IMR 800-X	Pat. Ctrl. 28		13.0/1190	10,300 psi	
Rem. 209P	IMR 800-X	Rem. PT28		13.5/1205	10,700 psi	
Rem. 209P	IMR 800-X	WAA28		13.5/1205	10,300 psi	
Rem. 209P	IMR PB	Pat. Ctrl. 28		13.0/1175	12,100 psi	
Rem. 209P	IMR PB	Rem. PT28		13.0/1185	12,500 psi	
Rem. 209P	IMR PB	WAA28		13.5/1205	12,300 psi	
Rem. 209P	SR-4756	Fed. 28S1		14.0/1140	10,300 psi	
Rem. 209P	SR-4756	Pat. Ctrl. 28		15.0/1165	9,900 psi	
Rem. 209P	SR-7625	Fed. 28S1		13.5/1185	12,400 psi	
Rem. 209P	SR-7625	Pat. Ctrl. 28		14.0/1200	11,700 psi	
Rem. 209P	SR-7625	Rem. PT28		13.5/1190	12,400 psi	
Rem. 209P	SR-7625	WAA28		14.0/1205	11,800 psi	
Rem. 209P	Universal	Rem. PT28		14.3/1200	10,200 psi	
Win. 209	IMR 800-X	CB 1034-28		13.5/1215	10,800 psi	
Win. 209	IMR 800-X	Fed. 28S1		13.0/1195	11,300 psi	
Win. 209	IMR 800-X	Pat. Ctrl. 28		13.0/1185	10,300 psi	
Win. 209	IMR 800-X	Rem. PT28		13.5/1210	11,100 psi	
Win. 209	IMR 800-X	WAA28		13.0/1185	10,400 psi	
Win. 209	SR-4756	Fed. 28S1		14.0/1160	11,500 psi	
Win. 209	SR-4756	Pat. Ctrl. 28		15.0/1200	11,200 psi	
Win. 209	SR-4756	Rem. PT28		14.0/1155	11,000 psi	
Win. 209	SR-7625	Pat. Ctrl. 28		14.0/1210	12,200 psi	
Win. 209	SR-7625	Rem. PT28		14.0/1200	12,500 psi	
Win. 209	SR-7625	WAA28		14.0/1210	12,200 psi	
Win. 209	Universal	Fed. 28S1		14.0/1200	11,400 psi	
Win. 209	Universal	WAA28		13.8/1200	10,600 psi	
WINCHESTER: COMPRESSION-FORMED AA TYPE				³/₄-OUNCE LEAD SHOT		
CCI 109	Herco	WAA28		14.0/1200	7,900 psi	
CCI 109	Unique	WAA28		13.0/1200	8,400 psi	
CCI 109	W 540	WAA28		17.5/1200	10,200 LUP	
CCI 109	W 571	WAA28	19.0/1200 20.0/1230	21.0/1260	11,100 LUP	

Section header row within table: REMINGTON: PREMIER & NITRO 27 & STS & UNIBODY (INTEGRAL PLASTIC BASE WAD) (CONT.)

Caution: Follow load recipes exactly; do not substitute components, exceed listed maximums or load less than listed minimums.

Primer	Powder Type	Wad	Powder Charge (grains) / Velocity (fps) Minimum		Maximum	Maximum Pressure	Load Notes
WINCHESTER: COMPRESSION-FORMED AA TYPE (CONT.)					³/₄-OUNCE LEAD SHOT		
Fed. 209	HS-6	WAA28			17.5/1200	10,300 LUP	
Fed. 209	SR-7625	WAA28			12.0/1100	10,600 psi	
Fed. 209	W 540	WAA28			17.5/1200	10,200 LUP	
Fed. 209A	IMR 800-X	CB 1034-28			12.5/1185	11,700 psi	
Fed. 209A	IMR 800-X	Fed. 28S1			12.0/1150	12,000 psi	
Fed. 209A	IMR 800-X	Pat. Ctrl. 28			13.0/1210	12,300 psi	
Fed. 209A	IMR 800-X	WAA28			12.5/1185	11,600 psi	
Rem. 209P	HS-6	WAA28			17.5/1200	9,600 LUP	
Rem. 209P	IMR 800-X	CB 1034-28			13.5/1200	10,200 psi	
Rem. 209P	IMR 800-X	Fed. 28S1			13.5/1205	11,500 psi	
Rem. 209P	IMR 800-X	Pat. Ctrl. 28			13.0/1200	11,400 psi	
Rem. 209P	IMR 800-X	WAA28			14.0/1200	9,700 psi	
Rem. 209P	SR-4756	CB 1034-26			14.0/1165	12,000 psi	
Rem. 209P	SR-4756	Pat. Ctrl. 28			14.5/1185	12,200 psi	
Rem. 209P	SR-4756	WAA28			14.0/1150	11,500 psi	
Rem. 209P	SR-7625	CB 1034-28			14.0/1190	12,300 psi	
Rem. 209P	SR-7625	Fed. 28S1			13.5/1170	12,400 psi	
Rem. 209P	SR-7625	Pat. Ctrl. 28			13.5/1170	12,000 psi	
Rem. 209P	SR-7625	WAA28			14.0/1205	12,300 psi	
Rem. 209P	Universal	Rem. PT28			13.2/1200	11,900 psi	
Win. 209	Herco	WAA28			14.0/1200	8,400 psi	
Win. 209	HS-6	WAA28			17.5/1200	9,800 LUP	
Win. 209	HS-7	WAA28			19.0/1200	10,100 LUP	
Win. 209	IMR 800-X	CB 1034-28			13.0/1190	11,200 psi	
Win. 209	IMR 800-X	Fed. 28S1			12.5/1175	12,200 psi	
Win. 209	IMR 800-X	Pat. Ctrl. 28			13.0/1205	12,000 psi	
Win. 209	IMR 800-X	WAA28			13.0/1195	11,400 psi	
Win. 209	Solo 1250	WAA28			13.0/1155	11,300 psi	
Win. 209	SR-4756	CB 1034-28			14.0/1170	12,200 psi	
Win. 209	SR-4756	Fed. 28S1			14.0/1155	12,500 psi	
Win. 209	SR-4756	Pat. Ctrl. 28			14.5/1190	12,000 psi	
Win. 209	SR-4756	WAA28			14.0/1150	11,400 psi	
Win. 209	Unique	WAA28			13.0/1200	9,400 psi	
Win. 209	Universal	Pat. Ctrl. 28			13.2/1200	11,900 psi	
Win. 209	Universal	WAA28			13.0/1200	10,800 psi	
Win. 209	W 540	WAA28			17.5/1200	9,900 LUP	
Win. 209	W 571	WAA28	19.0/1200	20.0/1230	21.0/1260	11,000 LUP	
Win. AATP	W 540	WAA28			16.5/1200	12,000 psi	Note 2
Win. AATP	W 571	WAA28			18.0/1200	11,600 psi	

Load Notes: 2 = This load duplicates ballistics of Winchester's AA target loading.

Caution: Follow load recipes exactly; do not substitute components, exceed listed maximums or load less than listed minimums.

Primer	Powder Type	Wad	Powder Charge (grains) / Velocity (fps) Minimum	Maximum	Maximum Pressure	Load Notes
FEDERAL: PLASTIC (PAPER BASE WAD)				7/8-OUNCE LEAD SHOT		
Rem. 209P	HS-7	Rem. PT28		19.5/1200	10,900 psi	
Win. 209	HS-7	Pat. Ctrl. 28		19.2/1200	10,700 psi	
FIOCCHI: PURPLE TARGET (HIGH BASE WAD)				7/8-OUNCE LEAD SHOT		
Rem. 209P	HS-7	Pat. Ctrl. 28		19.0/1200	10,100 psi	
Win. 209	HS-7	Rem. PT28		19.5/1200	11,100 psi	

END OF 28-GAUGE LEAD SHOT LOAD DATA

32-GAUGE 2½"   ½-OUNCE LEAD SHOT

Primer	Powder Type	Wad	Powder Charge (grains) / Velocity (fps)		Maximum Pressure	Load Notes
			Minimum	Maximum		
Fiocchi: Plastic				½-Ounce Lead Shot		
Fio. 615	Alliant 2400	SG32		**17.0/1220**	12,200 psi	

32-GAUGE 2½"   ⅝-OUNCE LEAD SHOT

Primer	Powder Type	Wad	Powder Charge (grains) / Velocity (fps)		Maximum Pressure	Load Notes
			Minimum	Maximum		
Fiocchi: Plastic				⅝-Ounce Lead Shot		
Fio. 615	Alliant 2400	SG32		**16.0/1200**	12,000 psi	

END OF 32-GAUGE LEAD SHOT LOAD DATA

Caution: Follow load recipes exactly; do not substitute components, exceed listed maximums or load less than listed minimums.

Primer	Powder Type	Wad	Powder Charge (grains) / Velocity (fps) Minimum	Maximum	Maximum Pressure	Load Notes
FEDERAL: PLASTIC (PAPER BASE WAD)				**½-OUNCE LEAD SHOT**		
Fed. 209	Alliant 2400	Fed. 410SC		**13.5/1200**	11,900 psi	
Fed. 209	Alliant 2400	Rem. SP410		**13.0/1200**	11,500 psi	
Fed. 209	Alliant 2400	WAA41		**13.0/1200**	11,300 psi	
Fed. 209A	AA 4100	Pat. Ctrl. 410		**13.5/1200**	9,600 psi	
Fed. 209A	AA 4100	Rem. SP410		**13.5/1200**	9,700 psi	
Fed. 209A	AA 4100	WAA41		**13.5/1200**	9,400 psi	
Fed. 209A	H 110	Fed. 410SC		**15.0/1200**	10,200 psi	
Fed. 209A	H 110	Pat. Ctrl. Orange		**15.5/1200**	8,500 psi	
Fed. 209A	IMR 4227	CB 1050-41		**17.5/1190**	12,200 psi	
Fed. 209A	IMR 4227	Fed. 410SC		**17.5/1195**	12,200 psi	
Fed. 209A	IMR 4227	Pat. Ctrl. 410		**17.0/1170**	12,500 psi	
Fed. 209A	IMR 4227	Rem. SP410		**17.0/1155**	12,000 psi	
Fed. 209A	IMR 4227	Trico No. 4		**17.0/1165**	12,000 psi	
Fed. 410	Alliant 2400	Fed. 410SC		**13.5/1200**	12,000 psi	
Rem. 209P	IMR 4227	Rem. SP410		**18.5/1180**	10,700 psi	
Win. 209	H 110	Pat. Ctrl. Orange		**15.5/1200**	8,400 psi	
Win. 209	H 110	WAA41		**15.0/1200**	9,700 psi	
Win. 209	IMR 4227	CB 1050-41		**18.0/1165**	11,300 psi	
Win. 209	IMR 4227	Pat. Ctrl. 410		**18.5/1215**	11,800 psi	
Win. 209	IMR 4227	Rem. SP410		**18.0/1200**	12,000 psi	
Win. 209	IMR 4227	Trico No. 4		**18.0/1170**	11,400 psi	
REMINGTON: PLASTIC				**½-OUNCE LEAD SHOT**		
CCI 209	Alliant 2400	Fed. 410SC		**14.0/1200**	10,600 psi	
CCI 209	Alliant 2400	Rem. SP410		**14.5/1200**	10,500 psi	
CCI 209	Alliant 2400	WAA41		**14.5/1200**	10,300 psi	
CCI 209M	Alliant 2400	Rem. SP410		**13.5/1200**	11,000 psi	
CCI 209SC	H 110	Rem. SP410		**15.0/1200**	9,700 psi	
Fed. 209A	IMR 4227	CB 1050-41		**18.0/1210**	12,500 psi	
Fed. 209A	IMR 4227	Fed. 410SC		**17.5/1195**	12,400 psi	
Fed. 209A	IMR 4227	Pat. Ctrl. 410		**17.5/1195**	12,500 psi	
Fed. 209A	IMR 4227	Trico No. 4		**17.0/1160**	11,900 psi	
Rem. 209P	H 110	Fed. 410SC		**15.0/1200**	9,500 LUP	
Rem. 209P	H 110	Pat. Ctrl. Orange		**16.5/1200**	7,000 psi	
Rem. 209P	H 110	Rem. SP410		**15.0/1200**	9,400 LUP	
Rem. 97*	Alliant 2400	Fed. 410SC		**13.5/1200**	11,400 psi	
Rem. 97*	Alliant 2400	Rem. SP410		**13.0/1200**	11,500 psi	
Rem. 97*	Alliant 2400	WAA41		**14.0/1200**	11,500 psi	
Win. 209	IMR 4227	CB 1050-41		**18.0/1160**	11,000 psi	
Win. 209	IMR 4227	Pat. Ctrl. 410		**17.5/1160**	11,200 psi	
Win. 209	W 296	Rem. SP410		**15.0/1200**	9,500 LUP	

Caution: Follow load recipes exactly; do not substitute components, exceed listed maximums or load less than listed minimums.

Primer	Powder Type	Wad	Powder Charge (grains) / Velocity (fps) Minimum	Maximum	Maximum Pressure	Load Notes
WINCHESTER: COMPRESSION-FORMED AA TYPE				**½-OUNCE LEAD SHOT**		
CCI 109	W 296	Fed. 410SC		**14.0/1200**	9,900 LUP	
CCI 109	W 296	WAA41	13.5/1150	**14.0/1200**	9,100 LUP	
CCI 209	Alliant 2400	Fed. 410SC		**13.0/1200**	12,100 psi	
CCI 209	Alliant 2400	Rem. SP410		**13.5/1200**	12,000 psi	
CCI 209SC	H 110	WAA41		**14.0/1200**	10,700 psi	
Fed. 209A	AA 4100	FC410SC		**13.5/1200**	12,600 psi	
Fed. 209A	AA 4100	Pat. Ctrl. 410		**13.5/1200**	10,700 psi	
Fed. 209A	AA 4100	Rem. SP410		**13.5/1200**	11,100 psi	
Fed. 209A	AA 4100	WAA41		**13.5/1200**	11,200 psi	
Fed. 209A	H 110	Pat. Ctrl. Orange		**15.0/1200**	9,000 psi	
Fed. 399	H 110	WAA41		**14.0/1200**	10,200 LUP	
Rem. 209P	IMR 4227	Trico No. 4		**17.0/1145**	11,600 psi	
Win. 209	H 110	Fed. 410SC		**14.0/1200**	9,100 LUP	
Win. 209	H 110	Pat. Ctrl. Orange		**14.0/1200**	9,500 psi	
Win. 209	H 110	WAA41		**14.0/1200**	9,900 LUP	
Win. 209	Alliant 2400	WAA41		**13.0/1200**	11,700 psi	
Win. 209	IMR 4227	Pat. Ctrl. 410		**16.5/1140**	12,300 psi	
Win. 209	IMR 4227	Trico No. 4		**17.0/1160**	12,400 psi	
Win. 209	W 296	Fed. 410SC		**14.0/1200**	10,300 LUP	
Win. 209	W 296	WAA41	13.5/1150	**14.0/1200**	9,800 LUP	
Win. AATP	W 296	WAA41	13.0/1145	**14.0*/1200**	10,700 psi	*Note 1

Load Notes: 1 = This load duplicates ballistics of Winchester's AA target loading.

   Caution: Follow load recipes exactly; do not substitute components, exceed listed maximums or load less than listed minimums.

⁵/₈-OUNCE LEAD SHOT

Primer	Powder Type	Wad	Powder Charge (grains) / Velocity (fps) Minimum	Maximum	Maximum Pressure	Load Notes
WINCHESTER: COMPRESSION-FORMED AA TYPE				⁵/₈-OUNCE LEAD SHOT		
Rem. 209P	IMR 4227	Fed. 410SC		18.5/1160	11,300 LUP	
Rem. 209P	IMR 4227	Rem. SP410		18.0/1160	11,000 LUP	
Rem. 209P	IMR 4227	Trico No. 4		20.0/1230	11,900 LUP	
Win. 209	IMR 4227	Fed. 410SC		17.5/1160	12,400 LUP	
Win. 209	IMR 4227	Rem. SP410		17.4/1160	12,400 LUP	
Win. 209	IMR 4227	Trico No. 4		18.8/1220	12,400 LUP	

¹¹/₁₆-OUNCE LEAD SHOT

Primer	Powder Type	Wad	Powder Charge (grains) / Velocity (fps) Minimum	Maximum	Maximum Pressure	Load Notes
FEDERAL: PLASTIC (PAPER BASE WAD)				¹¹/₁₆-OUNCE LEAD SHOT		
Fed. 209A	H 110	Fed 410SC		16.5/1200	12,600 psi	
Fed. 410	IMR 4227	Fed. 410SC		17.5/1125	11,000 LUP	
Fed. 410	IMR 4227	Rem. SP410		17.5/1125	10,900 LUP	
Fed. 410	IMR 4227	Trico No. 4		19.5/1215	11,800 LUP	
Win. 209	H 110	Pat. Ctrl. Orange		17.0/1200	11,000 psi	
Win. 209	IMR 4227	Fed. 410SC		17.5/1140	12,400 LUP	
REMINGTON: PLASTIC				¹¹/₁₆-OUNCE LEAD SHOT		
CCI 209M	H 110	Rem. SP-410		16.0/1200	12,300 psi	
CCI 209M	Alliant 2400	Rem. SP410		14.5/1135	12,200 psi	
Fed. 410	Alliant 2400	Rem. SP410		14.0/1135	12,700 psi	
Rem. 209P	H 110	Rem. SP-410		15.5/1135	10,600 psi	
Rem. 209P	IMR 4227	Fed. 410SC		18.5/1140	10,300 LUP	
Rem. 209P	IMR 4227	Rem. SP410		18.5/1135	9,800 LUP	
Rem. 209P	IMR 4227	Trico No. 4		20.5/1210	11,100 LUP	
Rem. 97*	Alliant 2400	Fed. 410SC		14.5/1135	12,600 psi	
Rem. 97*	Alliant 2400	Rem. SP410		14.5/1135	13,000 psi	
Rem. 97*	Alliant 2400	WAA41		14.5/1135	12,300 psi	
Win. 209	H 110	Pat. Ctrl. Orange		16.5/1200	12,100 psi	
Win. 209	H 110	WAA41		15.0/1135	10,800 psi	
Win. 209	IMR 4227	Fed. 410SC		17.5/1140	12,000 LUP	
Win. 209	IMR 4227	Rem. SP410		17.5/1135	11,500 LUP	
Win. 209	IMR 4227	Trico No. 4		19.0/1180	11,300 LUP	
WINCHESTER: COMPRESSION-FORMED AA TYPE				¹¹/₁₆-OUNCE LEAD SHOT		
Fed. 209A	H 110	Fed. 410SC		15.7/1200	13,000 psi	
Fed. 410	H 110	Fed. 410SC		14.0/1135	10,700 LUP	
Fed. 410	W 296	Fed. 410SC		14.0/1135	10,600 LUP	
Fed. 410	W 296	WAA41		14.0/1135	10,000 LUP	
Win. 209	H 110	WAA41		13.5/1135	10,900 LUP	

Caution: Follow load recipes exactly; do not substitute components, exceed listed maximums or load less than listed minimums.

Primer	Powder Type	Wad	Powder Charge (grains) / Velocity (fps) Minimum	Maximum	Maximum Pressure	Load Notes
WINCHESTER: COMPRESSION-FORMED AA TYPE (CONT.)				¹¹/₁₆-OUNCE LEAD SHOT		
Win. 209	H 110	WAA41		16.0/1200	12,900 psi	
Win. 209	W 296	Fed. 410SC		13.5/1135	10,800 LUP	
Win. 209	W 296	WAA41		13.5/1135	10,800 LUP	Note 1

Load Notes: 1 = This load duplicates ballistics of Winchester's Super-X loading.

END OF 410-BORE LEAD SHOT LOAD DATA

Caution: Follow load recipes exactly; do not substitute components, exceed listed maximums or load less than listed minimums.

STEEL SHOT LOAD DATA

This data is steel shot-specific; it does not interchange with data used for lead or any other non-toxic shot. Use only the components and amounts listed. Do not fire any steel shot loads in any gun that is not specifically certified by the manufacturer as safe for use with steel shot loads.

⁷⁄₈-OUNCE STEEL SHOT — 12-GAUGE 2³⁄₄"

Primer	Powder Type	Wad	Powder Charge (grains) / Velocity (fps) Minimum			Maximum	Maximum Pressure	Load Notes
WINCHESTER: COMPRESSION-FORMED AA TYPE						⁷⁄₈-OUNCE STEEL SHOT		
CCI 209M	Universal	BP STS	18.6/1200	19.8/1250	20.1/1275	20.5/1300	10,300 psi	
Win. 209	Universal	BP STS	19.0/1200	20.0/1250	20.6/1275	21.2/1300	11,000 psi	

1-OUNCE STEEL SHOT — 12-GAUGE 2³⁄₄"

Primer	Powder Type	Wad	Powder Charge (grains) / Velocity (fps) Minimum			Maximum	Maximum Pressure	Load Notes
ACTIV: ALL PLASTIC						1-OUNCE STEEL SHOT		
CCI 209SC	Universal	BP CSD-100		21.0/1250	21.6/1275	22.3/1300	10,900 psi	
CCI 209SC	Universal	BP STS	20.8/1200	22.0/1250	22.2/1275	22.5/1300	10,500 psi	
Win. 209	Universal	BP CSD-100				21.5/1250	10,600 psi	
Win. 209	Universal	BP STS	21.0/1200	21.7/1250	22.0/1275	22.3/1300	10,500 psi	
FEDERAL: GOLD MEDAL PLASTIC						1-OUNCE STEEL SHOT		
CCI 209SC	Universal	BP CSD-100	20.5/1200	21.0/1250	21.5/1275	22.0/1300	10,900 psi	
Fed. 209A	Universal	BP CSD-100	19.5/1200	20.0/1250	21.0/1275	22.0/1300	11,000 psi	
Fed. 209A	Universal	BP STS	21.5/1200	22.0/1250	22.2/1275	22.5/1300	11,400 psi	
FEDERAL: PLASTIC (PAPER BASE WAD)						1-OUNCE STEEL SHOT		
Fed. 209	Solo 1500	BP12234				29.5/1275	10,900 LUP	
FIOCCHI: PURPLE TARGET (HIGH BASE WAD)						1-OUNCE STEEL SHOT		
Fio. 616	Universal	BP CSD-100				18.7/1200	10,600 psi	
Fio. 616	Universal	BP STS	21.5/1200	22.0/1250	22.5/1275	23.0/1300	10,600 psi	
Win. 209	Universal	BP CSD-100				19.0/1200	10,900 psi	

Caution: Follow load recipes exactly; do not substitute components, exceed listed maximums or load less than listed minimums.

Primer	Powder Type	Wad	Powder Charge (grains) / Velocity (fps) Minimum			Maximum	Maximum Pressure	Load Notes
REMINGTON: PREMIER & NITRO 27 & STS						**1-OUNCE STEEL SHOT**		
CCI 209M	Universal	BP STS	**21.0/1200**	**21.5/1250**	**21.7/1275**	**22.0/1300**	11,000 psi	
CCI 209SC	Universal	BP STS				**19.5/1200**	10,100 psi	
Rem. 209P	Solo 1500	BP12234				**27.5/1275**	10,800 LUP	
Win. 209	Universal	BP STS				**19.5/1200**	10,800 psi	
VICTORY: PLASTIC						**1-OUNCE STEEL SHOT**		
Fio. 616	Universal	BP CSD-100				**18.7/1200**	10,600 psi	
Fio. 616	Universal	BP STS	**21.5/1200**	**22.0/1250**	**22.5/1275**	**23.0/1300**	10,600 psi	
Win. 209	Universal	BP CSD-100				**19.0/1200**	10,900 psi	
WINCHESTER: COMPRESSION-FORMED AA TYPE						**1-OUNCE STEEL SHOT**		
CCI 209M	Universal	BP STS	**20.5/1200**	**20.7/1225**	**20.8/1235**	**21.0/1250**	10,500 psi	
CCI 209M	Universal	BP STS				**19.0/1200**	11,000 psi	
Rem. 209P	Universal	BP STS				**18.8/1200**	10,600 psi	
Win. 209	Solo 1500	BP12234				**27.5/1275**	10,900 LUP	
Win. 209	Universal	BP CSD-100				**19.0/1200**	10,900 psi	
Win. 209	Universal	BP STS	**20.7/1200**	**21.3/1250**	**21.9/1275**	**22.5/1300**	11,000 psi	

12-GAUGE 2³/₄″   1¹/₈ OUNCES STEEL SHOT

Primer	Powder Type	Wad	Powder Charge (grains) / Velocity (fps) Minimum	Maximum	Maximum Pressure	Load Notes
FEDERAL: PLASTIC (PAPER BASE WAD)				**1¹/₈ OUNCES STEEL SHOT**		
Fed. 209	Solo 1500	BP12234		**28.0/1200**	10,900 LUP	
REMINGTON: PREMIER & NITRO 27 & STS				**1¹/₈ OUNCES STEEL SHOT**		
Rem. 209P	Solo 1500	BP Ranger Plus		**35.0/1350**	10,900 LUP	
WINCHESTER: COMPRESSION-FORMED AA TYPE				**1¹/₈ OUNCES STEEL SHOT**		
Win. 209	Solo 1500	BP Ranger Plus		**34.5/1350**	10,900 LUP	

END OF 12-GAUGE STEEL SHOT LOAD DATA

Caution: Follow load recipes exactly; do not substitute components, exceed listed maximums or load less than listed minimums.

Primer	Powder Type	Wad	Powder Charge (grains) / Velocity (fps) Minimum		Maximum	Maximum Pressure	Load Notes
Activ: All Plastic					³/₄-Ounce Steel Shot		
Rem. 209P	Alliant 2400	BP CS12D20	28.0/1170	29.0/1245	29.5/1275	10,500 psi	
Fiocchi: Plastic					³/₄-Ounce Steel Shot		
Fio. 616	Alliant 2400	BP CS12D20	28.0/1200	29.5/1255	30.0/1285	11,400 psi	
Remington: RXP					³/₄-Ounce Steel Shot		
Rem. 209P	Blue Dot	BP CS12D20	19.5/1270	20.0/1300	20.5/1330	12,000 psi	
Winchester: Compression Formed AA Type					³/₄-Ounce Steel Shot		
Rem. 209P	Blue Dot	BP CS12D20		19.5/1275	20.0/1300	12,000 psi	

END OF 20-GAUGE STEEL SHOT LOAD DATA

BISMUTH SHOT LOAD DATA

This data is bismuth shot-specific; it does not interchange with data used for lead or any other non-toxic shot. Use only the components and amounts listed.

10-GAUGE 3¹/₂" — 1⁷/₈ OUNCES BISMUTH SHOT

Primer	Powder Type	Wad	Powder Charge (grains) / Velocity (fps) Minimum	Maximum	Maximum Pressure	Load Notes
FEDERAL: ONE-PIECE				**1⁷/₈ OUNCES BISMUTH SHOT**		
Fed. 209A	HS-7	Rem. SP10		42.0/1225	10,900 psi	
REMINGTON: SP (SEPARATE YELLOW PLASTIC BASE WAD)				**1⁷/₈ OUNCES BISMUTH SHOT**		
Win. 209	HS-7	Rem. SP10		43.0/1250	10,600 psi	
WINCHESTER: POLYFORMED (SEPARATE PLASTIC BASE WAD)				**1⁷/₈ OUNCES BISMUTH SHOT**		
Win. 209	HS-7	Rem. SP-10		45.0/1275	11,000 psi	

10-GAUGE 3¹/₂" — 2 OUNCES BISMUTH SHOT

Primer	Powder Type	Wad	Powder Charge (grains) / Velocity (fps) Minimum	Maximum	Maximum Pressure	Load Notes
FEDERAL: ONE-PIECE				**2 OUNCES BISMUTH SHOT**		
Fed. 209A	HS-7	Rem. SP10		41.5/1175	10,200 psi	
Win. 209	HS-7	Rem. SP10		44.5/1225	10,300 psi	
REMINGTON: SP (SEPARATE YELLOW PLASTIC BASE WAD)				**2 OUNCES BISMUTH SHOT**		
Fed. 209A	HS-7	Rem. SP-10		40.8/1200	10,900 psi	
Win. 209	HS-7	Rem. SP-10		41.0/1200	10,500 psi	
WINCHESTER: POLYFORMED (SEPARATE PLASTIC BASE WAD)				**2 OUNCES BISMUTH SHOT**		
CCI 209M	HS-7	Rem. SP-10		40.0/1200	11,000 psi	
Win. 209	HS-7	Rem. SP-10		41.5/1200	10,600 psi	

END OF 10-GAUGE BISMUTH SHOT LOAD DATA

1¼ OUNCES BISMUTH SHOT   12-GAUGE 2³/₄"

Primer	Powder Type	Wad	Powder Charge (grains) / Velocity (fps) Minimum			Maximum	Maximum Pressure	Load Notes
FEDERAL: GOLD MEDAL PLASTIC					**1¼ OUNCES BISMUTH SHOT**			
Fed. 209A	HS-6	Rem. SP-12	30.0/1225	31.0/1250	32.3/1275	33.0/1300	10,500 psi	
Fed. 209A	HS-7	Rem. SP-12	33.0/1225	34.0/1250	35.5/1275	35.7/1300	10,600 psi	
Win. 209	HS-6	WAA12R	31.5/1225	32.0/1250	33.0/1275	33.5/1300	10,000 psi	
Win. 209	HS-7	WAA12R	34.0/1225	35.0/1250	35.5/1275	36.0/1300	10,200 psi	
FEDERAL: PLASTIC (PAPER BASE WAD)					**1¼ OUNCES BISMUTH SHOT**			
Win. 209	HS-6	WAA12R				36.5/1300	8,500 psi	Note 1
FIOCCHI: PLASTIC (LOW BASE WAD)					**1¼ OUNCES BISMUTH SHOT**			
Fio. 616	HS-6	WAA12F114				33.5/1300	10,400 psi	
Fio. 616	HS-6	WAA12R				34.0/1300	9,500 psi	Note 1
REMINGTON: PREMIER & NITRO 27 & STS					**1¼ OUNCES BISMUTH SHOT**			
Rem. 209P	HS 6	Rem. RP12	29.0/1225	29.1/1230	29.3/1240	29.5/1250	11,000 psi	
Rem. 209P	HS-7	Rem. RP12	32.5/1225	32.7/1230	33.0/1240	33.5/1250	10,100 psi	
Win. 209	HS-6	WAA12R	29.8/1225	29.9/1230	30.0/1240	30.2/1250	10,400 psi	
Win. 209	HS-7	WAA12R	33.0/1225	33.1/1230	33.3/1240	33.5/1250	10,300 psi	
VICTORY: PLASTIC					**1¼ OUNCES BISMUTH SHOT**			
Fio. 616	HS-6	WAA12F114				33.5/1300	10,400 psi	
Fio. 616	HS-6	WAA12R				34.0/1300	9,500 psi	Note 1
WINCHESTER: COMPRESSION-FORMED AA TYPE					**1¼ OUNCES BISMUTH SHOT**			
Win. 209	HS-6	WAA12R				29.0/1225	10,700 psi	
Win. 209	HS-7	WAA12R				32.0/1225	10,500 psi	

Load Notes: 1 = Add one 20-gauge, 0.135" card inside bottom of shotcup.

Caution: Follow load recipes exactly; do not substitute components, exceed listed maximums or load less than listed minimums.

12-GAUGE 2³/₄"   1³/₈ OUNCES BISMUTH SHOT

Primer	Powder Type	Wad	Powder Charge (grains) / Velocity (fps) Minimum		Maximum	Maximum Pressure	Load Notes
FEDERAL: GOLD MEDAL PLASTIC				1³/₈ OUNCES BISMUTH SHOT			
Fed. 209A	HS-6	WAA12R			30.0/1200	10,300 psi	
Fed. 209A	HS-7	WAA12R			32.0/1200	10,400 psi	
Win. 209	HS-6	WAA12R	30.0/1200	31.5/1225	33.0/1250	11,300 psi	
Win. 209	HS-7	WAA12R			33.5/1200	10,300 psi	
FEDERAL: PLASTIC (PAPER BASE WAD)				1³/₈ OUNCES BISMUTH SHOT			
Win. 209	HS-6	WAA12R			36.0/1300	9,600 psi	
FIOCCHI: PLASTIC (LOW BASE WAD)				1³/₈ OUNCES BISMUTH SHOT			
Fio. 616	HS-6	WAA12R			33.0/1275	10,700 psi	
Fio. 616	HS-7	WAA12R			37.0/1275	10,600 psi	
VICTORY: PLASTIC				1³/₈ OUNCES BISMUTH SHOT			
Fio. 616	HS-6	WAA12R			33.0/1275	10,700 psi	
Fio. 616	HS-7	WAA12R			37.0/1275	10,600 psi	

12-GAUGE 2³/₄"   1¹/₂ OUNCES BISMUTH SHOT

Primer	Powder Type	Wad	Powder Charge (grains) / Velocity (fps) Minimum		Maximum	Maximum Pressure	Load Notes
FEDERAL: PLASTIC (PAPER BASE WAD)				1¹/₂ OUNCES BISMUTH SHOT			
Win. 209	HS-6	WAA12R	34.0/1275	35.0/1300		11,400 psi	
Win. 209	HS-7	WAA12R			36.5/1250	10,500 psi	

Caution: Follow load recipes exactly; do not substitute components, exceed listed maximums or load less than listed minimums.

1 1/2 OUNCES BISMUTH SHOT — 12-GAUGE 3"

Primer	Powder Type	Wad	Powder Charge (grains) / Velocity (fps) Minimum	Maximum	Maximum Pressure	Load Notes
FEDERAL: PLASTIC (PAPER BASE WAD)				1 1/2 OUNCES BISMUTH SHOT		
Win. 209	HS-6	WAA12F114		34.0/1250	9,600 psi	
Win. 209	HS-6	WAA12F114		32.5/1200	10,200 psi	
Win. 209	HS-7	WAA12F114		38.5/1300	11,300 psi	
Win. 209	HS-7	WAA12R		37.0/1250	10,400 psi	
FIOCCHI: PLASTIC				1 1/2 OUNCES BISMUTH SHOT		
Fio. 616	HS-7	WAA12R		39.0/1300	10,200 psi	Note 1
Fio. 616	HS-6	WAA12F114		35.0/1300	10,900 psi	

Load Notes: 1 = Add one 20-gauge, 0.135" card inside bottom of shotcup.

1 5/8 OUNCES BISMUTH SHOT — 12-GAUGE 3"

Primer	Powder Type	Wad	Powder Charge (grains) / Velocity (fps) Minimum	Maximum	Maximum Pressure	Load Notes
FIOCCHI: PLASTIC				1 5/8 OUNCES BISMUTH SHOT		
Fio. 616	HS-6	WAA12R		34.0/1250	11,300 psi	
Fio. 616	HS-7	WAA12R		38.0/1250	10,800 psi	

END OF 12-GAUGE BISMUTH SHOT LOAD DATA

Caution: Follow load recipes exactly; do not substitute components, exceed listed maximums or load less than listed minimums.

Primer	Powder Type	Wad	Powder Charge (grains) / Velocity (fps)			Maximum Pressure	Load Notes
			Minimum		Maximum		
ACTIV: ALL PLASTIC					**1-OUNCE BISMUTH SHOT**		
CCI 209M	Universal	WAA16	18.0/1200	18.5/1225	19.0/1250	10,300 psi	
FEDERAL: PLASTIC (PAPER BASE WAD)					**1-OUNCE BISMUTH SHOT**		
Fed. 209A	Universal	Rem. SP16	19.5/1200	20.0/1225	20.5/1250	9,500 psi	
REMINGTON: PLASTIC					**1-OUNCE BISMUTH SHOT**		
Rem. 209P	Universal	Rem. SP16			18.0/1250	11,100 psi	
Win. 209	Universal	Rem. SP16			18.0/1200	10,300 psi	

END OF 16-GAUGE BISMUTH SHOT LOAD DATA

Caution: Follow load recipes exactly; do not substitute components, exceed listed maximums or load less than listed minimums.

1-OUNCE BISMUTH SHOT

20-GAUGE 2³/₄″

Primer	Powder Type	Wad	Powder Charge (grains) / Velocity (fps) Minimum	Maximum	Maximum Pressure	Load Notes
ACTIV: ALL PLASTIC				**1-OUNCE BISMUTH SHOT**		
CCI 209M	HS-6	WAA20F1		22.0/1200	9,700 psi	
CCI 209M	HS-7	WAA20F1		24.0/1200	8,900 psi	
Win. 209M	HS-7	WAA20F1		24.0/1200	9,200 psi	
Win. 209	HS-6	WAA20F1		22.0/1200	9,300 psi	
FEDERAL: PLASTIC (PAPER BASE WAD)				**1-OUNCE BISMUTH SHOT**		
Fed. 209A	HS-6	WAA20F1		22.0/1200	9,700 psi	
Fed. 209A	HS-7	WAA20F1		24.0/1200	8,700 psi	
WINCHESTER: COMPRESSION-FORMED AA TYPE				**1-OUNCE BISMUTH SHOT**		
CCI 209M	HS-6	Rem. SP20		18.5/1150	11,400 psi	
CCI 209M	HS-7	Rem. SP20		21.0/1150	11,300 psi	
Win. 209	HS-6	Rem. SP20		18.5/1150	11,300 psi	
Win. 209	HS-7	Rem. SP20		21.0/1150	10,600 psi	

Caution: Follow load recipes exactly; do not substitute components, exceed listed maximums or load less than listed minimums.

Primer	Powder Type	Wad	Powder Charge (grains) / Velocity (fps) Minimum	Maximum	Maximum Pressure	Load Notes
FEDERAL: PLASTIC (PAPER BASE WAD)				1-OUNCE BISMUTH SHOT		
Fed. 209A	HS-7	Fed. 20S1		26.5/1300	10,400 psi	
WINCHESTER: COMPRESSION-FORMED AA TYPE				1-OUNCE BISMUTH SHOT		
CCI 209M	HS-7	WAA20		26.5/1300	11,000 psi ·	
Win. 209	HS-7	WAA20		26.5/1300	10,800 psi	

END OF 20-GAUGE BISMUTH SHOT LOAD DATA

Caution: Follow load recipes exactly; do not substitute components, exceed listed maximums or load less than listed minimums.

Primer	Powder Type	Wad	Powder Charge (grains) / Velocity (fps) Minimum	Maximum	Maximum Pressure	Load Notes
FEDERAL: PLASTIC (PAPER BASE WAD)				³/₄-OUNCE BISMUTH SHOT		
CCI 209M	HS-6	Rem. PT28		17.5/1200	9,700 psi	
CCI 209M	Universal	Rem. PT28		13.5/1200	12,000 psi	
Win. 209	HS-6	Rem. PT28		17.5/1200	9,900 psi	
Win. 209	Universal	Fed. 28S1		13.5/1200	12,200 psi	
Win. 209	Universal	Rem. PT28		13.5/1200	11,200 psi	
FIOCCHI: PURPLE TARGET (HIGH BASE WAD)				³/₄-OUNCE BISMUTH SHOT		
CCI 209M	HS-6	Pat. Ctrl. 28		17.5/1200	10,200 psi	
CCI 209M	HS-6	Rem. PT28		17.5/1200	10,100 psi	
CCI 209M	Universal	Pat. Ctrl. 28		13.5/1200	11,900 psi	
CCI 209M	Universal	Rem. PT28		13.8/1200	11,200 psi	
Win. 209	HS-6	Pat. Ctrl. 28		17.5/1200	10,200 psi	
Win. 209	HS-6	Rem. PT28		17.5/1200	10,000 psi	
Win. 209	Universal	Pat. Ctrl. 28		13.5/1200	12,000 psi	
Win. 209	Universal	Rem. PT28		14.0/1200	11,800 psi	

END OF 28-GAUGE BISMUTH SHOT LOAD DATA

Caution: Follow load recipes exactly; do not substitute components, exceed listed maximums or load less than listed minimums.

Primer	Powder Type	Wad	Powder Charge (grains) / Velocity (fps) Minimum	Maximum	Maximum Pressure	Load Notes
FEDERAL: PLASTIC (PAPER BASE WAD)				⁵/₈-OUNCE BISMUTH SHOT		
Fed. 209A	H 110	Fed. 410SC		16.0/1200	12,600 psi	
REMINGTON: PLASTIC				⁵/₈-OUNCE BISMUTH SHOT		
Rem. 209P	H 110	Rem. SP410		17.0/1225	11,000 psi	
WINCHESTER: COMPRESSION-FORMED AA TYPE				⁵/₈-OUNCE BISMUTH SHOT		
Win. 209	H 110	Pat. Ctrl. Orange		16.0/1200	13,300 psi	

END OF 410-BORE BISMUTH SHOT LOAD DATA

Caution: Follow load recipes exactly; do not substitute components, exceed listed maximums or load less than listed minimums.

LEAD BUCKSHOT LOAD DATA

This data is lead buckshot-specific; it does not interchange with data used for any other types of lead or non-toxic shot. Use only the components and amounts listed. Avoid use in tightly choked guns (smaller than Modified) as poor patterns will result.

LEAD BUCKSHOT — 10-GAUGE 3½"

Primer	Powder Type	Wad	Powder Charge (grains) / Velocity (fps) Minimum	Maximum	Maximum Pressure	Buckshot Count
FEDERAL: PLASTIC				#4 LEAD BUCKSHOT		
Fed. 209	Blue Dot	Rem. SP10 + 20-gauge 0.270" card		45.0/1275	10,100 psi	40 pellets
FEDERAL: PLASTIC				#0 LEAD BUCKSHOT		
Fed. 209	Blue Dot	Rem. SP10 + 20-gauge 0.135" card		46.0/1300	10,000 psi	17 pellets
WINCHESTER: PLASTIC (POLYFORMED SEPARATE PLASTIC BASE WAD)				#4 LEAD BUCKSHOT		
Win. 209	Blue Dot	Rem. SP10 + 20-gauge 0.270" card		47.5/1275	10,000 psi	40 pellets
WINCHESTER: PLASTIC (POLYFORMED SEPARATE PLASTIC BASE WAD)				#0 LEAD BUCKSHOT		
Win. 209	Blue Dot	Rem. SP10		51.0/1300	9,500 psi	17 pellets

END 10-GAUGE LEAD BUCKSHOT LOAD DATA

Caution: Follow load recipes exactly; do not substitute components, exceed listed maximums or load less than listed minimums.

303

Primer	Powder Type	Wad	Powder Charge (grains) / Velocity (fps) Minimum			Maximum	Maximum Pressure	Buckshot Count
FEDERAL: PLASTIC (PAPER BASE WAD)						**#4 LEAD BUCKSHOT**		
Fed. 209	Blue Dot	0.135" card + 3/16" fiber + 0.135" card				37.0/1250	10,700 psi	34 pellets
Fed. 209	IMR 700-X	Rem. SP12 + 20 grains BP Shot Buffer				20.5/1225	10,800 LUP	24 pellets
Fed. 209	IMR PB	Fed. 12S4				25.0/1275	10,800 LUP	27 pellets
Fed. 209	SR-7625	Four BP BPGS Shot Buffer				30.0/1315	8,500 LUP	27 pellets
Fed. 209A	HS-6	Fed. 12S4	35.0/1300	36.0/1350	37.0/1375	38.0/1400	9,500 psi	27 pellets
Fed. 209A	Universal	Fed. 12S4				27.0/1300	9,900 psi	27 pellets
Fed. 410	IMR 700-X	Fed. 12S3				19.0/1200	10,900 LUP	27 pellets
FEDERAL: PLASTIC (PAPER BASE WAD)						**#3 LEAD BUCKSHOT**		
Fed. 209	IMR 700-X	Rem. SP12 + 20 grains BP Shot Buffer				20.5/1235	10,700 LUP	22 pellets
Fed. 209	IMR 700-X	Fed. 12S4				19.5/1190	10,500 LUP	25 pellets
Fed. 209	IMR PB	Four BP BPGS Shot Buffer				27.0/1375	10,900 LUP	23 pellets
Fed. 209	SR-7625	Four BP BPGS Shot Buffer				32.0/1375	8,600 LUP	23 pellets
FEDERAL: PLASTIC (PAPER BASE WAD)						**#1 LEAD BUCKSHOT**		
Fed. 209	IMR 700-X	Fed. 12S4 + 20 grains BP Shot Buffer				21.0/1300	10,900 LUP	12 pellets
Fed. 209	IMR 700-X	Four BP BPGS Shot Buffer				19.5/1200	10,900 LUP	15 pellets
Fed. 209	IMR PB	Three BP BPGS Shot Buffer				26.5/1315	10,800 LUP	15 pellets
Fed. 209	SR-7625	Four BP BPGS Shot Buffer				31.0/1355	9,100 LUP	15 pellets
FEDERAL: PLASTIC (PAPER BASE WAD)						**#0 LEAD BUCKSHOT**		
Fed. 209	IMR 700-X	Fed. 12S3				18.0/1255	7,800 LUP	6 pellets
Fed. 209	IMR 700-X	Fed. 12S4				18.5/1250	8,100 LUP	8 pellets
Fed. 209	IMR 700-X	Fed. 12S4 + 20 grains BP Shot Buffer				20.5/1285	10,700 LUP	8 pellets
Fed. 209	IMR 700-X	Four BP BPGS Shot Buffer				20.5/1345	10,200 LUP	9 pellets
Fed. 209	IMR 700-X	Rem. SP12 + 20 grains BP Shot Buffer				20.5/1230	10,600 LUP	10 pellets
Fed. 209	IMR PB	Fed. 12S4				28.0/1425	8,100 LUP	6 pellets
Fed. 209	IMR PB	Fed. 12C1				26.0/1355	8,200 LUP	8 pellets
Fed. 209	IMR PB	Four BP BPGS Shot Buffer				27.5/1410	9,200 LUP	9 pellets
Fed. 209	SR-7625	Four BP BPGS Shot Buffer				30.5/1405	6,400 LUP	6 pellets

Caution: Follow load recipes exactly; do not substitute components, exceed listed maximums or load less than listed minimums.

Primer	Powder Type	Wad	Powder Charge (grains) / Velocity (fps) Minimum			Maximum	Maximum Pressure	Buckshot Count
FEDERAL: PLASTIC (PAPER BASE WAD) (CONT.)						**#0 LEAD BUCKSHOT**		
Fed. 209	SR-7625	Four BP BPGS Shot Buffer				31.0/1440	7,700 LUP	8 pellets
Fed. 209	SR-7625	Four BP BPGS Shot Buffer				33.0/1445	7,400 LUP	9 pellets
FEDERAL: PLASTIC (PAPER BASE WAD)						**#00 LEAD BUCKSHOT**		
Fed. 209	Herco	0.135" card + (¹/₄" + ³/₁₆"+¹/₂") fiber				30.0/1325	9,400 psi	9 pellets
Fed. 209A	HS-6	Fed. 12S3	37.0/1300	39.0/1350	39.5/1375	40.0/1400	8,000 psi	9 pellets
Fed. 209A	HS-6	Fed. 12S4		38.0/1400	39.0/1425	40.0/1450	9,500 psi	9 pellets
Fed. 209A	Universal	Fed. 12S3	27.5/1300	28.0/1350	30.0/1400	30.5/1450	9,800 psi	9 pellets
FEDERAL: PLASTIC (PAPER BASE WAD)						**#000 LEAD BUCKSHOT**		
Fed. 209	IMR 700-X	Four BPGS + 20 grains BP Shot Buffer				23.0/1395	10,600 LUP	6 pellets
REMINGTON: PREMIER & NITRO 27 & STS						**#4 LEAD BUCKSHOT**		
CCI 209M	HS-6	WAA12R	30.5/1250	31.0/1275		31.5/1300	10,400 psi	27 pellets
REMINGTON: PREMIER & NITRO 27 & STS						**#00 LEAD BUCKSHOT**		
CCI 209M	HS-6	WAA12F114				31.0/1250	7,500 psi	9 pellets
CCI 209M	HS-6	WAA12F114	30.5/1300	31.3/1325		32.0/1350	9,500 psi	9 pellets
REMINGTON: RXP						**#00 LEAD BUCKSHOT**		
Rem. 97*	Herco	0.135" card + (¹/₄" + ³/₁₆") fiber				29.0/1325	10,100 psi	9 pellets
REMINGTON: UNIBODY (INTEGRAL PLASTIC BASE WAD)						**#4 LEAD BUCKSHOT**		
Rem. 209P	IMR 700-X	Rem. Fig.-8 + 18 grains BP Shot Buffer				17.0/1205	8,800 LUP	20 pellets
Rem. 209P	IMR 700-X	Rem. RXP12 + 18 grains BP Shot Buffer				17.0/1200	8,800 LUP	20 pellets
Fed. 209	IMR PB	Rem. RP12 + 23 grains BP Shot Buffer				22.5/1250	9,600 LUP	22 pellets
Fed. 209	SR-4756	Two BPGS + 25 grains BP Shot Buffer				28.0/1220	8,500 LUP	27 pellets
Fed. 209	SR-7625	Rem. RP12 + 20 grains BP Shot Buffer				29.0/1400	8,800 LUP	21 pellets
REMINGTON: UNIBODY (INTEGRAL PLASTIC BASE WAD)						**#3 LEAD BUCKSHOT**		
Rem. 209P	IMR 700-X	WAA12F114 + 19 grains BP Shot Buffer				17.0/1195	9,400 LUP	19 pellets
Fed. 209	IMR PB	Rem. RP12 + 23 grains BP Shot Buffer				23.0/1285	10,600 LUP	20 pellets
Fed. 209	SR-4756	Two BPGS + 25 grains BP Shot Buffer				28.0/1220	9,000 LUP	25 pellets
Fed. 209	SR-7625	Rem. RP12 + 20 grains BP Shot Buffer				29.5/1400	9,600 LUP	20 pellets

Caution: Follow load recipes exactly; do not substitute components, exceed listed maximums or load less than listed minimums.

Primer	Powder Type	Wad	Powder Charge (grains) / Velocity (fps) Minimum		Maximum	Maximum Pressure	Buckshot Count
REMINGTON: UNIBODY (INTEGRAL PLASTIC BASE WAD)					**#1 LEAD BUCKSHOT**		
Rem. 209P	IMR 700-X	WAA12F114 + 19 grains BP Shot Buffer			16.5/1185	10,000 LUP	12 pellets
Fed. 209	IMR PB	Rem. RP12 + 23 grains BP Shot Buffer			22.5/1270	10,200 LUP	12 pellets
Fed. 209	SR-4756	Two BPGS + 25 grains BP Shot Buffer			28.0/1230	9,400 LUP	15 pellets
Fed. 209	SR-7625	Rem. RP12 + 20 grains BP Shot Buffer			29.5/1405	9,500 LUP	12 pellets
REMINGTON: UNIBODY (INTEGRAL PLASTIC BASE WAD)					**#0 LEAD BUCKSHOT**		
Rem. 209P	IMR 700-X	WAA12F114 + 20 grains BP Shot Buffer			17.0/1185	9,900 LUP	8 pellets
Rem. 209P	IMR 700-X	WAA12 + 15 grains BP Shot Buffer			17.5/1205	9,400 LUP	9 pellets
Fed. 209	IMR PB	Rem. RP12 + 23 grains BP Shot Buffer			23.5/1310	10,100 LUP	8 pellets
Fed. 209	IMR PB	Rem. RP12 + 23 grains BP Shot Buffer			21.0/1170	9,900 LUP	10 pellets
Fed. 209	SR-4756	Two BPGS + 25 grains BP Shot Buffer			28.5/1255	9,400 LUP	10 pellets
Fed. 209	SR-4756	Two BPGS + 25 grains BP Shot Buffer			27.5/1200	9,800 LUP	12 pellets
Fed. 209	SR-7625	Rem. RP12 + 20 grains BP Shot Buffer			29.5/1410	9,000 LUP	8 pellets
Fed. 209	SR-7625	Rem. RP12 + 20 grains BP Shot Buffer			28.0/1320	9,500 LUP	10 pellets
REMINGTON: UNIBODY (INTEGRAL PLASTIC BASE WAD)					**#000 LEAD BUCKSHOT**		
Fed. 209	SR-4756	Two BPGS + 25 grains BP Shot Buffer			28.0/1220	8,500 LUP	8 pellets
Fed. 209	SR-7625	Two BPGS + 30 grains BP Shot Buffer			24.0/1175	9,300 LUP	8 pellets
WINCHESTER: COMPRESSION-FORMED AA TYPE					**#4 LEAD BUCKSHOT**		
Win. 209	Blue Dot	0.135" card + ³/₁₆" fiber + 0.135" card			39.0/1250	10,900 psi	34 pellets
Win. 209	HS-6	WAA12R	30.0/1250	31.0/1275	32.0/1300	10,000 psi	27 pellets
Win. 209	Universal	WAA12R			23.6/1250	10,400 psi	27 pellets
WINCHESTER: COMPRESSION-FORMED AA TYPE					**#00 LEAD BUCKSHOT**		
Win. 209	Herco	0.135" card + (2) ¹/₄" fiber			30.0/1325	10,000 psi	9 pellets
Win. 209	HS-6	WAA12F114	30.0/1250	30.5/1275	31.0/1300	8,700 psi	9 pellets
Win. 209	Universal	WAA12F114	24.0/1250	24.3/1275	24.6/1300	9,900 psi	9 pellets

Caution: Follow load recipes exactly; do not substitute components, exceed listed maximums or load less than listed minimums.

Primer	Powder Type	Wad	Powder Charge (grains) / Velocity (fps) Minimum			Maximum	Maximum Pressure	Buckshot Count
FEDERAL: ONE-PIECE						**#4 LEAD BUCKSHOT**		
Fed. 209A	HS-6	Fed. 12S4		35.0/1250	35.3/1275	35.5/1300	10,200 psi	34 pellets
Fed. 209A	HS-7	Fed. 12S4				38.0/1250	10,600 psi	34 pellets
FEDERAL: ONE-PIECE						**#00 LEAD BUCKSHOT**		
Fed. 209A	HS-6	Fed. 12S3	36.0/1250	37.0/1300	37.8/1325	38.5/1350	9,700 psi	12 pellets
Fed. 209A	HS-7	Fed. 12S3	38.0/1250	39.0/1300	39.8/1325	40.5/1350	9,900 psi	12 pellets
Fed. 209A	Universal	Fed. 12S3		28.0/1250	28.5/1275	29.0/1300	10,500 psi	12 pellets
FEDERAL: PLASTIC (PAPER BASE WAD)						**#1 LEAD BUCKSHOT**		
Fed. 209	Blue Dot	BP BPGS + BP12				37.0/1250	10,500 psi	33 pellets
FEDERAL: PLASTIC (PAPER BASE WAD)						**#4 LEAD BUCKSHOT**		
Fed. 209	Blue Dot	BP BPGS + BP12				36.0/1225	9,700 psi	18 pellets
FEDERAL: PLASTIC (PAPER BASE WAD)						**#0 LEAD BUCKSHOT**		
Fed. 209	Herco	RP12 + 20-gauge 0.200″ card				31.5/1275	9,800 psi	12 pellets
REMINGTON: SP (SEPARATE BLACK PLASTIC BASE WAD)						**#4 LEAD BUCKSHOT**		
CCI 209M	HS-6	Fed. 12S4				34.0/1250	10,500 psi	34 pellets
CCI 209M	HS-7	Fed. 12S4				37.0/1250	10,500 psi	34 pellets
REMINGTON: SP (SEPARATE BLACK PLASTIC BASE WAD)						**#00 LEAD BUCKSHOT**		
CCI 209M	HS-6	Fed. 12S3	34.5/1250	36.0/1300	36.5/1325	37.0/1350	9,900 psi	12 pellets
CCI 209M	HS-7	Fed. 12S3				37.0/1250	8,400 psi	12 pellets
CCI 209M	Universal	Fed. 12S3				28.0/1250	10,500 psi	12 pellets
REMINGTON: UNIBODY (INTEGRAL PLASTIC BASE WAD)						**#4 LEAD BUCKSHOT**		
Rem. 97*	Alliant 2400	BP BPGS + BP12				46.0/1250	9,400 psi	33 pellets
REMINGTON: UNIBODY (INTEGRAL PLASTIC BASE WAD)						**#1 LEAD BUCKSHOT**		
Rem. 97*	Blue Dot	BP BPGS + BP12				35.5/1225	9,800 psi	18 pellets
REMINGTON: UNIBODY (INTEGRAL PLASTIC BASE WAD)						**#0 LEAD BUCKSHOT**		
Rem. 97*	Herco	RP12 + 20-gauge 0.200″ card				29.5/1275	10,000 psi	12 pellets
WINCHESTER: COMPRESSION-FORMED AA TYPE						**#4 LEAD BUCKSHOT**		
Win. 209	Alliant 2400	BP BPGS + BP12				46.5/1250	9,000 psi	33 pellets
Win. 209	Alliant 2400	BP BPGS + BP12				49.0/1300	9,800 psi	33 pellets
Win. 209	HS-6	WAA12R		34.0/1250	34.8/1275	35.5/1300	10,100 psi	34 pellets
Win. 209	HS-7	WAA12R		37.5/1250	38.8/1275	40.0/1300	10,400 psi	34 pellets
WINCHESTER: COMPRESSION-FORMED AA TYPE						**#1 LEAD BUCKSHOT**		
Win. 209	Blue Dot	BP BPGS + BP12				34.5/1225	9,900 psi	18 pellets
Win. 209	Alliant 2400	BP BPGS + BP12				50.5/1300	9,200 psi	18 pellets
WINCHESTER: COMPRESSION-FORMED AA TYPE						**#0 LEAD BUCKSHOT**		
Win. 209	Blue Dot	RP12 + 20-gauge 0.200″ card				37.5/1275	9,900 psi	12 pellets
WINCHESTER: COMPRESSION-FORMED AA TYPE						**#00 LEAD BUCKSHOT**		
Win. 209	HS-6	WAA12F114	34.0/1250	36.0/1300	36.2/1325	36.5/1350	10,100 psi	12 pellets
Win. 209	HS-7	WAA12F114	37.0/1250	39.0/1300	40.0/1325	41.0/1350	10,100 psi	12 pellets
Win. 209	Universal	WAA12F114		28.0/1250	28.5/1275	29.0/1300	10,900 psi	12 pellets

END 12-GAUGE LEAD BUCKSHOT LOAD DATA

Caution: Follow load recipes exactly; do not substitute components, exceed listed maximums or load less than listed minimums.

20-GAUGE 2³/₄″   LEAD BUCKSHOT

Primer	Powder Type	Wad	Powder Charge (grains) / Velocity (fps) Minimum	Maximum	Maximum Pressure	Buckshot Count
FEDERAL: PLASTIC (PAPER BASE WAD)				**#1 LEAD BUCKSHOT**		
Fed. 209	Blue Dot	Rem. SP20 Petals removed		25.5/1275	10,100 psi	12 pellets
FEDERAL: PLASTIC (PAPER BASE WAD)				**#3 LEAD BUCKSHOT**		
Fed. 209	Blue Dot	Rem. SP20 Petals removed		24.0/1200	11,200 psi	24 pellets
FEDERAL: PLASTIC (PAPER BASE WAD)				**#4 LEAD BUCKSHOT**		
Fed. 209	Blue Dot	Rem. SP20		25.0/1275	9,300 psi	18 pellets
Fed. 209	Herco	Rem. SP20		19.0/1275	11,000 psi	18 pellets
WINCHESTER: COMPRESSION-FORMED AA TYPE				**#1 LEAD BUCKSHOT**		
Win. 209	Blue Dot	Rem. SP20 Petals removed		25.5/1275	10,400 psi	12 pellets
WINCHESTER: COMPRESSION-FORMED AA TYPE				**#4 LEAD BUCKSHOT**		
Win. 209	Blue Dot	Rem. SP20		24.0/1275	9,600 psi	18 pellets

20-GAUGE 3″   LEAD BUCKSHOT

Primer	Powder Type	Wad	Powder Charge (grains) / Velocity (fps) Minimum	Maximum	Maximum Pressure	Buckshot Count
FEDERAL: PLASTIC (PAPER BASE WAD)				**#3 LEAD BUCKSHOT**		
Fed. 209	Blue Dot	Rem. SP20		26.0/1220	7,800 psi	21 pellets
Fed. 209	Herco	Rem. RXP20		19.5/1220	8,400 psi	18 pellets
WINCHESTER: COMPRESSION-FORMED AA TYPE				**#3 LEAD BUCKSHOT**		
Win. 209	Blue Dot	Rem. RP20		25.0/1200	9,400 psi	21 pellets
Win. 209	Herco	WAA20F1		19.0/1220	9,500 psi	18 pellets

END OF 20-GAUGE LEAD BUCKSHOT LOAD DATA

Caution: Follow load recipes exactly; do not substitute components, exceed listed maximums or load less than listed minimums.

Lead Slug Load Data

This data is lead slug-specific; it does not interchange with data used for any other type of shot. Use only the components and amounts listed. For best results, do not use any slug load in a tightly choked barrel—Cylinder, Improved Cylinder or Modified chokes work best.

7/8-Ounce Cast Rifled Lead Slug — 12-Gauge 2³/₄"

Primer	Powder Type	Wad	Powder Charge (grains) / Velocity (fps) Minimum	Maximum	Maximum Pressure	Load Notes
FEDERAL: PLASTIC (PAPER BASE WAD)			**7/8-OUNCE CAST RIFLED LEAD SLUG**			
Fed. 209	Unique	0.135" card + (5/16" + 1/4") fiber + (2) 0.135" card		33.0/1570	10,000 psi	Roll Crimp
Fed. 209	Herco	0.135" card + 5/16" fiber + (2) 0.135" card		35.5/1570	8,000 psi	Roll Crimp
REMINGTON: RXP			**7/8-OUNCE CAST RIFLED LEAD SLUG**			
Rem. 97*	Unique	0.135" card + (2) 1/4" fiber + (2) 0.135" card		34.0/1570	10,800 psi	Roll Crimp
Rem. 97*	Herco	0.135" card + (2) 1/4" fiber + (2) 0.135" card		35.0/1570	9,700 psi	Roll Crimp
WINCHESTER: COMPRESSION-FORMED AA TYPE			**7/8-OUNCE CAST RIFLED LEAD SLUG**			
Win. 209	Unique	0.135" card + 1/4" fiber + (2) 0.135" card		34.5/1570	9,800 psi	Roll Crimp
Win. 209	Herco	0.135" card + 1/4" fiber + (2) 0.135" card		29.0/1570	8,600 psi	Roll Crimp

7/8-Ounce Slugmaster Lead Slug — 12-Gauge 2³/₄"

Primer	Powder Type	Wad	Powder Charge (grains) / Velocity (fps) Minimum	Maximum	Maximum Pressure	Load Notes
FEDERAL: GOLD MEDAL PLASTIC			**7/8-OUNCE SLUGMASTER LEAD SLUG**			
Win. 209	HS-6	BPGS + (2) 1/2" felt + 0.135" card		37.0/1450	10,200 psi	
Win. 209	Universal	BPGS + 1/2" felt + (2) 0.135" card		31.0/1500	10,100 psi	
FIOCCHI: PURPLE TARGET (HIGH BASE WAD)			**7/8-OUNCE SLUGMASTER LEAD SLUG**			
Fio. 616	Universal	0.135" card + 1/2" felt 0.135" card		31.0/1550	10,100 psi	
REMINGTON: PREMIER & NITRO 27 & STS			**7/8-OUNCE SLUGMASTER LEAD SLUG**			
CCI 209M	HS-6	0.135" card + 1/2" felt + 0.135" card		40.5/1550	9,500 psi	

Caution: Follow load recipes exactly; do not substitute components, exceed listed maximums or load less than listed minimums.

12-GAUGE 2³/₄″ — ⁷/₈-OUNCE SLUGMASTER (CONT.)

Primer	Powder Type	Wad	Powder Charge (grains) / Velocity (fps) Minimum	Maximum	Maximum Pressure	Load Notes
REMINGTON: PREMIER & NITRO 27 & STS (CONT.)			⁷/₈-OUNCE SLUGMASTER LEAD SLUG			
CCI 209M	Universal	0.135″ card + ½″ felt + 0.135″ card		29.0/1550	10,100 psi	
Win. 209	HS-6	0.135″ card + ½″ felt + 0.135″ card		40.0/1550	10,100 psi	
WINCHESTER: COMPRESSION-FORMED AA TYPE			⁷/₈-OUNCE SLUGMASTER LEAD SLUG			
Win. 209	HS-6	0.135″ card + ½″ felt + 0.135″ card		47.0/1500	10,300 psi	
Win. 209	Universal	(2) 0.135″ cards + ½″ fiber		29.5/1450	10,400 psi	

12-GAUGE 2³/₄″ — 1-OUNCE LEE PRECISION LEAD SLUG

Primer	Powder Type	Wad	Powder Charge (grains) / Velocity (fps) Minimum	Maximum	Maximum Pressure	Load Notes
FEDERAL: GOLD MEDAL PLASTIC			1-OUNCE LEE PRECISION LEAD SLUG			
Fed. 209A	Universal	Fed. 12S3		28.0/1450	10,200 psi	
Fed. 209A	HS-6	Fed. 12S3		40.0/1550	11,000 psi	
REMINGTON: PREMIER & NITRO 27 & STS			1-OUNCE LEE PRECISION LEAD SLUG			
Win. 209	HS-6	WAA12SL		36.0/1450	10,200 psi	
WINCHESTER: COMPRESSION-FORMED AA-TYPE			1-OUNCE LEE PRECISION LEAD SLUG			
Win. 209	HS-6	WAA12F114		36.0/1500	10,800 psi	

12-GAUGE 2³/₄″ — 1-OUNCE SLUGMASTER LEAD SLUG

Primer	Powder Type	Wad	Powder Charge (grains) / Velocity (fps) Minimum	Maximum	Maximum Pressure	Load Notes
FEDERAL: GOLD MEDAL PLASTIC			1-OUNCE SLUGMASTER LEAD SLUG			
Win. 209	HS-6	BPGS + (2) ½″ felt + 0.135″ card		35.5/1400	10,200 psi	
Win. 209	Universal	BPGS + ½″ felt + (2) 0.135″ card		29.0/1450	11,000 psi	
FIOCCHI: PURPLE TARGET (HIGH BASE WAD)			1-OUNCE SLUGMASTER LEAD SLUG			
Fio. 616	Universal	0.135″ card + ½″ felt + 0.135″ card		30.0/1550	10,200 psi	

Caution: Follow load recipes exactly; do not substitute components, exceed listed maximums or load less than listed minimums.

1-OUNCE SLUGMASTER (CONT.)

12-GAUGE 2³/₄"

Primer	Powder Type	Wad	Powder Charge (grains) / Velocity (fps) Minimum	Maximum	Maximum Pressure	Load Notes
REMINGTON: PREMIER & NITRO 27 & STS			1-OUNCE SLUGMASTER LEAD SLUG			
CCI 209M	Universal	0.135" card + ½" felt + 0.135" card		30.0/1500	10,900 psi	
Win. 209	HS-6	0.135" card + ½" felt + 0.135" card		36.0/1450	10,100 psi	
WINCHESTER: COMPRESSION-FORMED AA TYPE			1-OUNCE SLUGMASTER LEAD SLUG			
Win. 209	HS-6	0.135" card + ½" felt + 0.135" card		35.0/1450	10,200 psi	
Win. 209	Universal	0.135" card + ½" felt + 0.135" card		27.0/1400	10,500 psi	

1¹/₁₆-OUNCE LYMAN SLUG

12-GAUGE 2³/₄"

Primer	Powder Type	Wad	Powder Charge (grains) / Velocity (fps) Minimum	Maximum	Maximum Pressure	Load Notes
ACTIV: ALL PLASTIC			1¹/₁₆-OUNCE LYMAN SLUG			
CCI 209	Solo 1250	BP HCD24		27.0/1385	8,600 LUP	
FEDERAL: GOLD METAL PLASTIC			1¹/₁₆-OUNCE LYMAN SLUG			
Fio. 616	SR-7625	BP x 12X Gas Seal		29.5/1475	10,500 LUP	
FIOCCHI: PLASTIC (HIGH BASE WAD)			1¹/₁₆-OUNCE LYMAN SLUG			
Fio. 616	Green Dot	BP HCD24		25.0/1400	10,600 psi	
Fio. 616	Green Dot	BP HCD24		24.5/1400	10,100 psi	
Fio. 616	Unique	BP HCD24		28.0/1345	9,500 psi	
Fio. 616	Unique	BP HCD24		27.0/1290	8,540 psi	
Fio. 616	Unique	BP HCD24		28.6/1390	10,300 psi	
WINCHESTER: COMPRESSION-FORMED AA TYPE			1¹/₁₆-OUNCE LYMAN SLUG			
Win. 209	SR-7625	BP x 12X Gas Seal		29.0/1500	10,200 LUP	

1¹/₈-OUNCE BP DSG12 SLUG

12-GAUGE 2³/₄"

Primer	Powder Type	Wad	Powder Charge (grains) / Velocity (fps) Minimum	Maximum	Maximum Pressure	Load Notes
ACTIV: ALL PLASTIC			1¹/₈-OUNCE BP DSG12 SLUG			
CCI 209M	PB			32.0/1400	11,000 psi	
Win. 209	Solo 1250			30.0/1540	10,400 LUP	
Win. 209	SR-7625			32.0/1400	10,000 LUP	
Win. 209	WSF			32.0/1460	9,800 LUP	
Win. 209	Unique			32.1/1470	9,600 LUP	

Caution: Follow load recipes exactly; do not substitute components, exceed listed maximums or load less than listed minimums.

Primer	Powder Type	Wad	Powder Charge (grains) / Velocity (fps) Minimum	Maximum	Maximum Pressure	Load Notes
FIOCCHI: PLASTIC (LOW BASE WAD)			1¹/₈-OUNCE BP DSG12 SLUG			
Fio. 616	PB			32.0/1450	10,900 LUP	
Fio. 616	Solo 1250			30.0/1550	10,500 LUP	
Fio. 616	SR-7625			32.0/1390	10,000 LUP	
Fio. 616	WSF			32.0/1450	9,900 LUP	
Fio. 616	Unique			32.0/1460	9,500 LUP	

12-GAUGE 2³/₄″   448-GRAIN BP AQ SLUG

Primer	Powder Type	Wad	Powder Charge (grains) / Velocity (fps) Minimum	Maximum	Maximum Pressure	Load Notes
ACTIV: ALL PLASTIC			448-GRAIN BP AQ SLUG			
CCI 209	Green Dot	BPGS + (2) ¹/₄″ 12-ga. corks		26.4/1440	10,300 LUP	Roll crimp
Fio. 616	PB	BPGS + ¹/₄″ 12-ga. cork		31.0/1490	10,800 LUP	Roll crimp
ACT 209	Solo 1250	BPGS + ¹/₄″ 12-ga. cork		32.0/1550	9,500 LUP	Teflon wrap; roll crimp
Fio. 616	Unique	(2) BPGS + ¹/₈″ 12-ga. wool felt		32.0/1500	10,300 LUP	Roll crimp
FIOCCHI: PLASTIC (HIGH BASE WAD)			448-GRAIN BP AQ SLUG			
Fio. 616	Green Dot	BPGS + ¹/₂″ 12-ga. hard card		26.0/1400	8,600 LUP	Roll crimp
FIOCCHI: PLASTIC (LOW BASE WAD)			448-GRAIN BP AQ SLUG			
Fio. 616	PB	BPGS + 12-ga. ¹/₄″ cork		26.5/1450	9,500 LUP	Roll crimp
Fio. 616	Solo 1250	BPGS + 12-ga. ¹/₄″ cork		32.0/1560	9,700 LUP	Teflon wrap; roll crimp
Fio. 616	Unique	BPGS + ¹/₂″ 12-ga. hard card		29.0/1350	8,620 LUP	Roll crimp
Fio. 616	Unique	BPGS + (3) 0.125″ Nitro cards		30.5/1489	11,200 LUP	Roll crimp
WINCHESTER: COMPRESSION-FORMED AA TYPE			448-GRAIN BP AQ SLUG			
CCI 209	Unique	BPGS + ¹/₂″ 12-ga. hard card		1.0/1560	10,800 LUP	Roll crimp

Caution: Follow load recipes exactly; do not substitute components, exceed listed maximums or load less than listed minimums.

Primer	Powder Type	Wad	Powder Charge (grains) / Velocity (fps) Minimum	Maximum	Maximum Pressure	Load Notes
FEDERAL: PLASTIC (PAPER BASE WAD)				7/8-OUNCE CAST RIFLED LEAD SLUG		
Fed. 209	Herco	0.135″ card + (1/2″ + 3/8″) fiber + 0.135″ card		40.0/1570	10,500 psi	Roll crimp
REMINGTON: UNIBODY (INTEGRAL PLASTIC BASE WAD)				7/8-OUNCE CAST RIFLED LEAD SLUG		
Rem. 97*	Herco	0.135″ card + (1/2″ + 3/8″) fiber + 0.135″ card		37.5/1570	10,600 psi	Roll crimp
WINCHESTER: COMPRESSION-FORMED AA TYPE				7/8-OUNCE CAST RIFLED LEAD SLUG		
Win. 209	Herco	0.135″ card + 1/2″ fiber + 0.135″ card		37.5/1570	9,700 psi	Roll crimp

Primer	Powder Type	Wad	Powder Charge (grains) / Velocity (fps) Minimum	Maximum	Maximum Pressure	Load Notes
ACTIV: ALL PLASTIC				448-GRAIN BP AQ SLUG		
Win. 209	Green Dot	(2) BPGS + 1/2″ 12-ga. hard card		29.0/1490	10,700 LUP	Roll crimp
FIOCCHI: PLASTIC (LOW BASE WAD)				448-GRAIN BP AQ SLUG		
Fio. 616	PB	BPGS + (3) 12-ga. 1/4″ corks		36.0/1590	10,900 LUP	Roll crimp

END OF 12-GAUGE LEAD SLUG LOAD DATA

Caution: Follow load recipes exactly; do not substitute components, exceed listed maximums or load less than listed minimums.

20-GAUGE 2³/₄"   ⁵/₈-OUNCE CAST RIFLED LEAD SLUG

Primer	Powder Type	Wad	Powder Charge (grains) / Velocity (fps) Minimum	Maximum	Maximum Pressure	Load Notes
FEDERAL: PLASTIC (PAPER BASE WAD)				**⁵/₈-OUNCE CAST RIFLED LEAD SLUG**		
Fed. 209	Herco	0.125" card + ½" fiber + (2) 0.125" card		25.5/1570	9,800 psi	
WINCHESTER: COMPRESSION-FORMED AA TYPE				**⁵/₈-OUNCE CAST RIFLED LEAD SLUG**		
Win. 209	Herco	0.125" card + ½" fiber + (2) 0.125" card		25.5/1570	10,200 psi	

20-GAUGE 2³/₄"   ⁷/₈-OUNCE BP DGS20 SLUG

Primer	Powder Type	Wad	Powder Charge (grains) / Velocity (fps) Minimum	Maximum	Maximum Pressure	Load Notes
ACTIV: ALL PLASTIC				**⁷/₈-OUNCE BP DGS20 SLUG**		
Rem. 209P	Blue Dot			26.0/1370	10,370 psi	
Rem. 209P	Herco			19.0/1310	10,900 psi	
Fio. 616	Herco			19.0/1325	10,900 psi	
Fio. 616	Unique			18.0/1370	10,800 psi	

END OF 20-GAUGE LEAD SLUG LOAD DATA

Caution: Follow load recipes exactly; do not substitute components, exceed listed maximums or load less than listed minimums.

Common Bushings Charts

Caution: Read and understand the Instruction manuals for your reloading machine and tools. Shotshell reloading tool powder bushings and other fixed volumetric powder measures seldom throw the exact charge as suggested in the above tables. There are many reasons for these variations, including:

- Lot-to-lot powder density variations. Typical manufacturing tolerances for bulk density of most canister-grade smokeless powders is ±.025-gram per cubic centimeter.
- Usually a bushing chart lists the nominal weight of a powder charge based on normal packing as a result of free flow and nominal bulk density for that powder; alternately, some bushing manufacturers give ratings based upon the nominal bulk powder density.
- Various operators of any given tool will produce differing powder weights using identical tools, bushings and similar techniques. This variation results from differences in the force of operation and the amount of vibration transmitted to and through the tool.
- Variations in sizing force, resulting from differences in hulls, can produce differences in dropped charge weight owing to changes in tool vibration.
- Bushing manufacturing tolerances are always greater than zero!
- Tool manufacturing tolerances can have an effect.
- Mismarked bushings are possible.

Obviously, the handloader cannot expect his results to exactly match any bushing/powder/charge charts listing. These tables simply represent what the manufacturer believes to be the nominal charge thrown with the listed bushing and powder. Proper understanding of this is the key.

Never attempt to determine the charge that will be thrown by simply metering the powder bar back and forth and weighing the resulting charges. To produce the same amount of vibration and powder packing that will result during normal loading operations, the reloader must follow all usual loading procedures and then weigh the powder charges to determine the average thrown charge for that bushing or bar.

For powders not listed, refer to the latest tool manufacturer's data.

Bushings Chart for Hornady 366 and APEX 91 Presses
Range of bushing numbers apt to throw desired charge.

Powder	11.0	12.0	13.0	13.5	14.0	14.5	15.0	15.5	16.0	16.5	17.0	17.5	18.0	18.5	19.0	19.5	20.0	20.5
2400	256	266			291		300		312		324		330		339			
452AA					360		369		381		390		402		411		420	
473AA			327		339				348		357		369		381		390	
American Select									417		423		432		447		456	
Blue Dot													366		372		381	
Clays							414		429	435	441	447	456	462	468	474	483	489
Green Dot		363	378		390		405		420		435		447		456		468	
H 110			256		266													
Herco			357		369		381		393		405		414		426		438	
HS 6											300		309		318		327	
HS 7															318		330	
International	333	348	363		375		390		402	408	414	417	423	429	435	438	447	453
Nitro-100														414	420	426	432	438
No. 2 Improved													366,369		372,375	375,378	361,384	387,390
Red Diamond									435,438	441.444	447,450	450.453	459.462	465.468	468,471	474,477	480,453	486,489
Red Dot		384	393		405		423		438	453		468	480					
Royal Scot D										393,306	399,402	408,411	411,414	417,420	423,426	429,432	435,438	441,444
Scot 453										366,369	372.375	375,376	381,364	387,390	393,396	396.399	399,402	405,408
Solo 1000												444,447	447,450	453,456	459,462	465,468	471,474	477,480
Solo 1250			363,363	366,369	372,375	376,361	384,387	390,393	396,399	402,405	408,411	414,417	417,420	423,426	429,432	435,438	441,444	447,450
Solo 1500										364,387	390,393	396,399	402,405		406,411	414,417	420,423	426,429
Unique			342		354		369		381		393		405		414		423	
Universal			330		342		354		366	372	378	384	390	393	402	405	411	417
W 296			256		266													
W 540											300		309		318		327	
W 571															318		330	
WAAP											405	411	417	423	429	435	438	444
WSF								327	330	336	342	348	351	354				
WSL									333	339	345	348	354	360	363	366	372	378
WST											405	411	417	423	429	435	438	444

Powder	21.0	21.5	22.0	22.5	23.0	23.5	24.0	24.5	25.0	25.5	26.0	26.5	27.0	27.5	28.0	28.5	29.0	29.5
452AA	432		441		450		462		474									
473AA	399	408			414		426		435		444		450		462		474	
American Select	468		477		483													
Blue Dot	390		396		408	414			423		435		441		447		459	
Clays	495	501	507															
Green Dot	480		492		501		513		522		534				549		558	
Herco	450		462		471		477		489		498					513	522	
HS 6	336		345		351		360		366		375		381		387		393	
HS 7	339		348		357		363		369		378		384		390		396	
International	459	465	471	477	483	489	495	501	507									
Nitro-100	444	450	458	462	400	474												
No. 2 Improved	393,396	396,399	399,402	405,408	408,411	414,417	420,423	426,429	432,435	435,438	441,444	444,447	450,453					
Red Dot	489	498		510		519												
Royal Scot D	447,450	453,456	456,459	459,462	465,468	471,474	477,480	480,483	486,489		402,405							
Scot 453	406,411	414,417	420,423	426,429	432,435	435,438	441,444	444,447	450,453									
Solo 1000	489,492	495,496	501,564	504,507	510,513	513,516	516,510	522,525	520,531	534,537								
Solo 1250	453,456	459,462	465,468	471,474	477,480	480,483	486,489	492,495	495,498	498,501	504,507	510,513	516,519	522,525	525,528	531,534	534,537	537,540
Solo 1500	429,432	435,438	441,444	447,450	450,453	456,459	459,462	465,468	468,471	471,474	477,480	483,486	489,492	492,495	498,501	501,504	504,507	510,513
Unique	435		444		453		465		474		483		492		501			
Universal	420	423	429	432	438	441	447	450	456		468		480		489		501	
W 540	336		345		351		360		366		375		381		387		393	
W 571	339		348		357		363		369		378		384		390		396	
WAAP	450	456	459	465	471	477	480											
WSF									411	414	420	423	426	429	432	438	441	447
WSL	381	387	390	396	402	405												
WST	450	456	459	465	471	477	480											

Powder	30.0	30.5	31.0	31.5	32.0	33.0	34.0	35.0	36.0	37.0	38.0	39.0	40.0	41.0	42.0	43.0	44.0
Blue Dot	468		474		483	489	495	501	510	516	522	531	534	543	549	555	561
Herco	531				549	558	564	573		588	594						
HS 6	402		408		414	423	429	435	441	444	450						
HS 7	405		411		417	423	429	438	444	450							
Solo 1250	543,546	546,549	552,555	555,558	561,564	567,570											
Solo 1500	516,519	519,522	522,525	525,528	531,534	540,543	549,555	558,561	564,567	570,573	576,579	581,584	587,590	593,596	599,601	604,807	610,613
Unique	510																
W 540	402		408		414	423	429	435	441	444	450	459	465	471	477	483	489
W 571	405		411		417	423	429	438	444	450	456	462	468	474	480	486	492
WSF	450	453	456	459	462												

Powder	13.0	13.5	14.0	14.5	15.0	15.5	16.0	16.5	17.0	17.5	18.0	18.5	19.0	19.5	20.6	20.5	21.0	21.5	22	22.5	23
Royal Scot D								381,364	393,396	399,402	402,405	406,411	414,417	423,426	429,432	435,438	441,444	447,451	451,453	453,456	456,459
Scott 453								360,363	366,369	372,375	378,381	364,387	390,393	393,396	396,399	399,402	405,408	411,414	414,417	420,423	429,432
Solo 1000									426,429	429,432	435,438	441,444	447,450	453,456	459,462	465,468	471,474	477,480	483,486	489,492	495,498
Solo 1250	351,354	357,360	363,366	369,372	375,379	381,364	387,390	390,393	399,402	402,405	405,408	411,414	417,420	423,426	429,432	432,435	438,441	444,447	450,453	456,459	459,462
Solo 1500										384,387	387,390	393,396	396,399	402,405	408,411	414,417	420,423	423,426	429,432	435,438	441,444

Powder	23.5	24	24.5	25	25.5	26	26.5	27	27.5	28	28.5	29	29.5	30	30.5	31	31.5	32	33	34	35	36
Royal Scot D	462,465	465,468	471,474	477,480	483,486																	
Scott 453	429,432	435,438	441,444	444,447																		
Solo 1000	498,501	501,504	504,507	510,513																		
Solo 1250	462,465	465,468	466,471	474,477	480,483	486,489	492,495	498,501	501,504	504,507	510,513	513,516	516,519	522,525	525,528	528,531	534,537	537,540	546,549			
Solo 1500	444,447	456,453	456,459	462,465	468,471	471,474	474,477	477,480	480,483	486,489	489,492	492,495	495,498	501,504	504,507	507,510	510,513	516,519	522,525	534,537	540,543	549,552

Powder	Bushing Volume (cubic ins.)											
	0.30	0.32	0.34	0.37	0.40	0.43	0.46	0.49	0.53	0.57	0.61	0.66
452AA	2.6	2.7	2.9	3.2	3.4	3.7	3.9	4.2	4.5	4.9	5.2	5.6
473AA	3.1	3.3	3.5	3.8	4.1	4.4	4.7	5.0	5.4	5.8	6.3	6.8
Nitro-100	2.2	2.4	2.5	2.7	3.0	3.2	3.4	3.6	3.9	4.2	4.5	4.9
No. 2 Improved	2.9	3.0	3.3	3.5	3.8	4.1	4.4	4.6	5.0	5.4	5.8	6.3
Royal Scot D	2.3	2.5	2.7	2.0	3.1	3.4	3.6	3.8	4.2	4.5	4.6	5.2
Scot 453	2.8	3.0	3.3	3.4	3.8	4.1	4.3	4.6	5.0	5.4	5.8	6.2
Solo 1000	2.3	2.4	2.6	2.8	3.0	3.2	3.5	3.7	4.0	4.3	4.6	5.0

Powder	0.30	0.32	0.34	0.37	0.40	0.43	0.46	0.49	0.53	0.57	0.61	0.66
Solo 1250	2.4	2.8	2.7	3.0	3.2	3.4	3.6	4.0	4.3	4.7	5.0	5.3
Solo 1500	2.6	2.9	3.0	3.2	3.5	3.7	4.1	4.4	4.7	5.1	5.4	5.8
W 296	4.6	4.9	5.2	5.6	6.1	6.6	7.0	7.5	8.1	8.7	9.3	10.1
W 540	4.4	4.7	5.0	5.4	5.9	6.3	6.7	7.2	7.8	8.3	8.9	9.7
W 571	4.4	4.7	5.0	5.4	5.9	6.3	6.8	7.2	7.8	8.4	9.0	9.7
WAAP	3.6	3.8	4.0	4.4	4.8	5.1	5.5	5.8	6.3	6.8	7.3	7.9
WSF	3.6	3.8	4.0	4.4	4.8	5.1	5.5	5.8	6.3	6.8	7.3	7.9
WSL	3.5	3.8	4.0	4.4	4.7	5.1	5.4	5.8	6.3	6.7	7.2	7.8
WST	2.5	2.7	2.8	3.1	3.3	3.6	3.8	4.1	4.4	4.7	5.1	5.5

Bushing Volume (cubic ins.)

Powder	0.71	0.76	0.82	0.88	0.95	1.02	1.09	1.18	1.26	1.36	1.46	1.57
452AA	6.1	6.5	7.0	7.5	8.1	8.7	9.3	10.1	10.8	11.6	12.5	13.4
473AA	7.3	7.8	8.4	9.0	9.7	10.5	11.2	12.1	12.9	13.9	15.0	16.1
Nitro-100	5.3	5.6	6.1	6.5	7.0	7.6	8.1	8.7	9.3	10.1	10.8	11.6
No. 2 Improved	6.8	7.3	7.8	8.4	9.0	9.8	10.4	11.3	12.0	13.0	13.9	15.0
Royal Scot D	5.7	6.0	6.4	6.9	7.5	8.0	8.6	9.2	9.9	10.7	11.5	12.4
Scot 453	6.8	7.2	7.7	8.3	9.0	9.7	10.3	11.2	12.0	13.0	14.1	15.1
Solo 1000	5.3	5.7	6.2	6.6	7.1	7.7	8.2	8.9	9.5	10.2	11.0	11.8
Solo 1250	5.8	6.2	6.5	7.1	7.7	8.1	8.9	9.5	10.0	10.9	11.8	12.6
Solo 1500	6.5	6.8	7.2	7.8	9.5	9.1	9.8	10.4	11.4	11.9	13.0	13.8
W 296	10.8	11.6	12.5	13.4	14.5	15.6	16.6	18.0	19.2	20.7	22.3	24.0
W 540	10.4	11.1	12.0	12.9	13.9	14.9	16.0	17.3	18.5	19.9	21.4	23.0
W 571	10.4	11.2	12.1	12.9	14.0	15.0	16.0	17.4	18.5	20.0	21.5	23.1
WAAP	8.4	9.0	9.8	10.5	11.3	12.1	13.0	14.0	15.0	16.2	17.4	18.7
WSF	8.4	9.0	9.8	10.5	11.3	12.1	13.0	14.0	15.0	16.2	17.4	18.7
WS	8.4	9.0	9.7	10.4	11.2	12.0	12.9	13.9	14.9	16.0	17.2	18.5
WST	5.9	6.3	6.8	7.3	7.9	8.5	9.0	9.8	10.5	11.3	12.1	13.0

Bushings Chart for Lee Charge Bar
Approximate thrown charges in grains

Bushing Volume (cubic ins.)

Powder	.095	.100	.105	.110	.116	.122	.128	.134	.141	.148	.151	.155	.163	.171	.180	.189	.198
2400	21.0	22.1	23.2	24.3	25.6	27.0	28.3	29.6	31.2	32.7	33.4	34.3	36.0	37.8	39.8	41.8	43.8
452AA	13.3	14.0	14.7	15.4	16.2	17.1	17.9	18.8	19.7	20.7	21.1	21.7	22.8	23.9	25.2	26.5	27.7
473AA	16.0	16.8	17.6	18.5	19.5	20.5	21.5	22.5	23.7	24.9	25.4	26.0	27.4	28.7	30.2	31.8	33.3
Blue Dot	18.0	19.0	19.9	20.8	22.0	23.1	24.3	25.4	26.7	28.0	28.6	29.4	30.9	32.4	34.1	35.8	37.5
Clays	10.7	11.3	11.8	12.4	13.0	13.7	14.4	15.0	15.8	16.6	16.7	17.3	18.2	19.1	20.1	21.2	22.1
Green Dot	12.3	13.0	13.6	14.3	15.1	15.8	16.6	17.4	18.3	19.2	19.6	20.1	21.2	22.2	23.4	24.5	25.7
H 110	22.5	23.7	24.9	26.1	27.5	28.9	30.3	31.8	33.4	35.1	36.8	36.7	38.6	40.5	42.7	44.8	46.9
Herco	13.9	14.6	15.3	16.1	16.9	17.8	18.7	19.6	20.6	21.6	22.0	22.6	23.8	25.0	26.3	27.6	28.9
HS 6	21.9	23.0	24.2	25.3	26.7	28.1	29.4	30.8	32.4	34.0	34.7	35.7	37.5	39.3	41.4	43.5	45.5
HS 7	22.9	24.1	25.3	26.5	28.0	29.4	30.8	32.3	34.0	35.7	36.4	37.4	39.3	41.2	43.4	45.6	47.7
International	12.3	13.0	13.7	14.3	15.1	15.9	16.6	17.5	18.4	19.3	19.6	20.1	21.1	22.0	23.1	24.1	25.2
Nitro-100	11.3	11.9	12.5	13.0	13.8	14.5	15.2	15.9	16.7	17.6	17.9	18.4	19.3	20.3	21.4	22.4	23.5
Red Dot	11.0	11.6	12.2	12.8	13.5	14.2	14.8	15.5	16.4	17.2	17.5	18.0	18.9	19.8	20.9	21.9	23.0
Solo 1000	11.4	12.0	12.6	13.2	13.9	14.7	15.4	16.1	17.0	17.8	18.2	18.6	19.6	20.6	21.6	22.7	23.8
Unique	14.3	15.0	15.8	16.5	17.4	18.3	19.2	20.1	21.2	22.2	22.7	23.3	24.5	25.7	27.0	28.4	29.7
Universal	15.2	16.0	16.8	17.6	18.5	19.5	20.4	21.4	22.5	23.6	24.0	24.7	25.9	27.1	28.5	29.9	31.3
W 296	23.7	25.0	26.2	27.5	29.0	30.5	32.0	33.5	35.2	37.0	37.7	38.7	40.7	42.7	45.0	47.2	49.5
W 540	22.8	24.0	25.2	26.4	27.8	29.3	30.7	32.2	33.8	35.5	36.2	37.2	39.1	41.0	43.2	45.4	47.5
W 571	22.9	24.1	25.3	26.5	28.0	29.4	30.8	32.3	34.0	35.7	36.4	37.4	39.3	41.2	43.4	45.6	47.7
WAAP	12.9	13.6	14.3	15.0	15.8	16.6	17.4	18.2	19.2	20.1	20.5	21.1	22.2	23.3	24.5	25.7	26.9
WSF	18.5	19.5	20.5	21.5	22.6	23.8	25.0	26.1	27.5	28.9	29.4	30.2	31.8	33.3	35.1	36.9	38.6
WSL	18.4	19.3	20.3	21.3	22.4	23.6	24.8	25.9	27.3	28.6	29.2	30.0	31.5	33.1	34.8	36.5	38.3
WST	12.9	13.6	14.3	15.0	15.8	16.6	17.4	18.2	19.2	20.1	20.5	21.1	22.2	23.3	24.5	25.7	26.9

Bushings Chart for MEC Single-Stage Presses
Approximate thrown charge in grains

Bushing Designations

Powder	19	20	21	22	23	24	25	26	27	28	29	30	31	32	33	35	36
Nitro-100							15.9	18.6	17.2	17.9	18.5	19.2	19.9	20.6	21.3	22.8	23.5
No. 2 Improved		16.0	16.7	17.5	18.2	10.9	19.7	20.5	21.3	22.1	22.0	23.8	24.6	25.5			
Red Diamond																	
Royal Scot D				15.7	16.3	17.0	17.7	18.4	19.1	19.8	20.6	21.3	22.1	22.9	23.7	25.3	
Scot 453	16.0	16.7	17.5	18.2	18.9	19.7	28.5	21.3	22.1	22.9	23.8	24.6	25.5				
Solo 1000							15.6	16.2	16.8	17.4	18.1	18.7	19.3		20.7	21.4	
Solo 1250	12.6	13.2	13.8	14.4	15.0	15.6	16.2	16.9	17.5	18.2	18.9	19.6	20.3	21.0	21.7	23.2	24.0
Solo 1500						16.6	17.5	18.4	19.4	19.8	20.2	21.1	22.1	23.2	23.7	25.3	26.2

Bushing Designations

Powder	37	38	38A	39	39A	40	40A	41	41A	42	42A	43	43A	44	44A	45	45A
Nitro-100	24.3	25.1															
Red Diamond	22.1	23.1	23.8	24.5	25.3												
Royal Scot D	26.9																
Solo 1000		22.8	23.5	24.2	24.9	25.7											
Solo 1250	24.8	25.6	26.4	27.2	28.0	28.9	29.7	30.6	31.5	32.4	33.3	34.2	35.1	36.1	37.0	39.0	39.0
Solo 1500	22.4	27.8	28.8	29.8	30.7	32.1	32.8	33.5	34.5	39.1	36.3	37.8	39.5	39.6	40.4	41.7	42.5

Bushing Designations

Powder	10	11	12	12A	13	13A	14	15	16	17	18	19	20	21	22	23
2400	11.8	12.5	13.3	14.0	14.8	15.6	16.4	17.2	18.1	18.9	19.8	20.7	21.7	22.6	23.6	24.6
452AA	7.5	7.9	8.4	8.9	9.4	9.9	10.4	10.9	11.4	12.0	12.6	13.1	13.7	14.3	14.9	15.6
473AA	9.1	9.7	10.2	10.8	11.4	12.0	12.6	13.2	13.9	14.6	15.3	16.0	16.7	17.4	18.2	18.9
American Select	6.9	7.3	7.7	8.2	8.6	9.1	9.6	10.1	10.6	11.1	11.7	12.2	12.8	13.3	13.9	14.5
Blue Dot	10.8	11.3	11.9	12.5	13.1	13.7	14.4	15.0	15.7	16.3	17.0	17.7	18.4	19.2	20.1	21.0
Bullseye	8.6	9.1	9.6	10.1	10.6	11.2	11.7	12.3	12.9	13.5	14.1	14.8	15.4	16.1	16.8	17.5
Green Dot	6.7	7.2	7.6	8.0	8.4	8.9	9.3	9.8	10.3	10.8	11.3	11.8	12.4	12.9	13.5	14.0
H 110	13.5	14.4		16.4	17											
Herco	7.9	8.3	8.8	9.3	9.8	10.4	10.9	11.4	12.0	12.6	13.2	13.8	14.4	15.0	15.7	16.3
HS 6				15.5	16.1		17.9	18.8	19.8	20.7	21.6	22.6	23.7	24.7	25.8	26.8
HS 7					16.6		18.4	19.3	20.4	21.3	22.3	23.2	24.4	25.4	26.6	27.7
International									10.8	11.4	11.8	12.3	12.9	13.3	14.3	14.6
No. 2 Improved													16.2	16.9	17.6	18.1
Red Dot	6.3	6.7	7.1	7.5	7.9	8.3	8.7	9.2	9.6	10.1	10.6	11.1	11.6	12.1	12.6	13.1
Scot 453													16.2	16.9	17.6	18.1
Solo 1250													12.8	13.5	14.1	14.8
Unique	7.5	7.9	8.4	8.9	9.4	9.9	10.4	10.9	11.4	12.0	12.6	13.1	13.7	14.5	15.1	15.8
Universal								12.0	12.9	13.5	14.0	14.6	15.5	16.0	16.8	17.4
W 296	13.7	14.6	15.4	16.3	17.2	18.1	19.0	20.0	21	22	23.0	24.1	25.1	26.2	27.4	28.5
W 540	13.0	13.8	14.6	15.4	16.3	17.1	18.0	19.0	19.9	20.8	21.8	22.8	23.9	24.9	26.0	27.1
W 571	13.4	14.2	15.0	15.8	16.7	17.6	18.5	19.5	20.4	21.4	22.4	23.4	24.5	25.6	26.7	27.8
WAAP	7.9	8.3	8.8	9.3	9.8	10.4	10.9	11.4	12.0	12.6	13.2	13.8	14.4	15.0	15.7	16.3
WSF	10.9	11.5	12.2	12.9	13.6	14.3	15.0	15.8	16.6	17.4	18.2	19.0	19.9	20.8	21.6	22.6
WSL	10.6	11.2	11.9	12.5	13.2	13.9	14.6	15.4	16.2	16.9	17.7	18.5	19.4	20.2	21.1	22.0
WST	7.9	8.3	8.8	9.3	9.8	10.4	10.9	11.4	12.0	12.6	13.2	13.8	14.4	15.0	15.7	16.3

Bushing Designations

Powder	24	25	26	27	28	29	30	31	32	33	34	35	36	37	38	38A
2400	25.6	26.6	27.7	28.8	29.9	31.0	32.1	33.3	34.5	35.7	36.9	38.1	39.4	40.7	42.0	43.3
452AA	16.2	16.9	17.5	18.2	18.9	19.6	20.3	21.1	21.8	22.6	23.3	24.1	24.9	25.7	26.6	27.4
473AA	19.7	20.5	21.3	22.1	23.0	23.8	24.7	25.6	26.5	27.4	28.4	29.3	30.3	31.3	32.3	33.3
American Select	15.1	15.7	16.4	17.0	17.7	18.3	19.0	19.7	20.4	21.1	21.8	22.6	23.3	24.1	24.9	25.7
Blue Dot	21.9	22.8	23.7	24.6	25.5	26.4	27.3	28.2	29.1	30.5	31.6	32.7	33.8	35.0	36.1	37.3
Bullseye	18.2	18.9	19.6	20.4	21.2	21.9	22.8	23.7	24.6	25.5	26.4	27.3	28.2	29.1	30.1	31.0
Clays			14.6	15.2	15.9	16.3	16.9	17.5	18.2	18.9	19.4	20.1	20.7	21.4	22.2	
Green Dot	14.6	15.2	15.8	16.4	17.0	17.7	18.3	19.0	19.6	20.3	21.0	21.7	22.4	23.2	23.9	24.7
Herco	17.0	17.7	18.4	19.1	19.8	20.6	21.3	22.1	22.9	23.7	24.5	25.3	26.2	27.0	27.9	28.8
HS 6	27.9	28.9	30.3	31.2	32.6	33.6	35.0	36.2	37.8	39.0	40.4	41.1	43.0	44.4	46.2	
HS 7	28.9	29.9	31.2	32.3	33.6	34.7	36.2	37.4	38.9	40.1	41.5	42.4	44.4	45.7	47.4	
International	15.5	16.0	16.6	17.1	17.7	18.3	19.1	19.9	20.6	21.2	21.9	22.6	23.4	24.2	25.1	
No. 2 Improved	19.0	19.7	20.7	21.4	22.3	22.9	23.8									
Red Dot	13.7	14.2	14.9	15.7	16.4	17.1	17.8	18.5	19.2	19.9	20.6	21.3	21.9	22.7	23.3	24.1
Royal Scot D	16.0	16.5	17.5	18.1	18.7	19.3	20.2	20.9	21.9	22.4	23.2	23.9	24.7	25.7		
Scot 453	19.0	19.7	20.7	21.4	22.3	22.9	23.8									
Solo 1000			15.5	16.2	16.7	17.4	18.0	18.8	19.6	20.0	20.6	21.6	22.1	22.8	23.6	
Solo 1250	15.5	16.1	16.7	17.1	17.8	18.4	19.3	19.6	20.8	21.4	22.0	22.7	23.7	24.6	25.2	
Solo 1500	16.6	17.5	18.4	19.4	19.8	20.2	21.1	22.1	23.2	23.7	24.4	25.3	26.2	26.9	27.8	28.9
Unique	16.4	17.1	17.7	18.4	19.1	19.8	20.5	21.1	21.7	22.5	23.2	24.0	24.8	25.6	26.5	27.3
Universal	18.3	18.9	19.1	20.2	21.1	21.7	22.7	23.4	24.4	25.2	26.0	26.7	27.6	28.7	29.7	
W 296	29.7	30.9	32.1	33.4	34.6	35.9	37.3	38.6	40.0	41.4	42.8	44.2	45.7	47.1	48.7	50.2
W 540	28.2	29.3	30.5	31.7	32.9	34.1	35.4	36.6	37.9	39.2	40.6	42.0	43.3	44.7	46.2	47.6
W 571	28.9	30.1	31.3	32.5	33.8	35.0	36.3	37.6	38.9	40.3	41.7	43.1	44.5	45.9	47.4	48.9
WAAP	17.0	17.7	18.4	19.1	19.8	20.6	21.3	22.1	22.9	23.7	24.5	25.3	26.2	27.0	27.9	28.8
WSF	23.5	24.4	25.4	26.4	27.4	28.4	29.5	30.5	31.6	32.7	33.8	35.0	36.1	37.3	38.5	39.7
WSL	22.9	23.8	24.8	25.7	26.7	27.7	28.7	29.7	30.8	31.9	33.0	34.1	35.2	36.3	37.5	38.7
WST	17.0	17.7	18.4	19.1	19.8	20.6	21.3	22.1	22.9	23.7	24.5	25.3	26.2	27.0	27.9	28.8

Bushing Designations

Powder	39	39A	40	40A	41	41A	42	42A	43	43A	44	44A	45	45A	46
2400	44.6	46.0	47.4	48.8	50.2	51.6	53.1	54.6	56.1	57.6	59.2	60.7	62.3	63.9	65.6
452AA	28.3	29.1	30.0	30.9	31.8	32.7	33.6	34.6	35.5	36.5	37.5	38.5	39.5	40.5	41.5
473AA	34.3	35.4	36.4	37.5	38.6	39.7	40.9	42.0	43.2	44.3	45.5	46.7	47.9	49.2	50.4
American Select	26.5	27.3	28.1	28.9	29.8	30.7	31.5	32.4	33.3	34.2	35.2	36.4	37.0	38.0	39.0
Blue Dot	38.5	39.7	40.9	42.2	43.4	44.7	46.0	47.4	48.7	50.1	51.5	52.9	54.3	55.7	57.2
Bullseye	31.9	32.8	33.7	34.7	35.7	36.9	38.1	39.4	40.7	42.0	43.3	44.6	46.0	47.4	48.8
Clays	22.8														
Green Dot	25.4	26.2	27.0	27.8	28.6	29.4	30.3	31.1	32.0	32.8	33.7	34.6	35.5	36.4	37.4
Herco	29.7	30.6	31.5	32.4	33.4	34.3	35.3	36.3	37.3	38.3	39.3	40.4	41.4	42.5	43.6
HS 6	47.6														
HS 7	50.3														
International	26.9														
Red Dot	24.7	25.2	25.9	26.6	27.3	27.9	28.4	29.3	29.9	30.8	31.5	32.1	32.7	33.4	34.1
Solo 1000	24.5	25.0	25.8	26.7											
Solo 1250	26.9	27.8	28.8	29.6	30.0	31.1	31.8	32.9	33.7						
Solo 1500	29.9	30.7	32.1	32.8	33.5	34.5	35.1	36.3	37.8	38.5	39.6	40.4	41.7	42.5	

| | | | | | —Bushing Designations— | | | | | | | | | | | |
Powder	39	39A	40	40A	41	41A	42	42A	43	43A	44	44A	45	45A	46
Unique	28.2	29.0	29.9	30.8	31.7	32.6	33.5	34.5	35.4	36.4	37.4	38.4	39.4	40.4	41.4
W 296	51.7	53.3	54.9	56.6	58.2	59.9	61.6	63.3	65.0	66.8	68.6	70.4	72.3	74.1	76.0
W 540	49.1	50.6	52.1	53.7	55.2	56.8	58.4	60.1	61.7	63.4	65.1	66.8	68.6	70.4	72.2
W 571	50.4	52.0	53.5	55.1	56.7	58.4	60.0	61.7	63.4	65.1	66.9	68.6	70.4	72.3	74.1
WAAP	29.7	30.6	31.5	32.4	33.4	34.3	35.3	36.3	37.3	38.3	39.3	40.4	41.4	42.5	43.6
WSF	40.9	42.2	43.4	44.7	46.0	47.4	48.7	50.1	51.5	52.9	54.3	55.7	57.2	58.6	60.1
WSL	39.9	41.1	42.3	43.6	44.9	46.2	47.5	48.8	50.1	51.5	52.9	54.3	55.7	57.1	58.6
WST	29.7	30.6	31.5	32.4	33.4	34.3	35.3	36.3	37.3	38.3	39.3	40.4	41.4	42.5	43.6

Bushings Chart for Pacific Models DL 155, DL-105 and DL-155APF Presses*
Range of bushing numbers apt to throw desired charge.

| | | | | | | | | | | | —Grains— | | | | | | | | | | | | | | |
Powder	13	14	17	18	19	20	21	22	23	24	25	26	27	28	29	30	31	32	33	34	35	36	37	38
452AA			393	396	402	414	423	432	444	453	462													
473AA			351	363	372	381	393	399	405	417	426	435	444	453										
W 296	250	259																						
W 540				303			327	333	342	348		363	372	378	384		399	405	411	417	423	429	435	441
W 571					312	318	327		345	351	357	366	375	381		393	399		411	417	423	429	435	

*Pacific bushings are no longer manufactured. See Hornady charts for new powder series.

Bushings Chart for Pacific Model DL-266 Press*
Range of bushing numbers apt to throw desired charge.

| | | | | | | | | | | | —Grains— | | | | | | | | | | | | | | |
Powder	13	14	17	18	19	20	21	22	23	24	25	26	27	28	29	30	31	32	33	34	35	36	37	38
452AA			384	396	408	420	432	441	450	459	474													
473AA			357	366	378	387	396	402	411	423	432	438	450	456										
W 296	256	266																						
W 540			300	309	315	321	333	339	348	354	360	369	375	384	390	396	402	408	414	420	429	435	441	447
W 571					318	327	333	339	351	357	363	369	378	387	393	399	405	411	417	423	429	435	441	

*Pacific bushings are no longer manufactured. See Hornady charts for new powder series.

Bushings Chart for Pacific Model DL-366 Press*
Range of bushing numbers apt to throw desired charge.

| | | | | | | | | | | | —Grains— | | | | | | | | | | | | | | |
Powder	13	14	17	18	19	20	21	22	23	24	25	26	27	28	29	30	31	32	33	34	35	36	37	38
452AA			390	402	411	420	432	441	450	462	474													
473AA			357	369	381	390	399	408	414	426	435	444	450	462										
W 296	256	266																						
W 540			300	309	318	327	336	345	351	360	366	375	381	387	393	402	408	414	423	429	435	441	444	450
W 571					318	330	339	348	357	363	369	378	384	390	396	405	411	417	423	429	438	444	450	

*Pacific bushings are no longer manufactured. See Hornady charts for new powder series.

Bushings Chart for Texan Models GT, FW, LT, A, AP, D and DP Presses*
Approximate thrown charge in grains

| | | | | | | —Bushing Designations— | | | | | | | | | | |
Powder	101	102	103	104	105	106	107	108	109	110	111	112	113	114	115	116	117
473AA															17.2	18.0	18.6
W 296	13.5	14.1	14.6	15.3	16												
W 540							16.9	17.7	18.3	19.4	20.2	21.0	21.9	22.7	23.6	24.8	25.6
W 571									18.6	19.7	20.6	21.4	22.3	23.2	24.2	25.3	26.2

| | | | | | | —Bushing Designations— | | | | | | | | | | |
Powder	118	119	120	121	122	123	124	125	126	127	128	129	130	131	132	133	134
452AA		16.9	17.7	18.0	18.7	19.3	19.8	20.3	21.0	21.6	22.2	22.8	23.5	24.1	24.7	25.3	
473AA	19.4	19.9	20.8	21.4	22.2	22.9	23.5	24.2	25.1	25.9	26.6	27.3	28.1	29.0			
W 296	13.5	14.1	14.6	15.3	16.0												
W 540	26.7	27.5	28.8	29.4	30.5	31.6	32.4	33.5	34.6	35.6	36.6	37.5	38.6	39.9	40.9		
W 571	27.4	28.1	29.5	30.2	31.4	32.4	33.3	34.5	35.6	36.6	37.6	38.6	39.9	41.1	42.1	43.2	44.4

*Texan bushings are no longer manufactured. See alternate charts for new powder series.

Bushings Chart for Texan Model M Press*
Approximate thrown charge in grains

Powder	101	102	103	104	105	106	109	110	111	112	113	114	115	116	117	118	119
473AA														17.0	17.6	18.4	18.9
W 296	13.1	13.6	14.1	14.7	15.3	16.1											
W 540							17.4	18.3	19.2	19.9	20.8	21.6	22.5	23.6	24.4	25.5	26.2
W 571								18.9	19.6	20.4	20.6	21.3	23.4	24.3	25.2	26.3	27.0

Powder	120	121	122	123	124	125	126	127	128	129	130	131	132	133	134	135	136
452AA	17.1	17.7	18.3	18.8	19.5	20.1	20.7	21.2	21.8	22.4	23.0	23.6	24.3	24.9	25.3		
473AA	19.9	20.3	21.0	21.7	22.3	22.9	23.8	24.5	25.2	25.9	26.6	27.5	28.2	29.0			
W 540	27.4	28.1	29.1	30.2	30.9	31.7	33.0	34.0	34.9	35.9	36.9	38.1	39.0	40.1			
W 571	28.3	29.0	30.1	31.2	32.0	33.0	34.3	35.3	36.3	37.3	38.5	~39.6	40.7	41.8	42.9	43.8	45.2

*Texan bushings are no longer manufactured. See alternate charts for new powder series.

Bushings Chart for Ponsness/Warren Presses
Approximate thrown charge in grains:

Powder	1A	2A	3A	A	B	C	C1	D	D1	E	E1	E2	F	F1	F2	G	G1	H	I
2400		12.3	13.2	15.2	16.1	16.8	17.6	18.3	19.0	21.3	22.2	23.3	24.7	25.7	26.1	27.7	28.2	30.0	31.5
452AA												15.3	16.7	16.8	17.7	19.0	19.1	20.2	21.3
473AA									15.4	17.3	16.0	19.1	20.1	20.2	21.4	22.3	22.6	24.1	25.1
American Select																16.4	17.5	18.2	
Blue Dot									16.4	18.4	19.2	20.1	21.3	22.2	22.6	23.9	24.3	25.9	27.2
Bullseye										16.2	16.8	17.7	18.7	19.4					
Clays									11.7	13.1	13.7	14.4	15.2	15.8	16.1	17.1	17.3	18.5	19.3
Green Dot											11.7	12.3	13.1	13.6	13.8	14.7	14.9	16.3	16.7
Herco									12.3	13.8	14.4	15.1	16.0	16.6	16.9	18.0	18.3	19.5	20.5
HS 6				17.1	18.2	18.8	20.1	21.0	22.4	24.2	24.7	26.5	28.5	29.3		32.3	33.4	34.8	36.5
HS 7	13.7	14.8	15.6	17.5															
International						12.5	13.0	13.2	14.0	15.7	16.2	17.2	18.1	18.3	18.9	20.2	20.6	22.0	22.8
Nitro 100																		16.0	16.7
No. 2 Improved											16.1	17.0	17.2	18.9		20.7	21.0	21.9	22.2
Red Dot										11.6	12.2	12.9	13.4		13.7	14.5	14.7	15.7	16.5
Royal Scot D											15.5	16.2	16.4			18.2	18.5	19.4	20.4
Scot 453										16.1	17.0	17.2	18.9			20.7	21.0	21.9	22.2
Solo 1000																			17.4
Solo 1250									12.6	13.5	14.1	14.9	15.4	15.6		17.3	17.8	18.9	19.6
Solo 1500											16.5	17.4	17.9			10.2	19.7	21.0	22.2
Unique									12.6	14.2	14.8	15.6	16.5	17.2	17.5	18.7	19.0	20.2	21.2
Universal			15.3	16.8	17.6	18.5	19.6	20.4	21.3	23.5	24.0	26.1	27.5	28.3		31.2	32.7	34.0	34.4
W 296	13.6	15.0	16.0	18.2	19.3	20.0													
W 540				16.7	17.7	18.4	19.4	19.9	20.7	23.5	24.4	25.8	27.3	27.4	28.6	30.4	30.7	32.8	34.1
W 571				17.2	18.1	18.8	19.9	20.4	21.3	24.1	25.0	26.5	28.0	28.1	29.4	31.2	31.6	33.6	35.0
WAAP												15.0	15.9	16.0	16.5	17.7	17.9	19.1	19.8
WSF				14.0	15.1	15.7	16.7	17.0	17.8	20.0	21.1	22.1	23.2	23.5	24.6	26.0	26.3	28.0	29.0
WSL	10.2	11.2	11.8	13.5	14.3	14.9	15.7	16.3	16.6	18.7	19.6	20.4	22.0	22.1	22.7	24.5	24.7	26.2	27.2
WST												15.0	15.9	16.0	16.5	17.7	17.9	19.1	19.8

Powder	J	J1	K	L	M	N	O	P	Q	R	S	T	U	V	W	X	Y	Z
2400	32.2	33.1	33.7	35.5	37.1	39.8	40.2	41.1	42.0	43.8	44.5	47.5	49.8					
452AA	21.6	22.4	23	23.6	25.2	26.7												
473AA	26.1	26.8	27.2	28.3	30.1													
American Select	18.8	19.4	19.9	20.6	22.0													
Blue Dot	27.7	28.5	29.1	30.6	31.9	34.2	34.5	35.2	36.0	37.5	38.1	40.7	42.5	43.8	46.5	47.2	49.5	55.7
Clays	19.8	20.3	20.6	21.6	22.5	23.7	24.0	24.5	25.0									
Green Dot	17.0	17.5	17.9	18.8	19.6	21.1	21.3	21.8	22.3	23.2	23.6	25.3	26.5					
Herco	20.9	21.5	21.9	23.0	24.0	25.7	26.0	26.5	27.1	28.1	28.8	30.7	32.1	33.1	34.9	35.4	37.2	
HS 6	37.1	38.8	39.0	41.1	42.8													
International	23.9	24.5	24.8	25.7	26.8	28.2	28.5											
Nitro 100	17.2	17.6	17.8	18.7	19.7	20.8	21.0	21.5	21.9									
No. 2 Improved	23.7																	
Red Dot	16.1	17.3	17.6	18.5	19.4	20.7	20.9	21.3	21.9	22.9								
Royal Scot D	21.0	21.5	22.0	22.8	24.2	25.5												
Scot 453	23.7																	
Solo 1000	17.6	18.2	18.5	19.1	20.6	21.4	21.8	22.2	22.6	23.2	23.6	25.2						
Solo 1250	20.3	21.0	21.6	22.1	23.5	24.6	25.2	25.7	26.2	27.4	27.7	29.4	31.6	32.3				
Solo 1500	22.6	23.3	23.8	24.8	26.5	27.7	28.0	28.6	29.2	30.3	30.9	33.1	35.2	36.0	37.9	38.3	40.1	44.9
Unique	21.7	22.3	22.7	24.0	25.0	26.8	27.1	27.6										
Universal	35.5	36.9	37.1	39.5	41.2													
W 540	35.2	36.4	36.8	38.4	40.7	43.4	43.7	45.6										
W 571	36.2	37.3	37.7	39.4	41.8	44.5	44.8	46.7	46.8	48.7								
WAAP	20.5	21.3	21.6	22.5	23.8	25.5												
WSF	30.0	31.0	31.4	32.7	35.0	36.8	37.4											
WSL	28.2	29.0	29.4	30.6	32.6	34.8	35.0	36.5	37.7	38.1	38.6	41.3	44.0	45.0				
WST	20.5	21.3	21.6	22.5	23.8	25.5												